the psychology of he and health care

A CANADIAN PERSPECTIVE   FOURTH EDITIO

the psychology of health and health care

A CANADIAN PERSPECTIVE   FOURTH EDITION

GARY POOLE

UNIVERSITY OF BRITISH COLUMBIA

DEBORAH HUNT MATHESON

VANCOUVER ISLAND UNIVERSITY

DAVID N. COX

SIMON FRASER UNIVERSITY

Pearson Canada
Toronto

Library and Archives Canada Cataloging in Publication

Poole, Gary, 1950–
The psychology of health and health care: a Canadian perspective / Gary Poole, Deborah Hunt Matheson, David N. Cox.—4th ed.

Includes bibliographical references and index.
ISBN 978-0-13-703032-3

1. Medicine and psychology—Textbooks. 2. Medical care—Psychological aspects—Textbooks. I. Matheson, Deborah Hunt, 1966– II. Cox, David Neil, 1947– III. Title.

R726.7.P66 2012   610.1'9   C2010-906756-8

ISBN 978-0-13-703032-3

Vice-President, Editorial Director: Gary Bennett
Editor-in-Chief: Ky Pruesse
Editor, Humanities and Social Sciences: Joel Gladstone
Executive Marketing Manager: Judith Allen
Senior Developmental Editor: Madhu Ranadive
Project Manager: Imee Salumbides
Production Editor: Lila Campbell
Copy Editor: Judy Sturrup
Proofreader: Patricia Jones
Compositor: Aptara®, Inc.
Photo and Permissions Researcher: Lynn McIntyre
Art Director: Julia Hall
Cover Designer: Miguel Angel Acevedo
Cover Image: Masterfile/Jon Feingersh

For permission to reproduce copyrighted material, the publisher gratefully acknowledges the copyright holders listed on page 460, which is considered an extension of this copyright page.

1 2 3 4 5   15 14 13 12 11

Printed and bound in the United States of America.

For our families:

Marsha, Colleen, and Graeme Poole
Owen and Wyatt Matheson
Susan, Kelsi, Kieran, and Dylan Cox

Brief Contents

Contents

Preface

With each new edition of *The Psychology of Health and Health Care: A Canadian Perspective*, we as authors learn more and more about this fascinating field of health psychology. In writing this fourth edition, we have confirmed our belief that the field continues to mature and expand, learning from other branches of psychology and from other disciplines.

As learners and as authors, we continue to feel very fortunate to be able to work in a country in which issues, opinions, and data are so very accessible. In the late 1990s, when we first began conceptualizing this book, we were convinced that the topics of health psychology manifest themselves in unique ways in Canada. After writing this fourth edition, we hold fast to that conviction. While many psychological theories developed in the United States and elsewhere cross the border quite well, it is still the case that, when it comes to health and health care, our geography, demography, history, and health care system make Canadians unique, even in the face of significant reforms to the American health care system. Our experience in writing this edition continues to confirm that Canadians are very active in research that goes beyond descriptions of our health to explore the factors affecting it. Again, you will find hundreds of new references as this research is discussed throughout the book.

HOW BEST TO USE THIS BOOK

The fourth edition of *The Psychology of Health and Health Care: A Canadian Perspective* is organized into chapters and *focused modules*. Chapters are the traditionally used organizational elements. Focused modules present briefer treatments of more specific topics, inviting closer consideration. The chapters of this book present topics that are commonly found in most health psychology textbooks. Stress and coping, communication in medical settings, pain, chronic and life-threatening illnesses, and systems of the body are examples of such topics. However, this edition also contains chapters on some topics that are often covered in less detail by other texts. Examples include psychoneuroimmunology, health promotion, and health and physical activity. Also, with our chapter on the systems of the body, we have done more in this edition to link the discussions of anatomy and physiology to relevant topics in health psychology—topics that figure prominently in other chapters of the book.

Instructors are invited to use the book's chapters as they see fit for their educational context. For example, nursing and medical students may want to focus more on chapters such as Psychoneuroimmunology, Communication in Medical Settings, Hospital Stays and Medical Procedures, The Health Care Provider, Pain, and Chronic and Life-Threatening Illnesses.

Health psychology is essentially an applied discipline and each chapter of our book opens with a vignette intended to provide students with a realistic context for what they are about to read. In this way, we begin each chapter with an applied focus. Students will also find case studies throughout the book. In addition to the analysis we provide, students can discuss these case studies in lectures or seminars.

We hope that the focused modules will make the book even more flexible to use. Our conversations with instructors from across the country taught us that each has his or her own particular areas of emphasis. In some institutions, Aboriginal health is given considerable attention. In others, research methodology is an integral part of every course in the psychology curriculum. In still others, health issues are approached from multidisciplinary perspectives, and so people majoring in a field like psychology must be familiar with the language and concepts of more macroscopic disciplines like sociology. Hence, each of these is featured in a manageable focused module that can augment the chapters or be assigned for tutorials or other discussion forums.

We continue to enhance the layout and pedagogy of the text.

WHAT'S NEW IN THE FOURTH EDITION

The fourth edition includes new features that highlight the key concepts for each chapter. Key new review features for each chapter now include a set of Learning Objectives at the beginning of each chapter and a Chapter Summary and a set of Review Questions at the end of each chapter.

The chapter on Chronic and Life-Threatening Illnesses appears earlier in the book and new and revised topics include Personality and Stress (Chapter 3), Behaviour and Cognitive Therapy (Chapter 3), Stress and Cancer (Chapter 4), Biological Mechanisms to Explain Why Psychological States Affect the Immune System (Chapter 4), a feature on The Calgary-Cambridge Observation Guide (Chapter 5), Preparation for Surgery (Chapter 6), The Psychology of Colonoscopy (Chapter 6), and an update on Peter's Story: story of a heart disease patient (Chapter 9).

SUPPLEMENTS

The following instructor supplements are available for downloading from a password-protected section of Pearson Canada's online catalogue. Navigate to your book's catalogue page to view a list of those supplements that are available. See your local Pearson sales representative for details and access.

Test Item File: Available in Microsoft Word, the test bank includes a wide variety of questions that will help you create meaningful student tests and assessments.

PowerPoints: The PowerPoint presentations highlight the key concepts in each chapter and will enhance classroom lectures and discussion.

CourseSmart for Instructors: CurseSmart goes beyond traditional expectations—providing instant, online access to the textbooks and course materials you need at a lower cost for students. And even as students save money, you can save time and hassle with a digital eTextbook that allows you to search for the most relevant content at the very moment you need it. Whether it's evaluating textbooks or creating lecture notes to help students with difficult concepts, CourseSmart can make life a little easier. See how when you visit **www.coursesmart.com/instructors.**

CourseSmart for Students: CourseSmart goes beyond traditional expectations—providing instant, online access to the textbooks and course materials you need at an average savings of 60%. With instant access from any computer and the ability to search your text, you'll find the content you need quickly, no matter where you are. And with online tools like highlighting and note-taking, you can save time and study efficiently. See all the benefits at **www.coursesmart.com/students.**

MySearchLab offers extensive help to students with their writing and research project and provides round-the-clock access to credible and reliable source material.

Research

- Content on MySearchLab includes immediate access to thousands of full-text articles from leading Canadian and international academic journals, and daily news feeds from The Associated Press. Articles contain the full downloadable text—including abstract and citation information—and can be cut, pasted, emailed, or saved for later use.

Writing

- MySearchLab also includes a step-by-step tutorial on writing a research paper. Included are sections on planning a research assignment, finding a topic, creating effective notes, and finding source material. Our exclusive online handbook provides grammar and usage support. Pearson SourceCheck™ offers an easy way to detect accidental plagiarism issues, and our exclusive tutorials teach how to avoid them in the future. And MySearchLab also contains AutoCite, which helps to correctly cite sources using MLA, APA, CMS, and CBE documentation styles for both endnotes and bibliographies.

- Take a tour at **www.mysearchlab.com**. A MySearchLab access code can be provided at no extra charge with this text. Please order package ISBN 0-13-257214-1.

Acknowledgments

We are very grateful for the help we received from Sean Benay, who provided a very careful reading of our first edition; from Caroline Murphy of the University of British Columbia, who pointed us in the right direction regarding the content for the focused module on Health and the Internet; and from Dr. Colleen Poole for her consultation on our Systems of the Body chapter. Thanks also to Carol-Ann Courneya from the University of British Columbia, for her help with that same chapter.

We also continue to be very grateful to Peter Gibson for sharing and updating his remarkable story with us in Chapter 9. For their feedback on the first edition, we would also like to thank Lois Hunt, Dennis Krebs of Simon Fraser University, Tina Niwinska, Jody L. Bain of the University of Victoria, Kathleen A. Martin Ginis of McMaster University, Dean Tripp of Queen's University, and Angie MacKewn of the University of New Brunswick.

Pearson Canada and the authors would like to thank the following individuals for their reviews during the development phase of this title: Caroline Brunelle, University of New Brunswick; Peter Doherty, St Mary's College; Linda L. Hatt, University of British Columbia, Okanagan; Cameron Muir, Brock University; and Glen Paterson, Lakehead University.

Gary Poole
Deborah Hunt Matheson
David N. Cox

About the Authors

Gary Poole is an Associate Professor in the School of Population and Public Health in the University of British Columbia's Faculty of Medicine. He received his Ph.D. in Psychology from Simon Fraser University. He has won numerous awards for his teaching and he is currently the President of the International Society for the Scholarship of Teaching and Learning. In addition to his publications in the area of health psychology, he is the co-author of "Effective Teaching with Technology in Higher Education," (Bates, A.W. & Poole, G. (2003). *Effective teaching with technology in higher education: Foundations for Success* San Francisco, CA: Jossey-Bass.)

Deborah Hunt Matheson is Chair of the Department of Psychology at Vancouver Island University. She received her B.A. (Hons) from Simon Fraser University and did her M.A. and Ph.D. graduate work at the University of Victoria. Her research interests are in health psychology, especially on factors that motivate people to commit to an exercise program. In addition, she is interested in communication in the medical setting. Her research has been published in journals such as *Behavioral Medicine*; the *British Journal of Health Psychology*; the *Canadian Journal of Communication*; the *Journal of Nonverbal Behavior,* the *Journal of Sport and Exercise Psychology, Measurement in Physical Education and Exercise Science, Psychology and Health, Psychology, Health and Medicine*; and the *Psychology of Sport and Exercise.*

David Cox is in the Department of Psychology at Simon Fraser University where he just completed a term as the Director of Clinical Training. He received his M.A. and Ph.D. from the University of British Columbia in Clinical Psychology. His research interests currently focus on health psychology and on human performance and sport psychology. He recently served as a psychologist and member of the Mission Staff for the 2010 Winter Olympics. He is currently the Chairman of the Sport Medicine Council of British Columbia. His most recent research has been published in journals such as the *Journal of Clinical and Experimental Neuropsychology,*the *International Journal of Sports Physiology and Performance,* the *International Journal of Mental health and Addictions,*the *Journal of Pediatric Psychology,* and the *Journal of Adolescent Health.*

Chapter 1

The Development of the Field

CHAPTER OUTLINE

WHAT IS HEALTH PSYCHOLOGY?
THE DEVELOPMENT OF HEALTH PSYCHOLOGY AS A DISCIPLINE
WHY HAS HEALTH PSYCHOLOGY COME INTO PROMINENCE?
HEALTH PSYCHOLOGY TODAY
WORKING IN HEALTH PSYCHOLOGY

Learning Objectives

After studying this chapter, you will be able to

- Define health psychology

- Outline how the field grew in terms of important topics and theoretical perspectives

- Explain why health psychology has grown so quickly as a field

- Describe and apply fundamental theories in health psychology

- Describe different careers pursued by people who have studied health psychology

The British Columbia Cancer Agency's Vancouver Centre is a hive of offices, hospital rooms, meeting spaces, waiting areas, and other facilities. Today, a health psychologist arrives at the centre for a regular research meeting. The discussion will focus on finding research money, as it often does. These meetings are usually held in the second-floor boardroom, which looks deceptively like any room in a downtown office building. Today, however, the meeting is in a room on the fifth floor, a floor with hospital rooms. The elevator doors open to reveal a frail woman being weighed on a scale. She has lost her hair, and she is very thin, making it difficult to ascertain her age. She is helped off the scale and back to her room. For the health psychologist, the switch from the second to the fifth floor means much more than spending a bit longer on the elevator. Rather, the fifth floor gives the health psychologist a glimpse of the real world beyond the impersonal talk of funding and research, and provides a vital reminder of the real people all health professionals serve.

CASE 1-1 MATTERS OF THE HEART

Alan was admitted to hospital with classic heart-attack symptoms, though that wasn't how he explained his chest pain, breathing difficulties, and profuse sweating. He had been suffering from a cold for the past week and thought the virus had flared up badly. However, Alan was wrong. Tests revealed an *infarct*—tissue that has died because of a lack of oxygen. Other tests showed the reason for the infarct: a coronary artery was completely blocked. In fact, so were two others—not the stuff of viruses. Alan was advised that he needed emergency bypass surgery.

WHAT IS HEALTH PSYCHOLOGY?

After reading Case 1-1, ask yourself what might have caused Alan's heart attack. From the case study, we might conclude that the cause was the arterial blockage, and this would certainly be correct. But is that *all* that caused it? Why did bypass surgery like Alan's become so common in the latter half of the twentieth century? Did millions of people in North America develop blocked coronary arteries because of some colossal biological coincidence? No. To understand Alan's heart attack and the growth industry that bypass surgery has become, we must look beyond biology. We must consider psychological causes, such as Alan's outlook on life, his lifestyle, and his stress level. We must consider sociological causes, such as the nature of his employment and his social network. Finally, we must consider environmental causes, such as the air he breathes.

This collection of causes is relevant not only to Alan's heart; it is, indeed, at the heart of this book. The goal of this first chapter is to help you understand that health is best achieved through a partnership between medical and social science. We will explore, in detail, the contributions of the social science of psychology to this understanding.

Clinical psychologists have long recognized that there are psychological consequences associated with ill health, as well as physical consequences associated with many psychological disorders. It wasn't until the 1970s, however, that psychologists from other non-clinical subdisciplines began to recognize the many ways psychological principles could be applied to health and health care. It was out of this recognition that the fields of behavioural medicine and, ultimately, health psychology emerged.

Several names emerged for the new discipline linking psychology and health. These terms can be somewhat confusing, because some psychologists use them interchangeably while others believe they refer to distinctly different subcategories. We will begin our investigation of the field's development by trying to sort out some of the different labels.

The first formal definition of the field used the term **behavioural medicine**. The term, which was defined at the Yale Conference on Behavioral Medicine in 1977, stressed an integration of biomedical and behavioural approaches. Psychology achieved prominence among these behavioural approaches with the emergence of the term **health psychology**, for which Matarazzo proposed the following definition:

> Health psychology is the aggregate of the specific educational, scientific and professional contributions of the discipline of psychology to the promotion and maintenance of health, the prevention or treatment of illness, and the identification of etiologic and diagnostic correlates of health, illness, and related dysfunction. (Matarazzo, 1980)

Notice that this definition includes not just maintenance of health but also treatment of illness. Health psychology, then, is the compilation of all that psychology has to offer to the diagnosis and treatment of illness as well as to people's attempts to maintain health and well-being. In this context, the word *health* means more than just the absence of illness. As far back as the 1940s, the World Health Organization (WHO) promoted the notion that being "healthy" also means being able to enjoy a desired quality of life in terms of physical, mental, and social functioning. Today, WHO espouses the same definition it presented in 1946: "Health is a state of complete physical, mental and social well-being and not merely the absence of disease or infirmity" (WHO, 1946).

We can apply this notion of health to Alan, who has just had a heart attack. We can, with some accuracy, assess the extent of his tissue damage. However, what will it take to help Alan be *healthy* again, and what does this mean? If we adopt the World Health Organization's definition of health, our role as health psychologists becomes clearer. We must help Alan return to a level of functioning that restores his sense of quality of life. This may include addressing his fears of having another heart attack, helping him change his approach to life so that it is less hostile, and helping him develop the conviction that these changes are possible. In this example and in Matarazzo's definition of *health psychology,* we form an image of psychologists working at the interface of medicine and psychology. This work has been recognized by the Canadian Psychological Association in its creation of a section on health psychology, and by the American Psychological Association through its creation of Division 38, the Division of Health Psychology.

Another term common in the field is **psychosomatic medicine**, according to which a particular medical complaint is viewed as being the result of an underlying chronic emotional conflict that ultimately surfaces in the form of physiological symptoms. Specific symptoms are linked to particular kinds of conflict. Probably the most well-known example of this relationship between psychological conflict and physical symptoms is the understanding that essential hypertension (high blood pressure) is connected to an inability to express feelings of anger in an appropriate manner. Men who are prone to anger and who have untreated high blood pressure have significantly more plaque buildup in their arteries (Bleil et al., 2004).

As you might expect, psychotherapy is one of the treatment options in such cases because it aims to provide insight into the impact that unresolved conflicts have on a

behavioural medicine: a branch of medicine concerned with the relationship between health and behaviour. The focus is usually on remediation.

health psychology: the application of psychological principles to the diagnosis and treatment of illness as well as to people's attempts to maintain health and well-being.

psychosomatic medicine: approach in which a particular medical complaint is viewed as being the result of an underlying chronic emotional conflict that ultimately surfaces in the form of physiological symptoms.

particular individual's life, with the hope that such insight will enable symptom reduction. However, treatment of medical disorders based on this approach has not been successful. In comparison, treatment in behavioural medicine focuses on addressing the individual's current *behaviour*, which psychologists view as being strongly influenced by learning. In behavioural medicine, symptoms are important in their own right, and the emphasis is on defining those symptoms in observable and measurable terms.

In summary, many terms describe the work of psychologists in health-related areas. Some of these terms focus on behavioural interventions, some on enhancing people's abilities to maintain their own health. All these terms, however, relate to the same process—applying psychological principles to the understanding and improvement of our health.

THE DEVELOPMENT OF HEALTH PSYCHOLOGY AS A DISCIPLINE

A subdiscipline has truly "arrived" in psychology when the *Annual Review of Psychology* begins publishing articles summarizing its development. In such a way, Neal Miller's 1983 article on behavioural medicine (Miller, 1983) marked the arrival of health psychology. This article was followed over the years by a number of reviews that, taken collectively and in combination with other important reviews, provide a good overview of how the field has developed, especially in light of the topics given prominence.

The Early Stages of Health Psychology's Development: Applying the Principles of Behaviourism to Health

germ theory: the discovery that many illnesses are caused by the activity of micro-organisms, such as bacteria.

In 1983, Neal Miller traced the development of the biomedical perspective on illness, starting with the invention of the microscope and moving to the development of **germ theory**, which is based on the discovery that many illnesses are caused by the activity of micro-organisms, such as bacteria. From germ theory came the development of antibiotics to fight these germs. The biomedical perspective took full flight, realizing considerable success by reducing illnesses to a cellular level and treating them with medicines.

At least two important developments resulted from these discoveries. First, the success of antibiotics brought about a change in the profile of life-threatening illnesses, and lifestyle replaced infection as the number one killer. Second, an emphasis on the technical aspects of medicine replaced a consideration for emotional factors in health. The paradox is that technical medicine, so revered for its success in treating germ-based conditions, is relatively ineffective against health problems caused by lifestyle and other psychosocial factors. As a result, these two developments gave rise to behavioural medicine.

Psychologists adopting a behavioural perspective believe that our health is affected primarily by what we *do* rather than what we *think*. You will see later in this chapter how this perspective contrasts with theories such as the health belief model, which emphasizes the way our thinking can affect the decisions we make.

In Miller's article, the key issues of the day were explained using the language of behaviourism. For example, Miller identified *non-compliance* with medical regimens as an important problem. Today, we are more likely to use terms like *adherence* or *co-operation* to describe people's decisions to follow medical regimens. He explained non-compliance in terms of what he called a **gradient of reinforcement**. By this, he meant that the greater the lag time between behaviour and reinforcement, the weaker the behaviour will be. Non-compliance can be explained in these terms because the reinforcement for following a medical regimen is often delayed. When we exercise, we don't suddenly get fit. High blood pressure doesn't drop to a normal range after one low-sodium meal. These benefits take time to realize. Behaviourists call this time lag between behaviour and reinforcement **delayed gratification**. Returning to our case study, for example, Alan must contend with problems of delayed gratification as he recovers from his heart attack and tries to change his behaviour and thinking.

There is research support for the delayed gratification explanation of Miller's concept of non-compliance. Specifically, we know that compliance rates are higher for regimens bringing about a rapid reduction in symptoms than they are for those in which improvement takes longer. Lowest of all are compliance rates for conditions that are **asymptomatic**—that is, conditions accompanied by no palpable symptoms or sensations (Buckalew, 1991). For example, after one year, about 40 percent of people prescribed a medication for high blood pressure no longer take the medicine (Hong, Oddone, Dudley, & Bosworth, 2006).

The delayed gratification theory helps to explain why significantly more people will follow instructions to take an antibiotic to relieve a painful ear infection than will follow instructions to change their lifestyle to reduce hypertension. According to the behavioural explanation, this is because taking the antibiotic is reinforced almost immediately by pain relief. Lifestyle changes for the usually asymptomatic condition of high blood pressure are reinforced by longer life expectancy, which is far less immediate. This problem is further compounded by the fact that behaviours that worsen hypertension, such as eating a high-fat diet, are immediately reinforced—these foods taste good. Miller provided a similar analysis to explain why people find it difficult to quit smoking cigarettes.

Miller addressed a number of other conditions, including alcohol abuse, obesity, stress, and the Type A behaviour pattern that was first described in the late 1950s by two cardiologists who identified behaviour patterns that they claimed were more common among their cardiac patients than in the general population (Friedman & Rosenman, 1959). At the time of Miller's article (1983), psychologists believed that the entire constellation of attributes identified by the Type A pattern were linked to heart disease. These attributes included time urgency, achievement orientation, and hostility. Large-scale studies, such as the Framingham study, published around the time of Miller's article, showed that people exhibiting the Type A pattern were generally at greater risk for coronary heart disease (CHD) (Haynes, Feinleib, & Kannel, 1980). Other studies that followed large samples of men over a seven-year period found that those prone to anger were three times more likely to die from heart disease or suffer a non-fatal heart attack (Kawachi et al., 1996). We will review the balance of these findings in chapter 3 in our discussion of stress and coping. For now, it is important to understand that the Type A construct was a catalyst for general research attempting to link psychology with health.

Health Psychology Expands to Include Cognition and Personality Factors

Shortly after Miller's article, Krantz and colleagues (1985) published another major review that identified a number of key areas in which health psychology had made contributions and others in which more research was needed. By the mid-1980s, psychologists

gradient of reinforcement: the gradual weakening of a behaviour the further it gets in time from the reinforcement of that behaviour.

delayed gratification: term used by behaviourists to describe a situation in which there is a time lag between a behaviour and its reinforcement.

asymptomatic: conditions that are not accompanied by palpable symptoms or sensations.

Hostility, as identified by the Type A behaviour pattern, can take the form of road rage.

were working with physiologists and others to identify the mechanisms whereby stressful environments put people at risk for health problems. Further, Miller's behavioural perspective was expanded to study the cognitive and personality factors that cause some people to view a situation as being stressful while others may not.

As cognitive factors rose in prominence during this period, psychologists were also studying ways that stress could be reduced. For example, social support grew as a significant area of study, as did therapeutic interventions such as *cognitive restructuring,* which was aimed at changing people's stress-prone interpretations of events. (For a review, see Matarazzo et al., 1984).

Cognitive factors continue to be a central focus for health psychologists. Approximately 80 percent of the articles published in *Health Psychology* in 2002 emphasized cognitive processes (Montgomery, 2004).

Closely related to the investigations in the mid-1980s was the study of the relationship between behaviour and cardiovascular health. The link between cigarette smoking and disease had been sufficiently established, so the next logical step was to study the psychology of smoking. To this end, studies examined the ages at which people (usually young people) started smoking (Kozlowski, 1979; Pomerleau, 1979), how they maintained the habit (Kozlowski & Herman, 1984), and why smoking cessation programs were less successful than they might be (Schachter, 1981).

Eating disorders was another topic that rose to prominence in the 1980s, specifically obesity, anorexia, and cachexia (malnourishment). Obesity was studied from biological, behavioural, and social perspectives; today we call this a *biopsychosocial approach,* and it will be discussed later in the chapter.

Finally, Krantz and colleagues discussed communication issues as they related to compliance (as they called it) by introducing perspectives other than behaviourism. The work of Howard Waitzkin in the United States (Waitzkin, 1985), Philip Ley in Great Britain (Ley, 1977), and others showed that communication between physicians and their patients often lacked clarity and relevance. Through this work, physicians discovered that *their* impression of an interview with a patient could be quite different from the patient's impression. Specifically, less information was being conveyed and patients' understanding of that information was poorer than physicians realized. Communication in medical settings continues to be an important topic in health psychology (see chapter 5).

Thus, the study of compliance was also important because it led to a more in-depth study of the patient–physician relationship. Indeed, the term *compliance* has come under fire because of its implication that the physician–patient relationship is unidirectional (DiMatteo, 1991). Health psychologists criticized the expectation that the physician should give the orders and that patients should passively follow those orders.

More Attention Is Paid to the Ways People Cope

Four years after the review paper by Krantz and colleagues, Rodin and Salovey (1989) published another review of health psychology. By 1989, some new topics had emerged. For example, research attention was being paid to the ways in which people *coped* with illness and everything that went along with it, such as hospital stays and the impact of illness on relationships with others. At this time, health psychologists were attempting to identify **coping styles**—patterns in the ways people deal with difficult situations.

> **coping styles:** strategies that an individual employs to deal with stresses caused by ever-changing demands of the environment.

One good example of coping styles is Suzanne Miller's notion of *monitors* and *blunters* (Miller, 1980). **Monitors** are information seekers; **blunters** are information avoiders. The coping style of each type of person is consistent with that person's desire for receiving or avoiding information. This is just one example of how people differ in the ways they cope with illness and the challenges it brings. We will look more closely at these and other coping styles in chapter 6, when we talk about hospital stays and medical procedures, and again in chapter 8 in our discussion of chronic and life-threatening illness.

> **monitors:** people who seek information in their attempts to cope with illness and its accompanying challenges.
>
> **blunters:** people who avoid information in their attempt to cope with illness and its accompanying challenges.

The Introduction of Psychoneuroimmunology: Finding Links between Psychological and Biological Processes

In 1996, Cohen and Herbert approached health psychology by focusing exclusively on **psychoneuroimmunology (PNI)**. This is the study of the relationship between our psychological state and the functioning of our immune system, a relationship alluded to by Miller in 1983 and studied in more detail in recent years. The breakthrough in this area came with the development of techniques to quantify the status of our immune systems (called **immunocompetence**) through blood tests and saliva samples. This advance made PNI extremely important because it provided an opportunity for health psychology to produce empirical proof of hypothesized relationships between mind and body.

> **psychoneuroimmunology (PNI):** the study of the relationship between psychological states and the functioning of the immune system.
>
> **immunocompetence:** the extent to which our immune system is functioning properly to ward off micro-organisms.

In truth, PNI had been introduced well before the mid-1990s. In fact, a prominent book on the subject was published in 1981 (Ader et al., 1981). Since then, our knowledge of PNI has been significantly advanced by a number of researchers. One of the more prolific is Janice Kiecolt-Glaser, who has been publishing extensively on the subject of PNI since the mid-1980s. She has looked at such diverse psychological states and situations as marital conflict (Kiecolt-Glaser et al., 1987a) and caregiving for patients with Alzheimer's disease (Kiecolt-Glaser et al., 1987b) in terms of their effects on the immune system. (For a current review of Kiecolt-Glaser's work, see Glaser & Kiecolt-Glaser, 2005). We present a detailed examination of PNI in chapter 4.

An article by Andrew Baum and Donna Posluszny (1999) in the *Annual Review of Psychology* summarized the field of psychoneuroimmunology. Their paper provided an excellent overview of the ways in which all the major relevant topics since Miller's 1983 article had coalesced and evolved into the current perspective on health psychology. Baum and Posluszny covered the following topics, all of which we discuss in following chapters: stress and health (chapter 3), health-enhancing and health-impairing behaviours (chapter 10), and behaviours related to seeking and consuming health care (chapters 7, 8, and 10). A more recent review has focused on the contributions psychological theory can make to the self-management of chronic illness (Leventhal, et al., 2008).

Summary

When we compare these approaches to health psychology, it becomes clear that the topics being studied have changed much less than the ways in which we view them. From the strong behavioural roots of Miller and others, our thinking has expanded to include theories featuring a more cognitive approach. Today, health psychologists use interventions that combine behavioural and cognitive theories, evidence of which you will see in this book.

WHY HAS HEALTH PSYCHOLOGY COME INTO PROMINENCE?

The Health Psychology section of the Canadian Psychological Association (CPA) is one of the association's larger sections. There are many reasons for its importance, not the least of which are the changes in health and illness patterns in this country and elsewhere in the second half of the twentieth century.

Changing Profiles of Illness and Health in Canada

A comparison of mortality statistics over the course of the twentieth century reveals that the major causes of death today are quite different from those of just 50 or 100 years ago. In 1900, the most common cause of death in North America was acute, infectious disease—namely, respiratory diseases such as influenza and pneumonia (Sexton, 1979) (see Figure 1-1). By 1950, the leading cause of death in Canada had become circulatory disease (heart and cerebrovascular disease), while cancer had become the second leading cause, ahead of respiratory diseases (Wilkins, 1995). This was still true in 2003, with circulatory illnesses and cancer accounting for 60 percent of all deaths in Canada in that year (Statistics Canada, 2005).

When psychologists look at this change, they focus on the *preventability* of these diseases. As Neal Miller pointed out in 1983, it was around the middle of the twentieth century that lifestyle replaced microbiology as a major source of life-threatening conditions. Hence we see the rationale for behavioural medicine, which is concerned with the relationship between health and behaviour. It should also be noted, however, that comparing the Canadian death rates in 1950 and 1993 reveals a dramatic 57 percent drop in deaths from circulatory disease, a trend that continued to the end of the century. Much of this decline can be attributed to lifestyle change, so it becomes clear that the increased

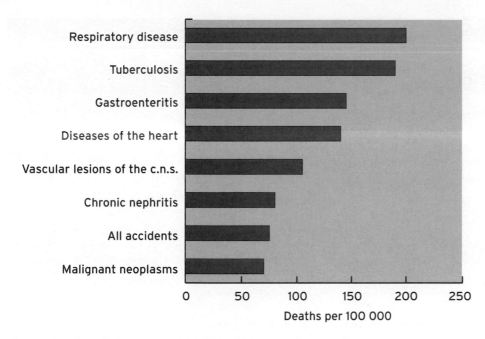

Figure 1-1 Death Rates per 100 000, 1900

Source: Sexton, M. M. (1979). Behavioral epidemiology. In O. F. Pomerleau & J. P. Brady (Eds.), *Behavioral medicine: Theory and practice* (pp. 3–22). Baltimore, MD: Lippincott, Williams & Wilkins.

propensity for diseases that are triggered by lifestyle can also be reduced by different lifestyle choices—lifestyle choices that are, in many ways, a psychological phenomenon. Returning once again to our case study, it is possible that lifestyle change will be the most pressing challenge facing Alan as he approaches life after his heart attack.

In Canada, 53 percent of men and 49 percent of women report being active or moderately active (Shields & Tremblay, 2008). This means that they engage in vigorous activities, such as calisthenics, jogging, racquet sports, team sports, dance classes, or brisk walking for a period of at least 30 minutes, three times or more per week. Men who are inactive by these criteria are 1.4 times more likely to be obese. Inactive women are 2.3 times as likely to be obese (Shields & Tremblay, 2008). Even with encouraging activity statistics, 23 percent of Canadian adults were obese in 2004, as measured by the Canadian Community Health Survey. In the United States, 30 percent of adults were obese (Statistics Canada, 2004).

While the data on adult activity levels does offer some encouragement, the data on childhood and adolescent obesity is now very worrisome. In 1978, three percent of children between the ages of two and seventeen were obese. In 2004, eight percent of that age group were obese (Shields, 2006). In Canada, this equates to 500 000 children (Statistics Canada, 2004). To demonstrate the behavioural and socioeconomic components of these statistics, research has shown that being overweight or obese is 39 percent more common among children who buy their lunch than among those who take a packed lunch to school from home (Canadian Institute for Health Information, 2005). Also, rates of obesity are increasing more rapidly among children from lower income families (Oliver & Hayes, 2008).

Comparing Canadian Health Status to Other OECD Countries

The Organisation for Economic Co-operation and Development (OECD) was founded by 12 countries in 1960. Currently, the OECD comprises 30 countries, all producing comparative research and publications on economic and social issues. OECD members are often used as comparison points for countries like Canada.

The Canadian Institute for Health Information (2005c) reports that, in 2001 and 2002, fewer Canadians died of cardiovascular disease than did people in most of the OECD countries. In those years, the cardiovascular disease death rate for Canada was 182 per 100 000 people. Only

3 of the 30 OECD countries had lower rates (Japan, France, and Spain).

On the other hand, the number of Canadians dying from lung cancer in 2001 and 2002 was higher than the OECD median (47 per 100 000 in Canada compared to an OECD median of 37). Female deaths from lung cancer in Canada were almost seven times higher than in 1960. For males in Canada, the rate has almost doubled since 1960—even though Canada has the lowest rate of daily smokers among OECD countries (17 percent in 2003).

If you have ever tried to quit smoking or make some other significant and lasting change to your lifestyle, it is likely that you encountered some psychological barriers along the way. Of those Canadians who have successfully quit smoking, the average number of attempts before stopping for good is 3.2 (Health Canada, 2004b). To successfully quit, you must *learn* new behaviours and *unlearn* old ones. You have to *believe* that you are capable of making the change. Other people might be involved who could make the change easier or more difficult. Even from this brief analysis, we can see that learning theory, cognitive psychology, and social psychology are all relevant to lifestyle change, which has become an integral part of our health and wellness in the new millennium.

Alan, from our case study, will be encouraged to learn new ways of thinking and behaving that will result in reduced stress, greater relaxation, and improved fitness. These changes will also have a social component, as family and friends will be called upon for support.

Multiple Perspectives Are Needed to Understand Health and Health Statistics

Another reason for the growth of health psychology is that it provides helpful ways to understand the statistics describing our health. For example, male deaths from cancer in Canada rose by over 35 percent in the second half of the twentieth century (Public and Population Health Branch of Health Canada, 2000; Wilkins, 1995). Which perspective provides us with the best way to respond to this new reality in ways that will affect that statistic? Biomedical research, for example, may focus on the biology of **malignant neoplasms**, cancerous growths that may be treated by radiation and chemical therapy. This is a valuable perspective, but is there more to the story? Just as we discovered when talking about Alan's heart attack, there are additional perspectives that will help us better understand cancer statistics.

malignant neoplasms: cancerous growths that may be treated by radiation and chemical therapy.

Perhaps we can learn more by looking at the *types* of cancer that account most for this 35 percent increase. Lung cancer had the highest mortality rate of all cancers, accounting for 26 percent of all cancer deaths in 2003 in Canada. This indicates that there is more at work than a random and unfortunate growth of neoplasms. Lung cancer is linked to a behaviour—smoking. Psychologists can make valuable contributions to the modification of this behaviour from what they know about attitude change, persuasion, and addiction. They can help reduce the number of smokers and thus reduce death rates resulting from lung cancer. And, in fact, lung cancer deaths for men fell slightly from 2002 to 2003.

We have shown that patterns of illness and health are changing in Canada. Also, there has been a change in emphasis from cure to prevention. To understand these changes and to improve health and health care, we need to acquire the knowledge of many disciplines. This is the essence of the **biopsychosocial approach** (Engel, 1977). As the term implies, this model considers biological, psychological, and social factors affecting health. We will take a close look at this approach in the next section. At this point, it is important to understand that psychology has much to offer in our attempt to understand as much as we can about health and illness.

biopsychosocial approach: a model that suggests that biological, psychological, and social factors are all involved in any given state of health or illness.

HEALTH PSYCHOLOGY TODAY

In this section, we will begin by introducing the most fundamental assumption of the field, as captured by the biopsychosocial approach. We'll then look at what this approach means for psychologists working in health care settings. From there, we'll move to an overview of prominent theories in the field today and conclude with a look at what people with training in health psychology actually do.

A Biopsychosocial Approach to Health

It is essential to understand that both good health and poor health can be attributed to a multitude of causes. Further, these causes are varied enough that they cannot be understood from any one perspective, whether in medicine or the social sciences. The biopsychosocial approach to health takes all of these various perspectives into account, acknowledging that biological, psychological, and social factors combine to influence our health.

The term *biopsychosocial* refers to three major perspectives on the causes of health and illness. As we move from the biological to the psychological to the social, we move from a microscopic perspective to a macroscopic one. For example, we can study cancer at a biological cellular level by analyzing neoplasms (new growths), at a psychological level by assessing patients' coping abilities and the correlations between stress and immune function, and at a sociological level by identifying government policies that affect environmental toxins or hospital regulations that affect the nature of treatment.

Why Is a Biopsychosocial Approach So Important?   Mortality statistics make it clear that many life-threatening conditions are preventable, in some cases by inoculation, in others by lifestyle changes, and in others by government policies such as seat-belt legislation. Only the biopsychosocial approach encompasses all these levels. Even the common cold has psychological and sociological causes. Our immune systems are affected by our psychological state (for a review, see Cohen & Herbert, 1996), so we are more likely to catch a cold when we have endured something stressful, and we often catch colds from people with whom we interact at work and in other social settings.

What Are the Implications of the Biopsychosocial Approach for Health Psychologists?

Today, the adoption of the biopsychosocial approach demands clear communication between health care practitioners and social scientists as well as a mutual respect for the potential contributions each can make to health and health care. It makes no more sense for a physician to downplay psychological factors affecting patients than it does for psychologists to say that viruses, tissue damage, and neoplasms are of little consequence.

Clear communication between practitioners and social scientists requires mutual understanding. This doesn't mean that social scientists must have all the knowledge of a physician or that physicians must be trained psychologists, but it does require a mutual appreciation for each other's potential contributions to the understanding of health and illness. For a number of reasons, however, achieving this mutual appreciation can be difficult because of the different ways in which health care professionals are trained.

biomedical model: an approach suggesting that health is best understood in terms of biology.

Medical practitioners are trained primarily in the **biomedical model**. According to this model, as the name implies, health is best understood in terms of our biology. Students of the biomedical model are taught that the model is precise and concrete, which might make this model easier to understand; however, it is a daunting task to learn enough human biology to be able to practise medicine. The time required often results in the exclusion of other models of health and well-being. It stands to reason, then, that the dedication required to cope with the reams of material presented in medical school also demands a strong belief in the efficacy of the biomedical model.

The end result, understandably, is that most medical school graduates are firmly entrenched in that model. Other approaches—for example, those from the social sciences—seem much less precise and far too abstract by comparison. The psychosocial causes of disease cannot be viewed under a microscope or measured directly via blood tests or a CT scan. This abstractness can undermine a physician's view of the credibility of disciplines like health psychology.

For their part, psychologists also have beliefs specific to their discipline that are not always considered legitimate by people outside the field. For example, psychologists are trained to believe that behavioural phenomena can be reliably measured, that correlations as small as 0.3 can be meaningful, and that there are attributes shared by large groups of people that go beyond how many kidneys or lungs they have.

The different emphases in training result in graduates with different perspectives, a conclusion that is well illustrated by health psychologist Robin DiMatteo, who describes a tour a physician gave her through a hospital's intensive care unit (ICU). The physician was justifiably excited by the recent acquisition of new equipment for the ICU. Dr. DiMatteo, on the other hand, had her attention drawn in different directions:

> I remember feigning interest in the newly acquired machinery, little of which I understood, and I congratulated everyone on this up-to-date facility. But as I looked around to where the loved ones of the intubated people were waiting, I tried to catch a glimpse of their faces. My concern was not with the tremendous technical advances in the intensive care unit (ICU). As a psychologist, my focus was on the loved ones of those in the ICU, people who were suddenly forced to have their lives revolve around the ICU, where they waited day after day for some news that their child, spouse, relative, or friend might survive and someday be normal again. (DiMatteo, 1995, p. 217)

Intensive Care Units feature impressive technology and intense psychology.

The point of this example isn't that the physician's focus was misguided in concentrating on the new equipment in the ICU but that many phenomena need attention in a place like the ICU. Robin DiMatteo and other health psychologists provide expertise that fills in other pieces of the puzzle implied by the biopsychosocial approach.

As we mentioned earlier, the biopsychosocial approach grew, in part, from a change in the causes of life-threatening illnesses. Psychological and behavioural factors became more significant, and it became clear that psychological causes and consequences are associated with *many* aspects of our health, not just those that result in mortality statistics. As a result, the way we train people to become psychologists working in health care needs to reflect the biopsychosocial approach (Levant, 2005).

Prominent Theories in Health Psychology

We began this chapter by defining health psychology. We then looked at how it developed from its early years and why it has grown so rapidly. Next, we looked at the overarching model in modern health psychology—the biopsychosocial approach. Now it is time to look into the "tool kit" of today's health psychologists. In it are a number of useful theories that help health psychologists understand health issues so they can help people recover from illness or injury and stay healthy.

Quite a few theories have emerged to help us understand, predict, and affect health behaviour. It is helpful to be able to group these theories into categories as Christopher Armitage and Mark Conner do in their review of social cognition models of health behaviour (Armitage & Conner, 2000). They present three categories: motivational models, behavioural enaction models, and multi-stage models. (Our list of theories will not be exhaustive at this point. Rather, we discuss some of the most prominent to give you a sense of the work that health psychologists do in research and intervention.)

To illustrate these models, we return to our case study of Alan, who, as you will see in Case 1-2, is home from the hospital and has been put on a rehabilitative recovery plan.

CASE 1-2 ALAN REVISITED: THE ROAD BACK

Alan spent five days in the cardiac care unit of the hospital. His moods swung between fear and frustration. He certainly didn't want another heart attack, but he had a business to run and countless other responsibilities. He felt that the people in cardiac care didn't appreciate this. They kept telling him to try and relax—easy for them to say.

Now that he was home convalescing, it was even harder to "relax." He had so much to do and think about. On top of it all, the cardiologist had given him a bunch of pills to take and a strict diet to follow. And then there was the Healthy Heart program that he was expected to start attending on a weekly basis at the hospital.

Health care professionals were asking Alan to rethink his life's priorities, change the way he ate, and start the Healthy Heart program. Would Alan do all these things? It is an important question, since Alan's life might depend on it. The theories we look at in this section will help us predict the answer.

Motivational Models   Motivational models of health behaviour are based on the assumption that behaviour follows *intention*—we must intend to do something before we will actually do it. For example, a study of pregnant women found that their intentions (whether or not they intended to breastfeed their babies and, if so, for how long) were predictive of their actual behaviour, in combination with their early breastfeeding experiences (DiGirolamo et al., 2005).

However, while there is some correspondence between intention and action, the fact that this correspondence is far from perfect is a source of criticism for these models, because they attempt to predict intention and not actual behaviour.

The Health Belief Model One of the most well developed and useful contributions psychology has made to the understanding of health is the **health belief model** (Becker, 1974; Rosenstock, 1974). This model represents a good entry point for our exploration of the psychological component of the biopsychosocial approach. A *health belief* is something we think to be true concerning our health. For example, we might believe that a low-fat diet will improve cardiovascular health or that modern medicine can cure most ailments. There are many different health beliefs.

The health belief model starts with the reasonable assumption that health behaviours are explained by our health beliefs. This is a good start, but we really need to know *which* specific health beliefs are most closely linked to behaviour if the model is to be of value.

To this end, the health belief model is valuable because it identifies a manageable number of relevant, measurable types of health beliefs that can predict health behaviour. In its most basic form, the model focuses on two beliefs—the belief that a health threat exists and the belief that a given course of action will affect the threat. Perceived threat is determined by our beliefs about vulnerability and the possible severity of an outcome.

Here is an everyday example. When the weather channel reports a 100 percent chance of rain on a day when you must go outdoors, you know you are personally vulnerable to rain, but the *consequence* isn't particularly severe so you don't believe a threat exists. On the other hand, if you read that one in three people will get cancer, you develop a belief regarding the likelihood that you could be that one (personal vulnerability), as well as a belief regarding how bad it would be to get cancer (severity of consequences). These beliefs affect your perception of threat and, in turn, affect your cancer-preventing behaviours, such as using sunscreen.

There are two types of beliefs that influence the fundamental confidence you have that a course of action will *reduce* a threat. First, there is something called a **response efficacy belief**. This refers to the extent to which you think a course of action (e.g., a preventive behaviour or treatment) will actually work. Second, there is a **cost–gain belief**, which refers to your assessment of the costs associated with this action (e.g., effort, discomfort, embarrassment, or inconvenience) compared to the benefit of the behaviour to your health. For example, if someone believes that the gains of exercise seem distant and minor compared to the costs, such as effort and short-term fatigue, then exercise behaviour is unlikely.

Table 1-1 contrasts the beliefs of two people (Person A and Person B). In this case, we use the model to predict condom usage. At the top of the table are two general beliefs: that a health threat exists and that a behaviour can affect the threat. Beneath that is a list of specific beliefs related to these general beliefs. The next two rows provide examples of those related beliefs for each of these fictitious people.

Person A believes himself to be somewhat vulnerable and that the consequences of contracting acquired immunodeficiency syndrome (AIDS) are severe (i.e., fatal). He also believes that condoms work and that the costs of using them are outweighed by the benefits. As a result, Person A uses condoms. In contrast, Person B feels little vulnerability, doesn't think AIDS is necessarily fatal, does not believe in the effectiveness of condoms, and thinks the personal costs of using them are high. Not surprisingly, this person doesn't use condoms.

health belief model: a model that analyzes health behaviour in terms of the belief that a health threat exists and the belief that a given course of action will affect the threat.

response efficacy belief: the perception that a threat-reducing strategy will work.

cost–gain belief: an individual's assessment of the costs associated with a course of action (e.g., effort, discomfort, embarrassment, or inconvenience) compared to the benefit of the behaviour to the individual's health.

Table 1-1 The Health Belief Model Applied to Condom Usage

General Belief	A health threat exists		A behaviour will affect the threat		Result
Related Beliefs	Beliefs regarding personal vulnerability to the threat	Beliefs about the severity of the consequences	The belief that a course of action will actually work or not	The assessment of the costs and benefits associated with this action	
Person A	"I could get AIDS."	"AIDS is a fatal disease."	"Using condoms will greatly reduce my chances of getting AIDS."	"I get embarrassed when I buy condoms, but they will reduce the risk of getting AIDS."	Condoms are used
Person B	"Other people might get AIDS but I won't."	"With new drugs, AIDS isn't as life-threatening as it once was."	"Condoms don't always work."	"I feel very embarrassed when I buy condoms and using them ruins sex."	Condoms are not used

The beliefs in this example have been intentionally polarized to make the contrast clear. In reality, a person may hold a range of beliefs working together in such a way that prediction of behaviour is more difficult. For example, a woman might believe that she could get cervical cancer and that it could be fatal. She might think the costs of screening are low but lacks confidence in the accuracy of the Pap test used in the screening, so she doesn't think screening is effective. What could we predict here? Perhaps sporadic Pap tests? It is difficult to be certain.

And what about Alan? The health belief model can help us predict the likelihood that he will attend the Healthy Heart program. To start, we need to know if Alan believes he is vulnerable to a second heart attack, and if so, whether he thinks its consequences would be severe. In fact, he does believe that people who have had one heart attack are at increased risk for a second and are much less likely to survive it.

Now we move to his beliefs regarding the behaviour that is supposed to affect that threat—the Healthy Heart program. We already know that he has considered the costs of attending. He is busy and thinks it will be inconvenient. And what about his efficacy belief? Does he think the program will reduce the threat of a second heart attack? If he does, then he might attend. The problem is that he must *keep attending*; therefore, his belief in the efficacy of the program must be strong enough to keep him going.

Health Beliefs and Health Values   The health belief model attempts to predict behaviour using a person's specific beliefs. There is one more important factor to consider, however: the extent to which the person values good health. Even if a person's beliefs appear to predict a particular behaviour, such as condom use or screening for cancer, the behaviour will not follow unless the person values his or her health.

It may be difficult to imagine that there are people who do not place a high value on their health. However, research indicates that people do indeed vary in terms of

According to the health belief model, this person felt vulnerable to SARS and believed that it was serious and that wearing a surgical mask would reduce his chances of contracting SARS at a Toronto Blue Jays game.

their health values. To understand this, we must view values as being relative to each other. For example, an adolescent might value health to a certain extent, but he or she might value group acceptance more. This person might take up smoking, in spite of the fact that it compromises health, to achieve the more valued outcome of group acceptance.

It is also possible that some people can *afford* to place health values high on their list while other people must be more concerned with basic survival. This does not mean that people living in poverty do not value their health. A study of homeless women, for example, found that health and self-respect were two commonly held values (Rosengard et al., 2001). In fact, women generally tend to value their health more than men do (Felton, Parsons, & Bartoces, 1997). Clear reasons exist, then, for individual differences in health values. These differences are important to consider because research has shown that the health belief model is most predictive for people who place a high value on their health (Lau, Hartman, & Ware, 1986).

How Well Does the Health Belief Model Predict Behaviour?   If the health belief model is to be useful, it must do a better-than-chance job of explaining and predicting health-related behaviour for those individuals who place a relatively high value on their health. For health psychologists, it is important to investigate the model's utility because the model has the potential to make significant contributions to the biopsychosocial understanding of health and illness. Given this importance, it is not surprising that a great deal of research has been conducted over the years testing the ability of the health belief model to explain and predict behaviour in a wide variety of

Table 1-2 The Health Belief Model Applied to the Decision to Have Back Surgery

General Belief	A health threat exists		A behaviour will affect the threat		Result
Related Beliefs	Beliefs regarding personal vulnerability to the threat	Beliefs about the severity of the consequences	The belief that a course of action will actually work or not	The assessment of the costs and benefits associated with this action	
Stan	*"I definitely have a back problem."*	*"I am in pain. I can't work and I can't enjoy my life."*	*"Surgery will correct this problem."*	*"I'm nervous about the possibility of being paralyzed but the risk is low."*	Surgery chosen

health-related contexts, from youth cigarette smoking (Li et al., 2003) to osteoporosis prevention (Silver Wallace, 2002).

One area in which the health belief model has been used extensively is in risky behaviours related to AIDS. DiFranceisco and colleagues (1998) used the health belief model to predict whether or not gay/bisexual men would complete a small-group program in HIV risk reduction. The health belief model has also been used to explain some of the variance in sexual risk behaviours among college students, such as having multiple partners and being intoxicated or high during sexual encounters. It was less helpful, however, when it came to predicting condom usage for this group (Lollis, Johnson, & Antoni, 1997).

The health belief model has also been used extensively in predicting behaviours associated with screening for cancer. In general, these behaviours can be analyzed reasonably well using the health belief model, given that important issues of perceived vulnerability and belief in the value of early detection fit well within the model. For example, a study in Ontario has shown that, consistent with the model, women with a relative who has had breast cancer are more likely to be interested in genetic testing for cancer than are women without this family history (Cappelli et al., 2001). The model is far less than perfect in this context, though, because of other psychological factors. Perhaps the most notable is the role that *emotion* plays in cancer screening. People might believe in the accuracy of a given screening technique and see cancer as a threat. However, they might not want to know if they have cancer (Cameron, 1997). Such a discovery would constitute too great a cost of the behaviour (e.g., Millar, 1997). For another example, see Table 1-2 for an application of the health belief model to the decision to have back surgery.

The Theory of Reasoned Action The **theory of reasoned action** (Ajzen & Fishbein, 1980; Fishbein & Ajzen, 1975) has a number of elements in common with the health belief model and adds some other considerations. The two main elements of the theory of reasoned action are a person's attitudes toward a behaviour and a person's beliefs regarding other people's thoughts about the behaviour. It is this introduction of other people's beliefs that most strongly differentiates the theory of reasoned action from the health belief model. In the language of the theory, other people's beliefs help us to develop **subjective norms**—what we think other people want us to do.

theory of reasoned action: a theory that behaviour is preceded by intention and that our intention is influenced by beliefs about the behaviour and subjective norms.

subjective norms: beliefs regarding what others think we should do and the extent to which we are motivated to go along with these people.

Baby Think It Over®: A Program Encouraging Teens to Rethink Their Chances of Getting Pregnant

One reason why teens might engage in unprotected sex is that they have an "it can't happen to me" belief regarding pregnancy. Using the language of the health belief model, they have low perceived vulnerability to pregnancy. But what if they had the chance to experience what it was like to look after a baby? Would this change their beliefs? Two researchers from the University of Windsor, Jennifer Out and Kathryn Lafreniere, have tested the effect of a program called Baby Think It Over®, which is intended to address these questions (Out & Lafreniere, 2001).

In this program, teens work with infant simulators (essentially, high-tech dolls) for two or three days to develop an appreciation for what it is like to have to look after a baby. After going through the program, a group of males and females aged 14 to 19 were more accurate at assessing the risk of unplanned pregnancy and at producing real examples of the consequences related to raising children than were a control group of teens. In other words, an experience that simulated the responsibilities of child rearing affected their perceptions of vulnerability to pregnancy and the consequences of having a child.

According to the theory of reasoned action, our attitudes toward a behaviour and our subjective norms determine our intention regarding the behaviour. As in the health belief model, we have related beliefs to consider for each of these two main elements of the theory of reasoned action. Specifically, our attitudes toward a behaviour are influenced by our beliefs regarding the *outcomes* that behaviour will yield and the extent to which we *value* that outcome.

Subjective norms are composed of beliefs regarding what others think we should do and the extent to which we are motivated to go along with these people. To put all this together and apply the theory to health, we will look at Table 1-3, which charts two people facing a decision regarding treatment of back pain. Person A believes that the surgery will work, so she sees a connection between the behaviour (surgery) and the outcome (pain relief). She values a pain-free existence. Her friends and family are in favour of surgery, and she wants them to have a favourable impression of her. These beliefs lead to a decision to choose surgery.

In contrast, Person B is not convinced of the efficacy of the surgery, nor does he place as high a value on being pain free. His subjective norms oppose surgery; namely, his wife favours exercise over surgery, and he values her opinion. Consistent with these beliefs, he does not choose surgery.

As we did with Table 1-2 in relation to the health belief model, in Table 1-3 we have presented two people with diametrically opposed views. In reality, our beliefs are more mixed than this. We may really want to engage in a health-related behaviour (be it surgery, a low-sodium diet, etc.) but find that our friends are opposed to it. The process by which we *choose* the people whose opinions we will consider can also be quite complicated (Kahneman & Miller, 1986). For example, we take into account such things as friendship and how similar these people are to us. This is part of the social component of the biopsychosocial approach.

Table 1-3 The Theory of Reasoned Action

General Beliefs	Attitudes toward the behaviour		Subjective norms		Result
Related Beliefs	Belief that the behaviour will produce given outcome	The value placed on the outcome	Beliefs regarding what other people think regarding the behaviour	Motivation to do what other people think should be a done	
Person A	*"Surgery will relieve the pain in my back."*	*"I would love to be pain free again."*	*"My friends and family think I should have the back operation."*	*"I want my friends and family to know I have the courage to have the operation."*	Surgery chosen
Person B	*"Surgery might not work. There's no guarantee."*	*"Being pain free isn't really possible. Everyone lives with some degree of pain."*	*"My wife thinks I should try bed rest before risking surgery."*	*"My wife is usually right."*	Surgery not chosen

How Well Does the Theory of Reasoned Action Predict Health Behaviour?   Modern research has used the theory of reasoned action to address many of the same phenomena as the health belief model. Thus, we find studies testing the power of the theory of reasoned action for predicting HIV risk and prevention behaviours (for a comprehensive review, see Crepaz & Marks, 2002), teen sexual behaviour (Frigon, 2004), and cancer-screening behaviours (e.g., Barling & Moore, 1996). (For a review of the applications of the theory of reasoned action, see Bogart & Delahanty, 2004.)

The literature indicates that the theory of reasoned action does a good job of predicting behaviours related to HIV and AIDS prevention. The addition of social norms tends to increase its predictive power compared to the predictive power of the health belief model. For example, the theory of reasoned action worked well to predict both intention and actual condom use among high-risk heterosexual teens (Morrison et al., 2000).

In terms of cancer-screening behaviour, the theory of reasoned action quite accurately predicts the intention to perform self-examination (breast and testicular) (Moore, Barling, & Hood, 1998). The theory has also been used to explain differences in women's intentions to be screened for cervical cancer via a Pap smear test (Barling & Moore, 1996). The theory of reasoned action has also been used to help understand gender differences in such health behaviours as sunscreen use (Abroms et al., 2003); females are more likely than males to use sunscreen (Campbell & Birdsell, 1994) and to be influenced by subjective norms as derived from family members. Abroms and colleagues found that young adults' beliefs about sunscreen use were divided along traditional gender lines. Females talked about the importance of skin care, which motivated them to use sunscreen. Males talked about skin care as being a feminine concern, and thus something that would not motivate them to use sunscreen.

perceived behavioural control: the belief that a specific behaviour is within one's control.

The Theory of Planned Behaviour   The predictive power of the theory of reasoned action is generally improved with the addition of the notion of **perceived behavioural control**

(Millstein, 1996). In other words, beliefs about the effectiveness and costs of a given behaviour are augmented by beliefs about one's ability to actually carry off the behaviour. This is consistent with the thinking of Fishbein and Ajzen, the psychologists who proposed the theory of reasoned action in 1975. In fact, Fishbein and Ajzen developed a hybrid theory that included perceived behavioural control and named it the **theory of planned behaviour** (Fishbein & Ajzen, 1975).

The only difference between the two theories is the addition of the belief that the person is actually capable of performing the behaviour. "Can I really quit smoking?" "Can I go through with the operation?" These are questions about perceived behavioural control. The answer must be "yes" for the theory of planned behaviour to predict that intention will follow belief.

The theory of planned behaviour can be a powerful tool to help explain variation in health-related intention and behaviour. For example, the theory helped predict binge drinking among university students (Johnston & White, 2003). In other words, the elements of the theory combine to correlate significantly with adolescents' reports of intention to drink. As one might expect, the theory of planned behaviour has been used as often as the theory of reasoned action to analyze a wide range of behaviours, including condom use and drinking and driving (Armitage, Norman, & Conner, 2002), and the use of dental floss (Lavin & Groarke, 2005). Also, interventions intended to help people with issues such as rehabilitation after cancer have been shown by researchers at the University of Alberta to be effective when perceived control was one of the targets of that intervention (Jones, Courneya, Fairey, & Mackey, 2005).

How can the theory of planned behaviour help us predict whether our case study subject, Alan, will attend the Healthy Heart program? To answer this question, consider each of the elements of the theory. First, like the health belief model, there are Alan's beliefs regarding the efficacy of the program and the value he places on not having another heart attack. Then there are the subjective norms. Would other people want him to go to the program? For example, his wife might really encourage him to attend, or she might see it as an unnecessary inconvenience, as Alan does. Also, we must know whether Alan is motivated to do what his wife thinks he should do or whether he would rather assert his independence and either not go or go in opposition to her wishes. Finally, there is perceived behavioural control. Does Alan really believe that he can do the things the Healthy Heart program will expect of him in terms of exercise, diet, tests, and so on? According to the theory of planned behaviour, the answers to these questions will determine whether Alan intends to go to the program. Research has shown that heart patients' beliefs about subjective norms and perceived behavioural control accounted for 69 percent of the variance in exercise rates (Prapavessis et al., 2005).

Behavioural Enaction Models   You may have heard the saying, "The road to ruin is paved with good intentions," implying that there is often a considerable gap between what we *intend* to do and what we *actually* do. For the most part, motivational models address intention, while behavioural enaction models attempt to improve our ability to predict and affect behaviour by addressing the gap between intention and behaviour. Behaviour enaction models add elements that bridge this gap.

Gollwitzer's Implementation Intentions Model   Gollwitzer's model (1993) contains many of the same elements as the motivational models but posits that people

theory of planned behaviour: behaviour is preceded by intention and that intention is influenced not only by subjective norms and beliefs about the efficacy of the behaviour, but also by the belief that one is actually capable of performing the behaviour.

who have an implementation plan are much more likely to engage in the behaviour. Such a plan indicates a higher level of commitment, just as when an organization strikes an implementation committee with a mandate to make something happen. Not surprisingly, research shows that such implementation plans do increase the likelihood that a behaviour will be enacted (Verplanken & Faes, 1999).

Bagozzi's Goal Theory Bagozzi's goal theory (1992) is similar to Gollwitzer's model but also considers a person's thoughts about the nature of the goal and the expression of intentions about the goal. Is the goal something I can attain—for example, reduced alcohol consumption (Murgraff, Walsh, & McDermott, 2000)? How would I feel if I succeeded? If I failed? You will recognize these as questions about perceived control and cost–gain analysis. This form of cost–gain thinking, however, entertains the possibility of fear of success and fear of failure.

Multi-Stage Models Multi-stage models provide a step-by-step explanation for how someone develops intention and then carries the intention through to behaviour, both short term and long term. Like all stage models, the ones that are used to analyze health behaviour are questioned regarding their rigidity. Do people have to go through these stages in this order? Can't someone skip a stage? Regress backward? And so on. In spite of these questions, stage theories have been influential in health psychology because they help us understand the progression of an individual's thinking and behaviour.

When we look at the topic of health promotion in chapter 12, we will see that an important challenge for health psychologists involves helping people make changes to their lives. In many cases, these changes involve aspects of lifestyle, as we have seen with Alan in Cases 1-1 and 1-2. In others, changes are forced upon us by illness, accident, or aging. Because change is such a major topic, models that describe the ways people go about effecting change (or not) are most helpful. Multi-stage models provide just such descriptions.

The Health Action Process Approach (HAPA) In HAPA, Schwarzer (1992) divides health behaviours into a motivational phase and a volitional phase. In the former, the person develops expectations regarding the outcomes being considered. Will I feel better if I engage in this behaviour? Will I be supported in my change? The person also perceives control. Am I capable of making this change? If the answers to these questions are positive, the person moves to the volitional phase, featuring planning, action, and maintenance of the change.

The Stages of Change Model The **stages of change model** (Prochaska & DiClemente, 1983; 1986), sometimes called the transtheoretical model, contains many of the same elements as HAPA, but provides six linear stages to help understand change: precontemplation, contemplation, action, maintenance, termination, and relapse. These stages are relatively simple to comprehend, and they can be valuable as a way to understand health behaviour—in particular, behaviour involving a lifestyle change. One of the most common applications of the stages of change model is to smoking cessation. Smokers in the precontemplation stage have not thought about quitting and see no need to do so. Smokers in the contemplation stage may have some symptom or nagging thought that has them considering quitting. In the next stage, they take action. Perhaps they visit their physician, or use patches, or make a pact with a friend. If the action works, then they must maintain their non-smoking behaviour. Eventually, after three

Stages of Change and Support for Government Quit-Smoking Programs

Researchers at the University of Toronto have applied the stages of change model to assess smokers' and former smokers' knowledge of the health consequences of smoking (Cohen et al., 2002). They hypothesized that the higher a person's stage in the model, the more knowledge the person would have regarding health consequences.

Remember that current smokers will be placed at one of two stages when it comes to quitting smoking: precontemplation or contemplation. Former smokers, on the other hand, could be placed at either of three different stages: action, maintenance, or termination. (Relapse was not included in this study.)

Cohen and colleagues provided operational definitions of each stage and then collected survey data from 846 people in Ontario to determine their knowledge of the health consequences of smoking. They asked questions about such things as smoking and lung cancer, chronic bronchitis, pregnancy complications, heart attacks, and environmental tobacco smoke. They did not stop there, however. They also reasoned that smokers' or former smokers' positions on the stages of change model would be related to their attitudes toward and support for government legislation regarding tobacco control measures. To test this, they also asked questions about these attitudes.

The researchers did indeed find that the further along the stage model the person was placed, the more knowledge the person had regarding health consequences. This was particularly true for the current smokers, who showed greater knowledge on seven of eight knowledge questions the further they were along the stages that applied to them. For the former smokers, this increase in knowledge across the stages applied to only two of the knowledge questions. The Cohen group also found that attitudes toward tobacco control and support for government control measures increased along the stages of the model.

These findings are interesting for at least two reasons. First, the study has implications for the health promotion programs designed to help people quit smoking. We will look closely at health promotion in chapter 12. It is simplistic to assume that smokers are not receptive to stop-smoking messages. Rather, precontemplative smokers are most likely to be unreceptive. Also, people in this category are the least well informed regarding health consequences. Second, this study extends the stages of change model. The model was originally introduced to help explain *behaviour*. Cohen and colleagues have used the model to help understand *cognition*.

years or more of abstinence, they would be considered to be in the termination stage (Gilpin, Pierce, & Parkas, 1997).

One of the most valuable contributions of the model is the acknowledgement of relapse as a stage rather than as failure. This allows people to deal with a bout of cigarette smoking as something that is part of the process, rather than as a sign that the entire lifestyle change has failed. They can then get back into the maintenance stage, rather than starting over.

Summary of the Models   You may have wondered, as you read through these theories, just how well they apply across different cultures. For example, the notion of internal perceived behavioural control tends to make more sense to people who have been raised in **individualist** rather than **collectivist** cultures (Hart & Poole, 1995; Triandis et al., 1988). Individualists focus on independence and self reliance, whereas collectivists see themselves as part of a greater whole in which individualism is less important than allegiance to the group.

The theory of reasoned action and the theory of planned behaviour have been tested with Latin American, English-speaking Caribbean, and South Asian participants (Godin et al., 1996). The study concluded that the theory of planned behaviour was more useful

individualist: one who focuses on independence and self-reliance rather than placing group needs above his or her own.

collectivist: one who considers him- or herself to be part of a greater whole and who considers individualism to be less important than allegiance to the group.

in these three cultures than the theory of reasoned action, even though these cultures would be considered more collectivist than most Western cultures. The theory of reasoned action has also been used successfully to analyze breastfeeding patterns in the United States and Colombia (Ramirez, Bravo, & Katsikas, 2005).

We introduced you to some of the major theories and models common to health psychology to give you an idea of some of the ways psychological theory has been applied to health and health care. The theories and models presented in this chapter grow, for the most part, from a cognitive perspective, with their focus on people's thought processes, attitudes, and beliefs. Of course, there are many other theories, some with a stronger behavioural emphasis, others more humanistic or psychodynamic. We refer to such models and theories throughout the remaining chapters of this book. We invite you to think critically about their utility and about ways in which they could be further developed to be even more useful.

WORKING IN HEALTH PSYCHOLOGY

Health psychology is a field that offers a number of interesting career opportunities, the vast majority of which require a graduate degree, usually a Ph.D. There are two main paths you can take when preparing for a career in health psychology: one is to be trained as a clinical or counselling psychologist, the other is to be trained as a researcher.

Clinical and Counselling Psychologists Working in Health Psychology

Clinical psychologists and counselling psychologists require different training and perform different roles in health psychology. Clinical psychologists must have either a master's or a doctoral degree, depending on the province or territory in which they are practising. The Canadian Psychological Association has recommended that all clinical psychologists hold a Ph.D. Clinical training usually involves a year of internship, and in some jurisdictions students must pass a certification exam in order to practise clinical psychology.

Counselling psychologists do not require a Ph.D., though some have one. The certification process for counselling psychologists tends to be less rigorous than for clinical psychologists. In fact, in some jurisdictions no formal training is required to call oneself a counsellor. Usually, however, counsellors working in health settings have formal training, at least at the master's level.

Clinical health psychologists work with people who are experiencing psychological problems that are either the result of illness or a cause of it. For example, they may work with cancer patients who are suffering from depression or breast reconstruction patients who are grappling with issues related to self-image. They may also work with people who suffer from anxiety and, as a result, are dealing with psychosomatic disorders.

Two major surveys have been conducted to learn more about the work these psychologists do. The first survey was conducted in 1982 (Arnett, Martin, Streiner, & Goodman, 1987), the second in 1999 (Humbke et al., 2004). A comparison of the two studies reveals a considerable increase over time in the number of psychologists working in acute-care hospitals. In 1982, 54 percent of acute-care hospitals employed at least one full-time psychologist. By 1999, that number had jumped to 68 percent (Humbke et al., 2004). This means that, in 1982, there was one psychologist for every 131 acute-care hospital beds. In

1999, there was one psychologist for every 53 beds (Humbke et al., 2004). One of many reasons for this increase in the number of psychologists working in health care is the growing emphasis on prevention and health promotion in Canadian health care (Kenkel, Deleon, Mantel, & Steep, 2005).

The three most common topics addressed by these hospital psychologists were pain, eating disorders, and cancer. Within those topics, mental health and rehabilitation were the most common areas where challenges were addressed. Over 80 percent of these referrals to psychologists came from physicians, and the majority of the hospital psychologists' work involved individual psychotherapy (Humbke et al., 2004).

Counselling psychologists work with people facing similar challenges. For example, a counselling psychologist might work with a family in which a member is seriously ill. Another might work with someone who is recovering from an injury or illness and is trying to integrate back into work and society. As is the case with clinical health psychologists, there is plenty of work for a skilled counselling psychologist in health-related settings. Counselling psychologists' salaries tend to be somewhat lower than those of clinical psychologists, though they can still do very well financially. Similar work might also be conducted by people in other helping professions, such as social work.

Research Careers in Health Psychology

Not all people working in health psychology have clinical training. Some are trained in other fields, such as social or developmental psychology, and they apply the theories of those disciplines to health and health care. Indeed, some of the major theories we introduced earlier in the chapter were forwarded by social psychologists. A good example is the theory of reasoned action developed by Fishbein and Ajzen. Instead of providing clinical services, psychologists from these other areas conduct research and consult with health professionals regarding aspects of health care delivery.

Most people conducting research in health psychology hold academic appointments at universities, though some are employed by other institutions, such as hospitals and cancer agencies. Most hold doctoral degrees. Those working in universities combine their research duties with teaching and other academic responsibilities. Of course, clinical work and research are not mutually exclusive; many people do both, within private practice, institutional appointments, or university positions.

CHAPTER SUMMARY

Health psychology is the application of psychological principles to the diagnosis and treatment of an illness as well as to people's attempts to maintain health and well-being.

Health psychology grew from behavioural and cognitive perspectives. The early focus was on affecting health-related behaviour. This expanded to include the relationship between people's thinking and their health. Behaviour, thought, and emotion have all been tied to physiological processes through the study of psychoneuroimmunology.

Health psychology has grown quickly as a field due to the changing nature of modern health problems. Over the last hundred years, the main causes of death have changed; today more people die from lifestyle choices than from bacterial infections. As a result, a comprehensive understanding of health requires a multi-disciplinary approach that includes social sciences such as psychology.

The Health Belief Model analyzes health behaviour in terms of the belief that a health threat exists and the belief that a given course of action will affect the threat.

The Theory of Reasoned Action posits that behaviour is preceded by intention and that intention is influenced by beliefs about the behaviour and subjective norms.

The Theory of Planned Behaviour is similar to the Theory of Reasoned Action but adds that intention is influenced not only by subjective norms and beliefs about the efficacy of the behaviour, but also by the belief that one is actually capable of performing the behaviour.

Career opportunities in health psychology include clinical psychologist (requiring a Ph.D.), counselling psychologist, and research psychologist. Some people with advanced degrees in health psychology work in hospitals; others work in higher education.

Review Questions

1. What is health psychology, and what other terms are used to describe the work conducted in this area?
2. How has health psychology developed over the years?
3. Why has the field of health psychology grown rapidly in recent years?
4. What is meant by a biopsychosocial approach to health?
5. What are the prominent theories used in health psychology?
6. What sorts of career opportunities are available in the field, and what training is required for them?

Chapter 2
Systems of the Body

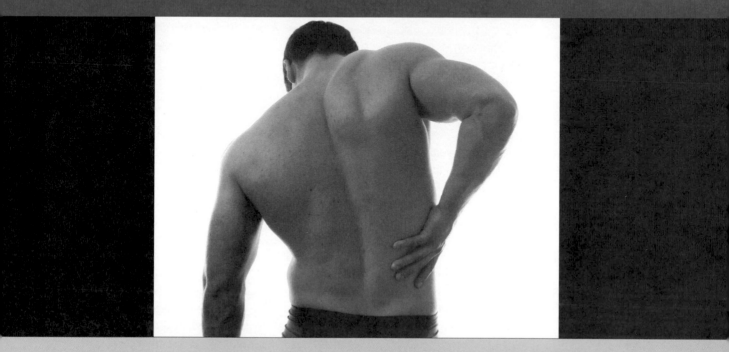

Learning Objectives

After studying this chapter, you will be able to

- Name the main components of the primary systems of the body and provide fundamental explanations of the functions they perform

- Give examples of what happens when each system malfunctions or is compromised

- Relate each system to at least one chapter of this Health Psychology text

Like most people, Pat did not like hassles. At work, he was happiest when he was left in peace to develop the spreadsheets his boss required for weekly sales meetings. He was certainly not very happy when his boss came by and complained that he needed more detail from Pat's reports, or that he needed them sooner, or that the column headings didn't make sense to anyone. To Pat, this felt like a barrage of criticisms raining down on him while he was trying to do his work. In fact, these interactions infuriated Pat. It was all he could do to keep himself from lashing out at his boss, saying something that he might regret or that might even get him fired.

Then one day, during a routine physical exam, Pat's doctor discovered that Pat's blood pressure had increased since his last physical. When he asked Pat about life at home and at work, Pat explained how angry he got at work and how this anger also surfaced when he drove in traffic or waited in line at the bank. Pat's doctor suggested that, at these times of intense anger, Pat's blood pressure might be spiking even higher. He recommended that Pat seek help to control his anger, for the health of his heart as well as for the sake of his happiness.

Health psychologists are concerned with the relationship between psychological states and biology, so they need to know how the biological systems of the body work. Pat's story demonstrates a relationship between emotional experience and blood pressure. As you read through this book, you will find many examples that demonstrate relationships like this one, like the work of University of British Columbia psychologist Wolfgang Linden, who uses the laboratory to simulate Pat's experience. Linden and his colleagues measure physiological responses, such as blood pressure, during these situations. Linden would probably agree with the physician's suggestion that Pat's blood pressure rose in response to his boss's criticisms (e.g., Anderson, Linden, & Habra, 2005).

To better understand what is happening to Pat, you need to know something about the cardiovascular system. It would also help to know something about other systems of the body, such as the endocrine system, which controls our hormone levels. In fact, each chapter in this book will make more sense if you know about the systems of the body that relate to the topics being discussed, whether that topic is pain, stress, immunology, or chronic illness such as cardiovascular disease and cancer.

For this reason, it is important to discuss systems of the body before launching into other topics central to health psychology. This chapter provides a basic introduction to these complex fields as they relate to health psychology. We begin with a look at *homeostasis,* which is a fundamental concept important to many of the body's systems and to health psychology. We then look at the major systems, relating each to topics in health psychology.

HOMEOSTASIS

For the systems of the body to function well, they must work within a stable internal environment. This stable environment is called **homeostasis**, involving such elements as body temperature and blood pressure, as well as levels of carbon dioxide and electrolytes (e.g., salt). In addition to *requiring* homeostasis in order to function properly, the systems of the body also share responsibility for *maintaining* this internal stability.

We describe homeostasis in terms of a stable internal environment, but that does not mean this environment never changes. On the contrary, when we go outside on a winter morning, for example, our body temperature drops. When we exercise, our temperature rises. In an attempt to maintain homeostasis, the systems of the body produce shivering (to warm the body) or sweating (to cool it). Thus, homeostasis requires a constant monitoring of our internal states and a response to changes, much in the way the thermostat monitors the temperature in your home. When the temperature falls below your preselected "ideal," that is, the temperature that you have indicated on your thermostat, the heat comes on (via your furnace or electric heaters). When the temperature rises above that setting, the furnace shuts off or a cooling system is activated. Your thermostat constantly monitors the temperature inside your home to maintain the temperature you have chosen. Like your home thermostat, the adjustments required by the body to maintain homeostasis might be short term and rapid, or they may be longer term in nature.

Psychological factors can also affect homeostasis, which represents a good starting point for a discussion of body systems. For example, emotions might be antagonistic to the systems of the body that are working to return your internal environment to normal levels. If the emotion is fear or anxiety rather than excitement, and if those emotions are common in your life, then this antagonism can be chronic and have negative effects on your health by causing, for example, increased blood pressure or blocked arteries (which occur when we mobilize our stores of fat during fight-or-flight responses).

homeostasis: the dynamic physiological response on the part of the body to maintain a stable internal state in spite of the demands of the environment.

THE NERVOUS SYSTEM

Homeostasis requires good communication systems within the body. The body communicates with itself in a number of ways, most commonly via electrical impulses conducted through nerve cells, or **neurons**. The nervous system consists of a remarkably complex collection of these neurons and other nerve fibres, as well as the brain and spinal cord. The nervous system is our primary communication system.

In terms of nerve cell function, an important distinction is made between neurons that take impulses to the brain, called **afferent neurons**, and those that take impulses away from the brain, called **efferent neurons**. Both afferent and efferent neurons communicate with each other via neurotransmitters that travel across a gap between neurons called the **synapse**. The biochemistry of *synaptic transmission* focuses on neurochemicals or neurotransmitters that are secreted or received by neurons, allowing for communication between cells (see Figure 2-1).

This is not a book on neurophysiology, so we will not be going into detail regarding cellular structure and activity. However, it is worth remembering that synaptic transmission is affected by our psychological state and, in reciprocal fashion, affects our psychological experience. Many diseases of the nervous system involve problems in neural transmission, and these diseases tend to be chronic and challenging in terms of coping.

neurons: nerve cells.

afferent neurons: nerve cells that conduct impulses from a sense organ to the central nervous system, or from lower to higher levels in the spinal cord and brain.

efferent neurons: nerve cells that take impulses away from the brain.

synapse: a gap between neurons that is crossed by neurotransmitters that neurons use to communicate with each other.

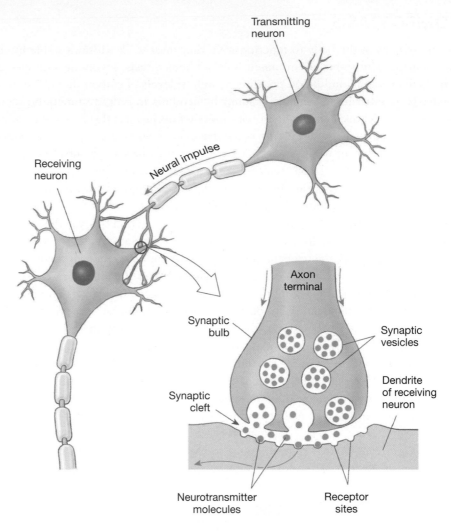

Figure 2-1 Neurotransmitter Crossing a Synapse

Neurotransmitters released by a transmitting neuron cross the synaptic gap and are taken up by receptor sites on the receiving neuron.

Source: *Invitation to Psychology,* Second Canadian Edition, by Wade, Tavris, and Poole, © 2006, p. 117. Reprinted with Permission of Pearson Canada.

central nervous system: the division of the nervous system that is composed of the brain and the spinal cord.

peripheral nervous system: the division of the nervous system that is made up of the somatic nervous system and the autonomic nervous system (which is further divided into the sympathetic and the parasympathetic nervous systems).

Examples include multiple sclerosis, in which nerve cells lose their outer layering (myelin sheath), and myasthenia gravis, which can be caused by an inability to produce certain neurotransmitters. People with multiple sclerosis may experience double vision, numbness, extreme fatigue, loss of bowel or bladder control, speech difficulties, and poor motor control. People with myasthenia gravis may have blurred vision, drooping eyelids, and difficulty eating because of problems with chewing and swallowing.

The cells of the nervous system are grouped within central and peripheral systems to work in harmony. The **central nervous system** consists of the cells that make up the brain and the spinal cord. The **peripheral nervous system** connects the central system to the outer reaches, or the periphery, of the body.

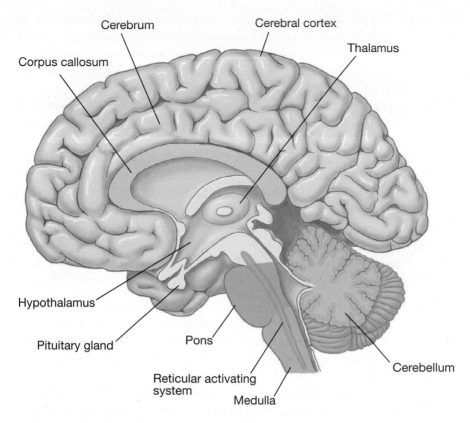

Cerebrum Cerebral cortex Thalamus
Corpus callosum
Hypothalamus
Pituitary gland Pons
Reticular activating system
Medulla Cerebellum

Figure 2-2 The Human Brain

This is a cross section of the human brain, showing the right hemisphere.

Source: *Invitation to Psychology,* Second Canadian Edition, by Wade, Tavris, and Poole, © 2006, p. 123. Reprinted with Permission of Pearson Canada.

The Central Nervous System (CNS)

You have probably heard important offices called the "nerve centre" of an organization. That metaphor is taken directly from the central nervous system. The main components of the CNS are neurons and **glial cells**. Glial cells make up about 90 percent of CNS cells (Sherwood, 2004), and they are the support system for neurons, providing nourishment and helping neurons maintain proper physical orientation to each other. (*Glia* means "glue" in Greek.)

In addition to the work of glial cells, the rather fragile cells of the central nervous system are protected by bone, membranes, and fluid. There is also a **blood–brain barrier** that acts as a sentinel for materials that enter the brain via the bloodstream. These protective mechanisms are very relevant to health psychologists, because diseases involving these mechanisms, including virtually all diseases of the nervous system, tend to be serious and very taxing on a patient's coping resources.

One such nervous system disease is **meningitis**, which is an inflammation of the membranes that protect the brain and spinal cord. It takes its name from the *meninges,* the membranes that provide further protection and keep the fluid contained within the CNS. There are three of these membranes, positioned between the protective bone layer

glial cells: make up about 90 percent of CNS cells and are the support system for neurons, providing nourishment and helping neurons maintain proper physical orientation to each other. (*glia* means "glue" in Greek).

blood–brain barrier: acts as a sentinel for materials that enter the brain via the bloodstream.

meningitis: an inflammation of the membranes that protect the brain and spinal cord. It takes its name from the *meninges,* the membranes that provide further protection and keep the fluid contained within the CNS. There are three of these membranes, positioned between the protective bone layer and nerve tissue.

and nerve tissue. The infection in meningitis can be either viral or bacterial. The distinction is important because bacterial meningitis tends to be more serious than viral meningitis. Viral meningitis often resolves itself without specific treatment, whereas bacterial meningitis can result in brain damage, hearing loss, learning disabilities, or death (Centers for Disease Control and Prevention, 2005).

The symptoms of meningitis in people over the age of two include high fever, headache, and stiff neck. In newborns and small infants, symptoms of meningitis can be difficult to detect. Babies with meningitis may appear inactive or irritable. They may vomit or not feed well (Centers for Disease Control and Prevention, 2005). Given the seriousness of the disease, babies under the age of three months who present with what is called "fever without a source" are now routinely tested for meningitis and infections of the bloodstream and urine. The test includes using a needle to take a sample of spinal fluid from the lower portion of the spine via a *lumbar puncture*, a painful procedure that both babies and parents find stressful. However, early detection of meningitis is very important, allowing for the correct identification of the particular bacteria involved and, thus, the correct treatment. Vaccines are also available to help reduce the risk of contracting infections that could lead to meningitis.

The Brain   If we depend upon communication among neurons to carry out all things human, then, in addition to this system of neurons spread throughout the body, it would make sense to gather many neurons together to maximize the number of synapses and the speed of those synaptic transmissions. We do, indeed, have this large bundle of neurons. It is called the brain.

The various neurons of the brain have specialized functions. They are grouped within the brain and on its surface according to these functions. Thus, we can map out the brain, which is important because it allows us to predict the result of damage or disease to particular areas of the brain and to know which areas are affected when we observe specific symptoms (see Figure 2-2).

At the base of the brain is an area called the **brain stem**, which connects the brain to the spinal cord. The brain stem controls some very basic functions, such as breathing and sleep–wake cycles. It is also involved in maintaining posture and balance. Above the brain stem is the **cerebellum**, literally meaning "little brain." Anatomically, the cerebellum looks like a miniature brain attached to the back of the larger structure. It contributes to our control of balance and the coordination of voluntary movement.

Sitting below the centre of the brain is the **hypothalamus**, an important structure even though it is only about the size of a lima bean. The hypothalamus is a central control mechanism for homeostasis. For example, the hypothalamus is responsible for maintaining a steady body temperature, and it also monitors hunger and thirst. The hypothalamus and the pituitary gland combine to form a significant communication point between neural and hormonal systems. This combination helps the hypothalamus control sexual behaviour and reproduction. Above the hypothalamus is the **thalamus**, which manages synaptic input to the brain, sending impulses to the appropriate part of the brain.

Capping these and other internal structures of the brain is the cerebral cortex (see Figure 2-3). *Cortex* means "surface." It is highly folded, substantially increasing its surface area and allowing for numerous neurons and more cerebral activity. The cerebral cortex is divided into *hemispheres*, or sides, and is also separated into four functional areas called *lobes*, which can be thought of roughly as corners (to the extent that something essentially round can have corners).

brain stem: an area at the base of the brain that connects the brain to the spinal cord. The brain stem controls some very basic functions, such as breathing and sleep–wake cycles. It is also involved in maintaining posture and balance.

cerebellum: the "little brain," the cerebellum appears above the brain stem. It contributes to our control of balance and the coordination of voluntary movement.

hypothalamus: portion of the brain that initiates the stress response in both the nervous system and the endocrine system.

thalamus: located above the hypothalamus, it manages synaptic input to the brain, sending impulses to the appropriate part of the brain.

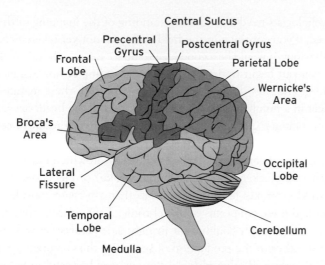

Figure 2-3 A Map of the Major Regions of the Brain's Cortex
This is a cross section of the human brain, showing the right hemisphere.

The **occipital lobes**, at the back of the brain, contain the visual cortex and are responsible for interpreting impulses that come in through light-sensitive receptors, the rods and cones in the eyes. The **temporal lobes** are on either side of the head, in the vicinity of the ears. This can help you remember that the temporal lobes are responsible for interpreting sound. The **parietal lobes** arc across the top back portion of the head, from the occipital lobes forward to the **frontal lobes**. The parietal lobes are responsible for processing sensory information other than hearing and vision, such as touch and temperature regulation. The frontal lobes are responsible for a number of main functions, including voluntary movement, language, thought processing, and emotion. The parietal and frontal lobes are separated by a deep channel called the *central sulcus*.

A ridge of tissue running across the top of the head, roughly from ear to ear and immediately in front of the central sulcus, is responsible for controlling voluntary movement. This is called the motor cortex. The motor cortex can be precisely mapped, identifying areas of the cortex responsible for movement of specific parts of the body. Generally, the lower part of the motor cortex, near the temporal lobes, is responsible for facial movement, and the upper portion of the cortex, at the top of the head, is responsible for limb and trunk movement. The hands are controlled by a large area in middle of the motor strip. It is not surprising that so many cells are dedicated to the hands, given the intricacy of hand movement.

The **sensory cortex** is another ridge of tissue running alongside the motor cortex, responsible for sensory activities in specific parts of the body as well as for processing sensations from the skin, muscles, and joints.

We should also note that each hemisphere of the motor strip controls the opposite side of the body—the left hemisphere controlling the right side, the right hemisphere controlling the left side.

Language and speech production are controlled by two cortical areas that, in most people, are located in the left hemisphere. **Broca's area**, located just in front of the base of the motor strip, controls the production of speech, while **Wernicke's area** (pronounced VER-nik-uh's), located at the junction of the occipital, parietal, and temporal lobes, controls the understanding and interpretation of language.

occipital lobes: contain the visual cortex and are responsible for interpreting impulses that come through light-sensitive receptors in the eyes.

temporal lobes: responsible for interpreting sound.

parietal lobes: responsible for processing sensory information other than hearing and vision, such as touch and temperature regulation.

frontal lobes: responsible for voluntary movement, language, thought processing, and emotion.

sensory cortex: responsible for sensory activities in specific parts of the body as well as for sensations from the skin, muscles, and joints.

Broca's area: the part of the brain that controls speech production.

Wernicke's area: the part of the brain that controls the understanding of language.

Health psychologists need a good understanding of the mapping of the brain and its functions. Indeed, if you continue in the field and have not yet taken a course dedicated to brain and behaviour, it would be a good idea to do so. Even with the quick tour we have provided here, you can begin to develop an understanding of how damage to the brain may manifest itself and how difficult it can be to cope with these manifestations. Brain damage can occur in a number of ways, including blows to the head, oxygen deprivation, or the growth of tumours. Oxygen deprivation may occur as a result of **cerebrovascular accidents**, known more commonly as strokes.

Strokes are a form of cardiovascular disease (CVD) in which blood flow to the brain is disrupted, either by blockage (called **ischemic stroke**) or blood vessel rupture (called **hemorrhagic stroke**). Strokes result in symptoms that can cause considerable disruption in a person's life, and these symptoms can be chronic. Thus, a stroke that deprives the left hemisphere of its blood supply could result in right-side paralysis as well as disruption in language abilities, either in the production of speech or the comprehension of language, or both. Speech therapy and other physical therapy may be useful in helping stroke victims regain at least some of their previous levels of functioning. Such therapy can, however, be a major test of perseverance and mood. Moreover, a stroke may cause a personality change, which can be difficult for the patient as well as for family and friends.

Strokes are just one of many ways in which brain function can be disrupted. We haven't even begun to talk about such things as dementia, Alzheimer's, cerebral palsy, or epilepsy, which we will discuss in chapter 8 and elsewhere in this book. Many psychological issues are associated with diseases and disorders of the brain, such as changes in cognition, memory impairment, perceptual disturbances, and disturbances in consciousness.

Psychologists have an important role to play in helping people cope with other problems of the CNS, such as spinal cord injury (SCI). Such injuries can result in the loss of leg movement (paraplegia) or, if the damage is high on the spine, the loss of movement of all limbs (quadriplegia). Obviously, the physical and psychological adjustments a person must make in coping with SCI are significant. Not surprisingly, more than 100 studies have been published in psychology journals investigating factors that affect coping among people with SCI (see, for example, Martz, 2005).

The Peripheral Nervous System

Spinal cord injury can cause paralysis in the limbs when a connection is severed between the central nervous system's spinal cord and the peripheral nervous system, interrupting the neural pathways that take impulses to and from the spine and the brain.

Earlier in this chapter, we said that pathways taking impulses to the brain are called *afferent*. These **sensory afferents** carry sensory information to the brain via the spinal cord—information about temperature, pressure, and pain (originating from the skin), or about body position and balance (from the muscles, joints, skin, and inner ear). They may also carry information regarding vision, hearing, taste, and smell directly to the brain without engaging the spinal cord. Sensory afferents are affected by psychological states. In chapter 11, we discuss theories of pain and the use of distraction and other pain-management techniques.

As we mentioned earlier, pathways taking impulses from the brain are called *efferent*. The efferent pathways of the peripheral nervous system can operate voluntarily or involuntarily. Voluntary activity is the responsibility of the **somatic nervous system**, which controls skeletal muscles. Involuntary activity is the responsibility of the **autonomic nervous system**,

cerebrovascular accidents (strokes): a form of cardiovascular disease (CVD) in which blood flow to the brain is disrupted.

ischemic stroke: a stroke that is caused by blockage.

hemorrhagic stroke: a stroke that is caused by blood vessel rupture.

sensory afferents: carry sensory information to the brain via the spinal cord.

somatic nervous system: responsible for voluntary activity and controls skeletal muscles.

autonomic nervous system: responsible for involuntary activity and controls the cardiac muscle of the heart, smooth muscle of the internal organs, and most glands. This system is very important in the maintenance of homeostasis.

which controls the cardiac muscle of the heart, the smooth muscle of the internal organs, and most glands. Because of what it controls, the autonomic nervous system is very important in the maintenance of homeostasis. This maintenance is achieved via **sympathetic** and **parasympathetic** systems within the autonomic nervous system. The sympathetic and parasympathetic systems work together in an *antagonistic* manner, in that while one will be working to increase an organ's activity, the other will be working to decrease it. Thus, these two systems allow the body to adjust to changes that require more or less activity.

For example, sympathetic stimulation increases your heart rate, whereas parasympathetic stimulation decreases it. Sympathetic stimulation disrupts the digestive tract, whereas parasympathetic stimulation aids digestion (Sherwood, 2004). Have you ever felt a bit queasy just before or during an exam or other stressful situation? The feeling of "butterflies in the stomach" is an example of sympathetic stimulation overriding parasympathetic stimulation of the digestive tract.

Generally, then, sympathetic stimulation is required to mobilize the body for stress or challenge. We discuss this notion of fight-or-flight further in chapter 3 when we discuss stress and again in chapter 4 when we talk about how stress affects the immune system. By contrast, the parasympathetic system returns the body to homeostatic levels of functioning and is most active when we are at rest. For this reason, it is often seen as the system that "calms" the body after its fight-or-flight response and has been called the regulator of the "rest-and-digest" response.

THE ENDOCRINE SYSTEM

The endocrine system is a collection of glands found throughout the body, from the brain to the genitals. These glands share one important trait: They secrete hormones. These hormones then travel via the bloodstream to their intended targets to regulate the targets' functions. The targets contain cells that respond to specific hormones. In this way, certain glands can control specific activities.

As we discuss the various systems of the body, keep in mind that there is considerable overlap among them. For example, the endocrine system, along with the nervous system, is considered one of the two major regulatory systems in the body. The main difference is that the endocrine system specializes in long-term control compared with the rapid responses afforded by the nervous system. Nevertheless, as we will illustrate further in chapter 3 when we talk about the physiology of stress, the endocrine system works with the nervous system to help the body cope with stressful situations. In addition, the endocrine system helps control such developmental phenomena as growth and metabolism.

The main control centres for the endocrine system are found in the brain: the hypothalamus, which we mentioned in our discussion of the brain, and the pituitary gland, which sits below the hypothalamus in the interior of the brain. The pituitary gland produces hormones that stimulate other glands rather than organs. Hormones produced to stimulate other glands are called **tropic hormones** (*tropic* means "having an affinity for"). One example of a tropic hormone that is relevant to psychology is the **adrenocorticotropic hormone**, or **ACTH**. ACTH is produced by the anterior (front) lobe of the pituitary gland; it stimulates the adrenal gland to produce cortisol, a hormone that is important in the stress response. In chapter 3 we show that, while cortisol aids in

sympathetic nervous system: the system responsible for the "fight or flight" response when triggered by the hypothalamus (e.g., faster heartbeat, increased blood pressure).

parasympathetic nervous system: the component of the autonomic system that re-establishes homeostasis in the system and promotes the reconstructive process following a stressful experience.

tropic hormones: hormones produced to stimulate other glands.

adrenocorticotropic hormone (ACTH): a tropic hormone produced by the anterior lobe of the pituitary gland; stimulates the adrenal gland to produce cortisol, a hormone that is important in the stress response.

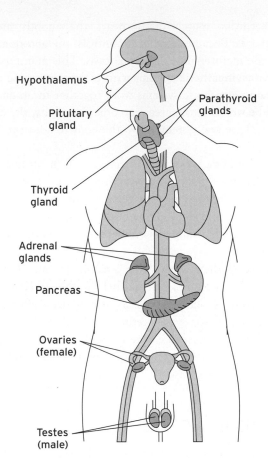

Figure 2-4 Major Glands of the Endocrine System for Males and Females

potentially adaptive fight-or-flight responses along with the nervous system, prolonged production of cortisol can be unhealthy.

The thyroid gland and the adrenal gland are two important glands in the endocrine system. The thyroid produces hormones that help regulate growth and immune function. The adrenal gland produces cortisol (among other hormones), which provides energy by helping the body convert stored proteins and fats into glucose. Other glands are shown in Figure 2-4, including those responsible for sexual function and reproduction.

While a given gland may produce a specific hormone that can stimulate a specific target, the full story is often much more complex than that. In fact, some glands produce more than one hormone. The pituitary gland is a good example: It produces eight. To make matters even more complicated, a given hormone may be secreted by more than one type of gland and may have more than one target cell. And a target cell may have a collection of receptors, making it responsive to more than one type of hormone. Somehow, in spite of these complexities and the fact that secretion rates vary over time, the endocrine system works, and correct hormone levels are usually maintained. However, this is not always the case. A common disease that results from a malfunction in the endocrine system is **diabetes**. Diabetes is caused by too little secretion (hyposecretion) of insulin, which is a hormone produced by the pancreas. Insulin aids in the body's ability to convert blood sugar to energy. More specifically, insulin lowers blood sugar levels, while glucagon raises them. As the disease affects the body's ability to regulate this balance, extreme fatigue becomes one of the symptoms of diabetes. In Chapter 8, we will discuss psychological issues related to diabetes, a disease that affects more than one million Canadians (*Diabetes in Canada*, 2003). For example, diabetics can have difficulty doing what is necessary to monitor and control insulin levels.

THE IMMUNE SYSTEM

The immune system is designed to monitor the invasion of micro-organisms in the body and prevent their spread and growth by eliminating them. Micro-organisms come in many different forms. In terms of the immune system, the relevant forms include bacteria, viruses, parasites, and fungi. These invading microbes are called **antigens**. The term *antigen* generally refers to any micro-organism that stimulates the production of antibodies. If these antigens have the potential to cause disease, they are called **pathogens**.

The immune system is our guard against infection and the growth of cells associated with disease. The immune system's first line of defence is a combination of skin and mucus, which stops most antigens. People who suffer serious burns are at risk for life-threatening infection because the skin's ability to prevent the invasion of pathogens is compromised and the internal components of the immune system are unable to deal with such a massive invasion. These internal components of the immune system work by producing cells that are designed to attack antigens and eliminate infected cells. In this section, we will provide a basic introduction to these immune-system cells. This will help you make sense of the research in psychoneuroimmunology that assesses the number and efficacy of these cells, which we will discuss in chapter 4.

When our immune system detects an antigen, it acts in one or more ways to eliminate it. This action can be specific or non-specific in nature. As the term implies, **specific immunity** refers to protection against a particular antigen. This immunity is acquired sometime after birth and is the result of exposure to the antigen, either by having contracted the disease or by having received an inoculation that gives the body a non-toxic dose of the antigen. This is called acquired immunity.

Specific immune function is the consequence of acquired immunity. There are three aspects to its effective functioning—memory, specificity, and tolerance (Seymour, Savage, & Walsh, 1995). **Immune system memory** refers to the ability of certain immune system cells to adapt to an antigen and to "remember" the antigen and work to eliminate it when it encounters the antigen again. Not only will the immune cells recognize the antigen, they will also react much more explosively upon subsequent exposure to it. For example, once you have had chicken pox, it is unlikely that you will contract the disease again because your immune system has acquired a *memory* for the virus that causes chicken pox.

It is for this reason that we are more susceptible to certain diseases when we travel to foreign destinations. We increase our chances of encountering a pathogen (in the drinking water, for example) for which we have no immune system memory. By contrast, the water doesn't bother the locals, because they have cells (B lymphocytes) that have a memory for the particular pathogen, and they produce the antibody to deal with it before it causes any trouble.

diabetes: a common disease that results from a malfunction in the endocrine system. Diabetes is caused by too little secretion (hyposecretion) of insulin, which is a hormone produced by the pancreas. (*See also insulin-dependent diabetes and non-insulin-dependent diabetes in the glossary.*)

antigens: micro-organisms that are foreign to our physiology.

pathogens: antigens that have the potential to create disease.

specific immunity: protection against a particular antigen.

immune system memory: the ability of certain immune system cells to adapt to an antigen, to remember the antigen when it encounters it again, and to work to eliminate it.

B lymphocyte cells: cells that, when re-encountering a specific pathogen, produce an antibody designed to eliminate the pathogen.

seroconversion: the production of antibodies by memory B-cells when exposed to a specific previously encountered and remembered antigen.

helper T-cells: cells that produce substances called *interleukins* that speed the division of B lymphocyte cells.

suppressor T-cells: cells that stop the production of antibodies after the antigen has been destroyed.

specificity: ability of certain immune system cells to remember an antigen and respond only to the remembered antigen.

tolerance: the ability of immune system cells to remember and respond to a remembered antigen while not reacting to the body's own cells.

non-specific immunity: general protection against antigens, rather than against one specific antigen.

A T-cell in action. In the first photo, the T-cell makes contact with the antigen. In the second, it creates holes in the antigen by hitting it with protein. In the third, little is left of the antigen.

B lymphocytes produce antibodies that attack antigens. A particular kind of B lymphocyte, called memory B-cells, develops a memory for a specific antigen after being exposed to it and acts only on that specific antigen by producing antibodies. The anti-tetanus antibody is an example. The production of these antibodies is sometimes called **seroconversion**.

B lymphocytes need help to produce antibodies. This help comes from T lymphocytes called **helper T-cells**. These helper cells produce substances called interleukins, referred to generally as *cytokines,* that speed up the division of B lymphocyte cells. Journal articles documenting research in psychoneuroimmunology often refer to interleukin-1 or interleukin-2. Interleukin production is a measure of how well our immune system is functioning (immunocompetence). These helper T-cells are also referred to in the literature as CD4. Interleukin-6, for example, is called a *pro-inflammatory,* because it aids in immune responses that result in inflammation. Our immune system also needs an "off switch" so that antibodies aren't produced unnecessarily after the antigen has been destroyed. This is the job of **suppressor T-cells** (sometimes referred to as CD8). B-cells and T-cells work together to maintain our immunity.

An important point to realize is that the process involved in this form of immunity takes time. In fact, it takes B lymphocytes five or more days to generate specific antibodies (Maier, Watkins, & Fleshner, 1994). Fortunately, in most cases the immune system generates antibodies faster than the antigen can multiply. There are many million different antigens, and the body simply cannot keep a plentiful stock of the antibody required for each. Instead, it keeps a small supply of each and relies on the B lymphocytes to generate an ample number when called upon to do so, which takes time. Fortunately, memory B lymphocytes allow this process to occur more quickly if we are re-exposed to the antigen. This is how the inoculations we receive before travelling work. Inoculations present the body with small dosages of a given pathogen so that we can produce antibodies and develop a memory for the pathogen. That way, if we do encounter the pathogen when travelling, our immune systems can produce cells quickly and deal with it while we relax on the beach.

Specificity implies that the B lymphocyte not only will remember this antigen, but also will respond to this antigen *only*. Having chicken pox does not make you immune to the mumps or the measles. **Tolerance** means that these cells will not react to the body's own cells—what is called "the self" in the language of immunity. Instead, immune cells react only to antigens, which are recognized as "non-self."

Non-specific immunity differs from specific immunity in that it relies on a system we are born with. Non-specific immunity works in a number of different ways. In one process, the immune system creates chemicals, called *antimicrobial substances,* that kill antigens. One result of this process can be seen by the naked eye: inflammation. An infected cut will usually become inflamed because fluids carrying white blood cells enter the area,

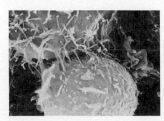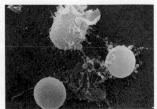

making it red as the fluids build up. In other words, inflammation is an indication that an immune system is working.

Lymphocytes, then, are important components of the immune system. They include B-cells, T-cells, and **natural-killer (NK) cells**. Natural-killer cells "seek and destroy" cells that are infected, cancerous, or altered in some other way.

When our immune system works well, it defends us against pathogens, removes cells that have ceased to function properly, and identifies and destroys abnormal or mutant T-cells that we have produced. When our immune system functions poorly, however, it not only "lets its defences down," but also can turn against itself to create allergies, which are the result of the immune system mistaking a harmless antigen for a pathogen. Or, it can cause **autoimmune diseases**, which occur when the immune system works against the body's own cells. One of the best-known autoimmune diseases is arthritis, which we discuss in chapter 8. The immune system can also attack organ transplantations, which is a problem that must be addressed for patients receiving kidneys, hearts, or other organs from donors (Sherwood, 2004).

natural-killer (NK) cells: cells that have the specific job of "seeking and destroying" cells that are infected, cancerous, or altered in some other way.

autoimmune diseases: occur when the immune system works against the body's own cells. One of the best-known autoimmune diseases is arthritis.

THE CIRCULATORY SYSTEM

In chapter 1, Case 1-1 introduced Alan, a hard-driving individual who had suffered a heart attack. Alan's case reminds us that the circulatory system, and in particular the heart, is extremely relevant to health psychology. Again, the circulatory system does not work in isolation. It is stimulated by the nervous system (or *innervated*), and is further regulated by the endocrine system.

The circulatory system consists of the heart, blood vessels, and blood. Like other systems of the body, this system is essential for life; however, we tend to associate life more directly with this system than any other, both medically and metaphorically. If the heart stops beating, the blood stops flowing, and the cells dependent upon that blood for nutrients and the transport of other materials die.

Blood circulates in two separate but equally crucial loops. One is a closed loop between the heart and the lungs in which blood is transferred from the heart to the lungs for the replenishment of oxygen. This is called pulmonary circulation. The other is a loop that links the heart to other body systems and returns oxygen-depleted blood. This is called systemic circulation. Blood is brought back to the heart by veins and taken away from the heart by arteries. Since both pulmonary and systemic circulation depends on the heart to pump blood through the loop, it is the heart that deserves most of our attention in this tour of the circulatory system.

The Heart

The heart is a hollow, muscular pump about the size of your fist, situated in the middle of your chest (not on the left side, as most people think). It is divided into two halves, left and right, by the *septum,* with the right half receiving and pumping blood low in oxygen and the left returning oxygen-rich blood to the body. Each half contains an upper and lower chamber. Thus, the heart has a total of four chambers. The upper two are called **atria** (atrium in the singular) and the lower two are called **ventricles**. Atria receive blood returning to the heart and transfer it to the ventricles, which pump the blood from the heart to either the lungs to receive oxygen (pulmonary circulation) or other parts of the body (systemic circulation).

atria: the upper two chambers of the heart. Atria receive blood returning to the heart and transfer it to the ventricles.

ventricles: the lower two chambers of the heart. Ventricles pump the blood from the heart to either the lungs or other parts of the body.

More specifically, the right-side atrium receives blood from the systemic circulation, which is low in oxygen (O_2) and high in carbon dioxide (CO_2). This blood flows to the right ventricle, where it is pumped through the pulmonary system via the pulmonary artery. In the lungs, this blood loses excess CO_2 and picks up O_2. It then returns to the left atrium via the pulmonary veins. You can probably guess what happens next. This oxygen-rich blood flows to the left ventricle, where it is pumped out via the systemic circulation. The main artery carrying this blood away from the heart is called the **aorta**. Other major arteries branch out from the aorta, taking blood to various parts of the body simultaneously. Because the left side of the heart pumps blood to the entire body, it must generate more pressure than the right side, which is just delivering blood to the lungs. As a result, the left side of the heart muscle is thicker and stronger.

The pumping activity of the heart consists of contraction, in which the heart is emptied, and relaxation, in which the heart is filled. Contraction is called **systole**, and relaxation is called **diastole**. The atria and ventricles go through separate cycles of systole and diastole.

Like any pump, the heart relies on the synchronized precision of valves to make sure the blood flows in the right direction. The valves of the heart open in response to pressure from blood being pumped through, and close when pushed back by blood that has entered the chamber (see Figure 2-5).

All of this happens because the heart is stimulated to contract and relax rhythmically through a process called **autorhythmicity**, which is the capacity of a cardiac muscle cell to fire by itself. The pulsing of the heart is regulated by autorhythmic cells, which in turn stimulate **contractile cells**, which work like other cells in the body—namely, they require stimulation from other cells in order to fire. As their name implies, contractile cells bring about the contraction that constitutes the work of pumping.

aorta: the main artery carrying oxygen-rich blood away from the heart.

systole: contraction of the heart during pumping, in which the heart is emptied.

diastole: relaxation of the heart during pumping, in which the heart is filled.

autorhythmicity: the capacity of a cardiac muscle cell to fire by itself. The pulsing of the heart is regulated by autorhythmic cells.

contractile cells: these cells require stimulation from other cells in order to fire. They bring about the contraction of the heart that constitutes the work of pumping.

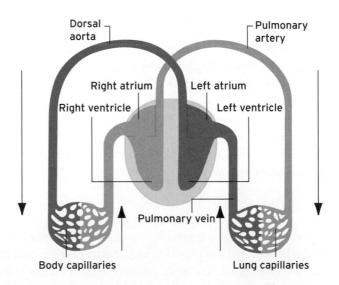

Figure 2-5 A Schematic Diagram of Pulmonary and Systemic Circulation

This diagram of the heart shows oxygen-depleted blood entering the right atrium from the body and being pumped from the right ventricle via the pulmonary artery to the lungs. From the lungs, the oxygen-rich blood returns to the left atrium via the pulmonary vein and is then pumped from the left ventricle to the body via the dorsal aorta.

Electrical activity of the heart is important to health psychologists because **arrhythmia**, or an irregular beating of the heart—such as rapid heartbeat or changing patterns of beating—can be caused by malfunction of the autorhythmic cells that are responsible for "keeping time." Such arrhythmias can be brought on by many factors, including anxiety, lack of sleep, caffeine, nicotine, alcohol, or a disease process (Sherwood, 2004). Moreover, the symptoms of arrhythmia can be *anxiety-inducing* in themselves, creating a problematic cycle of physical and psychological concerns for the patient.

Blood pressure is measured in terms of systolic and diastolic pressure and is reported as two numbers—systolic pressure over diastolic pressure. Systolic pressure is the higher of the two numbers. Blood pressure is usually measured via a device called a sphygmomanometer, which features an inflatable cuff and a scale that indicates pressure. It is used with a stethoscope so that blood flow sounds can be heard. When the cuff is inflated, blood flow is cut off and nothing is heard through the stethoscope. As the cuff is deflated, blood begins to flow again, and a thumping sound is produced. When this sound is first detected, systolic pressure is measured. As the cuff deflates further, the thumping will turn to a "swishing" sound. At the point when this sound stops, diastolic pressure is measured.

Abnormally high blood pressure is called **hypertension**. People with blood pressure in excess of 140/90 mm Hg are generally considered *hypertensive*. Abnormally low blood pressure is called **hypotension**. People with blood pressure below 100/60 mm Hg are generally considered *hypotensive* (Sherwood, 2004).

The circulatory system uses a complex process to monitor and automatically adjust blood pressure. Our blood pressure is primarily a function of cardiac output, the total resistance determined by the elements of the system transporting the blood and by characteristics of the blood itself. For example, blood pressure may increase as a result of a loss of elasticity in the arteries or when blood flow is restricted because of a buildup of plaque along the walls of the arteries. Thus, as a consequence of the aging process, or through the impact of diet and other lifestyle factors, blood pressure can increase. We also know that regular exercise can be an effective way to help combat mild hypertension. Exercise and diet are key issues for health psychologists, as you will see in chapter 9 when we look at the impact of physical activity on health.

Blood pressure is an important health consideration because there can be serious complications arising from hypertension. The heart must work harder in the event of increased peripheral resistance from fatty deposits, which reduce artery diameter, and this can result in congestive heart failure or heart attack. Also, hemorrhaging may occur if small vessels burst. In addition to these and other complications, hypertension is particularly dangerous because it is **asymptomatic**. Until a complication occurs, people with hypertension may have no symptoms to indicate that they have a problem. This is why it is important to have blood pressure checked routinely.

THE RESPIRATORY SYSTEM

Most of the time, we take our breathing for granted. However, when our ability to breathe normally is compromised we quickly become aware of just how important the respiratory system is to our continued functioning. As a respiration therapist working with patients who had serious pneumonia once said, "My job would be so much easier if people would just *breathe*."

The therapist's observation is based on the fact that the body needs oxygen in order to use (or *metabolize*) nutrients. As it does so, oxygen (O_2) combines with carbon (C) to

arrhythmia: an irregular beating of the heart, such as rapid heartbeat or changing patterns of beating.

hypertension: abnormally high blood pressure (i.e., in excess of 140/90 mm Hg).

hypotension: abnormally low blood pressure (i.e., below 100/60 mm Hg).

asymptomatic: conditions that are not accompanied by palpable symptoms or sensations.

produce carbon dioxide (CO_2). Thus, the respiratory system is responsible for getting oxygen into the body and carbon dioxide out of it as a waste product.

Physiologists refer to two kinds of respiration: internal and external. Internal respiration concerns cells using O_2 and producing CO_2. External respiration, which will be the focus of this section, refers to the taking in of O_2 from the external environment. External respiration involves breathing, the exchange of O_2 and CO_2 between the lungs and the blood, the transportation of O_2 and CO_2 by the blood, and an exchange of O_2 and CO_2 between blood and tissue.

The respiratory system consists of the airways to the lungs, the lungs themselves, and the anatomy of the chest that allows for the movement of air. The airways include the nose, throat (pharynx), windpipe (trachea), and esophagus (the tube through which food travels to the stomach), the very places where you would experience the symptoms of a cold. Remember this when you are reading chapter 4 on psychoneuroimmunology, where we talk about upper respiratory tract infections. It is this part of the respiratory system that is involved. Psychologists believe that when we are stressed we are more vulnerable to infections of the respiratory system as our immune systems are working at less than optimal levels.

Some of the components of the respiratory system serve dual functions. For example, the esophagus is involved in both respiration and digestion. This dual function requires mechanisms that close or open parts of the system depending on whether we are breathing or whether we are swallowing food.

Further down the airway from the nose and throat, the trachea divides into two main branches called the left and right **bronchi**. When each bronchus enters its respective lung, it continues to branch off, getting smaller and smaller, like the roots of a tree. The small branches are called **bronchioles**. At the ends of the bronchioles are many tiny air sacs called **alveoli**. The lungs contain about 300 million alveoli, and it is via these that gas (O_2 and CO_2) is exchanged between the air and the blood. The alveoli are encircled by a dense collection of **pulmonary capillaries**, which contain blood. Thus, the exchange of gases is facilitated by a vast number of alveoli surrounded by blood-bearing capillaries (see Figure 2-6).

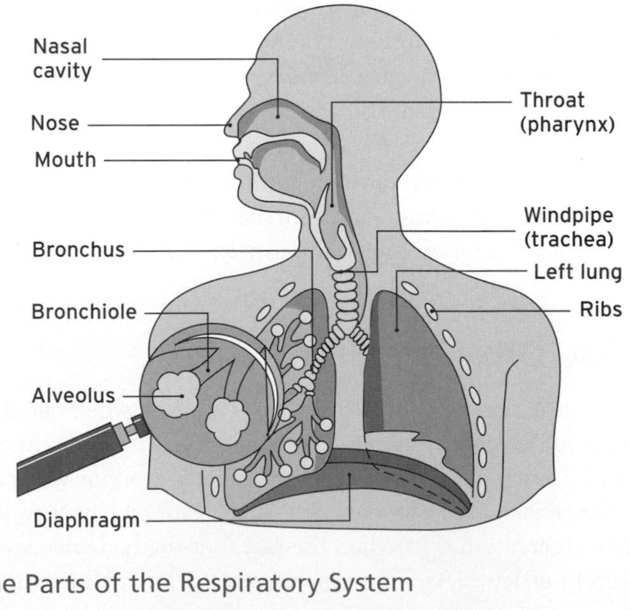

bronchi: the two main branches of the trachea, or windpipe.

bronchioles: the small branches of the bronchi.

alveoli: tiny air sacs found at the ends of the bronchioles. Gas (O_2 and CO_2) is exchanged between the air and the blood via the 300 million alveoli in the lungs.

pulmonary capillaries: a dense collection of blood-bearing capillaries that encircle the alveoli in the lungs, facilitating the exchange of gases in the lungs.

Figure 2-6 The Parts of the Respiratory System

The lungs themselves are relatively large. They are divided into five lobes, with the left lung having two lobes and the right lung having three. The lungs occupy most of the chest or thoracic cavity and are protected by the rib cage. The *intercostal* (i.e., between the ribs) muscles of the chest wall are used to expand the thoracic cavity, allowing for the intake of air. When relaxed, the pressure outside the lungs is greater than inside, allowing us to exhale. This is the act of breathing that the respiration therapist wanted all her patients to be able to do.

There are a number of conditions that could make breathing difficult for her patients. For example, one condition common among older people is **chronic obstructive pulmonary disease (COPD)**. The primary symptom of COPD is shortness of breath, a symptom that tends to worsen with time. The two most common forms of COPD are chronic bronchitis, which is an inflammation that irritates the airways and blocks them by producing extra mucus, and emphysema, which results from damaged or destroyed lung tissue. Emphysema causes large air pockets to be trapped in the lungs, making breathing difficult (Lung Association, 2004). The main cause of emphysema is cigarette smoking, although there are other causes, such as workplace exposure to chemicals and toxins (Public Health Agency of Canada, 2003). COPD accounts for approximately six percent of all deaths in people between the ages of 65 and 84.

The lung disease most associated with cigarette smoking, however, is lung cancer, for which the prognosis continues to be poor. In Canada, lung cancer accounts for 29 percent of all cancer deaths in men and 25 percent in women (Canadian Cancer Society, 2005). When you read about health-compromising behaviours in chapter 10, think about the respiratory system and how preventable some of the serious conditions that affect it are. These are conditions that we will discuss further in chapter 8, Chronic and Life-Threatening Illnesses.

Another common respiratory condition is asthma, a condition that is becoming quite prevalent among children and adults. According to the 1998/1999 National Population Health Survey, 2.5 million people in Canada had asthma, which amounts to 12 percent of children and 8 percent of adults (Public Health Agency of Canada, 2003). People who are predisposed to particular allergies and are then exposed to those allergens, or those who are exposed to environmental toxins, are at greater risk for developing asthma. As is the case with most respiratory conditions, difficulty in breathing is the primary symptom. People with asthma may also experience coughing, wheezing, and shortness of breath (Fraser Health, 2002). The two main causes of asthma are inflammation of the airways and narrowing of the airways caused by muscle tightening or spasm (Fraser Health, 2002).

Pneumonia is also a common respiratory condition. **Lobar pneumonia** occurs with the infection of an entire lobe of the lung, which causes an inflammation of the alveoli. This can be a serious condition in which the infection causing the inflammation spreads to other organs. The more familiar **bronchial pneumonia** is restricted to the bronchi and often occurs as a complication of other illnesses such as cold or flu.

Most of the conditions that cause respiratory difficulties are not as serious as pneumonia or COPD. Instead, we experience temporary symptoms that result from bacterial or viral infections, leaving us with coughs, colds, and flu-like symptoms. Some of the more serious forms of these include strep throat and whooping cough, two conditions that parents watch for when their children begin to suffer from cold symptoms. Strep throat produces a swelling of the throat, whereas whooping cough, so named for the distinctive

chronic obstructive pulmonary disease (COPD): the primary symptom of COPD is shortness of breath, a symptom that tends to worsen with time. The two most common forms of COPD are chronic bronchitis, an inflammation that irritates the airways and blocks them by producing extra mucus, and emphysema, which results from damaged or destroyed lung tissue, causing large air pockets to be trapped in the lungs, making breathing difficult.

lobar pneumonia: the infection of an entire lobe of the lung, which causes an inflammation of the alveoli. This can be a serious condition in which the infection causing the inflammation spreads to other organs.

bronchial pneumonia: pneumonia that is restricted to the bronchi and often occurs as a complication of other illnesses, such as cold or flu.

coughing sound of those with the disease, can migrate down the respiratory tract to the trachea and bronchi.

The distinction between bacterial and viral infections is an important one from the perspective of treatment. Antibiotics can treat the former but not the latter. Excessive use of antibiotics, however, can lead to the development of "super bugs" that become more and more resistant to the antibiotics themselves. Even more problematic is the use of antibiotics in the treatment of viral infections. Such use contributes to the "super bug" problem, and antibiotics are of no therapeutic value for viral infections. In spite of this basic biological fact, patients often insist on a prescription from their doctor when they are experiencing cold (i.e., viral) symptoms. Physicians observe that if they refuse to write a prescription, the patient often goes to another clinic and asks again. For some excellent information about the unnecessary versus recommended use of antibiotics, not just in medicine but in household products, check out the Do Bugs Need Drugs?® program at the University of Alberta (visit www.dobugsneeddrugs.org/index.html).

THE DIGESTIVE SYSTEM

Most people can tell stories of how their psychological state has affected their digestive system. We speak about having "butterflies in our stomach" while recognizing that the cause is psychological, and we attribute it to excessive tension, anxiety, or stress. We have already learned that this is due in part to the dominance of the sympathetic system during times of *fight or flight,* and this dominance disrupts digestion. It is the job of the digestive system to transform food into a form that the body can use, by breaking down food into smaller molecular forms that can be absorbed into the circulatory system.

The digestive system consists of the *digestive tract* and *accessory digestive organs.* The digestive tract is made up of the mouth, throat, esophagus, stomach, small intestine, large intestine, and anus (see Figure 2-7). The material travelling through the tract is referred to as **chyme**. The tract is best thought of as a long tube (about 4.5 m) that is sealed off from the rest of the body, and with good reason. There are biochemical processes required for digestion that could actually be quite harmful to the rest of the body if it were exposed to those processes. Powerful enzymes are used to process protein and could damage other tissue. The inner lining of the stomach produces hydrochloric acid, which is capable of dissolving a nail. In the lower intestine are millions of bacteria that are helpful in that region but, in some cases, lethal if exposed to other regions of the body—as might occur through a ruptured appendix (Sherwood, 2004).

The accessory digestive organs include the salivary glands, exocrine pancreas, and the biliary system (liver and gallbladder). These glands produce the materials used by digestive glands to break down food.

The digestive system is best understood by looking at its four basic processes: motility, secretion, digestion, and absorption.

Motility

The digestive system relies on muscle activity. At either end of the process, the muscles are skeletal and the movements are voluntary—chewing and defecation. The middle of the system, however, relies on smooth muscle contraction, which is involuntary.

chyme: refers to the liquid material travelling through the digestive tract.

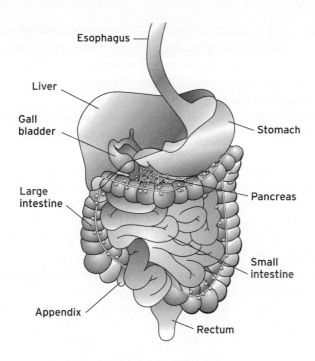

Figure 2-7 The Components of the Digestive Tract

Motility refers to the process of moving food through the system and mixing it with digestive juices. This process is particularly relevant to psychology because emotions affect motility. In general, emotions such as fear and sadness decrease motility and thus disrupt the digestive process.

At some places in the digestive system, movement of food is rapid—from the mouth down the esophagus, for example. In others, the movement must be slower, such as through the small intestine, which takes time because this is the major site of absorption. Thus, contractions of the smooth muscles in this area occur such that *propulsive movements* are slow.

The stomach plays an important role in managing the difference between the rapid flow of food through the esophagus and the much slower flow through the small intestine. It takes the food sent quickly via the esophagus and releases it slowly into the small intestine at a rate that allows the intestine to perform the task of absorption. While storing food, the stomach begins mixing it with hydrochloric acid and enzymes to begin the digestive process.

We tend to associate the stomach with vomiting, or **emesis**, because it involves the emptying of the stomach's contents. However, the process of vomiting is neither initiated, nor propagated, by the stomach. Instead, like most things, the process starts in the brain. The medulla contains a "vomit centre" that receives impulses causing it to initiate the process. In this process, the diaphragm, which normally aids in breathing, presses down on the stomach, which has actually relaxed at this point so that it can be compressed. The abdominal muscles press in on the stomach as well. The esophagus and other parts of the tract also relax, while other parts close in order to prevent material from entering the airways. The compression of the stomach by the diaphragm and abdominals forces material up from the stomach and out.

Vomiting may be caused by stimulation of the back of the throat; irritation of the stomach or duodenum (which connects the stomach to the small intestine); rotation or

motility: The process of moving food through the system and mixing it with digestive juices.

emesis: vomiting, or emptying of the stomach's contents.

acceleration of the head, producing dizziness; the ingestion of chemical agents; or psychological factors. Vomiting can also be caused by elevated intracranial pressure after a head injury. Vomiting in this instance must be treated seriously, since it could indicate swelling or bleeding within the cranial cavity. (See the discussion of concussion in chapter 9, "Health and Physical Activity.")

So, even though vomiting is not the most pleasant of topics, it is relevant to health psychologists. For example, in addition to being a symptom of concussion, it is an all-too-familiar part of life for cancer patients undergoing chemotherapy—so much so that it is not uncommon for cancer patients to vomit *in anticipation* of their chemotherapy treatment. To help reduce this problem, patients are sometimes given **antiemetics**, which are medicines designed to reduce nausea and the impulse to vomit. You will read about these in chapter 8. You will also read about vomiting in chapter 10 when we discuss eating disorders. People with bulimia access the connection between back of the throat stimulation and the vomit centre in the brain to induce vomiting after eating.

Another common condition associated with the stomach is the **peptic ulcer**. A peptic ulcer is so named because it involves a strong digestive enzyme called *pepsin*. The walls of the stomach and other parts of the digestive tract are protected from pepsin by mucous layers. However, in some cases this layer breaks down, perhaps because of the intrusion of bacteria called *H. pylori*, which are able to exist even in the highly acidic world of the stomach. *H. pylori* secrete toxins that bring about inflammation that weakens this mucosal protection. Once this happens, pepsin begins to erode the wall of the stomach, resulting in bleeding or the escape of gastric contents, which can damage tissue outside the digestive tract. Since the discovery—about 15 years ago—of *H. pylori*, a common bacteria that most, but not all, people tolerate well, the treatment of ulcers now includes the use of antibiotics. Psychological factors such as stress can also contribute to the development of ulcers by stimulating greater gastric secretion and, consequently, more pepsin.

Secretion

Along the digestive tract, glands secrete fluids that aid in digestion. These glands receive hormonal and neural stimulation, drawing the materials needed to produce these juices from the blood. When working well, the system returns these materials to the bloodstream for reuse. However, disruptions to the system, such as vomiting or diarrhea, deplete this fluid. Thus, there is the concern that people who suffer from prolonged diarrhea or vomiting will also suffer dehydration. This concern is underscored by the fact that water plays an important part in digestion by allowing enzymes to perform their functions.

Digestion

In the process of **digestion**, enzymes produced within the digestive system perform the biochemical breakdown of carbohydrates, proteins, and fats into molecular-size forms that allow for absorption. The biochemistry of digestion is complex, but a brief look at the major components will be helpful.

Carbohydrates come in a number of forms, including sugars and starch. In the process of digestion, carbohydrates are converted into simple sugars—glucose, fructose, and galactose. You may have heard that foods high in carbohydrates should be consumed before athletic competition or physical exertion. Such foods include breads, pasta, rice,

antiemetic medication: medication intended to reduce nausea and vomiting.

peptic ulcer: so named because pepsin, a digestive enzyme, begins to erode the wall of the stomach, resulting in bleeding or the escape of gastric contents, which can damage tissue outside the digestive tract.

digestion: the process whereby enzymes produced within the digestive system perform the biochemical breakdown of carbohydrates, proteins, and fats into molecular-size forms that allow for absorption.

and potatoes. This is, indeed, good advice for two reasons. The first is that the sugars derived from carbohydrates do provide a source of energy; the second is that carbohydrates move through the digestive system more quickly than do fats and proteins. Still, it is best to eat from one to four hours before exertion because you don't want to be calling on energy sources at the same time as you are trying to digest a meal.

Through digestion, proteins are broken down into the *amino acids* that constitute the proteins. Most fats are broken down from a *triglyceride* form (three attached fatty acid molecules) to a *monoglyceride* form (with just one fatty acid molecule attached), leaving two free fatty acid molecules.

Absorption

Absorption is the process by which nutrients move from the digestive tract to the blood-stream and the lymphatic system. Absorption occurs primarily in the small intestine. Motility, secretion, and digestion support absorption by working to move the chime along the digestive tract, break it down, and allow for the clearing of the tract in the small intestine so that it can continue its work unimpeded.

Problems with the absorption process can yield significant coping challenges. One such problem is **lactose intolerance**, caused by a deficiency of lactase, which is used to digest a milk sugar called *lactose*. The result of this deficiency is a buildup of lactose in the small intestine, which can cause an accumulation of water. Also, because bacteria in the large intestine can use lactose as an energy source, these bacteria move in and produce gases as they attack the lactose. The result is painful cramping and diarrhea.

Malabsorption, or the inability to efficiently absorb nutrients from the digestive system, may be caused by *gluten enteropathy*. If the small intestine is allergic to gluten, the intestine can become damaged. Symptoms of gluten enteropathy include diarrhea and weight loss. In some cases, a related skin condition can also develop. This problem is treated by modification of the diet to eliminate gluten. However, this is easier said than done, since gluten is found in wheat products, which are commonly used in food processing.

absorption: the process by which nutrients move from the digestive tract to the bloodstream and the lymphatic system. Absorption occurs primarily in the small intestine.

lactose intolerance: caused by a deficiency of lactase, which is used to digest a milk sugar called lactose, resulting in a buildup of lactose in the small intestine. Because bacteria in the large intestine can use lactose as an energy source, these bacteria move in and produce gases as they attack the lactose. The result is painful cramping and diarrhea.

malabsorption: the inability to efficiently absorb nutrients from the digestive system, which may be caused by *gluten enteropathy*.

THE URINARY SYSTEM

To understand the importance of the urinary system, we must return to the notion of *homeostasis*. As you have read about the other systems of the body, perhaps you were struck by the importance of fluids. Plasma (the liquid portion of the blood), glandular secretions, water, and electrolytes are some examples of these fluids. A vital element of homeostasis is the maintenance of the balance of chemicals in the body's fluids, and the urinary system plays an important role in that maintenance. The kidneys, a key element of this system, act as one of the body's filtering systems, removing waste products from the blood.

Kidney Functions

The kidneys are located just above the beltline on the back wall of the abdomen, one on either side of the vertebrae. Plasma flows through the kidneys, and, as it does, the kidneys monitor and adjust its fluid content. This is another one of those remarkable biological processes in which an organ is able to keep track of a delicate balance required for life, in this case extra-cellular fluids (ECF), and then maintain that balance.

The kidneys help us maintain our internal water balance, regardless of how much of it we drink or how much of it we lose via perspiration, vomiting, diarrhea, or bleeding. Normally functioning kidneys always know how much water to retain and eliminate via urine. In addition to controlling water levels, the kidneys control *electrolytes*, substances dissolved in water capable of conducting electricity. Salt (NaCl) is an example of an electrolyte whose levels are controlled by the kidneys.

By eliminating excess amounts of water and electrolytes, the kidneys help us maintain homeostasis. However, the kidneys cannot *produce* these substances if we are in short supply. Rather, they help us retain what we have until we can increase our supply in other ways. The kidneys also eliminate metabolic toxic waste materials from the body. To achieve this elimination process, a certain amount of water (about half a litre a day) must be eliminated through the urine, even if the person is not ingesting any water. Thus, people stranded in the desert without water may actually urinate themselves to death.

In all, the kidneys perform a number of functions that are essential for homeostasis and life itself. An imbalance can be dangerous. For example, excess quantities of potassium ions (K^+) can be harmful to the heart. The kidneys also play an important role in blood pressure regulation by controlling levels of water and salt in the blood.

The kidneys consist of millions of tiny functional units called nephrons. Physicians who treat kidney diseases are called nephrologists. Nephrologists must also understand the workings of the arteries and veins that flow into and out of the kidneys. These are called renal arteries and renal veins. Taken collectively, this part of the body is often referred to as the **renal system**.

renal system: the part of the body encompassing the kidneys, renal arteries, and renal veins.

Other Parts of the Urinary System

The other parts of the system are responsible for the elimination of urine (see Figure 2-8). Once formed, urine collects in each kidney and is channelled into the **ureter**. There are two ureters, one for each kidney, that carry urine to one storage space, which is the **urinary bladder**. The bladder is capable of expanding (*distending*) to hold more or less urine. Urine is emptied from the bladder to outside the body via the **urethra**. In females, the urethra is short and straight; in males, the urethra is much longer and extends through the prostate gland and the penis. The prostate gland sits just below the bladder and, because it encircles the urethra, can affect urinary flow if the prostate enlarges, which it can do, particularly as men get older.

The destruction of nephrons can gradually shut down the functioning of one kidney or both. Treatment for kidney diseases often involves using external devices to do the work of the kidneys. This is what happens during **kidney dialysis**. Of course, dialysis must be performed regularly, and so people on dialysis must use the machine often (daily in many cases) either at home or as outpatients in a hospital. This constitutes a major life adjustment, as patients must then plan their schedules around dialysis treatments. Another treatment approach is kidney transplant. All transplants carry inherent risks of rejection or infection, as well as the challenge of finding a suitable donor. Thus, health psychologists can make important contributions in helping people cope with the challenges of kidney disease.

ureter: carries urine from the kidney to the bladder. There are two ureters, one for each kidney.

urinary bladder: storage space for holding urine. The bladder is capable of expanding to hold more or less urine.

urethra: empties urine from the bladder to outside the body. In females, the urethra is short and straight; in males, the urethra is much longer and extends through the prostate gland and the penis.

kidney dialysis: uses external devices to do the work of the kidneys.

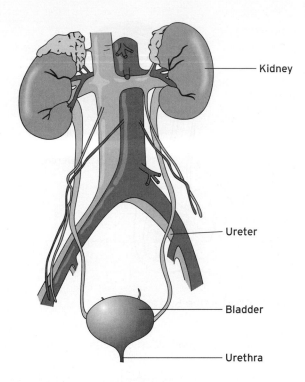

Kidney

Ureter

Bladder

Urethra

Figure 2-8 The Parts of the Urinary System

THE REPRODUCTIVE SYSTEM

The reproductive system is in close proximity to the urinary system and even uses some of the same parts (the urethra in males, for example). For this reason, diseases in this area of the body are often referred to as being genito-urinary (GU). For example, when cancer physicians (oncologists) discuss various sites for tumours, they might refer to the GU group when talking about prostate or ovarian cancer.

Unlike the other systems we have described in this chapter, the reproductive system is markedly different for males and females. Also, it is much less concerned with homeostasis than it is with the propagation of the species. Its reason for being, in a biological sense at least, is to provide the means by which reproductive cells, called **gametes**, can unite to form new life. Each gamete carries half of the chromosomes needed for this new life. The male gametes are spermatozoa, and the female gametes are ova, or eggs. The primary organs responsible for reproduction are called the **gonads**. In males, these are the testes and in females, the ovaries. In addition to producing their respective gametes, the gonads produce sex hormones—testosterone for males, and estrogen and progesterone for females. Testosterone and estrogen regulate secondary sexual characteristics, which are the outward signs of being male or female. These include such things as shoulder and hip width, breast development, and facial hair.

The male reproductive system consists of the testes; a collection of accessory sex glands, including the prostate gland, which aids in the production of sex hormones and secretions that allow for the transport of sperm; and the penis. The primary functions of

gametes: reproductive cells.

gonads: the primary organs responsible for reproduction. In males, these are the testes, and in females, the ovaries. In addition to producing their respective gametes, the gonads produce sex hormones—testosterone for males, and estrogen and progesterone for females.

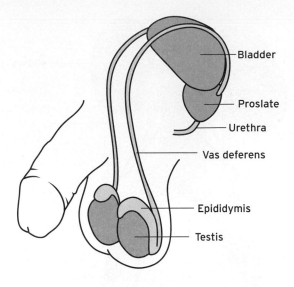

Figure 2-9 The Male Reproductive System

this reproductive system include the production of sperm and the transport of that sperm to the female (see Figure 2-9).

The female reproductive system is responsible for much more biological activity than that of the male. This system produces ova, receives sperm, transports sperm and ova to a site for fertilization, nourishes the fetus, provides an environment for its development, gives birth, and nourishes the infant once born via breast milk. The reproductive tract contains Fallopian tubes, which pick up ova and are the site of fertilization. The tract also includes the uterus, or womb, which provides the environment for the developing fetus. The vagina provides the passage between the uterus and the outside world. At the lowest portion of the uterus, the cervix makes the connection to the vagina and accepts sperm during intercourse. The cervix is capable of considerable dilation during childbirth, since

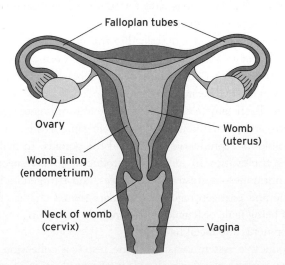

Figure 2-10 The Female Reproductive System

this is the exit point for the child at birth. The measurement of cervical dilation is one of the methods used to assess the progression of labour (see Figure 2-10).

Cancers of the Reproductive System

Some of the most common cancers are found in the reproductive system, including breast cancer, cervical cancer, and prostate cancer. We discuss these and other illnesses in more detail in chapter 8. Here, we want to make the link between these common cancers and this system of the body.

As of 1998, breast cancer was diagnosed in one in nine women in Canada (Health Canada, 2006c). The incidence continues to rise, though mortality rates from breast cancer have declined since the 1980s. Still, years of life lost due to breast cancer are greater than with some other cancers. In fact, it is because of breast cancer that cancer rates are higher for women between the ages of 30 and 39 than for men in that age range (Health Canada, 2006c).

The effectiveness of screening for breast cancer continues to garner much research attention. In chapter 6, we discuss the research on the effectiveness of mammography screening in reducing mortality rates due to breast cancer. Current research indicates that mammography can reduce mortality rates by approximately 15 percent (Gøtzsche & Nielsen, 2005).

One form of cancer that has been affected considerably by screening is cervical cancer. Health Canada estimates that effective screening for cervical cancer via a Pap smear test could prevent up to 90 percent of deaths from this disease.

According to the Canadian Cancer Society, prostate cancer is the most commonly diagnosed cancer in men; in 2005, over 20 000 men were diagnosed with this cancer while 4300 died from it. There are also screening tests for prostate cancer, including physical exams and a blood test for prostate-specific antigen, or PSA. Like mammography, the effectiveness of PSA tests is still the subject of considerable research due to questions about the accuracy of this screening tool.

CHAPTER SUMMARY

The nervous system is the body's communication system. It consists of the central nervous system and the peripheral nervous system. The former contains the brain and spinal cord; the latter the nerve pathways to the outer portions of the body. Efferent neurons take impulses from the brain to the body's organs and muscles. Afferent neurons conduct impulses from a sense organ to the central nervous system, or from lower to higher levels in the spinal cord and brain.

The endocrine system controls glandular activity in the body. Glands produce hormones that help control basic functions such as growth and immunity.

The immune system protects the body from infection and diseases that result from invading micro-organisms. The immune system consists of cells that detect invading micro-organisms and work to eliminate them. Certain immune system cells can remember previously encountered micro-organisms and quickly mobilize antibodies to destroy those micro-oganisms.

The circulatory system is responsible for the transporting of blood through the body and ensuring that the blood contains oxygen. The system consists of the heart, arteries, and veins. The heart accepts oxygen-depleted blood from the system, sends it to the lungs where it is re-oxygenated, receives this blood from the lungs, and then pumps it through the body.

The respiratory system is responsible for getting oxygen into the body and carbon dioxide out as a waste product. It consists of the airways to the lungs, the lungs themselves, and the anatomy of the chest that allows for the movement of air.

The digestive system is responsible for converting food into a form that the body can use, by breaking down food into smaller molecular forms that can be absorbed into the circulatory system. Components of the digestive system move food through the tract and help break it down into usable forms.

The urinary system plays a vital role in the maintenance of the balance of chemicals in the body's fluids. An important component of the urinary system is the kidneys that monitor and adjust fluid levels in the body's plasma.

The reproductive system, as the term implies, is responsible for human reproduction and sexual response. It is the one system discussed in this chapter that is different in men and women. The male reproductive system consists of the testes; a collection of accessory sex glands, including the prostate gland, which aids in the production of sex hormones and secretions that allow for the transport of sperm; and the penis. The primary functions of the male reproductive system include the production of sperm and the transport of that sperm to the female. The female reproductive system produces ova; receives sperm; transports sperm and ova to a site for fertilization; nourishes the fetus; provides an environment for its development; gives birth; and nourishes the infant once born via breast milk.

Many diseases are associated with malfunction of the nervous system. Some examples include multiple sclerosis, in which nerve cells lose their outer layering (myelin sheath), and myasthenia gravis, which can be caused by an inability to produce certain neurotransmitters.

One of the most common diseases associated with the endocrine system is diabetes. Diabetes is caused by too little secretion of insulin, which is a hormone produced by the pancreas. Insulin aids in the body's ability to convert blood sugar to energy.

Poor immune system functioning leaves a person susceptible to infections and other diseases brought on by invading micro-organisms. These include everything from the common cold to cancer. Also, the immune system can turn on the body itself. So-called autoimmune diseases include arthritis.

There are many health conditions associated with the circulatory system, including heart disease. One other common condition is hypertension, or high blood pressure.

One disease of the respiratory system is *chronic obstructive pulmonary disease* (COPD). The primary symptom of COPD is shortness of breath, a symptom that tends to worsen with time.

The digestive system might have a problem with *malabsorption*, or the inability to efficiently absorb nutrients from the digestive system. This may be caused by *gluten enteropathy*. If the small intestine is allergic to gluten, the intestine can become damaged. Symptoms of gluten enteropathy include diarrhea and weight loss. In some cases, a related skin condition can also develop.

Cancers of the urinary and reproductive systems have received considerable attention due to their prevalence rates. In men, prostate cancer and in women, breast cancer, have paraticularly high prevalence rates among cancers.

These systems of the body are relevant to all chapters of the book. Some prime examples include the chapter on stress and coping, which brings in the nervous system, the circulatory system, and the endocrine system. The chapter on psychoneuroimmunology, of course, relates to the immune system. The chapter on pain refers directly to the nervous system. The chapter on chronic and life-threatening illness refers to many of the body systems when it discusses diabetes, arthritis, and cancer.

Review Questions

1. Why should health psychologists have an understanding of basic anatomy and physiology?

2. What is homeostasis, and why is it a good starting point to develop an understanding of the systems of the body?

3. What are the divisions of the nervous system, and how do these work to communicate information throughout the body and help maintain homeostasis?

4. What is the endocrine system, and what part does it play in regulating body function?

5. How does the immune system work to ward off infection and help us stay healthy?

6. How does the heart work with the lungs to transport blood and oxygen through the body?

7. What are the fundamental elements of the digestive system, and what are the steps involved in digestion?

8. How does the urinary system work, and in particular, what part do the kidneys play?

9. What are the parts of the male and female reproductive systems, and how do they work in reproduction?

10. What are some of the diseases of the systems of the body, and how do these relate to things you will learn in other sections of this book?

Chapter 3
Stress and Coping

CHAPTER OUTLINE

ISSUES OF DEFINITION
THE PHYSIOLOGY OF STRESS
COGNITIVE TRANSACTIONAL MODELS
THE ROLE OF PERSONALITY IN STRESS AND COPING
COPING

Learning Objectives

After studying this chapter, you will be able to

- Define stress and coping

- Understand the physiology of stress

- Understand the cognitive components of stress

- Appreciate the role of personality in stress and coping

- Identify different coping styles

- Identify strategies for coping with stress

John, a young business executive, is awakened by his alarm. He hits the snooze button, but his relief lasts only 10 minutes. He snaps to attention, realizing that he is now running late. He was out until 1:00 a.m. at a social function, and although he understands that these events are important for his work, he wishes he had not had so much to drink and had come home somewhat earlier. He rushes to shower and shave and in his haste cuts his chin. Leaving his apartment, he runs to his car through heavy rain only to discover that he has left his briefcase back inside his apartment.

Once on the road he aims for his local coffee shop for his morning dose of caffeine. He arrives to find a long lineup, but the alternative, a commute without coffee, is not an option he would even consider. This is the first of approximately 20 cups of coffee he will have today, and he wants it to be a good one. His impatience is visible, and he curses under his breath at the woman at the head of the line who is having difficulty understanding the difference between a latte and a cappuccino. As the young executive leaps back into his car with his vente "dark" and a chocolate croissant, he spills coffee on his pants.

He endures the heavy rush hour by riding the bumper of the car in front of him and yelling at those around him who seem oblivious to his urgency. His cell phone is in constant use. Periodically, he has to slam on the brakes in order to avoid rear-ending the vehicle ahead of him. He has difficulty finding a parking spot and, after running through the rain, he arrives at his office 45 minutes late for an important meeting. His boss tells him not to bother coming into the meeting and suggests, in a somewhat sarcastic manner, that he should attend instead to some of the accumulated work on his desk.

He pours himself another coffee and sneaks a doughnut from a box in the coffee room. As he sits down at his desk his heart is racing, his stomach is churning, his jaw is clenched as he grinds his teeth, he is sweating profusely, he is hyperventilating, and he feels a muscle-tension headache coming on. He is so angry, frustrated, and worried by his boss's response to his lateness that he has difficulty focusing on the tasks in front of him. His enthusiasm for work has decreased dramatically. He longs to return home and curl up in his bed. There is nowhere to run to and no one to fight with.

ISSUES OF DEFINITION

Throughout this text, we provide many definitions for the terms we use. This is to ensure clarity regarding the meaning of the concepts presented. There is usually considerable agreement concerning the correct definition for a particular term. However, when it comes to the topics of this chapter, **stress** and **coping**, this is not the case. If we compared your definition of these terms with those of other students, there would likely be considerable variability. Definitions of stress and coping are highly personalized and reflect an individual's unique life experiences.

Brannon and Feist (1999) have compared the concept of *stress* to that of *love*. Everyone seems to know what the word means and the role it plays in their lives, and they are sure they know it when they feel it. Yet the concept is difficult to define. We do, however, have a commonsense understanding of these terms. When someone tells us they feel stressed, we empathize because we believe we have experienced similar feelings. Some of

stress: the non-specific mental or somatic result of any demand upon the body.

coping: strategies that an individual employs to deal with stresses caused by the ever-changing demands of the environment.

us would even describe ourselves as being "experts" in the field. We believe we have attained a high level of stress competency through one of the acknowledged avenues by which this can occur—personal experience.

A similar inconsistency exists with regard to how we define *coping*. To say we "cope with stress" is a highly individualized statement that also reflects the variability of human experience. There is obviously no "right" way to cope with stress, there are many different ways. Our stress is not your stress, for example, and our coping strategies are not yours.

Questions such as the following demonstrate that everyone does not experience stress in the same way: Is stress always a bad thing? Should positive events, such as getting married or having a child, be viewed as stressful? How much more stressful is it to lose a close relative than to receive a speeding ticket? Are the strategies one person uses to cope with stress applicable to another individual's world? Can some coping strategies actually increase the stress we experience? Why do we continue to use coping strategies that appear to be quite ineffective?

Given the number of times we use the terms *stress* and *coping* in describing our daily activities, it is remarkable how little consensus exists as to how to define them.

Our opening vignette reminds us that while stress and coping are concepts that have always existed, the sabre-toothed tigers of yesteryear have been replaced by the paper tigers of today's world. Only recently, however, have they been the object of research and systematic efforts at conceptualization. What we struggle with is what Smith (1993) described as **stress literacy**. He considers this an issue of considerable importance, as the alternative is confusion, and he suggests that the "popular culture provides volumes of conflicting bits of stress wisdom" (p. 5). For example, is it better to face your problems or ignore them? Do we perform better when we are "psyched up" or when we are relaxed? The contradictions are many, and Smith suggests that "stress literacy begins with a useful definition of stress" (p. 6).

One might expect that, in an empirical world, this issue would be somewhat more straightforward; however, considerable confusion exists. Haan (1993) addresses this concern directly. She believes that those studying stress are "handicapped by a lack of consensus on the meaning of these terms. The concept of stress is used and understood by laypersons, but its scientific study has proven difficult" (p. 256). Haan suggests that this same level of controversy and confusion is attached to definitions of coping. She argues that if we acknowledged "that our knowledge of stress arises from common, shared understandings and not from objective reality, the insight would be liberating" (p. 260).

The lack of consensus in defining these terms has led some researchers to ask if the concept of stress is worth retaining. Pearlin (1993) believes that the very nature of stress dictates that it is a diffuse, multidimensional phenomenon that cannot be reduced to one element. He believes that our efforts should be directed toward examining the interconnections between its multiple dimensions. This process is proceeding slowly, as it requires an interdisciplinary focus that is difficult to create. Pearlin laments that "firmly and actively engaged in his chosen research, each investigator is convinced that the manifestation of stress that he is examining represents 'real' stress" (p. 305). He argues that we should, instead, work with the concept of stress in an interdisciplinary fashion. It will be interesting to observe whether or not this kind of paradigm shift actually occurs.

Aldwin (1994) suggests that even through stress is difficult to define, the term should be retained. She writes that "stress refers to that quality of experience, produced through

stress literacy: the degree to which an individual (or community) understands the effects of stress.

a person-environment transaction that, through either overarousal or underarousal, results in psychological or physiological distress" (p. 22). DiMatteo and Martin (2002) conclude that as the concept of stress has developed and become more popular it has also become more imprecise.

Hans Selye, the originator of the biological concept of the term *stress* (see Focus on Canadian Research 3-1), defined it as "the nonspecific result of any demand upon the body, be the effect mental or somatic" (1993, p. 7). He also recognized that, for most people, stress is viewed as a negative experience that is equated with *distress*. To counter this position, he coined the term *eustress* to reflect a positive yet stressful experience. **Eustress** (like its related word, *euphoria*) is a state of physical and psychological well-being that is associated with increased motivation and the acceptance of challenge. Perhaps the ultimate expression of this positive state is found in the title of a book by the Canadian physician Peter Hanson, *The Joy of Stress* (1986). Selye argued that a sense of balance is essential, that we function best when stress is used to produce an optimal level of arousal. The implication is that too little stress can be as harmful as too much, that distress can result from being over- *or* understimulated. Selye believed that "stress is the spice of life" (1974, p. 83).

Lazurus and Folkman (1984) and more recently Lazurus (1999) have provided us with descriptions of stress and coping that have received wide acceptance in the field. *Stress is*

eustress: a positive yet stressful experience.

Focus on Canadian Research 3-1

A Great Canadian

Hans Selye has been described as "the grand master of stress research and theory." Born in Vienna in 1907, Selye lived and worked in Montreal for 50 years until his death in 1982. He first used the term *stress* in 1936 to describe the non-specific result, either mental or physical, of demands placed on the body. Close to 40 years later, Selye indicated that, if his English had been better at the time, he would probably have chosen the word *strain* to describe this response. He had taken the idea of stress from the field of physics, where it describes the force exerted by one body against another. The response to this tension is strain and, as what Selye was describing was a response, he acknowledged that he probably should have used this term. Rather than correct him, we have adjusted our definition to fit his model.

Selye initially observed a consistent pattern of responses in rats when these animals were exposed to diverse noxious stimuli. He called this a "stereotypic response," which he had first observed in human patients some 10 years earlier (the "general adaptation syndrome" or "biologic stress syndrome") and for which he now had experimental evidence. He also identified an initial "alarm reaction" in which the organism's defences were activated. If the organism survived this initial attack, Selye identified an adaptive phase or rebound effect that occurs, which he called the "the stage of resistance." Eventually, if the demands on the organism were of sufficient severity or length, a "stage of exhaustion" occurred.

In 1956 Selye published *The Stress of Life*, in which he translated the concept of stress for the layperson. He dedicated his life to the study of stress and wrote more than 1700 articles and 39 books on the topic. He was a scientist, trained as both a physician and an endocrinologist. He served as a professor and director of the Institute of Experimental Medicine and Surgery at the University of Montreal. He also served the non-scientific world through texts such as that mentioned above and *Stress without Distress* (1974), which he wrote to help us better understand the impact of the stress response on humans throughout their lifespans. He was made a Companion of the Order of Canada, the highest honour this country can bestow upon an individual, and has been described as a "Canadian resource to the world."

described in terms of a relationship that exists between a "person and the environment that is appraised by the person as taxing or exceeding his or her resources and endangering his or her well-being" (1984, p. 21). An individual's cognitive appraisal of a situation will determine the level of stress he or she will experience. It is interesting to note that Lazurus (2006), in discussing the development of stress as an interdisciplinary concept, suggests that overlapping terms such as *anxiety, frustration, conflict, trauma,* and *emotional distress* are unified under this rubric. He states that "stress became the dominant term for uniting these concepts, and for identifying the causes and emotional consequences of the struggle to manage the pressures of daily living" (p. 30). *Coping* is defined as "constantly changing cognitive and behavioral efforts to manage specific external and/or internal demands that are appraised as taxing or exceeding the resources of the person" (Lazurus & Folkman, 1984, p. 141).

homeostasis: the dynamic physiological response on the part of the body to maintain a stable internal state in spite of the demands of the environment.

fight-or-flight response: the body's complex autonomic reaction when faced with a perceived threat.

Central to our understanding of stress are the contributions of Walter Cannon. In 1939, he introduced the concept of **homeostasis**, which describes the body's attempt to maintain a stable internal state. This is a dynamic physiological response on the part of the body to the demands of the environment. The body seeks balance, and stress presents a challenge to homeostasis. It was Cannon who articulated the concept of the **fight-or-flight response** which describes a complex autonomic reaction to emergencies. The sympathetic nervous system and hormones secreted by the adrenal glands interact in an adaptive response developed through evolution. This response helps us to cope with potential attacks from a threatening world.

Cannon (1939) expressed concern about the implications for physical illness through the continuous activation of the fight-or-flight reaction in response to the chronic pressures and demands of the contemporary world. The actions implied by the term *fight-or-flight* are simply not always appropriate in our contemporary world. In fact, to engage in either of these responses in today's world could have disastrous consequences. Our young businessman could neither fight nor flee. He had to sit at his desk while his body experienced the same physiological responses as his ancestors (churning stomach, tightening muscles, pounding heart, soaring blood pressure, grinding teeth, hyperventilation, profuse sweating) while his emotions were running wild. It is not difficult to understand how the continual stimulation of this response could eventually result in physical illness.

A challenge to the universality of the fight-or-flight response has recently been put forth by Taylor et al. (2000), who propose that although the physiological component of the fight-or-flight response may be common to both males and females, the female behavioural component will also involve social and nurturant behaviours. These responses are described as "tend and befriend" behaviours. The implication is that the female response to stress has evolved to increase the likelihood of survival of both the self and offspring. *Tending* is associated with nurturing activities, and *befriending* involves establishing social networks. This attachment–caregiving response in females may be triggered by neuro-endocrine responses to stress. This theory is described as "a biobehavioural alternative to the fight-or-flight response" (Cannon, 1932), which has dominated stress research for the past five decades and has been "disproportionately based on studies of males" (Taylor et al., 2000, p. 422). Taylor (2006) states further that "we are affiliative creatures who respond to stress collectively, as well as individually, and these responses are characteristic of men as well as women" (p. 155).

Rice (1999) describes several distinct meanings attached to stress. One has to do with external causes. These are the environmental demands placed upon us that cause us to feel stressed. As such, these should be described as *stressors*, rather than *stress*. It is in response to these external stressors that we invoke coping strategies to reduce their impact. Stress is concerned with subjective responses and refers to the interpretive mental state of the individual. Stress allows us to react cognitively to diminish, augment, or distort the impact of external events. Another term used in this context is *strain*, which describes the long-term consequences of exposure to stress and can result in physiological problems, such as cardiovascular disease; psychological concerns, such as depression; and cognitive concerns (Francis & Barling, 2005).

The belief that stress is somehow "all in our minds" has been expressed by writers and philosophers throughout history. Epictetus, for example, said some two thousand years ago that "Humans are not disturbed by events, but by the view they take of them." Shakespeare wrote in *Hamlet* that "There is no such thing as good or bad, but thinking makes it so." Milton suggested in *Paradise Lost* that "The mind is its own place, and in itself can make a Heaven of Hell, a Hell of Heaven." And Mark Twain said, "I am an old man and have known a great many troubles—but most of them never happened."

Rice (1999) points out that even though stress may be a subjective experience, we frequently use physical terms to explain its impact. We speak of being on the "edge" of a breakdown, of feeling the "weight" of the world, of not being sure that we can cope with "the pressure" or of "exploding" if we are exposed to any more stress. Regardless of our personal views of what stress feels like, the fact is that stress imposes a physiological challenge which, if prolonged, can result in a decreased capacity to cope physiologically (Rice, 1999).

THE PHYSIOLOGY OF STRESS

There are two major components of the physical response to stress—the **nervous system** and the **endocrine system**. The nervous system is comprised of two divisions, the **central nervous system** and the **peripheral nervous system**. The former is made up of the brain and the spinal cord, while the latter is made up of the somatic nervous system and the autonomic nervous system, which is further divided into the sympathetic and parasympathetic nervous systems. The physiology of stress creates a highly complex response that begins when an individual perceives a (real or imagined) threat. The perception of stress mobilizes the body to act through two interrelated systems (Kemeny, 2005). One is the sympathetic adrenomedullary (SAM) system, in which the sympathetic nervous system and the adrenal medulla are most important. The second is the hypothalamic-pituitary-adrenal (HPA) axis, which initiates a response in the hypothalamus. The SAM system initiates the body's rapid *fight-or-flight* response to stress through the release of adrenaline and noradrenaline from the adrenal medulla as mediated by the sympathetic nervous system. The HPA system, on the other hand, is a delayed response to stress that attempts to minimize the initial impact of stress and restore the body to a balanced state. It involves activation of the adrenal cortex and the secretion of corticosteroids, the most important of which is cortisol. The levels of circulating cortisol in the blood and saliva frequently serve as a physiological indicator of stress. Prolonged or repeated activation of the HPA system can lead to dysregulation in the body's responses to stress, which can have both physical and psychological consequences.

nervous system: one of the two major components of the physical response to stress; made up of the central nervous system and the peripheral nervous system.

endocrine system: a system of the. body that controls glandular responses to stress; responds more slowly than the nervous system but the effects can persist for weeks.

central nervous system: the division of the nervous system that is composed of the brain and the spinal cord.

peripheral nervous system: the division of the nervous system that is made up of the somatic nervous system and the autonomic nervous system (which is further divided into the sympathetic and parasympathetic nervous systems).

hypothalamus: a portion of the brain that initiates the stress response in both the nervous system and the endocrine system.

More specifically, the stress response begins in the **hypothalamus**, which is located in the central core of the brain. It initiates the stress response in both the nervous system and the endocrine system. The hypothalamus helps maintain homeostasis in the body through its many regulatory functions. As well, it controls activities such as eating, drinking, and sexual behaviour, all of which are greatly affected by stress. The activities of the hypothalamus increase arousal in the sympathetic nervous system in the form of the previously described fight-or-flight response (Cannon, 1939). The heart beats faster and blood pressure increases at the same time as peripheral blood vessels, in areas such as the hands and feet, constrict to ensure sufficient blood supplies for the brain and skeletal muscles. Stored fats and glucose flow into the bloodstream to provide fuel for necessary actions. Respiration rate increases and the bronchial tubes dilate to help increase oxygen flow for the metabolism of fuel. Pupils dilate to allow more light to enter the eyes and improve vision. The efficiency of the process is demonstrated when non-essential activities, such as digestion, decrease.

adrenal medulla: the central portion of the adrenal gland; secretes catecholamines (containing both adrenaline and noradrenaline) when the hypothalamus initiates the stress response.

sympathetic nervous system: the system responsible for the "fight-or-flight" response when triggered by the hypothalamus (faster heartbeat, increased blood pressure).

As a part of this response, the hypothalamus causes the **adrenal medulla**, located above the kidneys, to secrete *catecholamines*, which contain the hormones adrenaline and noradrenaline (also known as epinephrine and norepinephrine). Catecholamines affect the response of the **sympathetic nervous system**, and the level of these two hormones increases with the severity of the stress. The actions of adrenaline and noradrenaline are different, however. The former is fast-acting and increases with mental stress; the effect of the latter is more prolonged and increases with physical activity.

Adrenaline has a powerful impact on heart function and blood pressure. Presumably it is this experience that finds expression in the phrase "adrenaline rush." It is interesting that this phrase is usually viewed in positive terms as something that people seek. We even go so far as to ascribe an addictive quality to it by describing people who purposefully seek the physiological "high" that adrenaline brings as "adrenaline junkies." These sensation-seekers may engage in extreme activities to purposefully initiate the fight-or-flight response and the flow of adrenaline.

limbic system: a system of the brain that is responsible, in part, for emotion in the stress response.

reticular formation: complex system running through the middle of the brain stem that serves as a communication network to filter messages between the brain and the body.

Also involved in the stress response is the **limbic system** of the brain, which adds an element of *emotion* to the response that goes beyond the identified dimensions of fight-or-flight. The feelings triggered by the limbic system include aggression, anger, fear, anxiety, sexual arousal, and pain. In addition, the **reticular formation** is a complex system running through the middle of the brain stem that performs several functions during the stress response. It serves as a communication network that filters messages between the brain and the body, which is most important when we consider the impact that the brain's perception of psychosocial stressors can have on physical systems in the body. The reticular formation receives input from all the sensory systems and influences which sensory information is processed or blocked.

Such selectivity results in increased efficiency in the system, which can become apparent to us in quite dramatic ways. For example, in high-arousal situations we may find ourselves remarkably able to selectively attend to a specific task while ignoring irrelevant distractions. A basketball player, given the opportunity to win a game by sinking a last-second foul shot, needs to focus his attention on the front rim of the hoop. He does not want to be distracted by the noise of the crowd and the movement of those behind the basket, who will often go to considerable extremes in an attempt to distract him. The reticular formation helps us attend to what matters and ignore what doesn't matter. It also serves an important role in modulating the brain's levels of arousal or alertness in preparation for action.

In contrast to the sympathetic nervous system, the **parasympathetic** component of the autonomic system is activated by the hypothalamus to re-establish homeostasis in the system and to promote the reconstructive process following a stressful experience. It is associated with a relaxed or hypometabolic state in which the heart rate slows and blood pressure drops. Muscle tension decreases and respiration is slow and easy.

The endocrine system responds to stress more slowly than does the nervous system, but the effects associated with it can persist for weeks. The **pituitary gland**, which is located in the brain close to the hypothalamus, is described as the "master" gland because of its controlling effect on other glands. Most of the hormones secreted by the pituitary gland have an indirect impact on stress. The most important of these is adrenocorticotropic hormone (ACTH), which acts on the adrenal glands and is eventually involved in the release of up to 30 stress hormones (Smith, 1993).

The **adrenal cortex** secretes **glucocorticoids** and mineralocorticoids. One of the glucocorticoids is cortisol, an important stress hormone that provides energy to the system by converting stored protein and fats into glucose. If stress is prolonged, glucocorticoids can adversely affect the body's ability to resist disease and recover from injury. Cortisol levels are often used as an index of stress. Aldosterone is an important mineralocorticoid that regulates minerals in the body during stress by increasing blood pressure.

The **thyroid gland** functions in the stress response by producing thyroxine, which increases the release of fatty-acid fuels that are metabolized in the stress process. Elevated thyroxine levels increase blood pressure and respiration rate. Mental processes are also affected, in that individuals feel more anxious or agitated.

The **pancreas**, which lies close to the stomach, secretes insulin and glucagon in response to blood sugar levels. Insulin decreases blood sugar by storing it, whereas glucagon stimulates increases in blood sugar, which is an energy source during times of stress.

The indication is that the autonomic nervous system responds rapidly in response to stress and the endocrine system responds more slowly, although its impact usually continues much longer. Acting together, these two systems provide a physiological response to stress that can be both adaptive and maladaptive.

The General Adaptation Syndrome

Initially, Selye conducted his research on laboratory animals. He observed that animals exposed to chronic stress demonstrated physical distress that included organic pathology and, ultimately, death. This work and that of others, such as Brady's work on executive monkeys (Brady, Porter, Conrad, & Mason, 1958), resulted in Selye's conceptualization of the **General Adaptation Syndrome (GAS)** (Selye, 1956). This is a three-stage response of the body to stressors. In the initial phase, the body goes into **alarm** as it mobilizes its defences against the stress. This involves many of the processes involved in the fight-or-flight response. As experience will often confirm, this acute response is usually enough to allow us to deal successfully with the impact of a stressor and then allow homeostasis to be re-established.

If a source of stress moves from acute to chronic, the body enters the second phase of adaptation, which Selye called **resistance**. Here the body mobilizes its resources over an

parasympathetic nervous system: the component of the autonomic system that re-establishes homeostasis in the system and promotes the reconstructive process following a stressful experience.

pituitary gland: a gland in the brain described as the "master" gland because it controls other glands through the hormones it secretes; most of these hormones have an indirect impact on stress.

adrenal cortex: the outer portion of the adrenal gland; at times of stress supplies hormones to the body that provide energy and increase blood pressure, but that can adversely affect the body's ability to resist and recover from disease.

glucocorticoids: substances released by the adrenal glands upon stimulation from the sympathetic division when one is under stress.

thyroid gland: an important gland in the stress response because it produces thyroxine, which increases blood pressure and respiration rate, and affects mental processes.

pancreas: a gland that secretes insulin and glucagon in response to blood sugar levels.

General Adaptation Syndrome (GAS): the three-stage response of the body to stressors as identified by Selye: alarm, resistance, and exhaustion.

alarm: the initial phase of Selye's General Adaptation Syndrome in which the body mobilizes its defences against a stressor.

resistance: a set of physiological responses that allow a person to deal with a stressor; the second phase of Selye's General Adaptation Syndrome in which the body mobilizes its resources if the source of stress moves from acute to chronic.

extended period of time. Initially, the individual will appear as normal. If the stress continues for too long, however, the body's resources are depleted and resistance decreases.

The result of neurological and hormonal changes can be what Selye described as **diseases of adaptation**, which include cardiovascular disease, hypertension, peptic ulcers, bronchial asthma, and the increased risk of infection.

The resources our bodies use to resist stress are clearly finite. Eventually, if the stressor is too severe or continues for too long, the body enters what Selye called **exhaustion**. This is an endpoint at which the body's ability to resist the stressor breaks down and might even result in death if a return to homeostasis is not possible.

An extension of the body's attempt to maintain homeostasis is the concept of **allostatic load** as described by McEwan and Stellar (1993). This "refers to the price the body pays for being forced to adapt to adverse psychosocial or physical situations, and it represents either the presence of too much stress or the inefficient operation of the stress hormone response system" (McEwen, 2000, p. 110). In this context homeostasis is seen as a mechanism that functions within an optimal physiological set point that is critical for survival, whereas allostasis promotes coping and adaptation by maintaining stability through change. If this adaptive process is called upon too frequently, or is not managed well, the consequence is allostatic load.

Criticisms of Selye's theory centre on its narrowness because it is concerned only with physical responses to stress and does not account for psychosocial factors that influence the human stress response. This emphasis may have derived from his initial work with animals; his critics suggest that he neglected those cognitive processes unique to humans (Brannon & Feist, 2007).

Other biologically based models have been proposed to explain our ability to resist the impact of stress. One emphasizes genetic influences that may predispose an individual to increased risk for specific diseases or to vulnerabilities or reductions in resistance that may be expressed under certain conditions. Closely linked to this is the **stress-diathesis model**, which examines the interaction between the environment and heredity, often referred to as *nature versus nurture*. This model proposes that people may be predisposed to experience a physical effect in the presence of stressful events. Thus, individuals with a genetic predisposition for a particular condition may never display signs of that condition if they are not exposed to the precipitating stress. However, high levels of stress may test the limits of invulnerability even in those who are genetically robust. There is a sense of adaptability or "survival of the fittest." The implication is that stress forces an individual to adapt and evolve or run the risk of being selected against. Certainly many of us, when we consider our own vulnerability to disease, are quick to blame or flaunt our genes. We boast to others that we will never develop cardiovascular disease no matter how much we abuse our bodies with environmental stressors such as a poor diet or lack of exercise, as we are blessed with "good genes." We develop an inappropriate sense of invulnerability. The stress-diathesis model (or diathesis-stress model, as Grossarth-Maticek and Eysenck call it) is also discussed in chapter 4 in our examination of psychoneuroimmunology.

COGNITIVE TRANSACTIONAL MODELS

Selye's popularization of the idea of stress can't be underestimated. It's hard to imagine where we would be today without the contributions he made to the field. However, as we have indicated, his theory may be limited by its reliance on physiological processes based

---

diseases of adaptation: health problems that are the result of long-term neurological and hormonal changes caused by ongoing stress.

exhaustion: the fourth stage in Selye's General Adaptation Syndrome; the body experiences fatigue and immunocompromise because of the severity or duration of a stressor.

allostatic load: the long-term physiological impact of chronic exposure to stress.

stress-diathesis model: model that examines the interaction between the environment and heredity, often referred to as *nature versus nurture*; this model proposes that predisposing factors in an individual may determine whether or not a physical effect is experienced in the presence of stressful events.

on an animal model of behaviour. In this regard, his theory fails to take into account those higher-level cognitive abilities that are distinctly human and allow us to interpret our vulnerability to a particular stressor both now and in the future. Compared to Selye's model, **cognitive transactional models** of stress hold far more appeal for psychologists. As indicated in the definition provided by Lazarus and Folkman earlier in this chapter (Lazarus & Folkman, 1984), these models, described more recently by Lazarus (2006), emphasize the relationship existing between individuals and the environment and the appraisal individuals make of that relationship. Personal **cognitive appraisals** determine whether or not an event will be perceived as stressful. These are based on an individual's unique social learning history.

Lazarus and Folkman (1984) describe the process of cognitive appraisal as one that is "largely evaluative, focused on meaning or significance, and takes place continuously during waking hours" (p. 31). They distinguish among three kinds of appraisal influencing the coping process: **primary appraisal, secondary appraisal**, and **reappraisal**. They acknowledge that these are somewhat unfortunate terms, as one form of appraisal (e.g., primary as compared to secondary) is neither superior to nor precedes the other.

Primary appraisals are concerned with the initial evaluation of a situation. Three kinds of primary appraisal are identified—**irrelevant, benign-positive**, and **stressful**. The first involves a cognitive process by which an event is appraised to have no implications for the individual's well-being; it is irrelevant and requires no response. Benign-positive appraisals involve outcomes appraised to be positive and that may increase well-being. They are associated with pleasurable emotions, such as happiness, joy, or love. The only demand benign-positive appraisals place on the individual is the awareness that these feelings will end.

There are three types of stressful appraisal—**harm/loss, threat**, and **challenge**. Harm/loss appraisals involve significant physical or psychological loss, such as might be experienced through a serious illness or the loss of one's job. Threat involves the anticipation of situations of harm or loss. When an individual has experienced harm/loss, threat is involved, as it has implications for the future. Perceptions of threat allow a person to anticipate and prepare for the impact of an event. Challenge appraisals involve events perceived to be stressful, but the focus is one of positive excitement and anticipation of the potential for growth contained in the situation. Having to speak in front of a class may be perceived as threatening by a person with anxieties about public speaking but as an opportunity to test one's public-speaking abilities by an individual who has worked on these skills. Clearly, it is possible to experience threat and challenge in the same situation. The confident speaker may experience some threat in the speaking opportunity, which is expressed in the form of anxiety and some fear; however, the dominant emotions are confidence and anticipation. The overall emotional tone is positive, and the individual actively employs available resources in preparing to meet the demands imposed by the presentation.

Secondary appraisal is concerned with people's evaluations of their ability to cope with a situation. After the initial evaluation of the nature of the event, which is *primary appraisal*, individuals consider their options. As Lazarus and Folkman (1984) make clear, this is not simply an intellectual exercise. It is "a complex evaluative process that takes into account which coping options are available, the likelihood that a given coping option will accomplish what it is supposed to, and the likelihood one can apply a particular strategy" (p. 35). They point out that this is very similar to the distinction Bandura (1985) makes between

cognitive transactional models: models that emphasize the relationship between a person and his or her environment and the appraisal that the individual makes of the situation.

cognitive appraisal: assessment of whether or not an event is stressful.

primary appraisal: the initial evaluation of a situation.

secondary appraisal: an individual's evaluation of their ability to cope with a situation following the primary appraisal.

reappraisal: a continuous experience in which existing appraisals of situations are changed or modified on the basis of new information.

irrelevant appraisal: a cognitive process by which an event is appraised as having no implications for the individual's well-being.

benign-positive appraisal: a cognitive process by which an event is appraised to involve outcomes that are positive and may enhance well-being.

stressful appraisal: a cognitive process by which an event is appraised to involve harm/loss, threat, or challenge at the time of the primary appraisal.

harm/loss appraisal: a type of stressful appraisal at the time of primary appraisal that involves significant physical or psychological loss.

threat appraisal: an appraisal at the time of the primary appraisal that involves the anticipation of harm or loss.

challenge appraisal: appraisal in which, though an event is perceived to be stressful, the focus is one of positive excitement and the potential for growth.

outcome and efficacy judgments. Bandura states that "efficacy and outcome judgments are differentiated because individuals can believe that a particular course of action will produce certain outcomes, but they do not act on that outcome belief because they question whether they can actually execute the necessary activities" (1985, p. 392).

The interaction between the secondary appraisals of coping options and the primary appraisals of the situation determines an individual's emotional reaction to the event. If the consequences of an event are perceived as important, individuals may experience considerable stress if they believe they cannot cope with the event; a state of helplessness may result. Conversely, *challenge appraisals* are more likely to result when an individual feels in control of the situation, even if this means overcoming extreme adversity.

We are all aware that some individuals, when faced with a devastating situation such as an illness or loss of a relationship, articulate their efforts to cope in very positive ways. They describe the challenge of *confronting* through their own behaviour what others would perceive as overwhelming odds. They know they may not ultimately have an outcome others would consider desirable, but they focus their attention on elements of the situation that are under their control. For example, they may talk of the challenge of coping with pain, either physical or psychological, to the best of their ability while recognizing that there are elements of the situation that are outside their control. Even though a situation may appear hopeless, they search for challenges.

Reappraisal is a continuous experience in which existing appraisals are changed or modified on the basis of new information. Reappraisal simply follows an earlier appraisal of an event and results in a new appraisal. What may vary is the direction of the outcome of the appraisal. For example, an irrelevant situation may now be perceived in terms of threat, or a harm/loss situation may now be appraised as a challenge. Lazarus and Folkman (1984) also identify what they call a *defensive reappraisal*. They describe this as a self-generated coping strategy in which an attempt is made to reinterpret past events more positively or to view current threats or losses as being less threatening.

Also of importance in the cognitive appraisal process is the concept of **vulnerability**, which reflects the adequacy of an individual's resources. This is a concept that, like so many in this area, is defined in the context of a relationship. With regard to physical issues, it is possible to think of vulnerability only in terms of resources. A physical injury can increase vulnerability to further injury. However, deficiencies in resources will result in a psychological vulnerability only when resource deficiency threatens that which is valued by the individual. Therefore, an individual may have resource deficiencies but not experience vulnerability, if the deficiencies do not threaten areas that are important to him or her.

The cognitive transactional model also identifies **person** and **situation** variables that influence appraisal. The impact of these variables is in the individual's assessment of the salience of an event, an individual's understanding of the event, the consequence of an event, and ultimately, the outcome of a particular encounter (Lazarus & Folkman, 1984). Person and situation variables are interdependent and involve transactions between individuals and their environments.

The person variables of importance are **commitments** and **beliefs**. *Commitments* are concerned with what is important to an individual. Commitments influence appraisal by determining the importance of a particular encounter and will affect the choices made to achieve a desired outcome. As well, they interact with concepts we discussed in the

vulnerability: physically, the adequacy of an individual's resources; psychologically, a threat to something that an individual values.

person variables: variables, particularly commitments and beliefs, that interact with situation variables to affect the appraisal of a situation's stressfulness.

situation variables: variables that interact with person variables to influence the appraisal of a situation.

commitments as person variables: values that influence appraisal by determining the importance of a particular encounter and that affect the choices made to achieve a desired outcome.

beliefs as person variables: pre-existing notions, both personal and cultural, that influence appraisal, and thus stress, by determining the meaning given to the environment.

context of primary appraisal, such as challenge, threat, benefit, or harm, to determine if an individual will engage in or avoid an encounter. *Beliefs* are pre-existing notions that determine the meaning given to the environment. They can be both personal and cultural. Their impact, which is often difficult to observe, is most obvious when there is a sudden change in the belief system.

Numerous factors influencing the appraisal process have been identified. **Novelty** refers to an individual's previous experience with a situation. **Predictability** identifies characteristics of the environment that can be learned or discerned. This allows an individual to prepare for an event and therefore reduce the stress involved. Of more relevance to appraisal, particularly in humans, is the concept of **event uncertainty**, which involves issues of probability. The observation is that high levels of uncertainty can be extremely stressful.

Temporal situational factors are also important in stress appraisal. **Imminence** concerns the time interval during which an event is being anticipated. Typically, the more imminent an event, the more intense the appraisal. **Duration** refers to the time period during which a stressful event occurs. The implication is that the longer the duration, the more stressful the event. This concept is reminiscent of Selye's General Adaptation Syndrome, in which the duration of stress plays an important role; continued exposure to stress compromises resistance and leads ultimately to exhaustion. **Temporal uncertainty** is concerned with the stress involved in *not knowing* when an event will occur.

A final concern here relates to the *timing* of stressful events in the context of the life cycle. This suggests that there are appropriate or "usual" times for events to occur in one's life. If these expectations are violated, it may result in the event being appraised as more stressful by some individuals. We have a sense of an order that we move through in our lives, and this master calendar allows us to develop expectations and prepare for events. When the timing is wrong, normal life events may become sources of stress. We can all think of people who have been affected by life events in this way, such as the couple who have a child unexpectedly later in life, or the athlete whose career comes to an abrupt end due to injury.

The model developed by Lazarus and his colleagues views stress as a complex, dynamic process in which individuals' experience of stress is determined by their own unique cognitive appraisal of the event and their coping abilities.

THE ROLE OF PERSONALITY IN STRESS AND COPING

If it were possible to prove that a particular temperament or set of personality traits predisposed an individual to a specific disease, then given the stable, enduring qualities of personality it might be possible to predict disease and intervene to reduce risk. There are several ways these interactions might occur (Rice, 1999). A specific personality profile might cause a specific disease to develop, as is the case with Type A personality and coronary heart disease. A second possibility is that a particular disease process could cause a particular personality profile—as when depression follows the diagnosis of a serious illness. The third possibility is that personality affects or filters the response to an illness. An individual receiving the news of a serious illness might respond in an optimistic and active manner compared to another person who responds passively and pessimistically. In the fourth possibility, personality interacts with the disease process in a feedback loop that affects the individual's physiology and may influence the disease process itself. Ultimately,

novelty: the extent to which an individual's previous experience with a situation influences the appraisal process.

predictability: a characteristic of the environment that allows an individual to prepare for an event and therefore reduce the stress involved.

event uncertainty: the inability to predict the probability of an event, which, as a result, increases the stress response

imminence: interval during which an event is being anticipated; the more imminent an event, the more intense the appraisal.

duration: situational factor involved in stress appraisal.

temporal uncertainty: lack of knowledge about when an event will occur, which can result in stress.

the question centres on whether there are personality traits that predict behaviours, such as smoking or alcohol use, or disease processes, such as cancer or coronary disease.

The most extensively studied set of personality traits in connection with disease is the **Type A behaviour pattern**. This personality type was first identified by two cardiologists, Meyer Friedman and Ray Rosenman, in 1974. They described individuals they saw frequently in their medical practice whom they believed were at a much higher risk for cardiovascular disease. Such "Type A" individuals display a sense of time urgency, are impatient and very competitive, and can be aggressive and hostile. They exhibit behavioural characteristics such as rapid, explosive, clipped speech; frequent interruptions of another speaker; speech-hurrying techniques (e.g., nodding the head while another person speaks); vehement reactions to time impedance; emphatic one-word responses; and finger-pointing to emphasize speech.

These individuals stand in comparison to "Type B" individuals, who give the impression of being relaxed and calm, are less competitive, are not overly reactive to time impediments, and rarely display hostility. Powerful empirical support has emerged for the suggestion that Type A behaviours are linked to an increased risk for coronary disease. Indeed, this set of behaviours has been identified as a risk factor for all forms of morbidity (Yakubovich, Ragland, Brand, & Syme, 1988). However, some inconsistencies in the findings have led to a search for the toxic core of Type A behaviours. This work initially identified the components of hostility and anger to be the crucial elements. Wright (1988) expanded it to describe a multi-causal pathway that identifies Type A behaviour in combination with family history, lifestyle risks, and anger as being the core risk factors. Williams et al. (2000) report that individuals with high anger-scale scores have a greatly elevated risk of heart attack in comparison to those with low scores. Also of interest is work summarized by Smith and Ruiz (2002) that has identified **social dominance** as a risk factor for coronary disease that is independent of hostility. Social dominance is described as "a set of controlling behaviours, including the tendency to cut off and talk over the interviewer" (p. 552).

Being able to identify the risk factors of coronary heart disease increases the likelihood of designing interventions that may successfully modify or eliminate destructive behaviours (Straub, 2001). These could involve a variety of activities such as making philosophical decisions about one's lifestyle, training in relaxation techniques, or specific behavioural management programs. The latter are designed to help people learn to modify emotional responses, such as hostility and anger, and control environmental conditions through techniques like practising time management, engaging in problem solving, beginning an exercise program, developing communication skills, and managing diet. You might find it relevant at this point to read "Peter's Story" in chapter 9 of this book. Peter would have been described as a Type A individual prior to having a heart attack. After surviving this scare he became involved in a hospital-based behavioural retraining program and has made significant lifestyle changes that have resulted in remarkable improvements to his health.

Interestingly, programs designed to change maladaptive behaviours are not usually described in terms of coping but are usually described as being programs in "stress management." This suggests that it is easier to sell the concept of *stress* than it is the concept of *coping*. The term *stress management* permeates our culture. We are taught to "manage" our stress rather than to cope. This sounds like an active, dynamic, even aggressive

Type A behaviour pattern: behaviours include impatience, time urgency, aggressiveness, hostility, and competitiveness; originally believed to be predictive of coronary heart disease.

social dominance: a risk factor for coronary disease that is independent of hostility; social dominance is described as "a set of controlling behaviours, including the tendency to cut off and talk over the interviewer."

response to the situation in which we will overwhelm the stress. Coping, on the other hand, suggests a more passive, reflective stance. To say that you are going to a stress management workshop implies that you are still in control of your situation and are learning techniques to help you maintain your position. A workshop in coping suggests that things have deteriorated for you and you are in need of help.

Research that examines the relationship between health outcomes and personality has focused primarily on negative traits (Kern & Friedman, 2008). In 1993 Friedman et al. suggested that conscientiousness, as measured in childhood, is predictive of longevity. Specifically, the indication is that higher levels of conscientiousness are significantly related to a longer life and more positive health behaviours.

A meta-analysis on 194 studies (Bogg & Roberts, 2004) indicated that "conscientiousness-related traits were negatively related to all risky health-related behaviors and positively related to all beneficial health-related behaviors" (p. 887). The behavioural contributors to mortality that were looked at include tobacco use, levels of physical activity, diet, alcohol use, sexual behaviour, vehicular behaviours, and illicit drug use, which are related to longevity through illnesses such as cardiovascular disease, cancer, AIDS, and accidental deaths. This may occur because a lack of conscientiousness is related to disinhibition and impulsive, reckless, present-centred behaviours as compared to the planned, risk-avoidant, long-term behaviours of conscientious individuals. Conscientiousness is also related to conventionality which such suggests that individuals displaying this trait are more likely to "uphold social norms and traditions (i.e. traditionalism), avoid trouble, and not let others down (i.e. responsibility)" (Bogg & Roberts, 2004, p. 890). Ultimately the value in this type of research may lie in interventions that focus on individuals who display a lack of conscientiousness or in attempting to enhance behaviours related to conscientiousness.

It appears that personality is an important determinant of health related behaviours and consideration should be given to how personality may positively or negatively affect our health. Kubzansky et al. (2009) conclude that a life course perspective "dovetails nicely with other research on personality and health which has posited cumulative effects via biological pathways, effects on stress, coping, and emotional responses, and health or illness behaviours" (p. 370). Again, the value of interventions which focus on early childhood characteristics is emphasized, particularly as it relates to the cumulative effect on adult health outcomes.

COPING

This discussion of the Type A behaviour pattern and its modification provides a transition into a discussion of specific coping behaviours. Sarafino (1998) states that as individuals make the "effort to neutralize or reduce stress, coping activities are geared toward decreasing the person's appraisal of or concern for this discrepancy. Thus coping is the process by which people try to manage the perceived discrepancy between the demands and resources they appraise in a stressful situation" (p. 133). These efforts may not necessarily improve the person's situation. As Rice (1999) points out, it has not always been clear whether we are talking about the process or outcome of coping. He cites research by Rudolph, Dennig, and Weisz (1995) that identifies three components of coping. They distinguish between a **coping response** and a **stress response**. A coping response is an

coping response: an intentional physical or mental act that is initiated in response to a stressor.

stress response: a response that reflects a spontaneous emotional or behavioural reaction to stress, rather than a deliberate attempt to cope.

intentional physical or mental act that is initiated in response to a stressor. It can be directed toward either external events or internal states. A stress response is defined as "any response that reflects a spontaneous emotional or behavioral reaction to stress, rather than a deliberate attempt to cope" (p. 329). The objective of a coping response, which is usually to reduce the impact of stress, is described as a **coping goal**. The specific or actual outcomes of a coping response are called **coping outcomes**.

Lazarus and his colleague have suggested that coping can serve two functions (Lazarus & Folkman, 1984). **Problem-focused coping** is concerned with changing the situation by defining the problem, looking at alternative solutions, evaluating the implications of the alternatives, and choosing the best one to act on. It is a rational approach, similar to problem solving. However, it also includes solutions that are focused inward as well as those directed at the environment. In our daily existence we use problem-focused coping strategies frequently as we take action to reduce the demands placed upon us. Students who feel overwhelmed with assignments may seek out the professor to discuss how they can reduce the impact of their workload. As part of this process, they might focus on what material to study, using time management to plan their study time more efficiently and reorganize their approach to preparing for the exams. Two types of problem-focused coping have been identified—*proactive coping* and *combative coping* (Aspinwall & Taylor, 1997). In proactive coping, potential stressors are anticipated and acted on in advance to either prevent or decrease their impact. In combative coping, people react to an unavoidable stress in a manner designed to help cope with the stress. For example, the relaxation technique described at the end of this chapter can be used as a combative coping skill to help deal with muscle tension.

Emotion-focused coping involves controlling emotional responses to an event. This could consist of using cognitive processes, such as avoidance or minimization, to decrease emotional distress, or using techniques to increase emotional intensity, as one might do in preparation for an athletic competition. Some forms of emotion-focused coping change nothing about the objective situation. They change only the manner in which an event is perceived and, as such, constitute reappraisal.

The emotional response to a situation can be regulated through both behavioural and cognitive strategies. Cognitive strategies change the way we think about a situation. There is a tendency to use emotion-focused coping when the individual believes nothing can be done to change the stressful situation. Lazarus and Folkman (1984) have indicated that problem-focused and emotion-focused coping strategies can be used at the same time and can either facilitate or impede each other in the coping process.

In their efforts to cope with stress, people call upon the **personal resources** available to them to help prevent the occurence of stressful events and to help them cope with stressful situations as they occur. The first of these personal resource mechanisms is **social support**. We discuss social support on a number of occasions in this book. In times of stress we have all benefitted from support received from friends, family, and institutions such as social agencies, the health care system, and the church. For example, it is reported that 80 percent of Americans believe prayer can have a positive impact on the course of an illness (Levin & Puchalski, 1997). In a general sense, spirituality is a frequent coping response to stress. Gall et al. (2005), in a recent review of the relevant literature, suggest that "the construct of spirituality is congruent with the basic tenets of the transactional model of coping. Specifically, this framework is seen to be dynamic and

coping goal: the objective of a coping response (which is usually to reduce the impact of stress).

coping outcomes: the specific outcomes of a coping response.

problem-focused coping: coping by actively addressing the stressors associated with a disease, such as cancer and its treatment.

emotion-focused coping: coping by focusing on ways to reduce the emotional impact of a disease without trying to cure it.

personal resources: resources that are available to people in their own lives to help them reduce the potential for stressful events and cope with stressful situations as they occur.

social support: a collection of interpersonal resources people have at their disposal to help them avoid or cope with difficult times in their lives.

relational, phenomenological, transactional, and process-oriented" (p. 90). We, in turn, provide assistance to family and friends when they are stressed. That we can turn to others and they to us is an expectation of the human condition and, as a first line of defence, it is a highly effective and widely used resource.

Social support takes different forms. **Emotional support** refers to being cared for and loved; **informational support** is the advice and information made available to us concerning a particular event; **tangible support** is the direct aid or services we receive to assist us in coping with stress. Each of these forms of support is more relevant at different times in the coping process. However, it is clearly the *perception* of social support rather than the *objective situation* that is most important (Coyne, Aldwin, & Lazarus, 1981).

Social support is believed to exert its effect on stress in one of two ways (Cohen & Wills, 1985). The **stress-buffering hypothesis** suggests that social support has an indirect effect and acts as a buffer to protect individuals from the negative effects of stress. This means that when people are exposed to stress, the social support they receive from others serves to buffer and therefore reduce the impact of the event. Social support acts between the event and the recipient, or between the response to the stress and the outcome. As a result, the effect of social support should be most noticeable at higher levels of stress, and social support should have little impact on lower levels of stress. Alternatively, social support may have direct effects that are independent of stress and serve to enhance an individual's general sense of well-being and self-esteem, thereby increasing their sense of control, decreasing anxiety, and increasing health-promoting behaviours—all of which help to reduce stress.

Kaplan, Sallis, and Patterson (1993) suggest that more complex models will ultimately be required to explain the relationship between social support and the impact of stress. One possibility is a direct-effect model incorporating the functional effects of the social support system (which may affect health either positively or negatively). These researchers "would expect that close, caring relationships would play a stronger role in reinforcing health behavior and in enhancing use of the health care system. At the other extreme, social isolation might contribute to disconnection with services, poor nutrition, and inadequate responses to emergency" (p. 145). It is clear that lack of social support is a risk factor for illness. For example, a lack of social support is reported to be as important a risk factor for cardiovascular disease as are cigarette smoking, poor diet, and inadequate physical activity (Kaplan, Sallis, & Patterson, 1993).

Another factor that may influence one's ability to cope with stress is a sense of **personal control**. Feeling in control of a situation appears to reduce the impact of stressful events. As Bandura (1985) has indicated, one's sense of control over events can be achieved either behaviourally, by taking actions to reduce stress, or cognitively, by believing in one's ability to control the impact of stressful events. Bandura points out that it is important to distinguish between these two forms of control, as the relationship between actual and perceived coping efficacy is often not perfect. He states that "there are many competent people who are plagued by a sense of inefficacy and many less competent ones who remain unperturbed by impending threats because they are self-assured of their coping capabilities" (p. 440).

Behavioural control has been demonstrated to greatly reduce the impact of stressful events. To have behavioural control over an event increases one's sense of predictability, which reduces stress. With regard to cognitive control, individuals who believe they can

emotional support: support provided by people who take the time to understand our fears and frustrations, who help calm us during anxious times, who help lift our moods, or who distract us from our worries.

informational support: the provision of information that might include such things as treatment options or typical recovery times from a treatment or injury.

tangible support: help with the demands of daily living, such as getting meals and rides to the doctor.

stress-buffering hypothesis: the theory that social support has an indirect effect and acts as a buffer to protect individuals from the negative effects of stress.

personal control: a factor that influences a person's ability to cope with stress; personal control can be achieved either behaviourally or cognitively.

effect control over stressful events have demonstrated that they will be less affected physiologically and behaviourally than those who believe they have no personal control over the situation. Bandura (1997) suggests that the "intensity and chronicity of human stress is governed largely by perceived control over the demands of one's life" (p. 262). He cites epidemiological and correlational evidence which suggests that a lack of behavioural, or even perceived, control over such demands increases our risk of infection, contributes to the development of physical disorders, and accelerates the rate at which disease progresses.

The role of perceived behavioural and cognitive control over stressful events is of importance to the emerging field of **positive psychology**, which encourages psychologists to use fewer negative, deficit-oriented, or problem-focused frameworks and to focus more on effective human functioning (Sheldon & King, 2001). The emphasis here is on what has been described as strength-based assessment (Tedeschi & Kilmer (2005).

Fundamental to this new interest is the concept of **resilience**, which Masten (2001) describes as "a class of phenomena characterized by good outcomes in spite of serious threats to adaptation or development" (p. 228). Research in this area attempts to understand better the process by which resilience is developed and can be enhanced (Karapetian et al., 2005). Positive emotions can have a powerful undoing effect on negative emotions and individuals should be encouraged to cultivate positive emotional experiences to help them cope with stress and adversity (Fredrickson, 2001).

Lyubomirsky (2001) discusses cognitive and motivational strategies that have been demonstrated to increase happiness and reduce the impact of stress. These include developing positive perceptions of one's self, learning to derive positive meanings from negative experiences, using humour and faith, not engaging in self-rumination, and using social comparison selectively in a manner designed to protect one's sense of well-being.

In their research on the relationship between positive emotions and health, Richman et al. (2005) conclude that "the consistency of effects across diseases that involve different physiological systems (cardiovascular, metabolic, and respiratory) strongly suggests broad-based effects of positive emotion on health. Moreover, the prospective analyses suggest the possibility of a protective role for positive emotion in the development of disease" (p. 427). The two positive emotions they examined were hope and curiosity, which were found to have a protective impact across multiple disease outcomes. They also concluded that the impact of positive emotions is not simply equivalent to "the absence of negative emotion" (p. 427), but rather there appears to be an increase in resilience and health promotion suggesting a unique protective role for positive emotions. Following an extensive review of the literature, Lyubomirsky et al. (2005) conclude that "happy individuals are more likely than their less happy peers to have fulfilling marriages and relationships, high incomes, superior work performance, community involvement, robust health, and a long life" (p. 846).

Social support and personal control are resources that increase one's ability to cope with stress. However, at times such resources are unavailable or insufficient to cope with high levels of stress. At these times, it is often necessary to seek the assistance of techniques that have been specifically developed to help people cope with stress either directly or indirectly. (Note that these are techniques that are considered adaptive compared to strategies such as alcohol or drug use, which, although effective in some ways, are *not* adaptive and ultimately increase stress.) Although adaptive techniques are coping techniques, they are often labelled **stress management techniques**.

positive psychology: approach that encourages psychologists to use fewer negative or problem-focused frameworks and to focus more on effective human functioning.

resilience: concept in positive psychology that describes "good outcomes in spite of serious threats to adaptation or development."

stress management techniques: techniques that have been developed specifically to help people cope with stress either directly or indirectly.

Some of the most widely used and effective interventions against stress are the various **relaxation techniques** that have been developed throughout history. These are strategies based on a simple principle—that we cannot be relaxed and tense at the same time. It is the antidote to the fight-or-flight response, which is under the control of the sympathetic nervous system, whereas the relaxation response is under the control of the parasympathetic nervous system. In a relaxed state, the heart slows, blood pressure drops, breathing is slow and easy, and muscle tension decreases. This response, described earlier as **hypometabolic**, is the opposite of the **hypermetabolic** fight-or-flight response. These responses reciprocally inhibit one another. One of the implications of understanding this inhibitory process is that it may allow us to gain some control over the autonomic nervous system, which has long been considered an involuntary system (i.e., outside of volitional control). Demonstrations of physiological control by highly trained individuals have provided support for this possibility and further expanded our understanding of physiological control.

East and West: Now the Twain Shall Meet

Since the mid-1960s, Western society has shown an increased interest in Eastern philosophies and meditative disciplines. This enthusiasm, shared by many, has largely focused on techniques designed to promote psychological and physical well-being; this interest forms an important component of the stress and coping literature. Many researchers have been intrigued by accounts of bodily control often difficult for us to comprehend (Brunton, 1972; Murray, 1980; Yogananda, 1946). Brunton, in a book first published in 1934, describes his travels to discover a "secret" India. He speaks of a culture described under the generic term of *Yoga* that "proffers benefits to mankind as valuable in their own way as any proffered by the Western sciences. It can bring our bodies nearer the healthy condition which nature intended them to possess; it can bestow one of modern civilization's most urgent needs—a flawless serenity of mind" (p. 6).

The philosopher Harvey Cox (1973) suggests that the "mystics and contemplatives have served as the guardians of that uniquely human realm called interiority" (p. 93). He believes that our renewed interest in this realm represents a survival instinct intended to turn our attention from without to within.

Our fascination with these traditions is important in a health psychology context, as it has caused us to question our understanding of the mind–body interaction. Our ability to control physiological processes was challenged by reports of individuals who claimed they could control or even stop their hearts, survive lengthy pit burials, regulate their body temperatures, or allow their skins to be penetrated without bleeding. It is quite reasonable to suggest that it was these early investigations that provided the foundation for many of the stress-management techniques we practise today. Techniques such as biofeedback and many of the secular relaxation strategies we use are firmly rooted in the belief that we can gain control of physiological variables previously thought to be outside our control.

Therese Brousse was a pioneer in this field. In 1935 she took a crude, portable electrocardiograph to India to record attempts by yogis to achieve voluntary control of cardiovascular activity. One of her published records indicates that for one individual, heart potentials and pulse waves recorded from the radial artery decreased almost to zero and remained there for several seconds. More than 20 years later, Wenger, Bagchi, and Anand

(1961) returned to India with more sophisticated equipment to record cardiovascular activity in four individuals who claimed to be able to slow or stop their hearts (including the person previously investigated by Brousse).

It was clear from the investigators' results that these individuals did not directly control the functioning of their hearts; rather, they used striate muscle control to produce changes in circulatory patterns. These yogis used a technique called the Valsalva manoeuvre, which involves an increase in muscle tension in the abdominal and thoracic muscles, closure of the glottis, and development of intrathoracic pressure. This interferes with venous return to the heart, so that heart sounds are diminished and masked by muscular sounds, and the radial pulse seems to disappear. The increased sophistication of the equipment in the study by Wenger and his colleagues indicated that normal cardiac activity continued to occur. The results Brousse had reported were an artifact of the crude recording techniques she used and did not take into account the impact of the Valsalva manoeuvre. Although these individuals did not stop their hearts, they did demonstrate a remarkable level of muscular control.

Anand and Chhina (1961) carried out a similar investigation with three yogis who claimed to be able to stop their hearts. Rather than supporting their claim, the electrocardiogram (EKG) indicated that their heart rate actually increased while the yogis held their breaths. This finding is supported by accounts of research done on Swami Rama at the Menninger Foundation (Luce & Peper, 1971). Physiological recordings indicated that when the Swami "stopped" his heart, his heart rate actually increased to approximately 300 beats a minute over a period of 17 seconds. This sudden atrial fibrillation, a dangerous cardiac condition that prevents the necessary volume of blood from being pumped to the body, would normally render a person unconscious and, if continued, would soon lead to death. Apparently the Swami was intrigued by this result, as he indicated that he experienced a "fluttering" in his chest. It is also reported that he was able to produce a temperature difference of 10 degrees between two spots on his hand.

An interesting extension of this work was done by Anand, Chhina, and Singh (1961a), who conducted experiments on Sri Ramanand Yogi while he was sealed in an air-tight box for two periods of eight and ten hours. It was reported that he was able to reduce his oxygen intake and carbon dioxide output beyond his requirements under basal conditions. Even when he was breathing air with decreased oxygen and increased carbon dioxide content, his heart rate did not increase, nor did his respiratory activity increase or deepen. The electroencephalograph (EEG) indicated brain waves suggestive of early stages of sleep, despite there being no evidence that he actually slept.

EEG measures can also be used to assess the ability to maintain attention without being distracted. Anand, Chhina, and Singh (1961b) used an EEG to test the assertion that, during meditation, highly trained yogis are oblivious to external stimulation. They examined four such individuals and found that they were indeed able to achieve this state. The yogis did not demonstrate the expected blocking of the EEG alpha waves in response to stimulation during meditation. Two of the subjects kept their hands immersed in cold water for 45 to 55 minutes with no apparent discomfort. During this experience, they displayed persistent EEG alpha wave activity, which is associated with a state of wakeful relaxation.

Swami Rama, while at the Menninger Foundation, experimented with EEG recordings and is reported to have produced alpha and theta waves with ease. The latter are slow waves associated with sleep states. He is also said to have entered a state he called "yogi sleep," which appeared, on the basis of the EEG, to be much like deep sleep, and yet he was able to repeat, almost verbatim, statements made to him during this state upon awakening 25 minutes later. Luce and Peper (1971), commenting on these findings, stated that "our idea of a 'normal' EEG is based upon the particular, limited, habitual use that a person makes of his brain. Swami Rama's agile and controlled transitions from one state of consciousness to another would, no doubt, be considered abnormal" (p. 43).

It is this final point that is important. As indicated earlier, this research raised questions about what our physiological and psychological limitations really are. When we think of stress and coping, we often think of physiological and psychological processes that are out of our control. It is our opinion that research such as that just described has considerable significance as it resulted in the development, over a very short period of time, of highly effective techniques oriented more to the Western mind and lifestyle. The impact of these techniques on our ability to regain control of our lives and effectively cope with stress has been profound.

Relaxation

There are many different relaxation techniques. One of the most popular is **progressive muscular relaxation (PMR)**. This technique originated in the 1930s with Edmond Jacobson, who spent 50 years of his life developing the technique. The literature abounds with variations on Jacobson's original relaxation strategies. For example, work done by Bernstein and Borkovec (1978) is widely cited. (We provide you with the opportunity to practise this technique through instructions provided at the end of this chapter.) Another method, autogenic training, is an imagery-based relaxation technique developed in Europe by Schutz and Luthe (1959). As well, Herbert Benson, as a result of his interest in transcendental meditation, developed a secular form of meditation that he described as being based on achieving the "relaxation response" (1975).

Although there are many different relaxation techniques, they share many similar features. To a large extent they require a quiet, undisturbed setting, where one can sit passively, usually with eyes closed, and allow the muscles to completely relax. It is of major importance that patterns of deep, rhythmical breathing be observed, although variations on breathing are often used.

Meditation has been used throughout history to reduce stress, and there are literally thousands of different forms of meditation practised throughout the world. Again, they usually share common features, such as positioning and attention to the *process* of thought rather than its *outcome*. There are differences in approach, though, particularly as many of these forms of meditation are based on religious belief systems. A system that has greatly influenced Western culture is **transcendental meditation (TM)**. An important aspect of TM is the extensive body of empirical research that has accumulated regarding the efficacy of the meditative practice. A consistent picture emerges indicating that the practice of TM has a beneficial physiological and psychological impact on an individual and that its benefits accrue with time (Dillbeck & Orme-Johnson, 1987; Alexander et al., 1994). Techniques such as this have important implications for stress and coping.

Biofeedback is another technique that has received significant attention with regard to the possibility of modifying physiological processes. This involves recording physiological measures with electronic instruments that provide immediate information or feedback

progressive muscular relaxation (PMR): a technique in which a person achieves relaxation by flexing and gradually relaxing muscle groups.

meditation: a form of relaxation in which one attempts to focus attention fully on a single thought or image.

transcendental meditation (TM): a technique of meditation to reduce stress introduced by Maharishi Mahesh Yogi in the late 1950s.

biofeedback: the recording of physiological measures through electronic instruments that provide immediate feedback concerning a subject's physiological state in an attempt to modify physiological processes.

concerning the subject's physiological state. The implication is that, since it has been shown that we may be able to exercise conscious control over aspects of our physiology, this feedback could allow us to make beneficial alterations where necessary.

This observation has led to the extensive development of a biofeedback technology aimed at controlling physiological variables, such as muscle tension, heart rate, blood pressure, brain wave activity, and skin temperature. For example, electromyography (EMG) has been widely used to record and modify muscle tension in specific muscle groups in the body. Temperature control of blood flow has been examined in the context of migraine headaches and Raynaud's disease (Blanchard & Haynes, 1975; Green, Green, & Walters, 1972). The initial enthusiasm for biofeedback was considerable; however, this enthusiasm has since been tempered by realistic evaluations of its efficacy. It appears that many of the effects attributed to biofeedback have more to do with the general state of relaxation, or the relaxation response, experienced during the procedure than the specific feedback provided (Straub, 2001). This development has been disappointing, particularly given the promise the technique held for teaching people to gain control of their physical and psychological states and thereby effect important changes in lifestyle.

Behaviour Therapy and Cognitive Therapy

In the fields of behaviour therapy and cognitive therapy, a wide array of strategies have been developed that have direct relevance for coping with stress. For example, Wolpe (1958) developed the technique of **systematic desensitization** to help people cope with fear and anxiety. It is based on the principle of reciprocal inhibition between the sympathetic and parasympathetic nervous systems and the position that anxiety and relaxation are incompatible responses. The client is initially trained in a relaxation technique and asked to construct a hierarchy of events that elicit increasing levels of anxiety. The client is then encouraged by the therapist to imagine or visualize these events from the least to the most anxiety-provoking. The technique assumes that imagining the feared event results in significant anxiety.

Our ability to create high levels of stress as a function of our thinking is a fundamental principle underlying our discussions in this chapter. Through cognitive exposure to the feared situation we enter into the process of *desensitization*. At the point at which the anxiety attached to imagining a particular event becomes unpleasant, the client is encouraged to use relaxation to decrease arousal. The process of pairing these two inhibiting responses can lead to a significant reduction in the stress associated with the situation, whether it is undergoing a medical procedure, such as an MRI or an injection, flying on an airplane, speaking in public, or writing an exam. It is clear that a crucial component of this process is the repeated exposure to the feared situation, which ultimately leads to fear reduction (Newman et al., 1994).

Modelling is another procedure that can be used effectively to reduce stress associated with fear-provoking situations. Bandura (1985, 1997), who has described this process in detail, points out that most human behaviour is learned through the observation of models. We acquire cognitive skills and new behaviours through observing others. The influence of a model can serve to instruct, inhibit, disinhibit, facilitate, enhance environmental effects, and arouse emotions. Individuals can learn to cope with stressful

systematic desensitization: a technique to help people cope with fear and anxiety by combining relaxation with gradual exposure to the fear-inducing stimulus.

modelling: a technique used to reduce stress associated with fear-provoking situations, in which observing a model coping well with a situation facilitates a similar response by the observer in a similar situation.

situations by observing models. The process is similar to that of desensitization in that observing a model coping well with an anxiety-provoking situation reduces fear.

In **participant modelling**, the individual observes a model coping with the anxiety-evoking situation. The individual is then encouraged to imitate the model and engage in the behaviour while receiving reassurance from the model (Ritter, 1968). The model may also be presented symbolically through videos or films. This procedure has been used effectively by Melamud and her colleagues to help reduce children's anxieties about hospitalization and medical procedures (Melamed & Siegal, 1975). It has also been used with adults to prepare them for the stress of aversive medical procedures. Bandura argues that modelling is an effective intervention because it increases the individual's sense of self-efficacy (1995).

In **cognitive restructuring**, maladaptive, stress-producing cognitions are identified and replaced with ones that are more appropriate. The most well-known approach to cognitive restructuring is based on the work of Albert Ellis, who developed *Rational Emotive Behaviour Therapy* (REBT) (Ellis, 1962, 1977). Ellis posits that it is our beliefs about events, not the events themselves, that create stressful emotional reactions. The sequence proceeds in the following manner: an event occurs, it is interpreted irrationally, and negative emotions and inappropriate behaviours follow. Ellis has identified specific logical errors that form the basis of this irrational thinking, such as overgeneralization, catastrophizing, and absolute thinking. To reduce the stress of the experience, it is necessary to identify the thoughts that are based on irrational beliefs, challenge the irrational beliefs, and replace them with thoughts based on rational beliefs. This approach has been used effectively in managing stress-related emotional states, such as anxiety, anger, fear, and depression, as well as in dealing with behavioural concerns, such as Type A behaviour and obesity.

The work of Beck is similar to that of Ellis in its emphasis on helping people to modify distorted cognitions (Beck, 1963, 1976). Beck describes his approach as *cognitive therapy*. Although it was initially developed to treat depression, cognitive therapy has now been applied to a wide variety of psychological problems. It differs from REBT in encouraging people to identify their dysfunctional beliefs and then to put these beliefs through a process of hypothesis testing, or what Beck calls "collective empiricism," to test their validity.

The final behavioural stress management technique we will consider here is based on the work of Donald Meichenbaum and is appropriately called **stress inoculation training** (Meichenbaum, 1977, 1985). This is a package of procedures designed to help people cope effectively with stressful events.

Initially, individuals are asked to examine how they conceptualize stressful events and are taught that those events can be reconceptualized in less stressful ways. They are encouraged to view coping as a process in which they can prepare for, confront, and cope with stressful events. In the second phase, they learn and rehearse coping strategies such as relaxation training, problem solving, and self-reinforcement. In the third phase, this reconceptualized approach, both cognitive and behavioural, is applied to relevant situations. This can be done initially through imagery and role-playing and then applied gradually to situations eliciting increasingly higher levels of stress.

Like many cognitive and behavioural strategies, stress inoculation training has been applied with success to a wide variety of problems within the health psychology realm. For example, Vocks et al. (2004) demonstrated that blood pressure reactivity was effectively reduced using a cognitive behavioural stress management program in comparison to

participant modelling: a technique used to reduce stress in which, subsequent to an individual's observing a model coping with an anxiety-evoking situation, the person is encouraged to engage in the behaviour while receiving reassurance from the model.

cognitive restructuring: a technique whereby maladaptive, stress-producing cognitions are identified and replaced with ones that are more appropriate.

stress inoculation training: a technique designed to help people cope effectively with stressful events; includes reconceptualizing events in less stressful ways, improving coping strategies, and applying the reconceptualized cognitive and behavioural approach to relevant stressors.

training in progressive muscular relaxation. The components of the program included the following: psychoeducation regarding stress and its impact, a behavioural analysis of individual patterns of stress-related behaviours, time management, cognitive restructuring, problem solving, assertiveness training, the use of positive affirmations, and the identification of short- and long-term stress management strategies.

Self-help manuals that provide do-it-yourself instruction in coping with stress abound in our culture today (e.g., Abascal et al., 2001; Romas & Sharma, 2004; Girdano et al., 2005). Although they provide evidence about the pervasiveness of stress in today's world, they serve a very useful function in allowing individuals to self-regulate their own behaviour and to actively engage in what is usually described as a positive process. Girdano et al. (2005) state that "stress is a gift of motivation and a compass to remind us we are off course. However, your whole life is your journey, so there is no need to hurry—if you miss this bus (or lesson) or if this bus takes you only part of the way, there will be another along shortly" (p. xix).

As part of this self-help process and as we bring this chapter to an end, we thought that, after speaking so much about stress and coping, we should give you the opportunity to experience the benefits of relaxation for yourself. So, read on.

The Relaxation Responses: A Personal Guide

You can have someone else read the relaxation script to you, you can make a tape of it, or you can commit it to memory and take yourself through it. We'll provide you with a general overview and the specifics of the technique. It's based on the original procedure developed by Jacobson in the 1930s and subsequently modified by Bernstein and Borkovec (1973), and Bernstein and Given (1984). A basic component of the procedure is learning to identify the sensations associated with muscular tension and relaxation through tensing and then relaxing different muscle groups in the body. It's important to realize that learning relaxation skills is like learning any other skill—no one else can do it for you; it's not a matter of desire, it's a skill that needs to be learned. This means learning the technique and practising it.

You will be asked to tense a specific muscle group initially to become aware of what muscle tension feels like and to be able to compare it to the experience of relaxation. As well, if the muscle group is tensed prior to relaxation a greater reduction in muscle tension will occur upon relaxation.

Rest in a comfortable position such as in a recliner or lying down, with support for your head and spine. Do not cross your legs or arms, and try to minimize body movements. Close your eyes so as to be less aware of your external surroundings and loosen any tight items of clothing. During the relaxation session, breathe slowly and regularly. Tense each muscle group for 5 to 7 seconds and relax it on cue for 30 to 40 seconds. If you have a tape of the procedure or someone is guiding you through it, a cue word such as "tense" can be used to signal the beginning of the tension phase and "relax" to signal the relaxation phase.

The tension phase need not be extreme and should not involve any pain to the muscle. If you feel pain or cramping, shorten the period of tension. You only need to tighten the muscles, not strain them. At the beginning of the relaxation phase, you should focus your attention on the sensations attached to the reduction in tension and the increase in relaxation in the muscles.

It's usual to relax each muscle group twice, although it's not inappropriate to continue the tension/relaxation sequence in a particular muscle group several times until a desired depth of relaxation is obtained. There are many variations on the sequence and methods used; the following is one example. As you practise and develop your relaxation skills, it's important to remember that you do not need to try to relax—you just let it happen. Increased effort is not the key to success; rather, you need to take a passive stance, let go, and enjoy the experience.

1. Dominant hand and forearm: make your hand into a tight fist, then relax.
2. Non-dominant hand and forearm; make your hand into a tight fist, then relax.
3. Dominant upper arm: bend your arm at the elbow and bring your hand toward your shoulder, then relax.
4. Non-dominant upper arm: bend your arm at the elbow and bring your hand toward your shoulder, then relax.
5. Forehead: raise your eyebrows and wrinkle your forehead, then relax.
6. Eyes: close your eyes tighter, then relax.
7. Lower face and jaws: clench your teeth and tighten the corners of your mouth, then relax.
8. Shoulders: raise your shoulders as if to touch your ears, then relax.
9. Chest: take a deep breath and hold it, then relax.
10. Abdomen: tighten the stomach muscles, then relax.
11. Legs one: point your toes downward, away from your body, then relax.
12. Legs two: bring your toes upward, toward your body, then relax.
13. Scan your body for residual tension: if tension is experienced in a muscle group, repeat the tension/relaxation sequence for that muscle group.
14. Take some time to enjoy the feelings of relaxation in your body.
15. You can end the session by counting backward from five to one, becoming more alert as you count down. When you get to one, open your eyes.

The procedure will take approximately 30 minutes. You should practise the technique regularly for optimal effectiveness; every day would be ideal. When you begin to learn a relaxation procedure, it's best to do so in a setting that is quiet and comfortable, where distractions are minimal, and in which you are not likely to be disturbed. This may require some preparation on your part, but it will make it easier to focus your attention on learning the technique.

As you become more skilled at relaxation, you'll want to generalize the learning experience to those places in your life where relaxation is most needed (e.g., your workplace, a performance activity, social situations). As you become more familiar with the relaxation experience, as indicated by greater levels of relaxation both during and outside the relaxation sessions, you can cut out the tension phase of the sequence and focus only on the relaxation of the muscle. Increased familiarity with the sensations of relaxation will make it unnecessary for you to have the feeling of tension to compare them to.

With time, you'll be able to combine muscle groups in obvious ways. For example, the four-group procedure involves the following groups: 1) hands and arms; 2) head; 3) chest, shoulders, and abdomen; and 4) legs. Combining muscle groups will reduce the time of the procedure to less than 10 minutes. Eventually, you should be able to achieve a relaxed state simply by recalling the sensations of the relaxed muscle groups together with deep breathing and a cue word such as "relax" or "let go." Ultimately, you should be able to achieve this relaxed state simply through a countdown in combination with deep breathing. When you have arrived at this level, you will have achieved the desired skill level. You should continue to practise and use this skill. It is a powerful resource for coping with stress.

CHAPTER SUMMARY

The terms *stress* and *coping* are somewhat difficult to define as they have a highly idiosyncratic meaning for each of us. My stress is not your stress and your coping strategies may not be the same as mine. It is important to achieve some consensus regarding the meaning of these concepts.

Central to our understanding of stress is the concept of *homeostasis* which describes the body's attempt to maintain a stable physiological internal environment. In this context Cannon articulated the *fight or flight response* which describes a complex autonomic response to perceived threat.

The physiology of stress involves a highly complex response to perceived threat that involves the *nervous system* and the *endocrine system*. The nervous system is comprised of the *central nervous system* and the *peripheral nervous system*. The former is made up of the brain and spinal cord while the latter is made up of the sympathethic and parasympathetic nervous systems. The endocrine system responds to stress more slowly but its effects may be persist for much longer.

The *General Adaptation Syndrome* describes a three-stage response to stress made up of *alarm, resistence,* and *exhaustion* which focuses essentially on physiological processes. Alternatively *cognitive transactional models* focus more on the role of *cognitive appraisals* in determining whether or not an event will be perceived as stressful.

It is possible that certain personality styles predispose an individual to specific stress responses and specific illnesses. A widely researched set of personality traits, the *Type A behaviour pattern*, has been identified as a risk factor for coronary cardiovascular disease.

Coping is the process by which individuals attempt to manage stress. This can be achieved through *problem-focused coping* or *emotion-focused coping*. The former involves identifying the problem and choosing a solution, whereas the latter focuses more on managing emotional responses to stress.

Highly effective procedures are available to help us cope, both physiologically and psychologically, with stress. These include strategies such as relaxation techniques, biofeedback, meditation, and behavioural and cognitive approaches to stress management.

Review Questions

1. Take some time to write down your definition of the two terms used in the title of this chapter—*stress* and *coping*. What do these terms mean to you?

2. What are the major sources of stress in your life at this time? A source of stress does not necessarily need to be a major event, such as a car accident; it may involve something less significant, although important to you, such as having recently received a speeding ticket.

3. What strategies do you use most frequently to cope with stress in your life? Some of these strategies will be more effective than others.

4. Each one of us tends to have characteristic behavioural responses that indicate stress is affecting us. Typical behaviours include nervous tics, nail biting, accident proneness, unusual mannerisms, absent-mindedness, increased alcohol consumption, changes in eating or sleeping patterns, and inappropriate emotional reactions. Take a moment to think about the signs that indicate stress is beginning to get the best of you.

CHAPTER OUTLINE

Learning Objectives

After studying this chapter, you will be able to

- Explain why psychoneuroimmunology (PNI) is important to health psychology
- Read and understand research papers on PNI
- Cite research evidence to show that there is a biological relationship between psychological state and health
- Explain fundamental biological mechanisms linking psychological state and health

Lori's last exam was scheduled for December 11. She was flying home the next day and was really looking forward to being home for a while. However, she expected she would spend the first few days with a bad cold or maybe the flu. Lori was a third-year student who was experienced with final exams and flying home, but didn't know why she got sick every year after final exams.

Was there something about being home that made Lori sick? That didn't seem likely. She got along well with her family and loved her parents' cooking. Maybe it was the airplane. She had heard about "bad air" on planes. But Lori played university volleyball and flew with the team all the time without ever getting sick.

Could it be the exams? That seemed more likely, since Lori often got sick right after April finals, too, and she didn't fly home until mid-May. Lori finally concluded that writing exams somehow affected her immune system.

Lori is not alone. Many university students get sick either during or just after exams. Indeed, research has shown that immune system functioning suffers during exam time (e.g., Glaser et al., 1993). Glaser and colleagues measured immune-system functioning in medical students one month before an exam period and then again on the last day of that exam period. They found significant declines in a number of indicators of **immunocompetence**—the extent to which our immune system is functioning properly to ward off micro-organisms that invade our bodies. More recently, researchers have found that self-hypnosis and massage therapy can actually reduce these exam-related effects on the immune system by reducing stress (Gruzelier, 2003; Kiecolt-Glaser et al., 2001; Zeitlin et al., 2000).

immunocompetence: the extent to which an immune system is functioning properly to ward off micro-organisms.

This sort of research raises a number of important questions for students of health psychology. How is immunocompetence assessed in studies like this? What biological mechanisms link a psychological state, such as stress, to immune-system functioning? How strong is this link? These are some of the key questions addressed by **psychoneuroimmunology (PNI)**, which is the study of the relationship between psychological states and the functioning of the immune system.

psychoneuroimmunology (PNI): the study of the relationship between psychological states and the functioning of the immune system.

The term *psychoneuroimmunology* is best understood by dividing it into its three component parts. Our psychology (*psycho*) affects nervous-system functioning (*neuro*), which, in turn, affects our immunity to disease (*immunology*). PNI is interested in the interaction among three of the body's systems we introduced in Chapter 2: the nervous system, the endocrine system, and the immune system (Glaser & Kiecolt-Glaser, 2005). In this chapter, you will learn how research has explored the interactions among these systems and how the systems are affected by a number of psychological states. We begin with an explanation of why PNI is so important to the discipline of health psychology.

THE IMPORTANCE OF PSYCHONEUROIMMUNOLOGY TO HEALTH PSYCHOLOGY

In chapter 1, we traced the development of health psychology from its roots. Many of the people participating in this early development cautioned that, while health psychology held considerable promise, it would be essential to avoid extravagant and unsubstantiated claims regarding what was known and what could be achieved in terms of improving health through psychological interventions. One important piece of the puzzle missing in those days was empirical proof that psychological states were directly linked to biological processes. Psychoneuroimmunology has uncovered that piece.

PNI research not only provides much-needed information linking psychology and health, but also provides data in a form that makes sense to people whose training is biomedical in nature. As such, PNI research represents an invaluable bridge between social scientists and health care providers and increases the credibility of health psychology in the eyes of health care providers.

HOW IMMUNE-SYSTEM FUNCTION IS MEASURED IN PSYCHONEUROIMMUNOLOGICAL RESEARCH

One of our main objectives in presenting this section on measuring immune-system function is to help you develop a familiarity with the language used in PNI research, without which the research can be confusing to read. With this objective in mind, we will focus on the *language* of PNI research as well as the *processes* involved in assessing immune-system function.

The *dependent variable* in an experiment is the variable we measure to determine if our treatment or manipulation has had any effect. In PNI research, dependent variables take the form of measures of immunocompetence. The manipulation, or *independent variable*, is usually some psychological state. This can be naturally occurring, as was the case with the stress caused by Lori's exams in our opening example, or it can be experimentally induced by putting people through stressful experiences or presenting them with stimuli aimed at eliciting positive moods, such as happiness.

For several reasons, measuring the impact of psychological state on immune functioning is a complex business. First, immune-system cells are located in a number of places throughout the body, such as the tonsils, appendix, small intestine, spleen, and bone marrow. This makes it difficult to just go to the source and measure activity. Instead, we must assess cellular activity in the bloodstream or mucus. Second, there are a variety of forms this cellular activity can take, and these operate independently of each other. So it is possible that a psychological state might influence one aspect of immune functioning and not another. This means that researchers must assess a number of immune-system cellular functions to ascertain the potential impact of a situation or mood state. It also means that two studies assessing the impact of the same psychological variable, such as exam stress, might come to different conclusions depending on which aspect of immune functioning is being assessed—that which fights off colds or that which kills tumour cells, for example.

Counting Cells to Measure Immunocompetence

You learned in Chapter 2 that immune-system function is dependent on the system's ability to produce, or *proliferate*, cells to do its work. One simple way of measuring immunocompetence is to count these cells (typically white blood cells) as they exist in the bloodstream. This cell counting is called an **enumerative assay** and is common in PNI research. In studies using cell counts, you will see lymphocyte measures taken from blood samples, counting such white blood cells as NK, T, and B cells. Researchers look for two things in these counts—a minimum number of cells for adequate immune function, and a balance between various cell types, such as different types of T cells (Herbert & Cohen, 1993).

enumerative assay: a lab test done to count cells (typically white blood cells) as they exist in the bloodstream.

In general, the better the immune system functions, the higher these counts are. Studies using cell counts will often report lower cell counts in blood samples taken from groups of individuals who have been exposed to a stressor, such as an exam.

Functional Tests of Immunocompetence: Measuring Cells in Action

Counting cells can be informative, but it is even more important to assess the immune system *at work*. This is what **functional tests of immunity** do (Cohen & Herbert, 1996). We can perform these functional tests inside the body, though this can be difficult because it is hard to localize the sites of the immune system. However, we can also measure cell functions by *removing* them from the body and incubating them with other cells to see how the immune-system cells respond. Functional tests performed on cells outside the body are called *in vitro* tests. Those performed inside the body are called *in vivo* tests.

In vitro tests of immunocompetence start with a blood sample that is combined with a substance called a **mitogen**. A mitogen is a substance that stimulates immune-cell activity as though the immune cell were acting against an invading cell, or antigen. Three of the most common mitogens used in PNI research are concanavalin A (Con A), phytohemagglutinin (PHA), and pokeweed mitogen (PWM).

A PNI study might say "people whose interactions with others were less confrontational showed greater lymphocyte proliferation in response to PHA." Translated, this means that blood samples taken from people who differed in the amount of confrontation they experienced in their interactions with others were incubated with PHA. From this, researchers discovered that the blood of people whose interactions were less confrontational produced more lymphocytes when exposed to PHA. Other studies using this general design might substitute Con A or PWM as the mitogen, or they might run a number of tests (or *assays* as they are sometimes called) using two or more different mitogens. In these studies, you will see data reported separately for each mitogen.

Natural Killer (NK) cell activity is also measured through *in vitro* techniques. Because NK cells perform a "seek and destroy" function, we measure their activity by exposing NK cells to diseased cells, usually tumour cells. For this reason, PNI research linking psychological variables to cancer often measures NK cell activity.

After exposure, NK cells are assessed in two ways. In one, *proliferation* is measured through cell counts taken after the introduction of tumour cells. In the other, NK cell *effectiveness* is assessed by measuring the destruction of the tumour cells. In PNI literature, this second method is often called an **NK cell cytotoxic activity** assay. This process of killing tumour cells is called **NK cell lysis** because to *lyse* a tumour cell means to destroy it. PNI researchers, especially those dealing with cancer, might talk of "a decrease (or increase) in NK cytotoxic activity," or "a significant effect on NK cell lysis." It is important to note that NK cells aren't the only immune-system cells capable of cytotoxic activity. However, they are commonly measured in PNI studies involving cancer.

There are also a number of *in vivo* functional tests of immunocompetence. Here, we will look at two of the more common types. One takes advantage of the fact that almost everyone carries herpesviruses. The other uses injections of small dosages of antigens.

Once you have been exposed to a herpesvirus you carry it with you for life. The virus is usually present in such small quantities that you don't experience any symptoms, but it

functional tests of immunity: tests done to assess the immune system at work.

mitogen: a relatively harmless substance that stimulates immune cell activity as though the immune cell were acting against an invading cell or antigen.

NK cell cytotoxic activity assay: a test in which the proliferation and effectiveness of NK cells is measured after they have been exposed to diseased cells.

NK cell lysis: destroying tumour cells by exposing them to NK cells.

is there all the same. There are many different types of herpesviruses, from cold sores to Epstein-Barr virus. One reason you don't have to spend much time worrying about herpesviruses is that your immune system does the worrying for you by producing antibodies (Ab) whose job it is to "flag" herpesviruses for destruction, thus keeping their numbers under control. Herpesviruses will multiply, however, when the immune system is suppressed, thus creating the need for more Ab. Therefore, we can determine immunocompetence by measuring Ab. Be careful when you read studies that use this measure, though. The more suppressed the immune system, the more herpesviruses, and thus the more Ab. This means that, when herpesvirus-specific antibodies are being measured, the *higher* the Ab count, the *poorer* the immune-system function.

Researchers can also introduce an antigen into the body and measure the specific Ab activity meant to deal with that intrusion. In these studies, small quantities of an antigen are introduced by injection or nasal spray. After this is done, scientists measure immune-system activity in two ways. In the simplest, the skin is observed at the site of the injection. If the immune system is working properly, there should be swelling and redness. Appropriate amounts of inflammation are signs of a properly functioning immune system.

We can also count antigen-specific Ab produced in response to the injection. This can be done through blood samples or mucous secretions that are measured most often in the saliva. One antibody commonly measured in the saliva or mucus is called sIgA, which stands for *secretory* or *salivary immunoglobulin* A antibody. Because it exists in saliva and mucus, it represents one of the body's first lines of defence against antigens (Tomasi, 1971). But measuring salivary sIgA isn't always as easy as it sounds. What happens when we want to measure sIgA levels during times of stress? Many people experience "dry mouth" at these times; that is, they don't produce much saliva.

Again, be careful when you read studies about tests that measure Ab production to assess immunocompetence. It is easy to get confused about the meaning of Ab counts, because they have opposite meanings depending upon whether the count is herpesvirus-specific or in response to an injection. In herpesvirus studies, higher Ab counts indicate *immunosuppression*. An increase in that virus comes about because of suppression of the immune system. In the case of injection studies, more Ab indicates *better* immunocompetence. In these studies, the antigen is introduced into the body. This means that Ab is being produced by a *competent* immune system that is dealing with an invading antigen. These herpesvirus studies have proven important, since this virus is linked to shingles, a painful condition found primarily in older adults (Irwin et al., 2003), and Epstein-Barr virus, considered a precursor to mononucleosis. In a study reminiscent of Lori's experience, medical students experiencing exam stress were more susceptible to Epstein-Barr virus than students not writing exams (Glaser, 2005).

Methodological Issues in the Measurement of Immune-System Function

As you read through the preceding section on measurement, did you wonder just *how* these blood samples were taken and *when*, given that the independent variable in much PNI work is often stress related? Can we casually draw blood from someone who is in the middle of an argument with her husband or studying for final exams? Hardly. In PNI research, a sophisticated knowledge of measurement techniques and biological processes is needed. Measurement of immune functioning is intrusive, and it requires skill. Certainly, conducting research in psychoneuroimmunology is not without its challenges.

Short-Term versus Long-Term Effects   In PNI research, we must make an important distinction between short-term and long-term effects. In laboratory research, it is common for a participant to be subjected to an **acute stressor,** which is to say one that is immediate in its duration and proximity. The effects of this acute stressor are then measured through blood samples taken just before, just after, and then some time (minutes to hours) after the stressor has been introduced. Studies of this nature measure how quickly the immune system reacts. As we will see in the next section, when we look at specific studies in PNI, short-term changes in immune-system function occur quite commonly in the face of these acute stressors. The complication here lies in the fact that acute stressors can actually enhance immune function by stimulating nonspecific, or innate, immunity while suppressing specific immunity (see chapter 2 for an explanation of these two types of immunity) (Moraska et al., 2002). Chronic stress, on the other hand, suppresses both nonspecific and specific immunity (Mercado et al., 2002).

acute stressor: a stressor that is immediate in its duration and proximity.

Not all psychological variables occur on an acute basis. Trait anxiety, job stress, marital problems, loneliness, and many other facts of life are *chronic,* or long-term. Their effects are more like a constant hum than a single blast. Psychoneuroimmunological research designed to measure the effects of chronic stressors cannot rely on well-controlled laboratory environments. Instead, field research must study people exposed to these stressors and compare their immune functioning to those who are not exposed (e.g., Barnett, Steptoe, & Gareis, 2005; Robles & Kiecolt-Glaser, 2003). It is much more difficult to ascertain definitive cause-and-effect relationships in these studies because there are so many other variables in field work that cannot be controlled.

Immune-System Function Takes Many Forms   As we mentioned earlier, there is no single accepted measure of immunocompetence. This is because the immune system does its job in a variety of ways depending on the nature of the antigen. Also, external factors and the internal states accompanying them will have different effects on the immune system depending on what those factors are. For example, studies with mice have shown that stress compromises their immune systems. However, the nature of this immunosuppression is different for stress created by intruders compared to stress created by physical constraint (Avitsur, Stark, Dhabhar, & Sheridan, 2002). As is the case with all biological systems, people differ in the ways their bodies respond to these factors.

For these reasons, PNI studies often report a multitude of dependent measures. This makes the work more difficult to wade through if you are a student of the field, but it also makes the findings more valid in that multiple measures increase the likelihood that an affected immunologic process will be identified.

Statistical Significance versus Clinical Significance   In any scientific endeavour, researchers need to be aware that data might be statistically significant without being clinically or socially significant. This fact is of great relevance to PNI studies attempting to determine if an aspect of the immune system has been affected by a person's psychology.

To prove that some aspect of immune functioning has been *affected,* we must be able to show that the difference in cell count or cytotoxic activity between groups of subjects is too large to have occurred by chance. In such a case, the results are said to be *statistically significant.* This means that there is a less than 1-in-20 chance that the differences detected would occur without the experimental manipulation. Applied to PNI research, statistical significance means that some psychological factor causes real immunologic effects.

Statistical significance may be scientifically important, but is it *clinically* important? In other words, do the statistically significant differences mean that people are actually more or less likely to *get sick*? Or are the differences, though statistically detectable, too small to affect our susceptibility to illness? These are important questions for PNI research, because it is entirely possible that our statistical tests are more sensitive to cellular differences than our bodies are.

In a concise review of some important PNI research, Kiecolt-Glaser and colleagues (2002a) observed that "future work should identify and examine immune measures that are directly relevant to particular health conditions" (p. 451). In other words, some studies show that psychosocial factors can make us sick or well, and others show that these factors can affect the immune system at the cellular level. What we need more of are studies that do *both*; that is, we need more studies that measure symptoms and immune functioning concurrently.

PNI researchers have responded to this call, although such studies are difficult to carry out for a multitude of reasons. If we want to study the link between immunocompromise and illnesses such as cancer that take a relatively long time to develop, then we must take our measurements regularly, on a longitudinal, prospective basis. This means that we must start with participants who are well, follow them over a long period, take regular assays, and compare the results for those who get sick with those who do not. This work isn't impossible, but it is expensive, intrusive, and fraught with extraneous variables that can account for health differences.

One way to get around these problems is to expose healthy people to antigens and psychological factors in the same study. Then we can observe the progression of symptom display while we monitor immune functioning. In studies that follow this approach, volunteers are exposed to a cold virus or similar pathogen, and the disease course is monitored for a two- or three-week period following exposure. Some of the volunteers in the study go through a stressful life event, such as an exam period, allowing researchers to monitor their immune cell activity as well as symptom progression.

RESEARCH IN PSYCHONEUROIMMUNOLOGY: PROVIDING EVIDENCE FOR A BIOLOGICAL LINK BETWEEN PSYCHOLOGY AND HEALTH

In the following overview of PNI research, we have organized the studies according to the psychological factors measured. Some factors, including depression, state anxiety, and short-term stress, are acute in nature. Others, including personality factors such as cynical hostility, coping styles, and social support, are more chronic or long-term. As you read through the summary of these studies, keep in mind the methodological issues discussed in the previous section. We have tried to select studies that not only are representative of the field of PNI but also use dependent measures and terminology consistent with those introduced earlier in this chapter. If you get confused at any point as you read this section, refer back to our explanations in the section entitled "How Immune-System Function is Measured in Psychoneuroimmunological Research."

Some of these students will catch a cold or flu after final exams are over because their immune systems have been compromised by stress.

The Effect of Stress on Immune Functioning

In the opening of this chapter, you read about Lori, a university student who regularly got either a cold or the flu just after exams. The assumption is that the stress of exams increased Lori's susceptibility to these illnesses by compromising her immune system. Health psychologists have studied students' immune functioning before, during, and after exams for some time (e.g., Jemmott et al., 1983; Kiecolt-Glaser, 1999; Wadee et al., 2001). The general finding has been that symptom complaint goes up at these times and that cellular measures of immune response indicate immunosuppression. Exams are examples of acute stressors. Chronic stress also affects immune functioning and has even been linked to premature aging (Kiecolt-Glaser, 2003), so Lori shouldn't spend her whole life writing exams!

Before we can link stress to disease using PNI research, we need to refer to the working definition of stress introduced in chapter 3. From that chapter, you might recall the work of Lazarus and Folkman (1984), who defined stress as an aversive condition in which the demands of a situation are perceived to be greater than our ability to cope with them.

The scientific study of the relationship between stress and disease was initiated in 1964 with the publication of a study by Solomon and Moos entitled "Emotions, Immunity and Disease: A Speculative Theoretical Integration." Since that time, a large number of studies have linked various types of stressors to a wide variety of diseases (see, for example, Bowler, 2001).

In the laboratory, volunteers have been exposed to acute, short-term stressors, such as having to make speeches or perform mental tasks under time pressure. At the same time, their immune functioning was monitored. Using designs such as these, researchers can learn about the immediacy with which a stressor can affect immune functioning. Such studies have discovered that, while it may take days for the immune system to react to an antigen, it takes as little as five minutes for a stressor to inhibit the ability of the immune system to engage that response (Herbert et al., 1994). Laboratory studies have also shown that the effect of stressors on immune functioning is stable over time for a given individual, leading to the conclusion that there are dispositional or personality factors that influence the extent to which a stressor affects immunity (Wadee et al., 2001). For example, laboratory research has demonstrated that people differ in their physiological reactivity to a stressor, as measured by cortisol levels. Not surprisingly, highly reactive people show the greatest incidence of such things as upper respiratory infections in the face of real-life stressors (Cohen et al., 2002).

In addition to laboratory studies of the effects of acute stressors, other work has investigated chronic, long-term stress as it occurs in real life. Boscarino (1997) conducted a 20-year follow-up of 332 Vietnam veterans who had presented symptoms of post-traumatic stress disorder (PTSD). He compared their health to 1067 veterans who did not suffer from PTSD. Post-traumatic stress disorder was reasoned to be evidence of severe stress exposure.

Boscarino discovered that the veterans who had suffered from PTSD were significantly more likely to suffer from a wide range of medical problems, including circulatory, digestive, musculoskeletal, and metabolic ailments. The worst problems were nervous-system disorders, which PTSD veterans were 2.47 times more likely to suffer from than non-PTSD vets, and non-sexually transmitted infectious diseases, which they were 2.14 times more likely to contract.

Two aspects of this study are particularly impressive. First, Boscarino controlled 14 other factors that could account for increased susceptibility to illness, including substance abuse, hypochondriasis, age, and smoking history. Controlling for these external variables makes it significantly more valid to attribute the higher odds of suffering from this wide variety of illnesses to the effects of the stress. Second, the long range of the follow-up (20 years) demonstrated that severe stress exposure can have long-term effects.

Studies based on the Canadian Community Health Survey have shown that people with PTSD have higher rates of respiratory disease, cardiovascular disease, chronic pain syndromes, gastrointestinal illnesses and cancer (Sareen et al., 2007). In the Netherlands, people who experienced PTSD after an explosion at a fireworks depot were more likely to subsequently experience vascular, musculoskeletal, and dermatological problems (Dirkzwager et al., 2007). Researchers in this study had access to people's health records from before the disaster, so they could compare pre- and post-disaster health data.

Research on clusters of symptoms experienced by veterans of the Gulf War has also implicated the immune system (Ferguson & Cassaday, 2002; 1999). These authors hypothesize that the illnesses commonly experienced by these veterans (sometimes called Gulf War Syndrome or Syndromes) are associated with the production of interleukin-1. The authors also hypothesize that these conditions persist, in part, because of classically conditioned associations triggered by such stimuli as smells and tastes.

Other research has shown that immune function is affected by exposure to natural disasters. Survivors of Hurricane Andrew in the United States, for example, showed disruption in their sIgA counts (Rotton & Dubitsky, 2002), and those who lived through an earthquake in Northridge, California, showed a positive correlation between immuno-compromise and the degree of distress experienced up to four months after the quake (Solomon et al., 1997).

In another study of real-life stressors and their effect on general health and the immune system, Kiecolt-Glaser and colleagues (1987a) took multiple measures of immune functioning from women who were recently divorced or separated (within the past year). They found that these women had significantly poorer functioning on five of the six immune-system measures compared to women who were neither divorced nor separated. In a subsequent study of men, it was found that those who initiated the divorce reported better health than those whose partner had initiated it (Kiecolt-Glaser et al., 1988).

It is clear from this collection of work that stress affects health through the immune system in acute and immediate ways, as well as on a long-term basis. (For a comprehensive review of 30 years of research linking stress to the immune system, see Segerstrom and Miller, 2004.) We turn now to a discussion of the link between specific illnesses and stress.

Stress and Upper Respiratory Infection Many people doing PNI research believe that, of all the medical conditions brought on or worsened by stress, **upper respiratory infection (URI)** might be the most common. Upper respiratory infection refers to a collection of common illnesses, such as colds, coughs, flu, and bronchitis. This is the category into which Lori's illness in our opening example would fall. If you have ever developed sniffles and sneezes or a nagging cough during or after exams, you may well have been a walking demonstration of the well-established relationship between stress and URI. You might also have been producing low levels of sIgA, which provides immune defence in the mucus and saliva (thus implicating sIgA when we come down with URI). In fact, research has shown that people who experienced high levels of stress over a two-year period had lower secretion levels of sIgA (Phillips et al., 2006).

In field studies, we can get self-report measures of the intensity of the stress being experienced, but we can't control the event. As such, we can't know for sure whether we are dealing with the kind of events most people would find stressful, or if we have a volunteer who is particularly vulnerable to stress. Is the variable a *situational* one that might affect most people the same way, or is it a *dispositional* one that can be generalized only to certain types of people? Some might argue that it doesn't matter—if a person reports stress, then there is stress. The fact that immune functioning clearly fluctuates with self-reports of stress supports the view that these subjective reports are a legitimate way of assessing stress for the purposes of PNI research.

Some people are more prone to stress than others. From the perspective of PNI, we should be able to learn something about the effects of stress by studying the URI experiences of these types of people. This is just what La Via and his colleagues (1996) set out to do. They studied 14 people with generalized anxiety disorder, a disorder characterized by excessive and chronic apprehension about a wide variety of aspects of life, such as work, family, and social contacts.

People with generalized anxiety disorder experience greater impact from stressful events, or, in the language of stress research, their **stress-intrusion scores** are high. La Via and his team members measured stress intrusion in these 14 people using the Impact of Events Scale. To measure immune functioning, they took *in vitro* measures of lymphocyte activity and kept track of the number of URI-related sick days the subjects reported. They began by confirming that the people with generalized anxiety disorder had higher stress-intrusion scores. The researchers discovered that the anxiety group had less lymphocyte activity and almost three times more sick days than a control group. In fact, the anxiety

upper respiratory infection (URI): one of a collection of illnesses, such as colds, coughs, and bronchitis.

stress-intrusion scores: a measure of the impact a stressful event has on a person's life.

Have You Had Your Flu Shot? Using Vaccinations to Measure Immune Responses within the Body

Many studies that investigate the relationship between stress and immune function use *in vitro* methods. While much has been learned from *in vitro* studies of this kind, concerns have been expressed about whether or not they reflect what is actually going on inside the body. In people's bodies, these cells exist in a biological milieu that is quite different from the lab dish (Fleshner & Laudenslager, 2004).

In response to this concern, a number of studies have introduced antigens into the body and then assessed immune function via blood samples (e.g., Smith, Kennedy, & Fleshner, 2004; Smith et al., 2004). These *in vivo* studies have the advantage of allowing immune cells to function in their normal internal environments, but how can researchers ethically introduce antigens into human participants? The answer is via routine vaccination. Vaccinations work by introducing nontoxic amounts of certain antigens into the body so that the immune system can develop specific immunities toward them. We know that poor immune responses to vaccination indicate a greater susceptibility to illness (Plotkin, 2001).

At the University of British Columbia and Carnegie Mellon University, Greg Miller, Sheldon Cohen, and colleagues have used this vaccination method. In one study (Miller et al., 2004), 83 first-year university students were given handheld computers to carry for two days before receiving a flu vaccine (not for H1N1) and then for ten days after. Four times per day, the computer would sound an alarm and students responded to a series of questions about mood state, perceived stress, health behaviours, and physical symptoms. On the day of their vaccination, a 20-mL blood sample was taken to be used as a baseline for immune system measures. Students also provided saliva samples (via a chewable cotton dental roll) on four of the thirteen days in order to assess cortisol levels.

After they received their flu shot, participants returned to the lab twice—after one month and again after four. In each of these visits, researchers took a blood sample to assess the immune system's response to the antigen presented in the flu shot.

Miller and colleagues had a measure of perceived stress, cortisol levels, symptom experience, and immune functioning. The hypothesis was that those students reporting higher stress and cortisol levels would exhibit poorer immune responses to the flu shot antigen. Their hypothesis was supported in that higher reports of stress were associated with lower levels of antibody production (though all students produced adequate responses to the shot for it to be an effective vaccination). This effect was not influenced by the health practices the students reported prior to receiving the shot, although it *was* related to reports of the amount of sleep the students were getting. Sleep reports were also correlated with stress reports.

Miller and colleagues discovered a critical period during which the stressors appeared to have the most detrimental effect on immune response. Specifically, stressors experienced before or on the day of the shot were not related to immune response. Instead, the effect started to be observed after the shot, peaking at between eight and ten days after the shot had been administered.

Other research using this same methodology has shown that students who score higher on measures of loneliness had lower antibody responses to vaccination (Pressman, 2005).

group averaged 24.8 URI sick days in a 12-month period, compared to only 9 days among the non-anxious control participants. The study showed that lymphocyte activity was correlated with URI sick days and with stress intrusion.

Research using flu vaccines (see Focus on Canadian Research 4-1) presents controlled and safe dosages of antigens. Doyle, Gentile, and Cohen (2006) have introduced another level of control—exposure to others.

It is possible that stress causes people to either seek out the company of others or hide away from them. In either case, exposure to viruses is significantly affected. For this reason, a number of studies have adopted a methodology whereby they intentionally expose volunteers to controlled dosages of URI-related viruses. These are called **viral challenge studies**.

In one viral challenge study, 327 participants were exposed to a safety-tested clinical dose of a virus via nasal drops. To control exposure to others, participants were quarantined for five days after exposure. Immune cells called cytokines were assessed in 234 people who developed infection. Those with what the authors called a lower positive emotional style had greater objective and subjective signs of illness and poorer production of particular interleukins. The viral challenge approach used in this study proves that stress-related increased susceptibility to upper respiratory infection cannot be explained solely by increased exposure to viruses at times of stress.

Thus far, we have assumed that stress works alone to influence URI. In the language of statistics, we have assumed a *main effects* model. However, while main effects models allow us to isolate a factor to determine its unique contribution to illness, they also oversimplify the realities of health and well-being. Stress rarely works in isolation. Instead, it *interacts* with other factors, such as social support, demographics, and personality.

In recognition of this fact, Miyazaki and colleagues (2003) have investigated the possible moderating effects of social support. Their predictor variables were perceived stress *and* perceived social support. They found that social support did help reduce the harmful effects of stress on the immune system. In particular, social support was positively correlated with NK cell production.

At least one study has found that *positive* life events can also increase vulnerability to URI (Evans et al., 1997). University students were asked to complete the Life Experience Survey as well as other measures, such as personality and stress experience. They were then monitored for just over six weeks for URI episodes, which were verified with body temperature readings. It was discovered that positive life events were most closely related to URI, independent of personality measures or health-related behaviours. This means that we need to consider the effect of *any* major event, not just the negative ones, when conducting PNI research.

What can we conclude about the extent to which stress puts us at risk for upper respiratory infection? Major life event stress often results in immunosuppression. If a person is exposed to a respiratory virus at the same time, it is likely that the person will get sick. These stressful events don't all have to be recent, though they probably have an additive effect if several of them "pile up" over time.

Stress and Autoimmune Disease When people have autoimmune diseases, their own immune systems becomes their worst enemy. These diseases cause the immune system to produce antibodies that attack the body's own tissue. In other words, the system fails at one of its hallmarks—*tolerance*. Autoimmune diseases include rheumatoid arthritis, insulin-dependent diabetes, and multiple sclerosis.

Research indicates that stress can put people at greater risk for contracting these diseases and for suffering more once they have contracted them (Homo-Delarches et al., 1991). Studies of children who have suffered abuse have found that the post-trauma stress that often accompanies that abuse is associated with higher rates of rheumatoid arthritis and other autoimmune disorders (Dickinson, deGruy, Dickinson, & Candib, 1999). It has been hypothesized that long-term secretion of cortisol is one of the culprits in these cases. Coincidently, children who have suffered long-term abuse tend to have a significantly smaller thymus gland, which is of central importance to the immune system (Fukunger et

viral challenge studies: studies in which volunteer subjects are intentionally exposed to controlled dosages of upper respiratory infection viruses and environmental stressors to measure the clinical progression of the virus and the response of the immune system.

al., 1992). These and other findings are cited in a comprehensive review of the health impact of childhood trauma by University of Western Ontario researcher Deanna Mulvihill (2005).

For those with arthritis not associated with trauma, both relaxation and hypnosis have been effective in reducing patients' physical pain, as has the use of analgesic medication (Gay, Philippot, & Luminet, 2002). Potential exists, therefore, for these therapies to be applied successfully to other autoimmune diseases.

Stress and Cancer   A great amount of research on the relationship between stress and cancer exists in the health psychology literature. Of course, many of these studies discuss the stress brought on by cancer rather than the possibility that the cancer was brought on by stress. However, others have looked at stress as a possible risk factor for cancer (Reiche, Morimoto, & Nunes, 2005). (See Kiecolt-Glaser et al., 2002, for a review of research linking stress to cancer and the immune system.)

One approach to understanding the relationship between stress and cancer is to conduct prospective studies: People who are cancer-free are followed over time, and their perceptions of stress and their incidence of cancer are measured. Another approach looks at the extent to which a diagnosis of, and initial treatment for, cancer are perceived to be stressful and then charts the progression of disease correlated with those preceptions of stress.

Using this latter approach, research has shown that patients reporting high perceived stress just after diagnosis and first treatment also showed poorer immune functioning (Anderson, 1998). Following this finding, Thornton and colleagues conducted longitudinal research in which they compared what they called the trajectory of stress following cancer diagnosis and early treatment with the trajectory of immune functioning (Thornton et al., 2007). Not surprisingly, Thornton found that the patterns, or trajectories, of stress and immune functioning were mirror opposites of each other. In some people, as the high stress associated with initial diagnosis and treatment subsided, immune functioning improved. In those whose stress did not subside, immune function remained compromised. Thus, those who could better cope with the stress of cancer and its treatment had better prognoses.

Remember that natural-killer (NK) cells are primarily responsible for seeking out and destroying abnormal cells. This function makes NK cells crucial in the body's ability to remain cancer free. Numerous *in vitro* studies have clearly established the relationship between stress (and other psychological factors) and NK cell activity (Herbert & Cohen, 1993). It is believed that hormones produced during stress, such as cortisol, may suppress the production of T-lymphocytes and NK cells (Maier, Watkins, & Fleshner, 1994; McEwen, 1998).

Consistent with Thornton and colleagues, two other studies found a positive relationship between severe adverse life events and cancer growth. In one (Ramirez et al., 1989), breast cancer patients with relapse had experienced significantly more of these events than had a group of matched patients who were in remission. In fact, patients who had experienced a family death or job loss were more than five times as likely to have had a relapse. In the other study (Geyer, 1991), women who had seen a physician to have a breast lump diagnosed were monitored for eight years. The study found that women who developed malignancies had experienced more stressful life events. Other research, however, has failed to find these links. A study of 204 breast cancer patients found no relationship between severe life events and relapse (Barraclough et al., 1992). In contrast to the Ramirez study, Barraclough used a *prospective* design, in which stressful events were measured *before* rather than *after* relapse.

These mixed findings indicate that the progression of cancer is not always adversely affected by major life stressors. One reason for this might be that the immune system cannot detect all tumour types. Spiegel and colleagues (1998) also point out that the cause-and-effect relationship between immune-cell activity and cancer progression isn't one way. That is, while compromised immune systems may put the body at greater risk for tumour growth, the presence of cancerous cells may also bring on immunosuppression. Spiegel and colleagues (1998) conclude that "the role of stress in immunosuppression and tumor progression may be central to *potentiating* existing tumor rather than *initiating* primary carcinogenesis" (p. 679). In other words, stress may worsen existing cancer but not make a person more susceptible to getting it. Further investigation is certainly warranted.

Stress-Reduction Interventions and Immune Functioning   Given the well-documented effects of stress on the immune system and illness and the clear biological links between stress response and immune function, it would make sense to study the potential immunologic benefits of psychological interventions designed to reduce stress. For example, Michael Antorini has presented a model that links the beneficial effects of cognitive-behavioural stress management to its effects on the immune systems of HIV-positive men (2003).

Greg Miller and Sheldon Cohen (2001) performed a meta-analysis using the results of 59 studies of stress-reducing interventions featuring more than 2000 participants, all of whom had chronic illnesses. Interestingly, Miller and Cohen discovered mixed results. Effects varied depending on the nature of the intervention and the form of immune response being measured. For example, interventions that featured relaxation techniques had a positive effect on sIgA production but not on any other elements of immune functioning. Hypnosis fared slightly better. Interventions using disclosure of emotions did not affect immune functioning. Furthermore, there was no *dose-response effect*, which in this case means that the length of the intervention was unrelated to its effect on the immune system.

Studies have also shown that pharmacological treatment of depression has a positive effect on NK activity (Frank, et al., 1999; Irwin et al., 1992; Ravindan et al., 1995; Scheilfer et al., 1999). In each of these studies, it was the reduction of depressive symptoms that correlated with improvements in immune function and not the mere presence of the medication in the system. Physical exercise and diet have also been shown to moderate the negative effects of depression on immune function to combat cancer and upper respiratory infection (Nieman et al., 1990).

The Effect of Depression on Immune Functioning

A body's physiological responses to stress may be adaptive in the face of the stressor, but in the long run stressors compromise its immune system. It is the *arousal* associated with stress that puts strain on our bodies. What effect, if any, do the opposite feelings associated with *under*-arousal, such as depression or sadness or loneliness, have on the immune system?

We have seen in our discussion of stress and immunity that so-called major negative life events affect immunity (see Figure 4-1). One reason for this is that these events are stressful. But another reason may relate to the impact of these events on mood (or *affect*), as they often elicit strong, unpleasant emotions, such as depression, sorrow, anger, grief,

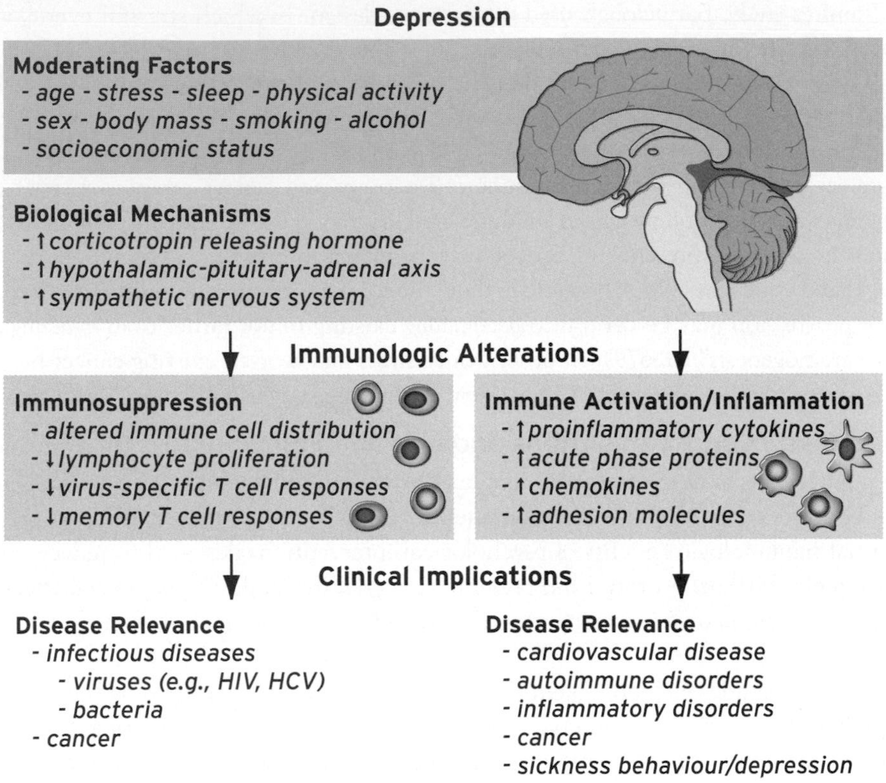

Depression

Moderating Factors
- age - stress - sleep - physical activity
- sex - body mass - smoking - alcohol
- socioeconomic status

Biological Mechanisms
- ↑corticotropin releasing hormone
- ↑hypothalamic-pituitary-adrenal axis
- ↑sympathetic nervous system

Immunologic Alterations

Immunosuppression
- altered immune cell distribution
- ↓lymphocyte proliferation
- ↓virus-specific T cell responses
- ↓memory T cell responses

Immune Activation/Inflammation
- ↑proinflammatory cytokines
- ↑acute phase proteins
- ↑chemokines
- ↑adhesion molecules

Clinical Implications

Disease Relevance
- infectious diseases
  - viruses (e.g., HIV, HCV)
  - bacteria
- cancer

Disease Relevance
- cardiovascular disease
- autoimmune disorders
- inflammatory disorders
- cancer
- sickness behaviour/depression

Figure 4-1 How depression affects health

Source: Irwin, M.R., & Miller, A.H. (2007). Depressive Disorders and Immunity: 20 years of progress and discovery. *Brain, Behavior, and Immunity, 21*(4), 374–383. Copyright 2007 by ELSEVIER SCIENCE & TECHNOLOGY JOURNALS. Reproduced with permission via Copyright Clearance Center.

and helplessness. The death of a loved one is a clear example of such a life event. Most health psychologists believe that coping with a seriously ill loved one brings on *stress*. Coping with their death, on the other hand, brings on *negative mood*. This is why studies that measure immune functioning of a caregiver when the loved one is very ill and then again if the loved one dies allow us to differentiate between stress and mood in terms of their impact on our immune system.

An early study (Irwin et al., 1987) measured immune functioning in three groups of wives: (1) wives whose husbands were in good health, (2) wives whose husbands were being treated for lung cancer that had spread to other parts of the body, and (3) wives whose husbands had died from lung cancer up to six months previously. It was discovered that this third group was the most depressed and also had the poorest immune functioning. A similar study of men whose wives were dying of breast cancer found that lymphocyte proliferation was better in pre-bereavement husbands than among those in the group whose wives had died (Schleifer, 1983).

Longitudinal work supports the conclusion that depression compromises the immune system. Having discovered that almost 25 percent of hospital patients had abnormally high depression scores, a group of researchers set out to measure the relationship between this depression and mortality. They measured depression in 454 people when they were admitted to hospital (Herrmann et al., 1998), and then monitored them for the next

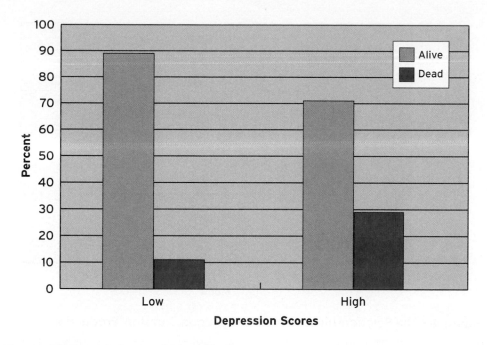

Figure 4-2 Depression and Mortality

Patients who scored high on a measure of depression were more than three times as likely to die within the next 22 months than those with lower scores.

Source: C. Herrmann et al., (1998). Diagnostic groups and depressed mood as predicators of 22-month mortality in medical patients. *Psychosomatic Medicine, 60,* 570–577. Adapted by permission from Wolters Kluwer Health.

22 months. Fifteen percent of them died. The strongest predictors of mortality were then identified through statistical analysis. After the expected variables of age and the nature of the illness, depression scores taken upon admission were the best predictors of mortality. When the other factors were controlled for, it was discovered that people scoring high in depression were more than three times as likely to die as those scoring low (see Figure 4-2). Kinder and colleagues (2008) looked at over 35 000 U.S. military veterans, discovering that depressed patients were at increased risk of dying over a period of five years.

By a wide range of cell counts, immune function is compromised by depression (Zorilla et al., 2001). However this effect is more pronounced in some people than others, suggesting that other factors also come into play. For example, the effect of depression on immunity appears worse for older adults (Andreoli et al., 1993). Also, NK cell counts are more severely affected in men with depression than in women with depression (Evans et al., 1992). Not surprisingly, depression interacts with stress to increase the negative effects of each (Irwin et al., 1990).

In the Herrmann study, depression increased mortality risk for all types of patients, regardless of their age or sex. However, depression had its strongest impact on patients with cardiopulmonary disease, which is consistent with research showing that depression increases mortality risk after myocardial infarction (heart attack). (See, for example, Parker et al., 2006.) Herrmann and colleagues also found that depression increased mortality risk for patients with hematological diseases and cancer.

These studies linking mortality rates and mood provide an important first step, but because they do not measure immune functioning, we cannot conclude from them that

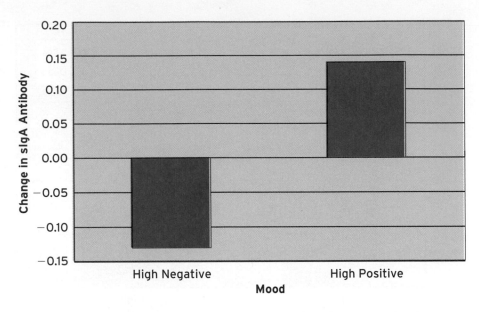

Figure 4-3 The Relationship Between Daily Mood and sIgA Production

Source: A.A. Stone et al., (1987). Evidence that secretory sIgA antibody is associated with daily mood. *Journal of Personality and Social Psychology, 52*(5), 988–993. Adapted by permission from the American Psychological Association.

the link is due to immunocompromise. However, other research has shown that certain components of the immune system do fluctuate along with mood (Stone et al., 1987). For example, the relatively short life span of sIgA makes it more susceptible to daily mood fluctuations. To demonstrate this, research subjects completed checklists of adjectives describing mood three times per week for eight weeks. Their responses were divided into positive and negative moods. Two weeks prior to all this, they started to ingest a harmless antigen. It was discovered that negative moods suppressed immune function and positive moods improved it (see Figure 4-3). More recent work has hypothesized that cytokines, specifically interleukin-6 (IL-6), may provide the pathway between mood and health (Kiecolt-Glaser et al., 2002b).

Negative Mood and Upper Respiratory Infection

One of the conceptual problems encountered when studying negative mood is that it can be difficult to distinguish between mood and personality characteristics. In other words, we must be sure that we are dealing with a "person who is down" rather than a "downer of a person." In the language of psychology, we are talking about a distinction between **states**, which are short-term conditions, and **traits**, which are enduring characteristics. This distinction might be particularly relevant if one of your dependent measures were symptom reporting, because increased reporting could just as easily be an indication of chronic complaining as it is of genuine symptom experience.

A study by Cohen and colleagues (1995) made the distinction between state- and trait-negative affect, including anxiety, anger, depression, and fatigue. The main purpose of the study was to sort out whether negative states or negative traits had more influence on the development of colds and flu.

At the start of the study, blood samples were taken to establish baseline measures of specific antibody levels. The participants were then exposed to either a cold or influenza virus by way of nasal drops (another viral challenge study). Measures of state- and trait-negative

states and **traits:** psychological concepts that distinguish between short-term conditions (states) and enduring characteristics (traits).

affect were also taken at the start of the study. To do this, participants filled out a scale called the Profile of Mood States (POMS). They did this twice—once for how they felt in the preceding 24 hours (state) and once for how they felt generally (trait).

The participants were then quarantined in hotel rooms for the duration of the study, and their URI symptoms were monitored daily via assessments of nasal secretions and self-reports of symptoms. Finally, a second blood sample was taken four weeks after exposure to the virus.

The researchers wanted to know to what extent symptom severity and frequency were related to negative affect. The answer is interesting, because it underscores the importance of drawing a distinction between state and trait affect. Both state- and trait-negative affect were correlated with symptom reporting; however, only state-negative affect was correlated with objectively confirmed symptoms. This means that higher state-negative affect at the outset of the study predicted the actual symptoms a person would experience upon exposure to a virus. It also means that people with high trait-negative affect reported symptoms that could not be verified objectively.

This illustrates why we must make the distinction between personality and state in this work. Interestingly, people who scored high on trait-negative affect didn't start complaining about symptoms until they actually started experiencing them; they weren't simply inventing them. Instead, their *cognitive bias*, as it is called, took the form of a *misinterpretation* of sensations once they started to feel the symptoms of a cold or the flu. The authors suggest that this misinterpretation is due to an inability to accurately discriminate between real symptoms and other sensations, rather than to an oversensitivity to actual URI symptoms.

At least three important points must be noted concerning the design of this study. First, the authors demonstrated statistically that state-negative affect and trait-negative affect are different things. Second, in their design they did not correlate antibody proliferation with symptoms. This means that we can only infer that the high-state-negative-affect people had compromised immune systems, although it is arguably a reasonable inference in this case. Third, this study used a *prospective* design, starting with healthy individuals and charting the course of their URIs. This is important because the relationship between mood and URI is bidirectional (Hall & Smith, 1996).

In subsequent work, Pressman and Cohen (2005) have looked at state and trait distinctions in positive emotions. In this work, the authors point out that trait-positive mood is more predictive of good health outcomes than is induced state-positive mood. In fact, the latter can have negative effects on immune function due to the physiological arousal accompanying it.

Depression and Cancer   At the beginning of this section on depression, we showed that depression was a significant predictor of mortality for a number of illnesses, including cancer. Here, we will take a closer look at the possibility that negative moods such as depression, hopelessness, and pessimism increase the risk of getting cancer or of shortening the patient's survival time. Of course, all research in this area must be prospective in nature. A diagnosis of cancer is depressing for most people. As such, we know about that causal direction. What we need to know is the impact of depression in causing or accelerating cancer.

Like research on the relationship between stress and cancer, prospective studies looking at depression and cancer take one of two forms. Researchers may begin with cancer-free people, measure their levels of negative mood, then monitor them for cancer onset;

or they may assess the moods of people with cancer and then monitor the *progression* of their cancer. In this latter type of study, researchers must control for the type and severity of cancer at the outset of the study in order to make meaningful comparisons among people regarding survival.

Interest in the relationship between depression and cancer progression was fuelled in the 1960s, when Arthur Schmale identified what he and George Engel called the "giving up–given up" complex (Schmale & Engel, 1967). This term referred to the accelerated rate of decline they observed in cancer patients after these patients gave up hope for survival. Because these observations were anecdotal rather than empirical, it is difficult to sort out cause and effect. Evidence for causal links between mood and cancer came some 15 years later from a study in which cancer-free participants were monitored for 17 years to assess the extent to which depression predicted cancer deaths (Shekelle et al., 1981).

In this large prospective study of male employees at the Western Electric Company in the 1950s, more than 2000 cancer-free men were administered a battery of psychological tests, including the Minnesota Multiphasic Personality Inventory (MMPI). The MMPI is a comprehensive measure that is often used in the diagnosis of psychological disorders. Its subscale, measuring levels of depression, provided the main predictor variable for this study. Once the study began, the men were given annual physical exams for each of the next 11 years. Then, 17 years after the start of the study, mortality statistics were collected from the sample.

The study discovered that men who showed evidence of clinical depression on the MMPI were 2.3 times more likely to have died of cancer at some point in the 17 years covered by the study than those who didn't (see Figure 4-4). This effect was independent

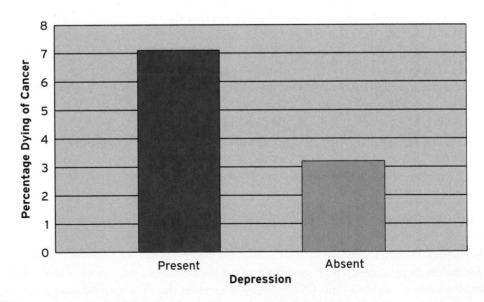

Figure 4-4 Cancer Deaths Over a 17-Year Period Categorized by Presence or Absence of Pre-Cancer Depression

In a 17-year prospective study, physically healthy men who showed signs of clinical depression at the start of the study were 2.3 times more likely to die of cancer.

Source: R.B. Shekelle et al., (1981). Psychological depression and 17-year risk of death from cancer. *Psychosomatic Medicine, 43,* 117–125. Adapted by permission from Wolters Kluwer Health.

of age, cigarette smoking, alcohol use, family history of cancer, occupational status, or type of cancer contracted. Further, depression was not related to any other cause of death. These results were replicated in a follow-up study 20 years later (Persky, Kempthorne-Rawson, & Shekelle, 1987). More recently, a study of women with abnormal results on a Pap smear found that depressive symptoms were associated with poorer immune system functioning, specifically lower CD3+ CD8+ cell counts (Savard et al., 1999), thus suggesting a biological link between depression and disease.

More recently, researchers have discovered that pessimism, independent of depression, is related to decreased survival rates among younger people who already have cancer (Schulz et al., 1996). A study involving patients who were receiving palliative radiation treatment for either recurrent or metastasized cancer showed that, for patients aged 30 to 59 years, pessimism was a significant predictor of mortality, regardless of type of cancer (see Figure 4-5).

Here again it can be difficult to distinguish between a psychological state and a personality trait. We all feel pessimistic from time to time (state), but that does not mean that we are *pessimists* (trait). This study does not lead to the conclusion that pessimists are more likely to get cancer for two reasons. First, the design did not begin with cancer-free participants. Second, pessimism was conceptualized more as a state than a trait.

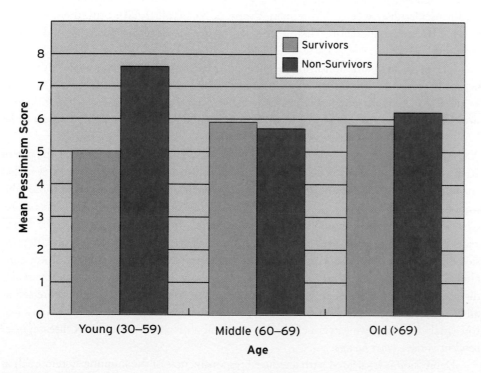

Figure 4-5 Pessimism Scores for Survivors and Non-Survivors of Cancer by Age

Younger patients who survived with recurrent or metastasized cancer had significantly lower pessimism scores than those in that age group who did not survive.

Source: Schultz et al., (1996). Pessimism, Age, and Cancer Mortality. *Psychology and Aging, II,* 304–309. Adapted by permission.

In summary, it is safe to say that depression and other negative mood states are related to increased risk of contracting cancer and of dying from it once it is contracted. It is also likely that immunocompetence provides one explanation for these increased risks. Some researchers have suggested that cancers related to viruses such as Epstein-Barr would be more susceptible to mood fluctuation than would cancers that are induced by chemical carcinogens, such as lung cancer (Kiecolt-Glaser et al., 2002a).

However, immunocompetence doesn't provide the whole explanation; we must remember that negative mood states are related to a number of other behavioural phenomena that can affect the experience of cancer, especially its progression. People experiencing depression or hopelessness are less likely to follow medical regimens and generally take care of themselves. Also, they tend to sleep poorly and have less energy (Jenkins, 1996). So it would be an oversimplification to say that the negative impact of mood on the immune system is the sole reason that negative mood is associated with increased cancer risk. However, whatever the actual mechanisms involved, health psychologists, counsellors, and others working in a psychosocial capacity with cancer patients must pay close attention to patients' moods and help patients to be optimistic and hopeful.

Depression and Heart Health   As we saw earlier in our discussion of research on negative mood, depression is often studied as an *outcome* rather than a *cause*. In this vein, researchers have suggested that depression, as an outcome, deserves more attention as an under-diagnosed problem for people with heart problems such as myocardial infarction or cardiovascular disease (e.g., Musselman, Evans, & Nemeroff, 1998). Still, there are some prospective studies indicating that depression is a risk factor for heart disease and related mortality.

One such study, after following people for 13 years, concluded that people with major depression had a 4.5 times greater risk of heart attack than those without depression (Pratt et al., 1996). Other studies measuring depressive symptoms as opposed to major depression estimated the risk of first heart attack for those with higher depression scores to be 1.5 to 2 times higher (Glassman & Shapiro, 1998).

Another prospective study followed more than 3700 adults who were over the age of 70 at the start of the study. The researchers made a distinction between what they called "new depression" and chronic depression. Newly depressed participants were those who were depressed at the outset of the study but had not been either three or six years before. Chronically depressed participants were depressed at the outset *and* either three or six years before. It was discovered that for men, "new depression" (but not chronic depression) increased the risk of contracting heart disease and dying from it. In fact, it was concluded that newly depressed older men were twice as likely to have a cardiovascular disease event than were men who were either chronically depressed or not depressed at all (Penninx et al., 1998). Because these studies statistically controlled correlated risk factors (including age), we can conclude that depression increases risk of heart disease, *independent of these other factors*.

Depression is associated with a reduced responsiveness of the immune system, such as lower lymphocyte proliferation (Maes, 1995). This, in turn, compromises the body's ability to deal with inflammation, which can be a good thing for the cardiovascular system as a short-term response, but if depression persists it can cause damage. This is but one of a number of ways in which the immune system is involved in cardiovascular health (Kop & Gottdiener, 2005).

Stress and Immune Function for Persons Living with AIDS

Leserman et al. (1999) have shown that HIV-positive men living with above-median stress for five or more years are two to three times more likely to progress to AIDS than HIV-positive men living with below-median stress levels. Thus, it makes sense that researchers at an Ottawa hospital have investigated the link between emotional states, such as stress and depression, on immune functioning among people living with AIDS (Balfour et al., 2003). Sixty-one people took part in the study, in which they were asked to complete the Perceived Stress Scale and a measure of depression. Outcome measures included HIV disease progression, and CD4 counts in particular. Remember that CD4 refers to helper T cells, and that these are believed to be particularly important in the progression of HIV.

It was found that stress and depression together accounted for 17 percent of the variance in CD4 counts, thus supporting a growing body of literature linking psychological state with symptoms associated with AIDS.

Depression and HIV Infection   Given what we know about the general effects of mood on the immune system, and given that AIDS is an immune-system disease, we might expect significant effects of negative mood on HIV infection and AIDS. There have been several fairly large studies in this area. For example, in a study of over 1700 HIV-positive women, depression was associated with shorter time to AIDS-related death (Cook et al., 2004).

Burack and colleagues (1993) measured depression in a group of 277 HIV-positive men. They then tracked T-helper-cell activity in these men for five years (T-helper-cell activity is an important predictor of prognosis for people who are HIV-positive). The depressed men showed a significantly greater decline in this cell activity than did the non-depressed men.

CASE 4-1 TWO DIFFERENT REACTIONS TO A DIAGNOSIS OF CANCER

Jack and Stephen had never met but found themselves sitting across from each other in a waiting room at the cancer clinic, leafing through magazines. Both had recently been diagnosed with prostate cancer and were very upset. However, from the moment their respective family physicians told them the news, each reacted quite differently. In this case study, we will describe these different reactions and speculate on the effect these reactions might have on the progression of the disease for each man. We will base our speculation on what we know from PNI research with cancer patients.

Both men were in their early sixties. Both were happily married. Jack kept in close contact with his two children, who were both married and had children of their own. Stephen didn't hear from his children much since they had started lives of their own. He saw them on major holidays, and that was about it.

The most significant difference between the two men was in the way they took the news that they had cancer. Jack was upset, of course, but he considered himself to be relatively young and determined. He went to the library and took out books on prostate cancer to learn more about the disease and what his options were. He also checked out the internet for information. He felt thankful that he wasn't in very much pain at this point, and he was confident that he could handle the treatment and that it would work.

Stephen responded differently. When he was told he had prostate cancer, he suddenly felt very old. He had heard of others with the disease and they were all in their seventies and eighties. He felt bitter that he had contracted a disease that put him in such an infirmed category. He decided that this would be the way his life would end—prematurely and terribly. Sure, he would go through with the treatments, but he had no confidence that they would work. He was convinced that his quality of life was about to decline, that the decline would be permanent, and that there was nothing he could do about it. He began to feel depressed much of the time.

Other aspects of these men's lives were different as well. When Jack told his wife about the diagnosis, she responded that the two of them were going to grow old together and that was that. She maintained an upbeat attitude and helped Jack through the times when he got discouraged or was in discomfort. Jack's friends and neighbours responded the same way.

Stephen had a different experience. His wife was devastated by the news that her husband had cancer. They had both just retired and had plans to travel and enjoy life. Now, in her mind, all of those plans would come to nothing. When Stephen would get depressed, he was difficult to be around. At these times, his wife would leave him alone. Stephen didn't have many friends, and he now felt awkward around those he had because he believed he had a horrible disease that made him different from them.

If Jack and Stephen were at the same stage of illness when diagnosed and were similar in all other aspects of their health, PNI research findings would suggest a more favourable prognosis for Jack. He had an optimistic attitude and believed in the efficacy of the treatment. These cognitions helped him avoid getting depressed, and depression has been shown to accelerate cancer progression. Jack also had a strong support system in the form of family, friends, and neighbours. This support is associated with better survival rates for cancer patients.

Stephen was on a much less encouraging course. His depression had the potential to suppress his immune system to the extent that his cancer could worsen over time. This, of course, would only depress him more. Stephen needed to get help for his depression in order to break this cycle. His social support network wasn't strong—another disadvantage—and Stephen needed to change his thinking in this regard as well. Perhaps if he gave his friends more of a chance, they would be more supportive of him, which would help him feel less depressed. Also, as difficult as it may have seemed for him, Stephen needed to be a more positive companion for his wife. For her part, she needed to persevere through the difficult times brought on by Stephen's depression and try to maintain an optimistic and positive approach to his treatment and their future together.

Although Stephen's response and that of his wife were understandable, such responses would not help Stephen. The couple had to try to make changes in the way they were reacting to Stephen's illness, which was easier said than done. Fortunately, there are counsellors who specialize in helping families cope with illness. We emphasize the need for such counselling here, because an improvement in Stephen's mood and thinking would likely increase the competence of his immune system and thus improve his chances of survival, not to mention his overall quality of life.

BIOLOGICAL MECHANISMS TO EXPLAIN WHY PSYCHOLOGICAL STATES AFFECT THE IMMUNE SYSTEM

We have reviewed studies indicating that psychological states and traits can influence our immune system in a variety of ways. This influence increases or decreases our susceptibility to a range of medical conditions and helps or hinders our ability to cope with these conditions once we have them. An important question remains to be answered, however: Just how does our biological makeup allow for this influence? When looking for mechanisms that link psychological factors to health, researchers tend to cite four possible sources—the endocrine system, which controls hormones; the sympathetic nervous system; the immune system; and behaviour. (See Kiecolt-Glaser et al., 2002a, for a concise review.)

In terms of the endocrine system, researchers have cited the hypothalamic-pituitary-adrenal (HPA) axis to help explain the biology behind the stress-immunity link (Kendall-Tackett, 2009). You may recall from chapter 2 that the hypothalamus and pituitary gland are located within the brain. When we experience stress, the hypothalamus releases a hormone that causes the pituitary gland to release yet another hormone which, in turn, causes the adrenal cortex to release cortisol. The immune system is affected by cortisol. Thus, this "axis" produces a chain of events that link stress to immune functioning.

When the stressor is particularly strong, as in the case of psychological trauma, the HPA axis is "chronically activated" (Kendall-Tackett, 2009, p. 37), as is the sympathetic nervous system, which has extensive nerve fibres in areas of high immune cell concentration (Evans, Hucklebridge & Clow (2003). This over-activity has adverse effects on the immune system, specifically by causing it to release an abundance of **cytocines**. Cytocines increase the system's capacity to produce inflammation and help heal wounds and fight infection. Cortisol usually helps keep the inflammatory response in check so that it doesn't go overboard and cause problems. Unfortunately stress reverses the effect of cortisol. Ultimately, severe stress results in excessive inflammation, which results in disease.

cytocines: increase the body's capacity to produce inflammation, and help heal wounds and fight infection.

Kendall-Tackett (2009) makes the case that excessive inflammation provides the explanation for many of the ways psychological state affects health, from coronary heart disease to impaired wound healing (e.g., Surtees et al., 2008).

Inflammation has also been cited to explain the relationship between depression and health. Another indicator of inflammation is C-reactive protein. Elevated levels of this protein have been found in depressed patients with heart disease (Surtees, et al., 2008; Taylor, et al., 2006). We also know that inflammation is an important contributor to coronary artery disease (Zouridakis et al., 2004). The important point here is that extreme stress can result in excessive inflammation, and that is bad for the heart.

Even some of the behavioural explanations of PNI can be traced back to inflammation. For example, disturbed sleep, which is not uncommon among people with depression, is associated with increased inflammation. To make matters worse, inflammation can disrupt sleep, thus creating a negative cycle (Suarez & Goforth, 2009). The good news is that stress, and inflammatory responses, can be affected by diet and exercise. Students with diets high in omega-3s (long-chain fatty acids) were found to have lower inflammatory responses to stress (Maes et al., 2000). One good source of omega-3 is fish oil. Exercise has also been shown to reduce excessive inflammatory response (Starkweather, 2007).

Remember that PNI distinguishes between the effects of acute and long-term stress on health. Short-term stress can actually enhance immune functioning, whereas long-term stress is most often detrimental. This is because long-term secretion of adrenalin (remember this is the output of the HPA axis) suppresses immunity (Song & Leonard, 2000). Specifically, lymphocyte proliferation is lower, and NK cells lose their ability to destroy cancerous cells (de Kooker, 2008).

The nature of cancerous cells also provides insights into the biological relationship between psychological state and disease. Cancer cells survive by mutation and proliferation, and spread. As a result, cancer becomes progressively more serious as the cells "escape" from the primary site and mutate, so that the immune system has difficulty tracking them down and destroying them (Ben-Eliyahu et al., 2007). Competent immune systems, which most people possess, deal effectively with these escaped cells. Compromised systems do not, resulting in the spread, or metastasizing, of the disease.

There are times during the cancer progression when a patient is at greater risk for metastatic spread. One such time is immediately following cancer surgery when there may be "shedding of tumour cells to circulation" (Ben-Eliyahu et al., 2007, p. 882). Other risky times are during exposure to carcinogens and during pregnancy. Ben-Eliyahu and colleagues suggest that these are times when it is particularly important to monitor and reduce the stress responses of cancer patients.

These explanations of the biological mechanisms linking psychological state and health are crucial to psychoneuroimmunology and, more generally, to health psychology. They prove that this link, which is at the heart of this book, stems from biological realities. The more we can learn about these mechanisms, the better we can help people stay healthy and cope with illness.

CHAPTER SUMMARY

PNI provides empirical proof that psychological states are directly linked to biological processes. This brings further credibility to the field of health psychology and provides the kinds of research evidence that biomedical practitioners understand.

Immunocompetence is measured in a number of ways. Some of the more common include counting cells that proliferate in the presence of an antigen or a substance that is foreign to the body. Functional tests of immunocompetence measure the extent to which these proliferated cells actually destroy, or lyse, the antigen. These measurements can be taken inside the body (*in vivo*) or outside (*in vitro*).

Research features a range of antigens, including Con A, phytohemagglutinin (PHA), and pokeweed mitogen (PWM). Cancerous cells might also be used in this research to assess the immunocompetence of natural killer (NK) cells. Alternatively, antigens, in the form of viruses, can be introduced into the body to track the progression of the virus.

Considerable research has linked stress with a range of illnesses, from upper respiratory infections to autoimmune disease to cancer. Depression has also been linked with a range of illnesses, most notably coronary heart disease.

One important mechanism linking psychological state and health concerns the body's ability to produce and control inflammatory responses. During stress and depression, this ability is compromised, often producing increased inflammation, which can result in disease.

In addition, the hypothalamus-pituitary-adrenal (HPA) axis works to link psychological state and health. During times of stress, this axis produces increased amounts of hormones that can compromise immune functioning, essentially by shifting the body's priority away from immune response to fight-or-flight response.

Review Questions

1. What is the relationship between our psychological states and our health?
2. Why is the study of psychoneuroimmunology so important to the work of health psychologists?
3. How does the immune system work to fend off infection?
4. How can researchers assess the effectiveness of someone's immune system?
5. What proof is there that the immune system is affected by psychological states and life circumstances?
6. What are the biological mechanisms linking these psychological states to our immune system?

CHAPTER OUTLINE

PERCEIVING AND INTERPRETING SYMPTOMS
SEEKING MEDICAL CARE
PHYSICIAN–PATIENT INTERACTION
ADHERING TO MEDICAL ADVICE

Learning Objectives

After studying this chapter, you will be able to

■ Describe key factors that influence our perception and interpretation of symptoms

■ Explain why people delay in seeking medical care

■ Provide an overview of different models of the physician-patient relationship

■ Outline both patient and physician characteristics that lead to poor communication

■ Define patient non-adherence and list contributing factors to non-adherence

■ Outline strategies to improve patient adherence

Lynn is visiting her physician, primarily because she has recently been experiencing a lot of stomach discomfort. However, this isn't Lynn's only complaint. In addition to her stomach problems, Lynn hasn't been sleeping, she has more blemishes on her face than usual, and her mother has recently been diagnosed with adult-onset diabetes. Lynn is quite concerned about her.

Upon visiting her physician, Lynn decides she will present her symptoms in order of ease of describing them. Lynn says, "My face has been worse than usual lately, I haven't been getting enough sleep, and I've had a lot of butterflies in my stomach these past few weeks." Lynn doesn't bother to mention her concern about her mother to the physician because she already has a lot of issues to discuss and knows the physician can't possibly help her mother during this visit. Lynn's physician dismisses the "butterflies" because Lynn has downplayed this symptom and hasn't reported any pain in her stomach. He also assumes Lynn hasn't been getting enough sleep simply because she has been busy lately.

The doctor therefore decides that Lynn is primarily there to seek help for her "worse than usual" face. He provides her with a prescription for a topical ointment and sends her on her way. The main reason for Lynn's visiting her physician, her upset stomach, is never discussed.

Compare Lynn's physician visit to the more positive experience that Alexander and his parents have when they visit the emergency ward:

Alexander is an 18-month-old toddler who just loves to run. However, running is a relatively new talent, and he sometimes forgets a few required details, such as looking where he's going. After Alexander has a head-on collision with the corner of a kitchen cupboard, resulting in a gash on his forehead, his parents take him to Emergency to get his cut sutured. As expected, there is a wait. Once Alexander sees a doctor, the stitch work begins. The physician, who seems to realize it is a stressful situation for the young family, quietly reassures Alexander that everything is going to be okay. Then the physician tells Mom and Dad how to care for the laceration and answers all their questions. Mom and Dad are allowed to stay in the room to lessen Alexander's anxiety, and when the suturing is complete, the doctor gives Alexander a "rubber glove balloon" and a Popsicle.

Most people have had both positive and negative experiences with physicians. Lynn's experience exemplifies a situation in which a patient isn't completely satisfied with the outcome of a physician visit. In this case, the physician didn't address all of Lynn's concerns during the physician–patient interview. Indeed, her primary concern, stomach problems, wasn't even mentioned by her physician. In contrast, Alexander's parents were very satisfied with their interaction with the emergency room physician. From the moment Alexander arrived at Emergency, it was obvious why he was seeking treatment. The doctor provided treatment for Alexander and answered all of the questions posed by Alexander's parents.

Effective communication contributed to the satisfaction Alexander's parents felt with the treatment they received from their physician. The *lack* of communication between Lynn and her physician, on the other hand, resulted in a negative experience for her.

Communication is central to the physician–patient relationship. In this chapter, we will discuss how both physician and patient behaviours contribute to faulty communication.

As well, we will outline the impact communication has on physician–patient relationships, adherence to medical advice, and health outcomes. However, before we begin our discussion of communication in the medical setting, we must consider the factors that lead someone to seek medical advice in the first place.

PERCEIVING AND INTERPRETING SYMPTOMS

How do we decide when to seek medical advice? Clearly, Alexander's parents knew they should seek medical care for their son. The cut on his forehead and the dripping blood were fairly obvious clues. But what led Lynn to see a doctor? Many of her symptoms were sensations that people experience every day; people have blemishes on their skin and stomach-aches from time to time. But most people don't seek medical advice every time one of these "symptoms" arises. How do we decide when to seek medical advice?

People have difficulty deciphering and even noticing some symptoms. People often don't notice even highly visible external symptoms, such as a mole-like lesion that may be melanoma (Miles & Meehan, 1995). It is, therefore, not surprising to learn that people also have difficulty accurately assessing their internal states. For example, people's estimates of their own heart rate are not well correlated with physiological indices (Pennebaker, 2000). These differences partly account for the considerable variability in individuals' decisions to seek medical advice.

Certainly, there are individual differences in the perception of symptoms. Have you ever noticed how some people seem to keep going no matter what, whereas others seem to adopt the role of patient the instant they are faced with a minor ailment? Some of these individual differences are constant over time. That is, individuals who pay a lot of attention to their internal states are consistently more likely than others to notice a symptom (Brink, Karlson, & Hallberg, 2002; Jurgens, 2006).

Other personal factors, including current mood, personality traits, and stress level, influence people's response to symptoms. People in a good mood, for example, view their own health more positively than do those in a bad mood. We have all experienced being in such a good mood that we didn't notice our normally aggravating aches and pains, as well as being in such a bad mood that we noticed every discomfort, no matter how minor. Research backs up these experiential observations. People in a good mood report fewer symptoms and fewer illness-related thoughts. In contrast, people in a bad mood report more symptoms, are less likely to believe that any behaviours they engage in will relieve symptoms, and assume they are more vulnerable to future illness (Gendolla et al., 2005; Leventhal et al., 1996; Salovey et al., 2000).

Given that people in a bad mood report more symptoms, it is not surprising that those with a mood-related disposition called negative affectivity (NA trait) have a greater proclivity to report symptoms than do those with low NA trait in the absence of any objective differences in health status (Pennebaker, 2000). In general, people with high NA trait experience consistently higher levels of distress and dissatisfaction over time and across different situations. According to Pennebaker (2000), "Those with high NA trait appear to be hypervigilant about their bodies and have a lower threshold for noticing and reporting subtle bodily sensations" (p. 306). Due to their pessimistic nature, such people are also more concerned about the implications of their perceived symptoms.

Stress is a personal factor that tends to elevate symptom reporting (Dorner, Stronegger, Rebhandl, Rieder, & Freidl, 2010). Stressful periods in people's lives can precipitate or aggravate the experience of symptoms. And people who have experienced a great deal of stress are more vulnerable to illness. People who believe they are more likely to contract an illness will also attend more closely to their bodies. This inward focus of attention may lead them to interpret stress-related physiological changes, such as accelerated heart rate or breathing, as symptoms of illness (Cameron, Leventhal, & Leventhal, 1995). However, those experiencing tremendous stress are more likely to seek health care than those under less stress, even with equal symptoms (Martin & Brantley, 2004).

In addition to personal factors, gender contributes to the perception of symptoms. Unfortunately, the research into which gender is most sensitive to internal bodily signals is equivocal. Some studies report that women are more sensitive to their internal state (Brannon & Feist, 2007), while others report that men are more sensitive (Pennebaker, 2000). We know that women seek health care more frequently than do men, but they may delay longer in seeking that care (Galdas, Cheater, & Marshall, 2005; Goldberg, Gurwitz, & Gore, 1999). Interestingly, men attribute minor symptoms to major problems more readily than women do (Martin et al., 2004).

There are also age differences in the reporting of symptoms and willingness to seek care. Elderly people frequently complain of physical symptoms that prompt them to seek medical intervention. There is evidence to suggest that older people perceive normal age-related bodily changes as illness (Gott et al., 1999; Haug, Musil, Warner, & Morris, 1997). Other researchers have suggested that the tendency for symptoms to increase as one ages may be partially due to the decreased cognitive performance that some adults experience as they age (Frisoni, Fedi, Geroldi, & Trabucchi, 1999). In other words, mild cognitive impairment is associated with the perception of poorer body functioning. These studies suggest that older adults may over-report their symptoms.

However, studies of cancer patients have discovered that older adults were less likely than younger adults to notice cancer symptoms—perhaps, in part, because they perceived less personal risk of developing the disease than did younger adults (Bish et al., 2005). One study (Ryan & Zerwic, 2003) found that older people with symptoms of acute myocardial infarction misattributed these symptoms to the pains of old age. Other studies report that older men delay seeking help for symptoms that might be viewed as embarrassing, such as those indicative of sexually transmitted disease (Gott et al., 2003; Pitts et al., 2000). Thus, the role of age differences in the recognition of symptoms is quite complex.

One of the most important factors in the interpretation of symptoms is the environment. When people are in environments that lack stimulation, they are more likely to pay attention to their internal states. Boring or tedious environments lead people to amplify bodily sensations (Pennebaker, 2000). Pennebaker (1983) relates many findings that are consistent with this view. He has observed, for example, that "individuals are more likely to notice itching or tickling sensations in their throats and emit coughs during boring parts of movies than during interesting portions" (p. 191). Similarly, environments that are isolated or that discourage interpersonal communication allow people time to ponder their bodily sensations—that is, in places where talking is discouraged (e.g., libraries) or where there is a great deal of noise (e.g., factories) (Pennebaker, 2000). This does not necessarily mean that these people are more accurate in their interpretation of sensations; in fact, they may overestimate changes in their physiological functions, such as heart rate and nasal congestion.

In contrast, when the environment is exciting or demands a great deal of attention or concentration, people are less likely to notice internal symptoms (Pennebaker, 2000). Internal symptoms are also likely to go unnoticed when an individual is engaged in physical activity (Pennebaker, 2000). This has been explained as the "competition of cues" and is consistent with the finding that distraction can serve as a useful short-term coping method (e.g., during sports competitions or visits to the dentist's office).

In summary, symptom recognition depends on several factors. The perception of symptoms is influenced by individual differences in body awareness as well as transitory situational factors. When attention is directed inward, symptoms are more likely to be recognized. When attention is directed outward, by physical activity or a distracting environment, symptoms are less likely to be noticed. Gender differences, age differences, personality differences, and current mood influence symptom recognition.

Once a symptom is perceived, it must then be interpreted. How a symptom is interpreted is influenced by a number of factors, including prior experience with the symptom. If, for example, your mother or your sister has had her appendix removed, you are more likely to consider appendicitis whenever you experience pain in your lower abdomen. Other people, who do not share this family history, would likely consider other causes for the pain before considering appendicitis.

A symptom's meaning is also influenced by how common it is among someone's family, friends, acquaintances, and culture (Croyle & Hunt, 1991). Symptoms that are perceived as commonplace are generally considered to be less serious than rare or unusual symptoms (Peay & Peay, 2000). As strange as it may seem, the simple fact that a symptom or condition is widespread may lead people to attach little significance to it, sometimes unwisely.

Cultural factors can affect how quickly someone recognizes symptoms and reports them. A study in Vancouver found that Chinese respondents were less likely to recommend enlisting emergency medical aid than English or Punjabi respondents in response to symptoms presented in a questionnaire study (Ratner et al., 2006). An international study (Alonso et al., 1998) noted that there are cross-cultural differences in the reporting of vision problems. Specifically, cataract patients in Canada and Spain were less likely to report vision trouble than were Danish or American patients. These reports could not be accounted for by either clinical or socio-demographic factors.

An important consideration in assessing reported symptoms is learning, because in a very real sense we *learn* how to experience symptoms. It is, therefore, likely that people in different cultures receive different "lessons" about the experience of symptoms.

For example, in Western culture men have traditionally been socialized to avoid complaining about emotional and physical symptoms of discomfort, as this is seen as a sign of weakness. Not surprisingly, men are less likely than women to report such symptoms (Nicholas, 2000). At a very young age, children are taught both directly and by example which symptoms are important and which are trivial. A parent's concern over a fever and seeming lack of concern over a superficial cut provide a child with powerful cues about which symptoms to attend to and which to ignore.

Our families contribute to our interpretation of symptoms in other ways, as well. We often consult our family and friends for help in interpreting the meaning of a symptom.

These advisers form a *lay referral system*, an informal network of non-practitioners who offer their own interpretations long before any medical treatment is sought (Skevington, 2004; Suls, Martin, & Leventhal, 1997). People in the lay referral system provide advice when someone mentions the symptoms, requests an opinion, or even if he or she simply looks sick. The friend or relative responds with personal views of what the symptom is likely to mean: "Connor and Liam each had a rash like that. It turned out it was a reaction to the new brand of bubble bath their mother had bought." The friend or relative provides advice about seeking medical attention: "Parker's temperature was getting quite high, and he ended up having convulsions. You'd better call your doctor." Some people may also recommend various home remedies: "Soak a wool sock in boiling water and vinegar, and then wrap it around your neck. Your sore throat will be gone in no time."

The advice provided by the lay referral network varies in its usefulness. Sometimes it is very helpful. For example, a study conducted at the Children's Hospital in Montreal determined that mothers who consulted their lay referral system about their child's symptoms were less likely to take their children to the emergency department unnecessarily. Although much of the advice provided by the lay referral network is helpful, lay persons are also far more likely than health professionals to recommend actions that worsen the condition or result in a delay seeking appropriate and needed treatment.

SEEKING MEDICAL CARE

When do people seek medical care? The answer to this question is more complex than simply stating that people visit their physician when they have experienced one or more symptoms. Studies of illness behaviour indicate that *when* a person seeks help is a function of the specific nature of the symptoms experienced as well as of the person's social and personal needs.

Perhaps the most obvious determinant of when a person seeks help is the type of symptoms experienced. Symptoms that are new, unexpected, painful, disruptive, highly visible, or that affect highly valued parts of the body are interpreted as more serious and are more likely to lead someone to seek medical care (Meechan, Collins, & Petrie, 2003; Skevington, 2004; Turk & Melzack, 2001). If the symptoms are recognizable from past experience and are believed to be unimportant or explainable, such as muscle aches after an athletic competition, they will probably be ignored. However, if the symptom interferes with daily activities such as job performance or participation in athletic events, medical care is usually sought. Symptoms also gain a person's attention if they attack a highly visible part of the body such as the face or eyes, or if they are important to one's self-identity (e.g., a lump in a woman's breast; Meechan et al., 2003). Above all, the symptom that leads a person to seek medical care most quickly is the experience of pain. Few of us enjoy pain and as a result we attempt to eliminate the painful experience as fast as possible.

Although symptom recognition is a major contributing factor to seeking medical care, Statistics Canada (Nabalamba & Miller, 2007) has identified a number of general trends regarding who seeks medical care in Canada. Specifically, females seek care more than males, the very old, and those who are of higher socioeconomic status. Interestingly, rural residents visit their family physicians more often than urban dwellers. In contrast, urban dwellers are more likely to consult specialists. Noting these trends should not detract from the fact that symptom recognition is what most often leads people to seek medical care.

Delaying Medical Care

Dean, the subject of Case 5-1, was lucky. He won his battle against testicular cancer. However, his odds of survival would likely have been better if he had not delayed so long in seeking medical advice. Delay in seeking diagnosis and treatment is clearly linked to increases in morbidity and mortality of cancer patients (Bish, Ramirez, Burgess, & Hunter, 2005). Perhaps Dean would have sought medical care sooner if it had been more obvious that his symptoms required medical treatment. In medical emergencies, such as when someone sustains a severe injury, people often seek help in a matter of minutes or hours. Referring back to Alexander, the little boy with the cut on his forehead in our opening vignette, we can assume that his parents wasted no time in getting him to the hospital.

CASE 5-1 DELAY IN SEEKING TREATMENT

One day after Dean returned from a four-hour bike ride, he noticed that one of his testicles was quite sore. He thought the sensation was odd, but quickly rationalized that he had just spent a considerable amount of time in the "saddle" and that this was likely responsible for his discomfort. The discomfort did not completely go away, but Dean, an aspiring professional cyclist, continued to spend a large amount of time on his bike.

About a month later he was thinking about his testicular soreness again. He realized that the discomfort wasn't subsiding. He vowed to visit a physician the next chance he got. Unfortunately, he was off to Dijon, France, in two days to try out for a professional cycling team and would likely have to wait until he returned to Canada before he could visit the physician. Three weeks later Dean returned to Canada. He hadn't experienced much discomfort in France because he was too caught up in the excitement of becoming a professional cyclist. However, back home in his own environment, he became aware that his discomfort was becoming more intense. Obviously, there was more wrong with him than simply spending too many hours training. He was extremely anxious as he made an appointment to see his family physician. The next day he visited his physician. This visit led to a number of medical tests to aid the physician in making a diagnosis. The physician felt it was likely that Dean had testicular cancer. Subsequently, this diagnosis was confirmed and the prognosis was not good. Dean was told that he had only a 50–50 chance of surviving because the cancer was at such an advanced stage.

Other emergency situations are more ambiguous (Brink, Karlson, & Hallberg, 2002). Most heart attack victims, for example, are initially confused by their symptoms and attribute them instead to a wide array of causes, including gas pain, ulcers, gallbladder disease, or even the common cold. Patients suffering from a myocardial infarction (more commonly referred to as a heart attack) typically arrive at the hospital or seek the care of paramedical staff between 2.5 and 4 hours after the onset of their symptoms (Walsh, Lynch, Murphy, & Daly, 2004), but the time from the onset of symptoms to the initiation of medical help varies between one hour and several days. And studies show that heart attack victims spend about 65 percent of that time trying to decide whether their symptoms require medical treatment. Even after they have correctly attributed the symptoms to a serious condition, such as a heart attack, people will waste a substantial amount of time before taking direct action to receive treatment.

What is responsible for such delay? In attempting to answer this question, researchers have developed a model to outline different stages of delay. They refer to **patient delay** as the period between an individual's first awareness of a symptom and treatment of that symptom. As illustrated in Figure 5-1, total patient delay occurs in a sequence of stages (Andersen, Cacioppo, & Roberts, 1995): (1) **appraisal delay**, the time it takes for a person to decide that a symptom is a sign of illness; (2) **illness delay**, the time between recognizing one is ill and deciding to seek medical care; (3) **behavioural delay**, the time that elapses between the decision to seek medical care and acting on this decision by making an appointment; and (4) **medical delay** (scheduling and treatment), the interval between making an appointment and first receiving medical care.

patient delay: the period between one's first awareness of a symptom and treatment for that symptom.

appraisal delay: the time it takes one to decide that a symptom is a sign of illness.

illness delay: the time taken between recognizing that one is ill and deciding to seek medical care.

behavioural delay: the elapsed time between the decision to seek medical care and acting on this decision by making an appointment.

medical delay: the time between making an appointment and first receiving medical care.

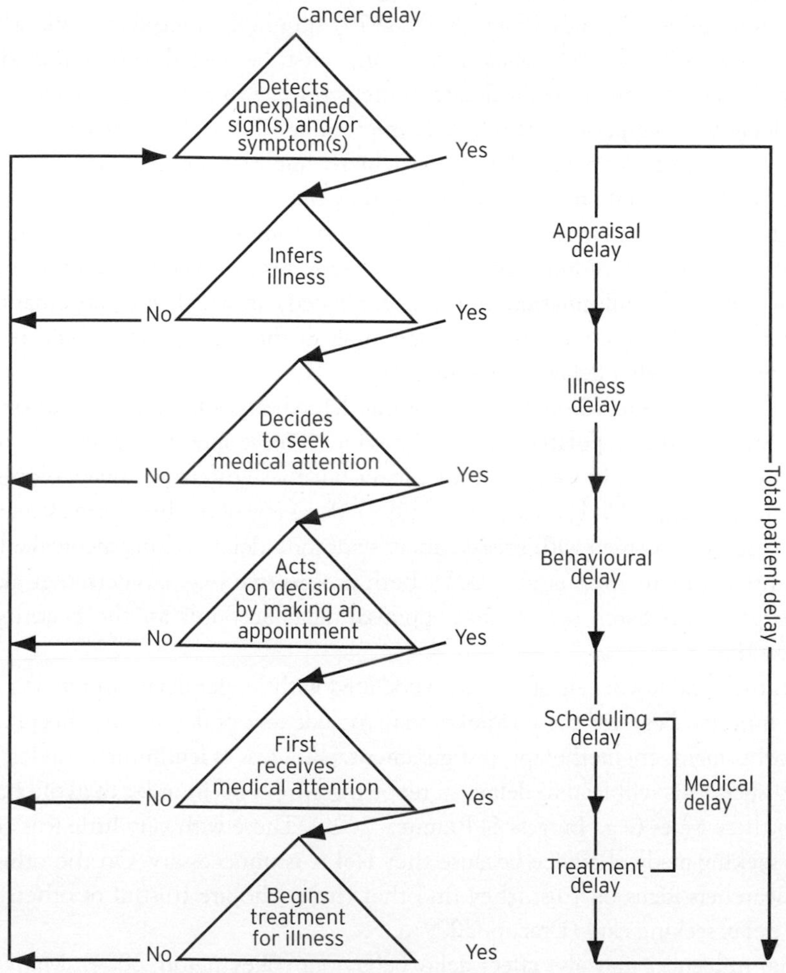

Figure 5-1 Stages of Delay in Seeking Treatment for Symptoms

Source: Andersen, B.L., Cacioppo, J.T., & Roberts, D.C. (1995). Delay in seeking a cancer diagnosis: Delay stages and psychophysiological comparison processes. *British Journal of Social Psychology, 34,* 33–52. Reproduced with permission from the *British Journal of Social Psychology,* © The British Psychological Society.

In a now classic study, Safer, Tharps, Jackson, and Leventhal (1979) identified stages of delay in seeking medical care. These researchers interviewed 93 patients who were waiting to see a physician at a hospital clinic or emergency room. They assessed patients' reactions to their symptoms and determined at what point these patients first interpreted their symptoms as illness, when they decided to seek medical care, and when they actually took steps to consult a medical professional. Not surprisingly, those who demonstrated the least delay were those in the greatest pain. The total delay in seeking care was significantly longer for patients who currently had other problems in their lives (such as a troubled marriage), who had read about their symptoms, who were older, and who had waited for the symptoms to go away. The best predictor of illness delay was whether the person had a new symptom. Patients were more likely to see an old symptom as normal and to tolerate it for a long period of time before deciding to seek medical care. Understandably, patients who imagined they were severely ill and imagined negative consequences of being ill had lengthy illness delays. And, not surprisingly, people who believed they could not be cured also delayed treatment.

The findings of this study (Safer et al., 1979) should be interpreted somewhat cautiously because of its methodological limitations. First, because the study included only persons who actually sought medical care, there is no way to generalize conclusions concerning delay to those persons who had a symptom but did not seek treatment. Second, the study uses retrospective data. This is particularly important, because the patients were asked to recall and specify the point at which they first noticed the symptom, when they first felt they were ill, and when they decided to seek treatment. Because the patients were asked to remember this information rather than report it as it was happening, there may be inaccuracies in the information. A prospective study, in which the participants maintain a diary of their symptoms and their appraisals of those symptoms, would be a more effective way of studying delay behaviours.

Much of the recent research investigating delay behaviours has focused on cancer patients. Studying this population's delay behaviour is most appropriate because, as previously mentioned, delays in treatment for cancer have a significant influence on survival rates (Ramirez et al., 1999; Richards et al., 1999). A review of the literature estimates that 20 to 30 percent of women with breast cancer symptoms delay seeking medical advice for three months or more (Bish et al., 2005). Both prospective (e.g., Andersen et al., 1995) and retrospective research reveals that appraisal delay accounts for the majority of the total delay time.

Both high and low levels of fear are associated with longer delays in reporting breast cancer symptoms. Fear, for these women, may include fear of doctors and hospitals, cancer, embarrassment, chemotherapy, disfigurement, pain, loss of femininity, and loss of control. And such fears will lead to delays in reporting symptoms in order to avoid having to deal with these issues (e.g., Burgess & Ramirez, 2006). Those with very little fear are likely to delay seeking medical advice because they feel it is unnecessary. On the other hand, when researchers focus on trust, they find that those who are trustful of others are less likely to delay seeking care (Dracup, 2009).

Social influences may also affect delay behaviour (Skevington, 2004). Many women believe that, if they are diagnosed with breast cancer their male partner, will abandon them (Facione & Giancarlo, 1998). And while a number of studies reveal that marital status is unrelated to delays by patients (e.g., Ramirez et al., 1999), there is support for the hypothesis that the role responsibilities of married women with children influence delay behaviour (Facione, Miaskowski, Dodd, & Paul, 2002). Women report that devoting time and attention to the needs of others, making domestic arrangements prior to the biopsy, arranging for child care during the summer and school holidays, and dealing with work-related demands all receive priority over discovered breast cancer symptoms.

Another factor that has been considered in delay behaviour is the age of the patient. This is often reported as having an effect on patient delay; however, findings haven't always been consistent. Many researchers (Ramirez et al., 1999; Richards et al., 1999; Sainsbury, Johnston, & Haward, 1999) report that older age is associated with longer symptom-reporting delay by breast cancer patients. Unfortunately, these investigators have not utilized the stages of delay model provided by Andersen and colleagues (1995) and outlined in Figure 5-1. These studies do, however, divide the time between onset of symptoms and start of treatment (total delay) into two main phases: delay by patients, defined as time between onset of symptoms and time of first medical consultation; and delay by providers, which is any delay between first medical consultation and start of treatment. Analysis based on this definition of delay reveals that many older women engage in patient delay (Burgess et al., 2006). However, some studies (e.g., Friedman et al., 2006) reveal that younger women also delay in reporting symptoms and, in addition, experience more delay by their health care providers (Ramirez et al., 1999). Based on the results of the study conducted by Richards and colleagues (1999), we can conclude that the health care providers were less likely to delay treatment of the older women because the older women were at a more advanced stage of cancer (likely resulting from their delay in seeking medical advice). Fortunately, delays by providers "do not seem to be associated with decreased survival in patients presenting with breast cancer" (Sainsbury et al., 1999, p. 1132).

Similar results have been found in studies with other patient populations. For example, a review of studies with acute myocardial infarction patients (i.e., heart attack victims) showed that women and older patients tend to delay seeking medical care longer (Nguyen et al., 2010). In Canada, close to 3.5 million people do not have a regular physician (Nabalamba & Millar, 2007). Undoubtedly, this will contribute to patient delay in seeking medical care as not only do the individuals need to seek treatment, but they must first determine who to seek treatment from.

In summary, there are a number of factors that contribute to patient delay, including characteristics of the symptom, age, gender, societal role obligations, and psychological attributes such as fear. Even physicians who are familiar with illness symptoms and know the importance of treating these symptoms promptly are not exempt from patient delay; consider the behaviour of Jorge, described in Case 5-2.

CASE 5-2 ONE SURGEON'S STORY: INVINCIBLE OR IN DENIAL?

What accounts for the delay behaviour of a 37-year-old male surgeon diagnosed as having a malignant, non-Hodgkin's lymphoma (cancer of the lymph nodes)? Jorge delayed identifying his symptoms as those of a possible serious illness even though he was trained to recognize the importance of such symptoms in his patients.

<Case Continued>

One morning, Jorge noticed a small lump on his jaw while shaving. He found the lump odd, but he certainly wasn't going to worry about it. As a general rule, physicians have a unique ability to think of themselves as invulnerable to the ailments and misery that they are exposed to each day. Jorge was in complete denial, and he ignored the lump. As time went by, the lump slowly enlarged and he casually showed it to his physician friends. He thinks they said not to worry but he really can't remember. Finally, at a dinner party one night, a woman with no medical training asked, "What is that thing under your jaw?" Jorge, still believing all was well, set up an appointment with a surgeon. He underwent surgery, five months of radiation treatment, and has lived to tell his story (Shlain, 1979).

PHYSICIAN–PATIENT INTERACTION

A final, extremely important factor contributing to people's decisions to use medical services is the quality of the relationship they have with their physicians.

Basic Models of Physician–Patient Interaction

A crucial element in the typical interaction between a patient and a health care practitioner is the nature of their relationship. A classic article in the field of health psychology by Thomas Szasz and Marc Hollender, written in 1956, outlines three basic models they believed characterized the nature of the physician–patient relationship.

active-passive model: situation in which patients are unable to participate in their care or to make decisions because of their medical condition.

The **active-passive model** describes a relationship in which patients are unable to participate in their own care or to make decisions for their own welfare because of the severity of their medical conditions. For example, when patients have severe injuries or are in a coma the physician is responsible for providing care and making decisions on their behalf; obviously, the patients are not in a position to provide any input. Consider the following situation:

Dennis gashed himself with a knife while camping in the bush. He cut an artery and the blood was spurting out. His buddies placed him in the back of their pickup truck and sped down the highway toward the nearest town. By the time they reached the hospital, Dennis was unconscious. A few seconds after they arrived at the hospital emergency ward, Dennis was placed on a gurney and wheeled to the operating room. Then Dennis's clothing was ripped off and the severed artery was found and tied. At the same time, others worked to find a vein that had not collapsed in order to put in an intravenous line. The entire emergency room staff worked with skill and speed. Dennis, who was unconscious, could neither participate in nor fight their efforts.

guidance-cooperation model: communication in which the patient seeks advice from the physician and answers the questions that are asked, but the physician is responsible for determining the diagnosis and treatment.

The **guidance-cooperation model** applies when patients seek advice from the physician. The patients answer the questions that the physician asks about their symptoms, but the physician is responsible for determining diagnosis and treatment. In essence, the physician is responsible for the thinking and decision making. This model would likely be followed if a person had an infection or a sprain. Consider the following example:

Henry was told by his physician to "take one of these little pills three times a day. If you do what I tell you to, you will be just fine." Henry was convinced that asking the physician questions would be challenging physician authority, so he simply nodded in agreement. Henry was to take the medication to control his hypertension. However, he couldn't seem to remember to take the pills. This may have been due to the fact that he didn't feel sick (hypertension is often referred to as "the silent killer"), or because he had never been told exactly what the medication would do.

In the **mutual-participation model**, the patient has more responsibility than in the other models. In this model, the physician and patient make joint decisions about every aspect of care, from deciding what diagnostic tests the patient should undergo to the choice and implementation of treatment. Input and responsibility are shared equally by physician and patient. The two work together in a partnership. Here's an example:

> *Patient*: I don't know how I'll be able to eliminate caffeine from my diet. That will be quite a challenge, especially if there needs to be an immediate reduction in my caffeine consumption.
>
> *Physician*: What do you think you'll be able to manage? Can you try to reduce your caffeine intake a little bit every day?
>
> *Patient*: I can try but it won't be easy. And you don't just mean reducing coffee drinking, do you? You also mean reducing the amount of chocolate I consume. I think I'm going to be pretty grumpy over the next while, perhaps you should warn my partner.
>
> *Physician*: Is there anything you can think of that I might be able to do to help you?
>
> *Patient*: Tell me again exactly why this is necessary. Also, is there anything else I should be doing to help my medical condition?

Do you think this scenario characterizes a typical interaction between a physician and patient? Or does the patient in this scenario seem unusually assertive? According to some researchers, assertiveness and active involvement on the part of the patient are the precursors of an effective partnership with the physician. The mutual-participation model is seen as the ideal relationship between physician and patient. However, the typical physician–patient relationship is one in which the physician possesses a greater degree of power than the patient.

Power is an issue that we will return to later in the chapter. For now, let's continue with our discussion of physician–patient relationship models. Szasz and Hollender (1956) were the first to provide a theoretical model of the physician–patient relationship, but they were not the last. Other models have been put forth over the years (e.g., Emanuel & Emanuel, 1992), but until recently none had used empirical techniques to determine whether patterns of interaction style in the physician–patient relationship corresponded to the theoretical approaches found in the literature.

Roter and colleagues (Roter, 2000; Roter et al., 1997) used audiotape analysis to describe communication patterns in 537 patients seen at 11 outpatient, private, and group primary care settings in the United States and Canada. Their analysis revealed five distinct communication patterns.

The first, **narrowly biomedical** communication patterns, were characterized mainly by biomedical talk (e.g., "The medication may make you sleepy"), closed-ended medical questions (e.g., "Are you in pain when you walk?"), and very little discussion of psychosocial topics (such as problems of daily living, emotions, and issues regarding social relations). The narrowly biomedical pattern occurred in 32 percent of the visits.

The second pattern was described as **expanded biomedical**. This pattern also included numerous closed-ended medical questions but had more moderate levels of biomedical

mutual-participation model: health care model in which the physician and patient make joint decisions about every aspect of care.

narrowly biomedical communication pattern: characterized mainly by biomedical talk, closed-ended medical questions, and very little discussion of psychosocial issues.

expanded biomedical communication pattern: includes numerous closed-ended medical questions and moderate levels of biomedical and psychosocial exchange between the physician and patient.

biopsychosocial communication pattern: suggests that biological, psychological, and social factors are all involved in any given state of health or illness.

psychosocial communication pattern: includes a substantial amount of psychosocial exchange between the physician and patient.

consumerist communication pattern: the use of the physician as a consultant who answers questions rather than asking them.

and psychosocial exchange for both physicians and patients. This pattern was common to 33 percent of the visits. The third pattern, **biopsychosocial**, reflected a balance of psychosocial and biomedical communication. The biopsychosocial pattern occurred in 20 percent of visits.

The **psychosocial** pattern was the fourth pattern identified by Roter and her colleagues. This pattern included substantially more psychosocial exchanges than the previous patterns. An example of such an exchange is the following: "It is important to get out and do something on a regular basis. The recreation centre is a great place to find the company of other seniors." Eight percent of visits are considered psychosocial. The final pattern was designated **consumerist**. This pattern of communication also represented 8 percent of visits. The consumerist pattern suggests the use of the physician as a consultant who answers questions rather than as one who asks them.

It is somewhat difficult to compare the model proposed by Roter and colleagues (1997; 2000) with that proposed by Szasz and Hollender (1956) because of the different terminology used in describing the models. However, it is clear that both models place the interactions on a continuum, where at one end the patient has little involvement in the decision-making process or in contributions to the interaction and at the other end is at least on par with the physician in guiding the interaction. Szasz and Hollender stated that the mutual-participation model was "essentially foreign to medicine." Now, more than 50 years have elapsed and this statement no longer seems to be true. Roter's (e.g., Bensing, Roter, & Hulsman, 2003; Roter et al., 2000) program of research suggests that while collaborative models do not predominate in North America, they are certainly evident in primary care practice. In Europe, where similar studies have been conducted, far fewer physician–patient interactions are active-passive or biomedically intensive (Bensing et al., 2003; Deveugele, Derese, De Bacquer et al., 2004).

Is the collaborative model the preferred model of physician–patient interaction? According to patients (Fraley & Altmaier, 2002; Roter et al., 1997), the collaborative model—or, in Roter's terminology, the psychosocial pattern—is preferred. Somewhat surprisingly, physicians were especially satisfied with the consumerist pattern, reporting that these visits made good use of their time. Patients were moderately pleased with these interactions, although they didn't receive the highest patient satisfaction ratings. Inasmuch as the patients who engaged in this pattern of communication were younger than others, there may be a cohort effect, suggesting that younger generations of patients will be consumerist in their relationships with physicians. In Roter and colleagues' study, the consumerist pattern occurred in only a small proportion of visits. We might speculate that this pattern will increase as younger cohorts get older and develop more chronic conditions and therefore become more frequent users of health services. The patterns least preferred by both patients and physicians were the biomedical patterns. Biomedical patterns of communication were used most often by younger, male physicians and by those physicians interacting with patients who were more sick, were older, and had a lower income.

In a national U.S. study (Graham Center, 2004), researchers investigated "what people want from their family physician." The people surveyed for this study mirrored the general population of the United States with regard to race, ethnicity, gender, age, and location. People deemed the 10 attributes identified in Figure 5-2 as those that most contributed to their satisfaction with their physician.

1. Always honest and direct
2. Listens to me
3. Encourages me to lead healthier lifestyle
4. Does not judge; understands, supports
5. Someone I can stay with as I grow older
6. Tries to get to know me
7. Acts as partner in maintaining health
8. Treats both serious and non-serious conditions
9. Attends to emotional and physical health
10. Can help with any problem

Figure 5-2 The Top 10 Physician Attributes Contributing to Patient Satisfaction in Rank Order

Source: Adapted from Graham Center One-Pager #26. Stock Keister, M.C., Green, L.A., Kahn, N.B., Phillips, R.L., McCann, J., & Fryer, G.D. (2004). What people want from their family physician. *American Family Physician, 69*(10), 2310. Copyright (2004) American Academy of Family Physicians. All rights reserved. This article was reprinted from the original article published in *American Family Physician*, a publication of the American Academy of Family Physician.

Focus on Canadian Research 5-1

Patient-Centred Care

Researchers at the University of Western Ontario (McWilliam et al., 2000; Stewart et al., 1995; Stewart, et al., 2000) have refined and tested a patient-centred model of physician–patient interaction that was first proposed by Levenstein (1984). This model highlights the need to integrate the conventional understanding of disease with each patient's unique experience of illness. The model is viewed as a total-person approach to patient problems. Six interconnected components are included in the model (Weston & Brown, 1995).

1. *Exploring both the disease and the illness experience.* Identification of disease, or problems in terms of abnormalities of structure and/or function of body organs and systems, takes place just as it would if a physician subscribed to the biomedical model. However, the patient-centred model focuses on four key dimensions of patients' illness experience: (i) what the patients believe is wrong with them; (ii) their feelings (e.g., fears) about being ill; (iii) the impact of the illness on their daily functioning, and (iv) how they believe the physician should proceed.
2. *Understanding the whole person.* The physician should come to understand both the patient's disease and the experience of illness in the context of the patient's life (e.g., the patient's cultural beliefs, stage of life, family situation, etc.).
3. *Finding common ground.* Physicians and patients must reach agreement in three principal areas if they hope to develop an effective management plan: (i) the specific problems and priorities; (ii) the goals of treatment; and (iii) the role of both the physician and the patient.
4. *Incorporating prevention and health promotion.* The physician and patient must work together to enable the patient to take the steps required to control and improve his or her own health.
5. *Enhancing the patient–physician relationship.* Every patient–physician interaction provides the opportunity to build rapport. The establishment of an effective relationship will aid the physician in recognizing the specific approach that should be taken with the patient in order to meet the patient's needs (e.g., recognizing vulnerability and offering support).
6. *Being realistic.* Physicians must recognize their own limits. They must manage their time and emotional energy in a way that provides the most benefit to their patients.

Physician–Patient Communication

Information-Giving   The collaborative model of physician–patient communication preferred by most patients requires their involvement in making decisions about their treatment. But in order to participate in these decisions, patients need information. Physicians provide information to their patients about a number of things, including the patient's diagnosis, possible causes of the problem, and methods of treatment. Information-giving is a very important element of the physician–patient interview, and yet researchers have found that "patients tend to be more dissatisfied about the information they receive from their physicians than about any other aspect of medical care" (Waitzkin, 1985, p. 83). For their part, when questioned about the amount of time they believed they spent giving information to their patients, physicians drastically overestimated the amount of time they were engaged in this task. Specifically, in an average 20-minute interview physicians estimated that they spent approximately nine minutes giving information to their patients. In reality, the physicians spent an average of one minute giving information to their patients.

Research consistently demonstrates that physicians underestimate patients' desire for information (Say, Murtagh, & Thomson, 2006). A number of studies have demonstrated that physicians sometimes choose to withhold information from their patients in an attempt to protect their patients from worry and because they find providing such information difficult (Rogg et al., 2009). Perhaps this is why patients who are elderly, have less education, or a poor prognosis receive less information from physicians (Ong, Visser, Lammes, & de Haes, 2000).

In one example, family doctors who had made a diagnosis of Parkinson's disease, a degenerative nerve disorder, were very concerned about protecting their patients (Pinder, 1990). Specifically, the physicians had difficulty deciding how, when, and whom to tell, and difficulty in deciding just how much information to share about the patient's diagnosis and prognosis. The physicians tended to be positive and overly optimistic. For instance, they avoided details about medications, were low-key about side effects, and did not explore the problems of long-term medication use.

Most patients, on the other hand, wanted to be given as much information as possible, including information about their medication and its side effects. Providing such information to patients results in lowered blood pressure and less psychological distress as well as improvement of symptoms when the information presented is coupled with emotional support (Roter, 2000).

Participation   Although the vast majority of patients would like to be informed about what their illnesses are and how to treat them, some want more details and involvement in decisions and some prefer less. Generally, healthier, younger, and better-educated patients prefer greater involvement in health-related decisions (Hall & Roter, 2007; Perneger, Charvet-Bérard, Perrier, 2008; Say et al., 2006). People in lower social classes tend to prefer a more passive role. Studies in the United States conducted along ethnic lines found that, compared to white patients, Hispanics and Asians are less satisfied with the involvement allowed them by their physicians (Bigby & Perez-Stable, 2004; Johnson, Saha, Arbelaez, Beach, & Cooper, 2004). African-American patients also experience less patient-centred care than do their white counterparts (Johnson, Roter, Powe, & Lisa, 2004).

Knowing patient preferences is invaluable. Research shows that providing the amount and type of participation that patients want in their health care enhances patients' adjustment to and satisfaction with medical treatment (Bennenbroek et al., 2002). Moreover, patients who report a preference for an active role in their treatment tend to recover faster than those who prefer an inactive role.

Just as patients differ in the amount of participation they want in managing their health, health professionals differ in the amount of involvement they are likely to encourage. As we might predict, some physicians are more inclined than others to share their authority and decision making (McKinstry, 2000; Say et al., 2006). A mismatch between the patient's and the physician's desire for participation can be detrimental to their relationship. Further, as we will discuss in more detail in the next chapter, mismatches of this type will frequently result in an increase in the stress experienced by patients during medical procedures. When determining how much information and involvement to provide each patient, health professionals clearly need to consider the needs of the patient.

General Patient Satisfaction   Considering the needs of the patient is certainly an important component of a physician's role. Most people can recall both positive and negative experiences they have had with physicians. When people talk about their negative experiences, they often mention the physician's hurried manner, insensitivity, lack of responsiveness, apparently faulty diagnoses, or useless treatment. However, most people can also provide details of an interaction with a physician that was exemplary. Patients praise physicians who don't rush and answer all their questions. Many of the positive attributes patients recount include personal factors about the physician. Patients show a strong preference for practitioners who have a warm and expressive emotional style as opposed to those who are emotionally neutral (e.g., Clowers, 2002; Coulter, 2002; Zachariae et al., 2003).

Patient satisfaction with medical care is primarily influenced by the quality of the physician–patient relationship. Nonverbal behaviours are more closely related to patient satisfaction than is verbal communication. A particularly important consequence of this is that patients often judge the competence of a physician by their emotional satisfaction with care. Physicians who appear more emotionally expressive in their facial expressions, eye contact, body posture, and tone of voice typically are viewed more favourably by their patients (Roter, Frankel, Hall, & Sluyter, 2006). The important implication of this finding is that patients who are satisfied with the emotional aspects of their care are more likely to want to return to that physician and are more likely to keep future appointments (Roter et al., 2006). The effect of nonverbal behaviour is so strong, in fact, that some researchers have found a relationship between tone of voice and medical malpractice suits (Ambady et al., 2002).

Patient Satisfaction, Communication, and Malpractice Claims   In Canada, most complaints by the public about physicians deal not with clinical competency but with communication (Richards, 1990; Simpson et al., 1991). Some estimate that 70 to 80 percent of medical litigation involves relationship or communication problems (Lussier & Richard, 2006). We should point out that the number of malpractice lawsuits is decreasing in Canada (CHSRF, 2006). In 1996, 1415 lawsuits were filed, the highest in Canadian history; however, the numbers have been declining ever since. By 2004, this number had declined by 23 percent to 1083. Lawsuits that go to trial increasingly favour the physician—84 percent of trials in 2004. Lawsuit rates have also been declining in the United States, but in both countries when a payment is made the sums are large. In 2004,

When physicians interact with patients in a warm, friendly, confident manner, they are viewed as both competent and nice.

payouts averaged $300 000 per case in Canada, which is an increase of 66 percent in 10 years (CHSRF, 2006).

As we have already mentioned, patients have preferences and expectations about their interactions with physicians. The physician's awareness of the patient's expectations during a visit is critical in achieving effective communication. And only with effective communication are patients likely to be satisfied with their medical care (Stewart et al., 2000). According to Lussier and Richard (2005), sources of patient dissatisfaction arising from poor physician–patient relations and inadequate communication include physicians' failing to prepare for meetings with patients, appearing to rush through the physician–patient interview, underestimating the seriousness of the symptoms patients report, and devaluing patient and family views. The combination of patient dissatisfaction and a bad outcome is said to be "a recipe for litigation." When patients and their families feel the physician is caring and compassionate, however, malpractice suits happen less frequently (Levinson, 1994).

Levinson and colleagues (1997) were the first to identify specific communication behaviours associated with malpractice claims based on direct observation of physicians' behaviour. Physicians and surgeons were randomly selected from the databases of companies providing malpractice insurance in Oregon and Colorado. Ten routine office visits were audiotaped for each of the 124 participants. Analysis of the conversations revealed significant differences in communication behaviours between physicians who had been subjected to malpractice claims and those who had not. Roughly half of the physicians were primary care physicians and the other half surgeons. "No-claims" primary care physicians gave more orienting statements about the flow of a visit (e.g., "First, I will examine you, and then we will talk about your condition"), laughed and used more humour, facilitated communication (e.g., asked patients for their opinions and checked that patients understood), encouraged their patients to talk, and spent more time with their patients

(18.3 vs. 15 minutes). Levinson and his colleagues found no behaviours that distinguished between claims and no-claims surgeons.

Undoubtedly, there is a link between communication, patient satisfaction, and malpractice claims. Although researchers have documented a number of components of poor communication possibly responsible for this link, further research is required to explain some of the anomalies (e.g., between physicians and surgeons). While studies investigating the link between communication problems and malpractice claims began relatively recently, research exploring more general communication problems during the physician–patient consultation began decades ago.

Physician Behaviours Contributing to Faulty Communication   Having exchanged introductions and established initial rapport, the next step for a physician is to determine what issues the patient wishes to discuss. What is his or her agenda for the consultation? Why has the patient come today? These are questions that cannot be addressed unless the practitioner listens to the patient. In a landmark study (Beckman & Frankel, 1984), physicians were found to interrupt their patients after only 18 seconds! In a span of 15 years, this behaviour improved only slightly; now patients are given 23 seconds to speak before they are interrupted (Marvel, Epstein, Flowers, & Beckman, 1999).

Research (Marvel et al., 1999; McDonald & Fedo, 2009) clearly demonstrates that even minimal interruptions to patients' initial statements can prevent other concerns from being mentioned at all or can make important complaints arise late in the consultation. By asking patients to provide further comment on any one problem, patients' options are restricted and they are prevented from expanding on other information. For example, a patient may have mentioned headaches but is interrupted before he or she can mention having experienced recent palpitations and marital problems. "Tell me more about your headaches" or, worse, "Where do you get the pain?" restricts the discussion to the headaches and limits both the patient's options and the effectiveness of the interview as a whole. Allowing patients to complete their opening statement without interruption should not be a difficult task for practitioners, as patients usually take less than 60 seconds to do this. In Beckman and Frankel's (1984) research, not a single patient took longer than 150 seconds to complete an opening statement, even when encouraged to continue. Yet in only 28 percent of the cases were patients given the opportunity to finish their explanations of concerns (Marvel, Epstein, Flowers, & Beckman, 1999). When patients are interrupted, they are given the opportunity to return to and complete their opening statement only two percent of the time (Frankel & Beckman, 1989).

Physicians seem to assume that the first complaint the patient mentions is the only one the patient has. However, patients come to an office visit with an average of three concerns they wish to express (Kaplan et al., 1995; Stewart et al., 1986). Further, the order in which patients present their problems is not related to their clinical importance; the first concern presented is no more likely than the second or third to be the most important, as judged by either the patient or the physician (Beckman & Frankel, 1984).

To make matters worse, patients and physicians do not always agree on the nature of the patient's chief complaint (Burack & Carpenter, 1983; Starfield et al., 1981). Recall Lynn from the beginning of this chapter. Her major complaint was not addressed by her physician. Lynn's primary reason for visiting her physician was to determine what was causing her stomach problems. However, this was not the first symptom Lynn described to her physician, because she also had some other concerns. Lynn left the physician's office still wondering what was responsible for her stomach ache. Stewart, McWhinney, and Buck (1979) discovered that 54 percent of patients' complaints were not elicited during the medical interview. These shocking findings have led researchers to devise interview methods, such as the Calgary-Cambridge method, that improve communication during the physician–patient interview (Kurtz, 2002; Kurtz, Silverman, Benson, & Draper, 2003; see Box 5-2 later in this chapter).

Medical Jargon Another factor that contributes to poor communication in the physician–patient interview is the physician's use of **medical jargon** and technical language. For example, the term *splenomegaly* conveys a considerable amount of information to health professionals, but very little to patients. Splenomegaly describes an enlargement of the spleen (a large glandlike organ situated in the upper left side of the abdomen that breaks down red corpuscles) often related to progressive anemia (reduction below normal in the hemoglobin, the volume of packed red blood cells) with no evidence of leukemia or disease of the lymph glands (DiMatteo, 1991). Even if the patient asks the physician for the meaning of *splenomegaly*, he or she is likely to need the physician to explain the explanation! Test *your* knowledge of common medical terms by attempting the quiz in Box 5-1.

There are a number of reasons physicians use medical jargon when talking to patients. One reason is because they tend to overestimate the amount their patients can understand (Guttman, 1993). A number of studies have tested patient knowledge of medical terminology (e.g., Castro et al., 2007). In a typical study, physicians and nurses make lists of medical words that they believe patients understand. When these same words are presented to patients, surprisingly few can define the terms accurately. For example, in the

medical jargon: technical language used by a physician that is sometimes unintelligible to the patient.

Box 5-1 Do You Know What These Medical Terms Mean?

The following 10 medical terms were used in Thompson and Pledger's (1993) study of patients' understanding of medical jargon. Match the terms with the definitions given below:

1. _____ malignant
2. _____ incubation
3. _____ acute
4. _____ abscess
5. _____ diuretic
6. _____ benign
7. _____ chronic
8. _____ cyst
9. _____ suture
10. _____ edema

A. A localized collection of pus in a cavity formed by the disintegration of tissue.
B. The accumulation of excess fluid in a fluid compartment.
C. Persisting for a long time.
D. The provision of proper conditions for growth and development.
E. Having severe symptoms and a short course.
F. Not recurrent: favourable for recovery with appropriate treatment.
G. An agent that promotes urine secretion.
H. A closed sac or capsule containing liquid or a semi-solid substance.
I. A joining together of separated tissue or bone, or material used to achieve this joining.
J. Any condition that, if uncorrected, tends to worsen so as to cause serious illness or death (e.g., cancer).

The answers are provided below. Did you obtain a perfect score? If you had been asked to define each of the terms rather than simply fill in the blanks with the provided answers, do you think you would have scored as well?

1–J, 2–D, 3–E, 4–A, 5–G, 6–F, 7–C, 8–H, 9–I, 10–B

---

study conducted by Thompson and Pledger (1993) less than half of the patients could adequately define the words *abscess, tumour, diuretic,* or *cyst.* Moreover, even simple everyday words can be ambiguous when used in a medical context (Hadlow & Pitts, 1991). For example, Mazzullo, Lasagna, and Griner (1974) showed that 52 percent of those interviewed thought that a medication prescribed "for fluid retention" would cause fluid retention. More recently (Castro et al., 2007), a sample of diabetic patients were asked about their comprehension of terminology (e.g., weight is stable) that was commonplace in audiotaped physician–patient interactions. The rates of comprehension never exceeded 38 percent.

Another reason practitioners use medical jargon when speaking to patients is because patients often believe that the sophisticated vocabulary of the physician represents intelligence. Perhaps they feel that they will be better taken care of by a physician who is obviously intelligent.

A more cynical view of the reason for using medical jargon was provided by the famous heart surgeon Dr. Michael DeBakey, who said, "Most doctors don't want their patients to understand them! They prefer to keep their work a mystery. If patients don't understand what a doctor is talking about, they won't ask him questions. Then the doctor won't have to be bothered answering them" (Robinson, 1973). Another famous physician, Howard Waitzkin (1985), explained jokingly that if you wanted to forestall any additional questions from the patient you could simply connect the term *itis* (meaning "inflammation of") to whatever organ was troubled (for example, *stomachitis*).

More commonly, however, health professionals may use medical jargon with their patients because they simply forget that their patients do not share the same medical vocabulary. Practitioners spent years in medical school learning this vocabulary, they use it when speaking with their colleagues, and they just naturally use the same vocabulary with their patients.

Unfortunately, when health care providers are aware that patients may not understand medical jargon, they sometimes go to the opposite extreme and engage in baby talk and simplistic explanations. One example comes from a surgeon who said to an elderly man, "We're just going to pop you into the operating theatre to have a little peek into your tummy." Toynbee noticed that the term *pop* was used quite frequently in the hospital by many of the hospital staff. Another physician said, "Nurse, would you just pop off her things for me? I want to examine her." Nurses also "popped" patients in and out of washrooms and wheelchairs, into and out of hospital gowns, beds, and bandages (Toynbee, 1977).

The ideal alternative to the use of medical jargon and baby talk is for practitioners to provide **non-discrepant responses** and **multilevel explanations** when speaking to their patients (Waitzkin, 1985). A non-discrepant response is one that uses the same level of vocabulary that the patient uses when asking the question. For example, if a patient asks about her "lump," the physician might reply by saying we have to remove part of the lump to determine if there is cancer in it. A multilevel explanation is one that initially uses medical jargon but then explains the jargon using everyday language. The use of multilevel explanations educates the patient in medical terminology, as seen in this example: "We'll have to conduct a biopsy to determine if the tumour is malignant. In other words, we'll have to remove the lump to determine if there is cancer in it." The use of medical jargon by health professionals is therefore appropriate if it is explained to the patient or if the patient is already familiar with the terminology (Thompson, 2000). Additional strategies such as asking patients to repeat information, drawing pictures,

non-discrepant responses: physician responds to the patient's questions using the same sophistication of vocabulary that the patient uses.

multilevel explanations: explanations that use medical jargon followed by further explanation using everyday language.

writing out instructions, or providing handouts are sometimes used by health care professionals to help with communication (Schwartzberg et al., 2007).

Time Factors   Another factor thought to limit a physician's ability to communicate effectively is the time available for the consultation. In our discussion of communication issues linked to malpractice claims, we mentioned that if patients felt rushed they were more likely to file a suit. Stewart and her colleagues (1999) reviewed the literature pertaining to communication and time, and maintained that "the literature is not clear on this subject perhaps because communication is defined and measured in many different ways" (p. 26).

A number of studies indicate that a long consultation is not required to communicate effectively with patients. Arborelius and Bremberg (1992) reported that positive consultations took less time than negative consultations. In this study, they defined a positive consultation as one where both physician and patient had a positive impression of the consultation; a negative consultation was one where both parties had a negative impression of the consultation. Further, during positive consultations, more time was devoted to patient ideas and concerns. Henbest and Fehrsen (1992) reported that consultations that were **patient-centred** did not take longer than those that were less patient-centred. Patient-centred approaches tend to include more open-ended questions by the physician, such as, "Can you describe when the pain is most severe?" compared to **doctor-centred** approaches in which physicians tend to ask questions that require only very brief answers. Referring back to Roter's (1997) classification of physician–patient relationships, we would say that patient-centred approaches most closely resemble psychosocial patterns of communication, whereas doctor-centred approaches are more similar to biomedical patterns. You may remember that patients tend to prefer the psychosocial pattern and that both patients and physicians like the biomedical pattern the least. Another study (Clark et al., 1998) found that physicians who were educated about communication issues were rated more favourably by their patients than physicians who did not take part in the education program. This occurred even though, on average, the physicians who had received communication training reported spending less time with the patients than the physicians who had not received such training. A trend toward lower patient satisfaction with longer visits has also been shown in other studies (e.g., Hornberger, Thorn, & MacCurdy, 1997).

In contrast, the results of some studies indicate that more thorough communication requires longer consultations. For example, studies by Hornberger et al. (1997) and Marvel (1993) concluded that there are tradeoffs among increasing the length of the consultation, the goals of the physician, the goals of the patient, and the many and varied issues that professional organizations counselling physicians deem as important. Howie, Porter, Heaney, and Hopton (1999) surveyed patients at the end of a consultation with their physicians and reported that patients were more satisfied on a number of dimensions after a long consultation than a short one.

Patient Behaviours Contributing to Faulty Communication   Both patient behaviours and physician behaviours contribute to faulty communication. In the next section, we discuss a number of patient behaviours that present challenges to efficient communication during physician–patient encounters.

patient-centred consultations: consultations in which physicians tend to ask open-ended questions that allow patients to elaborate.

doctor-centred consultations: consultations in which physicians tend to ask questions that require only very brief answers.

Patient Deception   Not surprisingly, patients also find some topics difficult to discuss with physicians. Both younger and older patients may experience difficulty and embarrassment discussing topics related to sexually transmitted diseases or sexual behaviours (Gott et al., 2003; Pitts, 2000). Patients may avoid the topic altogether, or if asked directly, they may give false information. Researchers at the University of Victoria (Lewis, Brimacombe, & Matheson, 2003) asked female patients attending a birth control clinic if they had falsified information during the preceding physician–patient consultation. Approximately one-half (46.4 percent) of female respondents admitted to withholding information or lying about their sexual histories to the physician during the consultation.

The list of topics that patients admit to lying about is long. Burgoon, Callister, and Hunsaker (1994) noted that 50 percent or more of the participants in their study admitted to lying "often" or "always" about adherence to medical regimens, exercise behaviours, the amount of stress they were under, and financial status. These participants lied about other topics with less frequency.

Lack of Information-Seeking Behaviours   Given that patients want information from their physicians, we would expect them to request additional information during the medical interview. Traditionally, however, patients do not engage in many information-seeking behaviours when communicating with their physicians (Beisecker & Beisecker, 1990). In a study conducted by Tuckett, Boulton, and Olson (1985, cited in Silverman, Kurtz, & Draper, 2005), 76 percent of patients said that they had specific doubts or questions during the interview that they did not mention to the physician. When asked why they did not ask the physician questions, patients gave the following reasons: (1) it was not up to them to ask questions, express doubts, or behave as if their view was important (36 percent); (2) they were afraid of being less well thought of by the doctor (22 percent); (3) they were frightened of a negative reaction from the doctor (14 percent); (4) they were too flustered or hurried to ask coherently (27 percent); (5) they doubted that the doctor could tell them any more at the moment (22 percent); (6) they forgot or were waiting until next time to ask, when they would be more certain of what they thought was reasonable to ask (36 percent); and (7) they feared the truth (9 percent). This behaviour, however, may be changing. Younger and better-educated patients tend to engage in more proactive behaviour, such as asking more questions and volunteering unsolicited information to the physician (Siminoff, Graham, & Gordon, 2006).

Trouble Remembering   Even if patients understand all the terminology the physician used, they may not remember everything that was said. In a review of the literature, Ley (1988) notes that, in the hospital setting, patients remember approximately 60 percent of the information a health care worker tells them. When Tucket and colleagues (1985) looked more closely at the information patients recalled, they found that only 10 percent of patients couldn't remember the key points they had been told. That is, most patients could remember the gist of what they heard even if they could not remember all the details.

Anxiety contributes to patients' inability to remember information from a medical interview. Specifically, when people are anxious (as they often are in medical situations) they find it difficult to concentrate and to process incoming information. Again, this is true even when patients understand the information they are being told. A physician describes her experience upon being told she had cancer in just these terms: She said that even though she knew exactly what her physician was telling her, as soon as she got the "news," she zoned out. She began thinking about what this would mean in terms of all the adjustments she would have to make in her life, whether she would survive, and so on, and in doing so she didn't hear another word her physician said to her.

Poor communication between physicians and patients is negatively correlated with patient adherence to treatment regimens. In the words of Moira Stewart and her colleagues at the University of Western Ontario, "Patient–doctor communication and patient adherence are inexorably linked because the interaction provides the context within which the recommendations to be complied with are delivered" (1999, p. 27). The next section of this chapter addresses the topic of adhering to medical advice.

ADHERING TO MEDICAL ADVICE

compliance or adherence: the degree to which patients carry out the behaviours and treatments that physicians and other health professionals recommend.

Traditionally, medical professionals have used the term **compliance** to mean the degree to which patients carry out the behaviours and treatments that physicians and other health professionals recommend. But because the term *compliance* can be interpreted as implying reluctant obedience, many health professionals prefer the term **adherence** (although some use the terms interchangeably). What does it mean to adhere to medical advice? Although we may immediately respond to this question by saying that being adherent means we take medication in the way a physician has prescribed, adherence is much more than that. Adhering to the advice of a health professional may mean maintaining healthy lifestyle practices, such as eating properly, avoiding stressful situations, getting enough sleep and exercise, abstaining from smoking, and limiting our intake of alcohol, as well as carrying out other behaviours that promote good health. Medical professionals use the term **non-adherence** to describe the practice of *not* following their advice.

non-adherence: failure to follow the advice of a health professional.

How prevalent is the problem of non-adherence? This question is actually more difficult to answer than one might first assume. Patients may fail to adhere to any of the different types of medical advice just outlined, and they can violate each of these types of advice in many different ways. Thus, failing to take one's medication as prescribed could mean taking medication in the wrong amount or at the wrong time, or discontinuing the medication before the prescribed time has elapsed.

creative non-adherence: a patient's intentional modifying or supplementing of a recommended treatment regimen.

Creative non-adherence is a particularly interesting form of non-adherence that is intentional and involves modifying or supplementing the recommended treatment regimen. These alterations are often based on private theories about a health problem and its treatment. For example, the patient may decide that particular symptoms meriting treatment were ignored by the health professional; he or she may then augment the treatment regimen, perhaps including over-the-counter medications or home remedies that interact with prescribed medication in unpredictable, even dangerous ways. Sometimes, however, these modifications are useful (Shine, 2002). For example, some patients are thought to have a better idea of how to control their blood glucose level than their health care provider does. Similarly, parents who adjust their child's asthma regimen can control asthma better than if they precisely follow a prescribed regimen. This is because there are often fluctuations in the severity of asthma (e.g., seasonal variability), and the parents can adjust the treatment in response to their child's needs at the time.

Assessing Adherence

To determine the prevalence of non-adherence, we must be able to assess the problem. There are at least seven methods researchers can use to measure patient adherence. They can (1) ask the health professional, (2) ask the patient, (3) ask other people, (4) watch for appointment non-attendance, (5) count pills, (6) watch for treatment non-response, and (7) examine biochemical evidence (Haynes, McDonald, & Garg, 2002; Turk & Meichenbaum, 1991).

One of the easiest ways to measure adherence is to ask the health professional who works with the patient to estimate it. Generally, though, health professionals' estimates of their patients' adherence are inaccurate, often only slightly better than chance (e.g., Gross et al., 2002; Miller et al., 2002). Typically, health professionals overestimate patient adherence. Another simple approach to measuring adherence is to ask the patient. However, patients also tend to overestimate their adherence, perhaps because they know they should follow "doctor's orders." Health professionals' and patients' reports of adherence are subjective and may be biased by lying and wishful thinking. The same bias may result when family members are asked to assess the patient's adherence.

More objective measures of patient adherence include pill counting and biochemical tests. In pill counting, the medication remaining in the dispenser is compared to the amount that should remain at this point in the treatment regimen to determine if patients have been following directions. However, even if the right quantity of medication is found, patients may not have been compliant. We would not know if the patients took the medication at the right times, in the correct amount, or if, wanting to please the health professional, they simply discarded some of the medication.

Some researchers (e.g., Kehr, 2004) have installed microprocessors in the lids of pill containers to record when the pill bottle is opened. Perhaps not surprisingly, data gathered from this device do not show high consistency with self-report (Garber, 2004). Biochemical tests can be conducted (on patients' blood or urine, for example) to determine if the patients have ingested a medication recently. This method of assessment is both time-consuming and expensive. In addition, there are problems with this technique, resulting from individual differences in absorption and metabolism of drugs (Liu et al., 2001). We should also point out that biochemical tests do not measure the degree of adherence; the presence of a drug simply identifies that the patients ingested some amount of the drug at some time. Such tests do not indicate that the patients took the proper amount at the proper time.

Frequency and Cost of Non-Adherence

Despite the difficulties in assessing adherence, researchers have been able to estimate the prevalence of non-adherence. A meta-analysis of more than 500 studies conducted over 50 years led Robin DiMatteo (2004b) to report that adherence ranges from 25 to 50 percent. However, the actual range of adherence to prescribed medications varies from zero to 100 percent (e.g., Haynes, McKibbon, & Kanani, 1996; McDonald, Garg, & Haynes, 2002). It is reported that at least 38 percent of patients do not follow short-term treatment plans (e.g., completing a prescription for medication; DiMatteo, 1994), and as many as 50 percent do not adhere to recommendations for long-term treatment (e.g., taking hypertensive medication; Wahl et al., 2005). Moreover, more than 75 percent of patients are unwilling or unable to follow suggested lifestyle changes, such as exercising regularly or eating a low-fat diet.

The cost of non-adherence is considerable. It is estimated that non-adherence costs Canadians several billion dollars annually (Coambs et al., 1995; MacLeod, 2002). Both direct and indirect costs are incurred when patients fail to adhere. Direct costs result from excessive hospital expenditures (e.g., for people admitted to hospital due to non-adherence regarding prescription medications); excessive nursing home expenditures (medication non-adherence is the primary reason that elderly patients must reside in nursing homes); and excessive treatment costs of ambulatory care (e.g., additional visits to a physician). Indirect costs result from reductions in worker productivity due to sick days taken, less efficient work due to illness, and costs associated with premature death.

As you can see, the monetary costs of non-adherence are enormous. But more importantly, the personal costs of non-adherence are also immense.

What Factors Predict Adherence?

Non-adherence often results in people becoming sicker or dying. Why, then, do people fail to adhere to medical recommendations? Although researchers are not completely sure how to answer this question, they have discovered a number of factors that are linked to non-adherence.

Illness and Characteristics of the Treatment Regimen Some medical recommendations require patients to change *longstanding habits*. For example, a physician may suggest that a patient go on a restricted diet, stop smoking cigarettes, begin a program of regular exercise, or avoid stressful situations. These changes can be thought of as lifestyle changes. Although some patients will adhere to these recommendations, particularly if they are at a high risk for serious illness (DiMatteo, 2004b), it is more likely that people will not make these lifestyle changes (e.g., Turk & Meichenbaum, 1991). Patients presumably do not make these changes because the effort involved seems greater than the health risks of not making such changes.

Both *complexity* and *duration* of the regimen prescribed also play a role in non-adherence. If you are told to "take one of these pills after meals, one of these other pills every eight hours, two of these pills at bedtime, and these pills as needed" you will likely have some difficulty following the "doctor's orders." As you might predict, the greater the variety of medications one must take and the more complex the schedule, the more likely people are to make an error, thereby failing to adhere to the medical regimen (Haynes et al., 2008).

Research exploring the impact of side effects on treatment is mixed. Not surprisingly, unpleasant *side effects* can lead to non-adherence. Research conducted with HIV-positive patients, for example, indicates that the more severe the side effects, the less likely the patient is to take the prescribed medication (Catz et al., 2000; Gellaitry et al., 2005). However, other research indicates that most people who engage in non-adherence do not consider side effects to be a very important factor.

As mentioned before, the longer the *duration* of the treatment the less likely people are to adhere to it. Researchers at McMaster University (Haynes et al., 2008) reviewed numerous studies comparing adherence rates to the length of treatment and concluded that, in most cases, non-adherence increases as duration of therapy increases. Often, long-term treatment programs are for illnesses that have no visible symptoms, such as hypertension. Understandably, people are less motivated to adhere to a treatment if there are no apparent symptoms indicating that they are unwell.

Because people are less likely to adhere to medical recommendations if they do not perceive symptoms of illness, it follows that *severity of an illness* will not lead to adherence unless symptoms are perceived by the patient. The more obvious a symptom is, the more likely people are to adhere to treatment.

The Patient's Personal Characteristics   Adherence is also linked to personal attributes of patients, such as their age, gender, and cultural background. The association between adherence and age is very complex. Adherence can either increase or decrease with age, depending on the specific illness, the timeframe, and the treatment regimen prescribed. Some research has revealed a curvilinear relationship between age and adherence. In a large-scale longitudinal study (Thomas et al., 1995) investigating colorectal cancer screening, those who adhered best were approximately 70 years old; the worst adherers were younger than 50 years of age or older than 80. Another study (Park et al., 1999) revealed a surprising pattern of medication adherence in arthritis patients. This study found an age-related cognitive decline among participants. Yet, the older participants actually adhered to their treatment regimen better than middle-aged patients. A busy lifestyle associated with middle age was found to be more of a determinant of non-adherence than was cognitive functioning.

Adherence rates are also related to age in children. Both cancer patients and diabetic children are more likely to adhere to treatment regimens at younger ages (e.g., until about nine years of age) (Jonasson et al., 1999; Manne et al., 1993; Miller & Drotar, 2003). These results may be explained by the decreasing responsibility parents have for their children's treatment as they get older.

Researchers have found very few gender differences in overall adherence rates (DiMatteo, 2004b). Some differences do emerge, however, when we look at adherence to specific medical recommendations. For instance, women seem to be better than men at adhering to dietary restrictions (Laforge, Greene, & Prochaska, 1994) and at taking medication for mental disorders (Sellwood & Tarrier, 1994). As well, young female pediatric patients are more adherent than males (DiMatteo, 2004b).

Cultural differences in adherence rates are rare but have also been noted (McDonald et al., 2002). Such cultural differences appear most often in patients who are from a culture that does not believe in modern medical recommendations and who prefer their own traditional healers (e.g., Novins, Beals, Moore, Spicer, & Manson, 2004). Ka'opua and Mueller (2004) note that native Hawaiians prefer holistic healing approaches that emphasize inclusion of the family. Native Hawaiians are also less likely to adhere to medical regimens prescribed to control diabetes and heart disease risk than other groups. But there are no notable differences in adherence rates by native Hawaiians in the complex pharmaceutical treatment of highly active antiretroviral therapy regimens (HAART) required to control HIV infection. Oggins (2003) provides narratives from minority group members that depict common misconceptions, often culturally based, that lead to non-adherence for other illnesses. Antshel (2002), and Hamill and Dickey (2005) outline how consideration of common elements in the minority member's culture improves treatment adherence.

Socioeconomic Factors   When considering the expense of medications, we see that seniors (4.6 percent) are less likely to report cost-related non-adherence than are young adults (8.7 percent) in Canada (Kennedy & Morgan, 2009). In the United States, studies report non-adherence due to cost to be at least three times higher than it is in Canada (Kennedy & Morgan, 2009).

Physician Characteristics   As we might predict, patients' adherence improves as confidence in their physician's competence increases (Gilbar, 1989; Wrath & Pathman, 2006). When patients lack confidence in their physicians, or are unsatisfied with the concern demonstrated by their physicians and even the friendliness of office staff, they are less likely to adhere to prescribed medical regimens (Wrath & Pathman, 2006). However, you may remember that the physician who is perceived as having positive attributes, such as kindness, is more likely to be perceived as competent than is one who is seen as unfriendly. It follows that people are more likely to adhere to medical recommendations if their physician is viewed as warm, caring, friendly, and interested in the welfare of patients (DiNicola & DiMatteo, 1984). When physicians exhibit a good bedside manner by providing encouragement, making eye contact, smiling, and even joking and laughing, patient adherence improves (Haskard Zolnierek & DiMatteo, 2009; Haskard, Zolnierek, DiMatteo et al., 2009). In contrast, when physicians are disrespectful to their patients the patients are less likely to adhere (Blanchard & Lurie, 2004).

Physician–Patient Interaction   Earlier in the chapter, we outlined a number of elements inherent in physician–patient communication and physician–patient relationships that can also influence patient adherence. For instance, if the patient does not understand instructions (e.g., due to the use of medical jargon), does not ask questions to clarify the instructions the physician provides, or does not remember those instructions, adherence is not possible. Indeed, there is a 19 percent higher risk of non-adherence among patients whose physicians communicate poorly compared to those whose physicians communicate well (Haskard Zolnierek & DiMatteo, 2009). When the interaction between physician and patient includes the discussion of benefits, risks, and barriers to adherence and allows patient involvement in decision making, then you have set the stage for maximum patient adherence (Haskard Zolnierek & DiMatteo, 2009). If a physician's expectations and a patient's expectations about what role each party should play in the interaction differ, patients are less likely to follow the physician's medical recommendations.

Improving Patient Adherence

In this next section, we will see a number of different approaches that can be used to increase a patient's medical adherence.

In their meta-analysis of published studies between 1949 and 2008 linking patient treatment adherence to physician–patient communication, Haskard, Zolnierek and DiMatteo (2009) state that providing physicians with communication skills training increases patient adherence by 12 percent. This effect is even greater when analyzing only studies that include pediatricians. However, there is less of an effect when a patient has a

Box 5-2 The Calgary-Cambridge Observation Guide

1. Initiating the session
   a. establishing rapport
   b. identifying reasons for the consultation
2. Gathering information
   a. exploration of problems
   b. understanding the patient's perspective
   c. providing structure, e.g., sequencing, summarizing
3. Building the relationship
   a. developing rapport
   b. involving the patient
4. Providing structure
   a. Summarizing what has been said
5. Explanation and planning
   a. providing the correct amount and type of information
   b. aiding accurate recall and understanding
   c. achieving a shared understanding, i.e., incorporating the patient's perspective
6. Closing the session

Source: Based on Silverman, Kurtz & Draper, 2005

more severe illness. As previously mentioned, when a patient has a serious illness, adherence is greater. Thus, one would assume that there would be less room for improvement. Interestingly, providing communication training that focuses specifically on achieving adherence does not seem to provide an additional increase in adherence rates. For an example of one framework for increasing communication skills see Box 5-2.

In addition to physicians becoming more skilled in communicating with their patients over the last several decades, patients have also begun to assert more power in the physician–patient relationship. One reason for this may be the increased level of education attained by people in Western society. The average person is better informed now than ever before about health. It is interesting to note that models of physician–patient relationships did not include a profile wherein the patient dominates until relatively recently. Roter and colleagues (1997) note that young patients often choose to interact with their physicians by controlling the consultation (e.g., asking the majority of questions). Whatever the cause of this change, it may necessitate health professionals to alter their style of social influence to maintain patient adherence. Moreover, there are additional strategies available to improve patient adherence.

Educational Strategies   Educational strategies to improve adherence are abundant. Health education is aimed at filling in the gaps in patient understanding about the need to follow medical recommendations (Ockene, 2001). Types of patient education vary considerably and include package inserts, written information sheets to reinforce verbal instructions, one-on-one counselling, small group sessions, lectures, demonstrations, and mailed information. In Canada, health education is provided by hospital, clinic, community, worksite, and private programs. As well, pamphlets and brochures are readily available to supplement and reinforce verbal instructions (Coambs et al., 1995).

Behavioural Strategies   Behavioural strategies can also be effective in increasing patients' motivation to adhere to their treatment regimens (Brondolo & Mas, 2001; DiMatteo & DiNicola, 1982; Ockene, 2001). Providing *prompts* and *reminders* as cues may encourage patients to perform recommended activities. These cues may include notes posted at home, reminder phone calls from a clinic, or even certain forms of drug packaging (e.g., dispensers with dated compartments or other built-in reminders).

Tailoring the regimen so that activities in the treatment are fitted to habits and routines in the patient's daily life may also help. For example, taking medication is easiest to do if it is tied in with another activity, such as brushing one's teeth in the morning. *Self-monitoring* is another way to encourage patient adherence; the patient keeps a written record of regimen activities, such as monitoring his or her resting heart rate or documenting foods eaten during the day.

Contingency contracting, wherein the patient and health professional (or parent, if the patient is a child) negotiate a series of treatment activities and goals as well as rewards based on the patient's fulfillment of these activities, can also help. For example, "a diabetic child and his or her parents may enact a contract that specifies a particular reward for each day the child does his or her insulin injection without argument" (Miller & Stark, 1994, p. 81). These techniques have a clear advantage in that the patient must actively participate in their design and execution. Further, the patient can usually carry out these strategies without assistance.

Social Support   Social and emotional support can provide much-needed motivation for patient adherence, particularly when the regimen is long-term or requires lifestyle changes. Family and friends can provide positive encouragement about the treatment activities and help to ensure they occur. Marital status, marital status of parents for children, and having a roommate increase adherence to medical regimens (DiMatteo, 2004a). Social support can also be provided by self-help groups, patient groups, and organizations established to help with specific health conditions. Patients who receive encouragement, inspiration, reminders, and aid in carrying out the regimen are believed to be more likely to comply than those who do not.

Research evaluating these strategies suggests that the more comprehensive the program of intervention, the more effective the outcome. Roter and colleagues (1998) contend that the most powerful interventions include combinations of all three strategies—educational, behavioural, and social or affective. Haynes and his colleagues have outlined which of these strategies is most effective for short-term (less than two weeks) and long-term treatment regimens (see Box 5-3).

A pill organizer such as this one can help ensure patient adherence.

Box 5-3 Methods of Increasing Adherence

Short-term treatments
Counselling about the importance of adherence
Written instructions about taking medicines
Reminder packaging (e.g., calendar packs, dosettes)
Reminders using personal phone calls or text messaging

Long-term treatments require combinations of the following for effective health outcomes:
Instruction and instructional materials
Simplifying the regimen (e.g., less frequent dosing, controlled release dosage forms)
Counselling about the regimen
Support group sessions

Reminders for medications and appointments
Manual telephone follow-up
Cuing medications to daily events
Reinforcement and rewards (e.g., explicitly acknowledging the patient's efforts to adhere)
Self-monitoring with regular physician review and reinforcement
Involving family members and significant others

Source: Based on Haynes, R. B., McDonald, H. P., & Garg, A. X. (2002). Helping patients follow prescribed treatment. *Journal of the American Medical Association, 288*, 2880–2883.

Health Outcomes

How important is it to adhere to medical recommendations provided by health care professionals? This is another question that is not easy to answer. By not adhering to treatment regimens, people increase their risk of developing health problems or of prolonging or worsening their current illnesses. Approximately 20 percent of hospital admissions are thought to result from patient non-adherence to medical recommendations (Ley, 1982). In general, studies show a strong relationship between loyal adherence and improved health. DiMatteo and colleagues (2002) reviewed studies of adherence involving more than 19 000 patients and concluded that 26 percent more patients experienced a good outcome by adhering than by not adhering to their treatment. This means the adherent patient's odds of having a good health outcome are three times higher than the odds for nonadherers.

This increase in health is essentially as effective as many well established medical interventions. Health outcomes were highest in studies of chronic conditions and of pediatric patient populations. Interestingly, a meta-analysis conducted by researchers (Simpson et al., 2006) at the University of Alberta noted that adherence to placebo treatment also led to lower mortality. There may be a **"healthy adherer" effect**, whereby adherence to drug therapy is indicative of overall healthy behaviour.

Another possibility to be explored in determining the importance of adherence is that complete adherence may not be necessary. Perhaps there are only certain levels of adherence that are required to obtain health benefits. If this is the case, it may explain why there are few differences between those who adhere completely and those who do not adhere. For example, consuming 80 percent of the medication prescribed has been described as the minimum rate of adherence necessary to treat hypertension effectively (Epstein & Cluss, 1982). Unhealthful non-adherence might then be defined as "the point below which the desired preventive or therapeutic result is unlikely to be achieved with the medication prescribed" (Parrish, 1986, p. 456).

In summary, non-adherence appears to be a fairly common phenomenon. There are a number of factors associated with non-adherence, including poor physician–patient communication; complexity and duration of the regimen; age, gender, and cultural

"healthy adherer" effect: greater adherence to health-promoting behaviours such as medication adherence is indicative of overall healthy behaviour.

background of the patient; and affective characteristics of the physician. Several strategies have been devised to increase adherence to medical regimens (e.g., educational and behavioural strategies), but researchers question their effectiveness. Furthermore, researchers have been unable to find a significant benefit to high levels of adherence. However, it may be that more moderate levels of adherence contribute to health benefits, thereby explaining the lack of differences between high- and low-level adherers.

CHAPTER SUMMARY

A number of factors influence our perception and interpretation of symptoms, including current mood or stress level. Being in a bad mood or experiencing stress both aggravate the experience of symptoms. Although the findings are not consistent, there do tend to be age and gender differences in the interpretation of symptoms.

There tend to be many types of delay in seeking medical care. Patient delay can occur at the stage of appraisal delay (deciding that a symptom is a sign of illness), illness delay (the time between recognizing that one is ill and seeking care), behavioural delay (the time between deciding to seek care and actually making an appointment), scheduling delay (the time between scheduling an appointment and receiving medical attention), or treatment delay (the time between receiving medical attention and beginning treatment).

A number of different models of the physician–patient relationship have been proposed. Szasz and Hollender outlined three basic models of the physician–patient relationship: active-passive, guidance-cooperation, and mutual-participation. Debra Roter and her colleagues outlined a model with five distinct communication patterns: narrowly biomedical, expanded biomedical, biopsychosocial, psychosocial, and consumerist. Other models have also been proposed including one entitled patient-centred care.

Communication in the physician–patient relationship has also been studied. Both patient and physician characteristics lead to poor communication. Physicians may interrupt their patients or in other ways receive little input from their patients, they may use medical jargon or baby talk when conversing with patients, they may give little information to their patients and they may appear hurried. Patients are not always forthcoming with information and they fail to ask questions of their physicians.

Patient non-adherence is the failure to follow the advice of the health professional. Certain patient characteristics also contribute to adherence. For example, children, females and those who have the socioeconomic means are most likely to adhere. When treatments are complex or when poor physician–patient communication occurs there is greater likelihood of non-adherence.

Adhering to treatment regimens results in better health outcomes. To improve adherence one should simplify the regimen, use reminders (calendar packs to manual phone calls from health care providers), engage in self-monitoring, provide reinforcements, engage in counselling about the importance of adherence, and involve family members and friends. A combination of strategies is often best.

Review Questions

1. What factors influence our perception and interpretation of symptoms?
2. Why do people delay in seeking medical care?
3. How have researchers conceptualized physician–patient relationships?
4. What patient and physician characteristics lead to poor communication?
5. How widespread is patient non-adherence?
6. How can we improve patient adherence to medical advice?
7. Does patient adherence lead to better health outcomes?

Chapter 6

Hospital Stays and Medical Procedures

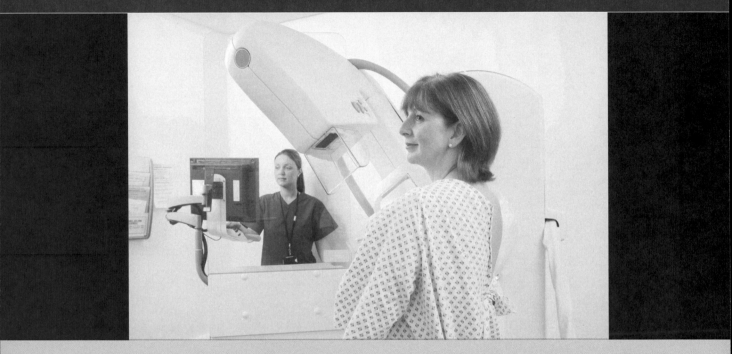

CHAPTER OUTLINE

THE HOSPITAL AS A DISTINCT CULTURE
THE PSYCHOLOGICAL IMPACT OF MEDICAL PROCEDURES
DAY SURGERY
IN THE HOSPITAL

Learning Objectives

After studying this chapter, you will be able to

- Explain specific ways in which the procedures and rules within a hospital affect patients' sense of control and their ability to cope with being in hospital
- Define "invasiveness" and use this definition to place various medical procedures on a continuum of invasiveness
- Describe ways in which the nature of care and preparation for medical procedures can help patients cope

- Describe psychological challenges associated with specific hospital departments (emergency, surgery, intensive care, discharge, and palliative care) and the coping and care needed to manage these challenges

As soon as Hanna walked into the hospital, she was reminded of all the hospital dramas she had watched on television. Staff members scurried through the halls with purpose and urgency. Families sat in waiting areas, talking quietly among themselves, some looking composed, others worried and anxious.

Today, Hanna was part of the drama. Her doctor had made an appointment for her to have a bone scan to screen for osteoporosis. Hanna had just turned 52, and the thought of having brittle bones that were prone to fracture made her feel old. Still, her mother had broken her hip when she was in her sixties, and Hanna's doctor felt that Hanna was at sufficient risk that a "bone mineral density" test was in order. She was expecting something like an X-ray, but she also knew of friends who had been tested using something called nuclear medicine. It sounded ominous.

Hanna finally found the radiology department after following a blue line on the floor that wound through the halls of the hospital. She was shown to a waiting room with a bunch of other people, some wearing what looked like discarded bed sheets. There were so many people. The nurses and technologists were obviously used to the crowds, though. They were moving people in and out very efficiently.

When Hanna's name was called, she jumped to her feet. She could feel the butterflies in her stomach as she went into the examination room. The procedure went smoothly, although Hanna was relieved when it was over. Fortunately, she had a technologist who seemed to know just how to empathize with her and make her feel at ease. Before she knew it, she was out in the hall, following the blue line back to the main entrance.

Most of us have been inside a hospital. However, unless you work in a hospital or have spent a considerable amount of time in one, you probably feel a bit out of place when you walk through the doors. People in unique garb might be wheeling unfamiliar machines through the halls, sometimes connected to other people. The place has its own collection of peculiar smells, and it's full of sick people, some of them dying. Indeed, a hospital is its own world, a world we will investigate in this chapter. If you ever walked through the halls of a hospital and wondered about the psychological impact the place has on patients, then you were thinking like a health psychologist.

Hanna's example reminds us not only that a hospital is an unfamiliar and somewhat dramatic place, but also that we usually encounter it when we are not at our best. We might be worried, or anxious, or just plain unwell. In this state we are put through procedures that can feel quite intimidating and that are designed to look for things we don't want to have in the first place.

In this chapter, we will start by looking at a hospital the way an anthropologist might look at a different culture. We will explore and attempt to understand the psychological impact of each department as we move through the world of a hospital.

THE HOSPITAL AS A DISTINCT CULTURE

Imagine being asked to spend a week in a place you have never been before. In this place, most of the people dress quite differently from you. They speak your language, but they also speak another language to one another. It is a language that you cannot comprehend. They will speak this language even when you are with them and they are talking about you. In fact, these people have very different rules of social interaction. They will ask you personal questions and expect detailed answers, even though they have just met you. They will wake you in the middle of the night. They will prevent you from getting out of your bed when you want to and will make you get up when you want to stay in bed.

And there are rituals. Many visitors to this place must first provide a small amount of their blood to the inhabitants before they are allowed to stay. These people take some of their visitors and make large incisions in their bodies, sometimes removing body parts. They may discard these body parts or keep them and study them. When it is time to leave, the visitors may be made to exit in a chair with wheels, even though they would rather walk.

Does this sound like the sort of place you would like to visit? Does it sound somewhat alien? The place we are describing is, of course, a hospital. When viewed as a distinct culture, with its own set of interaction patterns, rules, and rituals, it is easy to see why hospital stays can be quite disorienting and stressful.

In 2005, 8 out of every 100 Canadians were hospitalized. (Canadian Institute for Health Information [CIHI], 2005b), although across the country as a whole, inpatient hospitalizations declined by 13 percent between 1993 and 2003. At the same time, the average stay of those hospitalizations increased. But in 2004 and 2005, both those trends levelled off (CIHI, 2005b). Why would the number of people spending time in hospital go down while those who are admitted to hospital end up staying longer? The answer can be found in the changing nature of hospital treatment and health care funding.

For example, you might be surprised to learn that only one-quarter of all hospitalizations today involve surgery, and these do not account for the longest hospital stays. More than 40 percent of hospitalizations are categorized as "medical," including digestive disorders, respiratory diseases, heart diseases, and diabetes. Surgical patients stay in hospital an average of 5.4 days, whereas medical patients average 8.9 days per stay (CIHI, 2005b).

While some hospital stays can be difficult and lengthy, others are brief, like the one that Hanna experienced in our opening vignette. Hanna was an **outpatient**, meaning that she did not have to stay overnight. Her particular procedure, a bone mineral density scan, takes about 10 or 20 minutes and is **non-invasive**. This means that she did not have an incision or have anything inserted into her. Nor did she have to ingest substances to aid in the radiographic procedure. Even so, as we will see in a moment, a medical procedure such as this can engender its share of anxiety.

Other patients will be **day care patients**. This means they will be having a procedure that is more involved than Hanna's bone scan but still will not be staying overnight. They might be having laser surgery to remove cataracts from their eyes. Or they might be having tubes inserted in their ears to treat recurring infections. Day care patients might be put under general anaesthetic, and so they tend to be admitted early in the day and discharged by late afternoon. These patients usually need to be accompanied by someone who can be sure they get home safely and comfortably after the procedure. These patients will also get one of those identification wristbands that are a common part of hospital stays.

outpatient: a person who goes to the hospital for a procedure or test but does not stay overnight.

non-invasive: a term to describe any procedure that does not include piercing the skin or entering the body with an instrument.

day care patient: a person who goes to the hospital for a procedure or test that is more involved than, for example, routine radiography, but does not stay overnight.

Still other patients enter the hospital under emergency circumstances. They may enter by way of the emergency room and be treated and released from there in the same day. Others may be admitted through emergency and end up staying overnight or longer. Indeed, some may be unconscious when admitted and need to have their circumstances explained to them when they regain consciousness in some other part of the hospital. Clearly, this is a very different experience from that of day care patients or others who have had their procedure booked for a long period of time and have gone through the anticipation. Some will have gone through this waiting period only to be told just before their scheduled admission day that their procedure has been postponed. Sometimes the consequences of waiting are minor, amounting to frustration and inconvenience. But sometimes they are dire. In Canada in 2004, 242 people died while waiting for organ transplants. Keep in mind that approximately 1800 patients receive solid organ transplants in Canada in a year (CIHI, 2005b), a figure that has risen by 22 percent in the past 10 years.

Each of these admission patterns can have a different effect on the patient's psychological response to being in hospital. For some, it is a sign that something traumatic and frightening is going on. For others, there is a sense of relief that the waiting is over and something constructive is going to be done. Whatever the pattern of admission, it must be emphasized that the admission procedure often constitutes a patient's first encounter with the hospital. As such, it carries all the weight we would expect of a first impression in shaping the patient's perceptions of the hospital experience.

Studies dating back to the mid-1990s effectively capture the loss of control that often accompanies a hospital stay. Spencer and colleagues (1995) documented the case of a 30-year-old man who suffered a spinal cord injury and had to spend 116 days rehabilitating in hospital. You can imagine the challenges associated with learning to adapt to the disability incurred by a spinal cord injury. Interestingly, the investigators discovered through daily interviews with the patient that adaptation to his long-term hospital stay was almost as challenging. In fact, the injury and the hospital had a similar effect on the patient. Each took away some of the control he once had over his life. Adaptation to both hospital and injury meant regaining as much of that control as possible.

A Hospital Patient's Loss of Control

A study conducted in the Netherlands clearly showed that patients feel they relinquish control to others during hospital stays (Halfens, 1995). Seventy-two people were asked to complete the Health Locus of Control Scale, which measures their sense of internal control, external control (luck, fate, and circumstance), and control by powerful others, such as hospital staff. Participants completed the scale three times: nine days before admission, during their stay, and seven days after being discharged from the hospital. Figure 6-1 shows the significant increase in people's scores on the powerful-other subscale during their hospital stay.

More recently, a survey of women's hospital experiences identified three factors that were closely connected to their satisfaction with the experience (Polimeni & Moore, 2002). These were respect through communication, maintenance of dignity, and day-to-day control. The more these elements were compromised, the greater the level of dissatisfaction experienced. While most women reported being satisfied with their hospital experience, many still made reference to their perceived powerlessness. For many surgical

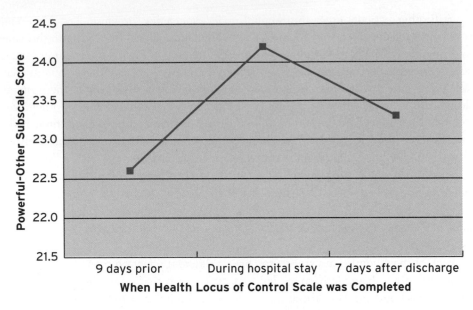

Figure 6-1 Change in Powerful-Other Control Beliefs during Hospital Stays

Source: Halfens, R.G., Effect of hospital stay on health locus-of-control beliefs. *Western Journal of Nursing Research, 17,* 156–7, ©1995. Copyright ©1995 by SAGE PUBLICATIONS INC. JOURNALS. Reproduced with permission via Copyright Clearance Center.

patients, hospital stays are improved when adequate information is provided about their surgery and their recovery, as well as general information about their upcoming stay and the sensations that will be part of it (Krupat, Fancey, & Cleary, 2000). The stronger a patient's need for control, the more he or she will value the information received.

For children entering a hospital, the feeling of loss of control can be even greater. This is especially true when the hospital stay involves medical trauma (Rennick, 2002). Researchers at McGill University have discovered that children whose hospitalization involved more invasive procedures felt they had less control over their health.

When hospitalized, the new patient enters what Erving Goffman (1961) describes as a **total institution**. In other words, the hospital takes control of virtually every aspect of a patient's life. Patients are expected to adapt to the hospital's schedule, to eat and sleep at specified times, perhaps to receive visitors only during designated hours, to conform to hospital procedures, and to make their bodies available for examination when requested.

How patients react to this loss of control in the hospital environment varies greatly from person to person. Yet some general patterns have been noted in patients' reactions to the hospital environment. As one example of a particularly traumatic kind of hospital experience, people faced with end-of-life decisions can be placed along a continuum in terms of the control they would like to maintain. At one end is the "activist" (Kelner, 1995), who wants total control. At the other end of the continuum is the "delegator" (Kelner, 1995), who wants to relinquish that control.

Generally speaking, people want to share the decision-making control with their physician. In one Canadian hospital, 49 percent of patients preferred this shared approach when the medical condition involved chest pain, whereas only 1 percent wanted totally autonomous decision-making control, and 50 percent wanted to give total control to the physician. Patients' preferences were linked to the trust they had in the physician—the

total institution: any institution, such as a hospital, that takes control of virtually every aspect of a person's day-to-day life.

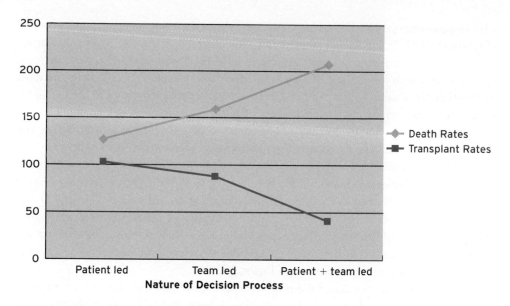

Figure 6-2 Health Outcomes x Decision Involvement

Patients who led the decision-making process regarding treatment for their kidney disease had lower death rates and higher transplant rates. (Death rates and transplant per 1000 patient-years living at risk.)

Source: Stack & Martin, (2005). Association of patient autonomy with increased transplantation and survival among new dialysis patients in the United States, *American Journal of Kidney Disease, 45*(4), 730–742. Copyright (2005) with permission from Elsevier.

more trust they felt, the more control they wanted the physician to have (Kraetschmer, Sharpe, Urowitz, & Deber, 2004).

Being involved in this decision-making process could lead to better outcomes for patients. A study analyzing decision-making control for patients with chronic kidney disease found better outcomes (lower death rates and higher transplantation rates) for those patients who led their decision-making process compared to those whose decisions were led by the medical team (see Figure 6-2) (Stack & Martin, 2005).

Practitioners' impressions of patients can also be affected by the patients' behavioural responses to a loss of control. Attempts to regain control can be misunderstood as attempts to be "difficult." One example of such a patient was a 74-year-old man who'd had his gallbladder removed and had post-operative psychological and medical complications. He "was labelled a problem patient by the surgeon, resident, intern, and day staff nurse" (Lorber, 1975, p. 218).

The behaviours of the "bad patient" are viewed as a form of **reactance** (Brehm, 1966), which is a response to an unacceptable challenge to one's freedom and which may arouse anger and must be resisted. Thus, the so-called problem patient's complaints and demands for additional attention may be angry attempts by the patient to re-establish at least a small measure of personal freedom. The person in this case was 74 years old. Generally, however, patients who are younger, better educated, or accustomed to more control over their environment are more likely to respond with reactance (Taylor, 1979).

Seligman (1975) investigated the idea that constant frustration can produce **learned helplessness**, the belief that nothing can be done to improve a difficult situation. The concept of learned helplessness has been applied to hospital settings as well, to explain

reactance: behaving counter to recommendations in response to the feeling that one has lost personal control over health behaviours; the non-compliant behaviours and attitudes of patients who perceive hospital rules and regimens to be unacceptable challenges to their freedom.

learned helplessness: a state in which a person, because of experience with previously uncontrollable stressful situations, learns to do nothing about a new stressor, rather than trying to cope constructively with it.

why **empowering care** yields independence and **disempowering care** yields dependence (Faulkner, 2001). It is Faulkner's contention that disempowering care results in learned helplessness, whereas empowering care results in learned mastery. He has demonstrated this in a study with hospitalized older adults (mean age 79 years). At mealtimes, patients were either given considerable aid (i.e., over-assisted) or told they were in control. This simple difference improved independence at mealtimes. As a follow-up, Faulkner placed half of the patients in the learned helplessness condition and the other half in the self-control condition and found that the latter group became more independent.

We have discussed how loss of control may cause reactance or helplessness in hospitalized patients. Neither behaviour is likely to be adaptive for the patient. Although good patients may be well liked by the hospital staff, they may be suffering from learned helplessness and may be at risk for norepinephrine depletion, general erosion of health, and the possibility of sudden death. Patients who respond with reactance, by contrast, are likely to experience anger, heightened secretion of stress hormones, and the possible aggravation of cardiovascular problems (Taylor, 1979).

We have already mentioned the link between control and the provision of information, but this crucial link deserves a closer look. Krupat and colleagues make the point that, about 30 years ago, many people facing surgery were poorly informed about their upcoming procedure. Some did not even know which organ was going to be the focus of the surgery. In response to this problem, a number of programs have been developed to train practitioners in the skills of information giving. A comprehensive study of patients from over 60 hospitals assessed the extent to which this provision of information affected patients' perceptions of their hospital stays. It was found that the provision of general information was the single best predictor of patients' satisfaction. This was also significantly correlated with patients' sense of control. These relationships were unaffected by other patient factors, such as age or desire for information (Krupat et al., 2000).

Numerous studies have reported the benefits of providing information to patients in preparation for surgery. However, unlike those in the Krupat et al. study, not all people have been shown to respond well to the provision of information. For example, some people, known as **monitors**, welcome information and seek it out, whereas others, called **blunters**, avoid it.

These concepts are well-demonstrated in a classic study by Suzanne Miller and Charles Mangan (1983), which showed how individual differences may affect responses to information about medical procedures. In this study, women about to undergo a diagnostic procedure for cervical cancer were divided into monitors and blunters based on their preference for information in a variety of naturalistic stress situations. Half the monitors and half the blunters were randomly assigned to either a high- or low-information group. Patients in the high-information group were given a 20-minute verbal and visual presentation explaining the procedure they were about to undergo. The other half of the monitors and blunters also spent 20 minutes with the research assistant but were given only minimal information about the upcoming procedure; the rest of the time was spent providing information on general nutrition. Measures of the patients' distress were taken in the form of pulse rates three times: before receiving the information, after receiving the information but before the examination, and after the examination. Patients who showed the least physiological stress in response to the exam were those who were given the amount of information that fit their preferences. In other words, monitors given a large amount of information showed low physiological stress and blunters given little information showed low physiological stress. Monitors who were given little information and blunters given a large amount predictably showed much greater stress.

We would expect that, in preparation for potentially stressful events such as hospital procedures, monitors and blunters would adopt different approaches. In terms of advice for practitioners, though, there is more to this story. Some practitioners and researchers argue that an informed patient simply copes better, and so all patients should receive information in their preparation for a hospital stay. Others have called this homogeneous approach to hospital preparation the **uniformity myth** (Kiesler, 1966; Miró, Turk, & Rudy, 1991).

The way patients are prepared for surgery has also received considerable attention. Information provision, or *psychoeducation*, as it is sometimes called, includes the provision of information about surgical processes and potential outcomes as well as about the patient's role in managing pre- and post-operative pain. Like the preparation for hospital stays, it would be a mistake to adopt a "one size fits" all approach to the provision of such information.

Good psychological preparation for surgery involves more than information provision, however. It includes other elements that should benefit all patients, regardless of their psychological state or characteristics. Brent Van Dorsten (2006) provides a number of helpful categories for such preparation. For example, pre-surgical treatment expectations need to be addressed. In the case of patients about to undergo surgery intended to lower chronic pain, patients can have unrealistically high expectations of the surgery's effect. Pre-operative preparation can help patients and practitioners come to a mutually agreed upon definition of "treatment success."

Practitioners must also consider how to manage and assess patients' emotions. Related to this is helping patients develop self-monitoring skills related to emotion, pain, and other symptoms. These skills help the patient recognize warning signs, as well as indications that they are getting better. Finally, there is relaxation training, which can have a positive effect on many of the other targets for pre-operative preparation.

While the Miller and Mangan study (1983) reminds us that health care providers should match the amount of information they provide with an individual's coping style, research has shown that *all* patients, regardless of their coping style, benefit from relaxation training prior to surgery (Miró & Rosa, 1999). Perhaps this is because monitors tend to experience greater stress and anxiety generally, as they scan for information and ruminate over the problem at hand (Ben-Zur, 2002; Miller, 1996). Thus, monitors benefit from the relaxation itself and blunters from the distraction it provides.

What can we conclude from all of this regarding preparation for surgery? All patients appear to benefit from relaxation training. This training appears to be most effective when the patients are encouraged to focus on distraction (e.g., "think of a very relaxing place") rather than physiology (e.g., "feel your muscles relaxing") (Miró & Rosa, 1999). Of course, all patients need a certain amount of information as well, or else they may be confused and disoriented by their hospital stays. Ideally, a practitioner would be privy to, and provide, the exact amount of information that matches the patient's coping style.

There are other ways of improving psychological control in patients. For example, researchers in Hamilton, Ontario, increased patients' perceptions of control by letting them choose to walk to the operating room rather than being transported on a stretcher

uniformity myth: belief that all patients should receive the same amount of information in their preparation for a hospital stay regardless of their personal styles of coping with stress.

(Porteous & Tyndall, 1994). During the study, 111 of 160 patients chose to walk to the operating room. Only two of these patients were not satisfied with their choice. The reasons given by these patients for their dissatisfaction included becoming uncomfortable waiting and believing that they "would have felt more pampered on a stretcher" (Porteous & Tyndall, 1994, p. 23). However, the majority of patients were satisfied with their decision, stating that as a result they "felt better, less like a sick person . . . more in control" (Porteous & Tyndall, 1994, p. 23). These examples suggest ways that hospitals can increase patients' perceptions of control with solutions that are fairly easy to implement.

Depersonalization   Feeling a lack of control is only one of the complaints patients have about hospitals. They also report experiencing **depersonalization** or **dehumanization**. Depersonalizing environments take away people's sense of individuality, making them feel more like objects than people. (You may have felt a bit like this at school when asked for your student number rather than your name.)

> **depersonalization:** taking away a person's sense of individuality.
>
> **dehumanization:** the tendency to see people as objects or body parts rather than human beings.

Depersonalization can result from many encounters in the hospital setting. For example, if you need to undergo even a fairly simple medical procedure it is likely that you will be required to follow a set procedure or routine and that the medical staff will also follow a routine. A pregnant woman may be required to undergo a glucose tolerance test to ensure that she has not developed gestational diabetes. Before this test begins, someone will explain to the woman that she must drink a very sweet "cocktail" and then remain in the hospital or lab for a number of hours so that her blood sugar can be monitored at various points. To aid the technologist and ensure all pertinent information is shared with the patient, it is likely that the technologist will run through a "spiel" (which he or she obviously has repeated many times), never seeming to pause for a breath. Although all the facts may be relayed to the patient during this interaction, it is unlikely that the patient will be able to retain all this information. The technician's routine is an example of an impersonal interaction.

Patients may also experience depersonalization when they are required to wear a hospital gown, when they are referred to by ailment rather than by name, and when their privacy is not respected, all of which do occur. However, hospitals are improving. Today, many hospitals encourage their patients to bring their own pyjamas and other personal effects. As well, patients are made as comfortable as possible.

How Patients Cope with the Hospital Culture

Patients mainly use two strategies to cope with loss of control and exposure to surroundings that are strange to them. One is by relying on other patients; the other is by adopting either a passive or an active approach to the stay.

In her book *Life on the Ward*, Coser (1962) analyzed how patients help each other cope, pointing out that the social support patients provide each other is based on their shared submission to what we now call "powerful others" (Wallston, Wallston, & DeVellis, 1978). This support is also based on shared disability and inconvenience. Even though these might be temporary conditions, patients are brought together like motorists in a snowstorm. They provide support by joking together about their conditions and generally building solidarity. Ironically, this social support probably helps patients cope with the hospital culture but may make it more difficult to adapt to life outside the hospital if the stay is a long one.

Coser's book was published in the 1960s, during a time when patients' experiences in hospitals were being studied extensively. By the 1970s, however, this level of study had diminished considerably. Zussman (1993) suggests that this was due, in part, to the nature of the modern hospital. In it, stays are short and technology dominates the medical landscape. To make his point, Zussman refers to intensive-care units (ICUs). In these facilities, which are taking up more and more of a hospital's floor space, "technical virtuosity" (p. 176) and relatively frequent deaths prevent patients from forming bonds with each other, and these factors also discourage staff from forming therapeutic bonds with patients.

Indeed, the ICU, with its strong orientation to physiology, can create the sense of depersonalization we discussed earlier. At the same time, we must emphasize that lives are saved in ICUs. Those who work in these units may argue that there is no point in forsaking technical intervention for personal care if it means the person is more likely to die. Clearly, the ideal is a balance between technology and the human touch.

For outpatient procedures and consultations, patients today may take advantage of social support by bringing a companion (Schilling et al., 2002). A study of 1300 patients ranging in age from 18 to over 65 found that companions were brought into examination rooms 16 percent of the time. The vast majority of these companions were family members. Both patients and practitioners saw advantages in having this third person involved. Specifically, the companion could help communicate the patient's concerns and help remember instructions and advice (Schilling et al., 2002). Patients reported that having a companion in the examination room was helpful 83 percent of the time.

The Role of Nurses in Hospital Culture

The hospital is populated by physicians, orderlies, administrators, technologists, and other staff. Arguably, though, a hospital's culture is affected most by its nurses—they are usually the largest group in the hospital, and nurses have the most person-to-person contact with patients. Indeed, nurses are called "patient advocates," in large part because they get to know the patients better than do other hospital staff and because they are most responsible for the day-to-day care of the patient. We will talk about the profession of nursing in more detail in chapter 7. Here, we look at the ways nurses affect hospital culture and patients' ability to cope with it.

Cultures have rituals and shared activities that take on meaning in terms of defining those cultures. Hospitals are no exception, and because of the importance of nurses to the hospital culture, nursing practice has been analyzed regarding the rituals common to it. Two general types of nursing rituals have been identified—**therapeutic rituals** and **occupational rituals**. Therapeutic rituals deal mostly with patient–nurse interactions. Occupational rituals concern the socialization of nurses into the profession. As such, they focus on interactions among nurses (Wolf, 1993).

People studying hospital culture (medical ethnographers) have identified administering medication and bathing patients as two important therapeutic rituals (Holland, 1993). Physicians prescribe the medication patients must take, but it is the nurse's job to see that the patients actually take the medication. Often, patients are very cooperative and nurses reward this with a show of appreciation. Sometimes, however, patients resist taking their medication, and the ritual changes to one that some nurse educators have

therapeutic rituals: in nursing practice, primarily activities that deal with patient–nurse interactions; for example, the administration of medication and bathing of patients.

occupational rituals: behaviours that indicate a person has been socialized into a profession; for nurses, these are communicated through interaction with other nurses.

called "assertive empathy." In these cases the nurse is effectively saying, "I know you don't like this, and I can understand why, but you must take it."

Patient bathing connotes a level of helplessness on the part of the patient and caring on the part of the nurse. Some patients are more comfortable with this relationship than others. Having the process ritualized makes it easier for the nurse to complete the task, maintaining a controlled and appropriate level of intimacy and, when necessary, a firm resolve that the job must be done.

Holland (1993) identifies at least three important components of occupational rituals. First, there is the uniform. Nursing uniforms vary from hospital to hospital and have become less prevalent in some hospitals, although they have a long history of meaning in relation to hospital culture and its association with religious institutions. Whatever the uniform may look like, the function is the same. It identifies the nurse as a member of the profession, subject to the codes of conduct and ethics that go with it.

The second component is the hierarchy of authority, both within the nursing profession and between professions, but primarily between physicians and nurses. Ritual in this context extends to the nature and direction of criticism allowed; namely, it rarely flows *up* the hierarchy. Authority and the power that accompanies it are key issues in the hospital culture.

The third component of occupational ritual is language. For language to define a culture, it must be unique to that culture. For example, nurses will describe a patient who is not allowed to eat or drink as being "nil by mouth" (Holland, 1993, p. 1466). This isn't the sort of phrase you would hear anywhere else but in a hospital. Language, in the form of euphemism, is also used to ritualize the delicate decisions surrounding death. A decision may have been made not to resuscitate a patient if heart or respiration stops. Nurses may call this situation a "no code." Much of this language is used when nurses communicate their change-of-shift reports (Wolf, 1993). This clearly ritualized activity for nurses helps to maintain the norms of the profession.

All patients have needs and expectations regarding the care they receive from nurses when they are in this strange world called a hospital. What are these needs and expectations, and how well do the rituals of nursing meet them? In answering these questions, the two types of care should be taken into consideration. These are **technical care** and **socioemotional care**. The former refers to the handling of prescribed medical procedures; the latter refers to the interpersonal skills required to help patients maintain a sense of optimism and psychological well-being.

Generally, patients aren't expert judges of technical care. Most are lay people and don't have much experience with medical procedures. Asking them to assess the technical expertise of their care would be like asking them to judge a figure skating competition when they don't know a Lutz from a triple toe loop. On the other hand, patients are good judges of socioemotional care. They know what a pleasant disposition looks like. They know what kindness and patience look like. They know when they have been treated with respect. For these reasons, patients often articulate their needs and expectations in terms of socioemotional care (Leiter, Harvie, & Frizzel, 1998).

There is an exception to this, however. Patients' satisfaction is determined by nurses' technical expertise when the patients' physical comfort and pain levels are involved. In one study, when nurses were asked what constituted the most important aspects of good nursing care, they cited listening to the patient. This answer acknowledges the value of

technical care: activities involving prescribed medical procedures, independent of the psychological needs of the patient.

socioemotional care: interactions that help patients maintain a sense of optimism and psychological well-being.

socioemotional care. In that same study, however, when *patients* were asked, they said the most important aspect of good nursing care was knowing how to give shots and IVs and manage equipment (Larson & Ferketich, 1993).

Whether patients' expectations focus on the technical or socioemotional care they receive from nurses, there is little doubt that their overall satisfaction with their hospital stay is determined, in large part, by the care the nurses provide. This relationship between patient satisfaction and nursing care is highlighted in a fascinating study conducted by researchers at Acadia University in Nova Scotia (Leiter, Harvie, & Frizzel, 1998) (see Focus on Canadian Research 6-1). In this study, Leiter and colleagues correlated patient dissatisfaction with nurses' self-reports of professional burnout. **Burnout** is a state that results from excessive patient loads, or as Leiter and colleagues put it, from nurses experiencing a "gap between expectations to fulfill their professional roles and the structure of the organization" (p. 1613). The most common symptoms of burnout include exhaustion, cynicism, a lack of belief in one's professional competence, and a low sense of accomplishment. Burnout is an all-too-common problem in health care that we will address further in chapter 7.

burnout: a condition that is similar to compassion fatigue and includes symptoms of physical exhaustion, depersonalization of patients, and feelings of discouragement and low accomplishment.

If patients' satisfaction is determined primarily by socioemotional care, then their satisfaction should be affected by the degree of burnout existing in the hospital unit in which they are treated. The question is, does nurse burnout show itself enough to be correlated with patient satisfaction? It is this question that Leiter and colleagues addressed. Focus on

Focus on Canadian Research 6-1

Burnout and the Capacity to Care

Title: *The correspondence of patient satisfaction and nurse burnout*

Researchers: Michael Leiter, Phyllis Harvie, and Cindy Frizzel

Purpose: To determine if there is a relationship between nurses' self-reports of burnout and patients' ratings of nursing care

Method: More than 700 nurses completed the Maslach Burnout Inventory to measure the extent to which they felt exhausted, cynical, and critical of their professional ability. Burnout is related to high demands created by such things as patient overloads. Nine hundred and thirty-one patients completed the Patient Judgments of Hospital Quality Questionnaire. This is a measure of their satisfaction with various aspects of their hospital stay. Of special interest was the subscale in which patients rate nursing care. Average scores for nurses working within a hospital unit were correlated with average nursing care ratings given by patients in that unit. A wide range of hospital units were used in the analysis.

Results: Strong correlations were found between nurses' reports of various aspects of burnout and patients' ratings of nursing care.

Nurse Self-Report	Correlation with Patient Rating of Nursing Care
Exhaustion	−.73
Cynicism	−.53
Intention to quit	−.53
Work meaningfulness	−.79

Conclusion: Patients' impressions of the care they receive from nurses is related to the nurses' feelings about their work as expressed in their self-reports of burnout. This is a correlational study, so we cannot draw conclusions regarding cause and effect. Having said this, it is worth exploring the very real possibility that burnout seriously affects nurses' capacity to provide socioemotional care for their patients. This study suggests that patients are sensitive to nurse burnout. This is a particularly important topic, given the vital role nurses play in helping patients cope with their hospital stays.

Canadian Research 6-1 describes a study in which a number of strong correlations were found between elements of burnout and patients' ratings of nurses. This study provides convincing evidence that patients' ratings of nursing care are based primarily on socio-emotional aspects of that care and that when nurses are overtaxed, their ability to provide that care is seriously compromised. Other research has found a similar correlation between nurse job satisfaction and patient satisfaction (Tzeng, Ketefian, & Redman, 2002).

Patient-Centred Care: An Ideal in the Hospital

In Zussman's words, hospital patients are more than just "the human backdrop for dramatic enactments of professional socialization" (Zussman, 1993, p. 173). Yet, in the traditional biomedical approach, the needs of health care professionals can become paramount (Ponte et al., 2003). Contrast this with **patient-centred care** in which patients and families become active members of the treatment team (Ponte et al., 2003).

patient-centred approach: approach in which patients and families become active members of the treatment team.

There are, of course, limits to how far we can go in dedicating resources to patients' psychosocial needs. In a San Francisco-area hospital, model units were created that featured homelike environments, art, and music. The nurses were specially trained to promote greater patient involvement in decision making, to provide more personalized care, and to increase the health education provided to patients. Not surprisingly, patients who were randomly assigned to these patient-centred units reported greater satisfaction with their stays (Martin et al., 1998). Administrators of Canadian hospitals must strike a balance between dedicating such extensive resources to patients' psychosocial needs and providing environments that address patients' fundamental biomedical needs.

THE PSYCHOLOGICAL IMPACT OF MEDICAL PROCEDURES

In our opening vignette, Hanna came to the hospital as an outpatient to undergo a medical procedure. Because so many people's experiences of hospitals come from outpatient procedures, we will investigate the psychological impact of some of these procedures. In this analysis, we will make the point that there is always more to a medical procedure than what meets the practitioner's eye. Patients attach meaning to the process that may go well beyond the biomedical purpose of the procedure. To illustrate this, we will look at two common procedures—colonoscopy and mammography—to learn about the psychological impact of such procedures.

The Psychology of Colonoscopy

In Canada, colorectal cancer is the second leading cause of cancer-related death (Marrett et al., 2008). The most common screening procedures for this type of cancer are colonoscopy and faecal occult blood test (FOBT). FOBT followed by colonoscopy (when FOBT yields positive results) has been estimated to reduce 10-year mortality due to colorectal cancer by 16.7 percent in Canada (Flanagan et al., 2003). In spite of these predictions, colonoscopy is under-utilized in Canada.

Colonoscopy decisions are affected by the kinds of cost-benefit analyses described in the health belief model (see Chapter 1). Like all screening procedures designed to detect potentially serious illness, the psychological costs of colonoscopy include the possibility that the test will yield worrisome results. This helps explain under-utilization. In addition, the procedure itself can be painful and anxiety producing. Pain ratings for colonoscopy tend to be higher for women than for men, explained in part by the fact that women have longer colons (Ylinen et al., 2009).

In Finland, where sedatives and pain medication are not routinely used for colonoscopies, about 58 percent of patients report at least some pain. Instead of sedatives, participants in a Finnish study were given what the authors called "peaceful talk," including calm and clear information regarding the procedure. Forty percent of patients receiving this during colonoscopy reported a significantly lower pain experience (Ylinen et al., 2009). In an American study of six patients undergoing colonoscopy, hypnosis was found to eliminate the need for sedation (Elkins et al., 2006).

The Psychology of Mammography

One valuable way to understand the potential negative psychological impact of a medical procedure is to consider its **invasiveness**. The term is self-explanatory, though it is worth noting that invasiveness has both physical and psychological components.

In a physical sense, health practitioners determine the invasiveness of a procedure by the extent to which it involves piercing the skin or entering the body with instruments—physically "invading" the body. In a psychological sense, a procedure is invasive if it has the potential to cause embarrassment, shame, or discomfort. This is often the result of procedures that intrude into intimate parts of the body (Weller & Hener, 1993). Not surprisingly, a patient's ability to adapt to a procedure is predicted, in large part, by the invasiveness of that procedure (Campbell-Heider & Knapp, 1993), although a procedure's potential results probably outweigh its invasiveness as a predictor of stressfulness (Kowalcek, Muhlhoff, Bachmann, & Gembruch, 2002).

Procedures can be placed on a *continuum* of invasiveness based on the definitions we have just introduced. If you have experienced a range of medical procedures in your life, you could probably rank them in terms of their invasiveness; even the different parts of a general physical examination vary in this way.

Mammography is, at most, moderately invasive. Nonetheless, there is considerable anxiety surrounding the procedure, not so much because of what is done but because of what might be found, as indicated by the finding that post-mammography anxiety levels are best predicted by pre-exam anxiety levels. The *idea* of such screening is anxiety-producing (Brain et al., 2008). Abnormal mammogram results can bring on fear, anxiety, and depression. This is also true for other screening tests, such as Pap tests for cervical cancer (Pasket & Rimer, 1995).

It could be argued that psychological distress is a necessary element of cancer screening and a relatively small price to pay for the lives that are saved by early detection. However, estimates vary considerably regarding just how many lives are saved by cancer screening, especially mammography. Evidence is far greater for the benefits of screening for other forms of cancer, such as cancer of the cervix (Sasieni, Adams, & Cuzick, 2003).

When calculating the cost–benefit ratio of mammography or any other screening procedure, we must take **false-positive** results into consideration. These are results that

invasiveness: a measure of the extent to which hospital procedures, in a physical sense, involve piercing the skin or entering the body with instruments or, in a psychological sense, have the potential to cause embarrassment.

false positive: result that indicates abnormality when none exists.

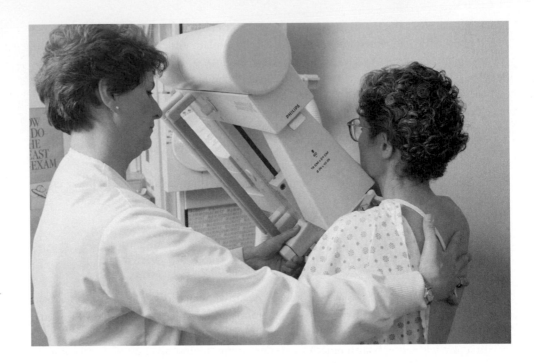

A woman undergoing mammography.

indicate abnormality when none actually exists. A perfectly reliable test has no false positives, but mammograms are not perfectly reliable. The rate of false positives for mammograms is generally considered to be quite high. A study in Europe estimated the rate of false positives to vary between 1 and 14 percent, depending upon the callback procedures of the clinic (Lynge, Olsen, Fracheboud, & Patnick, 2003). This rate of false positives creates a dilemma regarding mammography screening, since it can put women through unnecessary anxiety, though evidence indicates that anxiety related to false-positive results is more short-term than long-term in duration (Brain, et al., 2008).

Women who feel susceptible to breast cancer do not have their anxiety reduced by a normal mammogram (Absetz, Aro, & Sutton, 2003). These same researchers found that women who experienced false positives developed a greater sense of risk for breast cancer and increased their frequency of breast self-examination, but they lost confidence in their ability to perform the examinations well.

benign breast biopsy: when the results of a biopsy procedure show no evidence of malignancy.

One form of false positive is a **benign breast biopsy**. In this case, women with abnormal mammograms are called back for a biopsy procedure, and the results show no evidence of malignancy. Positive results from biopsies occur between 10 and 40 percent of the time (McCreery, Frankl, & Frost, 1991), so the majority are benign. A study of women after a benign breast biopsy showed greater short-term psychological distress than for those in a healthy control group (Andrykowski et al., 2002). If a woman learns that her test has yielded abnormal results and that she is to return for follow-up testing, she will likely see herself as a cancer patient until proven otherwise. And even if follow-up tests prove negative, she may well think it is just a matter of time before the cancer appears for real (Wardle & Pope, 1992).

Regardless of how distressing a callback or negative biopsy might be, women who experience these false positives are not more likely to stop regular screening. In fact, they may be *more* likely to attend regular screening appointments because they feel more susceptible to breast cancer. A study of over 2400 women in Vermont found that women experiencing false positives were 1.4 times as likely as women with true-negative results to return for a mammogram within 18 months (Pinckney, Geller, Burman, & Littenberg, 2003).

The vast majority of mammograms are performed on women. This does not mean, however, that the anxiety accompanying positive and false-positive results is a female phenomenon. To develop an understanding of how the nature of the machine can affect patients' psychological response to a procedure, we turn now to a slightly more invasive procedure that is common to both men *and* women.

The Psychology of Magnetic Resonance Imaging

Magnetic resonance imaging (MRI) has become a popular diagnostic tool. This is because the images produced are superior to those obtained through radiography and because the patient is not exposed to radiation (X-rays). The procedure is moderately invasive for at least two reasons. First, it is not uncommon for patients to require an injection of a contrast solution prior to their scan. Second, patients must enter a confined space, in some cases for 30 minutes at a time, for tests that can last more than two hours for a complete head and neck scan.

How confining is the space? Patients must enter a long cylinder, called a bore, that is either 55 or 70 centimetres in diameter. People with wide shoulders must pull them in to enter the bore. Once inside, patients must remain very still. To achieve this, the head may be held in place with Velcro straps. The temperature in the bore often reaches 27 degrees Celsius, and the machine makes a loud banging sound during the scan.

Claustrophobia is the greatest psychological concern for those undergoing MRI procedures. This is most prevalent for people who are having scans that require them to enter the bore headfirst. Before their scan, patients are asked, often repeatedly, if they have problems with enclosed spaces. The newest MRI scanners feature an open side so the patient isn't completely enclosed, thereby reducing claustrophobic reactions. At present, though, most hospitals use closed-bore models.

claustrophobia: an intense fear of enclosed spaces; a psychological concern for those undergoing MRI procedures.

It is important to acknowledge that the psychological effects of MRI can be either short-term or long-term. Short-term effects include anxiety and claustrophobia during the exam as well as something called **motion artifacts**. These are distortions to the MRI image caused by a patient's movement, sometimes referred to as "ghosts" because of the nature of the images produced (Constable, 2003). In some cases, these artifacts can make diagnosis difficult; in others, they can render the scan useless, thus requiring a re-scan. It has been estimated that up to 40 percent of all scans have motion artifacts to varying degrees, impairing the quality of the diagnosis 8 to 17 percent of the time. Some motion artifacts are caused simply by the patient's breathing.

motion artifacts: distortions to an MRI image caused by a patient's movement.

To assess short-term effects, researchers measured pre-exam worry in 297 patients over the age of 16 years who were about to undergo a headfirst MRI. They also asked them, after the exam, to indicate how anxious they had been during the exam (this was measured using the State Anxiety Inventory). In addition, motion artifacts were noted to determine if they were related to patient anxiety (Dantendorfer et al., 1997). Only 1.2 percent of the participants found the MRI "hardly bearable." On average, anxiety levels dropped from pre-exam to post-exam, and females experienced significantly more anxiety than did males. The size of the bore (55 or 70 cm) had no effect on anxiety. When asked what was most unpleasant about the experience, participants cited the fact they had to stay still, the banging sound, and the narrowness of the bore. Motion artifacts occurred in 17 cases. Twelve of these cases had expressed pre-exam worry. It should be noted, however, that more than 100 patients expressed pre-exam worry and the majority of these (88.5 percent) did *not* have motion artifacts.

Other studies have discovered that claustrophobic reactions are not uncommon during MRI procedures. Some researchers report such reactions in up to 20 percent of cases (Lukins, Davan, & Drummand, 1997). Others estimate that claustrophobia occurs about 5 to 10 percent of the time, although moderate to severe anxiety has been reported in 37 percent of cases (Katz, Wilson, & Fraser, 1994).

Long-term psychological effects have also been found, such as a newly formed apprehension of enclosed spaces that surfaces weeks or months after the MRI experience. In one study, 10 percent of patients reported feeling nervous in enclosed spaces one month after their scan (Kilborn & Labbe, 1990). Another study discovered that a small percentage of people had their first claustrophobic experience *after* having their MRI (Melendez & McCrank, 1993). McIsaac and her colleagues found that 30 percent of their participants' feelings of claustrophobia had increased one month after their MRI, and 33 percent said they were reluctant to have another scan (McIsaac et al., 1998).

Anxiety and claustrophobia are obviously linked in MRI procedures. For this reason, studies have attempted to apply what is known about claustrophobia to better understand the aversiveness of these procedures. One widely accepted view of claustrophobia is that it comprises two fears—**fear of suffocation** and **fear of restriction** (Rachman & Taylor, 1993). Studies have measured these fears in MRI patients to determine the extent to which they predict adverse reactions to the procedure (McIsaac et al., 1998). These researchers found a 0.41 correlation between fear of restriction and exam anxiety and a 0.57 correlation between fear of suffocation and anxiety. These researchers suggest that fewer problems would occur during the MRI if, prior to the exam, hospital staff administered a short version of the questionnaire that assesses these fears rather than simply asking patients if they are claustrophobic. It is interesting to note that, while other studies have found that claustrophobia worsens one month after an MRI, one study found that fear of restriction and suffocation improved if the MRI was completed without anxiety (Harris, Robinson, & Menzies, 1999). The general conclusion from this work is that most adults can get through an MRI, though many are made uncomfortable or anxious by the experience.

If an MRI exam has these effects on adults, how does it affect children? One study of pediatric oncology patients (children with cancer) found that 30 percent reported moderate to extreme distress during an MRI. The worst part for them, though, was not claustrophobia; rather, it was the insertion of an intravenous line (Tyc et al., 1995). This same study found that parents' estimates of their children's distress were higher than that actually reported by the children.

Just under 4 percent of the 491 children in another study were unable to complete the exam, although we should note that children under the age of eight years were routinely sedated for their MRI. In that study, children said that, apart from injections, the banging sound was the worst part of the MRI experience (Marshall, Smith, & Weinberger, 1995).

Sedation is one way to help children get through an MRI exam, although it is not an ideal technique. Other interventions have been introduced that reduce the need for sedation. For example, in a hospital in which children under the age of six were routinely

fear of suffocation: suffocation anxiety experienced due to the belief that one might die from the inability to breathe.

fear of restriction: anxiety experienced due to the inability to move when in a small, enclosed space.

sedated for MRI, 10 children with an average age of less than five years were given audio tapes containing music and a story that invited the children to create mental pictures. It was discovered that only 3 of these 10 children required sedation, compared to 8 of 10 in a matched control group (Smart, 1997). Other research has shown that a practice MRI conducted with an educational play therapist can help children get through an MRI procedure successfully (Hallowell, et al., 2007).

For adults, the intervention of choice is sedation, but it is not always effective. In fact, one study found that 13 percent of patients had taken medication to reduce their anxiety (called anxiolytic medication). In spite of having taken the anxiolytic medication, however, they were the very patients who reported the most pre-MRI anxiety (Katz, Wilson, & Fraser, 1994). This doesn't mean that the medication did not reduce their anxiety levels—we simply don't know what those levels were prior to their taking the sedative. What we do know is that sedation did not bring their anxiety levels down to the average.

In an analysis of sedative usage for MRI patients, Murphy and Brunberg (1997) found that more than 14 percent of 939 patients over the age of 18 years required sedation (of these, 36 percent were male and 64 percent were female). Murphy and Brunberg also discovered that sedation was more common for patients having MRI brain scans. Non-pharmaceutical interventions to help people cope with MRI include techniques such as hypnosis (Simon, 1999), relaxation, and distraction from the aversive properties of the MRI experience (Quirk & Wagner, 1995).

In summary, the clear images produced by MRI scans come with certain psychological costs, especially for people who enter the bore headfirst. Generally, about 70 percent of all people cope with the procedure reasonably well, though some may find that their general discomfort with enclosed spaces has worsened as a result of their MRI experience. Between 10 and 20 percent of patients find the MRI experience to be very difficult, and 3 to 5 percent cannot complete the exam. The open-sided design of new machines should make for a significant improvement in people's ability to cope with the procedure.

DAY SURGERY

The procedures we have described so far have varied in their invasiveness, but none have involved surgery. However, **day surgery**, also called *day care surgery*, is another common way in which people experience hospital settings. As the term suggests, this is surgery in which patients do not stay in the hospital overnight. They may have cataracts removed from their eyes through laser surgery, they may have urological procedures, such as cystocopies, to investigate urinary infections or widen the urethra, or they may have surgery to implant tubes in the ears to treat recurring ear infections. In fact, there are many procedures in which the patient does not have to stay in the hospital overnight. When this is handled well, there are considerable advantages, in terms of both hospital costs and patient welfare.

day surgery: surgery that does not require the patient to stay in the hospital overnight.

Research in Europe indicates that parents have very positive attitudes toward day surgery as an option, at least when their children's surgery is tonsillectomy. When called the day after the surgery, every parent stated that they were happy that their child had spent the night at home. In the two weeks following the tonsillectomy, 13 percent of patients visited a physician and 17 percent of the families called for information (Kanerva, Tarkkila, & Pitkaranta, 2003).

A British study (While & Wilcox, 1994) identified the three key elements to successful day surgery in pediatrics: (1) adequate preparation, in the form of information for parents and children; (2) timely (as opposed to premature) discharge; and (3) adequate home support. The study then assessed the extent to which these elements were in place. Data collected in British hospitals in 1992 indicated that there was room for improvement in these areas. Some of the information presented was inappropriate for pediatric day surgery patients—for example, "The patient must not operate heavy machinery for 24 hours." Often, there was no information given regarding post-discharge care. One of the results was that children experienced considerable emotional upset when they returned home. We can only speculate on the extent to which these findings apply to today's Canadian pediatric units. Regardless, they provide a valuable template for successful pediatric day surgery experiences.

IN THE HOSPITAL

hospital separation: a measure of hospital usage calculated as an overnight hospital stay for one person.

We now shift our focus to those people who spend at least one night in hospital. In the language of health statistics, this is called a **hospital separation**. In 2004–2005, there were 2.2 million hospital admissions in Canada (CIHI, 2005b).

The Emergency Department

The emergency department of a hospital deserves the attention of health psychologists for a number of reasons. First, it is a common point of entry for many patients. In Canada, 53 percent of all hospital admissions take place through the emergency department, and the people admitted this way tend to stay longer than those who have pre-arranged admissions (CIHI, 2005b). However, most people visiting an emergency department are not admitted to the hospital. In fact, one study found that 29 percent of patients presenting at emergency rooms were discharged without a specific treatment or investigative procedure (Cooke, Arora, & Mason, 2003). Surprisingly, of these discharged patients, 15 percent had arrived by ambulance.

The second reason a hospital's emergency department deserves the attention of health psychologists is that patients often come to emergency in a state of distress or even disorientation, depending on the nature of the problem. Their treatment needs are pressing, and they are in a setting where it is likely that many other people have equally pressing treatment needs. The way hospital staff members interact with these people from their first encounter in admission is very important.

In psychological terms, admission procedures are important because they constitute the patient's first impression of the hospital. Have you ever noticed that hotels spend a disproportionate amount of money on the architecture and furniture in the lobby and that the reception staff is trained to be extremely pleasant? Clearly, hotel owners have read the literature on first impressions. But Canadian hospitals are not hotels. The admissions area of emergency departments can get very hectic, and the questions that need to be asked are far more personal than those asked at the reception desk of a hotel. Still, patients' impressions of the care they receive in a hospital will be affected by the demeanour and efficiency of the admissions staff. This "personal touch" might be easier to implement for patients who are coming into the hospital for a planned procedure in which there is little sense of urgency and the patient is prepared to provide the information required. However, many hospital admissions are not planned. They occur through the emergency department, which is arguably the toughest test of a hospital's admission procedures and the one that can have the greatest impact on the patient, if he or she is conscious.

In order to meet the various psychological needs of emergency patients, the emergency department must, at the very least, have sufficient staff and organization to provide expert attention as soon as possible after the patient has entered the hospital. An important early step in emergency medicine is **triage** (Concheiro, Diaz, Luaces, Pou, & Garcia, 2001), which is the sorting and classifying of patients to determine priority of need and proper location and means of treatment. The admissions and other staff must also have the interpersonal skills needed to communicate a sense of caring. Asking questions while fixing one's gaze on a computer screen doesn't establish real communication. Neither does stoicism. Often all that is required is someone who will pay immediate attention to the patient-to-be, by indicating that a doctor or nurse will be with him or her as soon as possible. Patients and their families appreciate knowing if there is going to be a wait and why.

triage: the sorting and classifying of patients to determine priority of need and proper location and means of treatment.

It could be argued that the realities of emergency room work clash with the expectations of patient-centred care and that, in general, emergency departments are simply not the places where psychological issues can be given any priority.

There are, however, things that can be done to attend to patients' psychological experiences in emergency. These could start with the admission procedure, which some researchers have suggested should be taken away from the emergency area and be staffed by physicians and nurse practitioners who can send patients directly to the appropriate part of the hospital (Mayled, 1998). In addition, health practitioners need the skills required to provide clear yet brief explanations of diagnosis and treatment options (see chapter 5 on communication in medical settings).

Patients in emergency departments also benefit from **continuity of care**, in which a designated staff person (usually a nurse) takes primary responsibility for a patient for the duration of his or her stay in emergency.

continuity of care: arrangement in which a designated staff person, usually a nurse, takes primary responsibility for a patient during a hospital stay.

The most expensive considerations may well be architectural ones. Crowding in emergency departments reduces privacy and increases distress. Well-designed departments can reduce crowding and provide adequate spaces for consultation with patients while at the same time minimizing staff movement between treatment stations.

Recovering from Surgery

We have looked at people who enter the hospital for just one day to have some surgical procedure performed. Of course, there are also many people whose surgical procedures require hospital-based recovery. For a number of reasons, post-operative recovery can be a difficult time psychologically. In addition to having to cope with the unfamiliar surroundings of the hospital, post-operative patients must manage varying degrees of incapacitation, unfamiliar bodily sensations, actions that may be painful or uncomfortable (like forced deep breathing and coughing), and uncertainty about the expected rate of recovery.

We have seen that one way to help many patients through the post-operative period is to provide good pre-operative education. This is designed to clarify for the patient just what to expect in terms of sensations, recovery rates, instructions, and so on. This preparation is called *psychoeducational care* (Devine, 2003; Lenz & Perkins, 2000). When applied to the post-operative period, psychoeducational care refers to the provision of information regarding self-care practices, further procedures, and typical patterns of recovery.

Pain Management Following Surgery

One of the most important factors determining a patient's satisfactory recovery from surgery (and consequently the length of his or her hospital stay) is pain management. Pain affects mood, and mood (depression, in particular) affects length of stay for certain patients (Schubert, Burns, Paras, & Sioson, 1992; Zalewski et al., 1994). We will be discussing pain and pain management more generally in chapter 11. At this point, we will look specifically at patients recovering from surgery. Of course, pain levels vary, though moderate to intense pain is not uncommon following some surgical procedures. In these instances, pain is most often treated through pharmacological analgesics such as morphine, although relaxation and other non-pharmacological techniques are also used.

A number of challenges arise when providing pain medication for post-operative patients. One challenge is to ascertain correct dosage. Under-medication will discourage the patient and be ineffective. Over-medication may be harmful when strong drugs, such as opioids, are used. Another challenge is the psychological issue of control we discussed earlier in the chapter. Patients may not like being dependent on other people to relieve their pain. In asking for pain medication, patients might feel that they are being weak or "whiny." Finally, they might not want to give the impression that their recovery is not going well and thereby risk lengthening their stay in hospital (Taylor, Hall, & Salmon, 1996).

patient-controlled analgesia (PCA): analgesic administration that is independently controlled by the patient.

To deal with these challenges, in the 1980s hospitals introduced **patient-controlled analgesia (PCA)**. As the term suggests, PCA puts the control of analgesic administration in the hands of the patient (Alon, Jaquenod, & Schaeppi, 2003). This can be done a number of ways, from intravenous administration to oral tablet. One common way is to give the patient a device that, when pressed, releases a certain dosage of the prescribed analgesic intravenously. The device allows practitioners to set the dosage as well as the **lock-out interval**, which is the time period between allowable dosages.

lock-out interval: the time period between allowable dosages, when patient-controlled analgesia is used. A device is set by a practitioner to control this period.

What happens when the responsibility for analgesic administration is passed to the patient? In general, studies have had encouraging outcomes. For example, women who had undergone gynecological tumour surgery required lower dosages of analgesics post-operatively when using PCA (Standl et al., 2003). Colon surgery patients who were in the PCA group used less sedation and analgesia and enjoyed faster recovery times than did the group whose medication was administered by staff (Roseveare et al., 1998). Similarly, bone marrow transplant patients who were in the PCA group reported lower pain intensity and used less medication (Zucker et al., 1998). A study of cardiac surgery patients found that the PCA group reported less pain post-operatively but that they used more medication than the nurse-administered group did (Boldt et al., 1998). All of these studies were prospective in design, with randomized assignment to group.

Another study included a third group of patients who were in a patient-controlled condition but received a placebo rather than an analgesic (Stainer, Grond, & Maier,

1999). A placebo is a substance that does not contain active medication but might bring about desired effects for psychological reasons, such as the patient's belief that it will work. Patients in this "patient-controlled placebo" group administered twice the amount of medication as patients receiving opioid analgesic.

It has been suggested by some researchers that PCA would be more successful if patients received training in the procedure before surgery (Owen & Plummer, 1997). As a test of this, a group of patients was shown an educational videotape on PCA prior to surgery. This group had more positive attitudes toward PCA and greater pain control and satisfaction four and eight hours after surgery than did the group not shown the tape (Knoerl, Faut-Callihan, Paice, & Shott, 1999). Another study placed half of the PCA patients in a pre-operative tutorial group and half in a control group (Griffin, Brennan, & McShane, 1998). It turned out that both groups used the same amount of morphine and reported similar pain levels, but the tutorial group experienced less nausea between 6 and 24 hours after surgery.

The effectiveness of PCA might also be affected by staff attitudes toward it. For example, nurse–patient relationships can be strained if nurses feel that they should have the responsibility for analgesic administration (Taylor, Hall, & Salmon, 1996). This may be one reason why Fulton (1996) found that nurses' attitudes toward PCA ranged from being very in favour of it to rejecting it absolutely. Some nurses may believe that they are accountable for their patients' pain levels, and this belief may run counter to PCA. Other nurses may believe that they are being accountable by introducing PCA properly and providing good patient teaching regarding its use.

The research on PCA shows that it restores some sense of control for the patient and results in effective pain management in the majority of cases. It is not surprising, therefore, to find that PCA is commonly used in Canadian hospitals. The research is inconsistent, however, about whether the PCA approach results in more analgesic use than do staff-administered approaches. The differences between studies may be due to differences in the nature of the surgery featured in each. Also, it is possible that there are some patients who are not well suited to PCA. For example, researchers at Simon Fraser University, York University, and elsewhere have found that patients with a more passive or avoidant pre-operative coping strategy tend to self-administer more analgesic when using PCA than do people with more active coping strategies (Cohen, Fouladi, & Katz, 2005). Also, other York researchers have found that older patients tend to administer less analgesic medication than younger patients do (Gagliese, Weizblit, Ellis, & Chan, 2005). Among adolescents, higher pre-operative expectations of pain correlate with PCA use (Logan & Rose, 2005), although male and female adolescents don't differ in the amount of analgesic they administer via PCA (Logan & Rose, 2004).

While PCA does tend to reduce opiate consumption and increase patient satisfaction, errors can occur. To minimize these, practitioners are advised to have the patient be the only person to use the device. Well-meaning family members can unintentionally overdose the patient. Also, because education on the use of the device is important, PCA should be offered only to patients who are alert enough to follow the instructions. These cautions combine with other safety issues, such as adequate monitoring of the patient and careful checking that the right medications are used and that the device is properly programmed (Cohen & Smetzer, 2005).

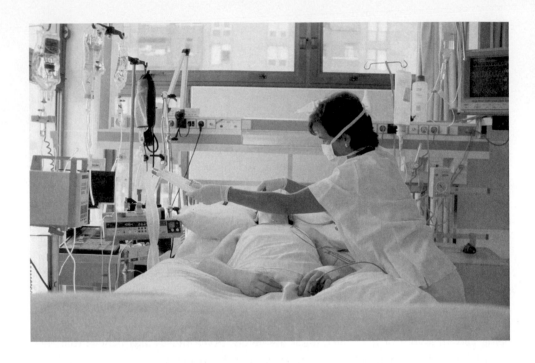

A modern ICU in which technology abounds.

The Intensive-Care Unit

Nowhere in the hospital is modern technology more prominent than in the intensive-care unit (ICU). It is the unit in which life-support machinery is used and where patients are closely monitored by a staff whose nurse-to-patient ratio is the lowest in the hospital. We made the point earlier in this chapter that the intensive-care units of hospitals are growing rapidly in terms of the number of beds dedicated to them. For these reasons, and also because the emotional consequences of an ICU stay can persist for up to a year after discharge (Rattray, Johnston, & Wildsmith, 2005), and because that emotional distress can be significant for family members as well (Wartella, Auerbach, and Ward, 2009), the ICU is an important area of study for health psychologists.

Interviews with patients after they have been in ICU have yielded some very interesting data regarding their experiences. Pallavicini-Gonzalez and colleagues (1995) discovered that patients in ICU go through three distinct stages. First, there is what the authors call the **incommunication stage**. In this stage, patients are either unconscious or barely conscious. Their memories of the experience are poor, but the memories they do have are somewhat strange. The equipment is imposing and the passage of time is unclear. The second stage is called the **readaptation stage**. At this point, patients become aware of their struggles to recover. It is during this stage that patients recognize their dependence on the machines, especially the ventilator, which helps them breathe. The equipment provides some reassurance, and patients perceive the staff as helpful. The final stage is the **reflection stage**, when patients try to piece together the details of the experience, wanting to know what happened to them.

Not all patients experience these stages, and some are moved out of ICU before they get through all three stages, which might explain why some patients have no recollection at all of their time in the unit. In fact, Russell (1999) discovered that 34 percent of the

incommunication stage: a period in ICU during which a patient is either unconscious or barely conscious.

readaptation stage: a period in ICU when a patient can sense a struggle to recover and recognizes his or her dependence on machines.

reflection stage: a period during which a patient who was in ICU tries to piece together his or her recent experience.

298 patients he interviewed had no memory of being in ICU, 42 percent had some memory of it, and 24 percent reported having clear memories of their ICU experience.

Upon discharge from ICU, patients can experience **relocation stress** (Beard, 2005), sometimes called **translocation stress** (Strahan & Brown, 2004). This is the stress caused by being separated from those things that were keeping patients alive—the one-on-one care and the technology.

Consistent with the readaptive stage identified by Pallavicini-Gonzalez, Russell's participants remembered that the close surveillance of technology and staff provided them with a sense of safety. Interestingly, though, they reported that the staff provided a feeling of safety more than the machines did. In fact, 76 percent of the participants had either a vague memory of the technology or no memory of it at all. Of those who did remember it, some found it reassuring, while others were frightened by it because of a lack of knowledge regarding what the machines were for. Many of these machines monitor vital physiological processes and can be set to sound an alarm if levels drop below or rise above a certain level. Not surprisingly, patients found these alarm sounds to be quite frightening when they did not know what they signalled. Much of this fear can be alleviated if nursing staff provide basic explanations of the machines' functions.

Indeed, the data from Russell's interviews suggest strongly that *communication* is a key factor in determining a patient's psychological reaction to ICU. However, there are a number of reasons why communication is sometimes poor in ICU. For instance, it has been found that nurses sometimes deliberately minimize communication with the patient in order to minimize their own anxiety (Leathart, 1994). Not talking to patients makes it easier to *dehumanize* them. This concept, taken from social psychology, refers to seeing people as objects rather than as human beings. Health practitioners may do this, not because they are uncaring but because it is easier emotionally to think of an ICU patient as "the acute MI in bed three" rather than as Mr. Chen, who has six grandchildren and may die.

Communication is also inhibited by the fact that patients in ICU tend to be unresponsive (Turncock, 1991). Some, of course, are unconscious. If they are conscious, they may have tubes inserted in their throats. Nevertheless, communication is still important. Just because a patient can't respond does not mean he or she can't *hear*. This is illustrated most graphically by the recollection of one of Russell's interviewees:

> I remember hearing a voice saying "His blood pressure's dropping, it's 60, 57, 55."
> Another voice saying, "Tell me when it is 50 and we can all knock off." I still think of
> that sometimes. (p. 789)

Overheard remarks like these carry a great deal of psychological weight for patients. Russell discovered that these remarks were remembered six months later and, as the quote suggests, may be remembered forever. These remarks were cited by Russell's participants as a major source of upset. Another patient recalled hearing one staff person telling another that they might as well pull the plug. It is doubtful that the staff member would have made that remark had he or she known the patient could hear.

When staff members do talk to patients, they tend to focus on procedure—what is going to be done—rather than on the patient's condition and progress (Baker & Melby, 1996). Information regarding progress may be very important for patients who have entered the readaptation stage and are aware of the struggle they face.

Russell also asked participants if they would want to go into ICU again if they were seriously ill or injured. Eighty percent said they would, 10 percent said they would leave that decision to the doctor, and 10 percent said they would not want to be a patient in ICU again, even if their condition warranted it. Studies report that between 14 and 27 percent of people experience post-traumatic stress disorder after their ICU experience (Cuthbertson, Hull, Strachan, & Scott, 2004). Russell also discovered that some patients need to revisit the ICU after their recovery to put the experience behind them. These revisits can be good for staff morale, too. Unfortunately, they can be difficult to schedule in a unit in which trauma is an everyday experience.

From the work of Russell and others, we can conclude that the psychological impact of ICU can be strong and lasting. Many patients credit the technology and staff with saving their lives, although recurring thoughts, dreams, nightmares (Minton & Carryer, 2005), or hallucinations (Magarey & McCutcheon, 2005) about the experience are not uncommon. As is the case throughout a hospital, communication is central to reducing the distress of being in ICU. Staff must assume that patients can hear them, and they must provide feedback regarding the patient's condition and progress.

This feedback must also be provided for the families of the patients, who, in the spirit of family-centred care, are essential to the patient's treatment. Family members experience the enormous stress of seeing the patient critically ill and in an unpredictable condition. They also see other patients who may be dying, and they hear alarms sounding on a regular basis (Lower, Bonsack, & Guion, 2003). A study of family members found that their need for information was one of the most often met. On the other hand, their need to talk about feelings of guilt and anger and the possibility of the patient's death were most often unmet (Browning & Warren, 2006).

Communication with family and visitors is often a low priority for ICU staff members, who are busy with critically ill patients (Greenwood, 1998). However, such communication is extremely important because the decisions made in ICU and NICU (neonatal intensive care unit) can involve end-of-life issues. These decisions are often fraught with ethical dilemmas. Who should make these decisions? Two prevalent, yet somewhat contradictory, models are called upon when answering this question (Leuthner, 2001). The **expertise model** implies that the physician and the intensive care team are best equipped to make end-of-life decisions. They are best informed and most objective. The **negotiated model** implies a sharing of the decision between the practitioners, patient, and family. Of course, in ICU, the patient is not always able to provide input, and so family and loved ones are left to represent the patient.

For ethical reasons, Leuthner and others argue in favour of the negotiated model because it reduces paternalism on the part of the practitioner and includes the family in one of the most important decisions they will ever face (Carter & Leuthner, 2002; Leuthner, 2001). A study of parents' wishes regarding end-of-life decisions in NICU has suggested that parents want the final call to be with the health care professionals because the burden of the decision is just too great for most parents to bear (Brinchmann, Forde, & Nortvedt, 2002). Having said this, the same authors advocate for keeping the family well informed and as involved as possible in this extremely difficult process.

We have looked at what it is like for adults to be in ICU with its collection of machines, tubes, and IV drips. But can you imagine a patient who weighs less than one kilogram (under two pounds) hooked up to all this, caught in a battle for life? These are

expertise model: model in which the physician and the intensive-care team are assumed to be best informed and most objective, and therefore best equipped to make end-of-life decisions.

negotiated model: decision-making model that allows decision making to be shared among the practitioners, patient, and family.

some of the patients in the neonatal intensive-care unit. Some have been born prematurely, and then taken quickly away from the delivery room to NICU. Other newborns (neonates) may be full-term births but suffering from a prenatal (before birth) or perinatal (during birth) condition that requires intensive care. It could be argued that the NICU is the most emotionally intense unit in the hospital, for both parents and staff.

CASE 6-1 THE PEDIATRIC INTENSIVE-CARE UNIT

Joy Tompkins (2005) was a nurse working in pediatric intensive care when a four-year-old girl was admitted with what would be diagnosed as Guillain-Barre Syndrome, a nervous system disorder in which paralysis gradually moves up the body, leaving the patient dependent on life-support. The condition tends to reverse itself in time, with movement and feeling gradually returning in reverse order of how paralysis had set in.

The nurse watched as her patient gradually became weaker and eventually motionless, requiring intubation and mechanical ventilation. Joy decided to plan out her patient's days as though they were that of a normal four-year-old, and to communicate these to her as she lay still, able to respond only by blinking. Joy provided tape recordings of music and the voices of the child's family (visiting was very limited when this patient was in pediatric intensive care).

Weeks passed this way. Finally, the paralysis began to recede. In Tompkins' words, "The disease left as silently as it arrived." Then came the day when that breathing tube could finally be removed:

> Our eyes were locked on one another's, we counted to three and the physician pulled the breathing tube out. She coughed, her eyes widened, her pupils dilated, and her hands trembled as she reached up to her face to feel where the tube was once secured. Her hands moved toward me, she reached out and abruptly slapped my face! I was stunned and momentarily taken back. But I knew, she knew, we understood. It was finally over. Then she grabbed me, we hugged, and we cried. For the first time I could hear her voice—a wonderfully froggy sound. Two decades have passed, and still, it is her eyes that I remember (pp. 424–425).

Parents' stress levels are often extremely high in NICU. One factor that predicts parents' stress is when and where they first see their baby (Shields-Poe & Pinelli, 1997). Even parents of full-term infants are shocked when they see the wiring, tubing, and blinking lights, combined with the noises the machines make in NICU (Jamsa & Jamsa, 1998). With this in mind, staff and psychologists can help prepare the parents by giving them a sense of what to expect and what is common in NICU. Family-centred care is obviously very important in NICU, as is *primary care*, which means that the same nurse cares for a given baby throughout the stay (Morris, 1999). Parent involvement is encouraged. They must learn to care for their new baby and may be able to notice subtle but important changes that the busy nursing staff could miss.

In working with parents, an approach has been advocated that goes by the acronym TEAM (Ward, 1999). In the TEAM approach, the practitioner will *teach*, by preparing the parents for the NICU and explaining the equipment, *empower* the parents by giving

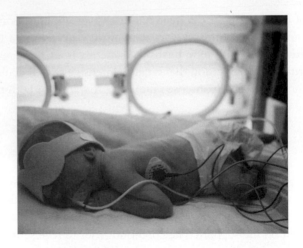

A prematurely born baby looks particularly vulnerable in a neonatal intensive care unit.

them tools to be involved in the care as soon as possible, *assess* the family's needs and develop a discharge plan, and *monitor* how well the program is meeting the parents' needs and how well the parents are coping. Health psychologists can play an important role in the TEAM approach, especially given that NICU can be a hectic place for nursing staff.

Discharge

For some patients, leaving the hospital involves more than simply gathering up their belongings and walking out the front door. It is often the case that further treatment or, at the very least, rest and general convalescence are required. As a result, there must be some form of support provided for patients after discharge. All of these considerations require **discharge planning**, a process in which post-hospital care is organized and risk is assessed (Tennier, 1997). By *risk*, we are referring to social problems, lack of support, and medical conditions that result in a high degree of dependency (Evans & Hendricks, 1993).

It is interesting to compare the impressions of practitioners and patients when it comes to discharge planning. A study in Switzerland found considerable discrepancies in this regard (Rentsch, Luthy, Perneger, & Allaz, 2003). When asked if their discharge was planned or being planned, 41 percent of patients reported that no discharge plan had been made. However, when the health care team members were asked the same question, only 27 percent of them felt that no discharge plan had been made. Also, the health care teams felt the discharge plans had already been discussed in 51 percent of the cases compared to patients' impressions that such plans had been discussed in only 41 percent of the cases.

Caring for a family member who has just returned home from the hospital can put a strain on family resources. Someone might have to take time off work, and expectations stemming from traditional roles within the family may provide challenges (Lemos, Suls, Jenson, Lounsbury, & Gordon, 2003). Lemos et al. discovered that male and female cardiac patients returning home tried to persevere with their traditional gender-typed roles.

In addition, there will be instructions to follow regarding such things as medication, diet, and activity levels. These can be complicated and can be made worse by a patient who stubbornly refuses to follow the regimen. Even patients who understand the purpose and pattern for their post-discharge medication might think they are taking

discharge planning: a process in which post-hospital care is organized and risks, such as social problems and lack of support, are assessed.

that medication correctly when, in fact, they are not (Kerzman, Baron-Epel, & Toren, 2005). All of these potential strains are magnified if home relationships are not strong to begin with. Good discharge planning tries to take as many of these factors into account as possible.

Imagine the possible sources of anxiety at discharge time for those parents whose babies spent the first weeks of their lives in NICU. Research in this area has discovered that parents' anxiety is related not only to the baby's condition (e.g., weight and central nervous system complications) but also the perceived personal and social resources of the parents (Auslander, Netzer, & Arad, 2003).

And what about the other end of the age spectrum? Elderly patients are likely to have a more difficult time at discharge because they have grown accustomed to hospital support and routine. Problems with discharge planning for elderly patients are compounded by the fact that the planning is time consuming, and so it must be started early. This means that discharge planning is taking place before the patient's medical condition has been clearly ascertained and effectively treated. One study that analyzed the discharge-planning process for 31 elderly patients discovered that, for 27 of the patients, their planning started before their medical status was clearly determined. As a result, discharge plans had to be altered in 26 of these 27 cases (Wells, 1997). As you can imagine, patients find these changes upsetting, especially when they lengthen the hospital stay. In fact, even the communication of early discharge decisions can be stressful because, at that point, some patients might doubt that they can manage at home. One attempt to reduce the stress associated with discharge plans involves conducting an accurate assessment of the patient's cognitive functioning upon admission to hospital (Sands et al., 2003). This level of functioning helps predict a patient's ability to cope when discharged.

There are other challenges involved with discharge planning for elderly patients. Elderly patients may, for example, have other functional problems that are secondary to the medical condition that's being treated but still very important to consider with regard to discharge. Can they walk unaided? Can they see and hear well? Also, what are the physical capabilities of the principal caregiver? This question is especially important if the caregiver is an elderly spouse. One way to take these functional limitations into account is to involve family members in the discharge-planning process. The study of the 31 patients mentioned above found that this involvement was sporadic (Wells, 1997), even though the staff regularly discussed discharge, or at least they thought they had (Rentsch et al., 2003). Thus, effective involvement of the family and good communication with them and among the multi-disciplinary health team can improve outcomes after discharge (Bauer et al., 2009).

The major dilemma in working with elderly patients is balancing adequate care with the patient's desire for autonomy. Patients may have realistic worries about "never being the same again" after their hospital stay (Keefler, Duder, & Lechman, 2001). To cope with these worries, elderly patients may shun assistance or attempt to veto discharge plans that create an impression of dependence rather than independence. Social workers, psychologists, health care workers, and family members must help the patient make discharge plans that achieve this balance between safety and autonomy, and they must do so without being patronizing or dictatorial. The key is to involve the patient in the discharge-planning process as much as possible, which requires a sensitive understanding of the patient, the options available, and the patient's health. This understanding can be achieved only if all involved adopt a team approach.

Palliative Care

Most patients are discharged from the hospital because their condition is improving and their prognosis is good. Some patients, however, have illnesses that are **progressive**, meaning the illness will continue to worsen in spite of treatment; when a progressive illness is **advanced**, it is at a stage where death is imminent. For these patients, care shifts from an attempt to cure the illness to a regimen intended to control pain and other symptoms. A primary goal of care, then, is to provide a good quality of life (as much as possible) for the time remaining. Other goals include controlling symptoms, supporting family and making sure they are satisfied, and staying focused on patients' perceptions of purpose and meaning in their lives (Kaasa & Loge, 2003). These are the goals and focus of **palliative care**. This care involves compassionate communication; an understanding of patient and family values and goals of care; the relief of suffering; management of pain, depression, delirium, and other symptoms; an awareness of the processes of grief; and sensitivity for the soon-to-be bereaved survivors (Abrahm, 2003).

In Victoria, British Columbia, Deanna Hutchings has proposed a model for palliative care. Based on the Theory of Human Becoming, it dovetails nicely with the fundamentals of palliative care. The model contains a number of important elements, including caring for the whole person and maintaining a necessary presence and dialogue with the dying person (Hutchings, 2002).

Once the decision has been made to move to palliative care goals, another important decision to be made is where the palliative care will be administered. There are three common choices: the hospital, the home, or a hospice. Hospice facilities represent a compromise between the comfort of home and the medical support of a hospital. We will focus more on the palliative care provided by hospitals, but it is important to note that hospital palliative care may also involve discharge planning and all the issues we discussed earlier in relation to that process, if the patient and family express a desire to move the site of care to the home or elsewhere. Because of this, palliative care is most successfully provided by multidisciplinary teams that include such people as physicians, nurses, social workers, chaplains, and psychologists. A review of studies assessing the effectiveness of such teams discovered that they yielded outcomes that were as good or better than those provided by individual planners with regard to patient and family satisfaction, patients being cared for as they wished, a reduction of family anxiety, less patient pain, and better symptom control (Hearn & Higginson, 1998).

Staff members working in palliative care face death on a daily basis. To cope with this, they must shed the prevailing belief shared by most acute care workers that death is tantamount to failure (Payne & Kalus, 1998). They must adjust their goals to make them consistent with those of palliative care. Moreover, they must come to grips with their own anxieties and fears about death. Perhaps this is why one study found that hospice nurses were less death avoidant and less concerned about their own death than were emergency room nurses (Payne, Dean, & Kalus, 1998).

While practitioners in acute care do everything they can to keep patients alive, practitioners working in palliative care must make difficult decisions that will actually result in a patient's death. Technology exists to keep patients alive virtually indefinitely—long after there is any hope that the patient will regain consciousness. Independent of debates about **euthanasia**, palliative care practitioners must decide when it has become futile to keep a patient artificially alive. It is a physician's responsibility to give a **Do Not Resuscitate order** (DNR) stating that CPR or other interventions will not be used if the patient stops breathing.

DNR decisions are complex. Most practitioners believe that seriously ill patients deserve the right to be involved in resuscitation decisions. However, how does the physician decide which patients are sufficiently "seriously ill" to warrant that discussion? When this decision is made, the patient moves from the world of the living to that of the dying (Teno & Coppola, 1999). In some palliative care units, these discussions are initiated with patients who are expected to live less than six months. At this point, palliative care units provide what has been called a **mixed management model of care**. They prepare the patient for eventual death while at the same time providing life-sustaining treatments (Teno & Coppola, 1999).

Do Not Resuscitate order: an order given by a physician indicating that CPR and other interventions are not to be used if the patient stops breathing.

mixed management model of care: the preparation of a patient for eventual death while simultaneously providing life-sustaining treatments.

CHAPTER SUMMARY

The procedures and rules of a hospital affect patients' sense of control and their ability to cope with being in hospital. Specifically, patients feel a loss of control in environments characterized as *total institutions*, in which many decisions are made for them. Patients sometimes respond to this loss of control with *reactance*: they disobey instructions in order to retain a sense of autonomy. Patients' sense of control is increased with the use of care plans that allow patients to be involved in decision making.

Medical procedures can be placed on a continuum of invasiveness. Invasiveness is defined in both physical and psychological terms. The procedures might physically "invade" the body or cause psychological distress in the form of embarrassment or anxiety. For example, both physiologically and psychologically, a colonoscopy would be considered more invasive than a mammogram.

The nature of care and preparation for medical procedures can help patients cope. An important example is the provision of information that matches a patient's need for such information. Also, providing patients with realistic expectations regarding recovery and treatment outcome is important, as is the introduction of relaxation techniques. Patients who are taught to self-monitor for emotions and symptoms will cope better with hospital procedures.

Specific hospital departments (emergency, surgery, intensive care, discharge, and palliative care) present their own challenges for the patient, and the coping and care needed to manage these challenges differs across departments. The emergency department is important as an entry point to the hospital and a place where patients may be in distress. Well-organized admission and triage procedures and adequate staffing are key factors in helping patients cope with this environment.

In addition to the list of considerations for good preparation, post-operative recovery focuses considerable attention on pain management. Patients can gain a sense of control over this via patient-controlled analgesics and other psychological techniques such as relaxation and distraction. Time spent in intensive care is often disorienting and, of course, anxiety producing for family members. A person's stay in ICU can be divided into stages, including the incommunication stage, the readaptation stage, and the reflection stage. The discharge process requires considerable planning, especially for the frail elderly. This planning must take into account the capacity of family members and others to care for the patient when he or she returns home. The potential stressors on the family at this time must also be addressed. In palliative care, the goals are to control symptoms, support the family, and focus on the patients needs. This requires an awareness of the grief process.

Review Questions

1. What are the psychological effects of high-tech medical procedures?

2. What is it like to be a patient in a hospital?

3. How does the experience of being a patient in a hospital differ from one department to another?

4. What are the factors affecting a person's ability to cope with a hospital stay, and what roles do staff play in that coping process?

5. In what ways does a person attempt to regain a sense of control when in hospital?

Chapter 7
The Health Care Provider

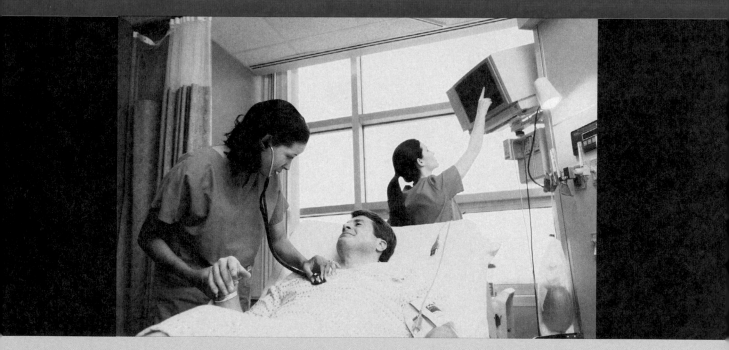

CHAPTER OUTLINE

PHYSICIANS
NURSES
OTHER HEALTH CARE PROFESSIONALS

Learning Objectives

After studying this chapter, you will be able to

■ Describe what students encounter during each year of medical school

■ List and explain the main sources of stress for health care practitioners, especially physicians and nurses

■ Explain the roles that nurses play in the health care system

■ Identify the major sources of stress experienced by nurses

■ Describe major gender-related issues in health care including patient preferences and practitioners' experiences with discrimination

- Outline important psychological issues related to physical rehabilitation and discuss the roles that physical therapists and occupational therapists can play in relation to these issues

- Explain how medical technologists can help patients cope with high-tech medical procedures

Jason's older sister was a doctor. He remembered how she had studied for an entire summer for her MCAT exams, a requirement for entrance to many medical schools. Then came the interviews and the anxious waiting. Jason also remembered very clearly the day his sister learned that she had been accepted into medical school. She was thrilled; her parents were thrilled. Even Jason was thrilled, even though he was only 10 years old at the time.

Jason remembered all this because he was now studying for his MCAT exams. Like his sister, he had given up an entire summer to study, putting in 40 or 50 hours a week. There were times, though, when he doubted whether it was all going to be worth it. When he talked to his sister recently, she made it clear that the practice of day-to-day medicine and the rigours of medical school weren't always as thrilling as that day when she found out she had been accepted into medical school. The work-load at that time was staggering. And when she became a physician, she discovered that her ability to actually cure people was more limited than she had expected.

On her more discouraging days, she felt as though her job was to help people cope with conditions that either never went away or went away only to come back. Certainly, medical science had no magical power to heal. And there was the pager. At first, it had seemed like a symbol of her success. Now it felt more like a ball and chain. It beeped at the most inconvenient of times, and she had to answer it. But despite all these negatives, Jason's sister said that she ultimately felt proud to be a physician and that she really did feel that she was helping people in important ways.

> Very little of my work was glamorous in the TV drama
> sense, but much of it was intense.
>
> A family physician (Coombs, 1998, p. 175).

It is important for health psychologists to understand the training health care providers receive as well as the stresses and joys they experience on a daily basis. For example, it is of little use to tell family physicians that they must spend more time listening to patients and explaining things to them if we have no appreciation for the number of patients those physicians must see in a given day. Similarly, a nurse may appear less compassionate than a patient would like simply because that nurse has a large patient load that includes some seriously ill people. In short, health psychology must be practised within the realities of the health care system.

In this chapter, we will look closely at what it is like to be a health care provider. Our main objective is to provide some understanding of the realities of the work. The hope is that, through this understanding, health psychologists can be effective members of inter-professional teams that provide modern health care.

In this chapter, we will present a series of profiles of health practitioners and the work they do. Since we are not physicians, nurses, physical therapists, or technologists (or other practitioners), we have relied on published research and first-hand interaction with practitioners and students to create these profiles. These profiles apply widely across the professions we will discuss. By the same token, we must never lose sight of the fact that there is considerable variation among practitioners. Some never experience stress or gender-related discrimination. Many find medical school to be quite straightforward and manageable. Others have been virtually paralyzed by these issues.

The research that studies health professionals is more likely to focus on challenges than rewards, and so in this chapter you will read about these challenges. We need to know about the stresses and problems practitioners face. However, the majority of people working in these professions find this work extremely rewarding. Every working day, no matter how long and demanding it might be, people in these fields can say they were dedicated to helping others. In order to truly understand what these professionals experience, we urge you to talk to people who work in health care to get first-hand accounts of their work.

PHYSICIANS

When we teach our health psychology classes, we often ask how many students aspire to a career in medicine. Sometimes as many as a third of the class will raise their hands, but almost always at least one person raises his or her hand. Perhaps you would have raised yours, if asked, "Do you plan to be a physician?" Perhaps you can relate to the people in the opening vignette. Few professions match medicine for responsibility and status. The ability to alleviate suffering and the responsibility for life itself can make a career in medicine both intensely satisfying and extremely stressful.

During the past decade in Canada, we went from a surplus to a shortage of physicians (Chan, 2002). Between 1993 and 2001, there was a 5.1 percent decline in the number of physicians practising in this country and a corresponding 7 percent increase in the workloads of general and family practitioners. While these trends might not translate into major changes to the way health care is delivered, they did raise some concerns (Watson, Roos, Katz, & Bogdanovic, 2003). More recent data are more encouraging, however. The Canadian Institute for Health Information (2005a) reports that the number of physicians in Canada increased by 5 percent between 2000 and 2004. Currently, there are 189 doctors for every 100 000 Canadians. Also, for the first time, more physicians returned to Canada than left to practise in other countries. In this section, we will explore reasons why people want to become physicians, and we will look closely at the medical school experience. We will then discuss some of the realities of day-to-day practice.

Choosing a Career in Medicine

The reasons people choose a career in medicine are not particularly surprising. A study in Britain found that students were drawn to medicine because of career opportunities, a desire to work with people and help patients, and the chance it provided to use their personal skills and pursue their interests in science (Crossley & Mubarik, 2002).

Who chooses medicine? Considerable research has looked at personality factors in medical students and practitioners. For example, medical students tend to score higher on measures of perfectionism than do first-year arts students (Enns, Cox, Sareen, & Freeman, 2001). Perfectionism, though, can be either adaptive or maladaptive. It is adaptive when it is associated with striving for achievement. It is maladaptive when it is associated with excessive concerns about being evaluated. Medical students who score higher on adaptive perfectionism had higher expectations for their academic success and were more conscientious. Conscientiousness is the best personality-related predictor of success in medical school (Ferguson, James, O'Hehir, & Sanders, 2003), although nothing predicts this success better than past academic performance, which explains about 23 percent of the variance in medical school grades (Ferguson, James, & Madeley, 2002). Students scoring higher on the measure of maladaptive perfectionism were more prone to distress in the form of depression and hopelessness (Enns et al., 2001).

Medical School

Because health psychologists need to understand what it is like to be a health care professional and because the intense training a physician receives is primarily biomedical rather than psychosocial, it is helpful for people studying health psychology to have an appreciation for the nature of medical school training. Such an appreciation may allow us to understand the comments of one medical student, who said of his sociology class, "I waited for half an hour for a *fact* to write down" (Sinclair, 1997, p. 166; author's emphasis). Or another student who said of his psychology class, "Psychology's interesting when she [the lecturer] is talking about [doctor–patient] interaction, but nothing much else" (Sinclair, 1997, p. 166).

There have been a number of good books written about medical school, some for premed students who want to know how to survive medical school, others by anthropologists and other social scientists trying to understand the culture of medical school. One book that actually does both is *Surviving Medical School*, by Robert Coombs (1998). Though over 10 years old, Coombs's book still makes a number of observations that apply well to medical schools today. Indeed, no other book has come along in recent years to challenge his observations. In his book, Coombs takes the reader through medical school, year by year. Of course, he discusses trends. Our experiences with medical students at various universities suggest that there are, in fact, noticeable trends, although they don't apply to all medical students.

First Year   In Canada, students enter medical school after already obtaining at least one post-secondary degree. All the same, they are called "undergraduates" in most medical programs. With few exceptions, these programs are four years in length. A notable exception is the University of Calgary, which offers a three-year program.

No matter how much warning incoming students may have had, they are almost always surprised by the workload in first-year medicine. The volume of work and the time pressures are overwhelming. One student said, "It's like trying to drink from a fire hose" (Coombs, 1998, p. 19). In fact, it is virtually impossible to learn everything that is presented, which causes some first-year students to wonder if they should have come to medical school in the first place. Their self-confidence might plummet. Yet despite the onslaught of material, few students fail first year. Somehow, they survive.

Second Year   The second year is often considered the most stressful academically. Having said that, students come to accept the fact that they can never know everything there is to know. They tell first-year students not to be upset that they can't possibly learn everything.

For second-year students, a transformation begins to take place. They tend to become more assertive and confident. They ask questions that show they are now focusing on what needs to be known for the patient's sake, rather than for the exam. Concurrently, second-year students begin to really feel the financial strain of medical school. Most don't feel they can continue to rely on their families for financial support, and costs continue to mount. A 2001 study found that medical students in Ontario anticipated carrying an $80,000 debt at graduation (Kwong et al, 2002).

The social relationships of many second-year students begin to take on a unique quality. A differentiation emerges between those on the "inside" and those on the "outside" of medical school. Second-year students report enjoying an elevated status among those on the "outside," yet loneliness is common. This is partly because many people on the "outside" don't understand medical school and are generally unsympathetic to students' complaints about it. They reason, "How hard can school be? You don't have to work for a living. And besides, you're going to be a doctor and make lots of money."

Third Year   In most medical programs, third-year students begin to gain clinical experience. They interact directly with patients in a hospital setting, which yields a whole new set of insecurities, because despite having learned a great deal in their first two years, they still do not know enough to take on the duties of a physician. A third-year student is not yet a physician but is expected to act like one. This becomes especially evident when third-year students must perform physical examinations. Students say that their lack of confidence was blatant when they were drawing blood or starting IVs, for example. Third-year students in clinical training are struck by the large gap between their textbooks and the real patients they are treating. Patients almost never lay out their symptoms as neatly as the textbook does. This leaves the student feeling uncertain and inadequate. Interestingly, Coombs reports that patients are usually quite accepting of these students.

In these clinical settings, it is imperative that students learn as much as they can. However, the teaching in these situations can be sporadic, given the demands of clinical work on the physicians. Students report that they are sometimes taught, but often just feel like they are getting in the way.

A number of challenging issues emerge for third-year students—issues that they must either come to grips with or be plagued by throughout their careers. For example, they must accept that they will make mistakes. They must strike a balance between clinical competence and unrealistic expectations of perfection. There is also the challenge of contagion. Few of us have to worry that we will get seriously ill from contact with people in our jobs. The physician, however, must deal with this all the time; physicians are exposed to many contagious diseases. One student admitted to spending less time than he should have with a typhoid fever patient because of fear of contagion. That student is not alone.

Closely related to this danger is the susceptibility to accidents that may compromise a student's health. In Canada in 2003, three percent of people working in health care suffered activity-limiting injury. This is about twice as many as those working in business and about half as many as those working in industry (Wilkins & Mackenzie, 2007). In a study of medical students at Washington University School of Medicine, 30 percent of third- and fourth-year students reported having had a needle-stick injury (Patterson, Novak,

Mackinnon, & Ellis, 2003). A study in France revealed that 38 surgeons per 100 per year had experienced a percutaneous (through the skin) injury (Denis et al., 2003). This study found no differences between practitioners and students in the incidence of blood-related accidents. A study conducted in England, Wales, and Northern Ireland found that there had been 588 of these injuries between July 1997 and June 2000. Of these, 200 were injuries to doctors and 210 to nurses and midwives (Evans, Duggan, Baker, Ramsay, & Abiteboul, 2001).

It is in the clinical training of third year that most students have their first encounter with critically ill patients. Students are taught to cope by immersing themselves in the work, using humour, and coming to realize that death is not always tantamount to failure. Dealing with death is in itself another major challenge. The practice of medicine can become a battle between death and medical science, and the sense of responsibility and emotion surrounding this can be daunting.

It is important to note that, while our discussion focuses on physicians, many of these challenges also apply to other health professionals. Nurses are an excellent example. In one case, a nurse was reported to have organized a memorial service for a patient who had died after a long hospital stay. No other nurses attended the service. When asked why, one nurse said that if she started to cry for this patient, she would cry for all the patients she had seen die and would never stop crying (Coombs, 1998).

Fourth Year
By senior year, students' socialization into the medical community is virtually complete. They will likely have developed a way to cope with the emotions associated with medical practice—that is, students are not so emotionally distant as to appear uncaring, but not so close as to suffer from the exhaustion of limitless caring, sometimes called **compassion fatigue**. Also, by this point most students have lost their sense of idealism regarding medicine, beginning to accept that there are limits to a physician's powers to heal and to always be correct.

compassion fatigue: a lack of energy among health care professionals, particularly nurses, who are constantly working in an environment in which suffering is common.

Residency
Residency is the time during medical training that bridges the attainment of a medical degree and the establishment of practice. It is during residency that MDs learn specialties. Residency typically lasts from two to five years, depending on the specialty, with further training after that for more advanced specialties.

Residents encounter a rather sudden increase in accountability, and a decrease in sleep. In the United States, the Accreditation Council for Graduate Medical Education passed regulations for medical residents (*Resident Duty Hours Language: Final Requirements*, 2003). According to these regulations, residents may work a maximum of 80 hours per week, with no shift longer than 24 hours, and with 10 hours of rest between shifts. These rules are equivalent to Canadian expectations for residents, with some variation between programs. Generally, residents are "on call" every fourth night. This usually means a work shift that can start at 8 a.m. and end at either 8 a.m. or noon the next day. Often, there is little opportunity for sleep during this period. A survey of residents found that, while they would appreciate shorter hours and more time to sleep, they appreciated the learning opportunities provided by these on-call shifts. This was particularly true for surgical residents, who work notoriously long hours (Green & Poole, in press).

To help residents cope with the demands of on-call nights, they are advised to prioritize their sickest patients, respond to their beepers quickly, and always try to prevent rather than treat (Peterkin, 1998).

This medical school graduate is one of a growing proportion of females entering the profession.

Physicians' Emotional Involvement in Their Work

At the beginning of this chapter, we quoted a family physician who said that his work wasn't as dramatic as television depictions but that it was still intense. It is important for health psychologists to learn to appreciate this intensity. One of the best ways to do this is to talk with physicians and get first-hand accounts. This, however, requires the physician to be comfortable disclosing some personal feelings and accounts, and we must remember that physicians themselves report a reluctance to discuss emotional aspects of their work. Another way to gain insights into what physicians face on an emotional level is to read sections of medical journals in which physicians write candidly about dilemmas they have faced. For example, try reading the section entitled "Salon" in the *Canadian Medical Association Journal*, "A Piece of My Mind" in the *Journal of the American Medical Association*, or "Filler" in the *British Medical Journal*.

In an issue of the *Canadian Medical Association Journal*, a physician describes one of his elderly patients. As you read this passage, contrast the clinical description provided in the first sentence and the information in the two sentences that follow:

> The history in her chart was all too familiar: 89-year-old woman from nursing home; Alzheimer's disease; inadequate oral intake; admitted with dehydration, hypernatremia and acute renal failure. She had a shock of frizzy white hair and a face crisscrossed with myriad fine wrinkles. Her eyes betrayed her confusion. (Hwang, 2006, p. 1138)

These sentences capture the very human nature of a physician's work.

In similar sections of medical journals, you may read articles like "No Pretending Not to Know," in the *Journal of the American Medical Association*, in which a physician recounts a case involving an ultrasound exam confirming that a woman's fetus had no skull or brain. At first, he grappled with the question of who should inform the woman about the results of the exam. In this case, the radiologist could have let her own doctor, or perhaps the resident obstetrician tell her, but the woman could sense something was wrong. There was no avoiding the truth, as the physician's description makes abundantly clear:

> "Did you see the baby's head?" Her question couldn't have been more to the point. My internal debate about who should tell her the results becomes academic. I pull up a chair next to her. "We've found something wrong with your baby, Mrs. J. Your baby's brain didn't develop." She is stunned, and for what seems like several minutes she says nothing. From her facial expression I can tell that she doesn't really understand. I try again to explain what is wrong with her baby. "What will happen when the baby is born?" she asks. I tell her that her baby will live a very short time and then die. She wants to know if there is any way her baby can live and even be somewhat normal: I have to tell her no. (Brown, 1988, p. 2720)

Few professions require such emotional conversations. Of course, not all conversations between patients and physicians involve negative emotions. Patients are elated by a normal childbirth and relieved when they are informed they are not seriously ill. The point is that such extreme emotional experiences are potentially exhausting and distracting. For this reason, most physicians find that they must learn to control their emotions, avoiding the peaks and valleys their patients may encounter. To do this requires the ability to distance oneself from a patient. It is difficult, however, to do this and still make it clear that the physician truly cares for his or her patient's well-being.

Physicians and Stress

The responsibility inherent in being a physician has the potential to cause great stress. In a 2008 study of family physicians in Canada, 42 percent reported high stress levels (Lee, Stuart & Brown, 2008). Researchers at the University of Saskatchewan found that emergency physicians, surgeons, and family practitioners reported the highest levels of stress (Lepnurm, Lockhart, & Keegan, 2009). In addition to the basic responsibilities that come with caring for patients, there are other aspects of a physician's work that can add to the problem. For example, physicians often work under time pressure (Richardsen & Burke, 1991). If you have ever sat in your doctor's waiting room for any length of time, you will probably have noticed how often the phone rings as people try to make appointments. Many of these people want to see the doctor as soon as possible, and so they are "fit in." While we appreciate this consideration as patients, it makes for a hectic day for the physician, who must try somehow to strike a balance between giving people ample time and moving patients through in a timely fashion. And all of this is thrown into chaos if an emergency occurs. It is not surprising that work overload is cited by physicians as a significant source of stress (Aziz, 2004; Burke & Richardsen, 1990). A large 1998 study in Canada found that 62 percent of physicians considered their workload to be too heavy (Sullivan & Buske, 1998). This situation persists today (Bergman, Ahmad, & Stewart, 2003).

Are There Enough General and Family Practitioners in Canada?

In their final year of medical school, students declare their preferences regarding residency—the time during their training in which they move from having a general medical degree to being a practitioner. These choices provide indications of the distribution of the kinds of physicians we can expect in Canada. In recent years, fewer and fewer students have been choosing family and general practice. In 2003, 25 percent of the residency positions available in family medicine were unfilled (Wright, Scott, Woloschuk, & Brenneis, 2004). In 2003, it was estimated that Canada was approximately 3000 general practitioners short of the population's needs (Gutkin, 2003). The number of general practitioners per 100 000 people in Canada has remained stable for at least the last 15 years, though the total number of physicians increased by 8 percent between 2004 and 2008, which was faster than the growth of the general population during those years (Canadian Institute for Health Information, 2008 (http://secure.cihi.ca/cihiweb/dispPage.jsp?cw_page=media_20091126_e. Accessed December 17, 2009).

What are the consequences of this shortage? For one thing, Canadians are having a harder time finding a family doctor. Thirty percent of our population has no family doctor, and 4.5 million people in the country tried unsuccessfully to find one between 2002 and 2003 (Gutkin, 2003).

Because the health of the population has been shown to improve with access to primary care physicians (Starfield, 1994), attempts are made to keep the ratio of general practitioners to specialists at 50:50 in Canada (Gutkin, 2003). There are factors, however, that make this ratio difficult to maintain. In fact, a recent study of medical students in Alberta and British Columbia revealed that only 20 percent of them planned to enter family practice (Wright et al., 2004). The authors identified a number of factors that explain the students' plans, including medical lifestyle (e.g., acceptable work hours), orientation to society (e.g., long-term relationships with patients), prestige, a focus on in-hospital care, and scope of patient problems. A person's values regarding these factors will influence choice regarding medical practice. Others have argued that, while the values students bring to medical school are influential, so too are the experiences they have as medical students (McPherson, 2005). Thus, if family practice is presented as an attractive option, more people will opt for it.

One other solution stemming from this position is to allow practising specialists who have grown dissatisfied with their practice to re-certify as family practitioners. In addition, the belief that family physicians are overworked and underpaid must change (MacKean & Gutkin, 2003).

Overload leads to **burnout**, a condition that was first identified among nurses but is now recognized in numerous health professionals, including physicians (Thomas, 2004). The symptoms of burnout have been well documented. They include emotional exhaustion, perceived ineffectiveness, cynicism, and dissatisfaction with relations with co-workers (Spickard, Gabbe, & Christensen, 2002). Those experiencing burnout perceive a lack of correspondence between what they think they should be doing and what they actually are doing (Maslach & Leiter, 1997).

burnout: a condition that is similar to compassion fatigue and includes symptoms of physical exhaustion, depersonalization of patients, and feelings of discouragement and low accomplishment.

The best way to prevent burnout is for health professionals to consider their own well-being throughout their careers. This can be done by spending more time with friends and family, focusing on spiritual and personal needs, finding meaning in work, setting limits at work, and maintaining a positive outlook (Weiner, Swain, Wolf, & Gottleib, 2001).

Of course, despite physicians' best efforts, some patients die, and physicians must face the stress of communicating bad news to patients and their families. This stressor is more common in some specialties, such as oncology. In a study of this source of stress, 38 physicians were asked to recall a time when they had given a patient bad news. They were then asked some questions based on their memory of the encounter. Most physicians followed published guidelines when giving bad news, though this did not eliminate the stress they felt when doing so. They felt that they had done an effective job of reducing their patients' distress but that their own discomfort and stress had started prior to the encounter and lasted beyond the end of the encounter. The conclusion of this research was that published guidelines on the giving of bad news are helpful in reducing patient distress, but more attention must be paid to the distress felt by the physician (Ptacek, Fries, Eberhartd, & Ptacek, 1999).

Good training in the communication skills that apply directly to the giving of bad news can help reduce this distress. In Canada, a survey showed that 88 percent of ophthalmologists favoured such training for medical residents (Zakrzewski, Ho, & Braga-Mele, 2008). Yet other studies show that less that one-quarter of residents receive such training in moderate or extensive amounts, and 37 percent receive none at all (Herber et al., 2009).

Considerable research indicates that male and female physicians experience stress differently. For example, one study showed that workload, *per se,* was not a predictor of psychological distress for women (Gareis & Barnett, 2002). Instead, manageability of hours or schedule fit was a predictor, which indicates that women physicians face a somewhat different set of stressors than men. Women face greater discrimination in the workplace and, in a larger context, experience strain between their work and family roles (Robinson, 2003). Still, female physicians tend to report higher degrees of job satisfaction than their male counterparts (Robinson, 2003), although an intergenerational comparison of female physicians whose mothers were also physicians found that daughters felt more stress and less satisfaction than their mothers had. This stress existed in spite of daughters' citing of more support mechanisms than their mothers had to help manage work–family conflicts (Shrier & Shrier, 2005). Perhaps this support is not keeping pace with increased expectations and workload.

There has been considerable research aimed at discovering the extent to which these stress levels put physicians at greater risk for suicide than the general public. One study in Britain reported that female physicians were more likely than females in the general public to commit suicide, whereas male physicians were *less* likely than males in the general population (Hawton, 2001). Based on this, Hawton concluded that female physicians were at greater risk for suicide. However, another author pointed out that, because rates of suicide are lower for females generally, in fact, the rates for male and female physicians were not significantly different from one another (Verberne, 2002).

Uncertainty as a Source of Stress   Another significant source of stress that is not always obvious to the general public is **uncertainty**. We like to think that medicine is a precise science, but it is not. In an article by Lurie and Sox (1999), the authors make two important points regarding uncertainty. First, "Clinical examinations and other diagnostic tests are imperfect" (p. 493); second, "The consequences of medical decisions are inherently uncertain at the decisive moment" (p. 493). This means that a given diagnosis is often accompanied by a degree of uncertainty, and **prognosis**, a prediction of how a medical condition will change in the future, is even more uncertain. Physicians work for the most part with probabilities rather than absolute certainties.

uncertainty: a significant source of stress for physicians, resulting from the fact that the consequences of medical decisions are uncertain.

prognosis: a prediction of how a medical condition will change in the future.

It is likely that the majority of patients do not have a good idea of how much uncertainty exists in medical decision making. In a study of this, patients were asked to estimate the accuracy with which diagnosis would be made for six different conditions (Hamm & Smith, 1998). Interestingly, the patients' estimates did not differ across conditions. This suggests that people have a general belief about the accuracy of medical science and that they apply that belief regardless of the condition in question. The medical truth is that some conditions are considerably easier to diagnose than others, and so certainty varies from one situation to the next.

Furthermore, the patients' estimates of accuracy were quite unrealistic. In particular, they underestimated the likelihood of a false-positive diagnosis. Taken collectively, then, this means that patients believe that diagnostic certainty is greater than it really is, regardless of the condition being diagnosed. It should be noted, though, that patients who had direct experience with a given condition were slightly better at estimating the diagnostic accuracy associated with it.

This level of faith in medical science only adds to the potential stressfulness of uncertainty for the physician. A patient thinks a physician should know and does know exactly what the diagnosis is and what the treatment should be, while, on the other side of the consultation, the physician is very aware of the level of uncertainty that exists. The physician's response to this situation ranges from communicating that uncertainty with a probability statistic through to denying the uncertainty altogether (Hamm & Smith, 1998).

When a group of physicians was presented with an identical video depicting an atypical breast case, half of them diagnosed benign breast disease, one-third identified breast cancer as the most probable initial diagnosis, six percent called it normal, and nine percent gave a diagnosis unrelated to breast disease (McKinlay et al., 1998). Generally, physicians' reports of certainty were high in this study.

Now, before you give up on medical decision making altogether, remember that the decision making simulated in this study is *preliminary* in nature. Further tests would likely be ordered to yield a more definitive diagnosis. However, diagnostic uncertainty may result in excessive testing, which is another source of stress for physicians and patients.

As we have already mentioned, medical tests don't completely eliminate uncertainty either. Tests differ in their **sensitivity** and **specificity**. Sensitivity refers to a test's ability to pick up true positives—actual cases of the disease. Specificity refers to a test's ability to pick up true negatives—cases where disease is definitely *not* present (see Lurie & Sox, 1999).

A final point to make about uncertainty in medical decision making is that it is more common among primary care physicians than it is among specialists. **Primary care physicians** include those in general and family practice. Differences between primary care physicians and specialists regarding certainty are not due to differences in skill levels. They exist because physicians of all types tend to solve problems through pattern recognition. Primary care physicians see a wider range of symptoms; therefore, they have far too many patterns to remember and often too few particular symptoms to even form a pattern in the physician's experience. Also, more problems are presented early to primary care physicians, before patterns have been well established. In contrast, specialists see a much narrower range of problems and symptoms, usually at a stage where the diagnosis has become clearer.

In spite of these differences between primary care physicians and specialists, patients usually report greater satisfaction with their primary care physician than with their

sensitivity: the ability of a test to correctly identify those who have a particular disease.

specificity: the ability of a test to correctly identify those who do not have a particular disease.

primary care physicians: those physicians in general and family practice.

specialist, because the former provides continuous, person-focused care. By contrast, the specialist tends to provide low-continuity, disease-focused care (Rosser, 1996). This may mean that patients are less concerned about specialized diagnostic certainty than they are about the nature of the relationship they have with the physician. Or, it may simply be that patients generally believe that levels of certainty are high and similar across diagnostic settings (Hamm & Smith, 1998).

Regardless of these patient perceptions, the most important points to remember here are that decision-related uncertainty is a significant source of stress for physicians, and that there is no easy solution to the problem. Perhaps this is why physicians sometimes cope by using rather dark humour. For example, DiMatteo (1991, p. 267) describes physicians telling one another that a patient has GOK, which stands for "God only knows."

Physician Impairment   The conditions accompanying stress are doubly problematic for a physician. These conditions compromise both the physician's own quality of life and the physician's ability to provide care to others. For these reasons, researchers looking at physician stress have coined the term **physician impairment**. It refers to a state in which stress-related symptoms interfere with the physician's ability to perform his or her job (Gold, 2004).

One of the most troubling causes of physician impairment is substance abuse. While alcoholism and drug addiction are no more prevalent among physicians, use of prescription drugs is, especially those drugs used to treat psychological distress. This is due in part to physicians' access to these drugs (O'Connor & Spickard, 1997; Ward, 2005). Issues of dependency have prompted a call to make alcohol and drug problems a health promotion issue for physicians (Brewster, 2001; Knight et al., 2002). Weir points out that it can be difficult for physicians to seek treatment because the admission of a drug or alcohol dependency can have implications for their licensing. As a result, physicians are more likely to deny their problems or suffer alone. By the time the problem surfaces in the workplace, it is probably well advanced. This reticence to seek treatment is unfortunate for many reasons, not the least of which is that recovery rates are around 80 percent when treatment is sought. This treatment is most effective when it is uninterrupted and residential, featuring family involvement and prudent return to practice with adequate follow-up and support (Weir, 2000).

physician impairment: a state in which stress-related symptoms interfere with physicians' abilities to perform their jobs.

Gender Issues in Medical Practice

No analysis of health care practitioners would be complete without a discussion of gender issues. Among physicians, men and women bring different attributes to their work, make somewhat different career choices, perceive their work differently, and communicate with their patients differently. Furthermore, patients' own gender influences their preferences for the gender of their physicians.

The "Feminization" of Medicine   In 1959, six percent of medical students in Canada were female. Thirty years later, that number had jumped to 44 percent. In 2003, 58 percent of medical students in Canada were female (Burton & Wong, 2004). In terms of practice, in 1997, 25 percent of physicians practising in Canada were women (CIHI, 2001). By 2004, that percentage had grown to 30 percent (CIHI, 2006). (See Figure 7-1.) In 2008, women made up more than half (52.1 percent) of the new general practitioners

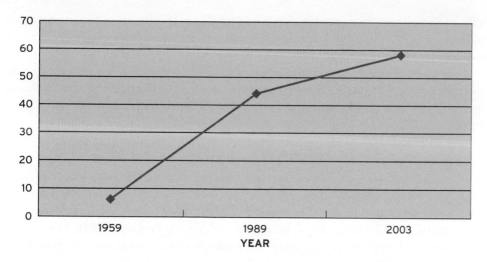

Figure 7-1 Percentage of Female Medical Students in Canada

The percentage of female students in Canadian medical schools has risen sharply in recent generations.

Source: Canadian Institute for Health Information. (2006). *Full-time equivalent physicians report: Canada, 2002–2003 and 2003–2004.* Ottawa, Canada.

in Canada and 45 percent of new specialists (Canadian Institute for Health Information, 2008 (http://secure.cihi.ca/cihiweb/dispPage.jsp?cw_page=media_20091126_e. Accessed December 17, 2009).

Regarding career choices, a study by researchers at L'Université Laval, where 74 percent of the medical students are women (Burton & Wong, 2004), discovered that female physicians place more importance on their private lives when making professional life decisions than do their male counterparts (De Koninck, Bergeron, & Bourbonnais, 1997). Interviews with female physicians yielded some clear statements about the way values affected their career choices: "What is important for women is not the size of their practice, the income, or publications, but the type of practice, personal satisfaction, fulfilling needs . . ." (De Koninck, Bergeron, & Bourbonnais, 1997, p. 1828). Another woman put it this way: "I didn't want to be just a doctor . . . I wanted a family, children . . . I wanted a life that I would call normal . . . I said to myself, if I go into neurosurgery, I'll never be able to" (De Koninck, Bergeron, & Bourbonnais, 1997, p. 1829).

In a study of medical students at the University of Toronto, 27 percent of the men said they would choose surgery compared to only 10 percent of the women (Baxter, Cohen, & McLeod, 1996). This difference was based, in part, on perceptions regarding the lifestyle demands of the work and the amount of interaction (or lack thereof) surgeons have with patients. Other research with medical students has found that men say they want to work longer hours than women do and that women are more likely to want to spend leisure time with their family and friends (McFarland & Rhoades, 1998). A study at the University of Alberta found that the gender gap in preferred work hours actually widened for pediatric residence between 1998 and 2006 (Shamseer et al., 2008).

Once they have made their career choice, female and male physicians have different perceptions of their work. Females are more likely to feel what is called **role strain**. This means that they feel torn by the demands of multiple roles—e.g., physician, mother, and

role strain: stress as a result of the demands of multiple social roles, such as health care practitioner and mother.

wife, to name a few—and they feel they are never able to handle any of them to their satisfaction, which is compounded by the fact that women report feeling a greater sense of responsibility to others (Gross, 1998).

The trend toward increased proportions of female physicians has led some theorists to speculate on the changes this will bring to the profession. The **feminization of medicine**, as this trend has been called, may bring about changes to the balance between cure and care we talk about later in the chapter in our discussion of nursing. This trend may also affect the nature of interactions between patients and physicians (Levinson & Lurie, 2004).

Female physicians are more likely to involve their patients as partners in care decisions (Roter, Hall, & Aoki, 2002). More generally, female physicians are considered to be skilled providers of patient-centred care (Levinson & Lurie, 2004), which has a positive impact on treatment outcomes (Stewart, 1995). These outcomes may be further enhanced when physician and patient are of the same sex (Franks & Bertakis, 2003). This is good news for female patients, as the number of female physicians grows, but not so good for males, who might have more difficulty finding a male doctor (Levinson & Lurie, 2004). Interestingly, an analysis of more than 70 000 patients at the Queen's University Family Medical Centre over a five-year period between 1988 and 1993 found that female residents in family medicine saw 68.4 percent of the female patients. This means that, in the final stages of their training, female physicians see significantly more female patients than male physicians do, at least in family medicine (Sabir, Godwin, & Birtwistle, 1997).

Given these trends, what do we know about patients' preferences for female or male physicians? It might stand to reason that patients' preferences regarding the gender of the physician would depend on the nature of the examination being conducted, given that some exams are more personally intrusive than others. With this possibility in mind, researchers looked at patients' perceptions of male and female physicians giving anal and vaginal exams (Van Elderen, Maes, Rouneau, & Seegers, 1998). Both male and female patients rated female physicians higher than males on a curing dimension for giving anal examinations. For vaginal exams, which were of course rated only by female patients, females were rated more highly on the curing dimension, the caring dimension, and a consulting dimension (see the "Nurses" section later in the chapter for more on curing and caring). Patient preferences are certainly more complex than simply men wanting male physicians and women wanting female ones.

Given that medicine has historically been male-dominated, it is not surprising that women physicians are more likely to perceive discrimination than men are (VanIneveld et al., 1996). A study of internal medicine house staff in Canada found that 70 percent of female residents said they had experienced discrimination by attending physicians, whereas only 23 percent of male residents reported such discrimination. Similarly, 88 percent of female residents reported discrimination from patients (38 percent of male residents reported this), and 71 percent of female physicians reported discrimination from nurses, compared to 35 percent for male residents (VanIneveld et al., 1996). Female physicians were also much more likely than male residents to state that they had experienced sexual harassment from attending physicians, peers, and patients. In a study of more than 450 female physicians in Ontario, 76 percent said that they had experienced sexual harassment from patients (Phillips, 1996).

Much of this work was conducted in the 1990s. Have things changed since then? An intergenerational study in 2007 of mothers and daughters who were both physicians

feminization of medicine: the trend toward an increased proportion of female physicians in the profession.

indicates they have not. In that study, daughters reported less discrimination than their mothers experienced based on race and ethnicity, but jut as much based on gender (Shrier et al., 2007). In addition to the overt expressions of discrimination, there are what have been called "micro-inequities" (Robinson, 2003). These might include fewer opportunities for career advancement, social isolation, and a lack of recognition for good work.

In summary, physicians deal with numerous stressors and challenges throughout their careers, however rewarding they might find them. Demanding caseloads and hours, emotionally challenging communication, high expectations, and other realities of medical practice are some examples. Men and women bring different approaches to medical practice and different ways to deal with its challenges.

NURSES

Modern nursing in Canada is a profession facing many challenges and opportunities. The constant changes in medical science demand that nurses stay absolutely current in their knowledge. The roles that nurses play in modern hospitals are expanding to include many advanced areas, such as transplant specialization and cardiac care. In fact, the area of advanced-practice nursing is expanding rapidly in Canada.

The Nature of Modern Nursing

When most lay people think of nurses, they think of people who are involved in **caring** for patients in hospital. This has been distinguished from the **curing** of people, which is more often associated with the physician's role (Barnes, 2005). In providing care, nurses make sure that medication is properly administered, that the patient's hygienic and dietary needs are taken care of, and that the emotional needs of the patient are considered as well. In general, nurses are patient advocates in the hospital setting. Of course, nurses work in settings other than hospitals, including community settings, as public health nurses, as home care nurses, and so on. All of these roles that we commonly associate with nursing have existed for many years.

There are those who believe that the caring side of health care is being eroded somewhat as modern medicine becomes more technical and specialized (Krebs et al., 1996). They feel that this shifts health care to a cure orientation. Curing patients is, of course, very important; however, when the cure–care balance is disrupted, the nurse's role can be devalued, which is a problem because the reality in health care is that care is more prevalent than cure. Nurses are using two strategies to make the importance of their role clear: first, they are emphasizing the importance of a care orientation; second, they are engaging in training and job re-definition so that they can become more actively involved in cure-related practice.

This advanced training and re-definition of roles in modern nursing has given rise to **advanced-practice nursing**. The Canadian Nurses Association (CNA) defines advanced practice as "the role of a nurse working within a specialty area where superior clinical skills and judgement are acquired through a combination of experience and education" (CNA, 1997a, p. 2). In advanced practice, nurses' roles expand to include teaching, consultation, and research. Concerns have been expressed, however, that this might come at the expense of their caring role (Donnelly, 2003) and that the challenges brought on by

caring: the role that most lay people think is the primary task of nurses.

curing: the role that most lay people think is the primary task of physicians.

advanced-practice nursing: nursing that includes teaching, consultation, and research within a specialty area where superior clinical skills and judgment are acquired through a combination of experience and education.

Modern nursing often requires advanced training and the ability to manage the stress of large patient loads.

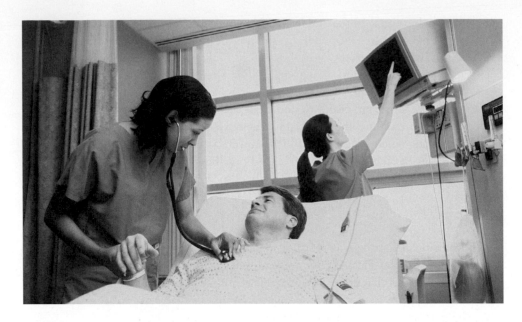

multiple roles within the practice will increase nurses' stress levels (Cummings, Fraser, & Tarlier, 2003; Musclow, Sawhney, & Watt-Watson, 2002). However, if these concerns can be dealt with, they need not outweigh the benefits of providing nurses with the opportunity to contribute more fully to the care and cure of patients.

There are a number of general categories of advanced nursing practice. One is the **clinical nurse specialist**. Nurses with this specialty hold a master's or doctoral degree in nursing and have extensive experience in a given clinical specialty. They may work with individual patients, families, and even in the areas of population health and policy (Canam, 2005). Another category is the **nurse practitioner**. The nurse practitioner might work in rural, remote settings, where physicians are often in short supply. As a result, the nurse practitioner performs functions that might otherwise be performed by a physician. The Canadian Nurses Association points out that, for the nurse practitioner, "caring and curing overlap" (CNA, 1997a, p. 4). The nurse practitioner combines medical knowledge with advanced nursing practice (McNamara, 2009). This category is formally recognized across Canada, with 1026 licensed nurse practitioners across the country in 2005 (CIHI, 2006). Sixty-four percent of these are found in Ontario. As is often the case when roles change and expand, there is debate in health care regarding the most appropriate scope and boundaries for the nurse practitioner. Experience has shown that nurse practitioners can make valuable contributions when the roles and responsibilities are clearly defined (Hass, 2006).

Nursing, then, is a profession in which ongoing education has become essential in order to keep up with advances in technology and nursing research. Many people entering the profession have a four-year bachelor's degree in nursing rather than a registered nursing degree that may take two to three years to attain. It is clearly a field with exciting challenges. At the same time, nursing can be a very stressful profession, as we will see later in this section, and funding cutbacks in health care affect nursing significantly. Thus, nursing is a profession in which the demands are high and the resources often inadequate.

The Canadian Nurses Association predicted a shortage of nurses in the order of 59 000 to 113 000 by the year 2001 (CNA, 1997b), with a 46 percent increase in demand for nurses. While there has been a small increase in the number of nurses practising in Canada since

clinical nurse specialist: a nurse with a master's or doctoral degree in nursing and extensive experience in a given clinical specialty.

nurse practitioner: nurses who often work in rural, remote settings, frequently performing functions that would be performed by a physician if available.

2001, a significant shortage still exists as a result of an aging (and thus retiring) workforce in nursing (O'Brien-Pallas, Alksnis, & Wang, 2003), turnover (Rondeau, Williams and Wager, 2008), and a lack of young people entering the profession. In addition, the population in general is aging, putting increasing demands on the health care system.

Why should all these aspects of modern nursing matter to health psychologists? First, increased demands combined with a shortage of resources is a recipe for stress. As we will see in this section, stress is a problem in nursing, for both nurses and patients. You may remember from our discussion of hospital stays in chapter 6 that we cited Canadian research indicating that patient satisfaction was correlated with nurses' self-reports of burnout (Leiter, Harvie, & Frizzel, 1998) (see Focus on Canadian Research 6-1). Burnout and stress are closely related.

The second reason that health psychologists should be concerned with the changes in nursing is that people in health care are not immune to lifestyle-related illnesses— illnesses they spend so much time treating. Third, a considerable amount of hospital research in health psychology involves nurses. Nurses may be asked to administer research protocols in addition to their regular duties. When conducting this research, it is essential to have some understanding of the demands such involvement places on nurses' already hectic schedules and the implications that our conclusions and recommendations will have for nurses' work.

Stress in Nursing

People who work in professions in which suffering is common are susceptible to compassion fatigue (Schwan, 1998). Even for the most caring of people, there are limits to the amount of energy someone can dedicate to other people's welfare. When those limits are exceeded, nurses with compassion fatigue must either become less compassionate or reduce the number of patients they treat. For nurses who work in trauma-related settings, the symptoms of compassion fatigue mimic those of post-traumatic stress disorder, including anxiety, exhaustion, and sleep disruption. Closely related to compassion fatigue is burnout, which we have already discussed in this chapter.

The consequences of stress and its related conditions—compassion fatigue and burnout—are significant. One study found a demonstrated relationship between patient incidents, such as falling and medication errors, and nurses' scores on a stress index (Dugan et al., 1996). Not only do patients notice burnout when being cared for (Leiter, Harvie, & Frizzel, 1998), but also nurses with burnout miss more shifts, so patients may miss the nurses entirely (Parker & Kulik, 1995). Worse still, nurses who suffer prolonged burnout tend to leave the profession altogether (Parker & Kulik, 1995). Turnover can be problematic, given the important role nurses play and the resources dedicated to nursing education (Hayes et al., 2006; Rondeau, Williams, and Wager, 2008). Moreover, nurse turnover is related to patient health outcomes. One study found that, with each loss of a full-time nurse in nursing homes, risk of infection increased by 30 percent and hospitalization by 80 percent (Zimmerman, 2002).

The causes of stress are numerous and begin as soon as nurses enter the profession from training. In fact, the transition from student nurse to practitioner can be the first major source of stress. This has been called **reality shock** (Kramer, 1974) and is defined as the reaction to the discrepancy between a training environment and an actual work

reality shock: the reaction to the discrepancy between a training environment and an actual work environment.

environment. Newly hired nurses report that they thought they had been adequately trained but quickly realize that they still have much to learn and that it must be learned quickly (Charnley, 1999). The sudden role shift from student to practising nurse can be frightening, since nurses now feel that they should know everything. They find it hard to cope with the volume of work and feel guilty when things don't get done in a timely way. New nurses sense a gap between the high standards of care they were taught and the lower standards that are the reality of nursing due to heavy demands and limited resources. One conflict many nurses must resolve is the one that exists between the nurturing, humanistic nature of nursing on one hand, and the high-tech, high-traffic demands of modern medicine on the other. Finally, there is the stress of "learning the system," from finding out where supplies are kept to developing relationships with colleagues (Charnley, 1999).

For experienced nurses, stress appears to come from a number of sources, from the work environment to job responsibilities (Santos et al., 2003). The sheer volume of a nurse's work responsibilities and the need for multi-tasking in modern nursing are also often-cited causes of stress. At any given moment, a nurse may be required to take numerous tests, manage supplies, complete paperwork, administer medications, and reassure worried family members (Flakus, 1998). Long hours can also be a problem as a number of hospitals have 12-hour shifts. Stress has been shown to be higher for nurses in these shifts compared to their 8-hour counterparts (Hoffman & Scott, 2003). Also, nurses interviewed by University of Toronto researchers talked about an "effort–reward imbalance" in which the long hours, multi-tasking, and patient loads are not duly recognized (Hall & Kiesners, 2005).

It would stand to reason that some nursing specialties are more stressful than others. For example, oncology (pediatric oncology, in particular) can be very demanding. A study in Australia found that 70 percent of oncology nurses reported moderate to high degrees of emotional exhaustion (Barrett & Yates, 2002). Booth (1998) has studied the intense stress that accompanies unexpected patient death during surgery. This is particularly stressful because the surgical staff may feel that the death was caused by the intervention (and they may be correct). Even if surgery was the only hope for the patient, staff are often left with the feeling that unexpected death during surgery was due to human error, whether it was or not. Few other professions combine doubts about one's own sense of competence with life-and-death situations.

Stress is a significant problem in nursing but is not an insurmountable one. There are ways in which nurses can cope effectively with the stressors of their job, and there are ways institutions can improve the work environment to reduce those stressors. For the nurses themselves, coping ability depends on social factors and personal factors (Boey, 1999). **Social factors**, as the term implies, refer to the nurse's social network—family, friends, and co-workers.

Personal factors include personality characteristics and coping strategies. For example, nurses with high self-esteem and a clear sense of control are less prone to stress. In terms of coping strategies, those who are more stress resistant tend to avoid negative, emotion-focused coping. Instead, they use problem-focused coping, trying to find ways to make their job more manageable rather than dwelling on the frustration and anxiety they may feel. Another important personal factor is **psychological empowerment**, which includes finding the work meaningful, having a sense of autonomy (Kramer & Schmalenberg, 2003), feeling competent, and having a positive impact. Research at the University of Western Ontario has found that nurses with this sense of empowerment are

social factors in stress: the elements of a person's social network, such as family, friends, and co-workers, that affect ability to cope with job stressors.

personal factor in stress: personal characteristics, such as high self-esteem and a clear sense of control, that enable some people to cope better with job stressors.

psychological empowerment in stress: a personal factor in stress that can include finding work meaningful, having a sense of autonomy, feeling competent, and having a positive impact.

more likely to stay in the profession and feel satisfied with their work (Laschinger, Finegan, Shamian, & Wilk, 2004).

The feeling of being in control that is so helpful in reducing stress can be greatly influenced by hospital management. Laschinger (2004) calls supportive management and policies *structural empowerment*. According to the **job strain model**, a job with high strain is one that features both high demands and low control (Karasek, 1979). Policies intended to enhance nurses' sense of control have indeed been shown to reduce stress and burnout. Such policies include group meetings, better communication up and down the hierarchy, and more say in job design (Felton, 1998). When these are in place, it is also likely that nurses will feel more committed to their institutions, which is another antidote to burnout (Hinds et al., 1998).

job strain model: a model that suggests a high-strain job is one that includes high demands and low control.

One of the grand ironies of work in the helping professions is that many people working in them spend most of their energy looking after other people and very little looking after themselves. After all, most people who are drawn to professions like nursing want to help others. The problem, of course, is that if nurses don't look after themselves they become more vulnerable to stress and burnout, and ultimately less effective at helping others.

In this vein, we are reminded of what airline flight attendants say to passengers before takeoff. It goes something like this: "In the unlikely event of cabin depressurization, a yellow mask will drop from the overhead compartment. Place the mask over your nose and mouth and begin breathing normally. *If you are travelling with young children or others who need assistance, put your mask on first, before assisting others.*" At the heart of this instruction is the reality that we can't help others if we pass out ourselves. This works as an excellent metaphor when teaching nurses the importance of maintaining their own health.

OTHER HEALTH CARE PROFESSIONALS

Physicians and nurses are not the only health care professionals deserving of a health psychologist's attention. In this section, we will look at two other health care professions in which psychology can play a central role. Certainly, our list of professions discussed in this chapter is far from exhaustive. You are invited to think of ways in which psychology can make constructive contributions to the work of others providing health care.

CASE 7-1 THE LONG ROAD BACK

May was extremely disturbed that she had no memory whatsoever of the event that left her so debilitated. One minute she felt fine, and the next she woke up in a hospital, having no idea how she got there. She did know, however, that something terrible had happened—she could feel nothing in her right arm or right leg, and she couldn't talk.

May, who was 61 years old, had suffered a stroke, or cerebrovascular accident (CVA) as it is known medically. During the stroke, the blood supply to the left side of her brain had been cut off due to a blockage in an artery. May's family had been told that no one could say for sure just how profound her disability would be. It would depend on biology, medicine, some luck, and May's motivation for rehabilitation.

<Case Continued>

The first few days in the hospital, May did show some improvement. Some of her speaking ability returned, much to the relief of her family, but she still found verbal communication enormously frustrating. And she was experiencing great difficulty with movement; getting up to go to the bathroom was a major undertaking. She wondered how she and her husband would ever manage outside the hospital. These thoughts were so discouraging for May that there were times when she wished the stroke had just killed her and put an end to everything.

That cloud began to lift, however, when May met Joyce. Joyce was the physical therapist assigned to help May on her long road to rehabilitation. Joyce's skill and encouragement became vital to May, who found herself working harder than she had at any time in her life. Soon May started to feel like a professional athlete, training for the biggest game of her career.

Physical Therapists and Occupational Therapists

Physical therapists and occupational therapists (or PTs and OTs, as they are often called) are important members of health care teams focused on rehabilitation. The roles of PTs and OTs overlap somewhat; however, occupational therapy is most often associated with the treatment or rehabilitation of physically or emotionally disabled people. Physical therapists might also help people with disabilities, though their patients may be coming to them for a broad range of reasons, from injury recovery to pain management and more.

In Case 7-1 you met May, a woman who had suffered a stroke that affected every aspect of her life. Many of the challenges that May and her physical therapist face as they work on May's rehabilitation are psychological in nature. In addition to knowing what May is capable of and what exercises to give her each day, Joyce must be sensitive to issues of motivation, adherence, mood, and social support.

Goal Setting   It is clear that physical therapists and occupational therapists must enter into a partnership with their patients if they hope to be successful. In other words, the relationship cannot be one in which the patient is passive and dependent upon the therapist. Nowhere is this more evident than in the area of goal setting (Barnes & Ward, 2000; Siegert & Taylor, 2004). We know from sports psychology that people are much more likely to work toward a goal if they have had a say in *choosing* that goal. This is not usually done by the athlete alone, nor should it be done by the patient alone. This is because the athlete and patient cannot be entirely objective regarding what is possible. In some cases, patients might let discouragement get the better of them and set goals that are not ambitious enough. In other cases, they may become impatient and set goals that cannot be reached in the short term, setting themselves up for frustration.

When setting goals for rehabilitation, it is important to acknowledge a difference between goals set in the hospital setting and those addressing integration back into the community (Playford et al., 2000). The former tend to be more short term and pragmatic in nature, relating to such things as mobility, hygiene, communication, and patient safety. The latter are more long term, addressing such things as social functioning.

The psychology of rehabilitation is as important for patients as sports psychology is for elite athletes.

Adherence   Closely related to goal setting is adherence (Sluijs, Kerssens, van der Zee, & Myers, 1998). The therapist cannot oversee all the work a patient must do. For improvement to occur, a patient like May must work diligently on rehabilitation on her own. She must adhere to the rehab regimen that she and the therapist have agreed on. All these factors are interrelated; for example, if May feels that she was part of the goal-setting process, she will feel more committed to achieving these goals and will be more likely to adhere to the regimen. Education, cognitive interventions, and behavioural interventions also affect adherence. (See Chapter 5 on Communication in Medical Settings for a more detailed discussion of adherence and factors affecting it.)

Behavioural Interventions   Most rehabilitation patients need some form of **external reinforcement**. That is to say, the physical therapist, friends, family, and other practitioners must encourage and praise the patient's successes. For May, improvement will not be measured on a minute-to-minute basis. She will need to be reminded of what she can do today that she could not do during the early weeks of her rehabilitation. Also, May will need to find ways for **self-reinforcement**. She must pat herself on the back and maybe even give herself tangible rewards for achieving certain goals. One of the best things about physical rehabilitation is that at least some of the success can be *measured objectively*. May can measure how much farther she has walked and how much more clearly she can speak as she progresses through the regimen. Objective criteria for success are the bread and butter of behavioural interventions. They allow for reinforcement to be directly contingent on desired behaviour and allow the patient and physical therapist to *shape* the program by gradually increasing observable standards. Perhaps this is why therapists tend to set goals for their patients that are physical in nature and thus objectively measurable. The downside is that psychological goals might be ignored by the practitioner adopting this focus (Wressle, Oberg, & Henriksson, 1999).

Cognitive Interventions   The power of effective behavioural intervention is clear in physical therapy. However, May's program cannot rely solely on behavioural strategies. It must also focus on her thinking, and that is the stuff of cognitive intervention. There are at least three areas in which this is crucial. First, May must be ready to make the necessary changes and to take on the challenges of rehabilitation (Wagner & McMahon, 2004). Recall the Stages of Change Model we discussed in chapter 1 and the Contemplative Stage.

Second, she must believe that she can reach an identified goal. You may remember also from chapter 1 that we call these **efficacy beliefs**. These beliefs can be tricky to instill. It isn't usually enough to simply *tell* people that they are capable of doing something. Those messages must be based on some *evidence* that the patient will accept as being reasonable. Efficacy beliefs, then, are often built on past successes. A classic example is an attained goal that the patient initially thought was unattainable. Also, it is possible that experienced physical therapists alter their patients' efficacy beliefs simply by the way they interact with them. In other words, they assume that the patient is capable, and the patient lives up to that assumption. More research needs to be done on the efficacy-enhancing strategies employed by physical therapists, however, to confirm this.

external reinforcement: the encouragement and praise from physical therapists, friends, family, and other practitioners needed by rehabilitation patients for their successes.

self-reinforcement: praising or rewarding oneself for accomplishments.

efficacy beliefs: the extent to which one thinks a course of action (e.g., a preventive behaviour or treatment) will actually work.

The third crucial target for cognitive interventions is the patient's **attributions**. These are the explanations people give for their successes and failures. In May's case, as with all patients, it will be essential that she attribute her success *internally* (Wiegmann & Berven, 1998). In other words, she must take credit for her improvement, citing things like her hard work and fighting spirit. If she tries to attribute her success to Joyce, her physical therapist, Joyce must politely deflect that back to May. So, if May says, "You're a saint, Joyce. I could never do this without you," Joyce should reply with something like, "Thanks for the compliment, May, but you're the one who's the great worker here."

Positive efficacy beliefs and internal attributions of success greatly increase the likelihood that May will adhere to her regimen when Joyce is not around. Most of all, these ways of thinking move May toward *independence*, which is an important goal of physical rehabilitation.

Pain Management   In our discussion of physical rehabilitation, we must address the issue of pain management, because pain is a common problem for many patients in rehabilitation. Chapter 11 addresses pain in detail, so we will not repeat the concepts presented there. At this point, it is important to remember the obvious—pain makes rehabilitation harder. This means that all of the pain management strategies discussed in chapter 11, such as relaxation, distraction, and interpretation of pain, are major topics for people working in physical therapy.

In our discussion of physical rehabilitation, we have not included a separate section for motivation. This is because motivation is involved in each of the sections we did include. Partnerships improve motivation, as do reinforcers and effective cognitive interventions. In fact, rehabilitation parallels athletics in terms of the importance of motivation. This makes sense, because there is considerable overlap between health psychology and sport psychology in the area of rehabilitation. You will note this overlap again when you read about recovery from athletic injuries in chapter 9, "Health and Physical Activity."

An excellent review of the literature on motivation and rehabilitation has placed this research into three categories (Maclean & Pound, 2000), depending on the assumed locus of motivation. Some research sees motivation in terms of personal traits the patient possesses. Other studies view motivation as something that is provided by the situation and the therapist. Still others combine these internal and external definitions. Maclean and Pound (2000) make the point that it is unfair and unhelpful to view motivation solely in terms of something the patient brings to the equation. The main problem is that when rehabilitation is difficult, this internal approach could lead to blaming the patient, even when there are many reasons why therapy could be difficult at that time. This notion of "blaming the patient" applies to all our work with patients and must be given serious consideration as we try to achieve a balance between helping them develop self-efficacy and unwittingly making them feel solely responsible when goals aren't being met.

Technologists

Much of the high-tech equipment found in hospitals and clinics is operated by technologists who go through two or more years of training. They learn how to operate the equipment

attributions: the explanations people give for events such as their successes and failures.

and about the biomedical assessments the equipment performs. Technologists, then, combine a desire to help others with an interest in technology. They often represent the human side of what has become a highly mechanized world of diagnostic and treatment procedures.

In diagnosis, experienced technologists can often tell a normal test result from an abnormal one, yet they are not allowed to pass on these impressions to the patient. This can be particularly difficult, because the patient might desperately want to know the technologist's opinion. Because many patients know that the technologist cannot provide a diagnosis, the patients may subtly probe the technologist with questions like, "Well, what do you think?" or "How does it look?" The technologist, in reply, must say, "The radiologist will go over your test results with you," or "We'll be sending the results to your doctor." The patient may interpret this evasion as an attempt on the technologist's part to avoid giving bad news, which can make the patient anxious.

As Case 7-2 shows, experienced technologists are very good at helping patients through procedures that may be physically or psychologically difficult. These include everything from nuclear medicine tests to radiation therapy for cancer. Technologists may help their patients by presenting **procedure-based information**, which addresses *what* will be done and why. They may also present **sensation-based information**, concerning what a procedure will feel or sound like and how long it will last. Or they might engage in **interpersonal small talk**, which has nothing to do with the procedure but helps distract patients from their anxiety (Poole & Kallhood, 1996).

procedure-based information: information given by a technologist at the time of a procedure that addresses what will be done and why.

sensation-based information: information given by a technologist at the time of a procedure that includes what a procedure will feel like or sound like and how long it will last.

interpersonal small talk: talk engaged in by a technologist during a procedure that has nothing to do with the procedure but passes the time and establishes rapport.

CASE 7-2 CAN HIGH-TECH BE HUMAN?

Chen consulted his doctor about a recurring pain on the right side of his abdomen. His apprehension level went up measurably when he heard the words "barium enema." He had never had one before, so he wasn't exactly sure what it was. All the same, it sounded embarrassing and awful. To make matters worse, the enema was only part of the examination he was to go through to discover the source of the pain. A machine was going to be pushed into his abdomen like it was some sort of balloon. And what was this pain, anyway? The very imposing machinery and embarrassing procedures made him feel as though he had something seriously wrong with him.

Thankfully, Chen met an experienced technologist who had a pretty good idea of what he was feeling. She told him just what the enema would involve. It didn't sound too pleasant, but at least he knew how long it would take and what it would feel like. She explained just what she was doing each step of the way. Just as important, she talked with Chen about things that had nothing to do with the test, giving him the sense that he was, indeed, a normal person going through a common experience.

In this chapter, we have taken a close look at the training and working lives of some of the people who provide health care. These people play crucial roles in society, and it is essential that health psychologists understand these roles as well as the challenges and rewards inherent in them.

CHAPTER SUMMARY

In their first year of medical school, students are surprised by the workload and must develop strategies to cope with it. In second year, students come to accept that they cannot possibly learn everything. Their social relationships can become divided between those on the "inside" and "outside" of medical school. In third year, students begin their clinical training. They often experience a tension between being expected to work like doctors and not having the training to adequately do so. By fourth year, students are socialized into the profession, generally learning how to cope with the emotions of medical practice. They also choose an area of specialization and apply to that area.

There are a number of sources of stress for health care practitioners, especially for physicians and nurses. Work overload is an often-cited source of physician stress. Other sources include decision-making uncertainty and the emotional nature of interactions with patients, especially when giving bad news. In the early stages of their career, nurses experience reality shock, which results from the realization that actual nursing practice is different from what they encountered in training. Work volume is another source of stress, especially in areas where nursing shortages and high turnover are experienced. Workload-related stress is exacerbated by a feeling that one has no control over one's work or work environment. Stress is alleviated by the creation of work environments that do give nurses a greater sense of control and by a problem-focused, rather than an emotion-focused, approach to coping with stress.

Nurses play essential roles in the health care system. They are "patient advocates." They interact extensively with hospitalized patients, looking after such things as medications, hygiene, and diet. Some nurses become acute care nurse practitioners, combining knowledge, advanced skills, and greater professional autonomy to provide a level of care that is typically greater than that provided by most nurses but not the same as that provided by physicians.

There are significant gender-related issues in health care, including patient preferences and practitioners' experiences with discrimination. With physicians in particular, a shift in gender balance has taken place as far more women have entered the profession. Discrimination, from co-workers and patients, is still an issue for female physicians. In addition, most female physicians fashion their careers in ways that allow them to exert more control over the hours they work.

Physical therapists and occupational therapists play important roles in relation to the important psychological issues involved in physical rehabilitation. Practitioners working in rehabilitation should work in partnership with patients to set mutually agreed-upon goals. Adherence to rehabilitation plans is important and can be enhanced by the effective use of behavioural and cognitive interventions. Pain management is another important psychological issue in physical rehabilitation.

Similarly, medical technologists can help patients cope with high-tech medical procedures. Skilled technologists use at least three techniques to help patients cope with procedures: (1) they clearly communicate what is going to be done and why (procedural information); (2) they explain what a procedure will feel or sound like (perceptual information); and (3) they engage in interpersonal small talk to establish rapport and distract the patient from unpleasant aspects of the procedure.

Review Questions

1. What is medical school like?

2. What are the common challenges and stressors in medical practice?

3. What are the possible consequences of excessive stress for a physician?

4. What do nurses do?

5. How stressful is nursing, and what are the factors affecting that stress?

6. What are the main gender-related issues in health care?

7. What are the psychological factors relevant to physical rehabilitation, and what role do physical therapists play in addressing those factors?

8. How do technologists help people cope with potentially stressful high-tech diagnostic and treatment procedures?

Chapter 8
Chronic and Life-Threatening Illnesses

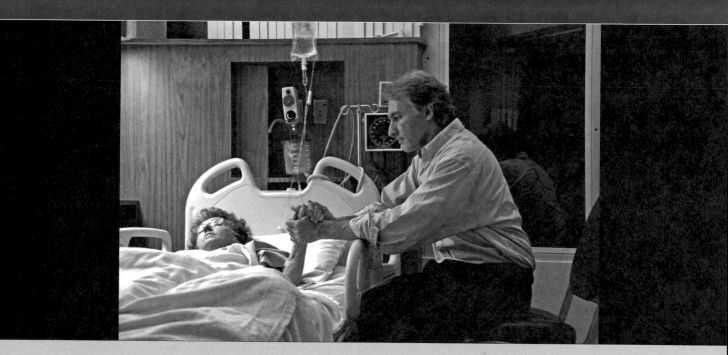

CHAPTER OUTLINE

CANCER
DIABETES
DISEASES OF THE CARDIOVASCULAR SYSTEM
HIV AND AIDS
OTHER CHRONIC CONDITIONS
QUALITY OF LIFE
DEATH AND DYING

Learning Objectives

After studying this chapter, you will be able to

- Present statistiics related to serious and chronic illness, including prevalence and mortality rates

- Describe common psychological challenges associated with specific serious and chronic illnesses, including cancer, diabetes, heart disease, and HIV/AIDS

- Explain ways in which professionals, family members, friends, and fellow patients can help people cope with these psychological challenges

- Define quality of life and explain its importance in the treatment of serious illness

- List and describe the elements of death and dying, as identified by Elisabeth Kubler-Ross

- List the steps involved in helping someone cope with bereavement

At first, Mario attributed his fatigue to a lack of sleep. However, his fatigue persisted, even on days when he had slept well the night before. And then there was the light-headedness, especially when he hadn't eaten for a while. Once, it got so bad that Mario actually felt disoriented.

After a trip to his doctor and after some blood tests, Mario found out that he had Type II diabetes. He was discouraged by the diagnosis. It sounded so serious. He had heard of people dying or going blind from diabetes. Just as discouraging was the fact that he was going to have to make significant and permanent changes to his life. This was because diabetes is a chronic condition. It doesn't go away or get better. Instead, people with chronic conditions must learn to cope with them on a daily basis.

Mario was going to have to change his diet and closely monitor it. He was going to have to lose weight, too. These major changes were going to be particularly diffi-cult for Mario to make because, for the first time in his life, he was feeling very depressed and fearful. Fortunately, his wife and friends were supportive, and there were some excellent information sessions put on by the hospital, so Mario did not have to feel alone in facing the daily challenges brought on by diabetes.

chronic condition: a condition that doesn't go away or get better.

acute illness: an illness with a defined beginning and end.

In this chapter, we will look at the psychology of **chronic conditions**, those that people live with for life, and *serious conditions*, which are life threatening and often accompanied by severe symptoms. For most of us, illness is **acute**, which means it is episodic in nature, having a defined beginning and end. But chronically ill people might not view their ill-ness in episodic terms, and this can make coping difficult (Gathchel & Oordt, 2003). It is not surprising that health psychology has dedicated a great deal of research effort to understanding chronic conditions, which are often accompanied by emotional distress. Mario's reaction to his diagnosis of diabetes is not uncommon. Many people feel anger, depression, and fear when they learn they must cope with serious or chronic illnesses. Moreover, in most cases these emotional reactions are not conducive to successful coping. Table 8-1 presents four different ways in which chronically ill patients may respond psych-ologically to physical symptoms. A chronically ill person may well experience a range of symptom patterns, resulting in a confusing mix of psychological responses.

In this chapter, we'll look closely at a number of conditions that are either chronic, seri-ous, or both. We'll also look at the factors affecting people's abilities to cope with these con-ditions and how people can be helped to cope better. You may remember that, in chapter 1, we made the point that major causes of death have changed since the beginning of the twentieth century. While viruses and bacteria were the main killers in 1900, diseases of lifestyle and environment—cancer and cardiovascular diseases—are now the main culprits. In this chapter, we are going to look closely at what it is like to have these and other diseases.

Table 8-1 The Range of Symptom-Related Experience for People with Chronic Illness

Symptoms that are	Produce
Constant	Discouragement and fear
Lessened or in remission	Hope
Unpredictably erratic	Anger and frustration
Relentlessly progressive	Exhaustion and a sense of being overwhelmed

Source: Goodheart, C.D., and & Lansing, M.H. (1997). *Treating people with chronic disease: A psychological guide.* Washington, DC: American Psychological Association. Reprinted with permission.

CANCER

Cancer is not one disease, but many. The experience of a patient with one form of cancer can differ radically from that of another patient with a different form. The study of and treatment of cancer is called **oncology**. Oncologists often specialize in a particular *site* where cancer occurs in the body. This specialization is further indication of the differences between types of cancer, or **sites of cancer**, as oncologists would refer to them. For example, one group of oncologists might specialize in cancers of the genitourinary system. These oncologists would treat prostate cancer. Others may focus on the central nervous system. The site at which the cancer occurs and the symptoms associated with it are significant factors in determining a person's psychological reactions to a diagnosis of cancer.

What all forms of cancer share is the uncontrolled growth of abnormal cells. General cell growth is, of course, common throughout the body. This growth is controlled as cells wear out and are replaced. Cancer cells are different. They grow in an uncontrolled manner and destroy normal cells in the process. When these abnormal cells form a mass, it is called a tumour. This tumour may be localized, or cells may spread to other parts of the body. When this happens, the cancer is said to have metastasized, or spread. Metastasized cancer is considerably harder to treat, since the treatment cannot be localized. Early detection of tumours reduces the likelihood that the cancer will have metastasized and thus increases chances of survival. In Case 8-1, Anna hopes that her physician detected the lump early, before the cancer had a chance to spread.

oncology: the study and treatment of cancer.

sites of cancer: types of cancer as defined by the location of the tumour.

metastasized: Spread (frequently used to denote the spread of cancer).

CASE 8-1 AN UNWELCOME DIAGNOSIS

Anna's life changed the day her physician discovered a lump in her breast during a routine examination. Then came the mammogram, the biopsy, and the result she had feared. She had a malignant tumour in her breast. Just the day before, she had been most concerned about her workload, her children's over-enthusiastic soccer coach, and her husband's reluctance to paint the kitchen. Suddenly, all of that seemed to pale in comparison to the questions that now had to be answered. Had the cancer spread? Could all the cancer be removed with a lumpectomy or would she require a mastectomy? How could she

<Case Continued>

cope with that? What would her husband think? There would be more tests and more procedures. She remembered a colleague at work who had died from breast cancer. Was Anna going to die? She could not answer any of these questions. All she knew for sure was that she had never been so afraid in her life.

Some Statistics

Approximately one in four Canadians will die from cancer: An estimated 171 000 cases of cancer and 75 300 deaths occurred in Canada in 2009. (Canadian Cancer Society, 2009). These numbers do not include cases of nonmelanoma skin cancer. It is also estimated that 40 percent of all Canadian women and 45 percent of men will develop cancer at some point in their lives. The leading cause of cancer death is lung cancer. Colorectal cancer is the second leading cause for men and third leading cause for women. Males generally have higher rates of cancer than women do, and with the exception of lung cancer, rates of all other cancers in women have dropped by 20 percent since 1979. Also, mortality rates due to prostate cancer are dropping, and survival periods for most cancers are increasing, so the news isn't all bad. For all cancers combined, the incidence rate has been stable since 1979. However, incidence rates vary from one cancer to another, with some increasing and some decreasing (Marrett et al., 2008). The Canadian Cancer Society has an informative website for those seeking more information at www.cancer.ca.

Whatever the site of the tumour, a diagnosis of cancer can have a profound effect. Some people will view it as a death sentence, others as the ultimate challenge of their lives. Many will go through strong denial in the early stages in an attempt to cope with trauma that is unprecedented in their experience. Even after receiving her diagnosis, Anna may deny that she has cancer.

Patients must cope with aggressive treatments that bring on side effects that are worse than the symptoms of many other diseases. They must face the real possibility that their lives will be shortened, and they must also face the possible stigma associated with serious illness. Friends and colleagues aren't always adept at providing support for the cancer patient. Their own fear and lack of familiarity with cancer can get in the way. There is evidence, though, that the stigma of cancer is diminishing and that people are becoming more adept at lending support to friends and family members with the disease (Bloom & Kessler, 1994). This might not apply as clearly to lung cancer, however, since its association with cigarette smoking increases the sense of "victim blaming," even when patients have never smoked (Chapple, Ziebland, & McPherson, 2004).

The nature of cancer patients' suffering has been described in many ways. Some have talked about being "at the mercy of the body, the consciousness, the illness, the treatment and the death" (Rydahl-Hansen, 2005, p. 217). Others have focused on cognitive interventions (Strasser, Walker, & Bruera, 2005) and coping strategies (Surtees et al., 2006) that reduce this sense of being at pain's "mercy," and thus reduce suffering while helping prolong life. Still others have categorized cancer suffering into three general areas—physical, psychological, and social (Kuuppelomäki & Lauri, 1998).

According to research in which cancer patients were asked to complete questionnaires about their suffering, approximately 60 percent of cancer suffering is related to physical factors (Kuuppelomäki & Lauri, 1998). These factors break down further into two subcategories—illness-caused and treatment-caused. The most common physical complaints are fatigue, pain (Ferrell, Smith, Cullinane, & Melancon, 2003), and the side effects of chemotherapy, which we will discuss later.

About 44 percent of suffering relates to psychological factors. The two most prevalent reactions are depression and fear. Depression is particularly prevalent at the initial diagnosis (Ferrell et al., 2003), when or if the cancer metastasizes, and when patients are in poor physical condition. About 13 percent of suffering relates to patients' social lives. The primary problem here is withdrawal.

Adolescents with cancer report cancer-related limitations as long as two years after they have been treated. Such limitations include being unable to play contact sports or, for one teen who had suffered a brain tumour 14 years earlier, experiencing fear every time he had a headache.

Physical Problems

As we have said, pain and fatigue have been identified as two of the most common physical problems faced by cancer patients (Ferrell et al., 2003). Pain management, then, is a major challenge for patients and for those providing treatment. One source of frustration in this regard is that cancer pain tends to be under-treated (Aiello-Laws et al., 2009). It has been estimated that more than 90 percent of cancer pain can be controlled by current treatments; however, these treatments are underused (Paice, Toy, & Shott, 1998). Why is this? Three types of explanations have been suggested: issues related to the health care system, issues related to health care practitioners, and issues related to patients and their families (Jacox, Carr, & Payne, 1994).

For example, patients' fears about building up a tolerance to analgesic medication and, to a lesser extent, becoming addicted to it, keep them from seeking adequate pain-relieving treatment (Letizia et al., 2004). Yet most of these fears are unfounded. Other patient-related barriers to taking analgesics for their cancer pain include forgetfulness, the belief that the pain should be tolerated, and concerns regarding side effects. For these and a host of other reasons, patients may be unwilling to report mild or moderate pain, making it difficult for practitioners to prescribe adequate medication (Thomason et al., 1998). (See chapter 11 for more on pain management.) We will discuss fatigue when we look at cancer treatment.

Psychological Distress

There are many different psychological reactions to the cancer experience. The most common and the most distressing for patients and their families are fear and depression. For example, breast cancer patients' most common concerns during the early stages of their illness include issues of body integrity, fear of radiation therapy, cancer relapse, and death (Monti, Mago, & Kunkel, 2005; Wu et al., 2001). You may recall from chapter 4 on psychoneuroimmunology that there are hypothesized links between psychological states and disease progression in cancer. These links continue to be investigated (Edelman, 2005), and research has found associations between psychological distress (stress and depression) and immunocompromise in the form of decreased natural killer cell activity and other immune cell functioning (Reiche & Nunes, 2005).

For some patients, fear and depression become chronic, even if cancer treatment is proceeding successfully. These patients may fear recurrence or that the cancer will metastasize (Bishop & Warr, 2003). They may fear the side effects of the treatment and the changes to their self-image (Pruzinsky et al., 2006).

Depression is a common form of psychological distress for cancer patients, and current estimates suggest that from 10 to 58 percent of patients experience depression, depending upon the form of cancer (Massie, 2004). For example, depression is diagnosed at a higher rate for pancreatic cancer, a disease that tends to have a poor prognosis (Zabora et al., 2001). Depression results in poorer quality of life, less compliance with medical treatment, longer hospital stays, and higher mortality rates (Di Matteo, Lepper, & Croghan, 2001; Sarna et al., 2002; Wenzel et al., 2002). Depressed patients also report greater pain intensity (Sist et al., 1998).

To compound the problem, a patient's depression is positively correlated with family caregivers' depression (Kurtz, Kurtz, Given, & Given, 1995), and depression persists even for some long-term survivors (McCorkle et al., 2006; Steinbach et al., 2006). Depression among survivors has become an important issue because there are now so many more of them. The number of people alive today after having had a cancer diagnosis at some time in their lives has more than tripled in the past 30 years (Hewitt & Rowland, 2002).

intrusive memories: unwanted thoughts, often visual in nature, related to thoughts that the patient has about cancer and death.

Analysis of cancer-related depression has shown that it is linked to **intrusive memories**. These are unwanted thoughts, often visual in nature, that are related to memories the patient has about cancer. They usually involve illness and death, often that of a friend, relative, or someone in a movie. These intrusive memories result in poor coping because they produce an anxious preoccupation with cancer, as well as a sense of helplessness and hopelessness (Brewin et al., 1998).

Brewin and colleagues studied 65 cancer patients who were either severely or mildly depressed, comparing them to a group of 65 non-depressed cancer patients. Thirty-two percent of mildly depressed patients and 43 percent of severely depressed patients reported intrusive memories, even though most of the participants had received their diagnoses years before. Only 11 percent of the non-depressed patients reported such memories (Brewin et al., 1998).

emotion-focused coping: coping by focusing on ways to reduce the emotional impact of a disease without trying to cure it.

problem-focused coping: coping by actively addressing the stressors associated with a disease, such as cancer, and its treatment.

The extent to which a person with cancer experiences depression and anxiety may be related to the person's coping style. For example, he or she may cope by focusing on ways to reduce the emotional impact of the disease. This is called **emotion-focused coping**. Alternatively, the person might engage in **problem-focused coping**. In this case, the person might seek information about the disease, closely follow treatment recommendations, and actively address the stressors associated with cancer and its treatment. One tendency in emotion-focused coping is to avoid thinking about possible stressors because to address them would be upsetting.

emotional-approach coping: coping by facing emotional responses to a disease and dealing effectively with those responses.

There has been a long-standing belief that problem-focused coping is superior to emotion-focused coping (Coyne & Racioppo, 2000). One assumption behind this belief is that problem-focused coping has been viewed as an *approach-oriented* strategy, in which problems are faced and dealt with. On the other hand, emotion-focused strategies have been seen as being *avoidance-oriented*. However, it has been pointed out that it is possible to adopt an approach orientation to emotion-focused coping (Austenfeld & Stanton, 2004). In this orientation, patients address their emotions, vent them, and deal with them. Thus, **emotional-approach coping**, in which patients

Table 8-2 A Comparison of Emotion-Focused and Problem-Focused Coping

	Emotion-focused coping	Problem-focused coping
Main objective	To reduce the experience of unpleasant emotions associated with the situation	To learn about the situation in order to affect factors that are causing the problem
Coping style	Avoidant	Active
Typical behaviours	Avoid thinking about the situation	Seeking information, following recommendations, and analysing factors involved

face their emotional responses and deal with them effectively, could be quite adaptive (Austenfeld & Stanton, 2004).

Although problem-focused coping may be associated with an enhanced sense of control over an illness, this control, and a related sense of responsibility, can be associated with state anxiety (Cousson-Gélie, 2005). At these times, patients might engage in self-blame, believing they should be able to control something that, in fact, they cannot. Self-blame has been shown to predict psychological distress in newly diagnosed breast cancer patients 7 to 12 months after diagnosis (Bennett, Compas, Beckjord, & Glinder, 2005).

In addition to the distinction between problem- and emotion-focused coping, other approaches have also been categorized according to fighting spirit, helplessness/hopelessness, denial, and avoidance (Petticrew, Bell, & Hunter, 2002). For example, prostate cancer patients who attended support groups were more likely than non-attendees to have adopted a coping style that was low in hopelessness and high in fighting spirit (McGovern, Heyman, & Resnick, 2002). In another study, patients who were considered to have adapted poorly to their cancer diagnosis showed low fighting spirit and high helplessness/hopelessness (Montgomery, Pocock, Titley, & Lloyd, 2003).

In summary, the cancer experience causes emotional responses and, in turn, is affected by those responses. People's psychosocial resources and the ways they think about their condition certainly affect coping. For example, optimism (David, Ruttenberg, & Bovberg, 2006) and having a sense of purpose in life (Pinquart & Frohlich, 2009) are positively associated with coping, and style of coping has implications for well-being.

Cancer Treatment

Cancer is most often treated through surgery, radiation therapy, chemotherapy, hormone therapy, or some combination of these. Anna, from Case 8-1, may have surgery to remove her tumour and possibly part or all of her breast. She may also have radiation therapy before surgery to shrink the tumour and chemotherapy after surgery to treat any cancer that may have spread.

Hormone therapy is used for cancers such as prostate and some breast cancers. When tumour growth is stimulated by the presence of certain hormones, the therapy reduces the existence of these tumour-stimulating hormones.

Prostate cancer patients on hormone therapy usually experience persistent fatigue. Moreover, their sex drive is severely diminished, and they may start developing female

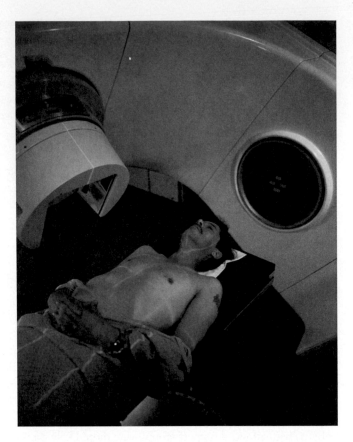

Machines like this radiation therapy machine deliver precise dosages of radiation designed to shrink tumours.

secondary sex characteristics, such as breast enlargement. Other forms of treatment also come with common side effects that can make coping difficult (Roesch et al., 2005).

Some patients also pursue complementary or alternative therapies, which we discuss in Focused Module C.

In chapter 6, Hospital Stays and Medical Procedures, we discussed recovery from surgery. In that chapter, we made the point that pain management is an important component of the recovery process, and this is particularly true for cancer patients recovering from surgery, but other psychological issues exist. One is the anxiety associated with the outcome of the surgery. Were all the cancerous cells removed? Was there evidence that the cancer had metastasized? How much normal tissue had to be removed? Will this affect normal functioning after the patient has recovered from the surgery?

radical surgery: cancer surgery that requires the removal of a considerable amount of normal tissue.

disfigurement: a potential physical result of cancer surgery that can have serious psychological consequences.

Cancer surgery that requires the removal of a considerable amount of normal tissue is called **radical surgery**. Radical surgery has the potential to change not only normal functioning but also appearance. Thus, another important issue in cancer surgery is **disfigurement**. Cancers of the head and neck, for example, may require surgery that changes facial shape (Pruzinsky et al., 2006). Throat cancer surgery may require the removal of the larynx, which is responsible for making speech sounds. Following this surgery a patient often requires the use of a prosthetic speech device that dramatically changes the sound of their voice. Colorectal cancer is one of the four most common cancers in Canada, afflicting 12 100 men and 9 900 women in Canada in 2009 (Colon Cancer Canada, www.coloncancercanada.ca/statistics_2009.php, Accessed February 4, 2010). If surgery is required to remove part of the colon, a patient may require a prosthetic replacement of the lower colon. This requires that the patient wear a colostomy bag to collect waste materials, and they may also lose control of the bowel. Patients undergoing radical mastectomy, in which part or all of a breast is removed, can experience depression and disruptions in sexual activity. One study has shown that this depression is unaffected by whether or not breast reconstruction occurs immediately after mastectomy (Holly, Kennedy, Taylor, & Beedie, 2003). However, patients tend to cope better following the much less radical lumpectomy surgery (Moyer, 1997).

Surgery, then, comes with considerable psychological and physical costs. Opting against surgery, however, creates the real risk of having the tumour grow and spread. For young patients, decisions regarding surgery are usually easier to make than for elderly patients, who might suffer more from the surgery than the cancer and who don't have as many years left to lose as the younger patient.

Radiation therapy is used to shrink tumours. It can be used prior to or following surgery or may be used on its own. Radiation therapy is usually administered on an outpatient basis, though patients' experiences with radiation therapy will differ significantly depending on the site of their cancer. A person may have just a few treatments or as many as 30 or more over the course of several weeks, as is the case with many prostate cancer patients.

radiation therapy: a form of cancer treatment in which radiation is used to shrink or destroy tumours.

Patients with head and neck tumours may have to undergo preliminary dental work before their radiation treatments can begin. They must also be fitted with a mask that will hold their heads in precisely the same position each time they come in for a treatment. Patients with tumours in abdominal regions may be fitted with a body mould that they are placed in before treatments to ensure accuracy. They may also be tattooed with small cross-hair target marks to help the radiation technologists line up the beams that position the treatment. Side effects from radiation therapy depend on the extent to which the radiation hits neighbouring cells and organs.

Surgery and radiation therapy are treatments intended to deal with specific sites as precisely as possible. In cases in which it is suspected that the cancer has metastasized, or to help prevent it from doing so, **chemotherapy** is used in addition to surgery and/or radiation therapy. It is called an **adjuvant therapy** when used in conjunction with other therapies in this way. Rather than attacking specific sites, the powerful drugs used in chemotherapy are distributed throughout the body (with the exception of the brain in some circumstances).

chemotherapy: treatment used in addition to surgery and/or radiation therapy when it is suspected that cancer has metastasized, or to help prevent it from doing so.

adjuvant therapy: therapy used in conjunction with other therapy.

As is the case with radiation therapy, the side effects of chemotherapy are caused by unavoidable harm being done to healthy cells. These side effects include fatigue, nausea, hair loss, erosion of oral and gastrointestinal mucosa, which can result in pain and diarrhea, and increased susceptibility to infection (Stuber, 1995). The number of side effects and their intensity vary depending upon the drug and the dosage. Fatigue is reported in up to 70 percent of chemotherapy and radiation patients (Dimeo et al., 1999) and, for many patients, is more problematic than pain (Curt et al., 2000). In some cases, fatigue is severe enough that the dosages have to be limited. It has been found, however, that exercise in the form of pedalling a stationary bike (in the supine position) (Dimeo, 2001, 2002) or moderately intensive walking (Mock et al., 2005) can significantly reduce fatigue in chemotherapy treatment.

Interestingly, of all the side effects associated with chemotherapy, 47 to 58 percent of breast cancer patients identified hair loss (called *alopecia*) as being the most difficult to deal with (Tierney, Taylor, & Closs, 1992). Both men and women find it difficult to cope with treatment-related hair loss. (Hilton et al., 2008). In fact, the thought of hair loss

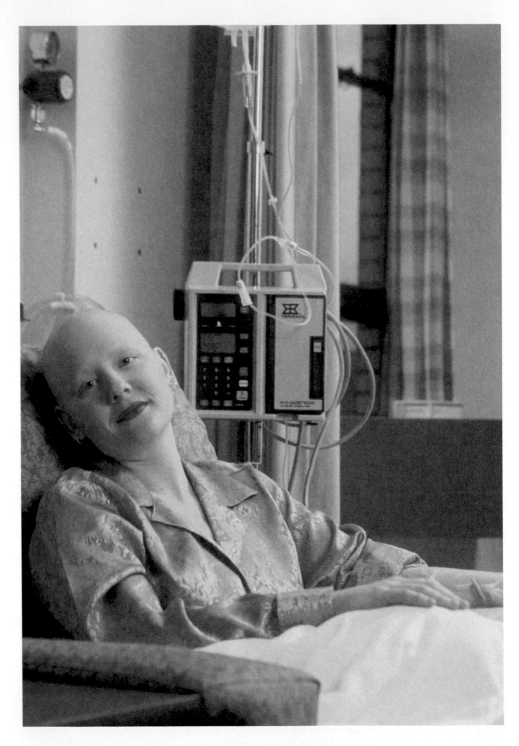

Hair loss can change the identity of patients undergoing chemotherapy. Some patients cover up with distinctive scarves and hats. Others display their new-found baldness comfortably.

might affect patients' willingness to pursue treatment that could be life-saving (Fawzy, Secher, Evans, & Giuliano, 1995). There are a number of understandable psychological reasons for this, many which relate to patients' sense of identity and many which have been shown to apply more to women than to men.

We look markedly different without our hair. It is a distinctive, defining characteristic for us. At the same time, hair loss signals a new identity—that of a cancer patient. Patients differ in how comfortable they are with this new identity. They may find that distinctive hats, scarves, and wigs help them re-establish a sense of uniqueness and normality. Others may pursue a program like Look Good . . . Feel Better (see www.lookgoodfeelbetter.org/). One of our students who had gone through chemotherapy chose not to cut his hair for years after it grew back.

The nausea and vomiting many patients experience as side effects of chemotherapy have received considerable study. Most chemotherapy treatments are administered in clinics on an outpatient basis or in physicians' offices. The patient then returns home to cope with the side effects. Patients might experience nausea and vomiting on the same day of the treatment, or after a delay of two to five days. Physicians and nurses have been shown to underestimate the frequency of delayed nausea and vomiting, which may occur in 50 to 60 percent of cancer patients (Grunberg et al., 2004).

It is not uncommon for patients to begin feeling nauseated *before* they receive their treatment. This is called **anticipatory nausea**, and it is explained in terms of classical conditioning (Jacobson et al., 1995) and also in terms of patients' expectations (Coiagluri et al., 2008; Montgomery & Bovbjerg, 2003). The setting in which the treatment is administered, the medical staff involved, and the smells of the room all become potential conditioned stimuli that bring on nausea in anticipation of the treatment. And to make matters worse, it is possible that immune suppression may be another conditioned response that accompanies anticipatory nausea.

anticipatory nausea: nausea that is felt before a chemotherapy treatment begins, explained in terms of classical conditioning.

When patients are given chemotherapy, they are also often given medication intended to reduce nausea and vomiting, called **antiemetic medication**. This can be administered before and after chemotherapy and radiation treatments. Studies have shown it to be effective for some patients (e.g., Dando & Perry, 2004; de Wit et al., 2004) but certainly not all (Hickok et al., 2003). Whether antiemetic medication is used may depend on the nature of the cancer and whether or not it could interfere with the effectiveness of the treatment (Muustedt et al., 1999).

antiemetic medication: medication intended to reduce nausea and vomiting.

Helping People Cope with Cancer

Social Support It is clear that cancer provides many challenges to a person's capacity to cope. It is also important to realize that virtually every cancer patient has a family and a collection of close friends who are also affected by the disease. With this in mind, those treating cancer patients adopt comprehensive **family-oriented cancer care**. In essence, the family becomes the patient. The lives of spouses and children can be changed dramatically when a family member is diagnosed with cancer. At the same time, family and friends will be called upon to provide much needed support for that person, and the strain on the family can be overwhelming (Sherwood et al., 2006). The family's ability to cope with cancer will be directly related to the extent to which they have learned in the past to be flexible in stressful situations (Goodheart & Lansing, 1997).

family-oriented care: in comprehensive cancer care, the family becomes the patient because for virtually every cancer patient there is a family and a collection of close friends who are also affected by the disease.

Modern medicine has sophisticated treatments for malignancies. It can also provide medication for depression and anxiety. However, when it comes to coping with cancer on a long-term basis, there is no substitute for a strong social support network (e.g., Holland & Holahan, 2003; Hoskins et al., 1996). We discuss social support a number of times in this book. We mention it here because of its importance as a mechanism for helping cancer patients and their families cope with serious illness. We know that social support is beneficial, but just how does it work? Those attempting to answer this question have taken a close look at the *social* nature of social support. What is it about some interactions that are so helpful and supportive?

We all know that sometimes it is enough to just "be there" as a sounding board for someone's concerns or to alleviate loneliness. Support can also be provided by helping with practical problems, like providing a lift to an appointment, doing some cooking, or taking out the garbage. Some forms of support, especially some forms of emotional support, require that people *communicate* with one another. This has been called **help-intended communication** (Goodman & Dooley, 1976) and is defined as communication that attempts to alleviate emotional distress (Goldsmith, 2004). The interesting thing about help-intended communication is that, despite its good intentions, it doesn't always work. In fact, sometimes it can be perceived by the person with cancer as being *un*helpful (Dunkel-Schetter, 1984).

To identify some of the differences between helpful and unhelpful communication, Pistrang, Barker, and Rutter (1997) analyzed conversations between recently diagnosed breast cancer patients and their husbands. They audiotaped the conversations and played them back for the participants to get their impressions of what had been helpful and what had been unhelpful. Many women felt that a husband's attempts to lighten the conversation were unhelpful because they suggested that he didn't empathize with what she was going through. Similarly, attempts to "look on the bright side" may be seen as unhelpful because they fail to acknowledge legitimate fears and concerns.

While microanalyses such as these can provide valuable insights into the interactive aspects of social support, they can also be somewhat daunting for those trying to provide this support. When we become preoccupied with "saying the right thing," we may become paralyzed and thus entirely unhelpful. The general conclusion to draw from work like that of Pistrang and colleagues is that support providers should acknowledge the person's concerns and fears as being legitimate while trying to help the person find effective ways of dealing with them. We can do this without dwelling on the intricacies of every word we say.

The fact that a patient's husband might think he is being helpful while she thinks he is being unhelpful indicates that perceptions are very important when it comes to social support. In fact, it may be that our beliefs about the *availability* of our support are as important as the actual support we receive (Komproe et al., 1997). The reassurance we get from knowing that support is out there if we need it has been shown to reduce depression and encourage cancer patients to actually seek support. This, in turn, reduces feelings of helplessness. This is reminiscent of what Vancouver residents say when asked how they can appreciate the city's mountains, which are so often obscured by cloud. They say, "It's important just knowing that they are there." When it comes to our social support networks, just knowing that they are there is very important.

Many patients also benefit from having a **navigator**. This person, often a nurse, community health worker, or social worker, can help people like Anna from Case 8-1

help-intended communication: communication that includes support, especially emotional support.

navigator: often a nurse, community health worker, or social worker who helps patients diagnosed with serious illnesses find their way through the sometimes complicated world of hospitals and treatment.

negotiate the sometimes complicated world of cancer treatment (Doll et al., 2005). The navigator can also help Anna prepare for her appointments in terms of knowledge and expectations (Doll et al., 2003). Research on the value of navigators for cancer patients is mixed, however, in terms of treatment outcomes and survival, and more research is called for in this important area (Well et al., 2008).

Empathy is an important element of support. Family and friends can provide some, but to truly empathize, two people must draw on similar experiences. For cancer patients, this means interacting with other patients in more formally organized support groups or being paired with volunteers who have had similar cancer experiences. For example, a well-timed visit from a volunteer can help breast cancer patients feel less isolated and more optimistic about the future (Dunn, Steginga, Occhipinti, & Wilson, 1999).

Community agencies and cancer centres coordinate such groups. In addition to providing empathy, these support groups can be good sources of information as new patients meet with others who have learned through experience how best to cope with various aspects of the disease. Studies have shown that support groups are of considerable benefit for prostate cancer patients. They help men feel more informed about the illness and more involved in the treatment (Gregoire, Kalogeropoulos, & Corcos, 1997; Kaps, 1994), and they provide opportunities to talk with other patients about difficult issues (Poole et al., 2001). In short, support groups provide good opportunities for problem-focused coping.

Having said this, it isn't necessarily true that support groups are good for all patients. Support groups often emphasize education, and so they suit people who cope best by being informed. You may remember from chapter 6, Hospital Stays and Medical Procedures, that these people are called *monitors*. Remember also that some patients cope best by blocking out information. These people are called *blunters* (Miller, 1980). It is very possible that blunters would have to change their coping style to benefit from support groups.

Social comparison processes may help explain why some people benefit from support groups while others do not (Bogart & Helgeson, 2000). When we engage in **social comparison**, we look to the opinions and experiences of others to determine what is right and wrong, normal or abnormal. We use this information to help guide us in our decision making (Festinger, 1954). This process is akin to the subjective norm component of the theory of reasoned action (Fishbein & Ajzen, 1975), which we discussed in chapter 1. When we engage in social comparison, we can compare *upward*, by looking at people who are better off than us, or we can compare *downward*, by looking at people who are worse off.

In support groups, upward comparisons are made with group members who are seen to be coping better than the person doing the comparing, and downward comparisons are made with those seen to be doing worse. Patients who view upward comparisons as evidence that they can get better or downward comparisons as reminders that they should be thankful because they could be worse off would be more likely to attend a support group. On the other hand, people who find upward comparisons discouraging because they feel worse off by comparison and downward comparisons depressing because they see themselves eventually declining to that state would not be likely to attend. For example, a person recently diagnosed with a brain tumour may attend a support group and meet people whose cancer has advanced to the point where they are terminally ill. The person could be thankful that her disease isn't that bad, or she could be frightened by the prospect that her disease will progress the same way. The majority of people attending support groups make downward comparisons and feel better for having done so (Bogart & Helgeson,

social comparison: monitoring the opinions and experiences of others to determine what is right and wrong, normal and abnormal; also subsequent use of this information to help with decision making.

2000). For Anna, then, a support group would be as beneficial as her thinking and coping styles allow it to be.

While cancer is undeniably distressing and can even lead to post-traumatic stress disorder (Kangas, Henry, & Bryant, 2002), it is not uncommon for cancer survivors to report positive outcomes from their cancer experience (Cordova, Cunningham, Carlson, & Andrykowski, 2001). These positive experiences fit in the category of **post-traumatic growth** (Tedeschi & Calhoun, 1995), which is often attributed to **benefit finding** (Katz, Flasher, Cacciapaglia, & Nelson, 2001; Lee & Poole, 2005), a term that refers to what might be called finding the "silver lining in the cloud." Growth can also stem from changing or affirming one's sense of spirituality (Gall & Cornblat, 2002), developing a greater appreciation of life, seeing new possibilities, and recognizing personal strength (Tedeschi & Calhoun, 1995).

Psychotropic Medication and Psychotherapy

For many cancer patients, the depression and fear they experience can be adequately managed with the help of social support, whether from family, friends, or a support group. Support networks may be readily available for the patient or may be created with the help of the hospital, community, or social worker. For some patients, however, more intensive intervention is needed. These people may need to work with a clinical psychologist, counselling psychologist, or psychiatrist.

Psychiatrists might prescribe antidepressant medication such as fluoxetine (Prozac), which has been shown to be effective in treating depression in people with advanced cancer (Bailey et al., 2005). However, it is possible that complications may arise from taking antidepressant medication in conjunction with other cancer-related treatments, and so drug interactions have to be taken into consideration when antidepressants are prescribed (Franco-Bronson, 1996).

Because of the concerns associated with the use of medication and because psychotherapy has been shown to be effective as a means of helping cancer patients (Jacobsen & Hann, 1998), psychotherapeutic interventions are not uncommon. Psychotherapy in these settings may focus on thoughts and behaviours (cognitive-behavioural approaches), and it may provide opportunities for the patient to express emotions and address anxieties (supportive expressive therapy) (Schneiderman et al., 2001).

Goodheart and Lansing (1997) have outlined a series of steps to follow when developing a psychotherapeutic treatment strategy for working with people who are chronically ill. These steps apply very well to cancer patients and their families. The first step is to *obtain sufficient medical information*. Some of this can be obtained from the patient. This may be difficult or burdensome for the patient, however, so the therapist must be able to communicate well with medical staff. Second, the therapist must *assess the person's psychological status and response to the illness*. In so doing, the therapist must weigh the demands of the illness against the coping resources of the patient. Also, the therapist must develop a sense of the person's psychological state before the illness. Third, the therapist must *integrate a theoretical orientation*. To probe the person's feelings and unstated anxieties, the therapist might adopt a psychodynamic orientation. To address functional quality-of-life issues, a behavioural orientation might be adopted. The key is to offer a range of interventions and then to match the intervention with the patient's most pressing needs.

Clinical psychologists, psychiatrists, and counsellors often work with people in groups. These therapeutic groups differ from support groups in that they are guided by a professional trained in psychotherapy, with the emphasis shifting somewhat from the

post-traumatic growth: positive psychological or lifestyle outcome resulting from an experience with a life-threatening illness.

benefit finding: attitude or technique often referred to as finding the "silver lining in the cloud," which appears to aid in post-traumatic growth.

provision of information to strategies to alleviate depression and anxiety. Therapy of this nature has been shown to reduce the physical and emotional distress associated with radiation therapy (Forester et al., 1993). Indeed, research reviews on the outcomes of group psychotherapy for cancer patients have identified considerable evidence that such therapy helps coping (Classen et al., 2001; Goodwin et al., 2001), though the effects of psychotherapy on survival rates remain contested (Coyne et al., 2009; Kraemer, Kuchler & Spiegel, 2009). Others argue that, while we might not have evidence of a direct effect of psychotherapy on the biology of cancer (via the immune system), treatment outcomes may nevertheless be positively affected by behavioural mechanisms such as improved adherence to treatments, improved diets, and increased physical activity (see Kissane, 2009, for a review).

Consistent with the notion of family-oriented care, psychotherapy is also often provided for families of the person with cancer. It has been estimated that 29 percent of family caregivers experience psychological distress severe enough to warrant clinical intervention (Rodrigue & Hoffmann, 1994). The roles of family members change when one of them is diagnosed with cancer. Household responsibilities must be shared, as one or more members become the principal caregiver. There can also be financial difficulties if the person with cancer must take an extended leave from work. Family members may need help managing the psychological burdens associated with taking on various caregiving roles and, in some cases, being a "midwife to death" (Brown & Stetz, 1999). In these cases, grief counselling may also focus on the entire family.

Given the prevalence of cancer and the myriad coping challenges associated with the disease, it is clear that health psychologists can make significant contributions to the quality of life of cancer patients and to the coping abilities of the patients' families.

DIABETES

Approximately two million people in Canada have diabetes, and the disease is more common among males (Public Health Agency of Canada, 2005a). About 17 people per 100 000 die from diabetes in a given year (*Diabetes in Canada*, 2003). Diabetes occurs when the pancreas produces too little insulin, which is needed to help the body use sugar for energy. People with **insulin-dependent diabetes (Type I)** produce very little or no insulin. According to Health Canada, about 10 percent of all diabetics are Type I. People with **non-insulin-dependent diabetes (Type II)** do produce insulin, but they either don't produce enough or they can't use their insulin effectively. There is a third type, called **gestational diabetes**, which is a temporary condition affecting two to four percent of all pregnant women.

Type I diabetes is more prevalent among people of Aboriginal, African, and Latin-American decent, and among people who have a history of diabetes in their families. Type II diabetes is more common among people over the age of 45, especially if they are obese. In fact, 10 percent of Canadians over the age of 65 have Type II diabetes, compared to 3 percent of those between the ages of 35 and 64 (Public Health Agency of Canada, 2005a). For people with Type I diabetes, symptoms usually come on quite quickly and are severe, including frequent urination, unusual thirst, extreme hunger, unusual weight loss, and extreme fatigue. People with Type II diabetes might also experience frequent infections, and cuts and bruises that take a long time to heal.

insulin-dependent diabetes (Type I): a condition in which a person produces very little or no insulin and as a result is required to take insulin on a daily basis, usually by way of self-administered injection.

non-insulin-dependent diabetes (Type II): a condition in which a person does not produce enough insulin or is not able to use insulin effectively.

gestational diabetes: a temporary condition affecting two to four percent of all pregnant women.

People with Type I diabetes must monitor their blood sugar levels very carefully and take insulin, usually by self-administered injection, on a daily basis. While the vast majority of Type I patients monitor their blood glucose levels, a large study in Germany found that only 41 percent do so as often as they should (Haupt et al., 1996). Research with children has found that their adherence to monitoring regimens varies considerably and is related to dynamics within the family. Not surprisingly, children with supportive parents who do not use nagging tend to control their diabetes better (Lewin et al., 2006). People with Type II diabetes do not have to take insulin; however, they must also monitor their blood sugar and maintain a well-controlled diet.

Diabetes and Psychological Distress

As is the case with most chronic illnesses, fear and depression are two of the most common psychological problems for people with diabetes.

Fear and Diabetes   Diabetic patients' fears tend to focus on the possible long-term consequences of the disease. These include amputation, cardiovascular disease, kidney failure (nephropathy), neurological problems, blindness (retinopathy), and stroke (Hendricks & Hendricks, 1998). These fears cause problems because they tend to get in the way of disease management for the patient and because stress-related hormones can interfere with insulin action (Wysocki, 2006). Consistent with the health belief model, diabetic patients who become fearful may doubt the efficacy of the management program in the face of these potentially terrible consequences.

People with Type I diabetes have other fears as well. They might fear self-injection or self-testing (Mollema, Snoek, Ader, Heine, & van der Ploeg, 2001). They might also have concerns when their blood sugar levels get out of balance. This condition, called **hypoglycemia**, brings on adverse physical symptoms, such as fatigue. Hypoglycemia can also be accompanied by disorientation, confusion, and negative mood. In extreme cases, hypoglycemia can lead to seizure or loss of consciousness.

The disorientation and negative mood states that sometimes accompany hypoglycemia can have upsetting social consequences. For example, a spouse, partner, or friend will often notice that a person is becoming hypoglycemic before the person notices it themselves. When the other person points this out, the suggestion might be met with anger and confusion (Ritholz & Jacobson, 1998). After the person gets his or her blood sugar stabilized, they may be discouraged by their inability to take quick action to remedy the condition and feel guilt about blowing up at someone who was only trying to help.

Type I diabetes often occurs in childhood. When it does, parents become very involved in disease management. Because of this, the parents' fears are just as relevant as those of the child. These fears include long-term complications, early death, and severe insulin reactions (Drozda et al., 1997). For example, parents of children who have had a diabetes-related seizure or loss of consciousness are significantly more afraid of hypoglycemia than are parents of diabetic children who have not suffered in this way (Marrero, Guare, Vandagriff, & Finebert, 1997). Parents must also find ways to help their children cope with daily routines that are usually much more structured than those of other children. These structures, and the symptoms of diabetes, can make diabetic children feel different from their healthy peers (Drozda et al., 1997). Family-oriented interventions have shown promise in supporting those dealing with the challenges of controlling diabetes by, for example, reducing the need for trips

hypoglycemia: low blood sugar.

Box 8-1 Diabetes among Canada's Aboriginal Population

Fifty years ago, diabetes was virtually unheard of among Canada's Aboriginal peoples. Today, the prevalence of Type II diabetes in this population is three to five times the national average. Diabetes is more prevalent for First Nations people living on reserves than for those living elsewhere, pointing to risk factors such as diet. The diets of Canada's First Nations people have been influenced significantly by non-Aboriginal trends. Fast foods and high-sugar products, such as pop and candy bars, are replacing more traditional foods in the diets of First Nations people. The result has been this high rate, and earlier onset, of diabetes. This trend is compounded by later detection; by the time the disease is diagnosed, it is more severe than it would be in other populations (*Diabetes among aboriginal [First Nations, Inuit and Metis] people in Canada: The evidence*, 2002). All of this has resulted in the conclusion that

diabetes has reached epidemic proportions among our Aboriginal peoples.

What can be done to address this problem? To find answers, Grams and colleagues (1996) held focus-group sessions with the Haida Gwaii living on the Queen Charlotte Islands, where 17 percent of the adults in one village suffered from diabetes. Through these discussions, it was discovered that the Haida found diabetes to be a very upsetting condition. They feared death and suffered grief from the loss of the things they loved to do and the things they loved to eat. They had a strong desire to regain personal control. The researchers concluded that attempts to help the Haida manage diabetes must not be dictatorial or prescriptive in nature. Rather, they must respect the way the Haida's feelings about the disease are manifest and work to give them a sense of control over their symptoms and valued aspects of their lives that suffer because of diabetes.

to hospital emergency departments (Ellis et al., 2005). (For an excellent review of the literature on families managing pediatric diabetes, see Lewin et al., 2006).

Depression and Diabetes Depression and discouragement are frequent psychological consequences of diabetes. Depression is twice as prevalent among diabetics as among non-diabetics, and it is estimated to affect 10 to 14 percent of people with diabetes (Anderson, Freedland, Clouse, & Lustman, 2001; Chyun et al., 2006). Diabetics often have trouble talking to others about hypoglycemia and the emotions associated with it. As a result, they may feel isolated or unsupported. Moreover, as we have already mentioned, they may have a difficult time accepting help when it comes during a hypoglycemic episode. It is not surprising, then, that depression is significantly related to a diabetic's quality of life (Chyun et al., 2006).

To complicate matters, depression and blood sugar are linked bidirectionally. Low blood sugar worsens depression and, in turn, depression reduces the likelihood that people with diabetes will monitor their blood glucose levels regularly. Not surprisingly, depression is also worse for people who suffer diabetes-related complications, such as cardiovascular problems, and it increases the risk for such complications (Lloyd, Mathews, Wing, & Orchard, 1992; Lustman et al., 1998a). For these reasons, it is very important to treat depression in order to break the cycle of depression and worsening symptomology.

Helping People Cope with Diabetes

There are at least two major goals of programs designed to help diabetics. The first is to ensure cooperation with the disease-management regimen. The second is to treat psychological distress. As you can probably tell, these two goals are closely related. Psychological distress decreases cooperation with the disease-management regimen. Also, poor management results in worse symptoms and complications, which in turn bring on more distress.

One way to break this cycle is through cognitive behaviour therapy (CBT). It is important to explore this option, because antidepressant medication can have unwanted side effects for diabetics. Fortunately, research indicates that CBT can reduce depression significantly (Jacobson & Weinger, 1998). Lustman and colleagues (1998b) randomly assigned diabetic patients to either a CBT group or a control condition. They discovered that 85 percent of the CBT group showed relief from depression compared to only 27 percent of the control patients. It was also encouraging to note that, at follow-up, 70 percent of the CBT group were still not depressed, compared to 34 percent of the controls. A systematic review of the literature in this area, however, has shown that this reduction in depression does not translate into better glycemic control by patients (Wang, Tsai, Chou, & Chen, 2008).

Educational and support groups are also provided for people with diabetes. This support is usually offered as part of a hospital education program that patients attend on a regular basis to learn more about the disease and its management, as well as to have their blood glucose and other indicators measured. At these sessions, patients can do much more than learn about nutrition and exercise. They also meet other patients, many of whom are coping well with their diabetes. This provides them with important information regarding efficacy—namely, that diabetes can be controlled. Patients also get "inside information" on disease control and emotional coping that can only come from other patients.

Family and friends of people with diabetes can help by being aware of the emotional side of the disease. The fears regarding long-term consequences are real. And when someone is experiencing hypoglycemia, it is important to remember that mood changes and disorientation might make him or her appear unreceptive to help. This does not mean that help shouldn't be offered.

DISEASES OF THE CARDIOVASCULAR SYSTEM

One in every three deaths in Canada has cardiovascular disease as the underlying cause (Heart and Stroke Foundation, 2003). When health psychologists work with and study people with heart and cardiovascular disease, they typically focus on three types of conditions.

myocardial infarction (MI): heart attack caused by lack of blood flow to the heart.

coronary artery bypass graft (CABG, or bypass surgery): a procedure in which healthy arteries from other parts of the body, often the legs, are grafted into the coronary artery system to bypass blocked arteries.

angioplasty: a procedure in which a bubble-like device is inserted into the artery at the point of the blockage, thus expanding the artery and allowing for better blood flow.

myocardial ischemia: a lack of blood flow to the heart muscle.

The first is heart attack, or **myocardial infarction (MI)** as it is known medically. Of particular interest are people who have had their *first* MI. The medical and psychological challenge for these people is to reduce the likelihood that they will have a second MI, which far fewer people survive. A second group consists of people who have had a **coronary artery bypass graft (CABG)**. This is commonly called bypass surgery, a procedure in which healthy arteries from other parts of the body, often the legs, are grafted into the coronary artery system to, as the term implies, bypass blocked arteries. The third group consists of people who have had **angioplasty**. In this procedure, a bubble-like device is inserted into the artery at the point of the blockage, thus expanding the artery and allowing for better blood flow. In a similar procedure, a cylindrical piece of metal called a stent is inserted to support the walls of the vessel. Other procedures, such as excimer laser coronary angioplasty, make use of laser technology (Karaca, Ilkay, Akbulut, & Yavuzkir, 2003; Topaz et al., 2003). Bypass surgery and angioplasty are used to treat a condition called **myocardial ischemia**, in which there is a lack of blood flow to the heart muscle..

Taken collectively, these conditions associated with MI and CABG represent coronary heart disease (CHD). Many of the risk factors for CHD are related to health psychology. Prominent among predisposing factors are those related to psychological distress, including depression, anxiety, social isolation, low perceived emotional support, hostility, and work-related stress (Hemingway & Marmot, 1999; Rozanski et al., 1999).

Cardiovascular Disease and Psychological Distress

Patients with cardiovascular disease often suffer accompanying psychological distress. This not only affects their quality of life when they have the disease, but also puts them at greater risk for developing CHD in the first place (Wulsin & Singal, 2003).

One common form of psychological distress accompanying cardiovascular disease is anxiety. Trait anxiety results in poorer quality of life for cardiac patients (Engebretson et al., 1999). A heart attack can be a frightening experience, so it is not surprising to find that some patients live in fear of having another one. As a result, these patients become crippled by their cardiac history; they curtail their activity levels far more than their disease status requires. This phenomenon, called **cardiac invalidism** (Riegel, Dracup, & Glaser, 1998), creates two major problems for the patient. First, the patient stops engaging in some of the things that enhance his or her quality of life, such as tennis, golf, or sexual activity. Second, the patient lapses into a sedentary lifestyle that is not conducive to good cardiovascular health.

cardiac invalidism: anxiety regarding a subsequent heart attack causes patients to curtail their activity levels far more than required by their actual disease status.

Anxiety is particularly strong for people who experience cardiac arrest, in which their heart actually stops beating and they must be resuscitated. In the first few weeks after cardiac arrest, phobic anxiety and panic symptoms are not uncommon (Ladwig & Dammann, 1997). An additional problem with these reactions is that panic symptoms often mimic heart problems or heart attack. This, in turn, fuels the sense of panic and a vicious cycle begins that further compromises the person's cardiac health. Fortunately, this anxiety stabilizes for most patients in time, though many experience intrusive thoughts about the event and try to avoid anything that might remind them of their resuscitation (Ladwig et al., 1999).

Perhaps the most common form of psychological distress associated with cardiovascular and heart disease is depression (Blane, Hughes, & McElnay, 2006). In fact, the incidence of major depression is three to four times greater for coronary artery disease patients than it is for the general population (Sheps & Rozanski, 2005). In addition, depression is a risk factor for the development of cardiovascular disease (Ward, Tueth, & Sheps, 2003; Wulsin & Singal, 2003) and for mortality after disease has been diagnosed, even for minor depression (Bush et al., 2002).

Five-year follow-up studies have shown that people with major depression are more likely to be hospitalized for cardiac problems than are patients with minor depression (Sullivan, LaCroix, Spertus, Hecht, & Russo, 2003). As well, depression predicts major adverse cardiac events (Frasure-Smith & Lespérance, 2008) and mortality after a diagnosis of cardiac disease (Frasure-Smith & Lespérance, 2003). Given these findings, it appears that there is a bi-directional relationship between depression and cardiovascular disease. It becomes imperative, therefore, to treat the depression and break this dangerous cycle.

There is evidence to suggest that this depression might be more problematic for women, especially those who are older (Naqvi, Naqvi, & Merz, 2005). It has been estimated that women are twice as likely as men to suffer post-MI depression (Frasure-Smith et al., 1993). One study found that 23 percent of female cardiac patients, including those with problems other than heart attack, were depressed.

Depression is particularly problematic for older cardiac patients. Patients over the age of 65 who are depressed are more than twice as likely to report difficulties with activities of daily living (ADL) (Steffens et al., 1999). Again, the consequences of depression appear to be somewhat more severe for women in this age group.

The physiological mechanisms by which depression increases risk of mortality for cardiac patients are not entirely clear (Grippo & Johnson, 2002). For answers, research is examining the autonomic nervous system (Carney, Freedland, & Veith, 2005) and the immune system (Kop & Gottdiener, 2005), especially in terms of inflammation (Surtees et al., 2008; Taylor et al., 2006).

CASE 8-2 SHORT-TERM REACTIONS TO FIRST MYOCARDIAL INFARCTION

One day when Lorne was mowing his lawn, he felt a strong pain in his chest that radiated to his shoulder and down his left arm. He began to sweat profusely and feel nauseated; had he not knelt down on the grass, he would surely have fainted. His wife found him in this position when she came out to do some gardening. She quickly got him to the car and to the hospital, where he was diagnosed as having had a heart attack.

When Lorne was settled in the cardiac care unit (CCU) of the hospital, he began to feel better. It struck him as ridiculous that he had actually had a heart attack, and he told the nurses so. Surely they had made a mistake. He told them that he should not be made to stay in the hospital, especially hooked up to a heart monitor. He was a busy man. He had a big meeting the next day and he needed to prepare. In fact, Lorne became a bit obnoxious as he lay in the hospital bed. The nursing staff did their best to calm him and tell him that he really needed to be right where he was.

Helping People Cope with Cardiovascular Disease

In addition to the support of family and friends, cardiac patients can benefit from rehabilitation programs and, where appropriate, psychotherapy. Modern rehabilitation programs for people recovering from heart attack, bypass surgery, or angioplasty are holistic in nature. That is to say, they address all aspects of the participant's life, from diet to exercise to psychological well-being (Lett, Davidson, & Blumenthal, 2005). See the story of Peter Gibson, Case 9-1 in chapter 9. Rehabilitation programs for people who have had one myocardial infarction have been shown to reduce mortality by 47 percent one year post-MI (Frasure-Smith & Prince, 1985) and improve psychological status in terms of reduced negative affect and state anxiety (Engebretson et al., 1999).

Rehabilitation programs may differ somewhat from location to location, but most share certain elements in common. Participants have their physical condition monitored. They are provided with education regarding their medication and the reduction of risk factors. They are also put on programs intended to reduce those risk factors, focusing on diet, exercise, and stress reduction. One such program, which featured three 75-minute sessions per week over 12 weeks, reduced levels of anxiety, depression, and confusion while increasing the participants' sense of vigour. This was particularly true for participants with high trait anxiety, which is a risk factor for further morbidity and poor quality of life (Engebretson et al., 1999). Another program tailored specifically to women yielded lower depression, anxiety, and hostility and increased exercise capacity and quality of life for the participants (Lavie, Milani, Cassidy, & Gilliland, 1999).

Another important psychological factor to address in therapy with cardiac patients is anger. Anger is a risk factor for CHD, especially when expressed as hostility; one episode of intensely expressed anger can trigger a fatal heart attack for people with severe CHD. Therapy intended to reduce anger features a number of components. Participants are taught to monitor their emotions so they can identify times when anger is a problem (Mayne & Ambrose, 1999). They are also taught relaxation skills. In terms of their thinking, participants go through what is called **cognitive reappraisal and restructuring**. In this, they learn to think differently about the things that tend to make them angry. For example, they may have been blaming other drivers for traffic jams or may mistakenly assume that people who frustrate them do so intentionally. Participants also spend time on behavioural change, in which they learn to control their voice tone, breathing, and so on.

cognitive reappraisal and restructuring: therapy sometimes used with cardiac patients, in which they learn to think differently about the things that make them angry, and to make behavioural changes such as learning to control their breathing.

With the proven benefits of holistic cardiac rehabilitation programs you might think that such programs are well attended, but they are not. In Canada, fewer than 20 percent of patients with coronary artery disease participate in such programs (Graveley-Witte et al., 2010; Suskin et al., 2003). Researchers at the University of Alberta have suggested that psychological factors affect these attendance rates. Such factors as self-efficacy, motivation, and social support may all be predictive of program completion (King & Teo, 1998). Again, this suggestion is consistent with the health belief model and the theory of reasoned action discussed in chapter 1. These theories predict that attendance would be

Focus on Canadian Research 8-1

Is Feeling Down Bad for the Heart?

Since the mid-1980s, Nancy Frasure-Smith and her colleagues at McGill University have led the investigation into the relationship between cardiovascular disease and depression. One of their studies (Frasure-Smith & Lesperance, 2003) followed patients for five years after they'd had a myocardial infarction. Frasure-Smith and her team administered a collection of self-report measures to assess such things as depression, anxiety, anger, and perceived social support soon after the participants had their heart attacks. The researchers then kept track of mortality statistics over the five-year period. The participants were 896 patients taken from 10 hospitals in the Montreal area. The purpose of the study was to determine the extent to which each of those psychological states helped predict mortality after heart attack.

They found that 155 people died during the five-year period. Of those deaths, 121 were cardiac-related. After taking factors such as sex and age into account, Frasure-Smith and colleagues then used correlation methods to determine which psychological factors best predicted mortality.

A number of psychological measures correlated significantly with mortality. These included depression and anxiety, as well as a more general measure of psychological distress (the General Health Questionnaire). Anger, stress, and social support were not significant predictors of mortality. Of all the measures, depression was the best single predictor of mortality.

higher for people who thought the program would work and who knew others who had either attended successfully or who encouraged them to do so.

For some patients, rehabilitation programs are not enough to help them overcome depression, and so medications are prescribed. For example, sertraline has shown promise for safe use as an anti-depressant soon after acute MI (Carney & Jaffe, 2002).

HIV AND AIDS

acquired immune deficiency syndrome (AIDS): a disease caused by the human immunodeficiency virus (HIV); after infection, the body's compromised immune system makes it susceptible to a host of other infections.

human immunodeficiency virus (HIV): a virus that gradually breaks down the body's immune system, making it susceptible to a host of other infections, eventually resulting in AIDS.

Acquired immune deficiency syndrome (AIDS) was first reported in Canada in 1982. By 2005, more than 20 300 cases had been reported in the country (Public Health Agency of Canada, [PHAC] 2006). (Since June 30, 2003, AIDS data have not been available from the province of Quebec.) The number of people diagnosed as positive for the **human immunodeficiency virus (HIV)** began to decline in 1995; however, this number began to increase again in 2000 and has more recently levelled off (see Figure 8-1). The number of people who die from AIDS continues to drop each year.

There are some groups that are at greater risk than others for contracting AIDS. These include men who have sex with men, injection drug users, those who receive blood and blood products, and our Aboriginal population (see Box 8-2).

The proportion of newly diagnosed cases of AIDS has dropped significantly among men who have sex with men—from 75 percent of cases diagnosed between 1985 and 1994 to 37 percent in 2005. However, among injection drug users, the rate has increased from 9 percent of diagnosed cases to 30 percent (Health Canada, 2002). Also, the female proportion of those with AIDS has increased sharply, from 6.6 percent in 1996 to 21.7 percent in 2005 (PHAC, 2006).

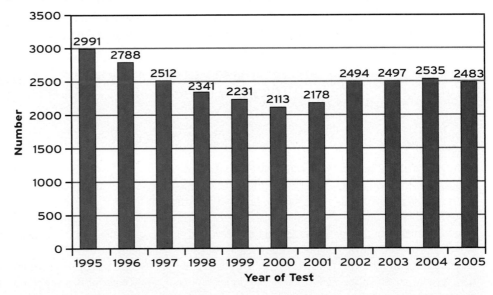

Figure 8-1 Reported Number of People Testing HIV Positive in Canada, 1995–2005

Source: *HIV and AIDS in Canada. Surveillance Report to December 31, 2005.* Figure 1: Number of positive HIV test reports by year of test (all ages), Surveillance and Risk Assessment Division, Centre for Infectious Disease Prevention and Control. Source: Public Health Agency of Canada, 2006. Reproduced with the permission of the Minister of Public Works and Government Services Canada, 2010.

Box 8-2 AIDS and Canada's Aboriginal Population

In 1993, two percent of everyone infected with AIDS were known to be Aboriginal persons. By 1999, that proportion had grown to ten percent (*HIV/AIDS among Aboriginal Persons in Canada: A Continuing Concern*, 2003). The proportion dropped during 2000 and 2001, but it climbed in 2002 to reach over 14 percent. Among these growing numbers, young people and women are disproportionately represented (*HIV/AIDS among Aboriginal Persons in Canada: A Continuing Concern*, 2003). In 2003, more than 60 percent of Aboriginal peoples testing HIV positive were injection drug users, making it the most common mode of transmission for this group (PHAC, 2005b).

AIDS develops at an earlier age within Canada's Aboriginal population. Twenty-five percent of the Aboriginal people living with AIDS (PLWA) are under the age of 30, compared to 17 percent for non-Aboriginal PLWA.

Twenty-three percent of Aboriginal PLWA are female, compared to just eight percent of the non-Aboriginal PLWA population. Females represented almost half of HIV diagnoses between 1998 and 2002, compared to 22 percent in the non-Aboriginal population. AIDS and HIV, therefore, are growing problems for Aboriginal peoples.

HIV is a so-called slow virus, with a long time delay between initial infection and the surfacing of serious symptoms. During this time period, CD4+ cells, which have receptors for the virus, cease to function and eventually die. Thus, the immune system is gradually compromised.

The symptoms of AIDS include persistent fever, swelling of the lymph glands on the neck and under the arms, frequent fatigue, diarrhea, sweating during sleep, and yeast infections in the vagina, ears, and tongue. Since these symptoms aren't unique to HIV, a person with concerns should see a physician.

HIV gradually breaks down the body's immune system, making it susceptible to a host of other infections, including neoplasms such as non-Hodgkin's lymphoma and Kaposi's sarcoma. Human immunodeficiency virus can be transmitted through unprotected vaginal or anal sex, through the sharing of needles, or during pregnancy or childbirth, when a mother can transmit HIV to her child. Prolonged HIV infection results in AIDS.

HIV/AIDS and Psychological Distress

HIV and AIDS are different from most other chronic and serious illnesses in a number of ways. First, though modern medicine has made encouraging strides in prolonging the lives of persons living with HIV and AIDS, there is still no cure for AIDS. In addition to a set of symptoms that can be difficult to endure, people living with AIDS often suffer from stigmatization (Joachim & Acorn, 2000; Rintamaki & Brashers, 2005). Their self-esteem and well-being suffer as they internalize this stigma (Lee, Kochman, & Sikkema, 2002).

Unlike many other serious illnesses, AIDS is contagious; in addition to which there are many myths about contagion. AIDS patients may feel personal responsibility or guilt regarding their illness. Additionally, many people with AIDS have lost people from their social network to the very disease they are trying to cope with. For all these reasons, people with HIV and AIDS must deal with a host of unique psychological challenges (Kelly, 1998). Generally, psychological distress is worsened if there is a lack of acceptance by family members; isolation is exacerbated if the patient does not attend a support group or know other people with HIV (Lee et al., 2002; Schmitz & Crystal,

2000). It is not surprising to find that over 54 percent of people living with HIV and AIDS in Canada experience depression (Williams et al., 2005).

Anxiety is a common problem for persons living with AIDS (Phillips & Morrow, 1998), even in the current era of life-prolonging therapies (Mkanta, Mejia, & Duncan, 2010). This anxiety stems from uncertainty about the future, the losses that are experienced, the social stigma, the prejudice that the offspring of people living with AIDS must endure, and the disease process itself (Phillips & Morrow, 1998). An HIV-positive diagnosis can be traumatic enough to elicit symptoms of post-traumatic stress disorder (PTSD), which is often related to major depression (Springer, Chen & Altice, 2009). One study discovered that 30 percent of HIV-positive gay and bisexual men showed symptoms of PTSD, and the onset of these symptoms in one-third of the infected men began six months or more after their HIV-positive diagnosis (Kelly et al., 1998). PTSD symptoms were more prevalent for men who had a history of PTSD prior to their HIV diagnosis.

Helping People Cope with HIV and AIDS

When providing psychotherapy for people who are HIV positive, a number of clinical issues must be considered (Smiley, 2004). Unlike other diseases, it can be difficult for HIV/AIDS patients to disclose their disease status to others. Telling someone you are HIV positive just isn't the same as telling that person you have a blocked artery. To compound things, persons living with AIDS have higher rates of bereavement and may have been caregivers themselves, especially if they are gay men or intravenous drug users (IDU). For these reasons, persons living with AIDS must often re-establish their social support systems. They must also make and maintain major changes in terms of risk-related behaviour and adhere to medical regimens that can be complex and extensive.

highly active antiretroviral treatment (HAART): a treatment for AIDS that has been shown to significantly increase life expectancy.

protease inhibitor: medication that can significantly prolong the lives of people living with AIDS.

Psychotherapy issues for persons living with AIDS have changed somewhat over the past few years due to advances in medicine that prolong life expectancies (Fox & Gourlay, 2000; Gushue & Brazaitis, 2003). **Highly active antiretroviral treatment (HAART)** (Gray, Chretien, Vallat-Decouvelaere, & Scaravilli, 2003) and **protease inhibitor** drug combinations are significantly prolonging the lives of persons living with AIDS. People living with HIV now live more than 10 years before developing AIDS (Health Canada, 2006a), and those diagnosed with HIV/AIDS live an average of 24 years after diagnosis, provided they receive the best care (Schackman, 2005). The psychotherapeutic issues are changing accordingly. Not surprisingly, psychological status is often related to disease-related milestones, such as the first notification of seropositive status, first symptoms, and first sign of AIDS-defining illness (Kelly, 1998).

Therapy for people dealing with these and other factors is often conducted in groups, which has proven effective (Smiley, 2004). The therapist must take into account the makeup of the group, given that AIDS affects many different types of people. For example, a group consisting exclusively of gay men is quite different from one in which there are gay men, intravenous drug users, and heterosexual women.

Groups may adopt a cognitive focus in which they help participants put a stop to intrusive thoughts or address irrational beliefs that lead to depression and anxiety. Groups can also take on a behavioural focus, looking at ways to cope with problems at home and at work, strategies for regaining social support, and ways to relax and manage stress. In general, psychological interventions for persons living with AIDS improve psychological status, and there is some evidence that therapy improves endocrine levels and immune system functioning (Schneiderman et al., 2001).

Those providing care to people living with AIDS are in need of considerable support. When AIDS patients are from the gay community, it is not uncommon for their caregivers to be from that same community. These caregivers may well have seen many of their friends and loved ones die. They may fear HIV infection themselves or know that they are, in fact, seropositive.

Finally, we must consider information presented in chapter 12, Health Promotion, to remind ourselves that *prevention* is a very important issue when it comes to HIV and AIDS. All the psychological principles discussed in chapter 12 apply well here. We cannot rely too heavily on fear appeals. Rather, we must convince people of the efficacy of safe sex and careful needle use while at the same time making salient the potential threat of AIDS.

A Final Word about Our Discussion of HIV and AIDS

It is important to note that our discussion of HIV and AIDS has been from a decidedly North American perspective. AIDS, however, is a world-wide disease that is experienced very differently depending upon geopolitical and socio-economic contexts. For example, survival rates based on "best" or "optimal" care may be relevant in parts of the world where such care is available but of little relevance in places where it is not. To develop an international perspective on HIV/AIDS see Volume 17, Issue 3-4, of the *Journal of Human Behavior in the Social Environment*. In that issue, you will find articles describing the AIDS experience of people in many countries.

OTHER CHRONIC CONDITIONS

Cancer, cardiovascular disease, diabetes, and AIDS are four of the most commonly studied chronic conditions in health psychology. There are, of course, other chronic conditions that are equally pressing for the people experiencing them. Included in this list would be Parkinson's disease and arthritis. More generally, many people live with physical and mental disabilities. Each of these conditions carries its own set of coping challenges.

For example, major depression occurs in 20 to 40 percent of all people with Parkinson's disease (Lieberman, 2006). This causes further problems in terms of memory, language, and motor performance. Not surprisingly, depression can also be a problem for people coping with the chronic pain of arthritis (Mangelli, Gribbin, Buchi, Allard, & Sensky, 2002), a disease that affects about one percent of the population and between five and seven percent of those over the age of 65. One study found that 36 percent of patients with arthritis (average age, 57 years) had scores indicative of clinical depression, which is above the norm for the general population (Walsh, Blanchard, Kremer, & Blanchard, 1999). As is the case with depression and most chronic conditions, the depression and disease symptoms tend to worsen together. Also, depression is related to feelings of isolation and self-blame and is worse for people who feel a lack of control over their illness (Murphy, Dickens, Creed, & Bernstein, 1999).

Additionally, many people cope with permanent physical disabilities that may impair their movement or sensory capacities. One of the main obstacles for people with disabilities is the attitudes of people *without* disabilities. These attitudes, which may range from pity to understanding to impatience, are often formed in childhood and might be based on stereotypes rather than first-hand experience (Bracegirdle, 1995; Harper, 1999).

The quality of life of people living with disabilities depends, in part, on their belief that they are engaged in meaningful activities. Another important factor is their sense of social integration, which is, of course, related to the extent to which they are accepted by others (Viemeroe & Krause, 1998). When trying to understand the psychological factors associated with coping with a disability, it is important to consider when the person became disabled. People who have recently become disabled may still be struggling with changes in their sense of self and re-evaluating their identity (Iwai, 1996; Mpofu & Houston, 1998).

Psychotherapy for people with physical disabilities has yielded encouraging results, although many psychotherapists neither see clients from this population nor specialize in the unique needs of people with physical disabilities (Hurley, Tomasulo, & Pfadt, 1998), which can include an accurate assessment of the person's physical capabilities and an understanding of the person's beliefs regarding his or her disability. Also, as is the case with many chronic conditions, there are caregivers to consider, who may be burdened by their responsibilities (Dumont, St. Onge, Fougeyrollas, & Renaud, 1998).

QUALITY OF LIFE

quality of life: the extent to which symptoms and treatment affect a person's physical, social, cognitive, and emotional functioning.

In this chapter on chronic and serious illness, we have made repeated reference to a patient's "quality of life." Just what does this mean? When we refer to **quality of life** in the context of serious and chronic illness, we are talking about the extent to which symptoms and treatment affect a person's physical, social, cognitive, and emotional functioning. Further, we are interested in how the patient *prioritizes* and *values* these functions, so that we can develop a more complete understanding of the impact the condition and treatment are having on the patient's life.

It may seem obvious that quality of life would be a primary concern in the treatment of people with serious and/or chronic illness. However, this has not always been the case. This is because treatments that might alleviate some of the medical symptoms of the disease can have very negative effects on other aspects of a patient's life. If the treatment plan is focused solely on biological factors, such as tumour size, it is easy to lose sight of the price the patient is paying for that treatment in a more holistic sense.

At least two issues become important when quality of life is made a priority as a treatment outcome. First, those providing treatment must be sensitive to the *tradeoff* between duration of life and quality of life. Second, the patient must be an integral member of the decision-making team, because quality of life is a *subjective* phenomenon (Gathchel & Oordt, 2003).

The Tradeoff between Duration and Quality of Life

The efficacy of treating a serious illness is often defined by the extent to which the treatment prolongs the life of the patient. For example, a person with throat cancer may have surgery that will prolong his life by five years. Without the surgery, he might live one year. Thus, the treatment is deemed reasonably efficacious because it has the potential to prolong the person's life by four years. Of course, after the surgery, which will very possibly involve the removal of the patient's larynx, a prosthetic device will be needed in order to talk. The patient's voice will not resemble his own and will sound somewhat mechanical. Also, there will be high levels of postoperative pain. In this case, the tradeoff is clear—five years with an artificial voice and pain versus one year with his own voice and much less pain. The fact that the two options are clear does not make the decision an easy one, however.

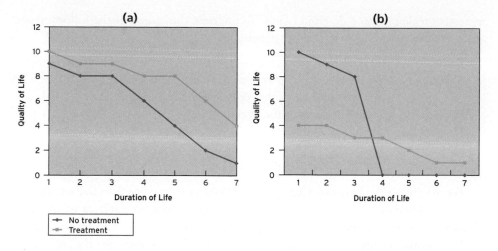

Figure 8-2 Treatment and Quality of Life

Figure 8.2a Treatment enhances quality of life

Figure 8.2b Treatment prolongs life but does not improve quality of life

Source: Based on P. Albertsen, "A competing risk analysis of outcomes associated with men treated conservatively for clinically localized prostate cancer." Paper presented at the Cancer Care: Quality of Life and Outcomes Symposium, Chicago, Illinois, (Nov. 13–14,1998). Adapted by permission.

The point of the example, of course, is that this decision must be based primarily on quality of life. If the person is an opera singer who cannot stand the thought of having a mechanized voice, then his quality of life would be compromised so severely by the surgery that it ceases to be a viable option. On the other hand, if the patient has a granddaughter who is getting married in 18 months and the patient dearly wants to be at the wedding, surgery is a good option because his quality of life is defined in terms of the wedding rather than his voice.

Figure 8-2 presents a graphic representation of what practitioners and patients must consider (Albertsen, 1998). In Figure 8-2a, the decision is quite straightforward. The therapeutic gain from the treatment is realized immediately from the time of treatment, as indicated by the distance between the treatment and no treatment lines at the start of the graph. Also, this gain is maintained for seven years, and the duration of life is equivalent with or without treatment. This would be analogous to the types of treatment gains typically found in coronary bypass surgery or angioplasty for older patients. The decision in Figure 8-2b is more difficult. Without treatment, the patient could live a high quality life for approximately three years. With treatment, she would live at least twice as long but at a much lower quality of life. It is not until those lines cross, at about 3.5 years, that any therapeutic gain is realized by the treatment. This graph is representative of the kinds of decisions some cancer patients must make.

Quality of Life as a Subjective Phenomenon

Quality of life must be measured **phenomenologically**—that is, by asking the patient directly to report on the phenomenon. In this respect, quality of life is like freedom. If someone says she is free, then she has freedom, regardless of whether she lives in an

phenomenologically: according to a person's own report on the phenomenon.

oppressive regime or on a deserted island. To illustrate this, consider the following conversation between a physician and her patient:

Patient: If I have this operation, will I be able to play competitive tennis again?
Physician: No. It will give you at least five more years of life, but your mobility will be restricted so that tennis would be very difficult.
Patient: Then I don't want the operation.
Physician: Because of tennis?
Patient: Yes.
Physician: But it's only a game!

For the physician, the notion that someone would rather not live than live without tennis is unthinkable, as it may be for you. However, what the physician thinks or what you and I think is irrelevant, because this is a quality-of-life decision, which is by definition subjective.

Most of the quality-of-life questionnaires in use today acknowledge the subjectivity of the phenomenon when they ask respondents to indicate not only if they are able to perform a given function, but how *important* the function is to the respondents. A good example is the Functional Assessment of Cancer Therapy (FACT) scales (Brucker et al., 2005; Cella et al., 1993). After completing each subscale, which assesses such things as emotional well-being, respondents are asked how important emotional well-being is to them. Research measuring the effects of psychotherapy and exercise use scales like the FACT to assess impact (Courneya et al., 2003).

There are others who have argued that the use of these scales, even when they do ask questions about importance, do not account for the subjectivity of quality of life (Clark, 1998). This is because the person designing the scale chooses the aspects to be included and also the language with which these aspects are described. This is like putting words in the patient's mouth. In focus groups, patients bring up things that are not featured in most scales (which tend to be quite biomedical in their focus). For example, 30 to 40 percent of a group of prostate cancer patients said they regretted their treatment choice (Clark, 1998), which is something that isn't explored in quality-of-life questionnaires as a rule.

Another consideration when measuring quality of life is whether the assessment is **multidimensional** or **global**. The scales we have been discussing have been multidimensional in that they assess different aspects of quality of life, such the ability to function physically, emotionally, and socially. A global approach would require just one question—for example, "How would you rate your quality of life today?" (Gough, Furnval, Schilder, & Grove, 1983). Generally, multidimensional approaches are favoured because they allow for an assessment of how an illness is affecting specific areas of a patient's life.

multidimensional measures of quality of life: assessment that includes specific aspects of quality of life, such as physical, emotional, and social.

global measures of quality of life: a general or overall assessment of quality of life without focusing on specific aspects.

DEATH AND DYING

Any attempt to help people cope with chronic and serious illnesses must address the prospect of premature death. In some cases, this prospect is very real.

Patients' Reactions to Death

Our thinking about death and the process of dying has been influenced greatly by the foundational work of psychiatrist Elisabeth Kübler-Ross (Kübler-Ross, 1969). Through her work, we moved from the belief that dying people did not want to know or talk about their death to the realization that they *did* want to talk about their impending death. Another important contribution was her theory identifying a series of reactions a person might experience when facing his or her own death. When her theory was first published, it was presented as a stage theory, which is to say that the reactions were postulated to occur in a particular sequence (Kübler-Ross, 1969). Now, it is believed that the reactions she identified may be common to many patients but that not all patients experience all reactions, nor do they do so in a particular order.

The first reaction identified by Kübler-Ross is **denial**. Denial is a defence mechanism we call upon when we are confronted with novel and severe trauma. The news that one is about to die certainly fits in that category. When people receive this news, they may think the physician is not being serious, or that some mistake has been made. They may make long-range commitments, ignoring the fact that their prognosis indicates they will not be alive to keep them.

denial: a coping strategy in which people deny that distressing events exist or that negative emotions are being felt.

Anger is a reaction that often follows denial. Patients might get angry at the medical system for being "incompetent" and for "all its fancy equipment and pills" being unable to prevent the patient from dying. They might get mad at the unfairness of it all. The anger may spread to family and friends. The dying person may become angry with them for not being helpful enough or trying to be too helpful, regardless of what they are actually doing. This can be difficult for family and friends to understand. Patients may also respond by **bargaining**, trying to do things that will buy more time. Perhaps they will volunteer for research or make strong commitments in terms of religiosity or spirituality. (This is not to say that all expressions of spirituality should be viewed as attempts at bargaining.)

anger: a reaction that often follows denial when people are confronted with novel and severe trauma, as identified by Kübler-Ross.

bargaining: a response, identified by Kübler-Ross, that may occur when a person is confronted with novel and severe trauma; includes trying to do things that will buy more time.

We have discussed depression quite extensively in this chapter, so it will come as no surprise to learn that Kübler-Ross identifies **depression** as a common reaction to dying. While understandable, depression is still problematic because it often means the person gives up, thus unduly hastening death.

depression: a common mental disorder of varying severity and impact that features depressed mood, loss of interest or pleasure, feelings of guilt or low self-worth, disturbed sleep or appetite, low energy, and poor concentration.

Finally, there is **acceptance**. If and when patients reach this point, they are likely to be at peace. Perhaps they view death as a relief. In fact, the patient might be considerably more peaceful than the family members and friends who are preparing for bereavement. Acceptance is emotionally very different from depression. Acceptance tends to come later than depression in the dying process and is not accompanied by a sense of despondency.

acceptance: the final stage of Kübler-Ross's theory of death and dying, in which someone achieves a peaceful acceptance of their own death.

Group therapy for people with serious illnesses must confront participants' feelings regarding death. If not, some of these people may die without the very important sense of reassurance that allows them to die peacefully (or, as people who work in palliative care might say, successfully). When patients do talk about death, a number of issues emerge (Hickman, Tilden, & Tolle, 2004). Patients are often concerned about loss of body functioning, being dependent on others, and being a burden, and they fear losing their decision-making capacity at a time when they feel they must make important decisions. In addition, existential and spiritual issues can be very important.

Given these issues and concerns, what are the most important assurances therapists can give to those who are seriously ill? Certainly, global assurances, like "Everything will be just fine," won't be very helpful. Molyn Leszcz and Pamela Goodwin, from the University of Toronto and Mount Sinai Hospital, respectively, have identified some key

Table 8-3	Reactions to Impending Death
Reaction	**Description**
Denial	Refusing to acknowledge the potential seriousness of a diagnosis or condition, perhaps to the point of making long-range plans in spite of a poor prognosis.
Anger	Often in response to feelings of unfairness, anger can be directed at health care professionals, family, or others.
Bargaining	"Buying more time" by taking on altruistic projects or striving to make self-improvements.
Depression	Can be associated with giving up, or feelings of helplessness and hopelessness.
Acceptance	Being at peace with one's situation and possibly viewing death as a relief.

Source: Kübler-Ross, (1969). *On Death and Dying.* New York: MacMillian.

assurances that can be offered (Leszcz & Goodwin, 1998). These include assurance that the person will not die lonely or alone, that the person's wishes will be respected, and that every effort will be made to minimize physical suffering. Of course, wishes must be clearly communicated in order to be respected, and this can occur only if the group doesn't collude to avoid discussions about death, fearing that discussing death will somehow bring it on (Leszcz & Goodwin, 1998).

Bereavement and Grief

bereavement: emotions attendant upon the loss of a close friend or loved one.

grief: deep sorrow, usually in response to bereavement.

It is also important to consider the family, friends, and loved ones who are left to cope with the patient's death. They are coping with **bereavement**, which is the loss of someone close to them. **Grief** is a common psychological response to bereavement. Vancouver palliative care physician David Kuhl has described grief as the feeling that accompanies the realization one will never again have something that one wants very much (Kuhl (2003). The bereaved are clearly an at-risk population (Walsh-Burke, 2000). They suffer higher death rates and suicide rates than the rest of the population. They also have a higher incidence of depression and substance abuse, and they have more medical problems.

There are a number of possible approaches that can be taken in grief therapy (Clements, DeRanieri, Vigil, & Benasutti, 2004). The therapist may pick one or a combination of them, depending on the needs of the participants and the preferences of the therapist. For example, there is the approach that acknowledges "the six Rs of mourning" which include recognition of the loss, reaction to the separation, recollecting and re-experiencing the relationship with the deceased, relinquishing old attachments, and readjusting to the new world without the deceased person in it (Rando, 1996, cited in Clements et al., 2004).

CHAPTER SUMMARY

Approximately one in four Canadians will die from cancer. An estimated 171 000 cases of cancer and 75 300 deaths occurred in Canada in 2009. These numbers do not include cases of nonmelanoma skin cancer. It is also estimated that 40 percent of all Canadian women and 45 percent of men will develop cancer at some point in their lives. Approximately two million people in Canada have diabetes, and the disease is more common among males (Public Health Agency of Canada, 2005a). About 17 people per 100 000 die from diabetes in a given year (*Diabetes in Canada*, 2003). One in every three deaths in Canada has cardiovascular disease as the underlying cause.

By 2005, more than 20 300 cases of AIDS had been reported in the country. The number of people diagnosed as HIV positive began to decline in 1995; however, this number began to increase again in 2000 and has more recently levelled off. The number of people who die from AIDS continues to drop each year. Some groups are at greater risk than others for contracting AIDS. These include men who have sex with men, injection drug users, those who receive blood and blood products, and Canada's Aboriginal population.

Serious and chronic illnesses, such as cancer, diabetes, heart disease, and HIV/AIDS, create psychological challenges. The most common psychological challenges associated with all these conditions are depression, anxiety and fear. All of these reactions can have detrimental effects on the patient, not only in terms of coping ability, but also on disease progression. Thus, there is the danger that problems will become cyclical, with the reactions worsening as the condition is, in turn, worsened by the reactions.

Professionals, family members, friends, and fellow patients can help people cope with these psychological challenges. Social support is very important for people coping with serious illness. This support can be emotional, practical, or informational in nature. Psychotherapy can also be helpful, usually in the form of cognitive behaviour therapy, which focuses on the ways people think about their condition (or learn to stop thinking about their condition), and the behaviours associated with successful coping, such as following medical regimens and continuing with activities that enhance daily life. Fellow patients can provide empathy and "inside information" that can only come from people who have first-hand experience with the condition.

Quality of life is an important consideration in the treatment of serious illness. Quality of life refers to the extent to which symptoms and treatment affect a person's physical, social, cognitive, and emotional functioning.

Elisabeth Kübler-Ross identified the following stages that typically accompany a terminal diagnosis: denial, anger, bargaining, depression, and acceptance. When in denial, the patient might believe that the diagnosis or prognosis is wrong. Anger might be expressed toward care givers and loved ones. Bargaining can refer to the hope that, if the person does certain good things, or generally tries to be a better person, then he or she will live longer. Acceptance comes when the person is finally at peace with coming death.

Helping someone cope with bereavement can involve the following steps: (1) recognition of the loss, (2) reaction to the separation, (3) recollecting and (4) re-experiencing the relationship with the deceased, (5) relinquishing old attachments, and (6) readjusting to the new world without the deceased person in it.

Review Questions

1. What are the most common examples of chronic and life-threatening illnesses?

2. What are the physical challenges posed by common chronic and life-threatening illnesses?

3. What are the psychological issues and sources of distress for people with chronic and life-threatening illnesses?

4. How can health psychologists and others help people cope with various chronic and life-threatening illnesses?

5. What do we mean by quality of life in this context, and why is it important when treating people with chronic and life-threatening illnesses?

6. What psychological reactions are common to people who face the real possibility of premature death?

7. How can we help people cope with the possibility of premature death, and how can we help family and friends when they lose a loved one to serious illness?

Chapter 9
Health and Physical Activity

CHAPTER OUTLINE

THE NATURE OF PHYSICAL ACTIVITY

PHYSICAL ACTIVITY AND THE FIVE COMPONENTS OF HEALTH

THE FIVE FORMS OF PHYSICAL ACTIVITY

PSYCHOLOGICAL BENEFITS OF PHYSICAL ACTIVITY

PHYSICAL BENEFITS OF PHYSICAL ACTIVITY

ADHERENCE TO PHYSICAL ACTIVITY

PSYCHOLOGICAL FACTORS AFFECTING PERFORMANCE IN EXERCISE AND SPORT

PHYSICAL ACTIVITY AND INJURY

Learning Objectives

After studying this chapter, you will be able to

- Define physical activity, exercise, and sport

- Describe the psychological benefits of physical activity

- Describe the physical benefits of physical activity

- Appreciate the importance of adherence to physical activity

- Understand some of the psychological issues involved in performance

Gerry thought of himself as an athlete, and in high school and university this was indeed the case. He excelled in basketball, and he enjoyed snowboarding and mountain biking. He went to university on a basketball scholarship where he fully immersed himself in the life of a student athlete. He trained hard, played well, and maintained a solid academic record.

In his fourth year all of this changed. He went skiing over the winter holidays and a seemingly minor collision on the ski hill resulted in an awkward fall. A visit to the local clinic revealed that he had torn his anterior cruciate ligament. This required surgery followed by several weeks on crutches and six months of rehabilitation. By the time it was over, the basketball season was well finished and he had graduated from university.

This experience was devastating for him, and he seemed to lose his interest in sport and physical activity as he sought to establish himself in the working world. He had less time to exercise and his eating habits were poor. He rationalized this shift in priorities as being necessary to advance in his job. Over a period of ten years he gained weight and did not handle stress well. Clearly his health had deteriorated.

In February of 2010 his life changed again when, like so many Canadians, he became completely absorbed in watching the Winter Olympics. He was mesmerized by the performance of Canadian athletes, particularly the snowboarders as this was a sport that he had once enjoyed. He watched North Vancouver's Maelle Ricker win the gold medal in snowboard cross and was amazed to discover that she'd had eight knee operations and frequently competes with braces on both legs. At the end of the second week he was again overwhelmed with emotion as he watched Quebec's Jasey Jay Anderson win the gold medal in alpine snowboarding. This time he was surprised to learn that Jasey Jay was 34 years old.

That evening he found himself thinking about how fortunate he was in that, although his health had deteriorated, he still had the option to change his situation. He had had seven fewer knee operations than Maelle and he was two years younger than Jasey Jay. The choice was his. The next day he watched the gold medal hockey game while riding an exercise bike at his fitness club. He made a decision to regain his health through regular exercise and good nutrition.

The personal choices that individuals make are among the most significant factors affecting health care and well-being. This chapter is about these decisions as they apply to health and physical activity. Most of us will admit that the first thing we sacrifice when overwhelmed by demands for our time is physical activity. We make comments like, "I won't be able to go for a walk today as I have too much work to do," or "I won't be able to attend my exercise class this evening as I need to spend more time with my family." The implication is that we have no choice in the matter. As in the examples given, we blame our jobs and our families for the fact that we will not exercise today; we are not even prepared to take responsibility for the decision. When it comes to priorities in our lives, physical activity is often low on the list. For many of us it does not occupy a line in our day planner. We tend to rationalize that "I'll do it if time allows, and if it doesn't, I can always do it tomorrow."

THE NATURE OF PHYSICAL ACTIVITY

In this chapter we focus on health issues relevant to physical activity, exercise, and sport. The literature indicates that one can attach quite different meanings to each of these terms. Biddle and Mutrie (2001) have promoted physical activity "in the belief that many forms of physical activity are healthy" (p. 3). They identify both exercise and sport as elements or sub-components of physical activity while recognizing that distinctions between these constructs are not always obvious and often overlap.

Dubbert (2002) points out that, although psychologists continue to be involved in the promotion of physical activity and exercise for disease prevention and rehabilitation, the research and intervention skills learned in these situations are now being applied to athletic performance. Hays (1999) suggests that, although exercise and sport may have different implications, the two fields are clearly related, and the effects of exercise are usually considered within the field of sport psychology.

Sport psychology focuses on the influence of psychological factors on sport behaviour, whereas **exercise psychology** is concerned with the influence that sport and exercise have on psychological behaviour. According to Hays, "Exercise psychology attends to the body-to-mind relationship, whereas sport psychology is directed toward the mind-to-body relationship" (Hays, 1999, p. 240). Anshel (2005) suggests that exercise and sport psychology differ primarily with regard to the populations served, the type of physical activity, and the goals of the activity. However, in noting these differences, Gill (2006) observes that applied sport psychology interventions are effective in enhancing exercise activities: "Behavioural strategies and social cognitive approaches that focus on recognizing health and fitness benefits, overcoming barriers and developing self-control and perceived competence in a supportive environment are particularly appropriate" (p. 611). It is interesting to note that in 1988 one of the major journals in the field, *The Journal of Sport and Exercise Psychology*, changed its title from *The Journal of Sport Psychology* in order to reflect its commitment to the emerging area of physical activity and exercise.

Gauvin and Spence (1995) define exercise as "leisure activity (as opposed to occupational physical activity) undertaken with a specific external objective, such as the improvement of fitness, physical performance, or health, in which the participant is advised to conform to the recommended mode, intensity, frequency, and duration of such activity" (p. 435). The intention of the activity is important in this definition. If we go to the gym to ride a stationary bike or play basketball to improve our fitness, this is considered exercise, but if walking is part of our work (e.g., a postal worker), it is not considered exercise as it is not being done to improve our fitness.

Understanding the purpose of the activity appears important in determining whether or not it is exercise. We can push a hand-mower, shovel snow, or chop wood to either get some exercise or to cut the grass, clear the driveway, or get some wood for the fire. The intention is different, but the outcome is the same. Alternatively, Casperson, Powell, and Christenson (1985) have suggested that **physical activity** can be a part of either leisure or work activities, as it is a function of bodily movements produced by skeletal muscles. Whether it is purposeful or without intention, it involves the expenditure of energy.

Gauvin, Levesque, & Richard (2001) have described four parameters of physical activity: type, frequency, intensity, and duration. *Type* identifies the physiological systems that are used in a particular activity such as aerobic, strength, endurance, and flexibility. *Frequency* is concerned with how much the activity is performed over a time period.

sport psychology: the study of the influence of psychological factors on sport behaviour.

exercise psychology: the study of the influence that sport and exercise have on one's psychology and behaviour.

physical activity: the expenditure of energy, either purposely or without intention, as a result of bodily movements produced by skeletal muscles as part of leisure or work activities.

Intensity describes the load imposed on physiological systems by an activity (e.g., strenuousness). *Duration* indicates the temporal length of a particular activity. More recently, Cox (2007) has drawn from the work of Morgan in suggesting that for "physical activity to be meaningful it must have a 'purpose.' The purpose must be more meaningful and immediate than wanting to be physically fit or lose weight" (p. 403). His examples include getting a dog and taking it for a walk each day or riding a bike to work in order to save gas.

Physical fitness refers to physiological functioning and describes attributes we have that influence the ability to perform physical activity (Casperson et al., 1985). Different forms of physical fitness have been identified (Hahn, Payne, Gallant, & Crawford, 2003; Kaplan, Sallis, & Patterson, 1993). These include cardiorespiratory endurance, muscular endurance, muscular strength, body composition, and flexibility.

Typical definitions of **sport** are often very inclusive, and it is difficult to distinguish among activities such as games, recreation, play, leisure activity, and sport. Wann (1997) suggests that most definitions of *sport* are too narrow and may exclude individuals often described as "weekend warriors." He defines sports as "activities involving powers and skills, competition and strategy, and/or chance, and engaged in for the enjoyment, satisfaction, and/or personal gain (such as income) of the participant and/or others (e.g., spectators), including organized and recreational sports, as well as sport as entertainment" (p. 3). The importance of including sports activities that fall outside the traditional realm of competition is supported by Biddle and Mutrie (2001). It is our sense that the most appropriate definition includes both the youngster playing recreational sport for the first time and motivated only by intrinsic enjoyment and the professional athlete who entertains others and makes his or her living in sport.

We now will consider the personal journey of Peter. In previous editions of this text he described his initial "heart attack" and the response he made at that time with regard to his commitment to his health and physical activity. In this edition, he brings us up to date on his health circumstances. This is not fiction but a Canadian's story told in his own words Case 9-1.

physical fitness: physiological functioning (including cardiorespiratory endurance, muscular endurance, muscular strength, body composition, and flexibility) that influences the ability to be physically active.

sport: an activity that involves rules or limits, a sense of history, an aspect of winning and losing, and an emphasis on physical exertion in the context of competition.

CASE 9-1 PETER'S STORY

In the Arms of the Angels

I have had two heart attacks in my life (March, 1995 and August, 2007). This vignette is about my existing health situation and how I am going about managing it.

I am the General Manager of a large sports club. It is a position that carries a certain amount of stress, responsibility, and a whole lot of satisfaction.

In November of 2009 my wife and I decided to vacation in Napa, California. We have become wine aficionados and we wanted to try some of the best that California had to offer. So off to California we went. We wanted a hotel that had amenities that were important to us, in particular, a gym and a pool. That way we could keep up our exercise program while on holiday.

We drove to California, which provided us with the time to actually converse with each other. We both work full time and it sometimes becomes difficult to keep up with the important things when you are more concerned with the day-to-day activities of life. Each evening we would go for a fairly long walk. This was something we did in Vancouver each night with our dog and we wanted to keep up with it. I noticed, however, that my breathing was getting difficult. I was sucking for air. Just before we left on the vacation I had been training at the club, and I had noticed that my breath was failing as well. I had originally blamed it on the flu, a cold, stress, or whatever. I never thought I may have some heart problems again. I had worked too hard to try and avoid this. For the next seven days we had a fantastic time and we enjoyed every minute of it. I was not feeling well on the drive back to Vancouver but we pushed on anyway. When we got home, I felt worse. I started vomiting and had diarrhoea as well. This continued for the next two days.

On Saturday morning, November 27, my wife took me to hospital. I was so dehydrated that I was put on a saline solution to get me back to normal. I was told by the doctor on duty to get some Imodium and go home. I got continually weaker and dehydrated. At 4:00 a.m. on November 28, I passed out in the bathroom. The noise of me hitting the floor wakened my wife. She phoned 9-1-1.

In a few minutes the paramedics were at the door. They took great care of me and transported me to hospital. The staff at the hospital started the process of rehydrating me again; however, an attending physician suspected that there might be something else going on. After some blood work, she determined that there may some problems with my heart. I was very concerned. Sitting in hospital not knowing what is going on is extremely stressful, frustrating, and demoralizing.

As I became hydrated again, I started to feel better, but the physician told me that I would be going to another hospital for an angiogram to determine the amount of blockage in my arteries and where the blockage was. The physicians would then determine the implications of the tests. The fix is drug therapy, the placement of a stent in the artery, or a bypass procedure.

After the angiogram, I was placed in a recovery area. A nurse was compressing my groin to ensure that the bleeding had stopped when the physician appeared. He informed me that I had blockages that could not be repaired by a simple stent. I required a triple bypass to allow my blood to flow properly. I was shocked and very, very frightened by the news. I was taken back to my local hospital to await a time to be scheduled for the required surgery. I was told it would take about a week.

The Support Network   Over the course of the next six days I was blessed to be visited by numerous friends and colleagues. It was a dreary and frightful time as I anticipated an operation that is very serious and one of the most invasive surgeries performed. I was continually visited by my wife and children. They were the pillars of strength I needed when I was feeling so down. Having friends and colleagues visit is as important, if not more so, than drug therapy or surgery. The mind is a wonderful part of the body. It is nurtured by words of positive encouragement. The body reacts when encouraged. I could feel warmth whenever anyone came to see me.

I was moved to the cardio ward. I think I must have been the youngest there. Not a good sign. I met a nurse who shared with me the experience I was about to go through. She did this with the most eloquent of words and a spirit of positivity. I was not so anxious any more. I wanted to know more about my situation and how I was going to cope with it. I asked her questions and she provided immediate feedback. It made me feel comfortable. I will always be grateful to her. I was also visited by many of our club members.   <Case Continued>

I was moved that they came to see me. Their visits meant a tremendous amount to me. Their spirit was unbelievable and their kindness incalculable. Words of encouragement were continual. They always told me how great I looked although I later found out that they only said I looked good to make me feel better. The trick worked because I did feel better whenever I heard those words.

The Crucial Time   On December 15, I was scheduled for surgery at 1:00 p.m. That morning my wife and I had a personal moment. I told her I was going to be okay. She told me that I had better be okay as there were a lot of things we had not done yet. My son had given me a letter the night before, although I was told not to read it until after the surgery.

The surgeon and his team gave me the final information before the surgery. The second lead informed me of the risks attached to this type of operation. I was informed that I had a two percent chance of having a stroke, a seven percent chance of dying from a reaction to the anaesthetic, and a five percent chance of dying from the surgical procedure itself. I was led down a corridor and into the operating room. The anaesthesiologists said something to me and the next thing I remember is waking in the post op room. As I awakened someone was removing something from my mouth. It must have been the tubes. The post op room is bright and white. I looked around wondering where I was. Someone walked by and I asked which side I was on. She said, "What did you say?" I repeated myself and she replied that she was a nurse and not an angel. I felt so relieved. For a while I felt I was in the arms of the angels. I know I was during the surgery. But for some unknown reason they said I was not ready to come with them and sent me back to my loving family. I am not a religious guy but I am very spiritual. I thank you, God, for not a second chance, but for a third.

Before long my wife and children were beside me. The look of desperation on their faces dissipated as they realized that I had survived. My wife was quiet, but I knew she was relieved. She had been through a lot and I knew she needed some rest. As I was being cleaned up, the fellow across from me was having problems from the same surgery. His family was beside him as he passed. My family witnessed this. There was a certain silence emanating from my bedside as we all had our thoughts on what had just happened and what could have been. I am a lucky guy.

The Healing Time   I was now on the road to recovery. I was so relieved to be in a ward with the rest of the Zippers (a Zipper is someone who has just had open heart surgery and has stitches along the breast bone). I started off just wanting to walk. I asked one of the nurses if I could and she said just a short distance. That was all it amounted to, but it was great to move. I read my son's letter. I was so moved that I cried the rest of the day. I could not get it off my mind. I still think about it today. My daughter brought me words of encouragement every day. She gave me the strength I needed to get on with my life. I wanted to go home so desperately and I pursued this with the nurses and doctors. I wanted to convince them that I was ready to go home. They soon agreed and I was released on the Saturday.

The Home Stay   I was now at home. I was propped up in a chair as the pain was so bad that I could not sleep in a bed. It did not matter, as I was home. My first visitors soon arrived. We drank wine and shared a few stories. There were many visitors over the next month, many of whom reminded me that I looked good and was getting better. My workout buddies came over to remind me that I was missing my workouts and that I had better get back in shape soon. It did not take long for them to tire me out. I had a visit from members of our Club Board. They assured me that it was important to take the time to heal properly and that the Board was all wishing me well. It was unbelievable how supportive the Board was and what impact it had on my recovery.

The Conclusion   Good friends and positive encouragement yield some unbelievable results. I received a Christmas card that was signed by about 200 of our members. I was so moved that my emotions got the best of me. It was a very Merry Christmas.

The most important item to a successful recovery is the love we share between us. My wife stuck with me through the whole process and never wavered in front of me. She was strong and passionate. I love her with all my heart (no pun intended).

Sometimes it takes difficult situations to force us into changing our lifestyle and rediscovering what it means to be alive. Make sure you enjoy each and every day on the right side of the ground as much as I do. Through trial and error, I have arrived at the following recommendations for living a healthy lifestyle: choose positive friends and discard the negative ones; read as much as you can about health, and share information with those who need and want it; take time for yourself; relax; thank your family and others who make a difference in your life; and be open to new experiences and new friends. In summary, I believe we can change if we want to.

PHYSICAL ACTIVITY AND THE FIVE COMPONENTS OF HEALTH

Peter's story (see Case 9-1) clearly demonstrates the importance of lifestyle change. For him, the alternative is unacceptable. The choices he faces and the decisions he must make touch on many of the issues connecting health psychology and physical activity.

Greenberg and Pargman (1989) describe a health–illness continuum anchored by four points: death, illness, health, and perfect health. Peter has moved close to the extremes of the continuum. To have been faced with the real possibility of death and to now be moving towards health demonstrates the power of personal change processes. For Greenberg and Pargman, each point on the continuum between death and perfect health is made up of five components: mental, physical, emotional, social, and spiritual health. Wellness is a function of the balance among the five components. The goal is to be well rounded in all areas.

Pargman (1998) believes that those involved in sport and exercise need to appreciate how physical activity can contribute to wellness. It is important not to invest in a particular area disproportionately, as wellness is achieved through balance. Each of these areas influences and is influenced by the others. This reciprocity is clearly demonstrated in Peter's story, in which growth in all five areas is evident. He has not only moved a significant distance on the continuum of health and illness, but also has achieved a greater sense of balance in his life. Clearly, his physical health has improved dramatically.

Conversations with Peter reveal that, in the other four areas, he feels that his life has also improved in positive ways. By his own admission he has in a sense been "reborn." Although these four components of health (mental, social, emotional, and spiritual) are active leisure: a positive experience that is associated with activities such as hobbies, playing a musical instrument, and exercise.

passive leisure: a positive experience that is associated with lack of activity (e.g., listening to music, daydreaming).

subjective and therefore difficult to quantify, they are perhaps the most important elements of change for him as they have the greatest impact on the quality of his life. He has discovered the joy of what Csikszentmihalyi (1997) has described as **active** rather than **passive** leisure. Active leisure is an extremely positive experience associated with activities such as hobbies, playing a musical instrument, and exercise. When people engage in activities such as these, they "tend to be more happy, motivated, concentrated, and more often in flow than in any other part of the day. It is in these contexts that all the various dimensions of experience are most intensely focused and in harmony with one another" (p. 39).

Levels of Physical Activity

It has been recommended that we should have at least 30 minutes of moderate exercise every day (Pate et al., 1995), although there is some debate over exactly what this means (Hahnet al.,2003). Dubbert (2002) has summarized recent advances in research into physical activity and exercise by concluding that "moderate-level activity has significant health benefits but that vigorous activity should also be encouraged for those who are able and willing to increase the intensity of their effort" (p. 527). Although an appropriate program of exercise is recognized as part of a prescription for physical and psychological health, it is clear that many individuals do not get sufficient exercise and that, for those who initiate a program of exercise, the levels of adherence are low.

A frequently cited statistic in this regard is based on early research by Dishman (1988). He found that 50 percent of those who began a structured exercise program discontinued it within the first six months. There appears to be consistency to these findings, as Estabrooks (2000) reported that while 30 percent of North Americans exercise on a regular basis, 50 percent of those who begin an exercise program stop within six months. We will return to the issue of adherence later; now we will focus on the incidence of physical activity in Canadians.

Statistics Canada (2007) reported that in the decade leading up to 2005 there was an increase in the number of Canadians aged 12 or older who are at least moderately active during their leisure time. This means that they achieved the equivalent of 30–60 minutes of walking per day or a one-hour exercise class three times a week. Essentially, half of the population (52 percent) was moderately active while 48 percent were described as "inactive" which means they got less than the equivalent of half an hour of walking each day. This is an increase of nine percent since 1996.

Men were more likely to be physically active than women and the proportion of individuals who were moderately active decreases with increasing age, although this is primarily due to declines in women's physical activity as they age. Those in higher socioeconomic groups were more likely to be physically active than those with lower socioeconomic status. Residents of British Columbia were the most likely to be physically active (59 percent) followed by people in the Yukon and Alberta. The positive health impact of physical activity was also noted: Those who were active were more likely to rate their health as being very good to excellent. They also reported lower levels of stress, were less likely to report high blood pressure, and were less likely to report being overweight or obese than those who were less physically active.

In people over age 15, there has been a decrease in involvement in sports, from 45 percent in 1992 to 28 percent in 2005 (Statistics Canada, 2008). This does not necessarily mean that Canadians are less physically active; individuals may be involved in exercise programs or physical activities such as jogging or walking. The reasons given for this decrease include an aging population, increased time pressures, careers, child rearing, and an increased interest in other leisure-time activities such as watching television and using computers. The Canadian Fitness and Lifestyle Research Institute reported that the most popular sports are, in order, hockey, soccer, golf, baseball and softball, racquet sports, basketball, volleyball, football or rugby, and curling.

It is interesting to note that in, 2005, fewer Canadian children participated in sports compared to the participation rate in 1992, with boys showing the largest decline (Statistics Canada, 2008). Parents, when asked about the potential barriers to their children's physical activity, cited, in order, cost of participation, lack of convenient facilities, child's preference for television and video games, lack of opportunities, homework, and traffic (Canadian Fitness and Lifestyle Research Institute, 2009).

THE FIVE FORMS OF PHYSICAL ACTIVITY

There are many different types of exercise and physical activity; however, physiologically we can identify five forms of exercise. Three of them—*isometric, isotonic,* and *isokinetic*—are based on the principle of resistance, which involves placing demands on, or overloading, the muscles in order to affect both muscle strength and endurance.

Isometric exercise involves contracting a muscle group against an immovable object without movement in the body. This may seem counterintuitive, as there is no noticeable body movement; however, the contraction of the muscles improves muscle strength, although it does little for endurance. **Isotonic exercise** is the form of exercise most of us associate with weightlifting or "bodybuilding." This involves using free weights or callisthenics to place resistance on the muscle by shortening or lengthening the muscle group. Most of the exertion occurs in one direction. Over time it can be expected that such a program will improve both muscle strength and endurance. **Isokinetic exercise** is the most efficient method of developing muscle strength and endurance as it involves placing resistance that overloads a muscle group through a complete range of motion. The difficulty is that training in this area requires specialized, often expensive equipment designed to vary the load placed on the muscle group according to muscle strength and position.

The two other forms of exercise are *aerobic* and *anaerobic*. Given that the word *aerobic* means "with oxygen," these can be defined in terms of the relationship between exercise and oxygen use. In **anaerobic exercise** intense effort is expended over a short period of time. The oxygen taken in is less than the oxygen required, creating a deficit that needs to be made up. A sprint to first base in a softball game, an all-out effort to catch a thrown football, or even an attempt to demonstrate how fast we can still run the 50-metre dash can leave us "gasping for air." Conversely, **aerobic exercise** involves an increased consumption of oxygen over an extended period of time. The oxygen being taken in is sufficient to replace that being used. Therefore, although the exercise may be strenuous it does not result in an oxygen deficit. It is the sustained nature of aerobic exercise that produces the health benefits associated with it, as the intensity and duration of the exercise stimulates the cardiovascular, pulmonary, and muscular systems, improving the efficiency with which the body uses oxygen. Common forms of aerobic exercise include jogging, swimming, cycling, cross-country skiing, paced walking, and activities done in a fitness

isometric exercise: contracting a muscle group against an immovable object without movement in the body.

isotonic exercise: exercise that uses weights or calisthenics to place tension on a muscle through the shortening or lengthening of the muscle group.

isokinetic exercise: exercise that places tension on a muscle group through a complete range of motion.

anaerobic exercise: exercise, such as sprinting, in which intense effort is expended over a short period of time, resulting in an oxygen debt.

aerobic exercise: exercise, such as jogging, that involves the increased consumption of oxygen over an extended period of time.

facility, such as "aerobics" classes or working out on equipment like a stationary bike, a treadmill, a rowing machine, or a stair-climber. Sports associated with high levels of aerobic fitness include soccer, ice hockey, cross-country skiing, marathon running, and triathlon.

PSYCHOLOGICAL BENEFITS OF PHYSICAL ACTIVITY

The psychological benefits of physical activity have been widely documented in both the empirical and lay literature. Central to this discussion is the integration of mind and body. As Mahoney (1996) points out in a textbook on exercise and sport psychology, "The body is back and so is the mind. They are not separate realms. They never were" (p. xv).

He suggests that psychology is in the midst of a "phase transition," in which new paradigms are being established that recognize the complexity of the mind–body integration, and that "One of the areas where such integrations and elaborations are particularly evident is that of exercise and sport psychology" (p. xv). Individuals who exercise frequently often make statements regarding their psychological well-being. We hear comments such as, "I exercise because it helps me cope with the stress of my work"; "When I run I leave the world behind and go into the zone"; "Exercise makes me feel good about myself." Or, conversely, "if I don't get my workout in, I get depressed." Pargman (1998) suggests that "People feel better about themselves when they believe they look better" (p. 116).

Although anecdotal evidence of the psychological benefits of exercise exists, concerns have been raised about methodological issues in the empirical evaluation of this relationship (Kircaldy & Shephard, 1990; Landers & Arent, 2001; Morgan, 1997; Pargman, 1989). One issue concerns the choice of experimental and control groups. The initial health status of the experimental group (i.e., whether they are normal, depressed, anxious, or recovering from a physical illness) will affect the impact of an exercise program and therefore the degree to which the results can be generalized. How an exercise program affects someone psychologically would be expected to be somewhat dependent on an individual's starting point.

A control group that is excluded from participation in an exercise program may not provide the appropriate comparison for a group that is assigned to an exercise condition and receives ongoing support to continue participation. Adherence to exercise programs has already been mentioned as an issue and may result in difficulties in evaluating those who remain in an exercise program as compared to those who drop out. Among those who continue with an exercise program will be individuals like Peter, who are committed to a lifestyle change that is independent of a particular form of exercise.

Evaluation of change may be difficult using standard clinical measures, particularly those originally designed to assess psychopathology rather than the more subtle changes one might expect through involvement in an exercise program. In this regard, the work of Ostrow (1996), who has developed an extensive directory of psychological tests appropriate to the sport and exercise field, is important.

Physical Activity and Sense of Self

Despite these concerns, there is an increasing body of evidence to support a correlation between involvement in physical activity and improvements in psychological health. For example, it has been postulated that participation in physical activity improves one's *self-concept.* In 1981, Folkins and Syme reviewed the existing research regarding physical fitness training and improvements on psychological variables related to perceptions of the self. They concluded that only about 15 percent of the studies reviewed were of an acceptable standard; however, those that were acceptable indicated that physical fitness training results in improved mood, work behaviour, and self-concept. They concluded that the "personality research with the highest payoff has been that which focuses on self-concept" (p. 380). What may be most important is the *perception* of change, which may occur quite independently of changes in physical fitness.

The Folkins and Syme review is discussed here as it is interesting to note that, in reviewing the literature on self-esteem and exercise 16 years later, Sonstroem (1997) came to essentially the same conclusion. More recently, Fox (2000) reviewed 36 studies published since 1972 and concluded that 78 percent of these indicated positive changes in physical self-esteem or self-concept in response to physical activity, although it is not clear what it is that makes people feel better about themselves. However, as Brannon and Feist (2000) have summarized, "It may not be necessary to know the exact variables responsible for improved self-esteem as long as increased feelings of self-worth and self-confidence are associated with an exercise program" (p. 491).

Exercise may indirectly influence one's self-esteem. Brannon and Feist (2007) conclude that "participation in an exercise program is strongly associated with feeling good about oneself" (p. 467). Spence, McGannon, and Poon (2005) reviewed 113 studies that met their selection criteria and examined the effect of participation in physical activity on global self-esteem. They found that small but significant improvements occurred and that this effect was larger for those who experienced actual increases in physical fitness.

One of the most widely cited psychological variables thought to affect performance in the realm of physical activity is **self-efficacy**, a construct that has been carefully articulated in the work of Bandura (1977, 1986, 1990, 1998) and summarized by Feltz and Lirgg (2001). Bandura defines perceived self-efficacy as "people's judgement of their capabilities to organize and execute courses of action required to attain designated types of performances. It is concerned not with the skills one has but with judgements of what one can do with whatever skills one possesses" (Bandura, 1986, p. 391).

self-efficacy: an individual's perception of his or her ability to succeed at a particular task at a specific time.

It is important to distinguish self-efficacy, a situation-specific belief that reflects an individual's perception of his or her ability to succeed at a particular task at a specific time, from self-confidence, which reflects a global trait associated with overall performance expectations. As Bandura (1990) points out, *confidence* as a colloquial term is an idea that permeates physical activity; however, it does not indicate direction. Individuals can be quite confident that they will be unsuccessful, but self-efficacy involves the affirmation of performance capabilities. The implication of the theory is that, provided an individual has the required skills and the appropriate incentives, self-efficacy will predict actual performance. Performers in all fields are frequently told that all they need is "a little more confidence" in their ability and they will realize their goals. So persuasive is this belief in the importance of confidence that it is often held out as the deciding factor in determining the outcome of one's actions. Individuals who have highly developed technical and physical skills are often believed to fall short of their goals because they are unable to use these skills in the relevant context, whereas those with limited technical and physical abilities often achieve well beyond their and others' expectations because they believe in themselves.

Every one of us can relate to those times when we thought we were well prepared for an event only to find our performance deteriorating due to what we perceive to be a "loss of confidence." As Jackson and Csikszentmihalyi (1999) have observed in discussing the challenge–skills (CS) balance, "It is not the objective skills that become critical in the CS balance, but rather how one perceives one's skills in relation to the relevant challenges. It is important to realize that what you *believe* you can do will determine your actual experience more than your actual abilities" (p. 17).

There is almost a mystical quality attributed to experiencing the upper reaches of performance achievements, or what Bandura (1989) has described as "transcendent accomplishments." This sense of transcendence is often expressed in terms of overcoming physical barriers that had seemed insurmountable. The most famous of these is the four-minute mile. Once considered a physical impossibility, it has become commonplace following the remarkable performance of Roger Bannister and John Landy at the Commonwealth Games in Vancouver in 1954, when they became the first individuals to run the mile in under four minutes in competition.

Prior to 1954, more than 50 journals contained articles predicting that it would not be possible for a human to run a mile in under four minutes. The next year, four more runners broke the four-minute barrier and many more have done it since then. Obviously, the athletes who followed so quickly in breaking the same barrier did not change physically or technically in this short time frame. What was different was their belief that it could be done. What had been overcome was a psychological barrier, not a physical one. Bannister, in describing the experience of breaking the four-minute mile, said, "The moment of a lifetime had come. There was no pain, only a great unity of movement and aim. The world seemed to stand still, or did not exist. The only reality was the next two hundred yards of track under my feet. The tape meant finality—perhaps extinction" (Bannister, 1955, pp. 213–14). The current world record for the mile is 3 minutes and 43.13 seconds, held by Hicham El Guerrouj, who set the record in 1999.

Researchers in the area (e.g., Bandura, 1998; Cox, 2007; Feltz, 1988; Hardy, Jones, & Gould, 1996) have described the exercise and sport field as an excellent arena in which to study self-efficacy. It provides a microcosm of relevance and immediacy. Bandura (1990, 1998) speaks specifically to the role of self-efficacy in the context of athletic performance. Athletes develop their skills to a high level of expertise and are often asked to execute these skills under situations of extreme stress against individuals who are also highly skilled. Skills performed with remarkable ease in practice often become fragile under the pressure of competition due to self-doubt. Successful athletes believe in their ability to focus on the task, ignore distractions, deal with mistakes and failures, cope with fatigue and pain, and ultimately to perform to the best of their ability in the circumstances in which they find themselves. They have succeeded in what Bandura (1990) has termed the "development of resilient self-efficacy."

Bandura (1998) has identified four sources of efficacy expectations: *performance accomplishments, vicarious experience, verbal persuasion,* and *emotional arousal.* **Performance accomplishments** or enactive attainments are the most influential source of self-efficacy, as they are based on actual experiences of mastery. Success increases self-efficacy and failure decreases it, although factors such as the perceived difficulty of the task, the effort expended, adverse external circumstances, and the temporal sequencing of events affect the strength of the relationship. For example, although early failure experiences may

performance accomplishments: actual experiences of mastery, considered to be the most influential source of self-efficacy.

decrease self-efficacy, initial setbacks—if eventually overcome by effort—can strengthen one's belief that even the most difficult of obstacles can be mastered. Improved self-efficacy will incorporate occasional failures with ease and will generalize to other situations, although the degree of similarity to the original task will determine the extent of the generalization process.

Vicarious experience, which is gained through observing or visualizing others perform a skill, can alert people to their own abilities and raise their sense of self-efficacy. How many times have we said to ourselves, "If they can do it, so can I." We follow the ski instructor down the hill observing every move, or we watch the tennis instructor's serve and then try to duplicate it. These models increase our sense of our own abilities and teach us better ways to do things. Conversely, observing an individual (whom we feel is competent) fail in a task may serve to decrease our own sense of ability. Although important in determining self-efficacy expectations, vicarious experiences are weaker than actual performance experiences. They may confirm our sense of inability, or they may cause us to persist despite performance failures and ultimately achieve success. We can all identify those moments when we persisted at a task despite repeated failure simply because we observed success in someone else and believed that eventually we would be able to do it. Our sense of determination is derived from our belief that, like the model, we will ultimately be successful.

Verbal persuasion refers to the commonly used strategy of attempting to persuade others or ourselves that the capability exists to achieve a desired outcome. Although considered a weaker strategy than performance accomplishments and vicarious experience, verbal persuasion can result in sustained and increased effort. However, the utility of this strategy is predicated on a sense of realism. To promote an unrealistic sense of competence in an individual who does not possess the necessary skills will likely result in a performance failure that serves to decrease self-efficacy and belief in verbal persuasion. Those involved in teaching others have to be cautious in their use of persuasion to improve performance. If it serves to remove self-doubts and allows existing skills to emerge, then it has served its purpose. However, if the results of an individual's actions serve to disconfirm your persuasive abilities, your credibility will be undermined.

The least powerful source of efficacy expectations is **emotional arousal**, or physiological state. Individuals evaluate their abilities, to a certain extent, according to their assessment of their physiological state. For example, high levels of arousal may be perceived as debilitating and predictive of failure and therefore result in a decrease in self-efficacy. The optimal level of arousal to perform a particular task will depend not only on the nature of the task but also on the causal inferences made about the arousal itself. Arousal may be interpreted positively or negatively according to the attributions we make about our physiological state. Strategies such as relaxation techniques may allow an individual to modify arousal levels in the desired direction. The high level of arousal we experience prior to engaging in a particular task might be interpreted either with anxiety and foreboding or with excitement and anticipation, depending on the attributions we make about our physiological state.

There is substantial research literature supporting the framework provided by self-efficacy theory in relation to performance in both exercise and sport. Research that demonstrates improved self-efficacy as a function of participation in exercise includes that of Bozoian, Rejeski, and McAuley (1994); Michalko, McAuley, and Bane (1996); McAuley and Courneya (1992); McAuley, Schaffer, and Rudolph (1995); and Rudolph and Butki (1998). In the sport domain, self-efficacy has been demonstrated to be an

vicarious experience: experience that is gained through observing or visualizing others perform a skill, which can alert one to one's own capabilities and raise one's sense of self-efficacy.

verbal persuasion: to verbally persuade others that they have the skills to perform a particular task—that is, to talk them into it.

emotional arousal: a source of efficacy expectation in which individuals assess their emotional level and evaluate their capabilities accordingly; for example, high levels of emotion may be thought to be debilitating and predictive of failure.

important discriminating factor in research by Feltz and Lirgg (2001); George (1994); Mahoney, Gabriel, and Perkins (1987); and Weiss, Wiese, and Klint (1989).

Physical Activity and Cognitive Functioning

Physical activity and exercise have also been examined in terms of their impact on information processing and cognitive functioning (Biddle & Mutrie, 2001; Etnier et al., 1997; Landers & Arent, 2001; Pargman, 1998; Tomporowski & Ellis, 1986). Does involvement in exercise have the facilitative effect on mental abilities that those who engage in exercise and sport frequently report? Does the ability to remember or discriminate improve? Based on their initial review of the existing literature, Tomporowski and Ellis (1986) concluded that the results to date were inconsistent, due mainly to a lack of a coherent methodology for examining the issue. They suggested that exercise, through its effect on the central nervous system, will initially improve attentional processes; however, as the intensity or duration of the exercise increases, this will be negated by the effects of increasing muscular fatigue. The implications for the assessment process are obvious. They concluded that "the dominant state determines the ability of subjects to perform tests of cognition. Thus, it may be possible for exercise to either facilitate or impair performance on the same cognitive test depending on the level of physical fitness of the subject and the point at which the subject is tested" (p. 344).

Subsequently, the meta-analysis by Etnier and colleagues (1997) further examined this relationship. They reviewed 134 relevant studies and concluded that exercise and fitness have a small yet positive impact on cognitive functioning. However, the indication is that acute exercise will have little impact on cognition, whereas chronic exercise that produces gains in fitness will improve cognition. This conclusion "would support the physiological mechanisms as explanations for the beneficial effects of exercise or fitness upon cognition" and "would suggest that the adoption of a chronic exercise program may be a useful intervention for enhancing cognitive functioning" (p. 267).

This improvement in cognitive functioning through exercise is supported in a review by Dubbert (2002). She also draws attention to the recent work of Kramer et al. (1999), which describes improvements in cognitive functioning in the elderly associated with regular aerobic exercise. With Canada's aging population, the positive effects of exercise in this area may have particular significance. This position is further confirmed by Landers and Arent (2007) who, while concluding that exercise is consistently "related to better cognitive functioning" (p. 473), also indicate that "experimental and longitudinal studies demonstrate a temporal sequence leading from exercise earlier in time to better cognitive functioning at a point later in time" (p.473). An issue for future research in this area is the possibility of a dose-response relationship between the intensity of exercise and cognitive functioning. Chang and Etnier (2009) suggest that this is indeed the situation with resistance exercise. The implication is that it may become important to identify the optimal exercise intensity at which benefits for cognitive functioning occur.

Physical Activity and Mood

An extensive body of literature has examined the impact of exercise and physical activity on mood states, particularly anxiety and depression. This research does have methodological problems, including the use of anecdotal versus empirical evidence, the assessment of mood states, the actual effect-size found, the representativeness of the data, and the mechanisms used to explain the findings. Despite these concerns, there is evidence that exercise is effective in reducing anxiety in some people (Hackfort & Spielberger, 1989; Landers & Arendt, 2001; Landers & Petruzzello, 1994; McAuley, Mihalko, & Bane, 1996; Raglan & Morgan, 1987; Salmon, 2000). This effect applies in particular to state, as compared to trait, anxiety.

The mechanism by which physical activity produces an anxiolytic effect is not clear. Morgan, who studied the effect of exercise on mood states for many years, has suggested that exercise provides a distraction or "time out" from the pressures and anxieties of daily living (Bahrke & Morgan, 1978). For many of us, this model will have considerable intuitive appeal. Our exercise time is a period of the day when we can leave the world behind. We are removed from our obligations or are at least less aware of them, are often inaccessible to others, and are completely focused on the task before us. Interestingly, Miller, Bartholomew, and Springer (2005) found that the affective response is mediated by preferred modes of exercise. They report that "participants reported greater improvements in positive affect following high preference exercise modes than for low preference exercise modes" (p. 270). This suggests that exercise preference contributes significantly to exercise enjoyment and needs to be taken into account when designing individual exercise programs.

Exercise can serve as an effective distraction; however, many activities can fulfill this function if this is all that is required. Is there a moderating effect that is unique to exercise? Tate and Petruzzello (1995) have demonstrated a differential pattern of anxiety responses for those engaged in exercise compared to those in a resting control condition. Research by McAuley, Mihalko, and Bane (1996) indicates that anxiety levels increase during exercise and then decrease significantly following exercise. These authors expressed the concern that anxiety and arousal are confounded in the measurement of state anxiety.

Research by Rejeski, Hardy, and Shaw (1991) indicates that anxiety decreases in a linear fashion during exercise, whereas arousal increases during exercise and decreases noticeably following exercise. This seems a reasonable position and helps explain what appear to be confusing results. Biddle and Mutrie (2001) conclude that exercise results in small to moderate reductions in anxiety, that the effect exists for both acute and chronic exercise and both state and trait anxiety, that anxiety is reduced both during and after exercise, and that individuals with high aerobic fitness display a reduced physiological response to psychosocial stressors. However, a recent meta-analysis by Wipfli, Rethorst, and Landers (2008) suggests that this effect is much larger that previous studies indicate. They indicate that exercise alone is as effective in reducing anxiety as psychotherapy and pharmacology. They conclude that their "finding supports the use of exercise as one of the frontline treatments for anxiety" (p. 401). The implications of exercise for the treatment of both anxiety and depression is also discussed.

The impact of exercise on depression has been the subject of research for a considerable length of time. As with research discussed previously, methodological problems limit the conclusions that can be drawn. However, there is evidence that physical activity can decrease *non-clinical* depression (e.g., Biddle & Mutrie, 2001; Jasnowski, Holmes, & Banks, 1988; Stein & Motta, 1992). With regard to clinically depressed individuals, initial research by Griest and his colleagues examined the effect of running as a treatment and reported decreased levels of depression in those involved in a running program, suggesting that exercise is an effective treatment (1984).

Reviews by Martinsen (1990, 1993, 1994), Martinson and Morgan (1997), and North, McCullagh, and Tran (1990) conclude that both aerobic and anaerobic exercise are effective treatments for depression, that exercise has *not* been shown to be effective with severe depression, that fitness levels are lower for clinically depressed individuals, and that there is no evidence that exercise can prevent relapse. Biddle and Mutrie (2001) provide an excellent summary of research in this area, again making the distinction between non-clinical and clinical depression. With regard to non-clinical depression, the conclusion is that there is an antidepressant effect associated with exercise that results in moderate decreases in depression, that this effect is present for both acute and chronic exercise and for groups different in age and gender, and that lower levels of depression are related to a physically active lifestyle.

With clinical depression the results are more equivocal; however, the conclusion is that the benefits are much greater than the risks, that the physical health benefits are important, and ultimately that "physical activity and exercise should be advocated as part of the treatment for clinically defined depression" (p. 219). In their recent review of the literature, Landers and Arent (2007) conclude that the anxiolytic and antidepressant effects of exercise are demonstrated with consistency. They go further in suggesting that, given the U.S. Surgeon General's criteria for therapeutic efficacy, the "experimental evidence for exercise as a treatment intervention exceeds this criteria for anxiety and both minor and major unipolar depression" (p. 482).

Recent research by Lin, Halgin, Well, and Ockene (2008) indicates that the effects of leisure-time physical activities such as exercise are associated with lower levels of depression, particularly in women, whereas this is not the case for physical activity related to household and occupational activity. This suggests that these effects may be specific to characteristics associated with exercise such as motivation, enjoyment, and control rather than just physical activity itself.

Stress is another area in which the psychological impact of exercise and physical activity has been evaluated, and indications are that physical activity may buffer the effects of stress. It has been demonstrated that "exercise plays a key role in moderating both psychological and physiological stress symptoms" Berger and Tobar, 2007, p. 603). (This topic was considered in more detail in chapter 3, Stress and Coping.) In their review of the impact of physical activity on mental health, Landers and Arent (2001) conclude that "exercise is related to, but does not cause, desirable changes to occur in anxiety, depression, stress reactivity, positive mood, self-esteem, and cognitive functioning. The overall magnitude of the effect on these variables ranges from small to moderate, but in all cases, these effects are statistically significant" (p. 759). Alderman, Rogers, Landers, Arent, and Johnson (2006), in a meta-analytic review of the literature, found support for the position, previously described by Biddle and Murtrie (2001), that aerobically fit individuals have a reduced psychosocial stress response. The physiological implication is that they may experience lower levels of stress for a short period of time.

PHYSICAL BENEFITS OF PHYSICAL ACTIVITY

The physical benefits of physical activity can be expressed in different ways. For some, they may be manifested in a high level of fitness and the physical appearance that goes with it. For others, it may mean the absence of disease and the promotion of health and longevity. For still others, it may simply be the expression of an optimistic, positive lifestyle. Kavussanu and McAuley (1996) found that highly active individuals are significantly more optimistic and less pessimistic than inactive individuals.

Numerous studies, some of which have been enormous undertakings, have demonstrated the positive benefits of exercise. For example, the longitudinal research of Blair and colleagues (1989) examined the role of physical fitness on mortality rates in more than 10 000 men and 3000 women over an average of eight years. Exercise appeared to reduce the risk of mortality from all causes, particularly cardiovascular disease and cancer. Some of the benefits attributed to physical activity include improved cardiovascular functioning and a reduced risk of cardiovascular disease; improved muscle strength and endurance; increased cardiorespiratory fitness; improved flexibility; improved weight control and fat metabolism; improved sleep; prevention of bone density loss; a reduction in poor health habits, such as cigarette smoking and alcohol consumption; reduced risk of injury; and increased energy. If involvement in exercise and sport can decrease mortality and increase longevity, they assume a most important status in our culture.

We will now focus our attention on the important role of physical activity in the prevention of cardiovascular disease. Since the 1950s, considerable evidence has accumulated to demonstrate that those who are physically active are less likely to develop and die from coronary heart disease (CHD). Miller, Balady, and Fletcher (1997) have stated that "a sedentary lifestyle carries approximately the same risk for the development of coronary artery disease as the more traditional risk factors of cigarette smoking, hypertension, and hypercholesterolemia" (p. 220). Early research examined the presence of CHD in individuals according to their occupation and the level of physical activity required in their work (Kahn, 1963). Individuals whose work involved a high level of physical activity appeared to be at a decreased risk for CHD (Brand, Paffenbarger, Scholtz, & Kampert, 1979).

The next level of evaluation involved the comparison of physically active and inactive individuals according to measures of energy expenditure. The most influential of these evaluative studies is the Harvard Alumni Study, carried out by Paffenbarger and colleagues. They assessed men who had graduated from Harvard University over a 50-year period according to their weekly expenditure of energy and divided them into two groups: high and low activity. They reported that men who were physically active had a 25 percent lower mortality rate from any cause and were 36 percent less likely to die from CHD (Paffenbarger, Wing, & Hyde, 1978).

The Framingham Heart Study evaluated CHD in both men and women and found that when the very active and very inactive groups were compared with regard to CHD, the risk for the latter group was approximately three times greater (Dawber, 1980). Also, exercise rehabilitation has been found to significantly decrease mortality in survivors of myocardial infarction (Haskell et al., 1994). Miller, Balady, and Fletcher (1997), after an extensive review of the literature, provide a series of summary statements that suggest a very positive role for exercise in the prevention and rehabilitation of cardiovascular disease. Biddle and Mutrie (2001) more recently concluded their research review by stating that "physical fitness (at least cardiovascular fitness) and habitual physical activity are both inversely related to CHD risk in adults" (p. 16).

It should be noted that the possible protective role played by physical activity with regard to illnesses such as stroke and cancer is still emerging. For example, with stroke, there is evidence that physical activity provides protection, particularly for those who are middle-aged and older (Abbot, Rodriguez, Burchfiel, & Curb, 1994). The impact of physical activity in protecting against cancer appears positive, particularly for men. For example, Lee, Paffenbarger, and Hsieh (1992) reported that participants in the Harvard Alumni Study who were physically active were much less likely to develop prostate cancer than those who were inactive. An international forum on physical activity and health held in Quebec in 1995 (*Research Quarterly for Exercise and Sport*, 1995) resulted in statements of consensus, including the following: whereas a sedentary lifestyle increases the risk of atherosclerosis, hypertension, and diabetes, regular exercise decreases it; physical activity benefits the musculoskeletal system, and decreases in functional capacity with age are due, in part, to insufficient physical activity; the risk of colon cancer and perhaps breast cancer is decreased through physical activity; and physical activity for all ages is a very effective strategy for improving health. Despite these statements, Biddle and Mutrie (2001) conclude that the relationship between the benefits derived from physical activity and how it relates to disease prevention and health promotion is still not well understood.

ADHERENCE TO PHYSICAL ACTIVITY

non-adherence: failure to follow the advice of the health professional; the inability to stay with an exercise program.

Despite the many psychological and physical benefits attributed to physical activity, the percentage of individuals exercising on a regular basis is disturbingly low (Dishman, 2001). For those who do exercise, a significant issue is **non-adherence**, an inability to stay with an exercise program. The most frequently cited statistic in this regard is based on the initial work of Dishman (1988), and more recently that of Estabrooks (2000), which indicate that approximately 50 percent of those involved in a physical activity program drop out within the first six months. This may seem counterintuitive, as we think of ourselves as being in the midst of an exercise and sports boom. Fitness centres are everywhere, fitness equipment is readily available, and sports participation seems to be increasing, particularly through the recreational and master's sports movements.

Taylor (1994) believes that the avoidance of exercise and sport is not difficult to understand, as exercise can be initially somewhat aversive and offers few immediate rewards. The environment can be unappealing, the activities monotonous, progress is often slow, a lack of expertise may be obvious, and social comparison with experienced exercisers can be unpleasant. The first experience in an aerobics class or an exercise room can be quite threatening. With regard to sports involvement, a lack of skills development and knowledge of rules, combined with an often highly competitive environment, can be a threat to self-esteem.

To a large extent, the positive benefits of exercise and sport emerge with time and will ultimately outweigh the initial impediments. Zifferblatt (1975) suggested some time ago that the likelihood of compliance is directly related to the visibility of the cues or reasons the individual should comply. When the reasons are vague or ambiguous the likelihood of compliance is low, whereas if they are specific, relevant, or salient the likelihood of compliance is high. The implication is that initial experiences in exercise and sport often do not provide enough reasons to continue. They may become obvious, but it will take time.

To better understand the factors affecting adherence to physical activity, numerous theoretical models have been used. Many of these were introduced in chapter 1 and include the health belief model (Becker & Maiman, 1975); the theory of reasoned action (Ajzen & Fishbein, 1980); the theory of planned behaviour (Ajzen, 1985); self-efficacy theory (Bandura, 1977); the transtheoretical model (Prochaska & DiClemente, 1983);

and the relapse prevention model (Marlatt & Gordon, 1980). These models were developed in the context of other behaviours, and it is still not clear how relevant they are to physical activity. Important predictors of adherence include physical proximity to the exercise area, availability of time, spousal support, group size and constitution, socioeconomic status, choice of exercise, and injury (LeUnes & Nation, 2002). It seems that the issue of salience is most important here. We need to know what rewards await us as a consequence of our sustained commitment to physical activity.

In a review of exercise adherence, Buckworth and Dishman (2007) indicate that subtle differences in the terms exercise, physical activity, and lifestyle activity impact how we measure and define adherence. They conclude that the "lack of progress in increasing adoption and adherence to regular physical activity may also be a consequence of limiting interventions to motivational and educational approaches directed to individuals and small groups" (p. 526). They also suggest that the concept of adherence needs to be reframed to take into account changes in patterns of physical activity that individuals may go through in their lifetime. Within this framework, it may be unreasonable to expect stability of adherence behaviour over the life span. In this context, Williams (2008) has suggested that self-paced exercise, as compared to prescribed intensity exercise, may produce a more positive affective response which will improve exercise adherence by enhancing anticipation of subsequent exercise sessions. Schneider, Dunn, and Cooper (2009) have extended this finding in adolescents, reporting that adolescents are more likely to engage in acute regular exercise if they experience a positive affective response during the experience.

Kirschenbaum (1998) has proposed that involvement in sport and the models that sport psychology has developed provide useful strategies for increasing adherence to physical activity. This may be important given the indications that health psychologists have achieved only modest success in this regard (Dishman & Buckworth, 1997). He uses a self-regulatory model to identify seven steps designed to improve athletic performance. He believes that this model is similar to that used by health psychologists to increase adherence and that sport can be used as a target for exercise adherence. By focusing on the commitment many individuals have to sport, psychologists can design strategies to increase adherence to exercise. The energy expended in sport can be considerable, and the modification of existing patterns could result in even greater expenditures. Kirschenbaum suggests that "not only could we target extant interest in sport as a goal in health psychology, but we could use sport psychology interventions to maximize involvement in such sports. These interventions could help participants enjoy their sports more fully, thereby sustaining their involvement in them" (p. 17). The extraordinary commitment that many individuals display to their sport can be used to indirectly increase their levels of physical activity and produce physical and psychological health benefits.

PSYCHOLOGICAL FACTORS AFFECTING PERFORMANCE IN EXERCISE AND SPORT

We will now examine developments in the sport psychology field that have implications for health psychology in general, and the choices individuals make regarding their health behaviour in particular. There are two principal areas of concern in sport psychology. One is performance enhancement as it relates to the development of psychological skills that can be used to optimize athletic performance. The second has to do with clinical issues, such as injury, depression, or eating disorders, any of which may compromise an athlete's performance.

We will focus initially on psychological skills as they can be applied to sport, physical activity, and life in general. This is important, for it recognizes that these are life skills as well as sport skills, and their utility extends beyond the domain of sport. This position is often recognized anecdotally by coaches who are aware of their impact on others, particularly young athletes, and view themselves as teachers of life skills.

Danish, Pettipas, and Hale (1993) developed a psychoeducational model for sport psychology that focuses specifically on the teaching of life skills, which they describe as "life development intervention." They suggest that sport is an effective and accessible analogy for the teaching of life skills. It is obvious that most young athletes will not go on to a career in sports; for these people, "growing up means further defining their identity, discovering other skills and interests, and, it is hoped, applying some of the valuable principles learned during sport participation to their adult pursuits. These transferable behaviours and attitudes are called *life skills*" (Danish, Nellen, & Owens, 1996).

An area of specific concern in this life-skills program is helping young people make appropriate decisions with regard to health-enhancing, as opposed to health-compromising, behaviours. Smith (1999) has addressed the assumption that sports skills will generalize beyond the athletic environment. In an athlete-centred program, sports skills are delivered in a manner that is developmentally appropriate and where "performance excellence is pursued only in the context of the athlete's overall health and well-being" (Miller & Kerr, 2002, p. 150). Based on research integrating sport and life-skills training, Papacharisis, Goudas, Danish, and Theodorakis (2005) conclude that the "program equips young athletes with knowledge and skills that are necessary for successfully coping with the complex realities of life" (p. 253).

In describing psychological skills training in sport, a distinction is often made between **psychological skills** and **psychological methods** (Vealey, 1988). Concerns such as arousal or

psychological skills in sport: arousal or attentional control implemented to enhance performance.

psychological methods in sport: techniques such as relaxation, goal setting, and imagery, which are used to develop psychological skills.

NBA MVP Steve Nash and Olympic gold medalist snowboarder Maelle Ricker are Canadians who embody health and excellence in both their professional and personal life.

attentional control relate to psychological skills, and issues such as relaxation, goal setting, and imagery are psychological methods; the latter serve to develop the former.

Others have suggested that the distinction should be made between "basic psychological skills," which can be used on their own, and "advanced psychological skills," of which the basic skills can be a component (Hardy, Jones, & Gould, 1997). In this discussion, we will focus on the basic skills, as they can be used in a psychological skills training program that can be applied both within and outside the sport and exercise domain. A recent edition of the *Journal of Applied Sport Psychology* concerned with the topic of excellence investigates the relationship between sport and business (Jones, 2002; Weinberg & McDermott, 2002); sport and the performing arts (Hays, 2002; Poczwarsdowski & Conroy, 2002); sport and acting (Martin & Cutler, 2002); and sport and police work (Le Scanff & Taugis, 2002).

These skills have application in models of stress management that have been adapted for sport. Examples would be Kirschenbaum's (1997) self-regulatory model, Meichenbaum's (1975) stress-inoculation training, Smith's (1980) cognitive-affective stress management training, and Suinn's (1972) visuomotor behaviour-rehearsal program. However, it has been suggested that rather than using specific programs such as these, the component skills of a psychological training program should be taught and used according to individual needs (Hardy, Jones, & Gould, 1997).

Relaxation

The ability to relax is an essential skill in coping with the pressure of athletic performance (Cox, 2002). Most individuals will acknowledge some degree of performance anxiety in anticipation of the demands of a task. **Relaxation skills** enhance one's ability to reduce anxiety to manageable levels, so that energy can be used to positively influence performance. Many of us experience "butterflies" prior to a performance, which is not a problem if we can teach them to "fly in formation." Relaxation skills assist in this process. It is also recognized that an effective performance, which is effortless and automatic, is more likely to occur in a relaxed state (Kirschenbaum, 1997; Taylor, 1996)..

Many successful athletes have developed relaxation skills on their own through a process of trial and error. However, there may be limitations to their ability to relax under pressure. Relaxation is viewed as a learned skill that needs to be applicable to the performance circumstances. For example, watching television or reading a book is relaxing; however, these activities, which are external to the individual, are not applicable to a performance situation. In this context we are describing an internal response usually described in either physical or mental terms.

The most widely practised form of relaxation in sport is the technique of progressive muscular relaxation (PMR) pioneered by Jacobson (1938) (see chapter 3). It involves focusing attention on different muscle groups within the body (e.g., the biceps, shoulders, or stomach) and progressing systematically through the entire body. With practice, one learns to initiate what Benson (1976) has termed the "relaxation response." It is important that, as familiarity with the technique increases, the ability to relax is generalized to the relevant performance domain. It seems that PMR is most effective in coping with the somatic or physiological components of anxiety, whereas strategies such as mental rehearsal and the management of self-talk may be more appropriate to coping with cognitive anxiety. It is also recognized that proper breathing is an effective strategy for

relaxation skills: techniques to reduce anxiety to manageable levels so that the energy can be used to positively influence performance; based on the principle that we cannot be relaxed and tense at the same time.

increasing levels of relaxation and successfully coping with anxiety. The deep, rhythmical breathing associated with relaxation can quickly replace the shallow, staccato breathing associated with tension and anxiety. Training in breath control can be most helpful in inducing and maintaining states of relaxation (Cox, 2007).

Self-Talk

self-talk: sport psychology concept to describe one of the methods athletes use to correct bad habits, focus attention, modify activation, increase self-confidence and efficacy, and maintain exercise behaviour.

Self-talk is a term used in sport psychology to describe one of the ways that people think (Cox, 2007). What do athletes say to themselves? It is a frequent observation that athletes talk to themselves a great deal, sometimes very negatively. Monitoring an athlete's self-talk gives us an opportunity to evaluate his or her perceptions and beliefs. We can identify cognitive distortions and irrational ways of thinking that might disrupt performance. It has been reported that patterns of self-talk can distinguish successful from unsuccessful performers (e.g., Orlick & Partington, 1988; Weinberg & Gould, 2003).

Williams and Leffingwell (1996) have identified different functions that self-talk can serve in sport, including correcting bad habits, focusing attention, modifying activation, increasing self-efficacy, and maintaining exercise behaviour. With regard to correcting bad habits, self-talk can be used to correct faulty technique. To focus attention, an athlete might say "watch the ball" or "execute." In modifying activation, the athlete might want to increase or decrease arousal levels. The self-talk might take the form of "relax" or "let go." Self-confidence may involve changing the tendency to call oneself a "loser" to saying "yes" to oneself. Given the importance attached to productive self-talk, interventions such as those described by Hardy, Roberts, and Hardy (2009) involving diaries and monitoring strategies designed to increase awareness of self-talk and the ability to change patterns of negative self-talk are important.

With regard to exercise behaviour, Gauvin (1990) suggests that those who maintain exercise have positive and motivating self-talk in comparison to the negative self-talk of non-exercisers. Once inappropriate patterns of self-talk have been identified, the concern is to modify this behaviour in the appropriate direction. This involves a restructuring process that replaces maladaptive cognitions with more adaptive ones.

The ongoing work of the eminent psychologist Albert Ellis (1975) in developing rational emotive behaviour therapy (REBT) is most relevant here. REBT involves the modification of irrational thoughts by identifying patterns of faulty reasoning. For example, in *absolute thinking*, events are viewed in all-or-none terms, such as "I must always do well." *Overgeneralization* involves drawing global conclusions on the basis of single events—for example, "I am never going to win a match." *Catastrophization* involves viewing minor concerns as disasters—for example, "Losing that match is the end of my career."

In REBT, irrational beliefs are actively disputed and individuals learn to substitute more rational ways of thinking. Ellis (1994) gave an invited address to Division 47, Exercise and Sport Psychology, at the 1993 American Psychological Association convention. His presentation was concerned with "The Sport of Avoiding Sports and Exercise." He believes that those who avoid exercise and sport have a low frustration tolerance that may be combined with a fear of failing. He states that "REBT helps them to discover and dispute their grandiose demands and absolutist musts" (p. 258). Ellis describes an intensive REBT program designed to help avoiders transform their inhibitions into healthy choices. In sport psychology, athletes are encouraged to restructure their self-talk and focus their attention on the task or process in a positive manner (e.g., Kirschenbaum, 1997; Rushall, 1984).

Imagery

The role of imagery in sport and exercise has been well documented (Hall, 2001; Weinberg & Gould, 2003). For instance, 99 percent of Canadian athletes who participated in the 1984 Olympic Games indicated that they had used imagery techniques to improve their performance (Orlick & Partington, 1988). Some of these athletes indicated that they had used imagery techniques for up to three hours in preparation for competition. There is a difference between *imagery* and *mental rehearsal* (Hall, 2001; Jones, Hardy, & Gould, 1997). The former is a sensory experience that is performed in the absence of external stimuli, whereas mental rehearsal is a technique that involves the use of imagery to mentally practise a skill.

A distinction is made between **external** and **internal imagery** (Hall, 2002). In external imagery, the individual is a passive and external third-person observer of his or her actions. Internal imagery is a much more active experience, in which the individual imagines being inside his or her own body, experiencing a situation as close to reality as possible.

external imagery: a technique in which an individual becomes a passive and external third-person observer of his or her own actions.

internal imagery: technique in which an individual imagines being inside his or her body, experiencing a given situation.

Several explanations have been given for the mechanisms underlying the relationship between imagery and performance (Gould & Damarjian, 1996; Hall, 2002). The psychoneuromuscular theory suggests that imagery causes the actual motor pattern to be rehearsed and therefore practised. According to symbolic learning, imagery provides the opportunity to symbolically practise an event. As one athlete said, "It felt like *déjà vu*, like I had done it before."

With regard to an imagery training program, Gould and Damarjian (1996) make several recommendations, including the following:

> Practice imagery on a regular basis, use all senses to enhance image vividness, use both internal and external perspectives, facilitate imagery through relaxation, use videotapes or audiotapes to enhance imagery skills, develop coping strategies through imagery, emphasize dynamic kinesthetic imagery, imagine in real time, use imagery in practice and competition. (p. 48)

Driskell, Copper, and Moran (1994) carried out a meta-analysis of the literature and concluded that mental practice has a "positive and significant effect on performance" (p. 481). They acknowledge, however, that although it is an effective strategy for improving performance, it is less effective than physical practice. They suggest that this makes mental practice most appropriate for difficult or dangerous training situations, for situations in which opportunities for physical practice are minimized, and simply as a strategy for supplementing normal training routines.

As Hall (2001) has indicated, we are still progressing in our understanding of imagery and how it can be used most effectively. To this end Murphy, Nordin, and Cumming (2008) recommend an integrative approach, such as functional equivalence, that focuses on the imagery process and "proposes that imagery draws on the same neural network that is used in actual perception and motor control and can also activate neural circuits used in memory and emotion."

Goal Setting

The final psychological skill we will discuss in this section is goal setting, a motivational strategy for improving performance (Barton, Naylor, & Holiday, 2001; Duda & Hall, 2001; Weinberg & Gould, 2003). Goal setting represents one of the most widely researched areas

ego orientation: a goal perspective that focuses on success and failure with success often coming at the expense of other people.

task orientation: a goal perspective in which individuals derive satisfaction from the sense of competence experienced as they improve; the focus is on effort and their own performance rather than that of others.

outcome goals: goals that are concerned with the results or outcomes of events and usually involve comparisons to others.

performance goals: goals that describe an outcome that can be achieved independently of others' performances.

process goals: goals that focus on specific processes that a performer will be concerned with during a performance.

in the field, as considerable research in goal setting in industrial and organizational fields has been applied to sports. The research on goal setting provided by Locke and his colleagues, beginning with his important paper in 1968, has been highly influential. Several important consistencies have emerged from this work. The indications are that higher levels of performance are achieved through difficult goals, specific goals, and a combination of both short-term and long-term goals (Locke, 1968; Locke & Latham, 1985; Locke & Latham, 1990).

Two different goal perspectives have been identified (Duda, 1992): **ego orientation** and **task orientation**. The former is focused on success and failure, with success often coming at the expense of others. In the latter, satisfaction is derived more from the sense of competence experienced through improvement. Their focus is on effort and one's *own* performance rather than that of others. These are not independent positions, and successful performers often make use of both of them (Duda & Hall, 2001).

Three different types of goals have been described in the literature (Hardy, Jones, & Gould, 1996). **Outcome goals** are concerned with the results or outcomes of events and usually involve comparisons to others. These goals might be expressed as a need to finish first in a race, where finishing second is equated with losing. **Performance goals** describe an outcome that can be achieved independently of others' performance; a novice marathoner may describe a desire to run her next race in less than four hours. **Process goals** focus on specific processes that a performer will be concerned with during a performance. A tennis player may indicate that during a match he plans to work on managing his self-talk.

Weinberg (1996) provides a number of goal setting principles based on his review of the relevant literature. They are as follows: "Set specific goals, set realistic but challenging goals, set both long- and short-term goals, set goals for practice and competition, 'ink it, don't think it,' develop goal-achievement strategies, set performance goals, set individual and team goals, provide support for goals, provide for goal evaluation" (p. 11).

Sebire, Standage, and Vansteenkiste (2009) compared the impact on exercise of intrinsic goals such as health improvement, skill, and relationship development, with extrinsic goals such as image enhancement and recognition. They report that intrinsic goals were associated with increased exercise engagement, physical self-worth, and well-being while anxiety decreased (p. 202).

This review of psychological skills training has focused on the four basic skills that are fundamental to understanding the more complex skills, such as attentional control, emotional control, confidence and self-efficacy, motivation, and coping with stress. As we discussed earlier, these are not skills unique to exercise and sport; however, in the context of physical activity, sport, and exercise, they can be useful in helping us to improve our performance and to enjoy ourselves. All indications are that we are more likely to continue to engage in exercise and sport if we enjoy it.

PHYSICAL ACTIVITY AND INJURY

The final issue we will consider in this chapter is of a more clinical nature—the psychological consequences of injury during physical activity, specifically sport and exercise. Clearly, injury is an event that occurs with an extremely high frequency in this context. Most of us will remember an injury we experienced while engaged in sport or exercise and could identify some of the psychological consequences of this event. We are also made very aware through the media of the injuries that regularly sideline our athletic heroes. Sometimes these are acute and sometimes they are chronic. The physical and psychological impact of these injuries is usually minimal; however, at times the impact can be very serious, extremely costly, and even career threatening (Cox, 2007; Weinberg & Gould, 2003; Williams, 2001).

A particular individual's reaction to a sports injury is a complex issue and will depend on numerous factors. These include the nature and severity of the injury, the role and importance of sport in the individual's life, and the response of the individual's support network. For example, athletes often state that the attention they receive from coaches and other support staff decreases dramatically when they are injured. Attention is given to those who can compete rather than those who cannot. An injured individual can also be a vicarious reminder of what can happen to others; for this reason, the uninjured may not want the injured athlete around them. The injured are also made painfully aware of what they are missing. One injury that has received considerable attention recently is concussion (see Box 9-1).

concussion (closed head injury): a bruising of the brain that can result in severe neurocognitive deficits, permanent disability, and even death.

acceleration-deceleration injury: a type of concussion that occurs when an immobile head is hit by a moving object or a moving head hits an immobile object.

rotational injury: a type of concussion resulting from a blow to the side of the head.

Box 9-1 Concussion

Athletes often describe it as "having your bell rung," while to the health professional it is known as a **closed head injury** or **concussion**. With disturbing frequency we read in our newspapers of the athlete whose career has been threatened by a blow to the head. After suffering a concussion during an NBA basketball game, an athlete stated, "The last thing I remember is checking into the game, then the next thing I remember is lying on the table and them asking me if I remember things. A long time elapsed between them. That's the scary part about it . . . that your mind can be altered like that" (Kingston, 1999).

Concussion is a bruising of the brain and is a serious injury. It can result in severe neurocognitive deficits, permanent disability, and even death. There is evidence that even mild concussion can result in neuropsychological impairments (Macciocchi et al., 1996). Two types of concussions are commonly described. An **acceleration-deceleration injury** occurs when an immobile head is hit by a moving object or a moving head hits an immobile object. A **rotational injury** usually results from a blow to the side of the head. A related concern in concussion is **second-impact syndrome**. This results when an athlete who has suffered a concussion returns to activity too soon and receives another blow to the head, which can result in much greater trauma to the brain than that initially experienced. **Post-concussion syndrome** is a term frequently seen in the press today. This describes a set of symptoms including memory problems and difficulties in concentration and complaints such as headaches, dizziness, and irritability.

It is important to remember that concussions can be experienced without the individual losing consciousness, and there is no visible physical evidence of concussion. The usual signs and symptoms of concussion include any period of loss of consciousness, confusion and inability to focus

attention, disorientation, slurred or incoherent speech, delayed verbal and motor responses, inappropriate emotional behaviour, memory deficits, and lack of coordination. Other signs include complaints such as headaches, dizziness, ringing in the ears, nausea/vomiting, impaired vision, seeing stars, and sensitivity to light.

Three grades of concussion have been identified. A **grade-one concussion** does not involve a loss of consciousness, although the individual may display transient confusion and should be taken out of the activity and examined for post-concussive symptoms. Someone with a grade-one concussion can return to the activity if any abnormalities or symptoms have cleared within 15 minutes. A **grade-two concussion** also does not involve a loss of consciousness; however, the concussion symptoms persist beyond 15 minutes. Such individuals should be taken out of the activity and not allowed to return. They should be seen the same day by a medical professional and should return to their sport only after one asymptomatic week and neurologic clearance by a physician. A **grade-three concussion** involves any loss of consciousness, brief or prolonged. The athlete may need to be taken to hospital by ambulance if still unconscious or if there are other concerns, such as neck pain. A neurologic evaluation is required initially, and further assessment will be necessary to determine when the athlete can return to the sport. Multiple concussions of any grade will further complicate the recovery process. The decision to return to activity should always be based on a physician's evaluation.

Concussion represents a serious problem in the sport and exercise field. With increasing public awareness of this problem, we have become more interested in understanding the nature of concussion and, most importantly, in the prevention of brain injury.

second-impact syndrome: results when an athlete who has suffered a concussion returns to activity too soon and receives another blow to the head that can result in much greater trauma to the brain than that initially experienced.

post-concussion syndrome: symptoms experienced subsequent to a concussion, such as memory problems, difficulties in concentration, headaches, dizziness, and irritability..

grade-one concussion: a concussion that does not involve a loss of consciousness, although the athlete may display transient confusion.

grade-two concussion: a concussion in which the symptoms persist beyond a 15-minute period but that does not involve a loss of consciousness.

grade-three concussion: any concussion that involves a loss of consciousness, whether it is extremely brief or prolonged.

When individuals suffer a sports injury, they may experience a wide range of emotions, such as anger, disbelief, frustration, fear, anxiety, guilt, panic, loneliness, and depression. A number of models have been proposed to help us better understand the psychological processes associated with an athletic injury. There are essentially two different kinds of approaches: those that focus on the stages of reaction and those that take a cognitive appraisal position. Stages-of-reaction approaches assume that individuals will pass through a series of stages in a set order. These approaches are frequently based on the model developed by Kübler-Ross (1969) to explain the experience of death and dying. She described five stages a dying individual goes through—denial and isolation, anger, bargaining, depression, and acceptance. In this context, the injury is considered to be similar to death and, indeed, many who suffer a debilitating injury view it this way. This model has been adapted to sport by Astle (1986) and Lynch (1988), who provide strategies for assisting those involved in the psychological rehabilitation of the injured person. The cognitive appraisal approach views an injury in the context of a stress and coping model (Brewer, 1994; Williams, 2001; Udry & Anderson, 2008). Individuals' emotional and behavioural responses to an injury will be determined by their personal appraisal of the event and their choice of coping strategies.

Brewer, Van Raalte, and Linder (1991) describe what they consider to be the primary responsibilities of a psychologist working with an injured athlete within a sports medicine context. The first involves an initial assessment of the individual's psychological status. The second is to facilitate, where necessary, communication between the physician and the athlete. The third is to provide the athlete with psychological skills to assist in the coping and rehabilitation process. These skills might include several we have discussed previously, such as relaxation training, goal setting, imagery and mental rehearsal, and cognitive restructuring. The fourth responsibility of the psychologist is to facilitate and provide social support for the injured athlete. The psychologist may be involved in actively seeking the assistance of others to develop a support network.

The role of the psychologist is being increasingly recognized as a crucial component in the intervention and management of injuries that occur in the context of sport and exercise (Brewer, 2001; Brown, 2005). Recently. Brewer (2010) described a biopsychosocial model of sport injury rehabilitation which identifies psychological factors such as cognitions, emotions and personality that impact the rehabilitation process and are important in designing psychological interventions. While acknowledging that, although there is over 30 years of work in this field, the position is taken that "inquiry on the role of psychological factors in sport injury rehabilitation outcomes is still in its formative stages' (p.58). It is clear that despite the demonstrated effectiveness of psychological interventions they are still rarely a part of the prevention and rehabilitation of sport injury (Brewer, 2009).

CHAPTER SUMMARY

The concept of physical activity is somewhat difficult to define; it is important to distinguish it from more formalized activities such as exercise and sport.

It is important to understand the relationship of physical activity to health, particularly in Canada where geography and climate can present challenges.

The psychological benefits of exercise relate to self-concept, self-esteem, and most importantly in this review, self-efficacy.

Physical activity is important, as it affects cognitive functioning and mood, particularly in relationship to anxiety, depression, and stress.

The physical benefits of physical activity have been demonstrated in regard to chronic illnesses such as cardiovascular disease and cancer.

Adherence, and long-term adherence in particular, is an issue of major concern with respect to physical activity, especially as it relates to exercise. Models for improving adherence are become increasingly relevant.

Performance-enhancing factors in both sport and exercise include relaxation techniques, management of self-talk, goal setting, and imagery techniques.

The psychological management of injury is an increasingly important component of rehabilitation in physical activity, sport, and exercise. A major issue has become the articulation of the significance of concussion and its impact on those who experience it.

Review Questions

1. How would you evaluate the balance in your life according to mental, physical, social, motivational, and spiritual well-being as discussed in this chapter?

2. Have you ever sustained an injury in sports, exercise, or another physical activity? How did it affect you psychologically?

3. Have you ever had a concussion? If so, what grade was it?

4. How would you describe your own adherence to health-enhancing activities? What factors affect people's adherence?

CHAPTER OUTLINE

SUBSTANCE ABUSE
UNSAFE SEXUAL BEHAVIOURS
OBESITY
EATING DISORDERS

Learning Objectives

After studying this chapter, you will be able to

- ■ Outline factors that contribute to smoking behaviour

- ■ Provide explanations for why indivuals drink alcohol or engage in illicit drug use

- ■ Inform others regarding how we can help people quit their smoking, alcohol or drug use

- ■ Outline factors that contribute to obesity in our society

- ■ Provide information about eating disorders

Jennifer began to smoke in high school. She was a bright girl who enjoyed the academic side of school but didn't always find the social side of school easy. When she began junior high school, also known as middle school, she noticed a radical shift in how her friends spent their time. Instead of playing sports and watching movies, her friends were now more interested in smoking, partying, and meeting guys. For a time, Jennifer resisted her friends' suggestions that she not be so uptight, that she learn to relax and start socializing at parties. However, Jennifer found that she was spending more and more time by herself and grew lonely. It seemed to her that the easiest way to fit in and regain friendships was to begin smoking. Both of Jennifer's parents smoked, so if she began it wouldn't cause much upset in the family. So she did begin and continued to smoke even after graduating from high school.

After high school, Jennifer went in search of a job. She wanted to work as a journalist or perhaps behind the scenes at a radio or television station. She was told that the best experience she could gain would be at a small-town radio or television station, where she would be expected to complete all the tasks of producing a story by herself; she'd have to find a story, write the story, and deliver the story on air.

Jennifer followed this advice. She found a job in a small town working for a local television station. In this new environment, Jennifer was able to give up smoking. Very few of the other people who worked at the television station smoked, and, of course, she no longer saw her high school friends, at least not on a regular basis. Jennifer was lucky. Unlike so many people who have a difficult time quitting, Jennifer was able to quit smoking on her own relatively easily.

Many years later, when Jennifer was going through the turmoil of a messy divorce, she began to smoke again. It all started when, after a lengthy meeting with her lawyer, she found herself craving a cigarette. After a couple of days she gave in to this craving and bought a package of cigarettes. She smoked a single cigarette and found that this did alleviate some of her stress—she welcomed the relief. Yet she knew smoking was unhealthy. She didn't want her children to model her behaviour and didn't want their health endangered as a result of her behaviour, so she never smoked indoors or let her children see her smoke. Fortunately, once the divorce was settled and she had obtained custody of her children, she was again able to kick the habit.

In this chapter, we will focus on specific health-compromising behaviours and the health hazards that are a product of these behaviours. Most of the behaviours we have chosen to focus on are behaviours that are voluntary in nature, at least initially. For example, we will examine the leading cause of premature death in Canada—smoking. We will also examine what is referred to as the obesity epidemic. And, in our discussion of disordered eating we will introduce you to a disorder that has been identified relatively recently—muscle dysmorphia. To begin, we will turn our attention to the most prevalent health-compromising behaviour in our society, smoking.

SUBSTANCE ABUSE

Smoking

Age and Gender Differences in Smoking
There are few habits as potentially deadly as smoking cigarettes. Smoking is the number one preventable cause of death and

These graphic images and warnings are among 16 that the Canadian government has required tobacco companies to include on all cigarette packaging.

their last cigarette and when they will smoke their next one. A highly addicted smoker deems the first cigarette of the day as most important and usually waits no more than 30 minutes before "lighting up" (Health Canada, 2005c). Addicted smokers have cigarettes with them at all times and usually keep at least one extra package "stashed away" for "emergencies." Research continues to support Tomkin's theory (e.g., Stevens, Colwell, Smith, Robinson, & McMillan, 2005).

Because different people have different reasons for smoking, strategies to quit smoking vary in their effectiveness. For example, people who smoke for pleasure show a sharp drop in the number of cigarettes they smoke when their cigarettes have been dipped in vinegar, whereas those who smoke for other reasons (e.g., addiction) do not. In contrast, people who smoke primarily from habit show a marked reduction in the amount they smoke when asked to keep a record of cigarettes smoked, whereas this is not the case for those who smoke for pleasure.

The psychological reasons for smoking are certainly important, but heredity may also play a role. Researchers have not definitively determined the link between heredity and smoking, but three possible explanations have been put forth. First, genetic factors may underlie certain personality traits associated with smoking (e.g., rebelliousness). Second, heredity may determine the extent to which people find tobacco pleasant or unpleasant. Third, genetically based differences in reaction to nicotine influence the degree to which people exposed to nicotine become dependent on it (Li et al., 2004; Ling, Niu, Feng Xing, & Zu, 2004; Munafo, Johnstone, Murphy, & Walton, 2001).

Once people begin smoking regularly, they become physiologically dependent on the nicotine in cigarettes, so it's important to understand how nicotine initially affects us. When a person inhales smoke from a cigarette, nicotine passes through cell membranes in the mouth and nose en route to the lungs, where alveoli absorb the nicotine and carry it to the blood. In a very short time, the blood has carried the nicotine to the brain. In the brain, nicotine triggers the release of various chemicals that activate both the central and sympathetic nervous systems, resulting in increases in heart rate and blood pressure. This entire process takes approximately 10 seconds (Health Canada, 2005c).

Health Consequences of Smoking

As previously mentioned, smoking is the number one preventable cause of death and disease in Canada. Research conclusively shows that smoking reduces life expectancy by several years. Ellison and his colleagues (1999) at Health Canada determined that the rate of premature death (before age 70) for lifelong smokers (both males and females) was twice that of people who had never smoked. Smoking also increases the risk of many illnesses, including cancer, cardiovascular disease, high blood pressure, high cholesterol, emphysema, pneumonia, gum disease, osteoporosis, cataracts, and sleeping problems (Health Canada, 2005c). And the more you smoke, the worse your odds become. Given this, it is not surprising that non-smokers are expected to live a higher proportion of their life without any disability (Statistics Canada, 2001).

On July 15, 2003, in an effort to protect Canada's citizens from the health hazards and economic burden of tobacco consumption and exposure to tobacco smoke, Anne McLellan, the Canadian Minister of Health at the time, signed the Framework Convention on Tobacco Control (FCTC). Member countries of the World Health Organization prepared the FCTC. Their goal was to aid in the prevention, cessation, and harm reduction of tobacco (Health Canada, 2003b).

Smoking and Cardiovascular and Cerebrovascular Disease

Together, cardiovascular disease (22.9 percent) and cerebrovascular disease (6.5 percent) were responsible for 66 600 deaths (29.4 percent) in Canada in 2004 (Statistics Canada, 2008). In general, the risk of dying of cardiovascular disease is about twice as high for smokers as for non-smokers. In a large-scale study that analyzed data from 52 countries, researchers from McMaster University's Population Health Research Institute determined that the risk of myocardial infarction (heart attack) increased by 5.6 percent for every cigarette smoked (Teo et al., 2006).

Smoking is thought to contribute to cardiovascular disease in a number of ways. There is some evidence that cigarette smoking increases the level of serum cholesterol and the size of plaque within the arteries. Amazingly, the progression of atherosclerosis in smokers is estimated to increase by as much as 50 percent during a three-year period (Howard et al., 1998). Nicotine itself may also contribute to heart disease. Nicotine has a stimulant effect on the nervous system, resulting in increases in heart rate, blood pressure, and cardiac output, combined with constriction of blood vessels. Fortunately, the risk of heart attack and stroke, like that of cancer, declines when people quit smoking (Critchley & Capewell, 2003; Teo et al., 2006).

Smoking and Cancer   Cancer is one of the leading causes of death in Canada. In 2004, 29.5 percent of deaths in Canada were attributed to various forms of cancer (Statistics Canada, 2008). Although almost 80 percent of smoking-related deaths in Canada result from lung cancer, smoking is also responsible for deaths from cancer of the lip, oral cavity, pharynx, esophagus, pancreas, larynx, urinary bladder, and kidney (Health Canada, 2006b). Researchers in the United States have documented the correspondence between the rise in lung cancer deaths and the prevalence of smoking since the 1930s. These researchers (e.g., Shopland & Burns, 1993) state that the rate of mortality from lung cancer began to rise approximately 15 to 20 years after the rate of smoking started to rise. These rates have paralleled each other since that time.

Smoking and Chronic Obstructive Pulmonary Diseases   Chronic obstructive pulmonary diseases (COPD) include a number of respiratory and lung diseases, such as chronic bronchitis and emphysema. They accounted for 10 000 deaths (or 4.4 percent of all deaths) in Canada in 2004 (Statistics Canada, 2008). Virtually all COPDs are experienced by smokers. In other words, these conditions are relatively rare in non-smokers. In general terms, smoking irritates and damages respiratory organs. This damage leads to reduced airflow when breathing and is particularly noticeable when trying to exhale with force.

Environmental Tobacco Smoke   We have looked at what happens to the health of people who smoke. What we have not considered is the number of people who are affected by **environmental tobacco smoke (ETS)**, also known as **second-hand smoke**. Most Canadians spend more time indoors than outdoors, and tobacco smoke is a key contaminant in indoor air quality. Breathing ETS is called **passive smoking**. The Public Health Agency of Canada estimates that approximately 800 Canadian non-smokers die each year from lung cancer caused by exposure to ETS (Public Health Agency of Canada, 2002). The number of non-smokers who die from cardiovascular disease as a result of ETS is likely much higher, given that researchers have estimated that at least 10 times the number of non-smokers die from ETS-related cardiovascular disease than they do from ETS-related lung cancer. Pregnant women, fetuses, and young children are especially susceptible. Health consequences include complications of pregnancy and low birth weight, increased risk of sudden infant death syndrome and ear infections, reduced lung development, and increased severity of asthma and other respiratory illnesses (Kuehn, 2006). In an effort to protect people, most provinces now have restrictions on smoking in public settings.

Quitting Smoking   The vast majority of current smokers state that if they had it to do "over again, they would not have started smoking" (Fong et al., 2004, p. S341). In fact, each year, almost half of all smokers attempt to quit (Reid & Hammond, 2009). Unfortunately, only about 12 percent of attempts to quit by 15- to 19-year-olds are successful. However, success rates increase with age and those 45 years and older have a success rate of 70 percent (Reid & Hammond, 2009). Additional information that might

environmental tobacco smoke (ETS) (second-hand smoke): smoke that is in the air we breathe because of others' smoking.

passive smoking: the breathing of environmental tobacco smoke.

motivate someone to quit smoking is that 60 percent of ever smokers have now quit (Reid & Hammond, 2009).

As previously mentioned, smoking is an **addiction**. That is, once people begin to smoke regularly most become physically or psychologically dependent on it. Therefore, people who want to quit smoking must go through a period of **withdrawal**. Withdrawal refers to the unpleasant symptoms that people experience when they stop using a substance they have become dependent on. When people reduce or eliminate nicotine intake, they experience short-term symptoms such as a reduction in concentration, attention, and memory, combined with an increase in anxiety, irritability, and moodiness (Health Canada, 2005c; Shadel et al., 2000). The good news is that if you do quit smoking, your odds of survival steadily improve. After 15 or 20 years as a non-smoker, your odds are similar to those of people who have never smoked (Critchley & Capewell, 2003; Teo et al., 2006). Although the benefits of quitting smoking are the same for everyone, the reasons why people choose to quit vary (see Figure 10-2).

addiction: the state of being physically or psychologically dependent on a substance.

withdrawal: the unpleasant symptoms people experience when they stop using a substance to which they are addicted.

Quitting on One's Own Approximately 10 percent of individuals interviewed about their attempt to quit smoking in the past year reported being abstinent for at least one month (Reid & Hammond, 2009). Most relapses occur in the first three months (Ockene et al., 2000). Almost half of those who attempt to quit smoking will do so on their own, without any professional help, self-help materials, or stop-smoking medications (Reid & Hammond, 2009). Why would so many smokers attempting to quit not seek help?

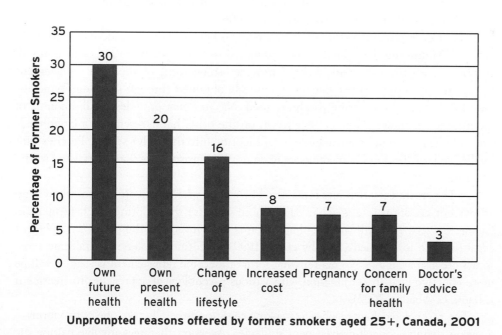

Unprompted reasons offered by former smokers aged 25+, Canada, 2001

Figure 10-2 Reasons for Quitting Smoking

Source: *Canadian Tobacco Use Monitoring Survey 2001: Quitting Smoking Among Adults,* Health Canada, 2003. Reproduced with the permission of the Minister of Public Works and Government Services Canada, 2010.

Canadians may be unaware of what help is available. When asked to recall tips or suggestions to help someone stop smoking, Canadian smokers could provide little advice: 14 percent of participants mentioned the nicotine patch or medication such as bupropion, 2 percent mentioned nicotine gum, and 16 percent said there was no way to help (Environics Research Group, 2001). In a more recent study, 24 percent of smokers from Ontario cited at least one cessation method with no evidence of effectiveness (i.e., hypnosis and acupuncture; Hammond, McDonald, Fong, & Borland, 2004). Perhaps, like smokers in other countries, Canadians do not believe in the effectiveness of nicotine replacement therapy (NRT) products. For example, a Swiss study revealed that only 16 percent of Switzerland's general public believed that NRT products assist people in quitting smoking (Etter & Perneger, 2001).

In Montreal (Kishchuk et al., 2004), college students expressed "uniformly negative" opinions about virtually all interventions—counselling, pharmacological aids, "Quit and Win" contests, self-help tools, media campaigns, environmental regulations, and social mobilization. These college students indicated that college life was already challenging and that they did not need more demands placed on them. To engage students, these authors suggest providing opportunities and support for exploration of, and commitment to, personal and social identities that exclude smoking, developing interventions that associate quitting with healthy outdoor environments and activities, and targeting friendship cliques with non-judgmental messages.

Quitting with Therapy   Some people who cannot quit smoking on their own do seek help from others. Most therapies include nicotine-replacement therapy, psychological interventions, or both. Therapies that combine both nicotine replacement and psychological interventions, known as multidimensional approaches, are considered most effective (Niaura & Abrams, 2002; Ranney et al., 2006).

nicotine-replacement therapy: a stop-smoking technique that provides some form of nicotine to replace that previously obtained through smoking.

Nicotine-replacement therapy was used by 40 percent of respondents to the 2008 Tobacco Monitoring Use Survey who attempted to quit smoking (Reid & Hammond, 2009). Nicotine-replacement therapy provides some form of nicotine replacement for the nicotine that former smokers previously obtained through smoking. Typically, nicotine gum or the nicotine patch are used. *Nicotine gum* provides small amounts of nicotine when chewed. The *nicotine patch,* on the other hand, resembles a large bandage and releases a small continuous dose of nicotine into the body's system. Patches with smaller and smaller doses of nicotine are worn until the person is no longer addicted to the nicotine.

A 23-percent cessation rate is achieved by people who use nicotine gum, whereas an 18-percent cessation rate is achieved by those who use the nicotine patch (American Cancer Society, 2006). If the drug bupropion is combined with the patch, a 35-percent cessation rate is obtained (Jorenby et al., 1999). Nicotine inhalers and nicotine nasal sprays are also available. No matter what form of nicotine replacement is used, it will be more effective used in conjunction with various psychological approaches to treatment (Niaura & Abrams, 2002).

aversion therapy: therapy that includes pairing the behaviour that one is attempting to eliminate with some unpleasant stimulus so that the undesired behaviour will elicit negative sensations.

The psychological approaches to smoking cessation generally take one of two forms—aversion therapies or self-management strategies. **Aversion therapies** involve pairing the behaviour to be eliminated, in this case smoking, with some unpleasant stimulus so that smoking will elicit negative sensations. The three most common forms of aversion therapies are electric shock, imagined aversive scenes, and rapid smoking.

Electric shock can be paired with smoking situations so that when a person smokes he or she is shocked and made uncomfortable. When *aversive scenes* are used, people are directed to think of an aversive scene that includes beginning to smoke, followed by something disgusting (e.g., you take the cigarette out of the pack and are about to light it when you suddenly vomit all over your cigarette, your hands, and the lighter. The smell is so foul you can hardly stand it. You drop the cigarette and the lighter and, as you turn away and head toward the bathroom to clean yourself up, you begin to feel much less nauseous). The third technique, *rapid smoking,* is seldom used. Rapid smoking involves placing the smoker in a small, enclosed room where he or she inhales from a cigarette rapidly every few seconds while concentrating on the smoke, the stinging burn in the throat, and other unpleasant elements. Aversion strategies may help in the initial stages of quitting smoking, but the effects are seldom long-term.

Self-management strategies are designed to help people overcome the environmental conditions that perpetuate smoking. *Self-monitoring* requires that people record each cigarette they smoke, the time of day, their location, who they are with, and their mood. Self-monitoring in itself reduces smoking, but the information obtained also aids in formulating other approaches to smoking cessation. *Stimulus control* strategies focus on removing the cues that lead a person to smoke. For example, if a person always smokes during a coffee break when sitting in the staff room, that person may want to go for a walk or have a coffee break in a different location. *Behavioural contracting* involves establishing a contract, according to which a person will be rewarded for fulfilling the contract or punished for failing to do so. These contracts often involve having the person deposit a large sum of money that he or she will lose if the contract is broken. These are only a few of the strategies that can be used to help people quit smoking.

self-management strategies: strategies used to help people overcome the environmental conditions that perpetuate smoking.

Interestingly, Reid and Hammond (2009) reported that the most common strategy used by those attempting to quit smoking over the last few years is simply to reduce the number of cigarettes smoked each day. Over 60 percent of individuals tried this approach in 2008, but this strategy was often used in combination with other strategies (Reid & Hammond, 2009).

Alcohol Use

Alcohol Consumption   About 76 percent of Canadians (80 percent of men and 73 percent of women) have consumed alcohol in the past 12 months (CCSA, 2009). Women are more likely than men to be non-drinkers (13.9 percent versus 9.1 percent). Men are more likely than women to report drinking alcohol at least once a week (55.2 percent versus 32.8 percent); to "binge" drink, that is, consume five or more drinks at a sitting (23.2 percent versus 8.8 percent); and to binge drink at least once a week (9.2 percent versus 3.3 percent). Men are also more likely to exceed the low-risk guidelines than are women (30.2 percent versus 15.1 percent) (CCSA, 2005).

What are the low-risk guidelines? The current guidelines were put forth in 1997 by what is now the Canadian Centre on Substance Abuse (CCSA). The low-risk drinking guidelines state that men should limit their weekly alcohol intake to no more than 14 standard drinks and women to no more than 9 standard drinks. A standard drink is a 5-ounce glass of wine, a 12-ounce glass of beer, or 1.5 ounces of spirits. Each standard drink contains 13.6 grams of alcohol. These guidelines are "designed to help people to enjoy the pleasurable effects of alcohol while minimizing the risk of health, social and family problems that may be caused by alcohol" (CCSA, 2008).

Additional demographic trends indicate that those 18 to 24 years of age and single persons were more likely to exceed the low-risk drinking guidelines than were their counterparts. Similarly, those in the highest income brackets are more likely to exceed the low-risk drinking guidelines (CCSA, 2005). This is a pattern that is in direct contrast to that found for smoking. You may remember that smoking rates decrease steadily with income level. There are, however, no alcohol-consumption differences observed according to level of education or based on living in a rural versus non-rural area. Aboriginal Canadian adolescents are reported as having a risk as much as six times greater than other Canadians for developing alcohol problems (CCSA, 1999).

ethanol (ethyl alcohol): the alcohol used in beverages.

The Effects of Alcohol The alcohol used in beverages is called **ethanol** or **ethyl alcohol**. This alcohol is a depressant drug, and, like other depressant drugs (e.g., tranquillizers and painkillers) it slows down the nervous system, which may cause drowsiness, induce sleep, or relieve pain. Even the initial apparent stimulant effect actually results from depression of centres in the brain that inhibit our actions and control our behaviour. After one drink, the majority of people report feeling more relaxed. With more than one drink, a person may feel more outgoing and self-confident, but some people will become aggressive, depressed, or withdrawn. At higher doses—even below a blood-alcohol concentration of 0.05, the legal limit for driving a car in Canada—thinking, judgment, and ability to estimate distance can be impaired and reaction times increased (Alberta Alcohol and Drug Abuse Commission, 2003; Canadian Health Network, 2005).

Excessive use of alcohol can have adverse effects on almost every system of the body, resulting in higher morbidity and shorter life expectancy (Statistics Canada, 2004a). For example, chronic alcohol abuse causes liver disease and damage to the stomach, pancreas, and intestines. Moreover, chronic drinking causes high blood pressure and depression of the immune system and is associated with coronary artery disease and cancer of the throat, larynx, mouth, esophagus, and liver (Alberta Alcohol and Drug Abuse Commission, 2003; Canadian Health Network, 2005).

Other consequences of drinking include blackouts, hangovers, and even death. Blackouts are periods of memory loss that occur while a person is drinking heavily. Hangovers, on the other hand, occur after drinking has stopped. Hangovers are caused by mild alcohol withdrawal and may be experienced 8 to 12 hours after a bout of heavy drinking. The symptoms of a hangover include fatigue, headache, nausea, and sometimes vomiting and shakiness.

Death may occur following moderate doses of alcohol taken together with other depressant drugs, such as sleeping pills and tranquilizers, or from an overdose of alcohol as a result of excessive consumption. This kind of consumption has been associated with events such as college fraternity initiations. For example, some college students have been known to participate in the dangerous behaviour of "funnelling," putting a funnel in someone's mouth and pouring liquor into the funnel. This method of drinking can be lethal because it easily provides too much alcohol.

In addition to harming oneself, one also harms others by drinking to excess. Violence and accidents due to alcohol consumption account for approximately 6000 deaths per year in Canada. Not surprisingly, motor vehicle accidents account for a large proportion of these deaths. However, alcohol is also responsible for "injuries and fatalities due to falls, drowning and fires; work-related accidents, absenteeism and illness; and crimes of violence including spousal abuse and physical assault" (Canadian Health Network, 2005, p. 10). Excess drinking also causes harm to society including job loss, relationship failure, disintegration of the family unit, and the contribution of deleterious drinking habits to ensuing generations. One of the most serious harms is damage to a growing fetus. **Fetal alcohol spectrum disorder (FASD)** is the name used to describe the range of disabilities caused by prenatal exposure to alcohol. These effects are permanent.

Although, as noted above, there are many dire negative consequences to excessive drinking, there may, in fact, be health benefits for light to moderate drinkers. Numerous studies (e.g., Gmel, Gutiahr, & Rehm, 2003; Gunzerath, Faden, Zakhari, & Warren, 2004) have reported that moderate drinking has survival advantages. Specifically, the relationship between alcohol consumption and mortality is depicted in a J-shaped curve, with the lowest mortality occurring when one to two drinks are consumed daily (Gmel et al., 2003; Gunzerath et al., 2004). These protective effects are primarily for coronary heart

fetal alcohol spectrum disorder (FASD): the name used to describe the range of disabilities caused by prenatal exposure to alcohol; these effects are permanent.

Binge drinking is the leading preventable cause of death among undergraduate students.

disease (CHD) and cerebrovascular effects (i.e., ischemic stroke). The relative risk of myocardial infarction is reduced by between 25 to 50 percent for men and 20 to 40 percent for women with moderate alcohol consumption, depending on the study cited (Gunzerath et al., 2004).

Researchers believe that consuming alcohol increases levels of high-density lipoprotein (HDL), which is responsible for a decreased risk of heart attacks. The risk of ischemic stroke is reduced for middle-aged and elderly adults, but there may be an increase in risk for young adults who are already more susceptible to hemorrhagic strokes. We should also note that women who drink moderately have an increased risk of death from other causes (e.g., breast cancer and cirrhosis). As well, we should point out that red wine was initially believed to have unique survival advantages; now we know that one kind of alcohol does not offer a particular advantage over another kind. Wine, beer, and liquor are all thought to produce the same advantages (Prickett et al., 2004). Most recently, large-scale studies are questioning the health benefits of moderate drinking, suggesting that the benefits may be overstated (Fillmore, Kerr, & Stockwell, 2006; Naimi et al., 2005).

Explaining Drinking Behaviour   It has been suggested that drinking is commonplace in North America because it is so widely accepted. But perhaps drinking is well accepted because it is so commonplace. Regardless, drunkenness or problem drinking is not acceptable, and it is therefore important to explain why this behaviour occurs. The **disease model** of problem drinking maintains that alcoholism is a disease brought about by the physical properties of alcohol. Jellinek (1960), a pioneer in the field of alcoholism, described a number of different types of alcoholism. For example, **gamma alcoholism** is loss of control once drinking begins, whereas **delta alcoholism** is the inability to abstain. This model, still common in medically focused treatment programs in North America, is closely linked to the 12-step program of treatment (Quinn, Bodenhamer-Davis, & Koch, 2004). The model is not as common in Europe, Australia, or in psychologically based treatment programs.

The **alcohol dependency syndrome model** states that at certain times and for a variety of reasons people do not exercise control over their drinking, and this leads to problem drinking (Edwards & Gross, 1976). A number of elements are said to be essential for alcohol dependency syndrome to develop, including a salience of drink-seeking behaviour (meaning that drinking begins to take priority over all other aspects of life) and an increased tolerance for alcohol. Someone with an increased tolerance for alcohol may gradually become accustomed to going about their daily routine "at blood alcohol levels that would incapacitate the non-tolerant drinker" (Edwards & Gross, 1976, p. 1059). Although this model remains popular in certain circles, it has been criticized because of its emphasis on the physical properties of alcohol and its neglect of the cognitive and social learning aspects of drinking (McMurran, 1994).

Cognitive-physiological models propose that people drink because alcohol influences cognitive functioning, allowing people to escape tension and negative self-evaluations. One of these models, the **tension reduction hypothesis**, maintains that people drink alcohol because of its tension-reducing properties. Although there is little empirical support for this theory, some research suggests that alcohol may lead people to avoid tension-producing behaviours or situations (Rutledge & Sher, 2001). The **self-awareness model** suggests that drinking inhibits the use of normal, complex information-processing strategies, such as memory and information acquisition, making people less self-aware (Hull,

disease model (of problem drinking): a theory suggesting that alcoholism is a disease resulting from the physical properties of alcohol.

gamma alcoholism: loss of control once drinking begins.

delta alcoholism: the inability to abstain from alcohol.

alcohol dependency syndrome model: a theory suggesting that for a variety of reasons people do not exercise control over their drinking, and this leads to problem drinking.

tension reduction hypothesis: the hypothesis that people drink alcohol because of its tension-reducing properties.

self-awareness model: the theory that drinking makes people less self-aware because it inhibits the use of normal complex information-processing strategies, such as memory and information acquisition.

1981, 1987; Hull & Bond, 1986). Decreased self-awareness leads to decreased monitoring of behaviour, resulting in the disinhibition and decrease in self-criticism that often occurs when people are drinking. Simply stated, some people may consume alcohol to avoid self-awareness.

A third cognitive-physiological theory developed to explain drinking behaviour is called **alcohol myopia** (Steele & Josephs, 1990). Alcohol myopia refers to a drinker's decreased ability to process information outside a narrow range (myopia). This effect also helps to lower inhibition of impulsive responses. Alcohol myopia is characterized by excessive behaviour (being more friendly or more aggressive, engaging in more risky sexual behaviour, etc.), the tendency to inflate self-evaluations, and *drunken relief* or a tendency to worry less and pay less attention to worries (Griffin, Umstattd, & Usdan, 2010).

alcohol myopia: a drinker's decreased ability to engage in insightful cognitive processing.

The **social learning model** proposes that people drink because they experience positive reinforcement for doing so (e.g., the taste or the effects of alcohol are pleasant) or because they observe others drinking and model this behaviour. For example, you may try drinking because your friends drink, and you may continue to drink in the company of your friends. Or, once you have tried drinking you may like the taste of the beverage or you may notice a change in your behaviour that you like (e.g., you feel less shy after having a drink). Recent research (Freeman, Friedman, Bartholow, & Wulfert, 2010) has discovered that the mere exposure to alcohol-related contextual cues (e.g., the sight or smell of alcoholic beverages) may reduce the threshold for engaging in behaviours that would otherwise be inhibited (e.g., physical aggression and sexual risk taking).

social learning model: this theory, when applied to drinking behaviour, proposes that people drink because they experience positive reinforcement for doing so or because they observe others drinking and model the behaviour.

Social learning theory can explain why people begin to drink, why they continue to drink in moderation, and why some people drink to excess. Excessive drinking may occur because of modelling (your friends are also drinking to excess) or because once you stop drinking you experience negative reinforcement in the form of a hangover or withdrawal symptoms. According to the social learning model, drinking behaviour is learned and can therefore also be unlearned. A number of treatment techniques to help people overcome excessive drinking habits rely on social learning principles.

Preventing and Treating Alcohol Abuse   Attempts to prevent alcohol abuse have taken a number of forms. Public policy and legal approaches include implementing age restrictions for individuals buying or consuming alcohol. Health promotion and education strategies incorporating social influence approaches have been useful in helping adolescents avoid drinking heavily. These may include discussions and films regarding how peers, family members, and the media influence drinking, or modelling and role-playing specific refusal skills (e.g., saying "No thank you, I don't drink") and how to deal with high-risk situations (e.g., Saltz, 2004–2005; Saltz, 2005).

The majority of people stop drinking without treatment (Cunningham, 1999). Authorities in the field of problem drinking prefer to use the term *unassisted change*. This term may be somewhat misleading, because support is likely provided to the individual by many people in an informal manner.

Those who do not obtain help when attempting to stop drinking are far more likely to relapse than those who do seek treatment (Moos & Moos, 2006). Many individuals do seek treatment, however, and the federal and provincial governments combined contribute $14 million annually to the provision of alcohol and drug treatment and rehabilitation (Health Canada, 2003b).

Twelve-step programs such as Alcoholics Anonymous (AA) are extremely popular (Quinn, Bodenhamer-Davis, & Koch, 2004). Yet this kind of program doesn't seem to be more effective than other formal treatments. Psychotherapy, drug therapy (e.g., disulfiram, commonly known as Antabuse), and aversion therapy (e.g., electric shock) have all been used with limited success (Schuckit, 1996). However, relapse is a persistent problem with all alcohol treatment approaches. Zwiak et al. (2006) have documented three distinct forms of relapse: negative affect, social pressure, and cue/craving. Women are most likely to have negative affect relapses, whereas men are most likely to relapse due to social pressure. Most often, a relapse will occur within three months after the end of treatment. After a year, only about one-third of those who complete the program are still abstinent.

Canada's Drug Strategy (Health Canada, 2000b) adopts the *stages of change* model for guiding both treatment processes and prevention goals. You may remember this model from chapter 1. If we apply the model to drug use, we note the stages an individual goes through in deciding to use a particular substance (Health Canada, 2000b, p. 34):

Pre-contemplation	Not considering use
Contemplation	Thinking about initiating use
Preparation	Intending to use
Action	Initiating use
Maintenance	Continuing to use
Relapse	

For anyone who is not considering alcohol use or anyone who is thinking about initiating use, primary prevention is the key. If, however, an individual is currently using or continuing to use alcohol, a harm reduction strategy is appropriate. An example of a large-scale harm reduction approach was initiated in Edmonton in the 1990s. The Alberta Liquor Control Board allowed early opening hours for a retail outlet in downtown Edmonton. The purpose of the extended hours was to reduce the use of potentially lethal non-beverage alcohol (e.g., shoe polish) by skid-row alcoholics. The objective was not to reduce the consumption of alcohol, but to increase their consumption of potable or safe alcohol (Single, 2005). Whatever an individual's current state, there are specific activities and messages that can be adopted (e.g., implementation of more intensive approaches for those in the preparation, action, or maintenance stages).

Drinking and Driving We mentioned previously that drinking influences our thought processes. Unfortunately, alcohol causes people to think less negatively about drinking and driving (MacDonald, Zanna, & Fong, 1995, 1998; Ortner, MacDonald, & Olmstead, 2003). In Canada, it is illegal to drive with a blood alcohol content of more than 50 mL of alcohol per 100 mL of blood (Health Canada, 2004a). The good news is that drinking and driving rates have been decreasing since the 1980s. Moderate drinkers are finding alternate forms of transportation. Unfortunately, heavy drinkers seem to be immune to the anti-drinking-and-driving programs that have been implemented; this group of drivers will get behind the wheel after consuming three or more times the legal limit (CCSA, 2008).

Because judgment and decision making are impaired, it is not surprising that intoxicated individuals are often involved in traffic accidents. However, while fewer people are driving after drinking, more drivers are testing positive for drugs. Approximately 8 percent of drivers test positive for alcohol, while just over 10 percent of night-time drivers

As of May 1, 2009, drivers in Ontario convicted of an impaired driving offence under the Criminal Code of Canada or suspended for registering a blood alcohol concentration of .05 to .08 three or more times in a five-year period will be required to install an ignition interlock device in their vehicle. The ignition interlock device is an in-car alcohol breath screening device that prevents a vehicle from starting if it detects a blood alcohol concentration over a pre-set limit of .02 (i.e., 20 mg of alcohol per 100 ml of blood). The device is located inside the vehicle, near the driver's seat, and is connected to the engine's ignition system (Ontario, Ministry of Transportation, 2009).

showed evidence of drug use, and 16.9 percent tested positive for drugs, alcohol or both. Despite perceptions that drug use is less harmful to drivers, there is growing evidence that drug impairment is also a major contributor to collisions (CCSA, 2008). Five percent of drivers have driven under the influence of cannabis, a drug that compromises visual ability and reaction time (CCSA, 2010). A study conducted in 2004 showed that drugs, often combined with alcohol, were detected in up to 30 percent of fatally injured drivers (CCSA, 2008).

Illicit Drug Use

Compared with those who succumb to the effects of smoking cigarettes and drinking alcohol, relatively few people die from the effects of illegal drugs. For example, cocaine, the most lethal of the illicit drugs, kills only one person for every 1000 killed by tobacco products (Rouse, 1998). Of course, even one death from illicit drugs is too many. Illicit drugs present certain risks not found with legal drugs, regardless of pharmacological effects. People purchasing illicit drugs may be told they are buying one drug but receive another; illegally manufactured drugs may be contaminated with toxic chemicals; and users never really know what drug or how much of a particular drug they are taking.

How prevalent is the use of illicit drugs? In Canada in 2009, the use of at least one of six illicit drugs (i.e., cannabis, cocaine or crack, speed, ecstasy, hallucinogens, or heroin) was 11 percent (Health Canada, 2010). The rate of use by males (14.7 percent) was almost double that for females (7.6 percent), and the prevalence of use was more than three times higher among youth (27.3 percent) than adults (7.9 percent) (Health Canada, 2010). Those with less education, those who lived in low-income households, and those who were single and were in younger age groups were more likely to be drug dependent. Of course, these factors do not occur in isolation. For example, young people are more likely to be single and to have comparatively low incomes. Those who were born in Canada were three times more likely than immigrants to be alcohol or drug dependent (Statistics Canada, 2004a).

Health Canada (2000a) reports that the use of illicit drugs is as great now as at any time in history. In fact, use of the most common illicit drug in North America, cannabis, is on the increase (Statistics Canada, 2004b). In 1989, 6.5 percent of Canadians reported using cannabis during the previous year; by 2004 the figure had risen to 14.1 percent, but has decreased to 10.9 percent (Health Canada, 2010). By 2008 almost half of all Canadians had used cannabis at least once in their lives (CCSA, 2010). Cannabis use is most prevalent in younger age groups and peaks at ages 18 and 19 (38 percent in 2004, but down to 26 percent in 2009).

The most recent survey of illicit drug use reports that in 2009 the most frequently used drug after cannabis in the previous 12 months was cocaine or crack (1.2 percent), followed by ecstasy (0.9 percent). Hallucinogens (e.g., LSD and PCP) have been used by 0.7 percent of the population, followed by speed (0.7 percent), and methamphetamine (0.1 percent) (Health Canada, 2009a). Those most likely to have tried other illicit drugs were 35- to 44-year-old adults (Statistics Canada, 2004b). The distribution was bell-shaped around this age group, with 25- to 34-year-olds the next highest age range, followed by 45- to 54-year-olds. We now turn our attention to the health problems associated with some of the more common illicit drugs.

Cannabis   Surveys indicate that youth are as likely to use cannabis as they are tobacco (Health Canada, 2000a). Cannabis, or marijuana, is composed of the leaves, flowers, and small branches of *Cannabis sativa*, a plant that grows in almost every climate. Delta-9-tetrahydrocannabinol (THC) is the intoxicating ingredient of cannabis. Is smoking cannabis a potential health hazard? Cannabis use leads to disturbances in short-term memory, judgment, and time perception (WHO, 2006). When large doses are consumed, heart rate is increased. A rapid heart rate may lead to health hazards for people who have coronary problems. Long-term use is associated with psychotic symptoms.

As well, smoking cannabis leads to many of the same respiratory problems as smoking tobacco, as both contain many of the same carcinonegens. However, those who smoke cannabis are exposed to unfiltered smoke, larger puffs, deeper inhalation, and breath-holding, suggesting that negative respiratory effects may occur sooner than when smoking filtered cigarettes (CCSA, 2010).

Cannabis has been used in medical situations because of its physiological effects. It has been used as an appetite stimulant for AIDS patients and has been used medically to treat glaucoma, to relieve pain, and to prevent the vomiting and nausea associated with chemotherapy (Ware, Doyle, Woods, Lynch, & Clark, 2003; WHO, 2006).

Why do people use cannabis in spite of the aforementioned side effects? They do so to experience euphoria, a sense of well-being, relaxation, and heightened sexual responsiveness. The psychological effects of cannabis seem to depend, in part, on the setting and on personal expectation. It is not surprising that those who attain these psychological effects are usually experienced cannabis smokers who expect to attain them.

Hallucinogens   LSD (lysergic acid diethylamide, commonly referred to as "acid"), PCP (phencyclidine), and MDMA (3,4-methylenedioxymethylamphetamine, most often referred to as "ecstasy") are drugs that are classified as **hallucinogens**. These drugs dramatically affect perception, emotions, and mental processes. As the name suggests, they can cause hallucinations. Hallucinations can elicit feelings of euphoria but can also cause one to feel threatened. This fear, anxiety, or panic can cause the user to behave quite violently. More often, however, users report a sense of well-being and heightened tactile sensations and emotions. The effects of MDMA usually last up to 8 hours and those of LSD up to 12 hours, while the effects of PCP may last as long as several days when taken in a single dose. However, the effects of high doses of PCP have been known in some cases to last from 10 days to 2 weeks (Alberta Alcohol and Drug Abuse Commission, 2002). *Salvia divinorum* is becoming popular with youth and its prevalence was examined for the first time in 2009. Approximately 1.6 percent of Canadians over the age of 15 had tried salvia, but 7.3 percent of youth had tried this legal hallucinogen (Health Canada, 2009a).

Short-term physiological reactions to hallucinogens include increased blood pressure, heart rate, and temperature; dilated pupils; impaired motor skills and coordination; dizziness; and nausea. Larger doses can cause convulsions, coma, and death. Persistent speech problems, memory loss, severe depression and anxiety, and social withdrawal have also been noted following prolonged use.

hallucinogens: drugs that dramatically affect perception, emotions, and mental processes; can cause hallucinations.

Cocaine   Cocaine is a **stimulant** drug, extracted from the coca plant indigenous to the Andes Mountains in South America. Cocaine is most often snorted through the nasal passages but is also smoked and "freebased"—that is, injected intravenously. Cocaine provides a sense of well-being, heightened attention, and a powerful euphoria. This effect lasts approximately 15 to 30 minutes. When the effects wear off, the user is often left with a feeling of fatigue, sluggishness, and a strong desire to "use" again. Increased doses do not make the euphoria last longer and can endanger the cardiovascular system.

Studies exploring long-term cocaine use among young adults have found mixed results regarding the relationship between heavy use of cocaine and various cardiovascular risk factors (Health Canada, 2009b). Using cocaine causes blood vessels to constrict, heart rate to increase, and blood pressure to speed up suddenly. It can also trigger cardiac arrhythmia. These factors may cause a stroke or myocardial infarction. Physiological withdrawal symptoms do not accompany cessation of cocaine use, but psychological dependence does seem to occur.

stimulant: a drug that increases alertness, decreases appetite and the need for sleep, and may produce intense feelings of euphoria and a strong sense of well-being.

Preventing and Treating Illicit Drug Use   Programs aimed at preventing teenage drug abuse are similar to those aimed at preventing smoking. Children and adolescents can be educated through the schools and mass media about the deleterious effects of drug abuse. These educational programs are based on social influence and life skills training methods that teach children and adolescents how to resist starting to use drugs (Fraguela, Martin, & Trinanes, 2003; Lloyd, Joyce, Hurry, & Ashton, 2000). A second preventive technique that is common in all Western countries is the use of laws to limit the legal access to drugs. Unfortunately, this approach may produce other social problems (e.g., a large criminal enterprise). Finally, encouraging parents to monitor their children has been found to reduce the likelihood that children will try drugs (Lloyd et al., 2000).

Treatment programs for drug abuse are similar to those for alcohol abuse. In fact, it's not uncommon for formal treatment centres to treat both forms of abuse. The most promising treatment approaches include both behavioural and cognitive methods, such as self-management techniques (NIAAA, 2000). Unfortunately, as with the treatment of alcohol and smoking, there is a high rate of relapse, and the first six months after treatment are critical. Many drug treatment programs now include follow-up or "booster" sessions to help people remain abstinent.

The use of drugs and alcohol directly results in numerous health consequences, including indirect health consequences. For instance, individuals who are intoxicated are more likely to engage in risky behaviours, such as unsafe sexual practices (e.g., MacDonald, Fong, Zanna, & Martineau, 2003).

UNSAFE SEXUAL BEHAVIOURS

The negative effects of unsafe sexual behaviours are numerous. In addition to unplanned pregnancies, unsafe sexual behaviours can lead to serious health consequences such as sexually transmitted diseases (STDs), infertility, and HIV infection. Results from the 2002 Canadian Youth, Sexual Health and HIV/AIDS Study (Health Canada, 2002) indicated that nine percent of grade 9 students and six percent of grade 11 students had used no birth control the last time they'd had sexual intercourse. Further, more than double that number of students chose birth control pills as their only means of contraception. Although more than 50 percent of these adolescents are using condoms, it is imperative that this number increase.

Similarly disappointing results are found with American youth. In a recent nationwide U.S. survey of high school students, 34.2 percent were currently sexually active and 38.9 percent of currently sexually active students had not used a condom during their last sexual intercourse (Eaton et al., 2010).

Why do people not use condoms when engaging in intercourse? A national survey of grade 9 and 11 students attempted to gain insight into this question (Health Canada, 2002). The students reported not using condoms because they did not expect to have sex; they already used some other method of birth control; they had too much alcohol/drugs; they did not want to spoil the moment; they did not like to or know how to use a condom; they did not have enough money to buy condoms; they had difficulty discussing condom use with their partner; they did not want to show distrust of their partner; or they felt they had a faithful (safe) partner.

A study of gay and bisexual males found that social anxiety was a contributing factor to unsafe sex (Hart & Heimberg, 2005). Another factor cited in previous studies for the failure to use condoms was insufficient knowledge of HIV/STDs (e.g., Boroditsky, Fisher, & Sand, 1995; Calzavara et al., 1999). Trevor Hart and his colleagues at York University report that recent immigrants to Canada are less knowledgeable about HIV than non-immigrants but engage in a similar amount of risky sexual behaviour as non-immigrants (Zhuk, Hart, & James, 2006).

We know that individuals who are intoxicated are more likely to engage in unsafe sexual practices (e.g., MacDonald, Fong, Zanna, & Martineau, 2003). This is, at least in part, due to the effect that alcohol has on decision making. People also state that they make poor decisions in the "heat of the moment." A recent study has examined the effect of sexual arousal on judgment and decision making. Ariely and Loewenstein (2006) had male college students indicate their willingness to engage in unsafe sex when sexually aroused (arousal was induced by self-stimulation). Participants were also asked how appealing they found a wide range of sexual stimuli and activities, and they were asked about their willingness to engage in morally questionable behaviour in order to obtain sexual gratification.

Ariely and Loewenstein report that sexual arousal acts as an amplifier of sorts. That is, a far wider range of activities was deemed sexually appealing when the participants were sexually aroused. In addition, the motivation to engage in sex decreased the relative importance of other considerations, including protecting oneself or one's partner against unwanted pregnancy or sexually transmitted disease.

A variety of theoretical approaches have been used in an attempt to understand sexual and reproductive health behaviours using a decision-making framework (see Fisher & Fisher, 1998, for a review of these theories). Some of these theories have been developed outside the domain of sexual and reproductive health and applied within it—for example, the health belief model (Rosenstock, Strecher, & Becker, 1994), the theory of reasoned action (Fishbein & Ajzen, 1975), the theory of planned behaviour (Ajzen, 1991), and the stages of change model (Prochaska & Velicer, 1997). You may remember reading about these theories in chapter 1. Other theories have been developed and applied specifically within the area of sexuality and reproductive health, including the sexual behaviour sequence model (Byrne, 1977), the AIDS risk reduction model (Catania, Kegeles, & Coates, 1990), and the information-motivation-behavioural skills model (Fisher & Fisher, 1999).

The **information-motivation-behavioural skills model** (Fisher & Fisher, 1999; Fisher, Fisher, & Shuper, 2009) maintains that there are a number of steps individuals must go through before they will engage in safe-sex practices. First, they must recognize and accept that they are sexually active. Second, they must create a "sexual and reproductive health agenda." In other words, individuals must be motivated to engage in safe-sex practices to prevent pregnancy and infection. Third, individuals must be capable of engaging in behaviours that fulfill this agenda. For example, they must be able to negotiate cooperation in contraceptive and condom use with a partner. If cooperation is not forthcoming, the individual must be able to exit the situation.

This model also acknowledges that it is frequently necessary to engage in public behaviour regarding sexual and reproductive health (e.g., condom purchasing, HIV testing). To maintain safe sexual practices over time, individuals must have this behaviour reinforced. Finally, individuals must be able to adjust sexual and reproductive health behaviour scripts appropriately as their needs change over time. For example, it may be appropriate to shift from condom use to non-use in a monogamous relationship after a window period, after mutual STD and HIV antibody testing, and after reaching an agreement about how to continue mutual monogamy and how violations of this agreement will be handled.

Of course, this change in practice can take place only if the individuals in the relationship are mature enough to accept the responsibilities and risks associated with this agreement. We cannot emphasize strongly enough that it is inappropriate to shift from condom use to monogamy as a strategy for safe-sex behaviour after a brief period of "getting to know" one's partner, or for younger couples whose relationships tend to be less stable and long lasting (Misovich, Fisher, & Fisher, 1996).

information-motivation-behavioural skills model: a theory maintaining that there are a number of steps one must go through to successfully achieve safe-sex practices.

OBESITY

Obesity has been recognized by the World Health Organization as one of the top 10 global health problems. It is predicted that obesity could have as great an impact on health as smoking (Kelner & Helmuth, 2003; Statistics Canada, 2002b). The Canadian Community Health Survey indicates that, in 2004, 23 percent of our adult population, or 5.5 million individuals, were obese (Statistics Canada, 2005a). And the number of obese Canadians is increasing rapidly. Since 1978, for example, the age-adjusted adult obesity rate has increased 10 percent. The rates for youngsters are also increasing dramatically with 6 percent of those ages 2 to 5, 8 percent of those 6 to 11, and 9 percent of those 12 to 17 classified as obese. Obesity has been increasing for every age group except one—those 65 to 74 years of age (Statistics Canada, 2005a). The lowest levels of obesity occur in urban areas of the country, most notably in Vancouver, Toronto, and Montreal (Statistics Canada, 2002b).

What exactly is obesity? **Obesity** refers to an excess of body fat, which normally accounts for about 25 percent of weight in women and 18 percent in men (Bray, 1998). The most commonly used measure of obesity is the **body-mass index (BMI)**. Obesity is defined as a BMI of 30.0 or greater (Health Canada, 2003a). To determine your BMI refer to Figure 10-3.

obesity: condition characterized by having an excess of body fat; Health Canada and the World Health Organization define obesity as a BMI of 30.0 or greater.

body-mass index (BMI): measure of obesity calculated by dividing one's weight in kilograms by height in metres squared.

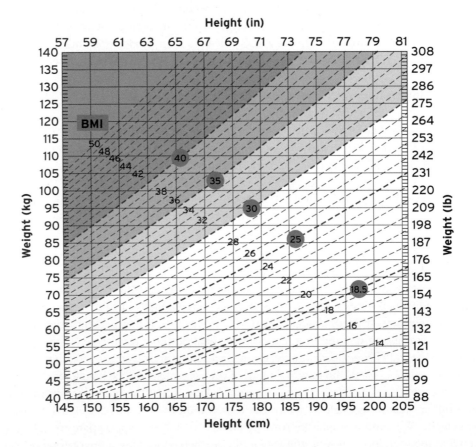

Figure 10-3 Body Mass Index (BMI) Nomogram

Source: Body Mass Index (BMI) Nomogram, 2003. Health Canada. Reproduced with the permission of the Minister of Public Works and Government Services Canada, 2010.

Table 10-1	Health Risk Classification According to Body Mass Index (BMI)	
BMI	**Classification**	**Risk of Developing Health Problems**
<18.5	Underweight	Increased
18.5–24.9	Normal weight	Least
25.0–29.9	Overweight	Increased
30.0–34.9	Obese class I	High
35.0–39.9	Obese class II	Very high
>40.0	Obese class III(Morbid obesity)	Extremely high

Source: Health Risk Classification According to Body Mass Index (BMI), 2003. Health Canada. Reproduced with the permission of the Minister of Public Works and Government Services Canada, 2010.

Keep in mind that, although the BMI estimates total body fat, it may not be accurate for selected populations (e.g., the elderly, certain ethnic groups, and persons with large muscle mass). For example, Arnold Schwarzenegger's BMI index might suggest that he is obese. However, we know better and we would suggest that he is fit rather than fat. More complex methods (e.g., densitometry) are available to professionals who require a more accurate measurement of body fat.

Generally speaking, as one's BMI increases so does one's risk of early mortality. A large prospective study following more than one million adults in the United States for 14 years documented that participants with a BMI of 40 or above had a relative risk of death two to six times that of their thinner counterparts with a BMI of 24 (Calle et al., 1999). Other studies report similar findings. For example, Bender and colleagues (1998) found that a BMI under 32 was not linked to premature death, a BMI of 36 was related to a slight increase in mortality rates, and a BMI greater than 40 more than doubled the risk of premature death. However, we must point out that the relationship between body weight (BMI) and increased risk of death is actually J- or U-shaped. That is, those who are underweight have a slightly increased risk of mortality compared to those classified as normal weight (e.g., Fontaine, Redden, Wang, Westfall, & Allison, 2003). In essence, the relative risk of death is highest among the thinnest and the heaviest individuals in our society.

Obesity helps create a burden that is economic and emotional as well as physical. The physical ailments associated with obesity that contribute most to premature death are hypertension, type 2 (adult onset) diabetes, and coronary heart disease (Statistics Canada, 2005). Obesity also predisposes people to arthritis, gout, gallbladder disease, sleep apnea, complications allowing surgery, and possibly also to various forms of cancer (Pi-Sunyer, 2003).

The economic burden of obesity was estimated to exceed $4 billion in Canada for the year 2005 (Public Health Agency of Canada, 2009). Personal costs are also prevalent. One prospective study documented that overweight adolescents were less likely to marry, had lower household incomes, and completed significantly fewer months of high school (despite equal grades) than their non-overweight counterparts (Gortmaker, Must, Perrin, Sobol, & Dietz, 1993). Prejudice and discrimination when seeking college admissions, employment, or a place to live are also consequences experienced by those who are overweight (Wadden, Womble, Stunkard, & Anderson, 2002).

Despite these obstacles, some studies report that there is no evidence of an effect of being overweight on self-esteem in the general population (Wadden et al., 2002). However, other studies report that overweight women are more likely to report being depressed or suicidal than are non-overweight women (e.g., Carpenter, Hasin, Allison, & Faith, 2000). Certainly, depression, anxiety, and binge eating are more common in those who are overweight and are currently seeking weight reduction (Wadden, Brownell, & Foster, 2002).

The statement "genes load the gun, the environment pulls the trigger" (Bray, as cited in Wadden et al., 2002, p. 512) summarizes the contributions of genetics and the environment to obesity. Genes are partly responsible for variance in BMI (Price, 2002). Genes also contribute to individual differences in basal metabolic rate (people with naturally lower basal metabolic rates burn fewer calories), in amount of weight gained after overeating, and in body fat distribution (Wadden et al., 2002). Some individuals are simply born with a genetic predisposition to obesity, and our current cultural environment contributes to its exhibition.

Biological Factors That Contribute to Obesity

Heredity   Twin studies, adoption studies, and family studies indicate that genes contribute to the development of obesity. The strength of the heritability of obesity is akin to the strength of heritability of height (Friedman, 2003). Maes, Neale, and Eaves (1996) reviewed the literature on the familial resemblance of BMI. Based on data from more than 25 000 twin pairs and 50 000 biological and adoptive family members, the following correlations were computed: 0.74 for monozygotic twins, 0.32 for dizygotic twins, 0.25 for siblings, 0.19 for parent–offspring pairs, and 0.06 for adoptive relatives. These figures provide convincing evidence that there is substantial heritability for obesity. Maes and colleagues conclude that genes account for approximately 67 percent of individual differences in BMI. The results of other studies corroborate these conclusions (e.g., Bulik, Sullivan, & Kendler, 2003).

Hormones and the Brain   The biological system that regulates our food intake and energy expenditure is extraordinarily complex and not well understood. Consider that over a period of 10 years, an average individual consumes approximately 10 million calories. Typically, a person will experience only a slight change of weight in that ten years. For such a slight weight variation, food consumption must be within 0.17 percent of energy expenditure over the entire decade (Friedman, 2003). Achieving this balance is quite an accomplishment; it is highly unlikely that a nutritionist counting calories could be so precise in matching food consumption with energy expenditure.

How does our body maintain such a constant weight? The **set-point theory** proposes that the body contains a set-point that works like a thermostat regulating heat in a home. When one gains weight, powerful biological control mechanisms diminish caloric intake. When one loses weight, similar mechanisms respond by increasing hunger levels until the person's weight returns to its ideal or target level. In 1994, a key element of this homeostatic system was discovered—the hormone **leptin** (Zhang et al., 1994). Leptin reports to the neurons of the hypothalamus (a key regulatory centre in the brain) whether there are sufficient fat stores in the body or whether additional energy is needed. Leptin is produced by fat cells; therefore, when fat stores increase, the body's level of leptin increases. This, in turn, suppresses the neurons that stimulate hunger and activates those that reduce food intake. When there is a decrease in body fat the reverse occurs—leptin levels decrease,

set-point theory: the idea that the body contains a set-point that works like a thermostat; when a person gains weight, biological control mechanisms diminish caloric intake; when a person loses weight, similar mechanisms increase hunger levels until the weight returns to its ideal or target level.

leptin: hormone that responds to weight loss by increasing hunger levels until the person's weight returns to its ideal or target level.

resulting in stimulation of appetite and a reduction of energy expenditure (Friedman, 2000, 2003).

If this homeostatic system can maintain weight within a relatively narrow range, why are some individuals obese and others are not? There appear to be individual differences in sensitivity to leptin. It may be that obese individuals are simply less sensitive to leptin or that they are leptin-resistant (Friedman, 2003). This would explain why obese people tend to have more leptin in their bodies. They must produce more of the hormone to compensate for their lack of sensitivity (Nakamura et al., 2000). In very rare conditions, individuals may lack the hormone leptin completely (see Case 10-1). Additional hormones (e.g., ghrelin) and neuropeptides are now being studied to determine their role in obesity (Hebebrand & Hinney, 2008).

CASE 10-1 HORMONES CONTRIBUTE TO REGULATION OF BODY WEIGHT

Two young English girls have become famous as a result of their obesity. The older, nine-year-old cousin had legs so large she could barely walk. The younger cousin could consume more than 1100 calories at a single meal. That's half of what the average adult will eat in a day! The girls were found to lack the weight-regulating hormone leptin. In order to treat their obesity, the girls were given leptin injections. After only a few such injections their calorie consumption decreased by a dramatic 84 percent. Their new appetites were now similar to those of other children their age. The outcome is amazing. Both girls are now at body weights considered normal for their size and are enjoying normal lives (Farooqui et al., 2002; Friedman, 2003).

Psychosocial Factors That Contribute to Obesity

Hunger and eating behaviour are not controlled solely by biological factors. In fact, our biology is now almost maladaptive in our environment of food abundance and sedentariness (Hebebrand & Hinney, 2009). Currently, social norms and values serve to reinforce behaviours that promote obesity (Herman & Polivy, 2005). We associate food with celebrations, rewards, and social occasions. Therefore, it is not surprising that we turn to food when anxious or depressed (Thoburn & Hammond-Meyer, 2004).

Stress and Eating   Stress affects people differently, and consequently it also affects people's eating behaviours differently. Approximately half the population will eat more when feeling stress, and the other half will eat less (Willenbring, Levine, & Morley, 1986). People of average weight who are not preoccupied with food often ignore or misinterpret physiological cues to hunger and therefore eat less. In contrast, stress can cause dieters to lose control, causing disinhibition or counterregulation and, consequently, overeating (e.g., Heatherton, Herman, & Polivy, 1992; Polivy, 1996).

Stress may also influence the food choices people make. Individuals experiencing daily hassles, ranging from a job interview or public talk to being late for a meeting or having an argument, report that their eating habits are compromised (O'Connor et al., 2008).

There is a tendency for people experiencing stress to increase their fat consumption and reduce their consumption of fruits and vegetables. As well, snacking increases in times of stress (O'Connor & O'Connor, 2004).

Sociocultural Factors That Contribute to Obesity

When we look through a broader lens, there is also clear evidence that our eating and activity habits are influenced by the people around us. When people move from a less developed country to a more modern country where food, particularly rich food, is plentiful, they tend to gain weight. For most immigrants to Canada, "the probability of being overweight or (for women) obese is lower on arrival than for comparable native-born Canadians, but increases gradually with additional years in their new country" (McDonald & Kennedy, 2005, p. 2479). The more likely a group is to acculturate, or take on characteristically Canadian ways of living, the narrower the new immigrants' health advantage with respect to comparable native-born Canadians. Chinese Canadian communities are the most geographically concentrated and least likely to acculturate. It follows then that immigrants of Chinese ethnicity exhibit little change in weight with increasing years in Canada.

On a more immediate level, we are influenced by our parents' eating behaviours (Keski-Rahkonen et al., 2005). Parents may influence their children's eating behaviours by encouraging them to overeat. Or, on a more positive note, parental presence at mealtime may lead to better food choices and less likelihood of adolescents skipping breakfast (Videon & Manning, 2003). The affluence of your family will also contribute to your weight, or it will if you are a female. In general, the more affluent a woman is, the less likely she is to be obese. For men, those in low to middle income households were the least likely to be obese (Statistics Canada, 2005).

Environmental and Hunger Cues   Most of us live a lifestyle that is laden with time pressures. We are exposed to an environment bursting with highly advertised, highly accessible foods (e.g., fast-food restaurants, buffet restaurants, food franchises in school cafeterias) (Hill et al., 2003). Is it any wonder that we respond to these cues by eating more prepackaged and fast foods? The way we respond to cues in our environment led Schachter (1971) to propose the **internality-externality hypothesis**. This hypothesis asserts that, in people of normal weight, feelings of hunger and satiety come from within in the form of internal stimuli (e.g., hunger pangs or feelings of fullness).

In contrast, obese people are more likely to respond to external stimuli (e.g., time of day, smell, or sight of food) in determining their level of hunger. Although highly influential, there has not been consistent support for this hypothesis. For example, Rodin (1981) discovered that internal sensitivity is not a characteristic unique to normal-weight persons. Likewise, externality can lead to overeating in everyone, regardless of weight category. Remick, Polivy and Pliner (2009) suggest that there may be an evolutionary explanation for these findings. To further understand the relationship between external stimuli and eating behaviour, Herman and Polivy have focused much of their research on this topic (see Focus on Canadian Research 10-2).

Another external stimulus that influences eating behaviour is the presence of others. There are three psychological explanations regarding the effects of the presence of others on food intake (Herman, Roth, & Polivy, 2003). Briefly, the **social facilitation approach**

internality-externality hypothesis: assertion that in people of normal weight, feelings of hunger and satiety come from within, in the form of internal stimuli (e.g., hunger pangs or feelings of fullness); whereas, obese people are more likely to determine their level of hunger in response to external stimuli (e.g., time of day, smell, or sight of food).

social facilitation approach: this approach states that people tend to eat more when in the presence of others.

suggests that when people eat in groups, they tend to eat more than when alone. The **modelling or matching effect** states that people tend to eat as much or as little as do those in their presence (Herman, Koenig-Nobert, Peterson, & Polivy, 2005). The **impression management approach** states that when people believe they are being observed or evaluated, they will suppress eating (Herman et al., 2003).

modelling effect: people tend to eat the same amount as those in their presence; this effect is sometimes referred to as the matching effect.

Focus on Canadian Research 10-2

Eating Behaviour: Can You Restrain Yourself?

Peter Herman and Janet Polivy, both of the University of Toronto, have spent more than y 30 years studying eating behaviour. In 1975, Herman and Mack proposed the **restraint theory** of eating behaviour. According to their theory, external sensitivity is linked to *restrained eating* (or strict dieting), rather than to body weight. When one is preoccupied with body-weight norms, food consumption will swing between restrained eating and overindulging.

In a typical study (e.g., Herman & Polivy, 1980), participants are classified as either high or low on restraint based on their responses to questions such as, "How often are you dieting?" and "Do you give too much time and thought to food?" Initially, the participants are given food to consume, for example a milkshake. Subsequently, participants take part in a "taste test," and they are allowed to "taste" as much food (e.g., ice cream) as they like from the selection that is offered. The researchers are interested only in the amount of food consumed, and each plate of cookies or dish of ice cream is measured after the participant is finished "tasting." The restrained eaters, who frequently think about food and are more likely to be dieting, consume more food than do the *unrestrained eaters* (those who are not trying to limit their food intake).

Subsequent studies have determined that restrained eaters are more sensitive to and reactive to food cues than are unrestrained eaters. Consequently, their appetites increase in response to these cues, and they will consume more food than if not exposed to such cues. Both cognitive and olfactory cues produce increased intake of food by restrained eaters compared to unrestrained eaters. Recently, Herman and Polivy (2008) proposed the sensory-normative distinction theory which states that sensory cues have a powerful effect on obese and/or restrained eaters, whereas normative cues (e.g., portion size) affect everyone (i.e., everyone eats more when the portion of food they are presented is large).

Variations on this research have discovered that restrained participants' own hunger ratings can be affected by fictitious hunger reports, but their actual food consumption remains unaltered (Herman, Fitzgerald, & Polivy, 2003). Another variation determined that restrained eaters who were led to believe that they weighed five pounds more than they actually did consumed more food during a subsequent "taste test" than did those who were provided with their true weight or a weight that was five pounds lighter than their actual weight. The authors contend that lowered self-worth and a worsening of mood experienced by those who were led to believe they were heavier than they really were led them to abandon their dietary control and overindulge (McFarlane, Polivy, & Herman, 1998).

Herman and Polivy's research also highlights the dynamic connection between dieting and overeating. One of their studies investigated the effect of anticipated food deprivation on food consumption in restrained and unrestrained eaters. Participants completed a taste test immediately after being assigned to either a diet condition (in which they expected to diet for a week) or a control condition (no diet). Unrestrained eaters consumed the same amount of food no matter what condition they had been assigned to. In contrast, restrained eaters had greater food intake when assigned to the diet condition than when assigned to the control condition. These and similar findings indicate that restricting one's eating or dieting to lose weight may have unanticipated deleterious effects (e.g., eating binges and preoccupation with food and eating). In a recent article, Polivy and Herman (2006) provide an evolutionary explanation for why restraint is a maladaptive strategy to lose weight. To oversimplify, we have evolved to abandon our self-control when foods are abundant or when there is no immediate shortage of food. They conclude that to avoid obesity, one should choose to eat foods in moderation, pay attention to satiety cues, and avoid overeating. In essence, a healthful, balanced diet is the best approach to "dieting."

Prevention and Treatment of Obesity

Clearly, prevention is the best way to attack the current obesity epidemic. Pi-Sunyer (2003) reports that education at two levels is essential. On one level, we must educate the public. Campaigns like those for smoking should be launched. As well, because we know that people consume more energy than they expend, Hill et al. (2003) advocate that only a small reduction in net energy input will prevent further increases in obesity rates.

Based on the average weight gain in the U.S. population of 1.8 to 2.0 pounds per year, Hill determined that on average people have an energy gap of 100 kcal a day. To reduce this energy gap, we should either reduce our caloric intake by 100 kcal or find a way to expend more energy. Adding 2000 to 2500 extra steps throughout the day would burn 100 calories for most people. Alternatively, eating 15 percent less a day by reducing portion sizes should accomplish the same goal.

Childhood obesity has become increasingly prevalent over the past 20 years; therefore, we should take extra steps to encourage children to make healthy food choices and to exert energy (Ball & McCargar, 2003). Programs that do exactly this are currently being implemented (e.g., the Action Schools! BC–Healthy Eating Program in British Columbia; Living Schools in Ontario, and others). On another level, Pi-Sunyer (2003) states that more health care professionals should become equipped to educate and treat obese people. These health care professionals must be provided the nutritional knowledge and counselling skills that will equip them to facilitate lifestyle changes in their patients.

For many, education about prevention of obesity comes too late, and treatment is required. Historically, dieting has been the most common approach to losing weight. At any given time, nearly 40 percent of women and 25 percent of men in the United States are trying to lose weight (Kruger, Galuska, Serdula, & Jones, 2004). Some individuals are motivated to lose weight because it reduces health risks, whereas others are motivated to lose weight to improve appearance (Polivy & Herman, 2006). The majority of people who try to lose weight do so on their own rather than following preset guidelines. Approximately 20 percent of people follow healthy guidelines that restrict their caloric intake and supplement their balanced diet with exercise (Powell, Calvin & Powell, 2007). Weight loss is usually successful following this approach.

Generally, when people do lose weight by dieting, they are not able to keep the weight off. Paradoxically, the more people try to control their weight, the more their weight increases in the long run (Polivy & Herman, 2006). Frequently people will lose the same 10 pounds over and over again. This repeated cycle of weight loss and gain is referred to as yo-yo dieting. Unfortunately, frequent dieting has a negative impact on psychological well-being and is often accompanied by compromised psychological functioning in the form of impaired concentration, food preoccupation, and binge eating (McFarlane, Polivy, & McCabe, 1999). The best approach to losing weight is to do so gradually and to make permanent lifestyle changes that can be maintained.

Pharmacological Treatment of Obesity

Both prescription and over-the-counter drugs are often used to reduce appetite and restrict food consumption (Bray & Tartaglia, 2000). Stimulants, such as amphetamines, have provided short-term weight loss. Stimulants result in weight loss because they increase metabolism and reduce appetite. However, to remain effective, ever-increasing doses must be consumed, which may result in physical dependence, a health hazard worse than obesity. Most currently available obesity drugs are not very effective and have negative side effects. The drug orlistat is effective in reducing weight and is available by prescription. This "diet" medication works differently than most in that it decreases dietary fat absorption, but it is accompanied by adverse effects including fatty, oily stools and oily leakage from the rectum. As well, there is concern that orlistat may decrease absorption of the fat soluble vitamins A, D, E, and K (Powell et al., 2007; Powers & Bruty, 2009).

Leptin, a hormone discussed earlier, is currently being tested in both animal and clinical trials; however, initial trials have been disappointing (Gura, 2003; Wadden et al., 2002). Investigators expect that additional research on the genetics of body weight regulation will provide new drug targets (Gura, 2003). However, the physiology of weight control is complex and "most researchers doubt that a pharmaceutical 'silver bullet' will be found that will allow us all to achieve healthy weights" (Komaroff, 2003).

Behavioural Treatment of Obesity   Behavioural treatments described previously in the context of smoking cessation have also been applied to reducing obesity. Behavioural treatment of obesity is at least as effective as pharmacological treatment (Wadden et al., 2002). Typically, individuals will take part in a program that lasts approximately 20 weeks. The program will likely include one or more of the following strategies (e.g., Stewart, Reilly, & Hughes, 2009):

- stimulus-control procedures that identify and modify external cues to eating (e.g., confining food intake to a particular place and time, such as in the dining room at mealtime)

- self-monitoring and record keeping of the type and quantity of food eaten each day; this provides awareness of the foods that are eaten and the situations in which one eats

- self-control techniques to control the amount eaten or to slow the act of eating (e.g., dieters can be instructed to place the proper proportion of food on their plate at one time, and once all of the food is on the plate to eat by putting down their forks after each bite)

- social support to help control stress that may arise (e.g., having a dieting "buddy," joining a program such as Weight Watchers, or enlisting the help of a friend or family member)

- contingency contracts, also known as behavioural contracts, that consist of rewards for achieving goals (or punishments for not reaching a goal); the contracts may be self-monitored or another person may be enlisted to monitor the behaviour and reward or punish accordingly

A behavioural treatment program usually leads to a loss of 8.5 to 9.0 kg, or approximately 9 percent of initial body weight (e.g., Wing, 2002). Regrettably, without further treatment (at least monthly), those who lost weight using behaviour therapies are likely to regain approximately one-third of the weight lost in the subsequent year (Powell et al., 2007).

Surgical Treatment of Obesity   Surgical interventions are a radical way to control extreme obesity (BMI > 40). In the 1960s, Drs. Mason and Ito developed a procedure called **gastric bypass** that is still widely used today. In this procedure a small pouch is created at the bottom of the esophagus to limit food intake. Food that enters the pouch

gastric bypass: radical surgical intervention to control extreme obesity; a small pouch is created at the bottom of the esophagus to limit food intake.

bypasses the stomach and part of the intestine. Those who undergo this procedure can expect to lose approximately 30 percent of their initial weight during the first 18 months. Approximately 25 percent of the weight loss will be maintained (Wadden et al., 2002).

gastric banding: a minimally invasive surgical procedure, involves placing a band around the stomach so that a person feels full after consuming only a small amount of food (Nickel et al., 2005). Positive changes in health-related quality of life have been noted after gastric band surgery. These changes are most dramatic in the first year after surgery but are still evident three years later (Nickel et al., 2005).

gastric banding: a minimally invasive surgical procedure that involves placing a band around the stomach so that a person feels full after consuming only a small amount of food.

EATING DISORDERS

CASE 10-2 BULIMIA NERVOSA IN TEENAGERS

Julia is an attractive girl of normal weight who has always been concerned with her appearance. If you ever want to know what clothes are trendy, take a look at what Julia is wearing. She can even tell you what colours of lipstick and fingernail polish are "in" this month. How does she know this? She reads magazines like *Elle* and *Cosmopolitan* religiously. Her friends are also very "up to date," and in junior high school they jointly began to engage in a behaviour they felt was "fashionable." As a group, the girls would go into the washroom and throw up. Julia says she was not all that concerned with losing weight, but she didn't want to gain any either. In fact, the purging began more because it seemed to be a "cool" thing to do rather than because of concerns Julia might have had about her own weight. Unfortunately, the purging changed from a group activity to something she did frequently on her own. It soon became a habit for Julia to vomit after eating—a very unhealthy habit.

bulimia nervosa: an eating disorder that involves recurrent episodes of binge eating followed by purging.

In Case 10-2, Julia's behaviour is indicative of an eating disorder known as **bulimia nervosa.** Bulimia nervosa involves recurrent episodes of binge eating followed by purging. The purging strategies used most frequently are vomiting and laxative use. This disorder can result in numerous medical problems, such as anemia, inflammation of the digestive tract, heart arrhythmias resulting from electrolyte imbalances (which may cause sudden death), and irreversible erosion of dental enamel (Mitchell & Crow, 2006; Polivy, Herman, & Boivin, 2005). Although some bulimics are overweight, most, like Julia, are of normal weight. Despite the fact that the behaviour may begin as a group activity, bulimics are typically aware that their behaviour is not normal and they are ashamed of it. Because of this, they usually try to hide their behaviour from others. In addition to reporting negative aspects of the disorder, such as shame and preoccupation with weight or shape, patients with bulimia nervosa also describe positive aspects of the disorder. These positive aspects include being able to eat and not get fat and as a way to combat boredom (Serpell & Treasure, 2002).

The binge portion of the bulimic episode is often impulsive, and bulimics are likely to engage in other impulsive and reckless behaviours as well (Fischer, Smith, & Anderson, 2003). For example, kleptomania is more common among bulimics than among the general population, although the items stolen are usually associated with the bulimic's binging and purging (such as food or laxatives). Bulimics are also more likely than the general population to engage in spending sprees or sexual promiscuity because of their impulsive nature (e.g., Matsunaga et al., 2000).

The number of patients diagnosed with eating disorders is increasing (Polivy & Herman, 2002). Although eating disorders are most common among adolescents and adults, even children suffer from eating disorders. Seventy percent of children with eating disorders are female. In the adolescent and adult eating-disorder population, 90 to 95 percent of those with eating disorders are female (Behar, 2006).

How prevalent are eating disorders? More than 500 000 Canadians reported suffering from an eating disorder in 2005 (Canadian Mental Health Association, 2005). A study conducted by the Douglas Mental Health Institute in Quebec found that nearly 15 percent of women sampled reported some type of eating disturbance (Gauvin, Steiger, & Brodeur, 2008). Approximately three percent of women will be affected by eating disorders in their lifetime (Zhu & Walsh, 2002). Although reports vary greatly, the average prevalence rate for bulimia nervosa is one percent and for anorexia nervosa ranges from 0.3 to one percent (Hoek, 2006; Su & Brimingham, 2003). There are reports that the number of patients with bulimia nervosa outnumbers the number with anorexia nervosa by at least two to one (Polivy & Herman, 2002).

Anorexia nervosa is an eating disorder characterized by a dramatic reduction in food intake and extreme weight loss. According to the DSM-IV (American Psychiatric Association, 1997), the diagnostic criteria for anorexia nervosa are maintaining a body weight at less than 85 percent of normal weight for one's age and height, an intense fear of fatness, disturbance in the way one's body weight or shape is experienced, and amenorrhea for at least three consecutive months. Anorexics are very fearful of gaining weight and consequently will refuse food and may engage in excessive exercise. Yet anorexics are extremely preoccupied with food and may spend a lot of their time cooking for others or engaging in other pursuits that revolve around food. The self-starvation in anorexia will lead to low blood pressure, heart damage or cardiac arrhythmias, and eventually death. At the point of near starvation, the person will lose the hair on his or her head, and fine hair growth (lanugo) will appear on the face and body. Anorexics are also at increased risk of osteoporosis (Mehler, 2003).

Anorexia is less prevalent in the general population than bulimia. Anorexia occurs most often in Caucasian adolescent females from the upper social classes and in those who dance, model, or are competitive in sports (Behar, 2006; Polivy, Herman, & Boivin, 2005; Ravaldi, Vannacci, & Zucchi, 2003). Yet anorexia is increasingly being seen in patients who are very young, male, less affluent, and in people of colour (Agras, 2004; Gard & Freeman, 1996; Story et al., 1995).

There are other eating disorders that are classified in the DSM-IV as "not otherwise specified" (American Psychiatric Association, 1994). **Binge eating disorder (BED)** is compulsive overeating or bingeing. Unlike with bulimia nervosa, with BED there is no compensatory measure or purge to counteract the binge (Stein et al., 2001). There will be noticeable distress around binge eating, and there may be attitudinal disturbance regarding eating and body image (Stein et al., 2001; Stein et al., 2007). Recurrent binge eating is reported to be as common in men as in women, as common in persons of colour as Caucasians, and is evenly distributed throughout adulthood (Streigel-Moore & Bulik, 2007; Wilson, Grilo, & Vitousek, 2007). Obesity is frequently a co-occuring problem and the typical patient often suffers from additional serious psychiatric disorders (e.g., major depressive disorder, anxiety disorder, alcohol use disorder, or personality disorder; Wilson et al., 2007).

anorexia nervosa: an eating disorder characterized by a dramatic reduction in food intake and extreme weight loss due to an extreme fear of gaining weight.

binge eating disorder (BED): compulsive overeating or bingeing; unlike bulimia nervosa, BED uses no compensatory measure or purge to counteract the binge.

Box 10-1 Mindless Eating

We often are not aware of exactly how much we are eating. Brian Wansink, a professor of marketing and nutritional science, has dedicated his career to understanding the environmental factors that influence food consumption. Package size, plate shape, food variety, accessibility of food, and even lighting can influence food consumption more than most people realize (Wansink, 2006).

Wansink (2004) demonstrates that atmospherics influence our food consumption. For example, dimmed or soft lighting leads people to be more comfortable in their environment and less inhibited. Consequently, these people consume more food. The smell of food can lead us to eat when we weren't planning on it (e.g., think of the smell of coffee brewing in the morning or of the delightful smells one encounters at a local fair or amusement park), whereas unpleasant odours tend to decrease our consumption (e.g., burnt toast or sour milk).

The variety of food available also alters consumption. That is, providing an assortment of food causes people to eat more (Kahn & Wansink, 2004). In fact, the subtle difference in an assortment of 300 M&M's candies in ten different colours rather than seven colours leads to the consumption of 43 percent more candies.

Another environmental factor that contributes to our consumption rates is portion size. Food packaging and portion sizes have steadily increased over the past three decades. Given this, it is not surprising that people are eating more. Studies indicate that people will help themselves to more food and consume more food when given a large plate rather than a small plate. Yet they argue that they have not eaten any more. What *is* surprising, however, is that people will consume more if given a larger portion even when the food doesn't taste good. That was the case when Wansink and Kim (2005) provided movie-goers with free 14-day-old popcorn in either a large or medium popcorn container.

People are often surprised at how much they consume. Wansink provides suggestions for altering one's personal environment to help curb "mindless eating" in his book of the same name (2006).

Biological, Cultural, and Psychological Contributors to Eating Disorders

Biological, cultural, and psychological factors may all be possible contributors to eating disorders. Twin studies have documented that both twins are more likely to suffer from eating disorders if the twins are identical rather than fraternal (Klump, McGue, & Iacono, 2000). A large study that included 31 406 Swedish twins reported a heritability estimate of 56 percent for anorexia nervosa (Bulik et al., 2006). Other studies have reported heritability estimates between 48 and 76 percent (Streigl-Moore & Bulik, 2007). Similarly, heritability estimates for bulimia nervosa range from 50 percent to 83 percent and those for binge eating disorder are approximately 40 percent (Streigl-Moore & Bulik, 2007).

Researchers at McGill University report that there is "a region on Chromosome 1 that differentiates people with and without anorexia. The abnormality on this chromome is linked to personality traits like compulsivity and anxiety" (Douglas Mental Health Institute, 2010) that are common in those with anorexia and bulimia. Neuroendocrine factors, which might or might not be genetic in origin, may contribute to eating disorders (Polivy & Herman, 2002).

In North American society, there is pressure on individuals to be thin and stay youthful. This expectation is learned at a very young age. When children reach puberty and naturally gain weight, many become distressed. Often adolescents will try to control their weight by dieting. Unfortunately, this strategy is sometimes carried too far, and this is when many eating disorders begin. Eating disorders are more likely to occur in individuals from families in which eating disorders, psychopathology, alcoholism, or sexual abuse exist or have taken place (Polivy & Herman, 2002). The media are also partly to blame for this pressure. Researchers (Stice, 1994) have documented that females who have greater exposure to media containing a high concentration of body images show more characteristics of eating disorders than do females with less exposure to these media. However, it remains unclear why most women exposed to thin media messages do not develop eating disorders (Polivy & Herman, 2004).

Psychological factors associated with eating disorders include issues of control, low self-esteem, extreme sensitivity to others' feelings, perfectionism, maturity fears, and distorted body image. Hilde Bruch (1973, 1978, 1982, 2001), who spent more than 40 years studying eating disorders, reported that anorexics typically are troubled female adolescents who feel incapable of changing their lives. These young women are from families that do not encourage autonomy and are perceived by the adolescent as overdemanding. More recent research corroborates this view and implies that insecure attachment is common in eating-disordered populations (Ward et al., 2000a, b). To exert some control in their lives, they exert control over the thing closest to them—their bodies. Many individuals who suffer from eating disorders do not perceive their bodies accurately, a condition referred to as **body dysmorphic disorder** (Chung, 2001). Women, in general, see themselves as one-fourth larger than they really are (Thompson, 1986). Men may also see themselves as larger than they really are, but they do so to a lesser degree, and, unlike women, many of these men may want to be larger (Geist et al., 1999; see Box 10-2). Both anorexics and bulimics tend to overestimate their body size to a greater extent than does the general population.

body dysmorphic disorder: condition in which individuals who suffer from eating disorders do not perceive their bodies accurately.

muscle dysmorphia: condition characterized by a belief that one's body is not sufficiently lean and muscular; clinically significant distress or impairment in social, occupational, or other areas of functioning; and a primary focus on being too small or inadequately muscular.

Box 10-2 Muscle Dysmorphia: The Body Dysmorphic Disorder Especially for Men

For men, the fear of being and looking like a "97-pound weakling" is not new, as a look through the ads in old comic books will attest. Yet today more than ever, many men fear that they are too small and skinny. In the words of Roberto Olivardia, "They feel like Clark Kent and long to be Superman" (2001, p. 254).

While conducting research on anabolic steroids, Olivardia and his supervisor, Harrison Pope, met several large and muscular bodybuilders who confided that they felt small and frail (Pope, 2001). Sometimes these people were referred to as experiencing "reverse anorexia" or "bigorexia," but the term most often used today is **muscle dysmorphia** (Olivardia, 2001). There is some debate as to whether muscle dysmorphia should be classified in the American Psychiatric Association's Diagnostic and Statistical Manual as a subcategory of body dysmorphic disorder or a subcategory of obsessive compulsive disorder, or whether it and anorexia nervosa should be in a category on their own (Chung,

2001). However, most people agree on the criteria for making a diagnosis of muscle dysmorphia (Olivardia, 2001, p. 255): (1) a preoccupation with the idea that one's body is not sufficiently lean and muscular; (2) clinically significant distress or impairment in social, occupational, or other areas of functioning; (3) a primary focus on being too small or inadequately muscular.

Due to their preoccupation with their bodies, individuals with muscle dysmorphia look at their bodies in the mirror many times a day. The need to look in the mirror becomes so strong that "one young man got into several car accidents because he compulsively checked a large hand-held mirror while driving to ensure that he wasn't getting smaller" (Olivardia, 2001, p. 255). Obviously, a preoccupation such as this can be detrimental. Many men with muscle dysmorphia are so obsessed with working out that they lose their jobs. Lawyers, doctors, and businessmen relinquish their careers so they can spend more time working

(*Continued*)

Box 10-2 (Continued)

out (Olivardia et al., 2000; Pope, 2001). A few specific examples include a lawyer who was fired because he often took three- to four-hour lunch breaks to fit in his workout, a student who missed a final exam because the time conflicted with his workout, and a man who missed the birth of his child so he could lift weights (Olivardia, 2001).

Some individuals with muscle dysmorphia react by hiding their bodies. These individuals are so ashamed of their bodies that they avoid situations where their bodies will be exposed to others. Many even refuse to take off their shirts at the beach (Pope, 2001). Unfortunately, those with muscle dysmorphia report anabolic-androgenic steroid use to increase their muscle mass (Pope et al., 2005; Rohman, 2009).

What causes muscle dysmorphia? Biological, psychological, and sociocultural explanations have all been put forth (Olivardia, 2001). There may be an underlying biological or genetic predisposition toward muscle dysmorphia. Those with muscle dysmorphia have higher rates of mood and anxiety disorders than those without muscle dysmor-

phia (Cafri, Olivardia, & Thompson, 2008). Also, low self-esteem and masculinity issues are typical in men with muscle dysmorphia. Achieving a body that is respected and admired by others may be a response to these psychological issues.

The explanation that has received the most attention, however, is sociocultural in nature. That is, boys and men are now experiencing appearance-related societal pressures similar to those that women have experienced for decades. The ideal male body in our culture is becoming increasingly more muscular. A look at either centrefold models in *Playgirl* magazine (Leit, Pope, & Gray, 2000) or male action toys such as G.I. Joe (Pope et al., 1999) confirms this. We also know that when exposed to muscular images, like those presented in advertisements, men will perceive a greater discrepancy between their own muscularity and the level of muscularity that they consider ideal (Leit, Gray, & Pope, 2002). Thus, it is likely that there are a number of factors contributing to muscle dysmorphia.

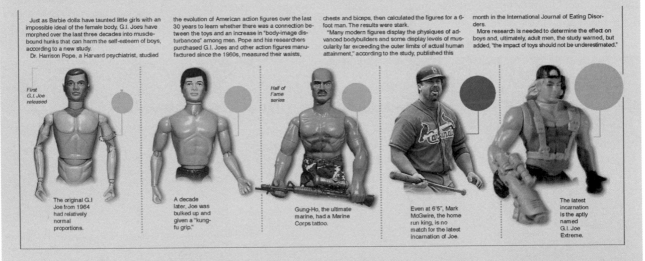

Just as Barbie dolls have taunted little girls with an impossible ideal of the female body, G.I. Joes have morphed over the last three decades into muscle-bound hunks that can harm the self-esteem of boys, according to a new study.
Dr. Harrison Pope, a Harvard psychiatrist, studied the evolution of American action figures over the last 30 years to learn whether there was a connection between the toys and an increase in "body-image disturbances" among men. Pope and his researchers purchased G.I. Joes and other action figures manufactured since the 1960s, measured their waists, chests and biceps, then calculated the figures for a 6-foot man. The results were stark.
"Many modern figures display the physiques of advanced bodybuilders and some display levels of muscularity far exceeding the outer limits of actual human attainment," according to the study, published this month in the International Journal of Eating Disorders.
More research is needed to determine the effect on boys and, ultimately, adult men, the study warned, but added, "the impact of toys should not be underestimated."

First G.I. Joe released

The original G.I Joe from 1964 had relatively normal proportions.

A decade later, Joe was bulked up and given a "kung-fu grip."

Hall of Fame series

Gung-Ho, the ultimate marine, had a Marine Corps tattoo.

Even at 6'5", Mark McGwire, the home run king, is no match for the latest incarnation of Joe.

The latest incarnation is the aptly named G.I. Joe Extreme.

G.I. Joe has become more muscle-bound over the last three decades. The latest doll, G.I. Joe Extreme, has a body that is unattainable by even the largest bodybuilders. Is the current North American cultural ideal of the male body so large and muscular that it represents an unattainable standard?

Treatment for Eating Disorders

Instruction and clinical experiences offered to Canadian psychiatry residents for the treatment of eating disorders is deemed insufficient (Williams & Leichner, 2006). Yet successful treatment for eating disorders is literally a matter of life and death. This is particularly true for anorexics, because there is such a high mortality rate within this population. Estimates vary but often indicate that between 5 and 10 percent of all anorexics die from their disorder—the majority from suicide (Brimingham, Su, Hlynsky, Goldner, & Gao, 2005; Wilson, et al., 2007).

Not surprisingly, anorexics are very difficult to treat because they believe that the only aspects of their environment they can control are their own bodies. As long as they refuse to eat, they maintain control. As starvation continues, anorexics eventually reach the point of exhaustion and possible physical collapse, so the first goal of treatment is to medically stabilize the patient and increase his or her weight.

Weight restoration is a step in the treatment process but is not a cure. Anorexics need to change both their body image *and* their eating habits. Cognitive behaviour therapy attempts to eradicate the irrational beliefs of patients while maintaining a warm and accepting attitude. For example, anorexics are encouraged to avoid absolutist thoughts like, "If I put on one pound, I'll go on to gain one hundred." Similarly, they are educated about nutritional facts. Superstitious beliefs like "laxatives prevent the absorption of calories" are dispelled. Patients are also encouraged to recognize that others do not have the same high standards for their behaviour that they do.

Cognitive behaviour therapy is often used in conjunction with pharmacotherapy, particularly antidepressants or selective serotonin reuptake inhibitors (SSRIs; Powers & Bruty, 2008). Most commonly, fluoxetine is used. Some studies report that when CBT and fluoxetine are used in combination, secondary outcomes, namely improvements in self-esteem, are produced in addition to weight gains (Stein et al., 2001). Yet other studies show that fluoxetine is not superior to either a placebo or CBT alone (Powers & Bruty, 2008; Walsh et al., 2006). Other pharmacotherapy treatments include second generational antipsychotics. These can be useful during the initial weight restoration phase of anorexia when clients have particularly severe obsessions, anxiety, or near delusional thinking (Powers & Bruty, 2008).

Pharmacotherapy as a sole treatment is not recommended as this results in a higher dropout rate than when used in conjunction with CBT (Halmi et al., 2005, Stein et al., 2001). CBT appears most useful in preventing relapse (Pike, Walsh, Vitousek, Wilson, & Bauer, 2003). Family therapy is often included in the treatment process. It has been found that family participation positively influences the results of therapy, although parents are typically more pleased with these sessions than are the patients (Eisler et al., 1999; Paulson-Karlsson, Nevonen, & Engstrom, 2006). The preferred format is to have the anorexic child and her parents attend different sessions (Wilson et al. 2007).

Bulimia is much easier to treat than anorexia, because bulimics are aware that their eating habits are not normal. As a result, they are motivated to change these behaviours. Psychological therapy is the most successful approach for treating bulimia (Chavez & Insel, 2007). Treatment for bulimia usually includes cognitive behaviour therapy (CBT). Typically, therapy begins by patients being instructed to monitor their eating habits. An individualized treatment program is then developed to help break down patterns of behaviour that maintain disordered eating. The program will include reinforcement, relaxation training, and cognitive restructuring (Thackwray, Smith, Bodfish, & Meyers, 1993).

Specific techniques might include increasing the regularity of meals, eating a greater variety of foods, delaying the impulse to purge for as long as possible, and eating foods in new settings not previously associated with binges (Agras et al., 1989; Kirkley, Schneider, Agras, & Bachman, 1985). The cognitive-behavioural techniques implemented should address the pathological concerns bulimics have about their weight and eating in addition to increasing perceptions of self-esteem. CBT may be combined with pharmacotherapy (Agras, 2004). Antidepressants are used in managing bulimia as it has been determined that they decrease the frequency of binges. However, drugs do not treat the cause of the problem and there is a lack of evidence supporting their long-term efficacy (Wilson et al., 2007). As such, they should be used to treat bulimia only in conjunction with other forms of therapy.

Psychological treatments are found to be most effective in treating binge eating disorder (BED), although pharmacotherapy is also utilized. Psychological treatments including CBT and interpersonal psychotherapy are useful in reducing bingeing over both the short and the long term. Pharmacological therapy is more prone to relapse on the part of the BED patient (Stein, 2001).

Unfortunately, as many as half of previously treated eating-disorder sufferers will continue to have eating problems. The difficulty in treating eating disorders effectively, coupled with their increasing prevalence, suggests that researchers should focus more on ways to prevent eating disorders rather than focusing almost exclusively on treating them after they have developed (Becker, Smith, & Ciao, 2006; Taylor, Bryson, & Luce, 2006).

CHAPTER SUMMARY

This chapter focused on health-compromising behaviours. Almost 1 in 5 individuals over the age of 15 in Canada smokes. Smoking is a preventable cause of death accounting for approximately 37 000 deaths each year. As socioeconomic levels increase, smoking levels tend to decrease. The highest rates of smoking occur among Inuit and First Nations people. People often begin to smoke because of parental modelling, peer influence, advertising or because of personality characteristics (e.g., rebelliousness). Those who become regular smokers tend to do so to increase positive affect and decrease negative affect, and then smoking may become habitual and addictive.

Smoking leads to cardiovascular and cerebrovascular disease, cancer, and chronic obstructive pulmonary disease. Those who do not smoke but breathe in the second hand smoke of others are also at increased risk for these illnesses. The federal government has attempted to prevent smoking by banning advertising and by including warning labels on tobacco products. More than half of those who begin to smoke attempt to quit at some later date. Quitting attempts take many forms including reducing the number of cigarettes smoked and using nicotine replacement therapy. Aversion therapies and self management therapies may also be useful.

More than 75 percent of Canadians have consumed alcohol in the last 12 months. Excessive use of alcohol can have adverse effects on almost every system of the body. Moderate consumption of alcohol may have protective health benefits, primarily by reducing the risk of cardiovascular and coronary heart disease. A number of theories have been put forth to attempt to explain drinking behaviour including the disease model, the alcohol dependency syndrome model, the tension reduction hypothesis, the self-awareness model, the social learning model, and alcohol myopia theory.

Attempts to limit drinking include implementing age restrictions for buying or consuming alcohol, anti-drinking and anti-drinking-and-driving campaigns. Treatments include 12-step programs, psychotherapy, drug therapy, aversion therapy, and multimodal therapies. Canada's Drug Strategy adopts the stages of change model for guiding both treatment processes and prevention goals.

More than 10 percent of the Canadian population admitted to using illicit drugs in the year preceding the survey. Cannabis is the most frequently used illicit drug. Treatment programs are similar to those used for alcohol abuse.

Many youths engage in unsafe sexual behaviours that can lead to serious health consequences. A variety of theoretical approaches have been used in an attempt to understand sexual and reproductive health behaviours using a decision-making framework e.g., information-motivation-behavioural skills model.

Obesity is becoming a significant health problem in Canada. Heredity, hormones, stress, and sociocultural and environmental factors all contribute to obesity. Treatment can be behavioural, pharmacological, or surgical. Eating disorders such as anorexia nervosa and bulimia nervosa are more common in women than men. Muscle dysmorphia, another body dysmorphic disorder, is more common in men. Treating eating disorders is very difficult, especially for anorexia and muscle dysmorphia, because the individuals don't admit to having a problem. Pharmacotherapy, cognitive behavioural therapy, and family therapy are all used with limited success.

Review Questions

1. What factors prompt adolescents to begin smoking?
2. How can we help people who are addicted to smoking, alcohol, or illicit drugs quit these habits?
3. Why do people engage in unsafe sexual behaviour?
4. What factors contribute to obesity in our society?
5. What are eating disorders and how does the incidence of eating disorders differ for men and women?
6. How can the stages of change model be applied to the prevention and treatment of health-compromising behaviours?

Chapter 11
Pain

CHAPTER OUTLINE

THE SIGNIFICANCE OF PAIN
PAIN PERCEPTION
THEORIES OF PAIN
NEUROCHEMICAL BASIS OF PAIN AND PAIN INHIBITION
ACUTE VERSUS CHRONIC PAIN
PSYCHOSOCIAL FACTORS AND PAIN
THE MEASUREMENT OF PAIN
PAIN CONTROL TECHNIQUES

Learning Objectives

After studying this chapter, you will be able to

- Explain the benefits of experiencing pain

- Describe theories that attempt to explain the phenomenon of pain

- Identify factors that contribute to the experience of and expression of pain

- Provide examples of how pain is assessed
- List and explain a variety of pain control techniques

At 22 years of age, Jake was a happy-go-lucky, athletic apprentice chef in an exclusive restaurant. He loved his job and took it very seriously. One day when the master chef was away, two boxes of chickens were delivered. Jake cut up the chickens and packaged them for the freezer. Not long after, he became very ill. Jake was finally diagnosed as having been infected with salmonella, caused by a bacterium that is usually present on raw chicken meat. Jake was quarantined in the hospital, where he spent 10 days and lost 30 pounds.

Upon his discharge from the hospital, Jake rapidly resumed his old activities—he went back to work and immediately returned to playing soccer. However, six weeks later, a host of new symptoms appeared: joint pain, urethritis (inflammation of the urethra), and conjunctivitis (inflammation of the eye). This triad of symptoms is indicative of Reiter's syndrome. Reiter's syndrome occurs in two to three percent of patients exposed to bacteria known to promote it (including that which produces salmonella). In North America, 30 in every 100 000 individuals will experience this syndrome at some point in their lives; the incidence rate is five times higher for males than for females. Although most people recover from this illness in six months, in some it "grumbles on" for a year or more, and a small minority develop unremitting and potentially disabling arthritis. Unfortunately, Jake was one of the unlucky ones. His physician told him his pain would increase over time and that he would eventually lose mobility—not an easy prognosis for anyone to accept and especially not for an active person at such a young age.

With his eternal optimism, Jake continued to embrace life. He made a career change and found a job where he would be interacting with others all day—he became a bus driver. This job was the perfect fit for Jake, because he loved people and almost everyone he came in contact with became an instant friend.

In the beginning Jake rarely exhibited any pain. He married and had two children. As the years passed, however, his pain increased, causing him to take more and more painkillers. The pain became more and more excruciating, until he was consuming 14 Tylenol Threes a day (far exceeding the recommended dosage). Then, 13 years after the initial diagnosis, he just couldn't keep it together any longer.

Jake became extremely depressed and began to experience anxiety attacks. He was off work for a few months, then returned to his jovial self. He returned to work, but after driving a bus for only three weeks he had to go on leave again. Emotionally, he was sinking deeper and deeper. He became suicidal and began abusing his medication, taking far more than the physician had prescribed. Secretly, he also began abusing alcohol. Jake was checked into a hospital where he would receive psychiatric help.

After a number of weeks in the hospital, Jake was discharged and seemed to be in better spirits. Unfortunately, he will have to live with physical pain for the rest of his life. He has tried, in his words, "every pain management technique available." In addition to pharmacological treatment, he has tried acupuncture, guided imagery, meditation, physical exercises, and massage therapy. He recently returned from a 10-day stay at a pain clinic. Jake said that the pain management techniques at the clinic ranged from group hugs to a few very painful procedures where he screamed louder than he had ever screamed before. Jake states that the most beneficial aspect of this visit was that he learned that he really wasn't "so bad off." Many of the other patients were currently experiencing more pain than he was, and the ordeals that they had gone through were heartrending. Currently, Jake continues to be in good spirits; he participates in aqua therapy and visits a massage therapist. He knows that he will be taking medication for the rest of his life, and very recently his physician told him he may have to give up the idea of ever driving a bus again.

The chronic (or long-term) pain that Jake experiences as a result of Reiter's syndrome has affected him in many ways. It has affected him emotionally. Jake can no longer work in the job he loves and is currently living on disability payments, a situation that is hard on his self-esteem. It is not surprising that depression and anxiety are often experienced by people with chronic pain. His social life has changed considerably, and for more than a year he didn't want to see even his closest friends. Obviously, the pain has affected him physically as well. Jake can no longer play soccer with his teammates. He only hopes that he will still be able to kick the soccer ball around with his children when they are old enough. It is true that pain of any kind usually leads people to change their activity level. As this chapter explains, such pain behaviours are an important component of the pain experience.

THE SIGNIFICANCE OF PAIN

After reading about Jake, the idea of a life without pain might sound rather appealing. You would feel no pain when falling down, when stubbing your toe, or when slamming your finger in the car door. Headaches would not exist. You would feel no pain while exercising, and giving birth might even be considered a pleasant experience. But before you conclude that life would be wonderful with no pain, consider the case of Miss C., a young Canadian woman who was a student at McGill University (Melzack & Wall, 1996). Miss C.'s father, a physician, suggested to his colleagues in Montreal that they should examine her. Miss C. was highly intelligent and seemed normal in every way except that she had never felt pain. As a child, she had bitten off the tip of her tongue while chewing food and had suffered third-degree burns on her legs after kneeling on a hot radiator to look out a window. In fact, Miss C. could not remember ever sneezing or coughing, and she had neither the gag reflex nor the corneal reflex that protects the eyes.

The physicians who examined Miss C. subjected her to tests that would have felt like torture to a normal person. They administered electric shocks to different parts of her body and immersed her limbs in hot water at temperatures that usually produce reports of burning pain. They immersed her limbs in cold water for prolonged periods and pinched tendons. She felt no pain. In addition, her heart rate, blood pressure, and respiration remained normal throughout the tests.

As a result of her inability to experience pain, Miss C. had severe medical problems, including pathological changes in her knees, hip, and spine. Melzack and Wall (1996) explain that insensitivity to pain can lead people to remain in one position too long, causing inflammation of the joints. Even worse, the failure to feel pain leads one to neglect injuries; as a result, healing is impeded. Injured tissue can easily become infected. These infections are very difficult to treat, particularly if they extend to the bone.

Rare disease makes girl unable to feel pain: Genetic disorder deprives kindergarten student Ashlyn Blocker of natural alarms.

Miss C. died when she was only 29 years old of massive infections that could not be brought under control. Miss C.'s insensitivity to pain directly contributed to the infections that killed her.

Thus, there are benefits to experiencing pain. Pain is known to serve at least three functions. First, the pain that occurs before serious injury, such as when we step on or pick up hot, sharp, or otherwise potentially damaging objects, has real survival value. It causes us to immediately withdraw, which prevents further injury. Second, the pains that prevent further injury serve as the basis of learning to avoid injurious objects or situations that may occur at a later time. Third, pains due to damaged joints, abdominal infections, diseases, or serious injuries set limits on activity and enforce inactivity and rest, which are often essential for the body's natural recuperative and disease-fighting mechanisms to ensure recovery and survival.

PAIN PERCEPTION

When a person comes in contact with injurious stimuli, signals of tissue damage follow a particular route from **afferent (sensory) neurons** of the peripheral nervous system to the spinal cord and then to the brain. The afferent nerve endings that respond to pain stimuli are called **nociceptors**. When activated, these nerve endings generate impulses that travel to the central nervous system. The afferent peripheral fibres that transmit pain impulses are **A-delta fibres** and **C-fibres**. A-delta fibres are associated with sharp, distinct pain. The A-delta fibres are small, myelinated fibres that transmit impulses very quickly. In contrast, C-fibres transmit impulses more slowly because they are unmyelinated. The C-fibres, which comprise over 60 percent of all sensory afferents, are involved when pain is diffuse, dull, or aching (Melzack & Wall, 1996).

The afferent fibres group together after leaving the periphery, and this grouping forms a nerve. The nerves then enter the dorsal horns of the spinal cord; these contain several layers, or laminae, each of which receives incoming messages from afferent neurons. The cells in the first two layers form the *substantia gelatinosa*, and it is here where sensory input

afferent (sensory) neurons: nerve cells that conduct impulses from a sense organ to the central nervous system, or from lower to higher levels in the spinal cord and brain.

nociceptors: the afferent nerve endings that respond to pain stimuli.

A-delta fibres: the afferent peripheral fibres that are associated with transmitting sharp, distinct pain.

C-fibres: the afferent peripheral fibres that are associated with transmitting diffuse, dull, or aching pain.

information is thought to be modulated. Sensory aspects of pain are strongly influenced by activity in A-delta fibres, which send messages through the thalamus on their way to the brain's cerebral cortex. Here the A-delta fibres signal sharp pain. The motivational and affective elements of pain appear to be more heavily determined by the C-fibres, which send pain messages to the brain stem and lower portions of the forebrain.

THEORIES OF PAIN
Gate Control Theory

gate control theory: suggests that a neural mechanism in the dorsal horns of the spinal cord acts like a gate that can increase or decrease the flow of nerve impulses from peripheral fibres to the central nervous system thereby influencing the sensation of pain.

In 1965, Melzack and Wall proposed the **gate control theory** of pain. This theory improved on earlier theories of pain by recognizing the contribution of psychological factors to our perception of pain (Melzack & Katz, 2004). According to the gate control theory, pain is not a sensation that is transmitted directly from the peripheral nerve endings to the brain. Instead, the theory emphasizes that sensations are modified as they are conducted to the brain by way of the spinal cord. They are also influenced by downward pathways from the brain that interpret the experience. Melzack and Wall propose that there is a structure in the dorsal horns of the spinal column, a gatelike mechanism that is able to control the flow of pain stimulation to the brain.

According to the gate control theory, information enters the dorsal horns of the spinal cord by way of primary afferent neurons. This information passes through the *substantia gelatinosa*, where the information is modulated by stimulation from the periphery as well as by feedback from the fibres descending from the brain. This then affects the activity of the transmission cells, causing them to either conduct (excitatory influence) or not conduct (inhibitory influence) pain sensations to the brain.

The gate control theory proposes that the experience of pain is affected by the balance of activity in the small and large nerve fibres. This activity determines the patterning and intensity of stimulation. Activity in the small A-delta and C-fibres causes prolonged stimulation in the spinal cord. This type of activity promotes sensitivity and opens the gate, which produces pain. In contrast, activity in the large A-beta fibres tends to close the gate.

central control trigger: in the gate control theory of pain, a specialized system of large-diameter, rapidly conducting fibres that activate selective cognitive processes that then influence, by way of descending fibres, the opening and closing of the gate.

The gate may be closed by activity in the spinal cord and also by messages descending from the brain. A specialized system of large-diameter, rapidly conducting fibres, called the **central control trigger**, activates selective cognitive processes that then influence, by way of descending fibres, the opening and closing of the gate. The experience of pain is thus influenced by past experience, attention, and other cognitive activities through the central control trigger. Consequently, affective reactions such as anxiety, depression, fear, or focusing on an injury can exacerbate the experience of pain by affecting the central control trigger, thus opening the gate. Intense involvement in other activities, or relaxation, or positive experiences can mute the pain experience by causing the gate to close.

Consider observations made by Beecher (1959) during World War II. An injury or wound sustained by a civilian produces pain (the gate is open). However, a soldier with the equivalent injury does not experience the same amount of pain, because the soldier is distracted by the environment (the gate is closed). Suppressing the pain of injuries allows individuals to defend themselves during attack and to escape from further harm. Evidence in support of this observation can be seen in the amount of analgesic requested by patients from each group. A civilian patient will ask for significantly more analgesic than will a soldier who sustained the same injury (Watkins & Maier, 2000).

This theory also explains how injuries can go virtually unnoticed. If sensory input is sent into a heavily activated nervous system, the stimulation may not be perceived as pain. A hockey player may fracture a rib during a game but not notice the acute pain because of excitement and concentration on the game. It isn't until after the game is over that the player notices the pain. At this time, the nervous system is functioning at a different level of activation, and the gate is more easily opened.

The gate control theory was arguably the leading theory of pain for over 25 years. And, in fact, the conceptual components of the theory have stood the test of time (Melzack & Katz, 2004). The theory continues to spur research and generate interest in the psychological and perceptual factors involved in pain. However, the gate control theory is not able to explain several chronic pain problems, such as **phantom limb pain** (see Box 11-1).

phantom limb pain: the experience of pain in an absent body part.

Neuromatrix Theory

Melzack (2001) has proposed an extension to the gate control theory—the **neuromatrix theory**. This theory places a greater emphasis on the brain's role in pain perception. According to this theory, a genetically determined neuromatrix or network of brain neurons "distributed throughout many areas of the brain, comprises a widespread network of neurons that generates patterns, processes information that flows through it, and ultimately produces the pattern that is felt as a whole body" (Melzack & Katz, 2004, p. 23). The neuromatrix-generated patterns are called *neurosignature patterns*. These patterns may be generated from sensory inputs; however, they may also be innately produced, such as in the case of phantom limb pain. The neurosignature patterns are responsible for producing a multidimensional experience of pain. Like the gate control theory, the neuromatrix theory maintains that pain perception is part of a complex process that is affected by sensory input, activity of the nervous system, and past experiences and expectations.

neuromatrix theory: an extension of the gate control theory, with greater emphasis placed on the brain's role in pain perception.

NEUROCHEMICAL BASIS OF PAIN AND PAIN INHIBITION

The gate control theory of pain asserts that the brain can control the amount of pain an individual experiences by transmitting messages down the spinal cord to block the transmission of pain signals (Melzack & Wall, 1965, 1996). There is evidence that supports this view. David Reynolds (1969) conducted a now-classic study in which he implanted an electrode in the midbrain portion of a number of rats' brain stems. The exact location of the electrode varied from one rat to the next. Then, he made sure that the rats could feel pain by applying a clamp to their tails. Not surprisingly, each rat responded by demonstrating pain.

Several days later, Reynolds tested whether stimulation through the electrode would block pain. At the same time the rats were electrically stimulated, he again applied the clamp. Those rats with electrodes in the area of the midbrain known as the **periaqueductal grey area** did not exhibit pain. Those rats that did not experience pain in response to having their tails clamped later had abdominal surgery performed on them

periaqueductal grey area: an area of the midbrain that is involved in pain reception.

Box 11-1 Phantom Limb Pain

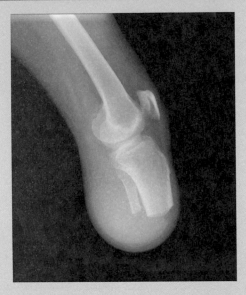

In 1866, the first account of phantom limbs was published. It appeared not in a scientific journal—as one might expect—but in the *Atlantic Monthly,* as an anonymously written short story. In "The Case of George Dedlow," the main character loses an arm to amputation during the Civil War. At one point, he awakens in the hospital after, unbeknownst to him, both his legs have also been amputated.

> [I was] suddenly aware of a sharp cramp in my left leg. I tried to get at it . . . with my single arm, but, finding myself too weak, hailed an attendant. "Just rub my left calf . . . if you please."
>
> "Calf? . . . You ain't got non, pardner. It's took off." (cited in Woodhouse, 2005)

The author happened to be Wier Mitchell, the foremost American neurologist at the time. Historians have proposed that Mitchell chose to publish this account in the *Atlantic Monthly* anonymously because he was unsure how his colleagues would respond to the concept of phantom limb pain. He feared that they would not believe that amputated arms and legs could be felt by their previous owners.

In fact, the phenomenon of phantom limbs is common to those who have undergone amputation. The limb is very vivid to the amputee, who can usually tell you the precise position of the phantom. A phantom limb behaves very much like a normal limb. Usually, a phantom arm hangs straight down at the side when the person sits or stands but moves in perfect coordination with other limbs during walking. Similarly, a phantom leg bends like a normal leg would when its owner sits; it stretches out when the individual lies down; it becomes upright during standing (Melzack, 1992).

Occasionally, the amputee becomes convinced the limb is stuck in an unusual position. Melzack (1992) noted that one man believed his phantom arm extended straight out from the shoulder, at a right angle to the body. Consequently, whenever the man walked through a doorway he would turn sideways so that his arm would not hit the wall. Another man slept only on his front or side because his phantom arm was bent behind him and got in the way when he tried to rest on his back.

The most extraordinary feature of phantom limbs is their reality to the amputee. The phantom limb may seem so real that the amputee might try standing up on a phantom foot or answering a phone with a phantom hand. A phantom limb can experience many sensations including warmth, cold, and pressure. A phantom limb can feel wet (as when an artificial arm is seen entering into a lake during a swan dive). It can also feel itchy, which can be very annoying. Fortunately, scratching the apparent site of discomfort can sometimes actually relieve the distress. It may sometimes seem that the phantom limb is sweaty, prickly, or even being tickled (Melzack, 1992).

Of course, the sensation in phantom limbs that causes the most distress to the sufferer is pain. Researchers (Ephraim et al., 2005; Richardson et al., 2006) have found that approximately 80 percent of amputees had phantom limb pain in the months and years following surgery. A national study deemed that the majority of amputees are "bothered" by the phantom (Ephraim et al., 2005). Yet general practitioners seem to underestimate both the prevalence and the severity of phantom limb pain (Whyte & Niven, 2004; Woodhouse, 2005). Unfortunately, this type of pain seems to be resistant to treatment (Hunter, Katz, & Davis, 2005).

Originally, it was believed that one must first possess and then lose a limb and the corresponding nerves to experience phantom pain. Certainly, there is good evidence indicating that cortical reorganization takes place following amputation, a possible cause of phantom limb pain (e.g., Grusser et al., 2001; Karl et al., 2004). However, there is now considerable evidence of phantoms in people born without limbs and in those who experienced limb amputation in very early childhood (e.g., Melzack, Israel, Lacroix, & Schultz, 1997; Woodhouse, 2005).

while the periaqueductal grey area of their brains was being electrically stimulated. Again, the rats did not feel any pain. This phenomenon has been termed **stimulation-produced analgesia (SPA)**. Reynolds' findings encouraged researchers to look for the neurochemical basis of pain. Subsequently, *endogenous opioids* were identified.

Endogenous opioids are naturally occurring opiate-like substances, produced in the brain, spinal cord, and glands, that regulate pain. They appear to relieve pain by slowing or blocking the transmission of nerve impulses—much like exogenous opioids such as heroin and morphine (Julien, 2005). Researchers have identified three main groups of these endogenous opioids: beta-endorphin, proenkephalin, and prodynorphin (Akil et al., 1998; Julien, 2005).

The system of endogenous opioids and their function in the body is very complex. Researchers do not have a full understanding of the mechanisms by which they work. However, it is apparent that having internal pain-relieving chemicals serves an adaptive function. It may be that because pain and emotions are closely linked, studies have found that psychological stress can trigger endogenous opioid activity (Turk, 2001). There is also evidence that intense physical exercise can trigger the release of beta-endorphin, resulting in natural, short-term pain suppression and subjective feelings of physical well-being. The release of endogenous opioids may help to explain how injured athletes in competition and soldiers on the battlefield continue to function after being injured, with little or no perception of pain.

stimulation-produced analgesia (SPA): freedom from pain as a result of electrical stimulation.

endogenous opioids: opiate-like substances produced within the body that regulate pain.

ACUTE VERSUS CHRONIC PAIN

Medical professionals make an important distinction between two main kinds of clinical pain—acute and chronic. Case 11-1 presents these two different types of pain in the examples of Riley and Michelle's individual experiences. Riley is suffering from **acute pain**. Acute pain seems to serve to warn of impending tissue damage or the need for convalescent rest. A toothache, the discomforts of childbirth, a broken limb, and postoperative pain are all forms of acute pain. Acute pain is by definition temporary, lasting less than six months (Turk & Winter, 2006). The physiological responses to acute pain seem partly proportional to the stimulus intensity. Acute pain can cause considerable anxiety and distress. Fortunately, painkillers can often ease the discomfort, and as the injury begins to heal, the anxiety subsides.

acute pain: pain that lasts less than six months and serves to warn of impending tissue damage or the need for convalescent rest.

CASE 11-1 ACUTE VERSUS CHRONIC PAIN

Riley is 28 years old and is just finishing his residency in anesthesiology. Recently, Riley received an invitation to his high school reunion. Riley had enjoyed high school and, in particular, his participation in school sports. He played volleyball and basketball, but the sport he enjoyed most was football. He decided that returning to his hometown for his high school reunion would be just the break he needed from life at the hospital.

The first night of the reunion weekend Riley met up with many of his former buddies and they reminisced about their football success. They really had been one of the greatest teams in the high school's history. In fact, six of the team members had gone on to play football in university, and four others had turned professional. The guys decided to get together for a scrimmage before the weekend was out.

<Case Continued>

On Sunday morning, 16 members of the former team gathered for a scrimmage. The guys played hard and even the spectators were impressed with the quick moves the players exhibited. After the game, the guys vowed to get together every year on the last weekend of August for a scrimmage.

Riley flew home on Sunday night. When he tried to rise from his seat at the conclusion of the flight, he experienced a sharp pain in his back. Slowly and carefully, he eased himself into a standing position. He had obviously overdone it at the scrimmage earlier that day. Riley knew he was going to be extremely stiff the next day. He decided that a walk before bed might help ward off some of the stiffness.

Compare Riley's experience of pain to that experienced by Michelle.

Michelle has been a professional pairs figure skater for almost 20 years. She and her partner have decided they will call it quits at the end of the current season. One factor that played a part in this decision is Michelle's pain. For the past few years, Michelle has found it increasingly difficult to land the jumps and throws that she and her partner practise over and over on a daily basis. After landing each throw and after landing each jump, Michelle experiences a sharp, searing pain in her knees. After each practice session, Michelle must ice her knees to help alleviate the pain, swelling, and tenderness. Not only does Michelle have a hard time landing her jumps, but she has also noticed that she is having some difficulty simply walking. It is likely that Michelle will be diagnosed with osteoarthritis. Although Michelle is going to miss skating, she hopes that a less physically demanding schedule will ease some of the pain she has been experiencing.

chronic pain: pain lasting for longer than six months.

But sometimes the pain lingers on. When it lasts longer than six months, pain is considered **chronic**. Any condition that is expected to bring only acute pain but continues for six months without resolution is considered to be chronic pain (Moulin et al., 2002). Michelle, like Jake in the chapter-opening vignette, is experiencing chronic pain. In Canada, estimates of those suffering from chronic pain range from 20 to 30 percent (Henry, 2008). These rates are similar to those found in other countries (Boulanger et al., 2007).

chronic recurrent pain: intermittent intense episodes of acute pain followed by relief.

Chronic pain can be intermittent or constant, mild or severe. It varies a great deal depending upon its type (Turk & Winter, 2006). **Chronic recurrent pain** does not become progressively worse. It is characterized by intense episodes of acute pain followed by relief. For example, a person who suffers from migraine headaches may have excruciating headaches lasting from hours to days, but then may have several pain-free weeks or months. By comparison, the person who has **chronic intractable benign pain** has pain all the time, with varying intensity. People who suffer from lower back pain generally experience their pain continually and find that they can do little to reduce it. Finally, **chronic progressive pain** involves continuous discomfort that gradually intensifies as the condition worsens. It is typically associated with malignancies or degenerative disorders, such as cancer and advancing arthritis.

chronic intractable benign pain: continuous pain that varies in intensity.

chronic progressive pain: continuous pain that gradually intensifies as a person's condition worsens.

In many types of chronic pain, the disease process is primarily responsible for the pain experienced. However, psychosocial factors may also play a role. Although tissue damage may result in the initial acute pain that the person experiences, subsequently, psychosocial factors may play a more prominent role. To clarify this process, we must distinguish between respondent and operant pain. **Respondent pain** refers to pain that occurs in response to noxious stimulation or tissue damage. In contrast, **operant pain** is pain that is reinforced by the person's environment.

Typically, people in pain will alter their behaviour in an attempt to reduce the pain. For example, a person may limp, guard a painful arm, avoid exercise, or even stay in bed to avoid pain. When such **pain behaviours** either reduce the pain or prevent it from getting worse, the tendency to continue the behaviour is reinforced. As the pain behaviours appear successful at preventing or reducing the pain, the person will continue to engage in these behaviours for fear that the pain will return if they are discontinued. Consequently, these behaviours are particularly resistant to change (Fordyce, 1976; Hadjistavropoulos & de C. Williams, 2004).

The verbal and behavioural expressions of pain also have a powerful effect on other people. When individuals complain of pain, display pain on their face, or exhibit an abnormal gait or posture, they may receive attention, concern, and even assistance from those witnessing these behaviours—this can further reinforce pain behaviour. Researchers have discovered that chronic pain sufferers who report higher levels of satisfaction with social support also exhibit higher levels of pain-related behaviours. Positive attention provided by supportive spouses in response to the expression of pain may build intimacy (Cano & de C. Williams, 2010) but it may also inadvertently maintain

respondent pain: pain that occurs in response to noxious stimulation or tissue damage.

operant pain: pain that is reinforced by a person's environment.

pain behaviours: alterations in behaviour by a person experiencing pain to either reduce the pain or to prevent it from getting worse.

An individual's experience of pain is often obvious to others.

or increase an individual's expression of pain and the experience of disability (Patterson, 2005).

One of the most common complaints described by those with chronic pain is the resulting sleep disturbance (American Pain Society, 1999; Breivik et al., 2006). A large majority (79 percent) of those experiencing moderate or severe chronic pain complain about the difficulties they have in falling asleep. As well, these individuals are frequently awakened as a result of the pain. In the morning, they wake up exhausted. They are tired and drained of energy, not merely from lack of sleep but also because the continuous pain wears them down. It is not surprising that these chronic pain sufferers also find themselves irritated by little things and trivial comments of those around them. These people recognize that they are snapping at their friends and family for insufficient reasons, yet they cannot seem to stop. This situation often leads those with chronic pain to withdraw from their families and friends.

The chronic pain sufferer who withdraws from family and friends experiences little social or recreational life. In addition, 59 percent of those with moderate or severe chronic pain have had to leave their jobs (American Pain Society, 1999). As a result, people's standard of living is reduced and an added strain is put on the family. In addition, both personal and career goals may be set aside because the sufferer's life is beginning to revolve around pain (Breivik et al., 2006). Ironically, if compensation is received for the pain experience because it resulted from an injury on the job or perhaps in an automobile accident, this may exacerbate the perceived severity of pain and distress (Turk & Okifuji, 1996).

All of the previously mentioned behaviours resulting from the experience of pain have an impact on one's emotional state. Many chronic pain sufferers are irritable, and many report being listless, unable to cope, and depressed (American Pain Society, 1999). In fact, people who suffer from chronic pain share many of the same symptoms as people who suffer from depression. Merskey (1986) reports that in almost all published studies of psychiatric and psychological test findings, chronic pain patients report mild but significant depression. Further, approximately 50 percent of hospitalized patients with depression report pain as a major symptom.

These are daunting statistics, especially considering that depression is known to exacerbate pain and pain-related behaviours (Tennen, Affleck, & Zautra, 2006). Fortunately, once pain is controlled there is a significant improvement in individuals' abilities and moods. For example, a national study in the United States found that 84 percent of chronic pain sufferers whose pain was now under control felt happy and upbeat; 41 percent provided this response before their pain was controlled (American Pain Society, 1999).

PSYCHOSOCIAL FACTORS AND PAIN
Gender Differences

Clinical research has documented that women are more likely than men to experience a variety of recurrent pain. Recurrent pain can result from many ailments, including migraine and other headaches as well as musculoskeletal, back, and abdominal injury (LeResche, 2000). In most studies, women report more severe levels of pain, more frequent pain, and pain of longer duration than men (Bingefors & Isacson, 2004).

Researchers agree that there are gender differences in the perception of and response to pain (see Fillingim, 2009; or Keogh, 2006, 2009 for reviews). The extent of these differences is under debate. Anita Unruh (1996) from Dalhousie University has identified three key issues surrounding gender differences and pain: (1) the manner in which women and men perceive and respond to pain, (2) the psychosocial and biological factors that may influence gender variations in pain experience, and (3) the response of the health care system to the pain presented by women and men.

Laboratory research has documented how men and women differ in their pain responses (Keogh et al., 2005; Sullivan, Tripp, & Santor, 2000). For example, Lowery, Fillingim, and Wright (2003) reported that women have a lower pain threshold and lower pain tolerance than men have. To determine a participant's pain threshold, researchers will inflict pain on the participant by one of a number of methods. A commonly used method is known as a "cold-pressor task." This entails participants submerging their hand in cold water until they experience pain. They indicate to the researcher, usually by pushing a button, when this point is reached. At this time participants are said to have reached their **pain threshold**.

Researchers are sometimes interested in identifying participants' *pain tolerance* levels rather than their pain threshold. The **pain tolerance level** is either the duration of time a person is willing to endure a stimulus beyond the point where it began to hurt, or the intensity of the stimulus a person will endure beyond that point. When the participants "can't stand it" any longer, they have reached their level of pain tolerance. Once the participants have indicated that they have reached their limit, they can remove their hand from the noxious stimuli. Laboratory studies investigating gender differences in pain threshold and pain tolerance generally suggest that women demonstrate a greater sensitivity to pain than men do (Keogh, 2006). Any inconsistencies in results are generally deemed due to the variety of noxious stimuli and measurement tools used by investigators (e.g., Giles & Walker, 2000; Hashmi & Davis, 2010; Keogh, 2006).

Another approach, taken by researchers at the University of Western Ontario (Rollman et al., 2005), indicates that individuals who have experienced greater pain in the past show lower pain tolerance. Given that women frequently have experienced high pain levels and demonstrate lower pain tolerance, we might consider whether these two factors are related.

Critics argue that apparent gender differences in response to pain are actually due to differences in reporting pain (e.g., Robinson et al., 2004). Some researchers (Robinson et al., 2001; Myers, Riley, & Robinson, 2003) believe that female participants in lab studies give a more unbiased report of their pain than do male participants. Men feel there is a social cost to admitting publicly that something hurts. Men are taught to "tough out" pain, and so in the lab they endure more discomfort. In contrast, women feel little pressure to endure unnecessary pain and therefore have no trouble admitting when something hurts.

It is plausible that societal beliefs about gender differences in response to pain are a product of different societal gender-role expectations (Robinson et al., 2004). Unruh (1996) points out that when we experience pain, we engage in a process of cognitive appraisal. That is, we determine what this experience means to us. To determine the meaning of an event

pain threshold: the point at which the intensity of a stimulus is perceived as painful.

pain tolerance: duration of time or intensity at which a person is willing to endure a stimulus beyond the point where it began to hurt.

we ask ourselves the following questions: "What does it mean?" "In what way does it affect me?" "Should I be concerned?" and "Is any action required on my part?"

Although psychosocial factors may influence pain perception, underlying biological differences in pain mechanisms may also predispose women to feel more pain. For example, there are known gender differences in brain chemistry, metabolism, physical structures, and hormones that may influence the biological mechanisms of pain transmission, pain sensitivity, and pain perception (Fillingim, 2009; Keogh, 2006). Wisenfeld notes that, after puberty, females are more sensitive to acutely painful stimuli than are males. Further, pain sensitivity may vary depending on the stage a woman is at in her menstrual cycle; however, the evidence is mixed (Fillingim, 2009; Wisenfeld, 2005). Pain sensitivity also appears heightened in women using estrogen replacement therapy (Fillingim & Edwards, 2001).

Both biological and psychosocial factors related to the experience and reporting of pain by men and women may lead to differences in the way men and women are treated by the health care system. For example, psychosocial factors, such as catastrophizing, may be responsible for women describing their pain in more detail and with more expressive and social language than do men. (See Focus on Canadian Research 11-1 for a more detailed discussion of catastrophizing.) As a result of these descriptions, women are more likely to receive a psychogenic interpretation of their pain by their physicians, particularly when the pain is not directly related to tissue damage. Unruh (1996) claims that these interpretations may "cause women to receive more attention for psychological aspects of pain but inadequate pain relief" (p. 159).

Women are also perceived by physicians and nurses as dramatizing or exaggerating their pain. As a result, they are provided less analgesia than are men (e.g., Chen et al., 2008; Hoffmann & Tarzian, 2001; Weisse et al., 2001). Men, on the other hand, are thought to minimize their pain and its consequences. This attitude may lead men to seek medical attention only when the pain characteristics have become more extreme, which may result in the pain being more difficult to treat. It is also true that men seem to implement fewer coping strategies than women in response to pain.

Cultural Differences

Pain is something that people all around the world experience, and ethnic differences in response to painful stimuli are believed to exist. For example, U.S. studies have indicated that whites show a greater tolerance to painful stimuli than do African Americans, and Asian Americans reportedly have the lowest pain tolerance (Campbell, Edwards, & Fillingim, 2005; Sheffield et al., 2000). Cultural background and social context will affect each person's experience, expression, and treatment of pain (Edwards & Fillingim, 2003; Edwards, Fillingim, & Keefe, 2001; Nayak et al., 2000; Riley et al., 2002; Zatzick & Dimsdale, 1990).

These differences result from the meaning each culture attaches to pain and from stereotypes associated with various cultural experiences. Consider, for example, members of certain African cultural groups who walk on burning coals and pierce their bodies with spikes yet show no outward appearance of pain. Similarly, in North America, body piercing and tattooing are commonplace in certain age and social groups. In both instances stoicism is expected, and expressions of pain might be ridiculed. In comparison, some Mediterranean peoples encourage the open expression of pain (Straub, 2007).

Catastrophizing

A group of Canadian researchers, led by Michael Sullivan at the University of Montreal, has been conducting research on pain catastrophizing for more than a decade. Pain catastrophizing involves a "negative emotional and cognitive response to pain involving elements of magnification, helplessness and pessimism" (Edwards et al., 2004, p. 336). In other words, people who spend considerable time ruminating about aspects of the pain experience become fearful of pain and adopt a form of helplessness. Specifically, they fear any movement that might be painful, and they also fear (re)injury; consequently, they engage in avoidance behaviour. Disuse, depression, and disability ensue, fostering the development of chronic pain problems.

The general conclusion that those who score high on the Pain Catastrophizing Scale experience greater pain intensity has been demonstrated numerous times (Bishop & Warr, 2003; Sullivan et al., 1995, 2001). For example, Pavlin, Sullivan, and colleagues (2005) asked a sample of patients who were to undergo anterior cruciate ligament repair to complete this scale presurgery. After surgery in the postanesthetic care unit, as well as one, two, and seven days after surgery, patients rated their pain on a scale of 0–10. Results indicated that those who scored higher on the Pain Catastrophizing Scale experienced greater pain postoperatively.

The relationship between catastrophizing and pain perception in a special subset of the population—that of ballet dancers—is not as clear. When examining the relationship between pain perception and catastrophizing in ballet dancers, Paparizos, Tripp, Sullivan, and Rubenstein (2005) noted that the relationship isn't simply that greater catastrophizing leads to a greater perception of pain. Ballet dancers, like athletes competing in competitive sports, are continually at risk for pain and injury. It seems that more experienced and highly skilled ballet dancers catastrophize less than ballet dancers who are less experienced and less skilled. Perhaps this trend is due to the rigorous training that a dancer must endure. Or, perhaps those who would have scored high on catastrophizing left dance earlier in their dance careers.

The literature germane to catastrophizing continues to grow. Recently, researchers have reported that high pain catastrophizers communicate pain more effectively when an observer is present (Sullivan, Adams, & Sullivan, 2004); high pain catastrophizers report using fewer cognitive coping strategies (Sullivan et al., 2004); and they perceive more intense pain in others than do low pain catastrophizers (Sullivan et al., in press). Further research exploring the concept of catastrophizing will continue to contribute to our understanding of the experience of pain.

If we focus on pain derived from one specific cause, such as cancer, we see that cultural differences still exist. For example, Europeans and North Americans consider pain to be a common experience for cancer patients, and pain experts state that pain is undertreated (Ferrell et al., 2001; Streltzer, 1997). In contrast, experts from Asian countries do not consider cancer pain to be as much of a problem. These different attitudes lead to differences in treatment—approximately 70 percent of patients in Europe receive opiates for cancer pain. In contrast, only about four percent of Asian cancer patients receive this medication. It is possible that these variations may be due more to physicians' beliefs than to patients' pain. Support for this idea is provided by a number of American studies that report that racial and ethnic minority groups often receive different diagnoses and less favourable care than do white Americans (Bonham, 2001; Rathmore et al., 2000).

Rollman (2004) aptly summarizes his review of ethnocultural variations in pain by stating that "it is misleading and potentially detrimental to generalize to all members of one group" (p. 174). In fact, there is stronger evidence of individual differences within ethnic groups than of differences between ethnic groups (Straub, 2007). In sum, health care practitioners should focus on the person before them rather than the ethnic group to which the person belongs (Korol & Craig, 2001).

THE MEASUREMENT OF PAIN

Pain is a challenge to assess because people have difficulty describing pain objectively. If you have cut your arm, you can point to the wound. Or, if you are concerned that you might have broken a bone, this can be determined by radiography. Pain lacks these objective referents. Yet assessing pain is very important in determining treatment for patients and evaluating the effectiveness of different pain-reducing methods. As a result, clinicians and researchers have developed many techniques for measuring the pain that an individual feels. These techniques include psychophysiological measures, behavioural assessment, and self-reports. Each technique has certain advantages and certain limitations.

Psychophysiological Measures

Pain has both sensory and emotional components that can produce changes in the autonomic nervous system as well as other physiological conditions. The physiological changes resulting from the pain experience can be assessed using psychophysiological measures (Flor, 2001; Turk & Melzack, 2001).

One psychophysiological measure researchers use for assessing pain is an **electromyograph**, or EMG. This measures the electrical activity in muscles, which reflects the level of muscle tension. Because muscle tension is associated with certain pain states, such as headaches and low back pain, we would expect that EMG recordings would be different for people experiencing pain and those not experiencing it (Levine & Levy, 2006). Measures of **autonomic activity**, such as heart rate, respiration rate, blood pressure, hand surface temperature, and skin conductance, assess generalized arousal, which may provide an emotional indicator of pain. Another instrument that measures pain is the **electroencephalograph**, or EEG. The EEG measures electrical activity in the brain. When a person's sensory system detects a stimulus, such as pressure on one's heel, the signal to the brain produces **evoked potentials** or a change in EEG voltage. The evoked potentials increase with the intensity of stimuli and decrease when people take analgesics (Chapman et al., 1985).

Even though psychophysiological measures objectively assess bodily changes that occur in response to pain, these bodily changes may also occur in response to other factors (e.g., attention, diet, and stress). Therefore, whenever possible, psychophysiological measures should be used in conjunction with other approaches in assessing pain.

Behavioural Assessment

Other measures of pain have focused on *pain behaviours*. Pain behaviours are behaviours exhibited when a person is in discomfort. They include non-verbal expressions (e.g., facial and vocal cues), distortions in movement and posture, irritability, and restrictions or avoidance of activity (Turk, Wack, & Kerns, 1985). Analyses of pain behaviours provide a basis for assessing how pain has disrupted the life of patients. Procedures have been developed for assessing specific pain behaviours in both daily activities and structured clinical settings.

Assessment of Pain Behaviour in Day-to-Day Activities   In assessing day-to-day activities, researchers and clinicians might be interested in the amount of time sufferers spend in bed, for example, or how many complaints they express. Do they bend over very carefully or not at all? Do they seek help in moving, walking, or climbing stairs? Do

electromyograph (EMG): an instrument that assesses pain by measuring electrical activity in muscles.

autonomic activity: physiological processes that cannot be consciously controlled, such as heart rate, respiration rate, blood pressure, hand surface temperature, and skin conductance.

electroencephalograph (EEG): an instrument that assesses pain by measuring electrical activity in the brain.

evoked potentials: electrical responses produced by stimuli.

they walk with a limp? Family members or significant others in patients' lives are often the best people to make these assessments. If these people are willing to help, they can be trained to make careful observations and keep accurate records. Fordyce (1976) documents a procedure for doing this, which has been refined by Turk (Turk et al., 1983).

Assessment of Pain Behaviour in Clinical Settings   Undertreatment of pain is a serious concern (Ferrell et al., 2001; Hadjistavropolous, 2004; Marquie et al., 2003). Laboratory studies indicate that, in general, health care professionals underestimate patients' pain (Prkachin, Solomon, & Ross, 2007). We might infer, then, that undertreatment of pain is due to the health care professionals' inaccuracy in assessing pain in the clinical setting. We must consider, however, that in a controlled laboratory environment, researchers limit the pain behaviours that are available to those making judgments. To further elucidate this point consider the following study. Kappesser et al. (2006) asked health care professionals to make their judgments of pain by viewing only the patients' faces. When they did so, their judgments underestimated the amount of pain experienced by the patient. However, when the patients' actual verbal description of their pain accompanied the facial expression, the judgment was more accurate.

In clinical settings, health care practitioners might include a measure of patients' pain behaviour to aid in their assessment. For example, in hospitals nurses may use the UAB Pain Behavior Scale (Richards et al., 1982) during routine care of patients. When using this scale, the nurse has the patient perform several activities and rates ten pain behaviours (e.g., mobility, medication use) on a three-point scale: "none," "occasional," and "frequent." These ratings are assigned numerical values and summed for a total score. A number of studies have focused on assessing discomfort in patients (Keefe, Williams, & Smith, 2001; Polatin & Mayer, 2001). These studies suggest that behavioural assessments of pain can be made relatively easily and reliably.

Self-Reports of Pain

The third and most obvious approach to pain measurement is to ask people to describe their pain, either in their own words or by filling out a rating scale or questionnaire. These are the most common types of pain assessment. In treating a patient's pain, health care practitioners ask where the pain is, what it feels like, how strong it is, and when it tends to occur.

Interviews   Interviews about pain can provide valuable information. In addition to a description of pain, such interviews can determine the history of the pain problem. The history would include when the patient first experienced the pain, how the pain developed, and the techniques the patient used for controlling it. Factors seeming to trigger or exacerbate the pain can be discussed. The patient's emotional adjustment and whether or how the patient's lifestyle has been altered can also be explored. The information obtained in these interviews can be supplemented with information provided by significant others in the patient's life (Turk, Monarch, & Williams, 2004).

Rating Scales   Rating scales are one of the simplest and most direct measures of pain. Therefore, it is not surprising that rating scales are the most frequently used measures of pain (Jensen & Karoly, 2001). These scales are usually used to measure pain intensity. Sometimes, patients are simply asked to respond verbally to the following statement: "On a scale from one to ten, with ten being the most excruciating pain possible, and one being

Visual Analog Scale:
Mark a point on the line to show how strong your pain is.

no pain   worst pain imaginable

Box Scale:
Rate the level of your pain by circling one number on the scale, where 0 means "no pain" and 10 means "worst pain imaginable."

| 1 | 2 | 3 | 4 | 5 | 6 | 7 | 8 | 9 | 10 |

Verbal Rating Scale:
Circle the phrase that best describes your pain.

Not Painful   Slightly Painful   Moderately Painful   Very Painful   Extremely Painful

Figure 11-1 Rating Scales for Pain Management

the lowest level of pain detectable, how much pain are you currently experiencing?" Or, the health care practitioner may ask the patient to respond to this statement on a scale of one to one hundred. In either of these cases, the basic question is really the same. However, the form of the scale can vary (see Figure 11-1).

The **box scale** is labelled at the ends with the phrases "no pain" and "worst pain imaginable." Patients are shown a series of numbers in boxes and must choose the number that best indicates the degree of pain they are experiencing. A second rating scale is the **verbal descriptor scale**, in which patients are asked to describe their pain by choosing the phrase that most closely resembles the pain they are experiencing. The **visual analog scale** is similar to the box scale in that the left end of the scale is anchored by the phrase "no pain" and the right by a phrase such as "worst pain imaginable." With this scale, however, people rate their pain by marking a point on the line provided. The VAS is deemed superior to scales using either word descriptors of pain (Rosier, Iadarola, & Coghill, 2002) or numerical ratings (Bigatti & Cronan, 2002).

Rating scales are quick and easy to use, allowing people to rate their pain frequently. Averaging ratings across time gives a more accurate picture of the amount of pain a person generally experiences than does a single rating. Turk, Meichenbaum, and Genest (1983) describe how this method can be used to identify patterns of pain in chronic pain patients. Multiple ratings provide a record to determine if the patient's pain is generally improving or getting worse. In addition, they allow patterns in the timing of severe pain to be recognized. For example, it may be that severe pain occurs most often first thing in the morning or later in the day. Or, it may be that on certain days the patient's pain is more severe. If these patterns can be identified, the patient may be able to alter his or her schedule or environment to accommodate or eradicate at least the most severe pain.

Pain Questionnaires   Pain questionnaires were developed to address the realization that pain is not one-dimensional. That is, the experience of pain is much more than a feeling of discomfort that can be described in terms of its intensity. Melzack asserts that

box scale: a scale on which people rate and report their pain by choosing the number that best indicates the degree of pain that they are experiencing from a series of numbers in boxes ranging from "no pain" to "worst pain imaginable."

verbal descriptor scale: a rating scale on which people are asked to describe their pain by choosing the phrase that most closely resembles the pain that they are experiencing.

visual analog scale: a rating scale on which people report their pain by marking a point on a line anchored by the phrase "no pain" and by a phrase like "worst pain imaginable."

describing pain on a single dimension is like "specifying the visual world only in terms of light flux without regard to pattern, color, texture, and the many other dimensions of visual experience" (1975, p. 278). In an effort to measure the multidimensional nature of pain, Melzack (1975) developed the McGill Pain Questionnaire (MPQ).

The McGill Pain Questionnaire (see Figure 11-2) offers patients the opportunity to describe their pain on three broad dimensions—sensory, affective, and evaluative. *Sensory* qualities of pain include its temporal, spatial, pressure, and thermal properties; *affective* qualities include fear, tension, and autonomic properties; *evaluative* qualities are the subjective overall intensity of the pain experience.

The MPQ has four parts. Part 1 consists of front and back drawings of the human body. Patients are asked to indicate on these drawings the areas where they feel pain. Part 2 consists of a list of 78 descriptive words, separated into a total of 20 subclasses. Patients are instructed to select a word from each subclass that most accurately characterizes their pain. The words are ordered in increasing intensity (e.g., *hot, burning, scalding,* and *searing*). Each word in each class has an assigned value based on the degree of pain it represents. In the

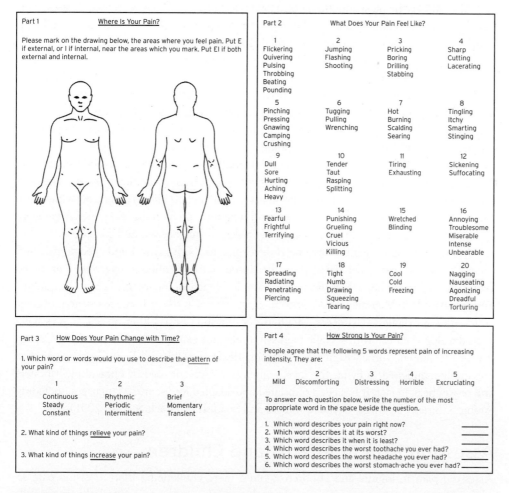

Figure 11-2 The McGill Pain Questionnaire

previous example, *searing* would contribute the largest number of points, and *hot* would contribute the lowest number. These points are summed across the 20 subclasses and the total score is called the "pain-rating index." This index is the most commonly used part of the questionnaire. Part 3 of the MPQ asks how patients' pain has changed with time. Part 4 contains a series of verbal descriptor scales. One of these scales inquires about the amount of pain the patient is experiencing at the present time. This scale provides a separate score called the Present Pain Intensity (PPI) score.

There are many advantages to the MPQ over previous instruments for measuring pain. The MPQ's largest contribution is its measurement of more than one dimension of pain. Also, patients suffering from similar pain syndromes often identify the same patterns of words from the MPQ to characterize their pain, just as those with different pain syndromes (e.g., cancer, arthritis, headaches, or phantom limb pain) identify different words to characterize their pain (Melzack & Wall, 1996). Yet there are drawbacks to the MPQ. For instance, because a fairly strong vocabulary is required to complete the questionnaire, the MPQ is not useful for assessing pain in young children or in people who do not have a strong grasp of the English language.

The MPQ is the most commonly used pain questionnaire. It has been used to assess pain in both clinical populations and in laboratory research (e.g., Gagliese & Katz, 2003; Sullivan, Lynch, & Clark, 2005). A short form of the MPQ is also available (Melzack, 1987).

However, the MPQ is not the only pain questionnaire available. The West Haven–Yale Multidimensional Pain Inventory (MPI) assesses many aspects of psychological and physical functioning and can provide a comprehensive assessment of the lives of pain patients (Kerns, Turk, & Rudy, 1985). The MPI comprises 52 items divided into three sections. The first section measures (1) pain severity, (2) pain's interference with patients' lives, (3) patients' dissatisfaction with their present functioning, (4) patients' view of the support they receive from others, (5) patients' perceived life control, and (6) patients' negative mood states. The second section measures patients' perceptions of the responses of significant others. The final section identifies how frequently patients engage in each of 30 different daily activities. The MPI is not without its problems, however, and long-term predictions of a patient's category of coping with pain have not been accurate (Broderick, Junghaenel, & Turk, 2004).

Many pain questionnaires have been developed for both general and specific uses and some for use with particular populations. For instance, the Dalhousie Everyday Pain Scale (von Baeyer, Baskerville, & McGrath, 1998) was developed for use with children; the Parents' Postoperative Pain Measure was designed to assist parents in the at-home assessment of their children's pain (Finley, Chambers, McGrath, & Walsh, 1999). Other questionnaires have been developed for use with specific pain syndromes, for example the Chronic Pain Coping Inventory (Jensen, Turner, Romano, & Strom, 1995). The McGill Pain Questionnaire, as previously mentioned, is by far the most common instrument used by clinical practitioners and researchers. In fact, it has been translated and adapted for use in 20 languages, including Arabic, Chinese, Japanese, German, Italian, and Spanish (Melzack & Katz, 2001).

Assessing Pain in Infants and Children

Assessing pain in infants and children is often more challenging than assessing pain in adults. Obviously, infants can not complete self-report questionnaires. Similarly, young children have difficulty expressing their experience of pain because of their limited language abilities and their level of cognitive development. Therefore, pain assessments conducted on these populations cannot follow the standard questionnaire format used with adults (McGrath & Gillespie, 2001; Stevens, 1997).

At one time, it was believed that very young infants were insensitive to pain (Gibson & Chambers, 2004). Currently, experts believe that infants are capable of feeling pain from the moment they are born (Stevens & Franck, 2001). If we cannot ask newborns whether they are in pain, or how much pain they are in, what should we do? A sample of 72 neonatal intensive-care unit (NICU) nurses were asked which indicators they used to interpret the experience of pain in the infants entrusted to their care (Howard & Thurber, 1998). The 10 pain indicators used by the NICU nurses, listed in decreasing order of frequency, were fussiness, restlessness, grimacing, crying, increasing heart rate, increasing respirations, wiggling, rapid state changes, wrinkling of forehead, and clenching of fist.

Canadian researchers (e.g., Hadjistavropoulos, Craig, Grunau, & Johnston, 1994; Hadjistavropoulos, Craig, Grunau, & Whitfield, 1997) have documented the relative importance of each of the cues available when judging infant pain. They have discovered that while cry characteristics seem to command attention, cues provided through infant facial activity are weighted more heavily in adults' judgments of newborn pain. These facial characteristics include a brow bulge, eyes squeezed shut, a taut tongue, and a deepened nasolabial furrow (the line or wrinkle that runs down from either side of the nose to the outer corners of the mouth). Facial characteristics also appear to convey more information to judges than does the infant's bodily activity.

Measurement of facial characteristics has been incorporated in the Neonatal Facial Coding System (NFCS). The NFCS was developed by Grunau and Craig (1987) to provide a detailed, anatomically based, and objective description of newborns' reactions to potentially painful stimuli. This instrument was developed primarily for use by researchers. It requires the researcher to assign a value of "1" or "0" to each facial action (brow bulge, eye squeeze, nasolabial furrow, open lips, vertical stretch mouth, horizontal stretch mouth, lip purse, taut tongue, and chin quiver). The scoring is completed by microanalyzing videotaped recordings of the infant. A similar system entitled the Child Facial Coding System (CFCS) was developed for use with preschool children (Chambers et al., 1996). As mentioned, these systems were created primarily for use in research settings although some have attempted to use them in clinical settings (Prkachin et al., 2002).

There are, however, a number of instruments that are available to assess pain in children in clinical settings (McGrath et al., 2009, Stevens, 2001). Children's behaviour can be observed and their pain rated by using scales such as the Dalhousie Everyday Pain Scale (von Baeyer, Baskerville, & McGrath, 1998). Self-report measures may also be used with children. However, these measures provide considerably less detail to the health professional than do self-report measures used with adults, in part because of the descriptors young children use to describe their pain. Elizabeth Job, a graduate student at the University of British Columbia, interviewed 106 children between the ages of three and six years. She discovered that the word *pain* didn't appear in the children's vocabularies until they were old enough to attend kindergarten. Instead, children tend to use words like *ouch, ow,* and *hurt* to describe their pain (Job, 2003). Preschool children may be asked to indicate the degree of their "hurt" by choosing from a scale of facial expressions (e.g., Faces Pain Scale Revised, Hicks et al., 2001; www.painsourcebook.ca). The Oucher scale displays six photographs of a child's face, showing increasing levels of discomfort. Pain questionnaires have also been developed for use with children. The Children's Comprehensive Pain Questionnaire (McGrath, 1987) is just one example of a pain questionnaire designed for use with children.

Assessing Pain in Older Adults

Interest in and research on pain in older adults is relatively recent (Gagliese, 2001). When comparing the usefulness of the numeric rating scale (NRS), the verbal descriptor scale (VDS), the visual analog scale (VAS), and the McGill Pain Questionnaire (MPQ) to assess pain intensity in surgical patients, Gagliese and her colleagues (Gagliese, Weizblit, Ellis, & Chan, 2005) discovered the NRS was best. Specifically, the NRS had lower error rates and greater validity than the other scales. The VDS also fared well; however, the use of the VAS led to high error rates and numerous incomplete or unscorable responses. Previous reports acknowledge that the failure rate of older adults on the VAS is as high as 30 percent (Gagliese & Melzack, 1997). Evidence suggests that the MPQ, with its emphasis on adjectival descriptors of pain, is a useful measurement tool for this age group; however, Gagliese (Gagliese & Melzack, 1997; Gagliese et al., 2005) deems the NRS superior.

Attempts to measure pain behaviours in this population have met with limited success (Gagliese, 2001). For example, a protocol was developed to simulate the movements of older adults' activities of daily living. However, many of the individuals were not able to complete the protocol because it triggered severe pain (Weiner et al., 1996). Using a different approach, a study was conducted to identify the accuracy of judgments of older adults' facial expressions of pain. Although this study resulted in higher pain ratings ascribed to older than to younger patients, it was unclear if the higher pain ratings were due to objective changes in facial expression, to preconceived notions held by the judges that older adults experience more pain, or if a combination of these factors was responsible for the results (Matheson, 1997).

Pain assessment in cognitively impaired persons and those with communication disabilities presents additional challenges (Hadjistavropoulos, et al., 2000; Hadjistavropoulos et al., 2001; Kunz et al., 2007, Prkachin, 2007). The Pain Assessment Checklist for Seniors with Limited Ability to Communicate (PACSLAC) was developed in response to this need (Fuchs-Lacelle & Hadjistavropoulos, 2004). Using PACSLAC to assess and manage the pain of individuals with dementia has resulted in improved pain management practices (Fuchs-Lacelle et al., 2008).

PAIN CONTROL TECHNIQUES

In addition to the many consequences of pain already mentioned, there is a consequence even more severe: death. Uncontrolled pain compromises immune function, promotes tumour growth, and can compromise healing—all factors that can lead to an early death (Lynch & Watson, 2006). Given the negative impact that pain has on the life of the sufferer the World Health Organization has declared that "pain relief should be a human right" (WHO, 2004). There are a number of pain control techniques available for those seeking pain relief but we must recognize that they are met with varying degrees of success.

Pharmacological Control of Pain

The traditional and most common method of controlling pain is through pain-relieving medications. At any given time, approximately seven million Canadians are taking pain medication to manage their pain (Lynch & Watson, 2006). **Peripherally acting analgesics**, also known as non-narcotic analgesics, are probably the most frequently used analgesics (Julien, 2005; Melzack & Wall, 1996). Included in this group are such common pain relievers as acetylsalicylic acid (e.g., Aspirin), acetaminophen (e.g., Tylenol), and ibuprofen (e.g., Advil). These drugs work by reducing inflammation at the site of tissue damage and inhibiting the synthesis of neurochemicals in the peripheral nervous system that facilitate the transmission of pain impulses. Peripherally acting analgesics provide substantial pain relief for a wide variety of pain conditions, especially arthritis and other conditions involving inflammation (Julien, 2005). Although peripherally acting analgesics are generally available over the counter, they do have side effects and may interact with other drugs. Used in recommended amounts, however, they are generally safe and are effective when dealing with mild to moderate pain.

peripherally acting analgesics: non-narcotic medications that decrease pain by reducing inflammation at the site of tissue damage; they also inhibit the synthesis of neurochemicals in the peripheral nervous system that facilitate the transmission of pain impulses.

Centrally acting analgesics are pain-killing medications called **narcotics**. Narcotics work by binding to opiate receptors in the central nervous system (Julien, 2005). These drugs are either derived directly from the opium poppy (e.g., codeine and morphine) or they are synthetically reproduced but based on opium molecules (e.g., heroin, methadone, and the brand-name drugs Percodan and Demerol). These drugs operate on the central nervous system by imitating the effects of the body's endogenous pain relief system. Specifically, the molecules in these drugs bind to receptors for endorphins and enkephalins in the brain and spinal cord, blocking the transmission of pain signals. They are considered the most potent pain relievers available. They are frequently used to alleviate labour pain, postoperative pain, and chronic progressive pain experienced by some terminal cancer patients.

centrally acting analgesics: pain-killing medications that operate on the central nervous system by imitating the effects of the body's endogenous pain relief system.

narcotics: pain-killing drugs that work by binding to opiate receptors in the central nervous system.

Although narcotics are extremely useful for relieving pain, they also have disadvantages: narcotics are known to be psychoactive; they depress respiration; they have tremendous potential to produce tolerance, so that higher and higher doses are needed to achieve the same effect; and they can be addictive (Aronoff et al., 2000; Julien, 2005).

There is considerable controversy about the likelihood of a patient becoming addicted to narcotics. Some researchers argue that this is a very real possibility, whereas others believe that this issue has been blown out of proportion (Aronoff, 2000; Dillard, 2002; Passik & Weinreb, 2000). Research suggests that, when allowed to self-administer narcotics, patients recovering from surgery use less medication than would have been given by hospital staff. For further discussion of this topic, refer to the section on patient-controlled analgesia in chapter 6.

Local anaesthetics, such as novocaine and lidocaine, make up a third category of chemicals for relieving pain. These medications can be applied topically but are much more effective when injected at the site where the pain originates. You would likely have received a local anaesthetic from your dentist before he or she began drilling or pulling a tooth. Likewise, you may have received a local anaesthetic before receiving sutures. Local anaesthetics work by blocking nerve cells from generating pain impulses (Winters, 1985). Although they work well to block impulses in pain fibres, they also block impulses in motor neurons. Consequently, you will have little or no control over your mouth, tongue,

local anaesthetics: pain-relieving chemicals that can be applied topically but are much more effective when injected at the site where the pain originates.

lips, and cheeks for several hours after a dental procedure if you received a local anaesthetic prior to it.

Other drugs affect pain indirectly. For example, **sedatives**, such as barbiturates, and **tranquillizers**, such as diazepam (Valium), are depressants; that is, they depress bodily functions by decreasing the transmission of impulses throughout the central nervous system (Julien, 2005). These drugs probably do not directly affect pain but rather reduce patient anxiety and help the patient to sleep (thereby escaping the pain for a while and resting so as to better tolerate the pain when awake). **Antidepressants** also help patients who are in pain by reducing the depression that frequently accompanies pain (Bair et al., 2004). In addition, it is believed that they affect pain-related neurotransmitters.

There has been a dramatic increase recently in research on drug combinations that enhance pain reduction (Dalal & Melzack, 1998). This research involves (1) drugs that have not traditionally been viewed as analgesics, such as antidepressants and sedatives; (2) drugs that have been viewed as effective analgesics in their own right, such as opioids and some anti-inflammatory drugs; and (3) combinations of both types, such as opioids and antidepressants. Combining drugs in the treatment of pain increases analgesia, either as a result of their interaction or as a result of their additive effects. For instance, opioid analgesia is enhanced when combined with the administration of amphetamines. Further, a combination of drugs may reduce their side effects because the amount of each drug administered is reduced, or because of the way the two drugs interact. For example, the general cognitive decline and drowsiness caused by opioids can be counteracted by introducing amphetamines.

Surgical Control of Pain

Surgical treatment of pain is the most extreme form of treatment available to pain patients. Surgery is considered only as a last resort, after all other treatment options have been exhausted (Cullinane, Chu, & Mamelak, 2002; Dillard, 2002). Surgical techniques include those that attempt to interrupt the transmission of pain from the periphery to the spinal cord, as well as those that disrupt the flow of pain sensations from the spinal cord to the brain. However, not all patients experience relief from their pain following surgery and, for those who do, relief may be temporary. We now know that the nervous system has regenerative abilities that enable pain impulses to reach the brain along a variety of neural pathways. As a result, surgical techniques that were once relatively common are now rarely performed.

Transcutaneous Electrical Nerve Stimulation

Transcutaneous electrical nerve stimulation (TENS) involves placing an electrode on the surface of the skin close to where the patient feels pain and applying electrical stimulation. This stimulation affects all nerves within approximately four centimetres of the skin's surface. Although stimulation is usually applied for approximately 20 minutes, the duration of pain relief reportedly lasts several hours and occasionally lasts for days or weeks. There is considerable individual variation in the amount of pain relief experienced, however, and the clinical effectiveness of TENS is controversial (Sluka

sedatives: medications, such as barbiturates, that affect pain indirectly by reducing anxiety and helping the patient to sleep.

tranquillizers: medications such as diazepam (Valium) that affect pain indirectly by reducing patient anxiety.

antidepressants: medications that reduce the depression and anxiety that frequently accompany pain; it is also believed that they affect pain-related neurotransmitters.

transcutaneous electrical nerve stimulation (TENS): a pain control technique that involves placing an electrode on the surface of the skin and applying electrical stimulation.

& Walsh, 2003). Researchers from New Zealand tested the effectiveness of TENS for pain relief in labour. Their conclusion was that "it probably does little good and they do not advocate its widespread introduction" (Thomas, Tyle, Webster, & Neilson, 2008, p. 182).

On the other hand, positive results can also be found. The effectiveness of TENS in reducing acute muscular and postoperative pain in the majority of patients is well documented (Bjordal, Johnson, & Ljunggreen, 2003). In a moving example, Chapman (1984) describes a nine-year-old boy who began receiving TENS while still unconscious from surgery. When the surgeon left the room the boy spoke casually with the others in the room. When asked whether there was anything he feared, he began to cry and confessed his terror of the expected operation that would remove his kidney. His surprised nurse tried to reassure him that the surgery had already been done, and that there was nothing to worry about. He refused to believe her. "But don't you remember?" she contended, "that's why they put you to sleep this morning—so they could do the operation." The little boy looked very threatened. "It's not true!" he shouted. "It's not true!" When asked why it couldn't be true, he asserted confidently, "Because I haven't got any bandages." He was asked to feel his belly. When he did, an expression of astonishment came over his face. At that moment, he declared he felt pain, and he began to cry.

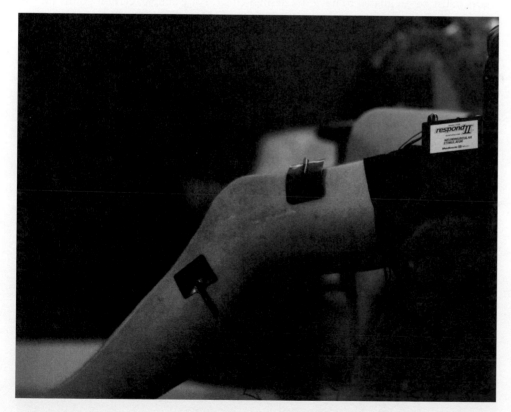

Transcutaneous electrical nerve stimulation (TENS) machines are easy to use and can help to relieve pain. Portable TENS machines allow individuals to engage in daily activities while their nerves are being stimulated.

Acupuncture

Acupuncture is an ancient Chinese pain control technique that has been in continuous practice for at least 2000 years (Turk & Winter, 2006). Basically, the procedure involves the insertion of fine needles (made of steel, gold, or other metals) through specific points in the skin then twirling or electrically charging them to create stimulation to the peripheral nerves. The effects of acupuncture are not immediate, and the needles must be stimulated for approximately 20 minutes to produce analgesia. In addition, the stimulation must be fairly intense and continuous. However, the analgesia can last for hours after the stimulation has ended.

The practice of acupuncture is part of a complex theory of medicine in which all diseases and pains are believed to be due to disharmony between *yin* (spirit) and *yang* (blood). In China, where this philosophy is more widely accepted, five to ten percent of surgical operations are conducted with the use of acupuncture as the only form of analgesia. The patients must volunteer for the procedure, and the surgeries using acupuncture analgesia are relatively straightforward, with little likelihood of complications. In Western countries, acupuncture is rarely used for surgery; it is seen instead as a treatment for less intense pain.

Laboratory studies have shown that acupuncture produces only mild analgesia in most people. Further, the degree of pain relief experienced is now known to be dependent on the intensity of the stimulation, rather than on the exact point of stimulation. Traditionally, it was believed that exact points on the body, outlined on acupuncture charts, must be stimulated to have the desired effect. For example, certain points on the

Stimulation of the peripheral nerves by acupuncture needles provides varying degrees of pain relief.

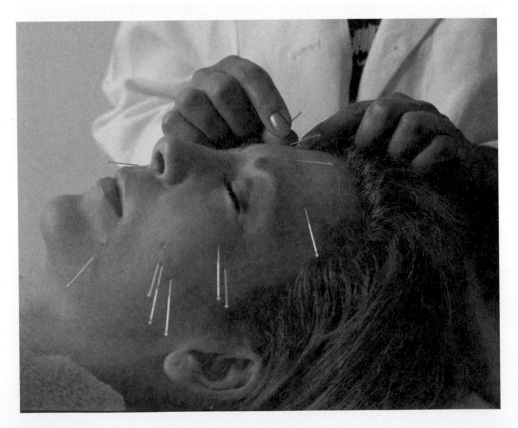

nose and ear were associated with the small intestine, whereas other points were associated with the kidneys heart, or abdomen. Interestingly, individuals who derive the most benefits from acupuncture are the same individuals who benefit most from hypnotism.

Acupuncture is becoming more widely practised in North America, and its popularity may continue to grow. A survey of health care professionals at two Cancer Care Ontario centres revealed that acupuncture was the nonpharmacologic strategy for the management of cancer pain that participants were most interested in learning more about (Sellick & Zaza, 1998). The National Institute of Health (NIH) acknowledges that acupuncture has been somewhat successful for pain conditions involving tissue damage or tenderness, such as that experienced in postoperative dental pain. In addition, the NIH asserts that there are many situations in which acupuncture may be useful as an adjunct treatment or possibly an acceptable alternative to traditional treatments (e.g., headache, myofascial pain, osteoarthritis, low back pain, neck pain, carpal tunnel syndrome, and tennis elbow) (Carlsson & Sjölund, 1994, 2001; JAMA, 1998; Kerr, Walsh, & Baxter, 2003; Lu, Lu, & Kleinman, 2001; Witt et al., in press; Zeltzer, 2002). Interestingly, a relatively recent review (Madsen, Gotzsche, & Hrobjartsson, 2009) of randomised clinical trials with acupuncture published in the *British Medical Journal* found considerable variability between studies and concluded that it is unclear if acupuncture reduces pain independently of the psychological impact.

Physical Therapy

Physical therapy involves a variety of treatment approaches to help patients who suffer from both acute and chronic pain. Patients usually work with a physical therapist to prepare an individualized treatment program. The program should provide daily or weekly goals that allow for gradual but steady progress. It should also progress rapidly enough to ensure the patient experiences a feeling of accomplishment but slowly enough to prevent overexertion or re-injury.

physical therapy: therapy involved in the rehabilitation of muscle, bone, joint, or the results of nerve disease.

In order to restore their range of motion, patients who have undergone surgery or experienced injury should exercise regularly. Exercise also benefits arthritis patients because it helps maintain joint flexibility and prevents joints from deteriorating (Minor & Sanford, 1993). In addition, exercising is extremely beneficial for low back pain patients who need to maintain flexibility and develop strength in key muscles to provide support for their spines (Hayden, van Tulder, & Tomlinson, 2005; Moffett et al., 1999). As part of an exercise program, patients are typically also taught body mechanics and proper posture to prevent further injuries.

Massage

Several years ago, a massage was considered a luxury. Today, massage therapy is one of the pain management techniques that Canadian physicians are keen to learn more about. A large-scale, primarily European survey revealed that the most common non-drug treatment for pain is massage (Breivik, 2006). Massage therapy is used to ease muscle pain and other pains, including that resulting from cancer. The procedure consists of systematic stroking and kneading of the body. The two main types of massage therapy are Swedish massage and Shiatsu massage. **Swedish massage** is a set routine of basic strokes to work the body and includes slow, gentle stroking movements, known as *effleurage*, to warm and

Swedish massage: slow, gentle stroking movements to warm and relax tissue and stimulate blood circulation.

relax tissue and to stimulate blood circulation. A deeper massage is also conducted with movements such as friction, percussion, and *pettrisage* (massage in which the muscles are kneaded and pressed). **Shiatsu massage** is based on the belief that there is a flow of energy through the body and that at times energy blockages develop. Consistent with this belief, energy blockages are released through the strong and sustained pressure of the massage at specific points on the body.

Both laboratory and clinical research indicates that massage is effective in reducing pain (Breivik, 2006; Frey Law et al., 2008). Research conducted with 32 hospital staff at a large teaching hospital investigated the usefulness of Swedish massage (Katz, Wowk, Culp, & Wakeling, 1999). Participants received either a series of eight 15-minute, on-site massage treatments or eight sessions of seated rest. Those in the massage group experienced significant reductions in pain and tension levels compared to the control group that received seated rest. This pain and tension relief persisted for up to a day or longer following the massage. An added benefit experienced by those who received the massage treatments was a lift in overall mood.

Relaxation

Many of the same relaxation strategies that are used to cope with stress (see chapter 3) are effective treatments for both acute and chronic pain. Relaxation is often used in conjunction with other pain management strategies and is thought to be an essential part of both biofeedback and hypnotic treatment. The rationale for relaxation training is straightforward: Continual muscle contraction is considered both a cause and an effect of pain. Researchers have found that muscle tension results in lactic acid buildup in muscles and also decreases blood flow to muscles. Both factors can significantly increase people's experience of pain.

As discussed in chapter 3, relaxation can be accomplished by many different techniques, including **progressive muscle relaxation** and meditation. Researchers (e.g., Carlson & Hoyle, 1993; Jacobs, 2001) report that progressive muscle relaxation is generally helpful in coping with stress-related disorders, such as migraine and tension headache, depression, hypertension, and low back pain. However, the actual effect size varies substantially from study to study, in part because of variation in the experimental procedures. Relaxation training was most effective when patients had participated in a sufficient number of training sessions, when they had been trained individually rather than in a group, when the patients used audiotapes to supplement their training, and when the patients had enough time to master the technique.

But how long do the effects of relaxation treatment for pain last? Edward Blanchard and colleagues addressed this issue in a five-year follow-up investigation of chronic headache patients (Blanchard, Andrasik, et al., 1987; Blanchard, Appelbaum, et al., 1987). These patients had all experienced an average of 18 years of headache, either muscle contraction (tension-type) headache or "vascular" headache, which includes both migraine and combined (migraine plus tension-type) headaches. These patients completed training for progressive muscle relaxation in ten sessions over eight weeks. Those patients whose headache pain had not improved by at least 60 percent were offered additional treatment in the form of biofeedback. The treatment effects endured over time. That is, five years after the initial treatment, patients reported headache pain at levels similar to those reported immediately after taking part in the treatment. The headache pain did not return to pretreatment levels.

Other research has supported this conclusion, with patients experiencing durable relief from both relaxation and biofeedback for at least two years (Blanchard, 1987, 2000).

Meditation is another form of relaxation. *Meditative relaxation*, developed by Herbert Benson and colleagues (e.g., Benson, Beary, & Carol, 1974), is derived from various religious meditative practices but has no religious connotations. With Bensonian relaxation, the patient attempts to focus attention fully on a single thought or image. Often a very simple syllable, such as "ohm" or "one," is repeated slowly over and over again with each breath. This process usually takes place in a quiet environment where the participant sits with eyes closed and muscles relaxed for a period of approximately 20 minutes.

Mindfulness meditation is a related strategy for achieving relaxation. This type of meditation has its roots in Buddhist practice. Participants engaged in mindfulness meditation do not try to ignore unpleasant thoughts or sensations. Instead, they are instructed to focus on any thoughts or sensations as they occur but to view these thoughts in a non-judgmental manner. As Kabat-Zinn (1993) explains, "Observing without judging, moment by moment, helps you see what is on your mind without editing or censoring it, without intellectualizing it or getting lost in your own incessant thinking" (p. 263). Brain imaging studies tell us that the right hemisphere of the brain becomes less active and the left more active during mindfulness meditation. With increased activation in the left hemisphere, a corresponding increase in positive affect is experienced (Davidson et al., 2003). A meta-analysis of mindfulness meditation studies indicates its effectiveness for stress- and pain-related problems and for those who are simply looking for a way to manage the everyday stresses in their lives (Grossman, Niemann, Schmidt, & Walach, 2004).

Guided imagery can be considered a form of relaxation and can also be classified as a technique that relies on distraction. With guided imagery, the participant is told to envision a calm, peaceful, and pleasant image. The image should be relatively unchanging, and participants are told to focus all of their attention on the image.

Guided imagery is a technique suggested to pregnant mothers for use in childbirth. Women in labour are told to choose a focal point, either real or imagined, that they can concentrate on when giving birth. The focal point may be the image of waves washing onto the beach, for example, or a picture of a loved one.

Children are also encouraged to use guided imagery when undergoing cancer treatment. One child described skiing down a mountain as fast as he could. He commented on the warmth of the sunshine but insisted that focusing on the speed with which he skied in and out of the gates was how he became most "absorbed" in his image.

When used to manage pain, guided imagery is most often used in conjunction with other pain-control techniques. Thus, the unique contribution of guided imagery is difficult to establish. Studies conducted on guided imagery suggest that it is superior to biofeedback in treating headaches (Evans & Penzien, 2003; Ilacqua, 1994); aids cancer patients in coping with the pain of treatments (Battino, 2000); and reduces postoperative pain and length of hospital stays for child surgical patients (Huth, Broome, & Good, 2004) and older adults (Antall & Kresevic, 2004).

Distraction

Like guided imagery, **distraction** involves focusing attention on something other than the sensation of pain. As we mentioned earlier, athletes, soldiers, and others who are "caught

meditation: a form of relaxation in which one attempts to focus attention fully on a single thought or image.

guided imagery: a form of relaxation that relies on distraction, in which the participant is told to imagine a calm, peaceful, and pleasant image.

distraction: a pain management technique in which the patient focuses attention on something other than the sensation of pain.

up" in what they are doing may not immediately notice when they have injured themselves. Although we sometimes engage in distraction unknowingly, it is also possible to consciously apply the technique of distraction to help control the experience of pain. We can distract ourselves by focusing on a completely different activity, such as listening to music, singing a song, playing a video game, doing arithmetic problems, or reading a book. Researchers at Dalhousie University note that when five-year-olds are watching a program on television during immunization, they experience lower levels of pain than when faced with a blank TV screen (Cassidy et al., 2002). Researchers at Washington University (e.g., Hoffman et al., 2006) have discovered a new way to help burn patients manage their pain—virtual reality pain control. This method of pain management relies on distraction to diminish severe pain (see Box 11-2 for more details).

Distraction can also involve reinterpreting the event that is resulting in pain. Bandura (1991) provides a description from an eight-year-old boy who is re-interpreting a painful event: "As soon as I get in the dentist's chair, I pretend he's the enemy and I'm

Box 11-2 Virtual Snowmen Alleviate Pain of Burn Victims

A can of gasoline placed too close to a campfire exploded, leaving 17-year-old Mark Powers with deep flash burns to 33 percent of his body. Mark was hospitalized in a regional burn centre, where he would receive skin grafting on his neck, chest, back, and stomach. The opioid painkillers that helped to alleviate his pain while he lay motionless in his hospital bed failed to relieve the excruciating pain Mark experienced when having his wounds cleaned. To help Mark and other burn victims control the severe pain experienced during wound care, psychologists David Patterson of the University of Washington's Harborview Burn Center and Hunter Hoffman of the university's Human Interface Technology Laboratory created a new psychological pain-control technique—virtual reality analgesia (Hoffman, 2004; Hoffman et al., 2006; Patterson et al., 2004).

Virtual reality analgesia relies on distraction to help reduce perceived pain intensity and unpleasantness. As we have discussed in this chapter, pain is not entirely determined by sensory input. Instead, as the gate control theory of pain suggests, the same pain signal can be viewed as more or less painful depending on what one is thinking about or attending to. We have a finite amount of attention that can be divided between tasks, so if we are immersed in a 3-D computer-generated environment, less attention is directed to the real world (Patterson et al., 2004) and consequently, less pain is experienced. In fact, the greater "presence" the virtual environment has for us, the less pain we experience (Hoffman et al., 2006).

SnowWorld was one of the first virtual reality software programs designed for the treatment of pain. To use this program, patients are outfitted with a virtual reality helmet that positions two miniature LCD screens in front of the viewer's eyes. These screens present patients with a view of the computer-generated world and prevent patients from seeing what is going on in the real world. As patients look around the virtual world, what they see changes. For example, as they look up, they will see an image of a virtual sky, and when they look down the image will change to an icy river and river canyon walls (Hoffman et al., 2006). Using a joystick, patients are able to shoot snowballs at snowmen, robots, and penguins. When hit, snowmen become puffs and penguins turn upside down, and these victories are accompanied by appropriate sound effects. The environment portrayed in SnowWorld is purposely cool and icy, a direct contrast to the "hot" unpleasant memories that most burn victims hold.

Patients participating in virtual reality treatments have been shown to have 50 percent less pain than patients in a no-distraction control condition (Hoffman, Patterson, et al., 2004). Treatment results using the virtual reality helmets are far superior to using distractive techniques in the form of Nintendo games, and the better the quality of the image presented on the screen, the better the analgesic effects (Hoffman, Sharar, et al., 2004). These researchers continue to develop new attention-grabbing virtual environments (e.g., ChocolateWorld), and they are optimistic that virtual reality analgesia will prove valuable for treating other patient populations in pain (e.g., for those undergoing cancer procedures, childbirth, dental work, and physiotherapy).

Box 11-2 (Continued)

Virtual snowmen help burn victims control pain psychologically.

A burn patient uses a water-friendly fibre-optic virtual reality helmet.

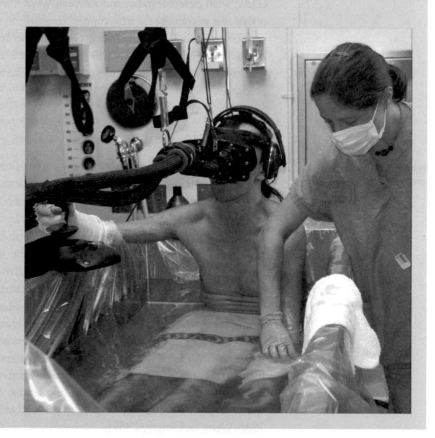

Multidisciplinary pain management programs represent a truly biopsychosocial approach to pain management. They can provide medical, psychological, physical, and occupational therapy. They can also improve chronic pain sufferers' psychological and physical functioning and reduce their pain, pain behaviour, and drug use.

CHAPTER SUMMARY

Pain is beneficial because it helps to prevent serious injury, teaches us to avoid injurious behaviours and forces us to limit our activity, thereby aiding in recuperation.

The gate control theory of pain emphasizes that both physiological and psychological factors contribute to the experience of pain. The neuromatrix theory of pain extends the gate control theory and suggests a greater role of the brain in pain perception.

Most research indicates that women have a lower pain threshold and lower pain tolerance than men. Cutural differences have been reported in both the experience and expression of pain; however, the strongest evidence indicates that there is more difference between individuals within each ethnic group than there is between ethnic groups.

Pain is assessed using (1) psychophysiological techniques such as an EMG or EEG, (2) behavioural measures, and (3) self-report. Various questionnaires (e.g., the McGill Pain Questionnaire) and rating scales (e.g., the Visual Analog Scale) are available to assist with the measurement of pain in both research and clinical settings.

A wide array of pain control techniques is available to the pain sufferer. Pain control techniques include pharmacological and surgical control, TENS, acupuncture, physical therapy, massage, relaxation strategies, distraction, biofeedback, hypnosis, and virtual reality programs. Multidisciplinary pain management programs use a combination of these techniques.

Review Questions

1. What are the benefits of pain?
2. Explain the gate control theory and the neuromatrix theories of pain.
3. How does acute pain differ from chronic pain?
4. Explain how factors such as age, sex, and ethnicity do (or do not) influence people's experience of, and response to, pain.
5. What are the different methods used to measure pain?
6. How does pain measurement differ in children and adults?
7. What are some of the pain control techniques available to pain sufferers?
8. Why are multidisciplinary pain management programs so successful?

Chapter 12
Health Promotion

CHAPTER OUTLINE

THE DEVELOPMENT OF HEALTH PROMOTION IN CANADA
IMPROVING HEALTH PROMOTION BY APPLYING PRINCIPLES OF PSYCHOLOGY
THE PRECEDE-PROCEED MODEL
ASSESSING THE EFFECTIVENESS OF HEALTH PROMOTION PROGRAMS
A FINAL WORD ABOUT HEALTH PROMOTION

Learning Objectives

After studying this chapter, you will be able to

■ Define health promotion.

■ Explain how health promotion has developed in Canada.

■ Apply the concepts of self-care and mutual aid to the goals of health promotion.

■ Apply the health belief model and the theory of reasoned action to the goals of health promotion.

- Apply theories of social psychology with the goal of improving the effectiveness of health promotion programs.

- Explain the Precede-Proceed Model.

- List the standards by which health promotion programs are evaluated.

A group of 12 teenagers is sitting around a table. They are watching a 60-second video. On the video, another group of teenagers is in a playground. A few are smoking cigarettes. Gradually, one of the teens on the tape begins to turn into a cigarette, much to the shock and horror of her friends. Fortunately, though, this terrible transformation helps them see the error of their ways. They throw away their cigarettes and start playing basketball. When they do, their friend morphs back to her old self.

After watching this tape, the group sitting around the table is asked to comment on it. They have been brought together as a focus group to provide insight into the impact of video campaigns such as this one. The teens are unimpressed by the video. They find it demeaning and ineffective. They highly doubt if this approach would make them or their friends quit smoking.

This is discouraging. Millions of dollars have been invested in the production and airing of this 60-second piece. Yet, if the focus group is to be believed, it will do nothing to reduce the number of teenagers who smoke.

Our federal government invested millions of dollars in this ad and others like it, in part because it is less expensive to convince people to look after themselves than to treat them medically when they do not. Focusing on prevention and self-care are the hallmarks of health promotion. However, the feedback provided by that focus group reminds us that health promotion is no easy task.

While many definitions of health promotion have been put forward, most refer to strategies intended to maintain or improve the health of large populations. The World Health Organization (WHO) defines **health promotion** simply as "the process of enabling people to increase control over, and to improve, their health" (1986). Yet even with this seemingly straightforward definition, health promotion takes many forms—from smoking-cessation programs to patient education, public awareness campaigns, and political activism—and this makes it difficult to state in concrete terms just what health promotion is (Ontario Health Promotion e-Bulletin, 2006).

health promotion: strategies intended to maintain or improve the health of large populations.

Health promotion strategies, like the quit-smoking campaign in our opening example, are often undertaken at a federal level of government. They are, therefore, usually very large, making their effectiveness difficult to measure directly. Furthermore, the challenges inherent in attempting to change attitudes and behaviour on such a large scale are daunting. Yet governments must persevere despite these difficulties, because effective health promotion is essential to our well-being.

Health promotion is also practised at an international level. The WHO Health Promotion Department uses political and sociological approaches to try to improve the health of the world's citizens. A good example of one of their initiatives is the *Mega Country Network*. This network attempts to affect health worldwide by involving the world's most populous countries. The program includes 11 countries with populations of

100 million or more, accounting for more than 60 percent of the world's population (for example, see www.who.int/school_youth_health/mega/en/). It includes such goals as the promotion of healthy diets and physical activity and the elimination of tobacco use.

Canada has played an active role in the WHO health promotion initiatives and has developed its own health promotion strategy. Here we begin by looking at the development of this work in Canada. This should provide you with a general sense of what health promotion entails.

THE DEVELOPMENT OF HEALTH PROMOTION IN CANADA

Canadian governments have actually been in the business of health promotion since the 1700s. Back then, the main task was regulatory in nature, coming up with regulations regarding sanitation and rules of operation for hospitals. In the early 1900s, once these regulations were firmly in place, the focus was shifted to educating the general public about the value of proper sanitation (Badgley, 1994).

In the first half of the 1900s, provincial health promotion programs were started in Ontario (1921), Manitoba (1929), Quebec (1943), and Newfoundland (1949). National programs followed—for example, *ParticipAction*, aimed at increasing Canadians' activity levels (started in 1971); the *Hole in the Fence* program, to curtail drug use (started in 1973); and *Dialogue on Drinking* (started in 1976).

Other examples of health promotion programs in Canada include the Aboriginal Head Start Program, Community Action Program for Children, and the many programs offered to all Canadians by the Public Health Agency of Canada—such as Stairway to Health, which encourages people to take the stairs rather than the elevator when at work.

In Canada, successful health promotion has been a clearly stated goal of federal governments since at least the mid-1970s. The kick-start came in 1974 from then Minister of Health and Welfare Marc Lalonde's paper, *A New Perspective on the Health of Canadians*. In it, he identified lifestyle as an important factor in health and well-being and, as such, an important target for health promotion and education.

In 1986, then Minister of Health and Welfare Jake Epp published *Achieving Health for All: A Framework for Health Promotion*(Epp, 1986). In it, Epp referred to the World Health Organization's definition of health promotion and applied it to Canada. Most importantly, in that paper Epp presented a very useful framework for health promotion.

We present this framework in Figure 12-1. Its categories sum up what health promotion is all about. Notice the scope of the goals; everyone in the country should find some relevance in the framework. Notice also the implications regarding locus of responsibility. All health promotion programs place the primary responsibility for good health on the individual rather than on medical staff or medical facilities.

Consistent with this emphasis on personal responsibility is the World Health Organization's reference to control in its definition of health promotion. Also note that self-care and mutual aid are cited as health promotion mechanisms in the Canadian framework. In other words, one goal of health promotion is to encourage people to look after themselves. Another is to encourage them to look after each other. A cynical view of these goals might suggest that they represent ways in which the government is shirking its responsibility to look after us. The reply to that cynicism is that there are limits to how much a government can do to look after its citizens, and having personal agency over one's health is, in itself, healthy.

In fact, some authors have argued that if health promotion is to be truly effective, it must be based on a social movement rather than a government edict (Labonte, 1990; O'Neill, Rootman, & Pederson, 1994). In other words, the real promoters of healthy choices must be the general public. For example, we know we are getting somewhere in terms of health promotion when parents won't start the car until every child's seatbelt is fastened. Another example of success can be found in the number of community-initiated programs that have been started independent of federal or provincial mandates.

Labonte (1987) provides a three-level framework for successful community-oriented health promotion. His analysis provides a useful taxonomy of health promotion and is very reminiscent of the biopsychosocial approach we introduced in chapter 1.

The first level identified by Labonte is **medical**. This level of health promotion is disease-based and the goal is disease treatment. For example, a community might develop a program to help people recover from heart attacks or devote funding to finding a cure for cancer. The second level deals with **public health**. This level is behaviour-based and the goal is disease prevention. A good example of a behaviour-based intervention would be the promotion of safe sex, or anti-drinking-and-driving programs. The third level is **socioenvironmental**. At this level, the orientation is toward social change and public health policy. Examples include such things as legislation to reduce poverty or school board policies to provide lunches for school children.

The second and third levels of Labonte's model are concerned with **social determinants of health**. These include such factors as income and social status, social support networks, education, employment/working conditions, personal health practices and coping skills, healthy child development services, gender, and culture (Public Health Agency of Canada, 2004). There is considerable evidence to indicate that these determinants have a greater impact on our population's health than does medical science (International Centre for Health and Society, 2003).

Of course, one of the goals of health promotion at the governmental level is to save those governments money on health expenditures. In Canada, where health care is socialized, total health expenditures are projected to reach $183 billion in 2009 (Canadian Institute for Health Information, 2009). This works out to $5452 per capita. When we consider that a great deal of that money is spent on treating conditions that are preventable, we can see why health promotion is important from a fiscal as well as a medical perspective.

medical level of health promotion: the orientation is disease-based and the goal is disease treatment.

public health level of health promotion: the orientation is behaviour-based and the goal is disease prevention.

socioenvironmental level of health promotion: the orientation is toward social change and public health policy.

social determinants of health: factors such as income, social support, education, working conditions, and culture that have a significant effect on health at the population level.

Aim	Achieving health for all		
Health challenges	Reducing inequities	Increasing prevention	Enhancing coping
Health promotion mechanisms	Self-care	Mutual aid	Healthy environments
Implementation strategies	Fostering public participation	Strengthening community health services	Co-ordinating healthy public policy

Figure 12-1 Canada's Framework for Health Promotion

Source: Epp J. (1986). Achieving health for all: A framework for health promotion. *Canadian Journal of Public Health, 77*, 393–430. Reproduced with the permission of the Minister of Public Works and Government Services Canada, 2010.

People who study health at the sociological level of the biopsychosocial approach will argue that saving money and saving lives are often accomplished by the same strategies. These strategies focus on prevention more than cure, and they feature messages that are intended to affect self-care behaviour, usually through attitude change. We now take a closer look at Canada's health promotion framework to develop an understanding of what forms these strategies can take.

The Goals of Health Promotion in Canada

In chapter 1, we traced the major topics of health psychology as they have developed over the years. As we work through Canada's framework for health promotion, you will see that a number of these same topics receive attention. Look for potential applications of research on coping, social support, and stress reduction as examples. You will also see that the level of emphasis is far broader than the purely biological. In keeping with the bio-psychosocial approach, you will find elements in the framework related to individual psychology (e.g., self-care), sociology (e.g., strengthening community health services), and geography (e.g., healthy environments).

Health Challenges   When Canadians think of their health care system, they are more likely to think of its equity than its inequity. It is, after all, a system designed to promote and provide equal access for all. However, the truth is that inequities exist and they pose a challenge for the Canadian health care system. These inequities may be based on differences in geography, culture, age, education, income, or labour-force status. For example, fewer than 6 percent of people in the highest income bracket in Canada rate their health as only fair or poor compared to 27 percent in the lowest income group (Tremblay, Ross, & Berthelot, 2002). These income-related disparities also apply to infant mortality rates and life expectancy (Wilkins, Berthelot, & Ng, 2002). Significant inequities also exist between Aboriginal and non-Aboriginal communities. A study of Aboriginal people living off reserves showed their self-reported health to be poorer than that of a non-Aboriginal population matched for socioeconomic level and health behaviours (Tjepkema, 2002).

The debate over the introduction of privatized health care options often involves issues of equity. Most Canadians would like to see surgical wait lists shortened, and one way to do that is to allow those willing to pay to enter a separate system, taking them out of the general wait list and providing them with more timely care. However, will this produce a two-tiered system in which those who can afford the private option receive the care they need while others do not? This debate is playing itself out in the courts, with cases such as the one brought to the Quebec Supreme Court by Dr. Jacques Chaoulli, a family physician in Montreal, and his patient George Zeliotis (*Chaoulli vs. the Attorney General of Quebec*). They argued that Mr. Zeliotis should not have to endure the painful wait for hip surgery because the province of Quebec (like other provinces) does not allow people to use private health insurance to pay for health services. After having their case turned down at the provincial level, Chaoulli and Zeliotis appealed to the Supreme Court of Canada. That court ruled in their favour by a vote of four to three. The outcomes of cases like these will shape the future of Canada's health care system and, subsequently, the health promotion strategies that accompany it.

Changing demographics provide another challenge for Canadian health care. As a population, an increasing percentage of us are in older age categories. We need to know

Do People with Higher Incomes Live Longer?

When it comes to health promotion research, Canada is a world leader. The primary sources of data for this research are the National Population Health Surveys. Other large national databases are also used, such as the Canadian Mortality Data Base and the Canadian Community Health Survey.

Researchers using the Canadian Mortality Data Base and census data from 1971 to 1996 have been able to assess income-based differences in mortality across the country. Causes of death were analyzed using international coding standards, though residents of long-term care facilities were excluded because census data that would indicate household income level do not apply well to institutions.

Income was divided into five equal categories, called *quintiles,* from richest to poorest. In these categories, total number of deaths and deaths by various causes were calculated. Using this methodology, it is possible to track changes in mortality rates for various groups over time. For example, researchers discovered that income-related disparities in life expectancy diminished by well over one year for both men and women between 1971 and 1996. Also, infant mortality rates for Canada's highest income bracket have dropped from 10.2 infants per 1000 births in 1971 to 4.0 in 1996. In the poorest quintile, infant morality has dropped over the same period from 20 to 6.4 per 1000 births. You can see some important trends here. First, there has been a significant drop in infant mortality rates overall. Second, that drop has been greater among those in the lowest quintile (Wilkins, Berthelot, & Ng, 2002).

about the ways in which our health needs change as we age (Chen & Wilkins, 1998). Age-related health concerns are not restricted to seniors, however. We know that our adolescent population has its own set of health promotion issues as well. Central among these are risk-related behaviours, such as cigarette smoking (Chen & Millar, 1998). As we saw in the example that opened this chapter, it is the job of health promotion to influence these behaviours. Another pressing age-related problem in Canada is childhood obesity. About one in six children in Canada is considered obese (Statistics Canada, 2002a).

The nature of people's occupations can be another source of health-related inequity. This is due, in part, to the differences in stress levels associated with various jobs (Wilkins & Beaudet, 1998). We also know that certain risk-related behaviours are more common among people in particular occupations. For example, in 1994 and 1995, 43 percent of people working in construction, transportation, and mining smoked cigarettes daily. By comparison, only 18 percent of people in so-called white collar occupations smoked every day (Gaudette, Richardson, & Huang, 1998). Equally pressing is the issue of second-hand smoke, which is a much greater problem in some occupations than in others—those who work in bars and pubs, for example, have been at greater risk than the general population. The laws that restrict smoking in workplaces are examples of health-promotion legislation (see Physicians for a Smoke-Free Canada, 2004).

Health Promotion Mechanisms

How can we best meet the health challenges laid out in the framework in Figure 12-1? This is the central question for people working in health promotion. The framework provides three answers: (1) we must be encouraged to look after ourselves, (2) we must be encouraged to look after each other, and (3) we must make our environments healthier by reducing pollution, improving safety, and reducing inequities.

As we review these health promotion mechanisms, notice again where the *locus of responsibility* is placed—squarely on the shoulders of the citizen. Remember that this is a key assumption of the health promotion process. Spending money to encourage people to look after themselves rather than having the government look after them costs considerably less and results in better quality of life. It has been estimated that obesity alone costs the Canadian health care system more than $4.3 billion a year. Inactivity costs a whopping $5.3 billion (Katzmarzyk & Janssen, 2004). Between 1981 and 1996, the prevalence of obesity more than doubled in both boys and girls (Canadian Health Network, 2003). Imagine the savings in money and the reduction of health problems if at least some of those people could be convinced to manage their diets in a healthier way.

Hence the rationale for an emphasis on **self-care**. Self-care refers to such things as exercise, diet, risk behaviours, voluntary screening, and regular medical checkups. Effective health promotion programs have measurable effects on these behaviours and, consequently, the general health of Canadians.

self-care: behaviours such as exercise, diet, voluntary screening, and regular medical checkups that people engage in to promote their health.

Utilization of effective screening programs is a form of self-care. In the late 1940s, the province of British Columbia became one of the first places in the world to introduce regular screening for cervical cancer (Wardle & Pope, 1992). The test used in this screening is called a **Pap test** (or Pap smear). When compared to screening tests for other kinds of cancer, the Pap test is considered to be among the most effective. By *effective*, we mean that it is an accurate early detection strategy that has significantly helped reduce cervical cancer mortality rates. The death rate from cervical cancer has declined by almost 50 percent since the Pap test was introduced. The current survival rate is estimated to be 74 percent over five years (Public Health Agency of Canada, 2009). However, older women, who are more at risk for cervical cancer than are their younger counterparts, do not receive Pap tests as often as they should (Lee, Parsons, & Gentleman, 1998).

Pap test: a test done to screen for cervical cancer.

The Canadian Pap test data illustrate a truism in health promotion—the work never ends. To be sure, there is tangible success; the majority of women in Canada do have Pap tests. In 1998 and 1999, 82 percent of women between the ages of 40 and 49 had received a Pap test in the previous three years (Cervical Screening in Canada, 1998 Surveillance Report).

The issue of smoking cessation also fits in the self-care category. In spite of what we know about the dangers of cigarette smoking, health promotion in this particular area of self-care runs into problems brought on by the social pressure and addiction that accompany smoking. Attempts to simply frighten people away from cigarettes have been discouragingly unsuccessful (Becker & Janz, 1987; Sutton & Eiser, 1984). The relative ineffectiveness of this approach obviously makes health promotion more difficult. Parading grim statistics or blackened lung tissue in front of people isn't enough to make them avoid smoking.

The good news is that smoking is on the decline in Canada, even among youth aged 15 to 19. In 1999, 28 percent of this age group smoked. By 2008, that number had dropped to 15 percent (Health Canada, 2010). Even with this trend, though, we have a long way to go with health promotion in this area, especially considering the fact that most smokers start when they are young. Programs must involve much more than simple appeals to fear. Later in this chapter, we will look more closely at the use of fear appeals and what must be added to make them effective.

Improving self-care among citizens is a fundamental objective of any health promotion program. But because people do not live in isolation from one another, in addition to looking after ourselves we must also look after each other. We have a responsibility to family, friends, loved ones, and for that matter, society as a whole when it comes to health and safety. This responsibility is highlighted in the Canadian framework by the promotion mechanism called **mutual aid**.

mutual aid: responsibility to family, friends, loved ones, and even society as a whole when it comes to health and safety.

A large body of literature in health psychology supports the framework's inclusion of mutual aid as an important promotion mechanism. The general conclusion of this literature is that it is healthy to have other people around (for a review, see Suls & Wallston, 2003). Mortality rates are lower in communities featuring a high level of social integration; close-knit communities are healthier.

Health psychologists are very interested in **social support**—that collection of interpersonal resources we have at our disposal to help us avoid or cope with difficult times in our lives. Social support is remarkably beneficial. Research indicates that strong support systems affect a number of health indicators, including how long a person can expect to live (Ross & Mirowsky, 2002).

social support: a collection of interpersonal resources that we have at our disposal to help us avoid or cope with difficult times in our lives.

In this book, we refer often to social support. It is an important resource when coping with stress, which we discussed in detail in chapter 3. Also, as we have mentioned, social support is a critical factor in people's ability to cope with serious illness, a topic we looked at in chapter 8.

It is important to know that social support doesn't always "just happen." Also, some people benefit from it more than others do. And social support comes in a number of different forms, some of which are easier to promote than others. We turn now to factors that affect the amount of support a person might receive, in an attempt to determine specific goals of health promotion strategies in the area of mutual aid.

Perhaps the most important point to make at the outset of this exploration is that social support is related to other elements of Canada's health promotion framework—most notably *reducing inequities*. For example, seniors who live on low incomes have less support than their more affluent counterparts. We also know that as people get older, their number of unmet needs increases in terms of health-related social assistance (Chen & Wilkins, 1998).

To understand how health promotion can be used to help reduce these inequities, we must divide social support into two general types, based on the source of the support. First, there is **naturally occurring support**. This is the support we get from friends, relatives, co-workers, and others in our own social networks. If you have just had triplets, you might have friends or family over to help out with meals or household chores, or to look after the babies so you can get some sleep. This would be an example of naturally occurring support.

naturally occurring support: the support we obtain from friends, relatives, co-workers, and others in our own social networks.

The other kind of support is called **agency-provided support**. This is support that is provided by agencies and organizations formed to fill the void when naturally occurring support is either lacking or unavailable. Imagine that you had those triplets just after moving to a new city where you didn't know a soul. You might be relieved to find that there was a support group for parents of multiple births in that city. This would be a group made up of people like you who help each other and find community resources to provide further help.

agency-provided support: social support provided by agencies and organizations that have been formed to fill the void when naturally occurring support is either lacking or unavailable.

When we study social support in the context of serious illness, we find that many people who are seriously ill don't have many people "like them" who share their illness. For example, wives of prostate cancer patients can be loving and extremely supportive, but they can't have had prostate cancer. For this reason, prostate cancer support groups are popular among men who want information and empathy that can come only from other patients. This is another important reason for agency-provided support.

What is the main job of health promotion here? In terms of mutual aid, health promotion campaigns must encourage the creation of support groups and attendance at them. This is especially true for segments of our population in which support is less available, as well as for people whose ability to cope can be improved by spending time with others who have similar illnesses or other health problems.

We have just seen that social support can be categorized in terms of its source. Social support can also be categorized by its type (for an application, see Cardenas, 2006). For example, we can receive **practical support**, sometimes called *tangible support,* which includes help with the demands of daily living—getting meals, going to medical appointments, mowing the lawn, and so on. Also, there is **informational support**, which could include such things as being told about treatment options, typical recovery times from treatment or injury, or what to do to speed recovery. Finally, there is **emotional support**. This is provided by people who take the time to understand our fears and frustrations, who help calm us during anxious times, who help bring our moods up, or who distract us from our worries.

When we know the types of support that people need, we can do a better job of providing that support. Imagine how you would respond if you found out that a close friend had just been diagnosed with cancer. You might know exactly what to do. On the other hand, you might have no experience with receiving this kind of news and so feel awkward. Do you call your friend right away or do you wait? If you call, what do you say? What should you do? What can you do to help? These are difficult questions that can paralyze us.

If you knew that people diagnosed with cancer need practical, informational, and emotional support, you might be better able to answer those difficult questions and provide support. Perhaps your friend needs a ride to an appointment. Maybe her kids need rides to school. Or perhaps there is something your friend needs to know, and you might be in a position to find out. In terms of emotional support, maybe you just need to be there to listen. The point is that we can use health promotion to educate people about these ways of providing support. Furthermore, we can promote the clear benefits of providing this support. In chapter 8, you found data from studies proving that mutual aid in the form of social support is of tremendous benefit to people with serious illnesses. For now, it is important to know that good health promotion programs can increase the likelihood that such support is forthcoming and that it will be effective by ensuring that it matches people's needs (Reynolds, 2001).

In examining Canada's health promotion framework, you will see that mutual aid isn't the only element for which social support is relevant. Consider also the two implementation strategies of *fostering public participation* and *strengthening community health services.* While these strategies clearly require the involvement of professionals from a variety of segments of the health care system, they also require the participation of the general public. Support groups obviously grow out of public participation, and they are commonly offered through community health service facilities.

In this section, we have used Canada's health promotion framework to provide some examples of the challenges faced by people working in health promotion. The number of health promotion programs that could be mounted in a country as vast and varied as Canada is virtually infinite. However, by using the framework, we can consolidate this number to a very manageable set of goals. We must find ways to promote self-care and

practical support: help with the demands of daily living, such as getting meals and rides to the doctor.

informational support: the provision of information such as treatment options or typical recovery times from a treatment or injury.

emotional support: support provided by people who take the time to understand our fears and frustrations, who help calm us during anxious times, who help bring our moods up, or distract us from our worries.

mutual aid, and we must reduce health-related inequities. These goals are not unique to Canada. Indeed, they are common to health promotion programs worldwide.

IMPROVING HEALTH PROMOTION BY APPLYING PRINCIPLES OF PSYCHOLOGY

Now that we know what the main goals and challenges are for health promotion in Canada, we will turn to the ways psychology can be used to help achieve these goals. In this section, we will draw on the major theories of health psychology that we introduced in chapter 1. We will also look closely at theories taken from social psychology.

Prominent Theories in Health Psychology Applied to Health Promotion

health belief model: analyzes health behaviour in terms of the belief that a health threat exists and the belief that a given course of action will affect the threat.

theory of reasoned action: posits that behaviour is preceded by intention, and that the intention is influenced by beliefs about the behaviour and subjective norms.

theory of planned behaviour: posits that behaviour is preceded by intention and that our intention is influenced not only by subjective norms and beliefs about the efficacy of the behaviour, but also by the belief that one is actually capable of performing the behaviour.

Much of health promotion is targeted at people's thinking. The assumption here is that one way to change behaviour is to change the beliefs relating to that behaviour. From chapter 1, you will recall that this line of reasoning is consistent with the **health belief model**, the **theory of reasoned action**, and the **theory of planned behaviour**.

These theories share two important elements: (1) the importance of people's beliefs regarding their vulnerability to a threat, and (2) the effectiveness of a given course of action to reduce that threat. In addition, it is important that people place a high value on their health. Because these beliefs and values are important to health-related behaviour, many health promotion programs are designed specifically to affect them.

Health promotion programs, then, must provide information regarding the likelihood that someone will suffer a health problem (vulnerability information) and advice on how one can reduce that likelihood (information regarding efficacy of preventive behaviours). Prominent theories in health psychology can inform decisions regarding content for health promotion.

For example, the theory of reasoned action and the theory of planned behaviour both acknowledge that people weigh the potential *costs* and *gains* of a given behaviour before adopting it. With this knowledge in mind, health promotion programs geared toward physical activity, such as Stairway to Health, focus on the gains rather than the costs of taking the stairs instead of the elevator. They emphasize the fun of exercise, not the fatigue that may result. These programs make the point that physical activity can be convenient, uplifting, and healthy. In so doing, they target people's beliefs regarding cost and gain. For some examples of these programs and messages, visit the Health Canada website and click on Healthy Living (www.hc-sc.gc.ca). The theories of health psychology are called on to form the foundation of health promotion programs. These programs also rely on research findings from the field of *social psychology*. This is because health promotion involves *persuasion*, which is a social phenomenon.

The Social Psychology of Health Promotion

persuasion: the attempt to change people's attitudes and beliefs.

attitude: a cognition in which a person evaluates some object or idea.

Persuasion is the attempt to change people's attitudes and beliefs. An **attitude** is a cognition in which a person *evaluates* some target. Attitudes involve words like *good* or *bad* and verbs such as *like* or *dislike*. Health promotion programs attempt to change attitudes when they try to persuade people that low-fat diets are *good*, and that people should *like* them. We might call this *health advertising*.

In chapter 1, we defined a *health belief* as something we think to be true concerning our health. More generally, beliefs are our personal encyclopedias of the world. They are the things we consider to be true. Beliefs are related to attitudes but different from them in that beliefs are not evaluative in nature. For example, we might hold the *belief* that yogurt contains less fat than ice cream, and this belief might support the attitude that yogurt is *good* for us.

Health promotion programs try to affect what people believe to be true and what they *like* and consider *good*. Over the years, social psychologists have conducted extensive research on persuasion (for a detailed review, see Olson & Maio, 2003). Well-proven principles have emerged from this research that can be applied to health promotion. Several examples follow.

The Elaboration Likelihood Model of Persuasion

Research investigating people's attitudes toward political candidates has discovered that there are basically two routes through which these attitudes are influenced (Petty & Cacioppo, 1981). The first, called the **central route**, refers to the use of logic, facts, and reason. Political campaigns using the central route present statistics and logical arguments in favour of a given candidate or perhaps in opposition to a candidate. Health promotion programs using this route will present statistics and medical facts.

central route to persuasion: the use of logic, facts, and reason to affect someone's attitude.

The second way that people's attitudes toward political candidates are influenced is called the **peripheral route**. This involves an appeal to emotion and general impression. Political campaigns using this route will focus on the looks and charisma of the candidate. Health promotion campaigns using the peripheral route feature healthy-looking people or show graphic depictions of the potential horrors resulting from risk behaviour.

peripheral route: attempts to affect attitude by appealing to emotion and general impression.

Research in social psychology shows that some people are influenced more by central routes and others more by peripheral routes. This means that health promotion campaigns must cover both bases. Statistical presentations, which make use of a central route, must be packaged well to appeal to people who are more influenced by peripheral routes.

A number of studies have applied the elaboration likelihood model to health promotion. In the area of AIDS prevention, for example, it has been suggested that there might be problems with programs focused exclusively on providing facts. People may become overloaded with information if it is not packaged in ways that arouse constructive emotional responses (Mulvihill, 1996). An example of this packaging is short films, which have been shown to be effective in engendering positive attitudes toward prevention behaviour (Igartua, Cheng, & Lopes, 2003).

Fear Appeals: An Example of Health Promotion by the Peripheral Route

One fairly obvious application of the peripheral route is the use of what are called **fear appeals**. The term is self-explanatory. The assumption, of course, is that we can change people's behaviour by presenting frightening accounts of what will happen to them if they continue a given behaviour (for example, smoking) or if they don't adopt a behaviour (for example, dental hygiene).

fear appeals: the attempt to change people's behaviour by presenting frightening accounts of what could happen to them if they continue a given behaviour or if they don't adopt a behaviour.

There is considerable theoretical support for this assumption. For example, main components of the theory of planned behaviour include *perceived threat* and *personal vulnerability*. Fear appeals are designed to intensify people's beliefs regarding this threat and

threat perception: the belief that a threat is real and that we are vulnerable to it.

drive-reduction theory: suggests we are driven to reduce the tension brought about by deprivation or other negative states.

the extent to which they are vulnerable. In other words, **threat perception**, the belief that a threat is real and that we are vulnerable to it, is more important than simple fear arousal.

Long before the introduction of the theory of planned behaviour, Hovland and colleagues' **drive-reduction theory** was used to explain fear appeals. Drive-reduction theory argues that we are driven to reduce the tension brought about by deprivation or other states to which we have an aversion (Hovland, Janis, & Kelley, 1953). According to this theory, fear appeals should work because we are driven to reduce fear, and when we are successful, the behaviour that we use to reduce the fear is reinforced.

However, if the fear arousal is *too high*, the person will respond in ways other than the recommended behaviour. There are a number of reasons for this, but the main one is that

Posters like this one take advantage of fear appeals.

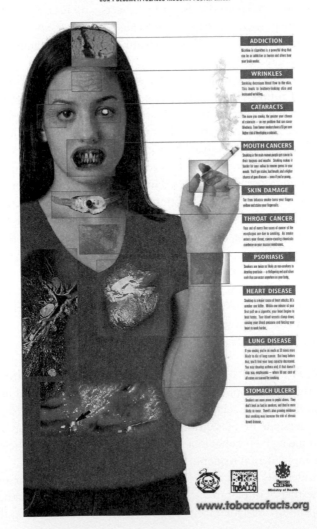

frightening messages present situations and outcomes that appear to be so awful that we don't think we can deal with them effectively no matter what we do. As a result, the recommended behaviour looks ineffective in comparison to the potentially catastrophic nature of the threat. For example, can I really prevent the devastating effects of cancer by eating broccoli? In answering this question, many people would see a mismatch in strength between the threat and the threat-reducing behaviour and so remain uninfluenced. They carry on with their old behaviour because the high-fear message makes the situation look too hopeless to do anything about. In this case, we don't believe in the *efficacy* of the behaviour to deal with the threat. Modern analysis of the mechanisms behind fear appeals indicates that the *efficacy beliefs* we talked about in chapter 1 might be more important than the amount of fear aroused by the message (Ruiter, Abraham, & Kok, 2001).

These efficacy beliefs take two forms—**response efficacy** (the belief that the behaviour will reduce the threat), and **self-efficacy** (the belief that one can carry out the behaviour). Another problem with high-fear messages is that our self-efficacy suffers when we are afraid. To illustrate this, ask yourself how reassured you would be by instructions on how to employ a backup parachute in the event that the main chute doesn't open. Imagine yourself listening to these instructions. In the event that you were plummeting to earth under the full force of gravity, are you confident that you would be able to carry out those backup instructions? Or would you be too afraid to remember the instructions and carry them out correctly? Confidence levels vary from person to person under such circumstances.

response efficacy: the perception that a threat-reducing strategy will work.

self-efficacy: an individual's perception of his or her ability to succeed at a particular task at a specific time.

Concerning health promotion, we might undermine people's confidence in their ability to perform self-examinations for cancer if we portray cancer in particularly frightening ways. This may be why 54 percent of women who were sent a reassuring letter listing "encouraging facts" about breast cancer made an appointment for a mammogram, whereas only 42 percent made an appointment after receiving an anxiety-arousing letter listing "worrisome facts." Interestingly, only 38 percent made an appointment when they received a standard letter listing no facts at all (Kendall & Hailley, 1993).

The point is that the effectiveness of fear appeals depends very much on people's *responses* while frightened. Efficacy beliefs represent one kind of response. **Self-accountability** represents another. As the term implies, self-accountability refers to the extent to which a person feels responsible for a given emotion or situation. This applies not only to fear appeals, but also to appeals to guilt and regret (Inman & Zeelenberg, 2002). Passyn and Sujan (2006) illustrate the distinction between fear and guilt appeals with a slogan used by the Partnership for a Drug-Free America: "Smoking pot may not kill you, but it will kill your mother"—a slogan aimed at guilt rather than fear.

self-accountability: the extent to which a person feels personally responsible for a given emotion or situation.

Appeals that feature guilt or fear demonstrate that we can frame a message in either positive or negative ways. **Message framing**, then, refers to the extent to which positive or negative aspects of an outcome are emphasized. Loss-framed messages emphasize the negative results of not engaging in a behaviour, and gain-framed messages emphasize the positive effects of engaging in the behaviour. A theory from cognitive psychology called *prospect theory* suggests that loss-framing will work best in some situations and gain-framing will work best in others (Tversky & Kahneman, 1981). Specifically, loss-framed messages are more effective when addressing risky behaviour, like getting a Pap test, which carries the risk of having cancer detected. Using sunscreen, on the other hand, is a behaviour that does not feature the risk of detection. Considerable research in health

message framing: the extent to which positive or negative aspects of an outcome are emphasized in a health promotion message.

Supermodel Christy Turlington represents a peripheral approach to health promotion.

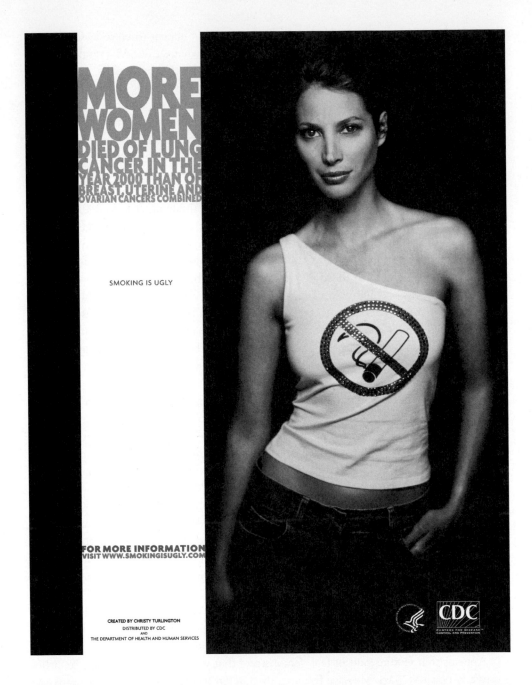

MORE WOMEN DIED OF LUNG CANCER IN THE YEAR 2000 THAN OF BREAST, UTERINE AND OVARIAN CANCERS COMBINED

SMOKING IS UGLY

FOR MORE INFORMATION VISIT WWW.SMOKINGISUGLY.COM

CREATED BY CHRISTY TURLINGTON
DISTRIBUTED BY CDC
AND
THE DEPARTMENT OF HEALTH AND HUMAN SERVICES

CDC
CENTERS FOR DISEASE
CONTROL AND PREVENTION

promotion has found that, indeed, loss-framed messages are more effective at promoting detection behaviours (Rivers et al., 2005), while gain-framed messages are better at promoting prevention behaviours (Kiene, Barta, Zelenski, & Cothran 2005). See Table 12-1 for examples of loss- and gain-framed messages.

What can we conclude from our analysis of fear appeals as a health promotion strategy? Clearly, messages that do nothing more than frighten people without addressing response efficacy, self-efficacy, or self-accountability are likely to be ineffective. On the other hand, if we arouse fear or guilt, send the message that the person is responsible for the existence of these emotions, and accompany that with a convincing argument that

Table 12-1	Examples of Loss-Framed and Gain-Framed Health Promotion Messages	
	Loss-Framed Message	**Gain-Framed Message**
High-Risk Behaviour (Detection)	Failing to detect cervical cancer early via a Pap test can cost you your life.	Detecting cervical cancer early via a Pap test can save your life.
Low-Risk Behaviour (Prevention)	By not using sunscreen, you could contract skin cancer and die.	By using sunscreen, you greatly reduce your risk of getting skin cancer.

Loss-framed messages emphasize the downside of not engaging in a health behaviour. Gain-framed messages emphasize the upside of that behaviour.

there are ways to address the problem within the capabilities of the people receiving the message, then we increase our chances of success. "Success" in terms of health promotion means that people will pay attention to our message, remember it, and behave in ways that are consistent with it by reducing health risks and increasing well-being. (For a detailed theoretical analysis of fear appeals, see Ruiter, Abraham, and Gerjo, 2001).

The Application of Other Social-Psychological Principles to Health Promotion

We know that the more often people hear a message the more likely they are to be influenced by it (Zajonc, 1968). Advertisers have known this for decades, as evidenced by the number of times we will see the same commercial in a 30-minute television program. Slogans take advantage of the repetition effect by being repeated in every different ad that appears in a given campaign. Health promotion campaigns could take greater advantage of slogans, just as advertisers do. Imagine the effect if a health promotion campaign had come up with the phrase "Just Do It."

Of course, advertising campaigns are far more than just repeated words and phrases. We must also consider who is saying those words. When we adopt a central route to persuasion, we want to use people who are credible, people who are seen as knowledgeable and believable. Not surprisingly, research has shown that sources perceived to be credible tend to be more persuasive than non-credible ones (Birnbaum, Wong, & Wong, 1976). If we are mounting an anti-smoking campaign, for example, we might want to put a physician on camera. If it is an anti-drinking-and-driving program, we could use a police officer who is often first on the scene of motor vehicle accidents.

If, on the other hand, we are using a peripheral approach, we will focus on the *attractiveness* of our speaker or we might want to pick someone who is famous. This is why anti-drug-abuse campaigns use professional athletes as speakers.

Good health promotion campaigns use both credible and popular speakers. As an example, imagine that you are asked to design a program to reduce the incidence of drinking and driving at high school graduations. In Ontario, 32 percent of the students in grades 7 to 13 reported being a passenger in a car driven by a drunk driver. Fifteen percent of those with driver's licences reported driving within an hour after consuming two or more drinks, and 20 percent reported driving within an hour after using cannabis (Adlaf, Mann, & Paglia, 2003). Your counterattack programs for high schools, aimed at affecting the drinking and driving behaviour, would be most effective if they combined messages from first-response police officers (because they are highly *credible*) and school presidents (because they are *popular*).

A health promotion program must consider the audience's *knowledge level*. When talking to small audiences, people in health promotion can make educated guesses about an audience's knowledge level. However, this is much more challenging when planning national campaigns. How much do people know about heart anatomy, for example? Early research found that people's knowledge of medical terminology was poor (Samora, Saunders, & Larson, 1961). A more recent update of that study showed that knowledge had improved somewhat, as people provided adequate definitions for 72 percent of a list of 50 commonly used medical terms (Thompson & Pledger, 1993).

Obviously, Canadians vary tremendously in their knowledge of medical language and procedures. For this reason, good health promotion campaigns must be basic enough to include as many people as possible without insulting anyone's intelligence. This can be a tricky balance to achieve.

Complicating the issue of knowledge is *literacy*. In Canada, those who report being in poor health are more likely to have low literacy scores, especially among the nation's senior citizens (Statistics Canada, 2005c).

In addition, there are people in Canada who are not fluent in English or French. According to Statistics Canada census figures, more than 450 000 people in Canada cannot understand spoken English or French. That figure represents 1.6 percent of our population. In British Columbia, 2.6 percent of the population cannot understand spoken English or French. Effective health promotion campaigns for these segments of our population must be either highly visual or multilingual.

Poole and Ting (1995) discovered that Indo-Canadian maternity patients scored lower on tests of knowledge of hospital procedures, baby care, and self-care than did Euro-Canadian patients. Language barriers are cited as a significant reason for these differences. It is clear, from studies such as this, that patient education and health promotion will be more effective when presented in a person's native language and, preferably, by people of the same cultural background.

In summary, we have seen that theories of psychology can and must be applied to the design and implementation of health promotion campaigns. When we consider these theories, we develop a greater appreciation for the complexities of health promotion. Changing the minds and behaviour of large groups of people is no easy task. The good news is that people who can be convinced to change their behaviour often come to endorse that behaviour and go on to carry out health promotion for others.

THE PRECEDE-PROCEED MODEL

People working in health promotion benefit greatly from a model that guides them in the planning of their programs. This provides not only structure and direction for the planning process, but also a set of criteria by which an existing program can be assessed. This is exactly what the precede-proceed model (Green & Kreuter, 1991) does. The model was designed as a way to facilitate and analyze health promotion programs from the planning stages through to their implementation and impact.

There are two key attributes to the model. One is the identification of components involved in the planning, implementation, and evaluation of health promotion programs. The other is the identification of causal pathways among these components. Table 12-2 presents the model. The "precede" phases of the model relate to the *planning* of health

Table 12-2 The Precede-Proceed Model of Health Promotion Planning, Implementation, and Evaluation

←PRECEDE

Phase 5	Phase 4	Phase 3	Phase 2	Phase 1
Administrative and policy diagnosis	Educational and organizational diagnosis	Behavioural and environmental diagnosis	Epidemiological diagnosis	Social diagnosis
Health promotion	Predisposing factors			
Health education	Reinforcing factors	Behaviour and lifestyle	Health	Quality of life
Policy regulation organization	Enabling factors	Environment		

Phase 6	Phase 7	Phase 8	Phase 9	
Implementation	Process evaluation	Impact evaluation	Outcome evaluation	

PROCEED →

Source: Green & Kreuter (1991). *Health promotion planning: An educational and environmental approach.* Mountainview, CA: Mayfield Publishing. Adapted by permission.

promotion programs. The "proceed" phases relate to the *implementation* and *evaluation* of that program. By examining Table 12-2, you can see that the model has an element of symmetry that helps clarify it conceptually. We begin by moving from right to left across the top of the model then proceed by moving from left to right across the bottom. In so doing, we end up where we started, with a focus on health and quality of life. We can walk through the phases of the model to develop an appreciation for its logic.

We begin in phase 1 by diagnosing quality of life. If there were no problems here, there would be no need to continue with our health promotion plan. However, there are always problems because no population is completely free of disease, disability, and accidents. In phase 2, we would conduct an epidemiological diagnosis to identify patterns of health and illness in our population. In terms of causation, the model assumes that these health patterns affect quality of life. Phase 3 requires a diagnosis of behavioural and environmental factors that explain our epidemiological data. We are now beginning to create a causal pathway from behaviour and environment, to health, to quality of life. In phase 4, we assess factors affecting behaviour and environment. What biological, psychological, or social factors influence behaviour? (This should remind you of the biopsychosocial model.) What factors affect environment? In phase 5, the final phase of planning, we would devise programs and policies meant to create optimal environments that are physically healthy and that reinforce healthy behaviours.

Now we are ready to "proceed," which is to say implement our plan and evaluate its effects. In phase 6, we would implement our education programs, new health policies, environmental regulations, and so on. These may take advantage of some of the psychological theories we discussed earlier in the chapter. To begin assessing the effectiveness of these programs, we would enter the process evaluation phase (phase 7). At this point, we evaluate the extent to which our programs affect the factors that predispose people to healthy behaviour and reinforce that behaviour. In addition, we may also be trying to bring about conditions that foster improvements in people's physical environments. In phase 8, we assess impact by measuring changes in behaviour, lifestyle, and environment since the program began. These changes should, in turn, bring about better health and, ultimately, better quality of life. This brings us back to where we started.

A good example of the implementation of the precede-proceed model is a program that was designed to increase the physical activity levels of senior citizens (Frankish, Milligan, & Reid, 1998). This program stems from the belief that health-related quality of life is influenced by active rather than sedentary behaviours and lifestyles. The next step (phase 4 of the precede-proceed model) is to identify factors that would predispose a person to activity and other factors that would reinforce it. Now we are ready to design a health promotion program that takes advantage of psychological theory to positively affect these factors.

When we move in the "proceed" direction, we would implement our program and evaluate the extent to which it brings about predisposing and reinforcing factors that favoured active living (phase 7). Next we would evaluate the extent to which these events actually had an impact on the seniors' behaviour and, more generally, their lifestyles—were people being more active (phase 8)? Finally, we would need to determine whether the seniors' health had improved and, along with it, their quality of life.

The precede-proceed model has been tested in more than 600 published studies, addressing everything from timely follow-up after an abnormal mammogram (Arnsberger et al., 2006) to the prevention of unintentional injury (Trifiletti, Gielen, Sleet, & Hopkins, 2005), making it the most widely tested model of its kind. One of the advantages of the

Community programs like Insite, operated by Vancouver Coastal Health, provide examples of the ways in which the precede-proceed model of health promotion planning can be applied.

model is that it works in conjunction with any other model or theory of health promotion design. For example, in phase 5, planners could use the health belief model as their guide, trying to educate people about their vulnerability and efficacy beliefs. The model has been criticized for being too individually oriented, with its emphasis on behaviour and lifestyle (Luschen, Cockerham, & Kunz, 1996). An expanded model might take the social and cultural context of that behaviour into consideration.

ASSESSING THE EFFECTIVENESS OF HEALTH PROMOTION PROGRAMS

Health promotion programs are labour-intensive initiatives that can be expensive. It is important, therefore, to find ways to assess their effectiveness. In health promotion, the magnitude of the interventions and the desired effects can make evaluation of impact difficult. Fawcett et al. (2001) identify no fewer than 12 challenges inherent in evaluating health promotion programs that are pitched at the community level. These authors point out that it can be difficult to identify just what is determining the health of the community, much less evaluating programs designed to affect those determinants. Furthermore, some of the endpoints of health promotion, such as "community capacity" or "quality of life," while important, are abstract in nature.

For example, getting definitive measures of changes in rates of child abuse and domestic violence on a population level can be difficult. For one thing, under-reporting is often a problem. And then there is the lag time between the implementation of a promotion program and the benefit that is realized. Some health promotion benefits, such as reduced cardiovascular disease, can take years to realize. These are just some of the challenges identified by Fawcett and his colleagues.

In spite of these challenges, health promotion programs must be evaluated, not just to satisfy the curiosity of policy makers, program planners, and researchers, but also for the good of the communities the programs are designed to support (Judd, Frankish, & Moulton, 2001). The key to effective evaluation of health promotion programs is to engage all relevant parties in the process. Judd and colleagues point out that an evaluation system that follows the values and goals of health promotion, as we have discussed them in this chapter, must be collaborative, democratic, participatory, and open.

Based on these goals, the standards applied to the evaluation of health promotion programs come in a number of forms, which have been nicely articulated by Judd and colleagues (2001). For example, **arbitrary standards** are based on decisions made by some outside body regarding what a community needs. Contrast these with community-based **experiential standards**, which are based on what experience has told the community it needs. There are **historical standards**, which are based on comparisons to other programs or to the program in question at an earlier time in its existence. **Normative standards** determine a program's impact by assessing national averages in areas such as literacy, mortality and morbidity, and self-reports of health. **Scientific standards** draw similar statistical comparisons but with data published in scientific literature. Finally, there are **propriety standards**, which take ethics and legalities into account, and **feasibility standards**, which are used to evaluate a program based on this practicality or sustainability (St. Leger, 2005).

Once standards have been identified to use for our evaluation, there are well-defined steps that can be followed (Rootman et al., 2001); see Table 12-3.

arbitrary standards: standards used to evaluate health promotion programs forwarded by a body that exists outside the community involved in the promotional campaign.

experiential standards: standards used to evaluate health promotion programs based on direct experiences of the community involved in the promotional campaign.

historical standards: standards used to evaluate health promotion programs based on comparisons to other programs or to the same program at an earlier time.

normative standards: standards used to evaluate health promotion programs using statistics, such as national averages, that describe the health issue being addressed.

scientific standards: standards used to evaluate health promotion programs using data published in scientific literature describing similar programs or health issues.

propriety standards: standards used to evaluate health promotion programs that take legal and ethical issues into account.

feasibility standards: standards used to evaluate health promotion programs based on the practicality or sustainability of the program.

Table 12-3 Steps involved in the Evaluation of Health Promotion Initiatives

STEPS	CONSIDERATIONS
Step 1: Describing the program	Develop a familiarity with the program you are evaluating in terms of its context, goals, and constituents.
Step 2: Identifying the issues and questions	What needs to be known about the program? What do the program's constituents mean when they ask "Is the program working?"
Step 3: Designing the data-collection process	Will qualitative and/or quantitative methods be used? What will your sources be?
Step 4: Collecting the data	Careful and systematic data collection is required.
Step 5: Analysing and interpreting the data	Will you be looking for themes? Is your analysis theory driven?
Step 6: Making recommendations	What can you confidently conclude from your analysis and what will you tell the constituents?
Step 7: Dissemination	Who should be made aware of your evaluation?
Step 8: Taking action	What should be done as a result of your evaluation?

Source: Based on Rootman recommendations, referenced from: Rootman, I., Godstadt, M., Polvin L., and Springett, J. (2001). A framework for health promotion evaluation. In Rootman, I., et al., (eds.). *Evaluation in health promotion: Principles and perspectives.* Copenhagen, WHO Regional Office for Europe, 2001 (WHO Regional Publications, European Sewries, No. 92, pp. 7–38).

In summary, while it is not easy, it is imperative to evaluate health promotion programs. The key is to apply appropriate standards that are consistent with the goals of health promotion and the needs of the community in question. These standards must be applied via careful steps, starting with a thorough knowledge of the program and leading to effective action informed by the evaluation.

A FINAL WORD ABOUT HEALTH PROMOTION

In this chapter on health promotion, we have made repeated reference to self-care and mutual aid, making the point that, with these goals in mind, the locus of responsibility for health is placed on individuals and groups. As you read through these sections, you might have wondered about the fairness of this locus of responsibility. If we lived in a world that featured perfect social justice, it would be reasonable to place major responsibility for health on the individual. However, we do not live in such a world.

Obviously, some people are in a much better position to engage in healthy behaviour than are others. Healthy diets tend to be more expensive than unhealthy ones. Opportunities for physical activity are not evenly distributed among Canadians. Health disparities can be mapped by postal codes, and an analysis of this shows that social determinants of health manifest themselves differently across these environments.

In this chapter, by referring to social determinants of health, health disparities, and personal responsibility for health, we are espousing what has been called a **co-production process** related to the promotion of health (Schmidt, 2009). By this we mean that the responsibility for health must be shared among centralized health bureaucracies, individuals, and communities.

co-production process:
a process whereby the responsibility for health is shared among centralized health bureaucracies, individuals, and communities.

CHAPTER SUMMARY

The World Health Organization defines health promotion as the process of enabling people to increase control over and to improve their health. Health promotion has a long history in Canada, dating back to the 1700s. Programs began developing at the provincial level in the 1920s with a focus on proper sanitation. From there, national programs began to flourish in the 1970s. An example is ParticipAction. Major documents have been produced by the federal government that have shaped the framework for health promotion. One example is "Achieving Health for All: A Framework for Health Promotion," published in 1986. A key goal for health promotion in Canada is the reduction of health disparities.

An important goal of health promotion programs is to have individuals and communities look after themselves and each other. A key mechanism for this is social support. This support, which can be naturally occurring or agency-provided, takes at least three forms: practical, informational, and emotional.

Major elements of most health promotion programs are drawn from the health belief model and the theory of reasoned action. They include perceived vulnerability, perceived seriousness, and cost/gain analysis. Health promotion programs communicate messages about how a given condition could affect anyone (vulnerability), could be serious and still easy to treat (low cost/high gain), and that treatment could be effective (efficacious).

Social psychological theories relevant to health promotion come from the study of persuasion. For example, the elaboration-likelihood model identifies central and peripheral routes to persuasion. Central routes present facts and figures, appealing to the cognitive dimension of attitudes. Peripheral routes appeal to emotion. Good health promotion programs follow both routes. The peripheral route sometimes features fear appeals. Such appeals are effective only if they are accompanied by ways in which the emotion can be reduced through dealing with the fear-arousing problem.

The precede-proceed model is a nine-phase model in which the first five phases (precede) describe the diagnosis of the problem and the design of a plan to address the problem. The remaining four phases (proceed) describe the implementation of the plan and the evaluation of the process and outcomes.

Health promotion programs are difficult to evaluate because they are often large in scale, and the outcomes can be abstract. The standards applied to the evaluation process may be arbitrary (some outside body decides what a community needs), experiential (based on the real experiences of the community), historical (based on the status of the community at an earlier time), normative (based on national averages), scientific (based on other research), or based on propriety (ethics and legalities) and feasibility.

Review Questions

1. How has health promotion developed in Canada?
2. What are the goals of health promotion?
3. How can the principles of psychology be applied to improve health promotion efforts?
4. How can we best evaluate the effectiveness of health promotion programs?

FOCUSED MODULE A
Conducting Research in Health Psychology

Health psychology is an **applied discipline**. This means that psychologists working in this field spend more time using theories to explain real-world phenomena than they do developing the theories. The applied focus in health psychology means that much of the research conducted in the field is applied research, which is designed to solve real-world problems.

Applied research comes with its own set of challenges. While basic researchers can study a phenomenon for its own sake, applied researchers usually need some practical outcome for their work—program improvement, improved coping, and wellness are goals of applied research. This is not to imply that one kind of research is better or more virtuous than the other.

In addition to requiring practical outcomes, applied research is challenging because it often takes place in the actual setting where the findings will be applied. In health psychology, this means doing a great deal of research in hospitals and clinics. Psychosocial research in hospitals can be intrusive. Imagine conducting a study in which nurses are asked to follow a script that differs from what they were used to. Now, in addition to concentrating on the patient, the nurses must also pay attention to this new protocol. Through all of this, patient care cannot be compromised. This means that close consultation must take place between practitioners and researchers before conducting hospital research that alters routine. To complicate matters, this consultation is time consuming, and practitioners usually don't have the luxury of spare time.

The intrusions of this research are not restricted to the practitioner—the patients must be considered as well. For example, just trying to enlist the participation of patients in hospital settings can be problematic. Patients might not be at their most receptive immediately before cardiac catheterization, in which a probe will be inserted into one of their coronary arteries. All the same, in order to guide practitioners and help patients cope, it is vital that we learn about the psychological factors relevant to patients undergoing such procedures (see chapter 6, Hospital Stays and Medical Procedures).

Perhaps the greatest challenge is that field research is never tidy; there are always going to be numerous variables that a researcher cannot control. Imagine being the researcher in the following example:

> A patient arrives 30 minutes early for her CT scan so that she can fill out your questionnaires. However, the clinic is running a bit ahead of schedule on this day and the patient is asked to come in for her scan before she has finished completing the questionnaires. She offers to finish them after the scan. Other patients in the study completed all the questionnaires before the scan, but you don't want to lose valuable data since so few patients fit the inclusion criteria for the study, so you take her up on her offer to complete them afterward. The patient returns from her scan 45 minutes later, willing to complete the questionnaires. Unfortunately, she was feeling a bit anxious just before her scan and so she was given a mild tranquillizer. Will her data still be of value?

In spite of challenges like these, good psychological research can be conducted in hospitals or other field settings.

OBSERVATIONAL METHODS: LEARNING BY LOOKING

One of the most fundamental ways to learn about phenomena in health psychology is to observe them. Observational research is almost always descriptive in its purpose. This method might seem straightforward on the surface, but there are many inherent challenges.

Imagine that you want to study communication between physicians and their patients. You might decide that the best place to start is with an observational design. To be of value, your observations must be made in real-life settings—that is, by observing actual consultations between physicians and their patients. Your first challenge presents itself: How do you make your observations without getting in the way? In the language of observational methodology, how can you be unobtrusive? Will you hide behind a screen? A one-way mirror? Not likely. These solutions are both awkward and unethical. The patients and physicians must consent to being observed, and so they will know their behaviour is being monitored.

Maybe technology can help. There is audio tape. This method is much less obtrusive but you would lose valuable visual information that might help you understand non-verbal behaviour. There is videotape. The camera is more obtrusive, but perhaps if you set it up inconspicuously enough people will forget it is there and you will get to observe some fairly natural behaviour.

If you do get good tapes, what will you do with them? When you begin to view them, you will realize that there is a great deal going on in them. Body positions are shifting, words are zipping back and forth between patient and practitioner, other non-linguistic sounds like *uh* and *mmm* are coming out, and it's all happening so fast. This is another challenge of observational research—knowing what to observe.

CASE STUDIES: ONE PERSON AT A TIME

Case studies are usually narrative in nature, providing details about one person's life (or, in some cases, comparing two or more individuals) that help us learn about some aspect of health psychology. **Case studies** present such things as individual histories, symptoms, specific reactions, or treatment outcomes (Cozby, 1993). They can also be used at a more sociological level. As such, they would present descriptions of programs or institutions.

A research group may want to trace the life of a prostate cancer patient to discover what role, if any, social support plays in his story. How does he describe his relationship with his wife? Did attending a support group represent some sort of turning point for him in his ability to cope with his prostate cancer?

Case studies can be valuable because they provide rich sources of data that are rarely obtainable using other methods featuring large groups. Also, the data become "personalized" rather than "dehumanized," which is important in a discipline like health psychology, which prides itself on its human focus. However, findings from case studies cannot always be generalized to other people.

case studies: narrative accounts of one person's health, including individual histories, symptoms, specific reactions, or treatment outcomes that inform some aspect of health psychology.

One form of case study is the *illness narrative*. As the term implies, an illness narrative is the complete story of a person's experience with a medical condition, told from the perspective of the person. To create illness narratives, an open-ended interview technique may be used in which the researcher provides a prompt like, "Tell me about your experience with multiple sclerosis from the time you first started experiencing symptoms." As you can imagine, these interviews may take two hours or more. The person's responses are usually audiotaped and then transcribed before being analyzed for themes and other important information.

SURVEY METHODS: TAKING SNAPSHOTS OF LARGE SAMPLES

Much of the data collected by social scientists working in health-related fields comes in the form of surveys. A well-designed survey can produce a wealth of information about a large group of people. Surveys are particularly useful for assessing trends in health behaviours and trends in the use of a health care system. For these reasons, you will find that much of the data available from sources such as Statistics Canada have been collected through surveys.

In British Columbia, the Adolescent Health Survey (conducted by the McCreary Centre in 1992, 1998, 2003, and 2008) has collected data on adolescent health and risk behaviours on four occasions from large numbers of youth in high schools throughout the province. By "large numbers" we mean over 69 000, making it one of the largest surveys of its kind in the world. The 2008 survey collected responses from over 29 000 people between grades 7 and 12 (Smith et al., 2009).

There are two fundamental questions that have to be answered at the outset of planning survey research: What do you want to know, and whom do you want to ask? It is amazing how often a research group goes over survey results only to have one of the group say, "If only we had asked _____!" This happens, in part, because it can be difficult to anticipate all the important questions the first time you administer a survey. For example, each administration of the Adolescent Health Survey includes most of the questions from previous versions of the survey, although a few items have been deleted and some new questions added. This has been done to reflect current issues among youth.

Of concern here is striking a balance between keeping the survey relevant, allowing for comparisons across different administrations of the survey, and keeping the administration within acceptable time limits—one high school period, in this case. Items that are deleted from one administration of the survey are lost for purposes of comparison, yet it is not possible to continuously add new items without deleting others. It can be a difficult trade-off.

CORRELATIONAL METHODS: LOOKING FOR THINGS THAT CHANGE TOGETHER

correlational research: studies including statistical analyses to determine if two variables change together, or *co-vary.*

For men with prostate cancer, we might hypothesize that coping is *positively correlated* with social support. This means simply that as social support satisfaction increases, so does coping ability. These two variables change together—they *co-vary.* To test this hypothesis, we would conduct **correlational research**. This means that we would use statistical analyses to determine if these variables did, in fact, co-vary. Of course, the main statistic we would rely on would be correlation. Not surprisingly, correlational research is common in health psychology.

Conceptually, correlations are not particularly complicated. For example, you need three things to do correlational analysis in our prostate cancer study. First, you need pairs of scores for a given individual. In this case, each man has a social support satisfaction score and a coping score. It would make no sense to correlate one man's satisfaction score with another man's coping score. Second, you need a large sample of these men, and it would be best if they varied on these scores. Third, you need variables with multiple levels, preferably measured on a continuum. For example, age works well in correlational analysis because you can measure it right down to the day, if necessary.

Once you have your pairs of scores on appropriate variables, you can calculate your correlation. There are three possibilities:

1. As one variable increases (or decreases), so does the other. This would result in a **positive correlation**. For example, we would hypothesize a positive correlation between social support satisfaction and coping.

2. As one variable increases, the other might decrease. This would result in a **negative correlation**. For example, we might hypothesize a negative correlation between social support satisfaction and illness progression. The better the support, the slower the illness progression (as measured by some biomedical indicator, in which higher scores meant more progression of illness).

3. The variables might be unrelated. For example, one person might be very satisfied with social support but be coping poorly. Another could be satisfied and coping well. Others may be coping well without any social support.

positive correlation: when one variable increases (or decreases), so does another.

negative correlation: when one variable decreases as another increases.

It is important to realize that correlational research does not allow us to draw conclusions regarding the cause–effect relationship between variables. For example, if satisfaction with support and coping are positively correlated, we cannot jump to the conclusion that support *caused* improved coping. There are at least two reasons why we cannot draw cause–effect conclusions from correlations.

The first is that both causal directions are possible. While it is possible that good social support causes better coping, it is also possible that those people who are coping better are more able to seek social support. If this is the case, then coping could affect social support scores. The point is that the correlation does not give us any definitive data regarding the direction of this relationship.

The second reason we can't draw cause–effect conclusions from correlations involves the possibility of third-variable explanations. It is entirely possible that social support and coping aren't causally related at all. Instead, there might be a third variable that affects both of them and, in so doing, results in a correlation. For example, it is possible that one's income could be related to both social support and coping. People who can afford cars go to support groups and get more support than people who can't. Also, a higher income might be affecting coping by allowing for the purchase of other things that make life more comfortable. In other words, income is a *third variable* that may be causally related to both support and coping.

In chapters 1 and 3, we discussed the Type A behaviour pattern. When it was first identified, the claim was that competitive, time-urgent, hostile people were at greater risk for heart disease. Further research has shown that it is hostility that is the most predictive factor in this list. *Factor analysis* can be used in research that identifies such patterns. **Factor analysis** compares a multitude of variables (factors) to find any patterns of occurrence that exist between them to create a larger, over-arching phenomenon.

EXPERIMENTAL METHOD: DRAWING CONCLUSIONS REGARDING CAUSE

Correlational researchers trying to learn about social support and prostate cancer do not control the amount of support the patients receive. They can only measure it. Similarly, researchers do not control the type of medical treatment the men receive. If we want to learn anything definitive about the extent to which variables cause certain health outcomes, we must be able to control those variables. When we control a variable and then observe changes in a specific health outcome, we can be much more confident when drawing conclusions about that variable causing the change. This is known as the experimental method.

The language of experimental design is somewhat different from that used in correlational research. The variables researchers manipulate are called **independent variables**. The outcome variables that are measured to determine the effects of the manipulation are called **dependent variables**. In its most basic form, then, the experimental method involves manipulating independent variables to determine their effect on dependent variables.

In the simplest version, one group gets the manipulation or treatment (the independent variable), and another group doesn't. The group that receives the manipulation is called the **experimental group**, while the group that does not is called the **control group**. The control group is used as a source of comparison to measure changes that can be attributable to the independent variable because, in theory, the independent variable is the only difference between the two groups. We say "in theory" because it is practically impossible to create groups that differ in only one way.

Individuals vary in many ways. Researchers using the experimental method take these individual differences into account by using **random assignment** to determine who will be in the experimental group and who will be in the control group. In this way, individual differences in such variables as intelligence and medical history, which might not be independent variables in a given study, should be evenly divided between the two groups because people have been placed randomly in the groups.

Main Effects and Interactions

A variable has a **main effect** if that single variable causes a significant change in a dependent variable. Main effects certainly do occur in health psychology research, but it is much more common to find that variables *combine* to produce an effect. For example, the effects of a person's social support may combine with the amount of stress that person is experiencing to have an effect on how well the person is coping with an illness—an effect that is different from the effect of either independent variable alone. We call this combined effect an **interaction**.

In chapter 1, we introduced a number of prominent theories in health psychology. Most of these theories assume an interactional model. For example, remember that the

factor analysis: analyzing a multitude of variables (factors) in order to find any patterns of occurrence that exist between them.

independent variables: the variables researchers manipulate.

dependent variable: in an experiment, the variable that is hypothesized to be measurably affected by the manipulation of the independent variable.

experimental group: participants in a study who receive the manipulation (the independent variable).

control group: participants in a study who don't receive the manipulation (the independent variable).

random assignment: determining randomly who will be in an experimental group and who will be in a control group so that individual differences should be evenly divided between the two groups.

main effects model: any scientific explanation that assumes an outcome is the result of the effects of a single variable.

interaction: when variables combine to produce an effect that is different from the effect of either variable alone.

two main elements of the theory of reasoned action are a person's attitudes toward a behaviour and her beliefs about what other people would do or would want her to do. To test this theory, we might want to manipulate these attitudes and beliefs to determine their effect on behaviour. Our assumption would be that these variables *interact*. In other words, the effect of a person's attitude toward the behaviour should depend on her beliefs about other people's thoughts regarding the behaviour.

QUASI-EXPERIMENTAL DESIGNS: TAKING OUR EXPERIMENTS INTO THE FIELD

Experimental methods using laboratory settings have the advantage of control but the disadvantage of artificiality. A method that allowed for control, yet could be conducted in real-life settings, would increase the ability to generalize results to applied settings. This is the objective of **quasi-experimental designs**. They are called "quasi" because researchers do relinquish some control by moving to real-life settings, but because researchers are still manipulating variables, they are using experimental methods. These studies are sometimes called **field research**, because they are conducted in real-life settings. Correlational studies can also fit into this broad category.

quasi-experimental designs: research done in real-life settings, but in which experimental methods (manipulation of variables) are used.

field research: research conducted in real-life settings.

Because they attempt to strike a balance between realism and control, quasi-experimental studies can be difficult to carry out. Researchers talk about "noise" that enters the data when they move to real-life settings. By "noise" they mean uncontrollable factors that can affect the results. For example, imagine asking an elderly patient to complete a questionnaire while in a waiting room at a hospital. She is accompanied by her daughter, who feels obliged to help her mother complete the questionnaire. As the researcher, you can urge her to let her mother complete the questionnaire alone. The daughter might even agree. Still, it is difficult to ensure that she will have no influence over her mother's responses.

Matching Groups

Remember that, in a proper experiment, participants are randomly assigned to groups to ensure that extraneous variables, such as age and IQ, are equally distributed among the groups. In this way, the groups can be closely matched on most variables so researchers can attribute the cause of changes in the dependent variable to their manipulation (the independent variable). In quasi-experimental designs, researchers don't usually have the opportunity to randomly assign people to groups.

For example, researchers wanted to assess the effects of relaxation training on children's respiratory health (Reid, Mackinnon, & Drummond, 2001). At first glance, this seems like a straightforward study. Create two groups—one that gets the relaxation training and one that doesn't—and make upper respiratory infection scores the dependent variable. However, these researchers weren't just interested in the effects of relaxation on infection-prone children. They also wanted to know if relaxation could benefit healthy children as well.

This introduced another variable—health status. Because of this, researchers now had an interactional design with four groups: (1) a group of healthy children getting the relaxation training, (2) a group of infection-prone children getting the training, (3) a group of healthy children not getting the training, and 4) a group of infection-prone children not getting the training. Even this isn't particularly difficult. However, there is the problem of matching groups.

The researchers cannot randomly assign children to the healthy or infection-prone groups. Therefore, they must be sure that the healthy and infection-prone children are similar in as many ways as possible. They must be matched for numerous variables, such as age, family income, family structure, and other health indicators, to name just a few. This matching procedure is logistically challenging for a number of obvious reasons. One is that it can be hard to get a sufficiently large sample size if researchers need to find a matching control for every experimental group participant. Another is that it can be difficult to decide how many variables need to be taken into account as matching criteria, given that the list is potentially endless. The researchers need to know which variables might be potential confounds, or "noise," and try to match control and experimental group participants on those.

RANDOM CLINICAL TRIAL STUDIES: ASSIGNING PARTICIPANTS TO GROUPS RANDOMLY

There are times when it is possible to randomly assign participants to groups even though the study is being conducted "in the field." In the study we just described, the health status of the children wasn't manipulated and randomly assigned, but the relaxation training variable was. In **random clinical trial studies**, participants are randomly assigned to treatment conditions. This eliminates the possibility that the treatment might work only because it attracted a certain type of person to it.

We can randomly assign people to treatment conditions, but we cannot control the medical conditions or other personal characteristics of people coming into a study. Instead, most quasi-experimental designs will stipulate a study's inclusion criteria. **Inclusion criteria** are those characteristics that make a person eligible for a study. These criteria represent another challenge for people doing field research. On one hand, it is important to establish sufficiently narrow inclusion criteria in order to limit the number of confounding variables. On the other hand, if the inclusion criteria are too narrow the researchers might never find enough people who fit them. Also, it is important to note that the results of a study cannot be generalized beyond the inclusion criteria. For example, if your inclusion criteria stipulate children between the ages of 10 and 12 with no history of other illness, then you cannot draw conclusions about younger or older children, or children who have a host of medical conditions.

LONGITUDINAL VERSUS CROSS-SECTIONAL RESEARCH

Researchers must decide if they are going to follow one group of people for a long period of time, or if they are going to look at a number of groups of people, each at a different stage of life. In the first approach, they must decide on the basic order of their work. Will they measure the variables they are interested in, then monitor people to see how these variables affect their lives? Or will they find people in varying degrees of good and ill health and look back to see what variables might have brought them to this state?

random clinical trial studies: research in which participants are randomly assigned to treatment conditions.

inclusion criteria: characteristics that make a person eligible for a study.

Following one group over time is called **longitudinal research**. Using numerous groups that differ according to stage is called **cross-sectional research**. For example, if a research group was interested in how the needs of prostate cancer patients changed over time, they could conduct longitudinal research, collecting data from a group of newly diagnosed men and then continuing to collect data from that same group every six months. Alternatively, they could test a wide variety of men who varied in terms of their time-since-diagnosis. They would then group these men according to stage (in six-month intervals) and compare the groups in terms of their social support needs. This would be a cross-sectional approach.

The relative advantages and disadvantages of each approach are fairly obvious. Longitudinal research features fewer confounding variables than does cross-sectional research. This is because, in cross-sectional designs, there will be more differences between the groups than just time-since-diagnosis. Since it is impossible to randomly assign people to these groups, researchers have to do their best to keep track of these other differences, such as age, severity of disease, marital status, and so on, by either matching their groups carefully or perhaps taking these variables out of their analysis. On the other hand, researchers using a longitudinal approach will compare the same group of men at six months, one year, and so on. While there will be some changes within the group in terms of severity of disease, marital status, and other variables, the differences across time will be fewer than would be expected between groups in the cross-sectional design. Also, in the longitudinal study the group will *age together*. This means that historical events, medical breakthroughs, and so on will occur at the same time for all participants.

On the other hand, longitudinal research is much more time consuming, logistically difficult, and more expensive. It is time consuming, of course, because many health problems take a long time to develop. This is good for our health but not so good for our research. Also, people don't live their lives for the convenience of longitudinal studies. They move from one city to another, they marry and change their names, they may even go to jail. For these and many other reasons, keeping a cohort together can be difficult. Just ask someone who has tried to organize a high school reunion.

Of course, one major reason for attrition in longitudinal cohorts is that people die. Researchers doing longitudinal research need to know the circumstances of these deaths. Exactly when did they occur, and what were the official causes? If you were trying to answer these questions, you would need access to death certificates and possibly other medical records. Imagine trying to contact one of your participants for his six-month data collection in the prostate cancer study only to find that he had died, and then, when you ask his wife for the cause of death she says "old age," or "he lost his will to live." When pressing these individuals for further details, such as whether the cancer had metastasized (spread), there is no guarantee that they will be forthcoming, and this lack of information can come after monitoring the patient for years. Certainly, you wouldn't give up at this point, but you can see that data collection can become very labour intensive.

If we wish to monitor people's health over long periods of time, longitudinal research is the ideal, though it requires rather extensive resources. There is, however, a shortcut that can save time and effort: starting at the *end* of the timeline and moving *backward*—in other words, taking people who have developed medical conditions, or who have died from them, and tracing their histories to find variables that might explain how they came to have that condition. This is called **retrospective research**. Its advantages are clear in

longitudinal research: experimental design in which researchers follow one group over time to chart their changes.

cross-sectional research: comparison of two or more groups that differ according to stage of life.

retrospective research: researchers study people who have developed medical conditions, or who have died from them, and trace their histories to find variables that might explain how they came to have that condition.

terms of convenience. Unfortunately, though, like so many shortcuts in research, there is a tradeoff between convenience and scientific rigour.

A classic example of this trade-off surfaces when researchers attempt to determine a possible causal relationship between mood and cancer. If it were discovered that cancer patients are more likely to be depressed, who would be surprised? The most likely assumption is that having cancer makes people more depressed. If this work is to provide evidence for the opposite causal direction—that mood increases risk for cancer or makes cancer progress more quickly—it simply cannot be retrospective. Instead, it must be *prospective*. This means that the researchers must conduct a longitudinal study in which participants begin disease-free (or are newly diagnosed).

COMMON FLAWS IN HEALTH PSYCHOLOGY RESEARCH

It is entirely possible that people change their behaviour when they know they are in a psychology study. They try to assess what is expected of them and either comply with that expectation or violate it. The implicit expectations that participants hold are called **demand characteristics** (Orne, 1962; Whitehouse, Orne, & Dinges, 2002). They refer to participants' beliefs about how they are "supposed" to respond. For example, what might be the demand characteristics when measuring patients' anxiety in a waiting room before they go in for a procedure in nuclear medicine? Possibly, such patients might think that a strong and mature person doesn't experience anxiety. Then, when you ask these patients to complete an anxiety questionnaire that features direct-item questions like "Do you feel tense?" they may say, "No" because that is consistent with the perceived demands of the situation. On the other hand, the patients might think, "This is obviously a study about anxiety in waiting rooms, and this nice person who has asked me to complete this questionnaire is looking for anxiety, so I'll cooperate and say that I am experiencing it." Either way, the *validity* of the measure is compromised, because it is not measuring anxiety any more. Now it is measuring people's perceptions of what is expected. Demand characteristics are reduced by creating less direct measures and by assuring the participant that a wide range of responses is expected and that their responses will be kept confidential.

It is possible that simply *receiving attention* is medicinal. If this is true, then it poses some problems for researchers, since every experimental group in health psychology research receives attention. To account for the extent to which the effect of an intervention is due to the *placebo effect* of attention, researchers often include a **placebo condition**. In this condition, people are given general attention but not the specific intervention that constitutes the independent variable.

The potential for **experimenter bias** exists when a person who knows the hypothesis interacts with participants or interprets qualitative data. It means simply that this knowledge affects participants' responses or qualitative data interpretation. It is especially problematic when the researcher has a *vested interest* in the outcome of the study. If a researcher believes that anxiety is a problem for people about to go through medical procedures, then he or she can interact with the participant in such a way that anxiety is either induced or at least expected. This won't necessarily be done consciously, but it can have a powerful effect all the same.

demand characteristics: beliefs held by people when they know that they are in a psychology study; beliefs about what is expected of them or how they are "supposed" to respond.

placebo condition: a study condition in which participants are given general attention, and perhaps an inert pseudo-medication, but not the specific intervention that is the independent variable of the study.

experimenter bias: an experimental construct flaw; the person who interacts with participants or interprets qualitative data has knowledge that affects participants' responses or the interpretation of qualitative data.

Some of the most extensive longitudinal, prospective research investigating cancer-prone personality types has been criticized because the principal investigators did much of the interviewing that yielded the personality types (Amelang, 1997). Attempts to replicate studies substantiating the claim that there is a cancer-prone personality have often been unsuccessful. The original investigators have countered that the collection of personality data at the outset of the study must be done in a particular way for it to yield information on the cancer-prone type (Grossarth-Maticek, Eysenck, & Vetter, 1997). The reply to this claim, of course, is that the personality typing is the result of experimenter bias rather than of interviewer skill. The way to avoid experimenter bias is, whenever possible, to use people to collect data who are *blind* to the hypothesis or at least blind to which group a participant has been placed in. In this case, *blind* simply means unaware.

People who take part in health psychology research must consent to do so. This is essential for ethical reasons. Nonetheless, it can result in a problem called **sampling bias**. This means that some variable or factor is shared by the people who agree to take part in the study, which makes them somehow different from the population the researchers are studying. The most common form of this bias occurs because there is a certain type of person who is more likely to volunteer for a particular study, making some sampling bias unavoidable. The best that can be done is to have a large sample of participants and hope that the sample is representative, or to somehow ascertain characteristics of those who choose not to participate so that you can show that they do not differ in important ways from those who did take part.

sampling bias: situation in which the people who take part in a study are different somehow from the population the researchers are studying.

ETHICAL CONSIDERATIONS IN HEALTH PSYCHOLOGY RESEARCH

Throughout this module, we have made reference to the ethics of research. All research must be conducted ethically, and this is especially true for research with people concerning their health. Universities and other institutions supporting this kind of research have research ethics boards (REBs). A research ethics board is defined by the Canada's Tri-Council for research funding as "a multidisciplinary committee established by an institution to undertake the ethics review of research projects involving humans developed or undertaken within that institution." (Tri-Council Policy Statement: Ethical Conduct for Research Involving Humans). One of the best places to learn about research ethics is the Tri-Council's Policy Statement (TCPS) tutorial on research ethics. You can find this at www.pre.ethics.gc.ca/english/tutorial/welcome.cfm. The tutorial lists the following important considerations:

- *Requirement for Free and Informed Consent.* Individuals are generally presumed to have the capacity to make free and informed decisions. Free and informed consent should be sought from potential research subjects or their representatives.

- *Respect for Vulnerable Persons.* Individuals with diminished competence and/or decision-making capacity are considered vulnerable. The interests of the vulnerable individuals should be protected.

- *Respect for Privacy and Confidentiality.* The access, control, and dissemination of personal information of research subjects should be protected.

- *Respect for Justice and Inclusiveness.* The benefits and burdens of research should be fairly distributed across society. Ethics review should have fair standards and procedures.

- *Balancing Harms and Benefits*. The foreseeable harms associated with the research should not outweigh the anticipated benefits.
- *Minimizing Harm*. Harm to research subjects should be avoided, prevented, or minimized.
- *Maximizing Benefit*. The benefits of research for the subjects themselves or for society as a whole should be maximized.

Each of these considerations is very relevant to research in health psychology. In health care settings, for example, people are considered vulnerable and in some ways "captive." Informed consent, confidentiality, and privacy must be managed carefully. In these settings, people must be assured that the quality of their care will be unaffected by their decision to participate in research. At the same time, the *nature* of that care might constitute one or more of the variables being studied. As such, the potential benefits and harms must be clearly explained before consent is given and people cannot feel coerced to participate.

As you were reading about randomized clinical trials, did you wonder about the people who were randomized into the control group? Would they be missing out on a potentially beneficial treatment by the luck of randomization? Conversely, would those in the treatment group potentially be exposed to a treatment that might be harmful? These are some of the important ethical considerations for this kind of study. It is why the progress of people in the treatment condition is carefully monitored. If the benefits are proven, then people in the control condition are typically offered the same treatment. On the other hand, if the treatment is proving harmful, the study might be stopped by the researchers.

FOCUSED MODULE B
Epidemiology: What Can Be Learned from the SARS Outbreak in Canada?

On February 23, 2003 a 78-year-old woman took a flight from Hong Kong to Toronto. When she did, what would normally have been an everyday occurrence changed the lives of many people living in Canada. This was because the woman was suffering from Severe Acute Respiratory Syndrome (SARS). When she arrived in Toronto, she became the first case of SARS in Canada. What followed was an outbreak of this infectious disease that, in Canada, resulted in 250 probable cases and 40 deaths by mid-June of 2003.[1]

An outbreak such as this, featuring an illness that is new to the country and virtually new to the world, demands fast and decisive action. Before cures can be found, the nature of the disease itself must be determined. The detective work on this falls primarily to epidemiologists, who are trained to trace disease patterns and draw conclusions regarding the cause of the disease and how it is spread.

Epidemiology literally means "the study of epidemics." More specifically, it is the study of incidence rates, prevalence rates, and locations of health-related phenomena. Epidemiologists chart *patterns* of health and disease (primarily disease) across populations and geographic areas, studying the origin and distribution of health problems (Cockerham, 1998). Epidemiology is truly biopsychosocial in nature. People working in the field include everyone from sociologists to physicians to meteorologists (for such things as air pollution data). Psychologists also work with epidemiological data. As we will see in this module, a basic understanding of illness patterns is very helpful to health psychologists.

THE LANGUAGE OF EPIDEMIOLOGY

To do their work, epidemiologists often start with a single case and trace it back to its starting point. From there, they determine how widespread the problem has become. They then try to identify factors that all people with that problem share. The goal is to identify causes so the problem can be eliminated or at least controlled. In doing this work, epidemiologists use terminology that health psychologists need to understand.

For example, a **case** is one instance of the problem. The **index case** is the first identified case. In the SARS outbreak, the 78-year-old woman who arrived from Hong Kong was the index case. When she was admitted to hospital, she was visited by her family. As a result, six of them contracted SARS. Three of these family members visited their physician, who was then infected as well. One of the family members (Case B) went to a hospital emergency department on March 7, 2003. During his treatment in ER, he transmitted the disease to two paramedics, a firefighter, and four hospital staff. Three members of Case C's family also contracted SARS.

case: one instance of a medical problem.

index case: the first identified instance of a medical problem.

---

[1]Details regarding the SARS outbreak in Toronto have been taken from a Health Canada Report entitled "Epi-Update: Interim Report on the SARS Outbreak in the Greater Toronto Area, Ontario, Canada, April 24, 2003." Accessed on November 26, 2006, from www.phac-aspc.gc.ca/sars-sras/index.html

incidence rate: the number of new cases of a health problem in a set period of time.

prevalence: in epidemiology, the total number of cases that exist at any given time.

point prevalence: the number of cases of a medical problem found at a given point in time.

lifetime prevalence: the total number of people who have ever had a particular medical problem, even if the problem went away or they died from it.

Soon, other hospitals became involved, as did groups of people who were believed to have been exposed to probable cases outside hospital settings. As a result, the number of cases in Toronto increased dramatically over a short period of time. In the language of epidemiology, this meant an increase in the **incidence rate**, which is the number of new cases of the problem in a set period of time. For example, if an epidemiologist says that there were 30 cases of X reported in the past two weeks, that would be its incidence rate.

Epidemiologists use incidence rates to determine whether a problem is on the rise or if it is waning. The word *outbreak*, as in SARS *outbreak*, often refers to incidence rates. On the other hand, **prevalence** refers to the total number of cases that exist at any given time, including existing and new cases. **Point prevalence** refers to prevalence at a given point in time. **Lifetime prevalence** refers to the total number of people who have ever had the problem, even if the problem went away or if they died from it. Cancer rates are often reported in terms of lifetime prevalence, which presents the proportion of people who have ever had the disease, for example, as the number of cases found per 100 000 people.

There are many important psychological issues related to outbreaks. For example, it is often the case that the general public exaggerates the danger, creating a certain degree of hysteria. For the SARS outbreak, Canada decided to report both *probable* and *suspect* cases. The former refers to people who are showing all the defining symptoms and have been exposed to the disease. The latter refers to people who are displaying some of the symptoms but very possibly have not been exposed. Suspect cases rarely become probable cases. In British Columbia, there were four probable cases and 46 suspect cases. Because of this reporting strategy, the general public is presented with numbers that inaccurately reflect the risk of the disease. Also, the media might report lifetime prevalence numbers. These numbers would include people who had SARS and are recovered. This also results in an inflation of the magnitude of the problem.

This is not to say that SARS was not serious. It just wasn't as serious as some members of the general public came to believe. Some people began wearing surgical masks to protect themselves from a disease they had very little chance of being exposed to and despite the fact that the masks probably did nothing to protect the wearer.

As we learned in chapter 12 (Health Promotion) fear does not always motivate people to engage in healthy behaviours. In the case of outbreak-induced panic, there is no guarantee that people will report symptoms promptly. Instead, they may try to carry on with their normal lives and risk the health of others by riding public transit and coming into contact with many other people.

THE STEPS INVOLVED IN EPIDEMIOLOGICAL RESEARCH

agent: in epidemiology, the means by which a disease spreads.

host: in epidemiology, the carrier of an agent of disease.

The first step in epidemiological research is to establish a pattern of the problem and identify **agents** (Cockerham, 1998). These are the means by which the problem spreads. There are five types of agent: biological, nutritional, chemical, physical, and social/behavioural. For SARS, the agent was biological (coronavirus).

After an agent has been identified, epidemiologists look for **hosts**. These are the carriers of the agents. In human disease, human hosts are those people who are most susceptible to a given agent. Epidemiologists can determine if a given agent is travelling through a certain age group or perhaps through people who have been in a certain area. For SARS, older people were most vulnerable. The 78-year-old woman who represented the index case had come recently from the Metropole Hotel in the Kowloon district of Hong Kong. This hotel was the site of many cases of SARS.

In addition to hosts, there are other ways that agents are transmitted. For example, there are **vectors**, which are living organisms that can transfer an agent from one host to another (Prescott, Harley, & Klein, 1999). A good example of a vector is the *Anopheles* mosquito, which carries malaria. Also, there are **vehicles**—non-living media involved in the transmission of an agent (Prescott, Harley, & Klein, 1999). Biologists and epidemiologists describe transmission by way of vehicles as being water-borne, food-borne, or air-borne, depending on the vehicle. For example, tuberculosis adheres to dust and then becomes air-borne (Prescott, Harley, & Klein, 1999). SARS could be transmitted through air-borne droplets.

vector: in epidemiology, a living organism that can transfer an agent from one host to another.

vehicle: in epidemiology, a non-living medium involved in the transmission of an agent.

The final step epidemiologists take is to propose strategies for control of the agent. Quarantine is a common step. After the final step, the process starts again to see if there are other agents and hosts or if the control measures have worked.

TRACING THE SPREAD OF AIDS

We have looked at some of the epidemiology of SARS. AIDS is another disease that epidemiologists have played an important role in attempting to control. The first known cases of AIDS emerged in New York, San Francisco, and Los Angeles in 1979 (Cockerham, 1998). These cases attracted attention in part because they were defined by rare forms of cancer, such as Kaposi's sarcoma, and a particular type of pneumonia called *Pneumocystis carinii*. By 1981, physicians' reports about the disease were coming into the Centers for Disease Control in Atlanta, Georgia, and epidemiologists went to work identifying hosts and agents (Cockerham, 1998). At this time, the *prevalence* was about 50 cases. However, through the early 1980s, the *incidence* rate began to skyrocket. Within three years, the number of cases went from 50 to over 4900 in the United States. By 1995, the number had risen to over 500 000 (Cockerham, 1998).

At first, it was thought that the *agent* was a drug used by some gay men to enhance sexual experience, but interview data ruled this out when it revealed that men who used the drug were not infected with AIDS (Cockerham, 1998). Then, when a number of intravenous drug users and one transfusion patient (a baby in San Francisco) contracted AIDS, the search for an agent became biological; that is, epidemiologists started suspecting a virus. The tracing of sexual partners as hosts supported this hypothesis. This tracing of sexual partners of those first showing symptoms of AIDS in North America led back, eventually, to one person. This was the so-called patient zero, a flight attendant from Canada named Gaetan Dugas (Taylor, 1999). After being located, Dugas estimated that he had had 2500 sexual partners in the 10 years prior to being identified (Taylor, 1999).

An analysis of the dramatic spread of the AIDS epidemic in sub-Saharan Africa, where, in 2007, 68 percent of all HIV-positive individuals lived (*AIDS Epidemic Update*, 2009), illustrates how sociological and anthropological factors can help to explain epidemiological data. In Africa, unlike North America, AIDS is spread primarily through sexual intercourse among heterosexuals. The economy of central Africa is such that there are many male migrant workers (Cockerham, 1998). Their movement from place to place facilitates the spread of the virus. In general, women in central Africa do not have the power to demand condom use or abstinence. From this analysis, we can see that economic, geographic, social, and cultural factors explain the proliferation of AIDS in central Africa (Cockerham, 1998). The good news is that programs to curb the AIDS epidemic are making headway by addressing these and other factors. For example, the national HIV prevalence rate has declined in two sub-Saharan countries—Kenya and Zimbabwe (Joint United Nations Programs on HIV/AIDS, 2006).

FOCUSED MODULE C
Complementary and Alternative Medicine (CAM)

Tyrell Dueck was a boy from Saskatchewan who died of cancer when he was 13 years old. For religious reasons, Tyrell's parents refused the treatment prescribed by oncologists, which would have involved chemotherapy and possible leg amputation. A Saskatchewan court ordered them to follow the oncologist's treatment, but they refused. Instead, they took Tyrell to a clinic in Tijuana, Mexico, where he received treatments using laetrile and shark cartilage. Unfortunately, the treatments were unsuccessful, and Tyrell returned to Canada, where he died in a Saskatchewan hospital.

The story of Tyrell Dueck reminds us that not everyone embraces the Western medical establishment. The use of medical treatments that are not the product of what has been called conventional medical science continues to grow in popularity. For this reason, health psychologists must develop an understanding of the many issues associated with the use of complementary and alternative therapies.

THE LANGUAGE OF CAM

Defining what is meant by *complementary* and *alternative* is no easy task. At one point, these were defined as therapies that were not normally part of medical school curricula, but these curricula have changed enough to make that definition obsolete (Thorne, Paterson, Russell, & Schultz, 2002). More comprehensive definitions contrast complementary and alternative medicine (CAM) with that which is dominant within a health care system or culture (Achilles, 2000). Such definitions say more about what CAM is *not* than what it is.

A number of different terms have been used to identify treatments that fall outside normative Western medical practice. Each carries its own set of connotations and implied set of values. As such, the terminology of the area makes for a good starting point.

We have used the terms *complementary* and *alternative* in the heading to this module. They are the terms that are commonly used to describe the field but, although the terms are used together, they do not mean the same thing. **Complementary treatment** is used in conjunction with so-called conventional treatments (National Institute of Health, 2002). This definition of complementary treatment implies that patients must be aware of potential interactions between the conventional treatment and the complementary one, since they are being used simultaneously.

Alternative treatment is the term given to treatments that are used instead of conventional treatments (National Institute of Health, 2002). Its use implies that the patient has either rejected conventional treatment, given up on it, or perhaps is ignorant of it. Some may infer that the term *alternative* carries a certain attractive value, as in "viable alternative," or even "better alternative." In keeping with this, it has been suggested that proponents of such treatments were the ones to coin the term (Beyerstein, 1997). In contrast, others may consider the term to be pejorative, implying that such treatments are not mainstream and, as such, are marginalized. In other words, the implication is that they are not a patient's best choice, but are an "alternative."

complementary treatment: treatment that is used in conjunction with allopathic treatment.

alternative treatment: any intervention or treatment that is not allopathic.

Others make the distinction between *traditional* and *non-traditional* treatments. However, this distinction is usually rejected by anthropologists because it implies that there is a single tradition—that is, conventional Western medicine. This contradicts the fact that many remedies called "alternative" have been around for centuries. Still others distinguish between *conventional* and *unconventional* therapy (UT). Some authors have argued that *unconventional* is the least pejorative of all the terms used to describe these treatments (Fitch et al., 1999). Not everyone interprets the word *unconventional* in neutral terms, however. A term that has come into use more recently to describe complementary or alternative therapies is **holistic therapy** (Schreiber, 2005). While it is possible for conventional treatments to be holistic in nature, this term is commonly used to contrast it with *biomedical* treatments.

Finally, it has been suggested that the most useful dichotomy is between treatments that work and those that don't. From this point of view, other terms, such as *alternative*, *unconventional*, *traditional*, or the less-often-used *frontier* are unnecessary.

The conclusion that we can draw from this dilemma is that there is probably no single term that everyone is going to be comfortable with regarding such therapies. We have chosen the CAM terminology because, at the very least, those terms draw a useful distinction between treatment followed in conjunction with conventional Western regimens and treatment used instead of conventional Western regimens.

holistic therapy: a term that has come into use to describe complementary or alternative therapies that acknowledge treatment of the whole person.

HOW PREVALENT IS CAM?

If complementary and alternative therapies were rarely used, they would not be such an important topic of discussion; however, this certainly isn't the case. A study conducted in 1999 revealed that 70 percent of Canadians had used one or more natural health products in the past six months (de Bruyn, 2000). Forty-six percent of patients with inflammatory bowel disease reported using CAM (Hilsden, Verhoef, Best, & Pocobelli, 2003) compared to 35 percent of patients with fractures (Sprague et al., 2007). There is a discrepancy, though, between the number of people pursuing CAM and the number consulting a CAM practitioner. Only 24 percent of Canadians did the latter in 1999 (de Bruyn, 2000). For serious illnesses, such as head and neck cancer, it has been shown that 23 percent of patients had sought CAM for their cancer and 39 percent had used CAM more generally (Warrick et al., 1999). Another study found that 46 percent of parents whose children had cancer were using CAM for their child (Gagnon & Recklitis, 2003).

A study of brain tumour patients in southern Alberta found that 24 percent of them were using complementary therapy (Verhoef et al., 1999). Interestingly, the researchers in this study became interested in CAM when they discovered that some of their patients had a distinctive orange colour on their hands. It turned out that these patients were using beta carotene as a complementary treatment.

From all these studies, we can conclude that CAM is anything but rare. Indeed, it is likely that these figures represent an under-reporting of CAM use. The Canadian study of CAM use among people with fractures discovered that 55 percent did not discuss their CAM use with their orthopaedic surgeon (Sprague, et al., 2007). In the southern Alberta study, 45 percent of the patients said their doctors were aware of their alternative therapy use. This means that practitioners and health psychologists need to know more about CAM in terms of its perceived effectiveness and the reasons why patients pursue it, from what some patients call "personal luxuries" (Bishop, Yardley & Lewith, 2008) to what is perceive to be a last hope. This need is underscored by evidence that the use of CAM is increasing steadily (de Bruyn, 2000). Also, CAM is big business. In Canada, it has been estimated that $3.8 billion was spent on CAM in 1996 and 1997 (de Bruyn, 2000).

SOME EXAMPLES OF CAM

It is important to realize that CAM covers a diverse collection of treatments. These range from the conservative, such as certain lifestyle changes (exercise and relaxation training), to what Beyerstein (1997) has called the "patently absurd" (p. 149), such as crystal healing. Of the many substances that may be prescribed as part of CAM regimens, some are herbal (such as echinacea), some are animal or vegetable derivatives (such as shark cartilage or mushrooms), some are macrobiotic, and others are vitamins (as in the beta carotene used by brain tumour patients). Some other CAM procedures do not require the ingestion of substances. These include such treatments as acupuncture and various forms of homeopathy (Verhoef et al., 1999).

HOW EFFECTIVE IS CAM?

Research on the effectiveness of complementary and alternative therapies varies considerably in its rigour and comprehensiveness from one therapy to the next. In general, these therapies are not well researched in terms of methodology or number of studies. This is gradually changing, however. The "gold standard" by which therapies of any type tend to be judged is the random clinical trial (RCT), and we are now seeing more RCT studies published assessing complementary and alternative therapies (Holdcraft, Assefi, & Buchwald, 2003; Weiger et al., 2002). (See Focused Module A, Conducting Research in Health Psychology, for a review of RCT logic.) There are those, however, who argue that RCT methodology does not always provide a valid assessment of the potential benefits of CAM (Verhoef et al., 2005; Verhoef, Casebeer, & Hilsden, 2002).

There has been a great deal of research on the vitamins A, C, and E and their potential role in the prevention and treatment of cancer (though considerably more on prevention than on treatment) (Kaegi, 1998a). Since it is widely accepted that a diet rich in fresh fruits and vegetables reduces the risk of some cancers and that these foods contain vitamins A, C, and E, it seems reasonable to investigate the potential of supplements of these vitamins as cancer treatments. Further indirect support for their use in cancer treatment comes from studies that have reported an enhancement in immune functioning associated with them. These effects are more common for vitamins A and C than for E. It also must be noted, however, that the dosages required to bring about real therapeutic effects, as opposed to measurable immune system enhancement, might be too high to be practical or even safe (Weiger et al., 2002). It appears that more research is required in this area.

For practitioners, some helpful literature reviews have been produced (Weiger et al., 2002). Also, resources such as the Cochrane Collection produce many useful reviews (see www.cochrane.org). The conclusions from these reviews can be placed generally into one of three categories: (1) a therapy has been proven beneficial and should be encouraged or prescribed, (2) a therapy has been proven harmful and should be discouraged, or (3) a therapy has not been proven beneficial or harmful. Among the harmful therapies are those that interact poorly or even dangerously with other therapies. For example, high-dose vitamin therapy can cause problems when taken concurrently with radiation or chemotherapy (Weiger et al., 2002).

The last conclusion, that a therapy is neither harmful nor beneficial, is a very common one in CAM studies. In these cases, the practitioner is left to decide if there are non-medical benefits to the patient's use of the therapy. We will discuss these in the next section when we talk about reasons why people choose CAM. Often, there are such benefits in terms of the patient's sense of control and optimism, though false hopes can be a justified concern for practitioners.

A paper in the *Canadian Medical Association Journal* entitled "A Patient's Guide to Choosing Unconventional Therapies" (Kaegi, 1998b) generated debate among its readers. In it, Kaegi provided detailed advice for the potential consumer of what she called "unconventional therapies." For example, she cautioned people to do the research before choosing, to ask practitioners for their credentials, to check for possible interactions with conventional therapy before committing to unconventional therapy, and to know one's comfort level regarding such therapy. This all seems like sound advice except that, for patients, doing the research isn't as easy as it sounds. Kaegi herself generally concluded that the research on the treatments she reviewed was still inconclusive. Others have argued that patients usually aren't assertive enough to ask for a practitioner's credentials or, if shown them, don't have the expertise to evaluate them (Tannock & Warr, 1998).

WHO USES CAM AND WHY

Warrick and colleagues' (1999) analysis of head and neck cancer patients found more use in patients who were younger, had post-secondary education, and were in upper income brackets. These findings are consistent with other similar analyses (e.g., Sprague, et al., 2007). In their study of brain tumour patients in southern Alberta, Verhoef and colleagues (1999) found that alternative therapy was more commonly used among younger patients.

Why do patients pursue alternative therapies? The reasons for using alternative therapies will, of course, vary considerably from person to person and from condition to condition. The Alberta brain tumour patients tended to talk about needing to take charge of their treatment, and pursuing alternative therapies provided them with the feeling they were doing that (Verhoef et al., 1999). Other studies have also found that increasing one's sense of personal control is a motivating factor in alternative treatment choice (e.g., Seidl & Stewart, 1998; Sprague et al., 2007). Menopausal patients have said that some alternative therapies are more natural and holistic. On a related theme, these same patients expressed concerns with the possible side effects and risks associated with Western scientific paradigms. Still others reported that they have found CAM to be a more user-friendly approach to health (Seidl & Stewart, 1998).

Taken collectively, these reasons depict a patient who is interested in self-care and wants to manage it. As such, the use of CAM is not merely the result of rejection of conventional medicine (Thorne et al., 2002; Verhoef & White, 2002). This is an important point for practitioners to keep in mind.

Other research (Nam et al., 1999) indicates that people who attend support groups may be more likely to use complementary or alternative therapy. The study looked at men who either had prostate cancer or were considered at high risk for the disease, as defined by family history and abnormal prostate specific–antigen (PSA) scores. Among the high-risk men, 80 percent of those attending support groups were using complementary therapies, compared to 26 percent who were interviewed in a clinic. Of all the patients using CAM, 24 percent did not tell their urologist they were doing so.

One explanation for the effect of support group attendance on CAM usage might be that information about CAM is more available to support-group attendees. Consistent with this possibility, another study of prostate cancer patients discovered that attendees of support groups were significantly more likely to cite fellow patients as their main source of informational support; non-attendees, however, cited medical staff in this category (Poole et al., 2001).

Psychology is not the only social science that has made a significant contribution to our understanding of health and health care. Anthropology, economics, geography, and sociology, just to name a few, have also done so. In this module, we look at the sociology of health and illness, which dovetails well with psychology to help us understand the forces that shape our health.

Sociology is "the study of social causes and consequences of behaviour" (Cockerham, 1998, p. 1). Sociologists study groups, institutions, and society. According to Clarke (2000), medical sociology is "the study of the ways the institutionalized medical system constructs what it deems to be illness out of what is recognized as signs and symptoms, and constitutes its response to such 'illness' through the treatments it prescribes" (p. 4).

Health psychologists, who tend to study health-related phenomena on a more individual level, can work well with medical sociologists. For example, in chapter 4 we explored psychoneuroimmunology (PNI), which is the study of the ways in which our psychological states might affect our health. Research in PNI reveals physiological reasons why stress can be unhealthy. It focuses on the cellular level—specifically, the workings of the immune system.

But what about some of the causes of that stress? Knowing what you know about PNI, would it surprise you to learn that illness tends to follow unemployment trends? Probably not. However, as soon as we introduce trends of this type into the analysis, we are no longer working at a microscopic level. Now we are working at the level of medical sociology. Clarke (2000) asks why there is a moratorium on silicone breast implants in the United States and Canada (Holmich et al., 2003; Muller, 1996). Is it because of a biomedical discovery or because of mass social action? Medical sociologists would say that this development is due more to the latter than the former because, in fact, while certain risks have been clearly identified, biomedical research has not yielded conclusive findings regarding the relationship between systemic illnesses and breast implants (Health Canada, 2005a).

THE SICK ROLE

Roles are sets of behaviours, attributes, and expectations that are institutionally defined. For example, the institution of family yields the roles of father, mother, daughter, son, and so on. According to well-known sociologist Talcott Parsons (1951), the medical institution has created something called the **sick role**. People who legitimately adopt the sick role are temporarily exempt from their other roles. Because sick people can no longer perform their other roles adequately, the sick role was created to prevent social breakdown. We say that people adopting the sick role are *temporarily* exempt because the role is defined in such a way that people can't opt out of their other roles permanently and still keep the social organization functioning. Therefore, one defining characteristic of the sick

sick role: a status that, when temporarily and legitimately adopted, exempts people from their other roles.

role is that it can't be assumed indefinitely. Anyone who tries to do so will be given a different label—like *malingerer,* for example (Slovenko, 2006).

Roles carry with them certain rights and duties. People adopting the sick role have two duties. First, they must be trying to get well. Second, they should be seeking technically competent help and cooperating with the prescribed regimen. If someone were to shirk one of these duties, he or she would lose the rights of the sick role. There are two such rights. First, as we have said, a person adopting the sick role is temporarily exempt from other responsibilities. Second, the person is not responsible for his or her condition, and so can't be blamed for his or her incapacitation.

Parsons' notion of the sick role has come under criticism over the years, though it has been argued that the construct is still of value (Williams, 2005). One criticism addresses the fact that the extent to which a person is held responsible for his or her incapacitation varies by condition. Also, with today's emphasis on health promotion and healthy lifestyles, people are being held more personally responsible for their health. This should mean that fewer people can legitimately adopt the sick role. Also, some people associate certain diseases with a person's moral worth; thus, people with such diseases might have a more difficult time adopting the sick role. Indeed, it is generally the case that people with socially stigmatized diseases (such as sexually transmitted diseases) are not afforded sick-role status (Clarke, 2000).

You will remember that people must be trying to get well to be given sick-role status. But what about those people who may want to get well but cannot? These people must make long-term adaptations and in so doing come to take on another role, such as "disabled," or "impaired," or "chronically ill."

Sociologists refer to a person's *master status.* This is the status that reflects the person's most prominent position in society. This may stem from such things as his or her occupation, family role, or position in the community. A person's disease status should not become his or her master status, because the sick-role status normally intervenes. However, because AIDS is stigmatizing and chronic, people with this disease often find that their disease status does become their master status. Disease status overwhelms other aspects of their identity, and this can make coping with the disease all the more difficult.

Criticism of the sick role construct has also been levelled at the duty to cooperate with technically competent help. This duty is often interpreted in such a way that, to be granted sick-role status, a person must accept the biomedical model. According to this interpretation, people seeking what are currently called complementary or alternative treatments would not be afforded the sick role. If the Western medical establishment is the gatekeeper of sick-role status, then this institution becomes even more powerful and dominant.

Indeed, from the perspective of medical sociologists, the medical establishment is seen as an agent of social control. There are at least two forms that this control takes. First, it dictates the conferring of sick-role status. Second, from this perspective, sickness is viewed as a form of deviation from the norm, and sick people need to be brought back to that norm. In what is often called Western society, the medical establishment holds the responsibility for doing this. As an indication of this, think of conditions that are viewed today as illnesses that were once considered to be religious or legal transgressions. (Hint: some of the best examples come from psychiatry.)

CONFLICT THEORY AND THE RIGHTING OF INJUSTICES

conflict theory: school of thought in sociology claiming that structures do not simply exist; rather, they exist *in conflict*.

Another school of thought in sociology argues that structures do not simply exist; rather, they exist in *conflict*. This is an important assumption of **conflict theory**. This theory has a long history in medical sociology. As early as 1845, Friedrich Engels, a collaborator with Karl Marx, made the point that inequality in living conditions and the emergence of capitalism in England had negative effects on people's health. To maximize profits, companies paid their workers poorly, forcing them to live in slums. These living conditions became breeding grounds for infectious diseases, such as typhoid. Conflict theory, then, can be very useful when trying to understand socioeconomic differences in health status.

Modern multinational corporations have been accused of exploitation that is not dissimilar to that practised by their nineteenth-century counterparts. Clarke (2000) points out that the Great Lakes, which supply drinking water for over 40 million people in Canada and the United States, also serve as a dumping site for industrial and municipal waste. Clarke also reminds us that it is the poor, those who cannot afford to drink bottled water or move to affluent suburbs well removed from toxic locations, who suffer the worst health effects of this pollution. Proponents of conflict theory might also argue that the state tends to deflect responsibility for ill health away from itself and focuses it on the individual. Health then becomes a "commodity with a certain value in the marketplace" (Clarke, 2000, p. 28). These theorists would argue that research conducted by and funded by institutions within that marketplace, such as pharmaceutical companies, cannot be expected to produce findings that are self-critical—hence the need for health-related research from the social sciences and humanities.

SYMBOLIC INTERACTIONISM: UNCOVERING SUBJECTIVE MEANING IN HEALTH AND HEALTH CARE

symbolic interactionism: sociological theory that people's interpretations of their interactions and the events of their lives go well beyond the actual words used, or in the case of health-related events, the diagnosis they are given.

transcript analysis: recordings of interactions with patients that are transcribed to paper and analyzed; often used by medical sociologists adopting a symbolic interactionist perspective.

Sociologists also take a more microscopic look at social factors by analyzing the interactions between people and by interviewing people to determine the meaning they attach to events. When these researchers adopt the perspective of **symbolic interactionism**, they are assuming that people's interpretations of their interactions and the events of their lives go well beyond the actual words used or, in the case of health-related events, the diagnoses they are given. As is the case with much of sociology, another assumption here is that reality is *socially constructed* rather than objective. In other words, we piece together our version of the world by interacting with others and construing our own interpretation of that world.

Medical sociologists using symbolic interactionism often use **transcript analysis** in their research. As the term implies, they record interactions with patients, then transcribe them to paper. They are particularly interested in the pauses between turns in a conversation, which can be very meaningful in an interaction between a physician and a patient. Another research method is the in-depth interview. For example, a person with arthritis may be interviewed at length to determine the meaning the person attaches to having that illness. It may be associated with aging, frustration, loss of control, or being pitied by others. The possibilities are numerous. The point is that it is *the person with the illness* who determines the meaning.

Researchers adopting this approach make a distinction between disease and illness. **Disease** refers to the physical pathology. **Illness** refers to the subjective experience of having that pathology. From this perspective, it is possible for two people to have the same disease but different illnesses. This distinction is rarely made in medical settings. It is the *illness* that sociologists try to understand. For example, two people with very similar tissue damage from a heart attack may have very different subjective experiences as a result. One may be motivated to re-prioritize his or her life and make the most of each day; another might live each successive day in fear and become an invalid unnecessarily.

Psychologists who use the theory of reasoned action, introduced in chapter 1, may do well to consider the tenets of symbolic interaction. You may remember that one important component of the theory of reasoned action is social norms—the collection of beliefs regarding what other people would do and would want us to do. Sociologists would remind us that, by interacting with others to establish these social norms, we are also constructing a social reality. The person then decides on a course of action based on this constructed meaning of the illness.

disease: physical pathology.

illness: the subjective experience of having a disease.

FEMINIST THEORY AS APPLIED TO HEALTH AND HEALTH CARE

In chapter 7, we discussed gender issues related to health care, specifically from the perspective of the practitioner. We could have adopted a more sociological perspective on those issues by applying feminist theory. In terms of health care, feminist theory focuses on at least three important topics. First, it makes salient the fact that women's health concerns are both biologically and socially different from men's. For example, stress-related medical conditions are different for women because the causes of their stress can be different. Women's stress is more likely to stem from **role strain**, in which a woman is expected to perform two or more roles that compete for her time and, in addition, may be in conflict with one another. This is compounded by the social fact that women still find themselves in subdominant positions, with little control compared to men.

role strain: stress as a result of the demands of multiple social roles, such as health care practitioner and mother.

A second topic concerns the fact that socially constructed meanings of health experiences have historically been male dominated. For example, one measure of the seriousness of an illness is the number of days a person misses from work. This is fairly easy to assess if that work takes place outside the home and is salaried. On the other hand, "days missed" are harder to quantify when the work is being done in the home. Traditionally, this situation has applied to women more than to men. More to the point, women may well argue that, when it comes to tasks like child rearing, there is no such thing as a "day missed," regardless of one's health.

Third, we know that the health care system has been male dominated. This can make it more difficult for women to find practitioners who can empathize with and legitimize their health concerns. Feminists have been vocal in their attempts to raise awareness regarding these three issues and to change the health care system accordingly. As a result, feminist theory has had a tangible impact on health care and, indeed, on health psychology. A good example is childbirth. Feminist theory would advocate for a system in which decisions regarding childbirth, such as whether to have a Caesarean section, are the domain of the woman giving birth (Beckett, 2005).

SUMMARY

Now that you have been introduced to medical sociology, think of the ways in which health psychologists and medical sociologists can collaborate. In what ways are the two fields similar? In what ways are they different? Clearly, they share a mutual concern for the improvement of health, as the World Health Organization defines health—not just the absence of disease, but the ability to live a life of reasonable quality. We hope that you can appreciate how sociologists and psychologists differ in their *unit of analysis*. For psychologists, it is the individual; for sociologists, it is people in groups, organizations, and societies. This isn't to say, of course, that psychologists aren't interested in social phenomena. However, the "bottom line" for psychologists tends to be how these phenomena affect the individual.

FOCUSED MODULE E
Aboriginal Health

In chapter 8, Chronic and Life-Threatening Illnesses, we made specific reference to Aboriginal health issues as they pertained to diabetes and HIV/AIDS. In this module, we will explore a wider range of Aboriginal health issues. There are many inequities and serious challenges that are revealed by this exploration—indeed, far more than we can adequately cover here.

WHO ARE CANADA'S ABORIGINAL PEOPLES?

Canada's Aboriginal population is not homogeneous. In fact, the term *Aboriginal* refers to a variety of groups in Canada. The language that is used, both officially and colloquially, to describe these groups carries its own collection of connotations. The language we will use here is derived from documents produced by Health Canada. These documents make reference to four groups under the general heading "Aboriginal"—First Nations people, who include North American Indians registered under the Indian Act; North American Indians not registered; Métis people; and Inuit people (*The Need for an Aboriginal Health Institute in Canada*, 2003). Some of the issues discussed under the heading of "Aboriginal Health" apply to all these groups. Some, however, do not. The population of Aboriginal groups is growing faster than the general population in Canada. The Aboriginal population is generally younger as a result. Thirty-eight percent of that population is under the age of 15, compared to 21 percent of Canada's general population. Many of the health challenges faced by our Aboriginal peoples, therefore, relate to youth.

HEALTH CHALLENGES

The health of all Canadians is affected considerably by what have been called **social determinants of health**. These include factors such as living conditions, education, and economics. Table E-1 lists nine prominent social determinants. In chapter 12, Health Promotion, we discussed health inequities existing in Canada today. Many of these inequities relate to social determinants of health. Thus, social determinants go a long way to explain why the health of our Aboriginal population is considerably poorer than that of other segments.

Figures from 2004 reveal that life expectancy for First Nations males is seven years shorter than for non-Aboriginal males, and First Nations females live an average of five years less than their non-Aboriginal counterparts (*Health Canada*, 2004). General violence, physical abuse, and sexual abuse are more common in Aboriginal communities, as are accidental deaths and injury among children. Add to this list infectious diseases, such as tuberculosis, which is ten times more prevalent in First Nations and Inuit populations (Health Canada, 2004). Further challenges are presented in the form of substance abuse, which members of Aboriginal communities recognize as a serious problem (*Literature Review: Evaluation Strategies in Aboriginal Substance Abuse Programs: A Discussion*, 2002).

All of these challenges are significant, though two have received increased attention because of their severity: children's health and diabetes. We looked at diabetes in the

social determinants of health: factors such as living conditions, education, and economics that affect the health of all Canadians.

Table E-1 Prominent Social Determinants of Health in Canada

- Income inequality
- Social inclusion and exclusion
- Employment and job security
- Working conditions
- Contribution of the social economy
- Early childhood care
- Education
- Food security
- Housing

Source: Public Health Agency of Canada. (2004). "The Social Determinants of Health: An Overview of the Implications for Policy and the Role of the Health Sector."

Aboriginal population in chapter 8 (refer to Box 8-1). Add to those statistics a University of Manitoba study showing that Type 2 diabetes is four times as prevalent among First Nations people in that province (Martens et al., 2002). Children's health is a particular concern in Aboriginal communities, where 50 percent of children live in poverty (*The Need for an Aboriginal Health Institute in Canada*, 2003). The good news is that infant mortality rates are declining in these communities, though they are still well above the Canadian average (*The Need for an Aboriginal Health Institute in Canada*, 2003). Injury and accident-related death rates are four times greater than for non-Aboriginal children. And suicide rates are significantly higher.

As we have mentioned, substance abuse is another major problem, though this varies depending upon which Aboriginal population is being studied. In some cases, general consumption of alcohol might be lower for a given group compared to the non-Aboriginal population; however, a concentrated percentage of that Aboriginal group might be drinking to excess (*Literature Review: Evaluation Strategies in Aboriginal Substance Abuse Programs: A Discussion*, 2002). Solvent use is a problem particular to youth. Recent data on solvent use are hard to come by, though studies in the mid-1980s conducted in Manitoba and Quebec revealed that two to three percent of Aboriginal youth were using solvents beyond an experimental level and that their median age was 12 to 13 years (Layne, 1987).

SOLVING THE PROBLEMS

What is being done to help Canada's Aboriginal population meet their health challenges? This is not a problem that governments can simply "throw money at," although funding is certainly necessary. Rather, solutions will be found by building partnerships among government, Aboriginal peoples, and Canada's population at large. These partnerships must work at the community level because the Aboriginal tradition is such that the well-being of the individual is rooted in the health of the community (*Volume III: Gathering Strength*, 1996). Many programs focused at the community level have been called for and initiated by such national organizations as the First Nations and Inuit Health Branch (FNIHB) and the Assembly of First Nations Health and Social Secretariat.

When you peruse Table E-2, you will find early childhood development is one of the priorities identified by the Assembly of First Nations. Programs addressing this priority could provide information regarding fetal alcohol syndrome (FAS) and fetal alcohol effect (FAE), problems that stem directly from the substance abuse problems we discussed earlier. FAS can result from alcohol consumption during pregnancy. It is manifest in a number of ways, including pre- or postnatal growth retardation, central nervous system abnormalities, and facial abnormalities (Robinson, Armstrong, Brendle-Moczuk, & Loock, 1992). FAE is typically less severe, featuring behavioural problems, such as hyperactivity, social problems, and learning disabilities. In fact, prenatal exposure to alcohol is now thought to be associated with more subtle problems in judgment and reasoning in people of otherwise normal intelligence (Robinson et al., 1992).

Table E-2 Assembly of First Nations Health Policy Areas

Area	Description
Diabetes	Promotion of awareness, including risk factors and the importance of healthy lifestyle.
Early Childhood Development(ECD)	Work with First Nations regions to address the need for Early Childhood Development funding and programs.
HIV/AIDS	Support Peer Youth Education and help coordinate activities at a national level.
First Nations' Research and Information Governance	Support and improve e-health and tele-health initiatives. Improve Regional Health Surveys. Ensure ownership, access, control, and possession of all First Nations health data.
Health Renewal	Ensure culturally relevant, efficient, effective, and sustainable health services and programs for First Nations.
Home and Community Care	Build better awareness of the continuing care needs of First Nations people.
Injury Prevention	Develop a coordinated approach to First Nations injury prevention and control activities.
Non-Insured Health Benefits	Protect and advance the rights of all First Nations citizens to quality health services and drug coverage.
Public Health Advisor	Develop policies and procedures that feature holistic and culturally appropriate plans for pandemic influenza and other communicable disease outbreaks.
Suicide Prevention and Mental Health	Establish linkages with suicide prevention programs and improve access to mental health services in order to reduce the unacceptably high rate of suicide among First Nations, especially among youth.
Tobacco Control Strategy	Working at the community level, encourage smoking prevention, cessation, and treatment programs.
AFN Health and Social Communications	Using such vehicles as media releases, talking points, fact sheets, and speeches, provide communications support to policy analysts in all program areas.

Source: Assembly of First Nations Health and Social Secretariat. (2006). Health Policy Areas. www.afn.ca/article.asp?id=1647 (Accessed June 28, 2006).

Another priority of the Assembly of First Nations is called Health Renewal, involving the building of a framework to provide sustainable and effective health services. This priority could be supported by trained paraprofessionals within these communities, and it must be ensured that their roles are clear and valued by other health professionals (Minore & Boone, 2002). Bruce Minore and Margaret Boone, from the Centre for Rural and Northern Health Research at Lakehead University, have studied the work of Aboriginal paraprofessionals working in the communities of northern Ontario.

A study of these communities reminds us that Canada's Aboriginal population lives in every possible setting within the country. Unlike their urban counterparts, Inuit and First Nations people in northern Ontario often live in remote and small communities. Some might have one nurse, with physicians and others flying in once a month or so. Other communities share one nurse who works with paraprofessionals within these communities. These are local people who have received training at institutions such as Nunavut Arctic College. Originally, indigenous paraprofessionals filled a variety of roles, including community health representative, mental health worker, and addiction and alcohol program worker (Minore & Boone, 2002). Today, they are limited to health promotion and prevention activities (Minore, et al., 2009).

According to Minore and Boone, the success of the paraprofessional model depends upon the establishment of role clarity and consistency for these workers, clarity that is harder to achieve given the limitations to their roles and concerns regarding liability (Minore, et al., 2009). It also depends upon the attitudes of the health professionals who work in these communities. While training programs seem quite good, the reality is that, when paraprofessionals enter their jobs, they are often unsure of their exact roles. A good example concerns patient confidentiality. In some cases, in an attempt to adhere strictly to confidentiality, paraprofessionals not only do not discuss a case informally with members of the community, but also might fail to share important information with a health care professional (Minore & Boone, 2002). One of the keys here is the education of rural health care workers. They must be helped to develop an awareness of the roles played by Aboriginal paraprofessionals in order to appreciate their contributions and to make them contributing members of the team.

SUMMARY

This brief exploration of Aboriginal health cannot do justice to the scope of the problems and the efforts being taken to address them. However, we hope that you can develop some appreciation for each and for the reasons why we must continue our commitment to helping Canada's Aboriginal peoples improve their health and general well-being.

FOCUSED MODULE F
Health and the Internet

Internet use is is having a significant impact on the way people think about their health and how they consume health services. In 2010, when we "Googled" the word *diabetes*, the internet found 67 600 000 sites in 0.24 seconds! When we did this in 2003, we got 6 350 000 hits. These numbers are going up daily.

In terms of the percentage of the population using the internet, Canada ranks second in the world. Only Sweden has a higher percentage of internet users (*How Canadians Find Health Information on the Internet*, 2003). What do these countries have in common? Both are relatively affluent, and both must deal with geographic challenges, either in terms of distance or terrain. These challenges are very relevant to health, given what we know in Canada about disparities in health associated with distances people must travel to access a physician (Ng, Wilkins, Pole, & Adams, 1997).

The internet is particularly relevant to health in Canada. Geography provides challenges for health care access, computer technology is relatively more available than in many other countries (though disparities still exist within Canada in this regard), and a wealth of information is available on the internet. Thus, the internet has the potential to have a positive impact on the health of Canadians.

In this module, we make reference to a number of health-related websites. Where appropriate, we also indicate the date we last accessed that site; however, websites and their addresses are subject to change. In fact, a recent study of website attrition found that, of 184 websites studied, 59 percent of those that existed in 1999 could not be found using the same web addresses in 2002 (Veronin, 2002).

While it is likely that some of the sites mentioned in this module will be active for a long time, it is possible that some will be eliminated or that, perhaps, their addresses will change. Even if this is the case, we hope they will stand as good examples of the phenomena we discuss.

SEARCH ENGINES' PRIORITIZING OF HITS

We have already discussed **search engines**. This is an internet service that scans the web with remarkable speed and thoroughness. Given the overwhelming amount of information available on the internet, search engines are essential to effective use. If one types the word *diabetes* into a search engine, a list of more than 67 million hits is generated. Have you ever wondered how it is determined which sites appear in that first-page listing of 10 sites? As you can imagine, this is a very important question for people who want their sites to be prominent.

One answer, of course, is relevance. But how does a search engine determine relevance? The search engine looks for key words in the site and matches them with the word or words you have put in the search field. Thus, designers of sites might try to present key words that mirror the kinds of language people use when doing their searches. There is more to it than that, though. In fact, there are companies that offer consultation in "search engine positioning" or "search engine optimization."

search engine: internet service that scans the web with remarkable speed and thoroughness to find where desired information is stored.

EXAMPLES OF HEALTH-RELATED RESOURCES AVAILABLE ON THE INTERNET

Not only is there a great deal of health information on the internet, it also covers a wide range of topics. What follows is a description of some of the more commonly accessed resources.

Medical Articles and Reports

Health Canada is a rich source of health information. Visit www.hc-sc.gc.ca and have a look around. If you did this in March of 2010, as we did, you would find a list of advisories and warnings covering everything from eating sprouts to the purchase of children's jewellery. Some of these articles are written for the general public, others are targeted to health care professionals. Good articles are not only well written, they are also well referenced. Claims and statistics are linked to sources that the reader can find and assess. Of course, this is no different from good articles in any medium. It becomes more of an issue with the internet, though, because of its widespread use and potential misuse.

The home page of Health Canada (or the Health on the Net foundation) features a wealth of information.

Another example of an informative Canadian site is the Centre for Health Evidence, affiliated with the University of Alberta and the University of Manitoba (www.cche.net/CHE/home.asp, accessed March 29, 2010). The purpose of this site is to support evidence-based practice, thus supporting medical decision making that relies on research findings and not just on intuition. As such, it is intended for patients, practitioners, and policy makers and geared primarily for practitioners and practitioners-in-training. Publications found on this site include a User's Guide to Evidence-Based Medicine, which contains information about how to calculate the benefits and risks of health decisions and interventions.

Yet another good Canadian site is run by the Canadian Institute for Health Information (CIHI) (www.cihi.ca, accessed October 24, 2010). The information found here is particularly helpful for researchers, policy makers, and practitioners. A number of the reports also provide useful information for the general public. Throughout this book, you will see information drawn from the CIHI site.

Services

Imagine the following story:

> Shortly after moving to Halifax, Maureen and her husband had triplets. Needless to say, this changed everything for them. At times, they found it difficult to cope, especially since they knew very few people in town. One day, while working on her computer, Maureen typed the following into her search engine: "Parents of multiple births, Halifax, Nova Scotia." This yielded 19 900 hits! The first site listed was for the Parents of Multiple Births Association—Halifax Region. There she found information on support groups and a list of activities and events for families with multiple births.

Other organizations, like the Alzheimer Society of Canada, provide valuable information and services across the country. For example, if you lived in Manitoba, you could use the society's website to discover that there are offices in Winnipeg, Brandon, Winkler, Portage La Prairie, Dauphin, and Whitemouth. Each comes with contact information, including an email address. The Society's **URL** is www.alzheimer.ca (accessed March 29, 2010).

Still other internet-based services help people make treatment-related decisions. Using the tools provided by these sites, people can view interviews with practitioners and other consumers and obtain information pertaining to the specific decision they face (Schwitzer, 2002). These tools have considerable potential to provide help with difficult decisions, when used in concert with one's own physician.

URL (uniform resource locators): locations where desired information is stored that can be accessed from a computer.

HEALTH INITIATIVES AND HEALTH PROMOTION

Not surprisingly, the internet is a widely used vehicle for health promotion (see chapter 12). The Health Canada home page in July of 2003 featured something called "SummerActive 2003," a name that sounds very much like the now defunct ParticipAction program. SummerActive ran from 2003 to 2009 and was "designed to increase awareness about the importance of physical activity, healthy eating, and tobacco-free lifestyles to health." SummerActive contained information about such health-promotion activities as World Blood Donor Day and Stroke Awareness Month. There was also information on Seniors' Month and Environment Week.

The World Health Organization website features health initiatives on a global scale (www.who.int, accessed March 29, 2010). Good examples from 2010 include World Health Day and World No Tobacco Day.

If you have ever tried to quit smoking or know someone who has, you might know that you would come up with no fewer than 12 billion hits from a Google search using the words *quit smoking*. Some of these sites promote tobacco-free living, some provide free quit-smoking support, some sell smoking cessation products, and still others get you into chat rooms and newsgroups.

Surveys

Canada does a good job of surveying its population on issues relating to health. More important, a considerable amount of the data from these surveys is available on the web free of charge. These sites contain a collection of tables presenting statistics on such things as health expenditures and pregnancy outcomes. Of course, we have accessed many sites like these in writing this book.

On a provincial level, websites like the one for The McCreary Centre Society, which addresses the health of young people in British Columbia, describe numerous health initiatives for that population. You can read about the McCreary Centre Society in Focused Module A, where we discuss survey methodology and the Adolescent Health Survey. This initiative is documented on the McCreary Centre Website (www.mcs.bc.ca, accessed March 29, 2010).

Support

While there are numerous services providing support on the web, there are also groups of individuals engaged in email conversations and blogs that take place outside the purview of any formal support service. It is quite possible that someone caring for a person with Alzheimer's disease could "meet" someone halfway around the world engaged in the same challenges. These relationships can be extremely important to the individuals involved (Wright & Bell, 2003).

ASSESSING THE QUALITY OF HEALTH INFORMATION ON THE INTERNET

The quantity of information available on the internet is unparalleled. The *quality* of that information can vary considerably, however. How, then, can we assess quality? One way is to rely on others to provide that assessment. Organizations such as the Internet Trade Bureau provide what might be called seals of approval for business-related internet sites. Services like this one monitor complaints against sites and provide a list of these upon request.

Services also exist that provide accreditation or "seals of approval" for health-related websites. One such example is Health on the Net (HON) (www.hon.ch, accessed March 29, 2010). The HON code of conduct allows for the display of the HON code icon by websites meeting HON quality criteria, which are based on principles outlined in Table F-1 (*HON Code of Conduct for Medical and Health Websites*, 2006). These criteria are consistent with those recommended by other bodies, such as the World Health Organization, the Canadian Health Network (which is maintained by the federal government), and the American Accreditation Health Care Commission.

Table F-1 Health on the Net Foundation Principles Used to Assess Quality in Health-Related Web Sites

Principle	Description
1. Authority	Advice is given by those who are medically trained and qualified, unless it is made clear that other forms of qualification apply.
2. Complementarity	The purpose of the site is to support relationships with health practitioners, not replace them.
3. Confidentiality	Any health data presented or information provided by visitors to the site is kept strictly confidential.
4. Attribution	Sources of data and claims are clearly provided.
5. Justifiability	Claims are supported by appropriate and balanced evidence.
6. Transparency of authorship	Contact addresses, including that of the Webmaster, are provided so that further information can be sought.
7. Transparency of sponsorship	Any organizations, public or private, contributing funding are identified.
8. Honesty in advertising and editorial policy	The advertising policy of the site is described. Advertising will be presented so that it is clearly distinguishable from other site content.

Source: Health on the Net Foundation, http://www.hon.ch, accessed July 1, 2003.

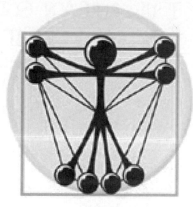

Health on the Net Foundation   medCIRCLE

These symbols indicate that a health website has been reviewed and approved by the Health on the Net Foundation or medCIRCLE.

IMPLICATIONS FOR PATIENT–PHYSICIAN RELATIONSHIPS

Internet use is having a considerable impact on the way people interact with their doctors. A study of 266 oncologists found that 98 percent of them felt they were spending increasing amounts of time discussing information that patients derived from the internet. The oncologists estimated that this has added about ten minutes to each patient consultation, compared to five years ago (Helft, Hlubocky, & Daugherty, 2003).

A study in the United States found that 12 percent of patients receiving radiation for cancer had purchased complementary therapies over the internet (Metz et al., 2003). That same study recommended that radiation oncologists familiarize themselves with internet-based resources available to their patients.

Patients' increased usage of the internet is also affecting their expectations of the health care system. A study at Princess Margaret Hospital in Toronto (Chen & Siu, 2001) discovered a gap between the number of people who wanted as much information as possible about their cancer (86 percent) and the number who believed they were getting enough information from health care professionals (54 percent). The internet provides one way to close this information gap. Of the 191 cancer patients surveyed in the Toronto study, 88 percent felt their doctors were willing to discuss information the patients found on the internet.

While patients in the Toronto study felt their doctors were receptive to discussions of internet information, there were differences in patients' and physicians' views about that information. For example, of the 410 oncologists who took part in the study, only 6 percent thought their patients used internet information correctly. Perhaps this helps explain differences in opinion regarding the helpfulness and potential negative impact of this information.

Glossary

A

A-delta fibres the afferent peripheral fibres that are associated with transmitting sharp, distinct pain

absorption the process by which nutrients move from the digestive tract to the bloodstream and the lymphatic system; absorption occurs primarily in the small intestine

acceleration-deceleration anjury a type of concussion that occurs when an immobile head is hit by a moving object or a moving head hits an immobile object

acceptance the final stage of Kübler-Ross's theory of death and dying, in which people achieve a peaceful acceptance of their own death

Acquired Immune Deficiency Syndrome (AIDS) a disease that develops as a result of the human immunodeficiency virus (HIV); the body's compromised immune system makes it susceptible to a host of other infections

active leisure a positive experience that is associated with activities such as hobbies, playing a musical instrument, and exercise

active-passive model situation in which patients are unable to participate in their care or to make decisions because of their medical condition

acupuncture an ancient Chinese pain control technique that involves the insertion of fine needles to create stimulation to the peripheral nerves

acute illness an illness with a defined beginning and end

acute pain pain that lasts less than six months and serves to warn of impending tissue damage or the need for convalescent rest

acute stressor a stressor that is immediate in its duration and proximity

addiction the state of being physically or psychologically dependent on a substance

addictive smokers smokers who develop a psychological dependence on smoking and are keenly aware when they are not smoking

adherence the degree to which patients carry out the behaviours and treatments that physicians and other health professionals recommend

adjuvant therapy therapy used in conjunction with other therapy

adrenal cortex the outer portion of the adrenal gland; at times of stress supplies hormones to the body that provide energy and increase blood pressure, but that can adversely affect the body's ability to resist and recover from disease

adrenal medulla the central portion of the adrenal gland; secretes catecholamines (containing both adrenaline and noradrenaline) when the hypothalamus initiates the stress response

advanced illness stage of illness at which death is imminent

advanced-practice nursing nursing that includes teaching, consultation, and research within a specialty area where superior clinical skills and judgment are acquired through a combination of experience and education

aerobic exercise exercise, such as jogging, that involves the increased consumption of oxygen over an extended period of time

afferent (sensory) neurons nerve cells that conduct impulses from a sense organ to the central nervous system, or from lower to higher levels in the spinal cord and brain

agency-provided support social support provided by agencies and organizations that have been formed to fill the void when naturally occurring support is either lacking or unavailable

agent in epidemiology, the means by which a disease spreads

alarm the initial phase of Selye's General Adaptation Syndrome in which the body mobilizes its defences against a stressor

alcohol dependency syndrome model a theory suggesting that for a variety of reasons people do not exercise control over their drinking, and this leads to problem drinking

alcohol myopia a drinker's decreased ability to engage in insightful cognitive processing

allostatic load the long-term physiological impact of chronic exposure to stress

alternative treatment any intervention or treatment that is not allopathic

alveoli tiny air sacs found at the ends of the bronchioles; gas (O_2 and CO_2) is exchanged between the air and the blood via the 300 million alveoli in the lungs

anaerobic exercise exercise, such as sprinting, in which intense effort is expended over a short period of time, resulting in an oxygen debt

anger a reaction that often follows denial when people are confronted with novel and severe trauma, as identified by Kübler-Ross

angioplasty a procedure in which a bubble-like device is inserted into the artery at the point of the blockage, thus expanding the artery and allowing for better blood flow

anorexia nervosa an eating disorder that is characterized by a dramatic reduction in food intake and extreme weight loss due to an extreme fear of gaining weight

anticipatory nausea nausea that is felt before a chemotherapy treatment begins, explained in terms of classical conditioning

antidepressants medications that reduce the depression that frequently accompanies pain; it is also believed that they affect pain-related neurotransmitters

antiemetic medication medication intended to reduce nausea and vomiting

antigens microorganisms that are foreign to our physiology

aorta the main artery carrying oxygen-rich blood away from the heart

applied discipline any field in which researchers spend more time using theories to explain real-world phenomena than they do developing the theories

appraisal delay the time it takes one to decide that a symptom is a sign of illness

arbitrary standards standards used to evaluate health promotion programs forwarded by a body that exists outside the community involved in the promotional campaign

arrhythmia an irregular beating of the heart, such as rapid heartbeat or changing patterns of beating

asymptomatic conditions that are not accompanied by palpable symptoms or sensations

atria the upper two chambers of the heart; atria receive blood returning to the heart and transfer it to the ventricles

attitude a cognition in which a person evaluates some object or idea

attributions the explanations people give for events such as their successes and failures

autoimmune diseases occur when the immune system works against the body's own cells; one of the best-known autoimmune diseases is arthritis

autonomic activity physiological processes that cannot be consciously controlled, such as heart rate, respiration rate, blood pressure, hand surface temperature, and skin conductance

autonomic nervous system responsible for involuntary activity and controls the cardiac muscle of the heart, smooth muscle of the internal organs, and most glands; this system is very important in the maintenance of homeostasis

autorhythmicity the capacity of a cardiac muscle cell to fire by itself; the pulsing of the heart is regulated by autorhythmic cells

aversion therapy therapy that includes pairing a behaviour that one is attempting to eliminate with some unpleasant stimulus so that the undesired behaviour will elicit negative sensations

B

B lymphocyte cells cells that, when re-encountering a specific pathogen, produce an antibody designed to eliminate the pathogen

bargaining a response, identified by Kübler-Ross, that may occur when a person is confronted with novel and severe trauma; includes trying to do things that will buy more time

behavioural delay the elapsed time between the decision to seek medical care and acting on this decision by making an appointment

behavioural medicine a branch of medicine concerned with the relationship between health and behaviour; the focus is usually on remediation

beliefs as person variables pre-existing notions, both personal and cultural, that influence appraisal, and thus stress, by determining the meaning given to the environment

benefit finding attitude or technique often referred to as finding the "silver lining in the cloud," which appears to aid in post-traumatic growth

benign breast biopsy when the results of a biopsy procedure show no evidence of malignancy

benign-positive appraisal a cognitive process by which an event is appraised to involve outcomes that are positive and may enhance well-being

bereavement emotions attendant upon the loss of a close friend or loved one

binge eating disorder (BED) compulsive overeating or bingeing; unlike bulimia nervosa, BED uses no compensatory measure or purge to counteract the binge

biofeedback the recording of physiological measures through electronic instruments that provide immediate feedback concerning physiological state in an attempt to modify physiological processes

biomedical model an approach suggesting that health is best understood in terms of biology

biopsychosocial approach a model that suggests that biological, psychological, and social factors are all involved in any given state of health or illness

biopsychosocial communication pattern communication patterns between a physician and patient that include a balance of psychosocial and biomedical topics

blood-brain barrier acts as a sentinel for materials that enter the brain via the bloodstream

blunters people who avoid information in their attempt to cope with illness and its accompanying challenges

body dysmorphic disorder condition in which individuals who suffer from eating disorders do not perceive their bodies accurately

body-mass index (BMI) measure of obesity calculated by dividing one's weight in kilograms by height in metres squared

box scale a scale on which people rate and report their pain by choosing the number that best indicates the degree of pain that they are experiencing from a series of numbers in boxes ranging from "no pain" to "worst pain imaginable"

brain stem an area at the base of the brain that connects the brain to the spinal cord; the brain stem controls some very basic functions, such as breathing and sleep-wake cycles and is also involved in maintaining posture and balance

Broca's area (of the brain) the part of the brain that controls speech production

bronchi the two main branches of the trachea, or windpipe

bronchioles the small branches of the bronchi

bronchial pneumonia pneumonia that is restricted to the bronchi and often occurs as a complication of other diseases, such as cold or flu

bulimia nervosa an eating disorder that involves recurrent episodes of binge eating followed by purging

burnout a condition that is similar to compassion fatigue and includes symptoms of physical exhaustion, depersonalization of patients, and feelings of discouragement and low accomplishment

C

C-fibres the afferent peripheral fibres that are associated with transmitting diffuse, dull, or aching pain

cardiac invalidism anxiety regarding a subsequent heart attack causes patients to curtail their activity levels far more than required by their actual disease status

caring the role that most lay people think is the primary task of nurses

case one instance of a medical problem

case studies narrative accounts of one person's health, including individual histories, symptoms, specific reactions, or treatment outcomes that inform some aspect of health psychology

central control trigger in the gate control theory of pain, a specialized system of large-diameter, rapidly conducting fibres that activate selective cognitive processes that then influence, by way of descending fibres, the opening and closing of the gate

central nervous system the division of the nervous system that is composed of the brain and the spinal cord

central route to persuasion the use of logic, facts, and reason to affect someone's attitude

centrally acting analgesics pain-killing medications that operate on the central nervous system by imitating the effects of the body's endogenous pain relief system

cerebellum meaning "little brain," the cerebellum appears above the brain stem; it contributes to our control of balance and the coordination of voluntary movement

cerebrovascular accidents (strokes) a form of cardiovascular disease (CVD) in which blood flow to the brain is disrupted

chemotherapy treatment used in addition to surgery and/or radiation therapy when it is suspected that cancer has metastasized, or to help prevent it from doing so

chyme the liquid material travelling through the digestive tract

chronic condition a condition that doesn't go away or get better

chronic intractable benign pain continuous pain that varies in intensity

chronic obstructive pulmonary disease (COPD) the primary symptom of COPD is shortness of breath, a symptom that tends to worsen with time; the two most common forms of COPD are chronic bronchitis, an inflammation that irritates the airways and blocks them by producing extra mucus, and emphysema, which results from damaged or destroyed lung tissue, causing large air pockets to be trapped in the lungs, making breathing difficult

chronic pain pain lasting for longer than six months

chronic progressive pain continuous pain that gradually intensifies as a person's condition worsens

chronic recurrent pain intermittent intense episodes of acute pain followed by relief

claustrophobia an intense fear of enclosed spaces; a psychological concern for those undergoing MRI procedures

clinical nurse specialist nurse with a master's or doctoral degree in nursing and extensive experience in a given clinical specialty

cognitive appraisal assessment of whether or not an event is stressful

cognitive reappraisal and restructuring therapy sometimes used with cardiac patients, in which they learn to think differently about the things that make them angry and to make behavioural changes, such as learning to control their breathing

cognitive restructuring a technique whereby maladaptive, stress-producing cognitions are identified and replaced with ones that are more appropriate

cognitive transactional models models that emphasize the relationship between a person and his or her environment and the appraisal that the individual makes of the situation

collectivist one who considers him- or herself to be part of a greater whole and who considers individualism to be less important than allegiance to the group

commitments as person variables values that influence appraisal by determining the importance of a particular encounter and that affect the choices made to achieve a desired outcome

compassion fatigue a lack of energy among health care professionals, particularly nurses, who are constantly working in an environment in which suffering is common

complementary treatment treatment that is used in conjunction with allopathic treatment

compliance the degree to which patients carry out the behaviours and treatments that physicians and other health professionals recommend

concussion (closed head injury) a bruising of the brain that can result in severe neurocognitive deficits, permanent disability, and even death

conflict theory school of thought in sociology that claims that structures do not simply exist; rather, they exist in *conflict*

consumerist communication pattern the use of the physician as a consultant who answers questions rather than asking them

continuity of care arrangement in which a designated staff person, usually a nurse, takes primary responsibility for a patient during a hospital stay

contractile cells these cells require stimulation from other cells in order to fire; they bring about the contraction of the heart that constitutes the work of pumping

control group participants in a study who don't receive the manipulation (the dependent variable)

coping (styles) strategies that an individual employs to deal with stresses caused by ever-changing demands of the environment

coping goal the objective of a coping response (which is usually to reduce the impact of stress)

coping outcomes the specific outcomes of a coping response

coping response an intentional physical or mental act that is initiated in response to a stressor

co-production process a process whereby the responsibility for health is shared among centralized health bureaucracies, individuals, and communities

coronary artery bypass graft (CABG, commonly called bypass surgery) a procedure in which healthy arteries from other parts of the body, often the legs, are grafted into the coronary artery system to bypass blocked arteries

correlational research studies including statistical analyses to determine if two variables change together, or *co-vary*

cost-gain belief an individual's assessment of the costs associated with a course of action (e.g., effort, discomfort, embarrassment, or inconvenience) compared to the benefit of the behaviour to the individual's health

creative non-adherence a patient's intentional modifying or supplementing of a recommended treatment regimen

cross-sectional research comparison of two or more groups that differ according to stage of life

curing the role that most lay people think is the primary task of physicians

cytocines increase the body's capacity to produce inflammation and help heal wounds and fight infection

D

day care patient a person who goes to the hospital for a procedure or test that is more involved than, for example, routine radiography, but does not stay overnight

day surgery surgery that does not require the patient to stay in the hospital overnight

dehumanization the tendency to see people as objects or body parts rather than human beings

delayed gratification term used by behaviourists to describe a situation in which there is a time lag between a behaviour and its reinforcement

delta alcoholism the inability to abstain

demand characteristics beliefs held by people when they know that they are in a psychology study; beliefs about what is expected of them or how they are "supposed" to respond

denial a coping strategy in which people deny that distressing events exist or that negative emotions are being felt

dependent variable in an experiment, the variable that is hypothesized to be measurably affected by the manipulation of the independent variable

depersonalization taking away a person's sense of individuality

depression a common mental disorder of varying severity and impact that features depressed mood, loss of interest or pleasure, feelings of guilt or low self-worth, disturbed sleep or appetite, low energy, and poor concentration.

diabetes a common disease that results from a malfunction in the endocrine system; diabetes is caused by too little secretion (hyposecretion) of insulin, which is a hormone produced by the pancreas; *see also insulin-dependent diabetes and non-insulin-dependent diabetes*

diastole relaxation of the heart during pumping, in which the heart is filled

digestion the process whereby enzymes produced within the digestive system perform the biochemical breakdown of carbohydrates, proteins, and fats into molecular-size forms that allow for absorption

discharge planning a process in which post-hospital care is organized and risks, such as social problems and lack of support, are assessed

disease physical pathology

disease model (of problem drinking) a theory that suggests that alcoholism is a disease resulting from the physical properties of alcohol

diseases of adaptation health problems that are the result of long-term neurological and hormonal changes caused by ongoing stress

disempowering care patient care that yields dependence and can result in learned helplessness

disfigurement a potential physical result of cancer surgery that can have serious psychological consequences

distraction a pain management technique in which the patient focuses attention on something other than the sensation of pain

do not resuscitate order an order given by a physician indicating that CPR and other interventions are not to be used if the patient stops breathing

doctor-centred consultations consultations in which physicians tend to ask questions that require only very brief answers

drive-reduction theory a theory that suggests we are driven to reduce the tension brought about by deprivation or other negative states

duration temporal situational factor involved in stress appraisal

E

e-journal a journal that is accessible through the internet

efferent neurons nerve cells that take impulses away from the brain

efficacy beliefs the extent to which one thinks a course of action (e.g., a preventive behaviour or treatment) will actually work

ego orientation a goal perspective that focuses on success and failure with success often coming at other people's expense

electroencephalograph (EEG) an instrument that assesses pain by measuring electrical activity in the brain

electromyograph (EMG) an instrument that assesses pain by measuring electrical activity in muscles

emesis vomiting, or emptying of the stomach's contents

emotion-focused coping coping by focusing on ways to reduce the emotional impact of a disease without trying to cure it

emotional-approach coping coping by facing emotional responses to a disease and dealing effectively with those responses

emotional arousal a source of efficacy expectation by which individuals assess their emotional level and evaluate their capabilities accordingly; for example, high levels of emotion may be thought to be debilitating and predictive of failure

emotional support support provided by people who take the time to understand our fears and frustrations, who help calm us during anxious times, who help lift our moods up, or who distract us from our worries

empowering care patient care that yields independence and results in learned mastery

endocrine system a system of the body that controls glandular responses to stress; responds more slowly than the nervous system but the effects can persist for weeks

endogenous opioids opiate-like substances produced within the body that regulate pain

enumerative assay a lab test done to count cells (typically white blood cells) as they exist in the bloodstream

environmental tobacco smoke (second-hand smoke) smoke that is in the air we breathe because of others' smoking

ethanol (ethyl alcohol) the alcohol used in beverages

eustress a positive, yet stressful, experience

euthanasia the deliberate ending of a patient's life to relieve suffering

event uncertainty the inability to predict the probability of an event which, as a result, increases the stress response

evoked potentials electrical responses produced by stimuli

exercise psychology the study of the influence that sport and exercise have on one's psychology and behaviour

exhaustion the fourth phase of Selye's General Adaptation Syndrome; the body experiences fatigue and immunocompromise because of the severity or duration of a stressor

expanded biomedical communication pattern includes numerous closed-ended medical questions and moderate levels of biomedical and psychosocial exchange between the physician and patient

experiential standards standards used to evaluate health promotion programs based on direct experiences of the community involved in the promotional campaign

experimental group participants in a study who receive the manipulation (the independent variable)

experimenter bias an experimental construct flaw; the person who interacts with participants or interprets qualitative data has knowledge that affects participants' responses or the interpretation of qualitative data

expertise model model in which the physician and the intensive care team are assumed to be best informed and most objective, and therefore best equipped to make end-of-life decisions

external imagery a technique in which an individual becomes a passive and external third-person observer of his or her own actions

external reinforcement the encouragement and praise from physiotherapists, friends, family, and other practitioners needed by rehabilitation patients for their successes

F

factor analysis analyzing a multitude of variables (factors) in order to find any patterns of occurrence that exist between them

false positive result that indicates abnormality when none exists

family-oriented care in comprehensive cancer care, the family becomes the patient because for virtually every cancer patient there is a family and a collection of close friends who are also affected by the disease

fear appeals the attempt to change people's behaviour by presenting frightening accounts of what could happen to them if they continue a given behaviour or if they don't adopt a behaviour

fear of restriction anxiety experienced due to the inability to move when in a small enclosed space

fear of suffocation suffocation anxiety experienced due to the belief that one might die from the inability to breathe

feasibility standards standards used to evaluate health promotion programs based on the practicality or sustainability of the program

feminization of medicine the trend toward increased proportions of female physicians in the profession

fetal alcohol spectrum disorder (FASD) the name used to describe the range of disabilities caused by prenatal exposure to alcohol; these effects are permanent

field research research conducted in real-life settings

fight-or-flight response the body's complex autonomic reaction when faced with a perceived threat

frontal lobes (of the brain) responsible for voluntary movement, language, thought processing, and emotion

functional tests of immunity tests done to assess the immune system at work

G

gametes reproductive cells

gamma alcoholism loss of control once drinking begins

gastric banding a minimally invasive surgical procedure that involves placing a band around the stomach so that a person feels full after consuming only a small amount of food

gastric bypass radical surgical intervention to control extreme obesity, in which a small pouch is created at the bottom of the esophagus to limit food intake

gate control theory suggests that a neural mechanism in the dorsal horns of the spinal cord acts like a gate that can increase or decrease the flow of nerve impulses from peripheral fibres to the central nervous system thereby influencing the sensation of pain

general adaptation syndrome the three-stage response of the body to stressors as identified by Selye: alarm, resistance, and exhaustion

germ theory a theory based on the discovery that many illnesses were caused by the activity of micro-organisms, such as bacteria

gestational diabetes a temporary condition affecting two to four percent of all pregnant women

glial cells make up about 90 percent of CNS cells and are the support system for neurons, providing nourishment and helping neurons maintain proper physical orientation to each other (*Glia* literally means "glue")

global measures of quality of life a general or overall assessment of quality of life without focusing on specific aspects

glucocorticoids substances released by the adrenal glands upon stimulation from the sympathetic division when one is under stress

gonads the primary organs responsible for reproduction, in males, the testes and in females, the ovaries; in addition to producing their respective gametes, the gonads produce sex hormones—testosterone for males and estrogen and progesterone for females

grade-one concussion a concussion that does not involve a loss of consciousness, although the athlete may display transient confusion

grade-two concussion a concussion in which the symptoms persist beyond a 15-minute period but that does not involve a loss of consciousness

grade-three concussion any concussion that involves a loss of consciousness, whether it is extremely brief or prolonged

gradient of reinforcement the gradual weakening of a behaviour the further it gets in time from the reinforcement of that behaviour

grief deep sorrow, usually in response to bereavement

guidance-cooperation model communication in which the patient seeks advice from the physician and answers the questions that are asked, but the physician is responsible for determining the diagnosis and treatment

guided imagery a form of relaxation that relies on distraction, in which the participant is told to imagine a calm, peaceful, and pleasant image

H

habitual smokers smokers who smoke without the awareness that they are doing so

hallucinogens drugs that dramatically affect perception, emotions, and mental processes; can cause hallucinations

harm/loss appraisal a type of stressful appraisal, at the time of the primary appraisal, that involves significant physical or psychological loss

health belief model a model that analyzes health behaviour in terms of the belief that a health threat exists and the belief that a given course of action will affect the threat

health promotion strategies intended to maintain or improve the health of large populations

health psychology the compilation of all that psychology has to offer to the diagnosis and treatment of illness as well as people's attempts to maintain health and well-being

"healthy adherer" effect greater adherence to health-promoting behaviours such as medication adherence is indicative of overall healthy behaviour

help-intended communication communication that includes support, especially emotional support

helper T cells (T lymphocytes) cells that produce substances called interleukins that speed the division of B lymphocyte cells

hemorrhagic stroke a stroke that is caused by blood vessel rupture

highly active antiretroviral treatment (HAART) a treatment for AIDS that has been shown to significantly increase life expectancy

historical standards standards used to evaluate health promotion programs based on comparisons to other programs or to the same program at an earlier time

holistic therapy term that has come into use describe complementary or alternative therapies that acknowledge treatment of the whole person

homeostasis the dynamic physiological response on the part of the body to maintain a stable internal state in spite of the demands of the environment

hospital separation a measure of hospital usage calculated as an overnight hospital stay for one person

host in epidemiology, the carrier of an agent of disease

Human Immunodeficiency Virus (HIV) a virus that gradually breaks down the body's immune system, making it susceptible to a host of other infections, eventually resulting in AIDS

hypermetabolic state a physiological state in which the metabolic rate is higher than normal as occurs in the fight-or-flight response

hypnosis an altered state of consciousness

hypoglycemia low blood sugar

hypertension abnormally high blood pressure (i.e., in excess of 140/90 mm Hg)

hypometabolic state a state of the body in which the heart slows, blood pressure drops, breathing is slow and easy, and muscle tension decreases

hypotension abnormally low blood pressure (i.e., below 100/60 mm Hg)

hypothalamus a portion of the brain that initiates the stress response in both the nervous system and the endocrine system

I

illness the subjective experience of having a disease

illness delay the time taken between recognizing that one is ill and deciding to seek medical care

imminence interval during which an event is being anticipated; the more imminent an event, the more intense the appraisal

immune system memory the ability of certain immune system cells to adapt to an antigen, to remember the antigen when it encounters it again, and to work to eliminate it

immunocompetence the extent to which an immune system is functioning properly to ward off micro-organisms

impression management approach when people believe they are being observed they will eat less than when they believe no one is watching

incidence rate the number of new cases of a health problem in a set period of time

inclusion criteria characteristics that make a person eligible for a study

incommunication stage a period in ICU during which a patient is either unconscious or barely conscious

independent variables the variables researchers manipulate

index case the first identified instance of a medical problem

individualist one who focuses on independence and self-reliance rather than placing group needs above his or her own

information-motivation-behavioural skills model a theory maintaining that there are a number of steps one must go through to successfully achieve safe sex practices

informational support the provision of information that might include such things as treatment options or typical recovery times from a treatment or injury

insulin-dependent diabetes (Type 1) a condition in which a person produces very little or no insulin and as a result is required to take insulin on a daily basis, usually by way of self-administered injection

interaction when variables combine to produce an effect that is different from the effect of either variable alone

internal imagery technique in which an individual imagines being inside his or her body, experiencing a given situation

internality-externality hypothesis assertion that in people of normal weight, feelings of hunger and satiety come from within, in the form of internal stimuli (e.g., hunger pangs or feelings of fullness); whereas, obese people are more likely to determine their level of hunger in response to external stimuli (e.g., time of day, smell, or sight of food)

interpersonal small talk talk engaged in by a technologist during a procedure that has nothing to do with the procedure but passes the time and establishes rapport

intrusive memories unwanted thoughts, often visual in nature, that are related to memories that the patient has about cancer and death

invasiveness a measure of the extent to which hospital procedures, in a physical sense, involve piercing the skin or entering the body with instruments or, in a psychological sense, have the potential to cause embarrassment

irrelevant appraisal a cognitive process by which an event is appraised as having no implications for the individual's well-being

ischemic stroke a stroke that is caused by blockage

isokinetic exercise exercise that involves placing tension on a muscle group through a complete range of motion

isometric exercise exercise that involves the contraction of a muscle group against an immovable object without movement in the body

isotonic exercise exercise that involves using weights or calisthenics to place tension on the muscle through the shortening or lengthening of the muscle group

J

job strain model a model that suggests a job with high strain is one that includes high demands and low control

K

kidney dialysis uses external devices to do the work of the kidneys

L

lactose intolerance caused by a deficiency of lactase, which is used to digest a milk sugar called *lactose*, resulting in a buildup of lactose in the small intestine; because bacteria in the large intestine can use lactose as an energy source, these bacteria move in and produce gases as they attack the lactose; the result is painful cramping and diarrhea

learned helplessness a state in which a person, because of experience with previously uncontrollable stressful situations, learns to do nothing about a new stressor, rather than trying to cope constructively with it

leptin hormone that responds to weight loss by increasing hunger levels until the person's weight returns to its ideal or target level

lifetime prevalence the total number of people who have ever had a particular medical problem, even if the problem went away or they died from it

limbic system a system of the brain that is responsible, in part, for emotion in the stress response

lobar pneumonia the infection of an entire lobe of the lung, which causes an inflammation of the alveoli; can be a serious condition in which the infection causing the inflammation spreads to other organs

local anaesthetics pain-relieving chemicals that can be applied topically but are much more effective when injected at the site where the pain originates

lock-out interval the time period between allowable dosages, when patient controlled analgesia is used; a device is set by a practitioner to control this period

longitudinal research experimental design in which researchers follow one group over time to chart their changes

M

main effects model any scientific explanation that assumes an outcome is the result of the effects of a single variable

malabsorption the inability to efficiently absorb nutrients from the digestive system, which may be caused by *gluten enteropathy*

medical delay the time between making an appointment and first receiving medical care

medical jargon technical language used by a physician that is sometimes unintelligible to the patient

medical level of health promotion the orientation is disease-based and the goal is disease treatment

meditation a form of relaxation in which one attempts to focus attention fully on a single thought or image

meningitis an inflammation of the membranes that protect the brain and spinal chord; takes its name from the *meninges*, the membranes that provide further protection and keep the fluid contained within the CNS; there are three of these membranes, positioned between the protective bone layer and nerve tissue

message framing the extent to which positive or negative aspects of an outcome are emphasized in a health promotion message

metastasized spread (frequently used to denote the spread of cancer)

mitogen a relatively harmless substance that stimulates immune cell activity as though the immune cell were acting against an invading cell or antigen

mixed management model of care the preparation of a patient for eventual death while at the same time providing life-sustaining treatments

modelling a technique used to reduce stress associated with fear-provoking situations, in which observing a model coping well with a situation facilitates a similar response by the observer in a similar situation

modelling effect people tend to eat the same amount as those in their presence; this effect is sometimes referred to as the matching effect

monitors people who seek information in their attempt to cope with illness and its accompanying challenges

motility the process of moving food through the system and mixing it with digestive juices definition

motion artifacts distortions to an MRI image caused by a patient's movement

motor cortex responsible for controlling voluntary movement such as facial movement, limb and trunk movement, and hand movement

multidimensional measures of quality of life assessment that includes specific aspects of quality of life, such as physical, emotional, and social functioning

multilevel explanations explanations that use medical jargon followed by further explanation using everyday language

muscle dysmorphia condition characterized by belief that one's body is not sufficiently lean and muscular; clinically significant distress or impairment in social, occupational, or other areas of functioning; and a primary focus on being too small or inadequately muscular

mutual aid responsibility to family, friends, loved ones, and even society as a whole when it comes to health and safety

mutual-participation model health care model in which the physician and patient make joint decisions about every aspect of care

myocardial infarction (MI) heart attack caused by lack of blood flow to the heart

myocardial ischemia a lack of blood flow to the heart muscle

N

narcotics pain-killing drugs that work by binding to opiate receptors in the central nervous system

narrowly biomedical communication pattern characterized mainly by biomedical talk, closed-ended medical questions, and very little discussion of psychosocial issues

natural-killer (NK) cells cells that have the specific job of "seeking and destroying" cells that are infected, cancerous, or altered in some other way

naturally occurring support the support we obtain from friends, relatives, co-workers, and others in our own social networks

navigator often a nurse, community health worker, or social worker, who helps patients diagnosed with serious illnesses find their way through the sometimes complicated world of hospitals and treatment

negative-affect smoker a smoker who smokes to reduce negative affect, such as anxiety, distress, fear, or guilt

negative correlation when one variable decreases as another increases

negotiated model decision-making model that allows decision making to be shared between the practitioners, patient, and family

nervous system one of the two major components of the physical response to stress; made up of the central nervous system and the peripheral nervous system

neuromatrix theory an extension to the gate control theory, with greater emphasis placed on the brain's role in pain perception

neurons nerve cells

nicotine-replacement therapy a stop-smoking technique that provides some form of nicotine to replace that previously obtained through smoking

NK cell cytotoxic activity assay a test in which the proliferation and effectiveness of NK cells is measured after they have been exposed to diseased cells

NK cell lysis the destroying of tumour cells by exposing them to NK cells

nociceptors the afferent nerve endings that respond to pain stimuli

non-adherence failure to follow the advice of the health professional; the inability to stay with an exercise program

non-discrepant responses physician responds to the patient's questions using the same sophistication of vocabulary that the patient uses

non-insulin-dependent diabetes (Type 2) a condition in which a person does not produce enough insulin or is not able to use insulin effectively

non-invasive a term to describe any procedure that does not include piercing the skin or entering the body with an instrument

non-specific immunity general protection against antigens, rather than against one specific antigen

normative standards standards used to evaluate health promotion programs using statistics, such as national averages, describing the health issue being addressed

novelty the extent to which an individual's previous experience with a situation influences the appraisal process

nurse practitioner a nurse who often works in rural, remote settings, frequently performing functions that would be performed by a physician if available

O

obesity condition characterized by having an excess of body fat; Health Canada and the World Health Organization define obesity as a BMI of 30.0 or greater

occipital lobes found at the back of the brain, they contain the visual cortex and are responsible for interpretation of impulses that come in through the light-sensitive receptors, the rods and cones, in the eyes

occupational rituals behaviours that indicate one has been socialized into a profession; for nurses, these are communicated through interaction with other nurses

oncology the study and treatment of cancer

operant pain pain that is reinforced by a person's environment

outpatient a person who goes to the hospital for a procedure or test but does not stay overnight

outcome goals goals that are concerned with the results or outcomes of events and usually involve comparisons to others

P

pain behaviours alterations in behaviour by a person experiencing pain to either reduce the pain or to prevent it from getting worse

pain threshold the point at which the intensity of a stimulus is perceived as painful

pain tolerance the duration of time or intensity at which a person is willing to endure a stimulus beyond the point where it began to hurt

palliative care care intended to maintain the best possible quality of life for a patient who is in the advanced stage of an illness; focuses on the control of pain and other symptoms as opposed to the cure of the illness

pancreas a gland that secretes insulin and glucagon as a function of blood sugar levels

Pap test (or Pap smear) a test done to screen for cervical cancer

parasympathetic nervous system the component of the autonomic system that reestablishes homeostasis in the system and promotes the reconstructive process following a stressful experience

parietal lobes responsible for processing sensory information other than hearing and vision, such as touch and temperature regulation

participant modelling a technique used to reduce stress in which, subsequent to an individual observing a model coping with an anxiety evoking situation, the person is encouraged to engage in the behaviour while receiving reassurance from the model

passive leisure a positive experience that is associated with lack of activity (e.g., listening to music, daydreaming)

passive smoking the breathing of environmental tobacco smoke

pathogens antigens that have the potential to create disease

patient-centred consultations consultations in which physicians tend to ask open-ended questions that allow patients to elaborate

patient-controlled analgesia (PCA) analgesic administration that is independently controlled by the patient

patient delay the period between one's first awareness of a symptom and treatment for that symptom

patient-centred care approach in which patients and families become active members of the treatment team

peptic ulcer so named because pepsin, a digestive enzyme, begins to erode the wall of the stomach, resulting in bleeding or the escape of gastric contents, which can damage tissue outside the digestive tract

perceived behavioural control the belief that a specific behaviour is within one's control

performance accomplishments actual experiences of mastery, considered to be the most influential source of self-efficacy

performance goals goals that describe an outcome that can be achieved independently of others' performances

periaqueductal gray area an area of the midbrain that is involved in pain reception

peripheral nervous system the division of the nervous system that is made up of the somatic nervous system and the autonomic nervous system (which is further divided into the sympathetic and the parasympathetic nervous systems)

peripheral route (to persuasion) attempts to affect attitude by appealing to emotion and general impression

peripherally acting analgesics non-narcotic medications that decrease pain by reducing inflammation at the site of tissue damage; they also inhibit the synthesis of neurochemicals in the peripheral nervous system that facilitate the transmission of pain impulses

person variables variables, most importantly commitments and beliefs,, that interact with situation variables to affect the appraisal of a situation in terms of its stressfulness

personal factors in stress personal characteristics, such as high self-esteem and a clear sense of control, that make some people better able to cope with the job stressors

personal resources resources that are available to people in their own lives to help them reduce the potential for stressful events and cope with stressful situations as they occur

persuasion the attempt to change people's attitudes and beliefs

phantom limb pain the experience of pain in an absent body part

phenomenologically according to a person's own report on the phenomenon

physical activity the expenditure of energy, either purposely or without intention, as a result of bodily movements produced by skeletal muscles as part of leisure or work activities

physical therapy therapy involved in the rehabilitation of muscle, bone, joint, or nerve disease

physical fitness physiological functioning (including cardiorespiratory endurance, muscular endurance, muscular strength, body composition, and flexibility) that influences the ability to perform physical activity

physician impairment a state in which stress-related symptoms interfere with physicians' abilities to perform their jobs

pituitary gland a gland located in the brain; described as the master gland because it controls other glands through the hormones it secretes; most of these hormones have an indirect impact on stress

placebo condition a study condition in which participants are given general attention, and perhaps an inert pseudo-medication, but not the specific intervention that is the independent variable of the study

point prevalence the number of cases of a medical problem at a given point in time

positive-affect smoker a smoker who smokes to attain positive affect (e.g., increased stimulation, relaxation, or gratification of sensorimotor needs)

positive correlation when one variable increases (or decreases), so does another

positive psychology approach that encourages psychologists to use fewer negative or problem-focused frameworks and to focus more on effective human functioning

post-concussion syndrome symptoms experienced subsequent to a concussion, such as memory problems, difficulties in concentration, headaches, dizziness, and irritability

post-traumatic growth positive psychological or lifestyle outcome from an experience with a life-threatening illness

practical support help with the demands of daily living, such as getting meals and rides to the doctor

predictability a characteristic of the environment that allows an individual to prepare for an event and therefore reduce the stress involved

prevalence in epidemiology, the total number of cases that exist at any given time

primary appraisal the initial evaluation of a situation

primary care physicians those physicians in general and family practice

problem-focused coping the altering of a situation or the creating of conditions in which stress and danger are reduced; a rational approach that involves changing the situation by defining the problem, looking at alternative solutions, evaluating the implications of the alternatives, and choosing the best one to act on; coping by actively addressing the stressors associated with a disease, such as cancer, and its treatment

procedure-based information information given by a technologist at the time of a procedure that addresses what will be done and why

process goals goals that focus on specific processes that a performer will be concerned with during a performance

prognosis a prediction of how a medical condition will change in the future

progressive illness a condition that will continue to worsen in spite of treatment

progressive muscle relaxation (PMR) a technique in which a person achieves relaxation by flexing and gradually relaxing muscle groups

propriety standards standards used to evaluate health promotion programs that take legal and ethical issues into account

protease inhibitors medication that can significantly prolong the lives of people living with AIDS

psychological empowerment in stress a personal factor in stress that can include finding work meaningful, having a sense of autonomy, feeling competent, and having a positive impact

psychological methods in sport techniques such as relaxation, goal-setting, and imagery, which are used to develop psychological skills

psychological skills in sport arousal or attentional control implemented to enhance performance

psychoneuroimmunology (PNI) the study of the relationship between psychological states and the functioning of the immune system

psychosocial communication pattern includes a substantial amount of psychosocial exchange between the physician and patient

psychosomatic medicine approach in which a particular medical complaint is viewed as being the result of an underlying chronic emotional conflict that ultimately surfaces in the form of physiological symptoms

public health level of health promotion the orientation is behaviour-based and the goal is disease prevention

Q

quality of life the extent to which symptoms and treatment affect a person's physical, social, cognitive, and emotional functioning

quasi-experimental designs research done in real-life settings, but in which experimental methods (manipulation of variables) are used

R

radiation therapy a form of cancer treatment in which radiation is used to shrink or destroy tumours

radical surgery cancer surgery that requires the removal of a considerable amount of normal tissue

random assignment determining randomly who will be in an experimental group and who will be in a control group so that individual differences should be evenly divided between the two groups

random clinical trial studies research in which participants are randomly assigned to treatment conditions

reactance behaving counter to recommendations in response to feeling that one has lost personal control over health behaviours; the non-compliant behaviours and attitudes of patients who perceive hospital rules and regiments to be unacceptable challenges to their freedom

readaptation stage a period in ICU when a patient can sense a struggle to recover and recognizes his or her dependence on machines

reality shock the reaction to the discrepancy between a training environment and an actual work environment

reappraisal a continuous experience in which existing appraisals of situations are changed or modified on the basis of new information

reflection stage a period during which a patient who was in ICU tries to piece together his or her recent experience

relaxation skills techniques to reduce anxiety to manageable levels so that the energy can be used to positively influence performance; based on the principle that we cannot be relaxed and tense at the same time

relocation stress (translocation stress) the stress caused by being separated from those things that were keeping patients alive—the one-on-one care and the technology

renal system the part of the body encompassing the kidneys, renal arteries, and renal veins

resilience concept in positive psychology that describes "good outcomes in spite of serious threats to adaptation or development"

resistance a set of physiological responses that allow a person to deal with a stressor; the second phase of Selye's General Adaptation Syndrome in which the body mobilizes its resources if the source of stress moves from acute to chronic

respondent pain pain that occurs in response to noxious stimulation or tissue damage

response efficacy belief the perception that a threat-reducing strategy will work

restraint theory an explanation for eating behaviour that claims that external sensitivity is linked to *restrained eating* (or strict dieting), rather than to body weight, and that overeating is more likely in people who restrain their eating

reticular formation complex system running through the middle of the brain stem that serves as a communication network to filter messages between the brain and the body

retrospective research researchers study people who have developed medical conditions, or who have died from them, and trace their histories to find variables that might explain how they came to have that condition

role strain stress as a result of the demands of multiple social roles, such as health care practitioner and mother

rotational injury a type of concussion resulting from a blow to the side of the head

S

sampling bias situation in which the people who take part in a study are different somehow from the population the researchers are studying

scientific standards standards used to evaluate health promotion programs, using data published in scientific literature based on similar programs or health issues

second impact syndrome the result when an athlete who has suffered a concussion returns to activity too soon and receives another blow to the head that can result in much greater trauma to the brain than that initially experienced

secondary appraisal an individual's evaluation of their ability to cope with a situation following the primary appraisal

sedatives medications, such as barbiturates, that affect pain indirectly by reducing anxiety and helping the patient to sleep

self-accountability the extent to which a person feels personally responsible for a given emotion or situation

self-awareness model the theory that drinking makes people less self-aware because it inhibits the use of normal complex information-processing strategies, such as memory and information acquisition

self-care behaviours such as exercise, diet, voluntary screening, and regular medical checkups that people engage in to promote their health

self-efficacy an individual's perception of his or her ability to succeed at a particular task at a specific time

self-management strategies strategies used to help people overcome the environmental conditions that perpetuate smoking

self-reinforcement praising oneself or rewarding oneself for accomplishments

self-talk sport psychology concept to describe one of the methods athletes use to correct bad habits, focus attention, modify activation, increase self-confidence and efficacy, and maintain exercise behaviour

sensation-based information information given by a technologist at the time of a procedure that includes what a procedure will feel like or sound like and how long it will last

sensitivity the ability of a test to identify correctly those who have a particular disease

sensory afferents carry sensory information to the brain via the spinal cord—information about temperature, pressure, and pain (originating from the skin), or about body position and balance (from the muscles, joints, skin, and inner ear); may also carry information regarding vision, hearing, taste, and smell directly to the brain without engaging the spinal cord

sensory cortex (of the brain) responsible for sensory activities in specific parts of the body as well as for sensations from the skin, muscles, and joints

seroconversion the production of antibodies by memory B cells when exposed to a specific previously encountered and remembered antigen

set-point theory the idea that the body contains a set-point that works like a thermostat; when a person gains weight, biological control mechanisms diminish caloric intake; when a person loses weight, similar mechanisms increase hunger levels until the weight returns to its ideal or target level

shiatsu massage sustained massage pressure on specific points of the body; according to the beliefs of practitioners, Shiatsu massage releases blockages in the flow of energy through the body

sick role a status that, when temporarily and legitimately adopted, exempts people from their other roles

sites of cancer types of cancer as defined by the location of the tumour

situation variables variables that interact with person variables to influence the appraisal of a situation

social comparison monitoring of the opinions and experiences of others to determine what is right and wrong, normal and abnormal; also subsequent use of this information to help with decision making

social determinants of health factors such as income, social support, education, working conditions, and culture that have a significant effect on health at the population level

social dominance a risk factor for coronary disease that is independent of hostility; social dominance is described as "a set of controlling behaviours, including the tendency to cut off and talk over the interviewer"

social facilitation approach this approach states that people tend to eat more when in the presence of others

social factors in stress the elements of a person's social network, such as family, friends, and co-workers, that affect ability to cope with job stressors

social learning model this theory, when applied to drinking behaviour, proposes that people drink because they experience positive reinforcement for doing so or because they observe others drinking and model the behaviour

social support a collection of interpersonal resources that people have at their disposal to help them avoid or cope with difficult times in their lives

socioemotional care interactions that help patients maintain a sense of optimism and psychological well-being

socioenvironmental level of health promotion the orientation is toward social change and public health policy

somatic nervous system responsible for voluntary activity and controls skeletal muscles

specific immunity protection against a particular antigen

specificity the ability of a test to identify correctly those who do not have a particular disease

specificity (of immune system cells) ability of certain immune system cells to remember an antigen and respond only to the remembered antigen

sport an activity that involves rules or limits, a sense of history, an aspect of winning and losing, and an emphasis on physical exertion in the context of competition

sport psychology the study of the influence of psychological factors on sport behaviour

stages of change model model in which change is broken down into six stages: precontemplation, contemplation, action, maintenance, termination, and relapse

states and traits psychological concept that distinguishes between short-term conditions (states) and enduring characteristics (traits)

stimulant a drug that increases alertness, decreases appetite and the need for sleep, and may produce intense feelings of euphoria and a strong sense of well-being

stimulation-produced analgesia (SPA) freedom from pain as a result of electrical stimulation

stress the non-specific mental or somatic result of any demand upon the body

stress-buffering hypothesis the theory that posits that social support has an indirect effect and acts as a buffer to protect individuals from the negative effects of stress

stress-diathesis model model that examines the interaction between the environment and heredity, often referred to as *nature versus nurture*; this model proposes that predisposing factors in an individual may determine whether or not a physical effect is experienced in the presence of stressful events

stress inoculation training a technique designed to help people cope effectively with stressful events; includes reconceptualizing events in less stressful ways, improving coping strategies, and applying the reconceptualized cognitive and behavioural approach to relevant stressors

stress-intrusion scores a measure of the impact a stressful event has on a person's life

stress literacy the degree to which an individual (or community) understands the effects of stress

stress management techniques techniques that have been developed specifically to help people cope with stress either directly or indirectly

stress response a response that reflects a spontaneous emotional or behavioural reaction to stress, rather than a deliberate attempt to cope

stressful appraisal a cognitive process by which an event is appraised to involve harm/loss, threat, or challenge at the time of the primary appraisal

subjective norms beliefs regarding what others think we should do and the extent to which we are motivated to go along with these people

suppressor T cells (CD8) cells that stop the production of antibodies after the antigen has been destroyed

Swedish massage slow, gentle stroking movements to warm and relax tissue and stimulate blood circulation

symbolic interactionism sociological theory that people's interpretations of their interactions and the events of their lives go well beyond the actual words used, or in the case of health-related events, the diagnosis they are given

sympathetic nervous system the system responsible for the "fight or flight" response when triggered by the hypothalamus (e.g., faster heart beat, increased blood pressure)

synapse a gap between neurons that is crossed by neurotransmitters that neurons use to communicate with each other

systematic desensitization a technique to help people cope with fear and anxiety by combining relaxation with gradual exposure to the fear-inducing stimulus

systole contraction of the heart during pumping, in which the heart is emptied

T

tangible support help with the demands of daily living, such as getting meals and rides to the doctor

task orientation a goal perspective in which individuals derive satisfaction from the sense of competence experienced as they improve; the focus is on effort and their own performance rather that that of others

technical care activities involving prescribed medical procedures, independent of the psychological needs of the patient

temporal lobes found on either side of the head, near the ears; responsible for interpreting sound

temporal uncertainty lack of knowledge as to when an event will occur, which can result in stress

tension reduction hypothesis the hypothesis that people drink alcohol because of its tension-reducing properties

thalamus located above the hypothalamus, the thalamus manages synaptic input to the brain, sending impulses to the appropriate part of the brain

theory of planned behaviour posits that behaviour is preceded by intention and that our intention is influenced not only by subjective norms and beliefs about the efficacy of the behaviour, but also by the belief that one is actually capable of performing the behaviour

theory of reasoned action posits that behaviour is preceded by intention, and that the intention is influenced by beliefs about the behaviour and subjective norms

therapeutic rituals in nursing practice, primarily activities that deal with patient-nurse interactions; for example, the administration of medication and bathing of patients

threat appraisal an appraisal at the time of the initial evaluation of the primary appraisal that involves the anticipation of harm or loss

threat perception the belief that a threat is real and that we are vulnerable to it

thyroid gland an important gland in the stress response because it produces thyroxine, which increases blood pressure and respiration rate, and affects mental processes

tolerance (of immune system cells) the ability of immune system cells to remember and respond to a remembered antigen while not reacting to the body's own cells

total institution any institution, such as a hospital, that takes control of virtually every aspect of a person's day-to-day life

tranquillizers medications such as diazepam (Valium) that affect pain indirectly by reducing patient anxiety

transcendental meditation (TM) a technique of meditation to reduce stress introduced by Maharishi Mahesh Yogi in the late 1950s

transcript analysis recordings of interactions with patients that are transcribed to paper and analyzed; often used by medical sociologists adopting a symbolic interactionist perspective

transcutaneous electrical nerve stimulation (TENS) a pain control technique that involves placing an electrode on the surface of the skin and applying electrical stimulation

triage the sorting and classifying of patients to determine priority of need and proper location and means of treatment

tropic hormones hormones produced to stimulate other glands

type A behaviour pattern behaviours include impatience, time urgency, aggressiveness, hostility, and competitiveness; originally believed to be predictive of coronary heart disease

U

uncertainty a significant source of stress for physicians resulting from the fact that the consequences of medical decisions are uncertain

uniformity myth belief that all patients should receive the same amount of information in their preparation for a hospital stay regardless of their personal styles of coping with stress

upper respiratory infection (URI) one of a collection of illnesses such as colds, coughs, and bronchitis

ureter carries urine from the kidney to the bladder; there are two ureters, one for each kidney

urethra empties urine from the bladder to outside the body; in females, the urethra is short and straight; in males, the urethra is much longer and extends through the prostate gland and the penis

urinary bladder storage space for holding urine; the bladder is capable of expanding to hold more or less urine

URL (uniform resource locators) locations where desired information is stored that can be accessed from a computer

V

ventricles the lower two chambers of the heart; ventricles pump the blood from the heart to either the lungs or other parts of the body

vector in epidemiology, a living organism that can transfer an agent from one host to another

vehicle in epidemiology, a non-living medium involved in the transmission of an agent

verbal descriptor scale a rating scale in which people are asked to describe their pain by choosing the phrase that most closely resembles the pain that they are experiencing

verbal persuasion to verbally persuade others that they have the skills to perform a particular task—i.e., to talk them into it

vicarious experience experience that is gained through observing or visualizing others perform a skill, which can alert one to one's own capabilities and raise one's sense of self-efficacy

viral challenge studies studies in which volunteer subjects are intentionally exposed to controlled dosages of upper respiratory infection viruses and environmental stressors to measure the clinical progression of the virus and the response of the immune system

visual analog scale (VAS) a scale on which people rate and report their pain by marking a point on a line anchored by the phrase "no pain" and by a phrase like "worst pain imaginable"

vulnerability physically, the adequacy of an individual's resources; psychologically, a threat to something that an individual values

W

Wernicke's area (of the brain) the part of the brain that controls the understanding and interpretation of language

withdrawal the unpleasant symptoms people experience when they stop using a substance to which they are addicted

References

A

Abascal, J.R., Brucato, D., & Brucato, L. (2001). *Stress mastery: The art of coping gracefully.* New Jersey: Prentice Hall.

Abbott, R.D., Rodriguez, B.L., Burchfiel, C.M., & Curb, J.D. (1994). Physical activity in older middle-aged men and reduced risk of stroke: The Honolulu Heart Program. *American Journal of Epidemiology, 139,* 881–893.

Abrahm, J.L. (2003). Update in palliative medicine and end-of-life care. *Annual Review of Medicine, 54,* 53–72.

Abramson, L., Garber, J., & Seligman, M.E.P. (1980). Learned helplessness in humans: An attributional analysis. In J. Garber & M.E.P. Seligman (Eds.), *Human helplessness: Theory and applications* (pp. 3–34). New York: Academic Press.

Absetz, P., Aro, A.R., & Sutton, S.R. (2003). Experience with breast cancer, pre-screening perceived susceptibility and the psychological impact of screening. *Psycho-Oncology, 12*(4), 305–318.

Achilles, R. (2000). *Defining complementary and alternative health care.* Ottawa: Strategies and Systems Health Directorate, Health Promotions and Programs Branch, Health Canada.

Ader, R., Felton, D.L., & Cohen, N. (1981). *Psychoneuroimmunology.* New York: Academic Press.

Adlaf, E.M., Mann, R.E., & Paglia, A. (2003). Drinking, cannabis use and driving among Ontario students. *Canadian Medical Association Journal, 168*(5), 565–566.

Aiello-Laws, L., Reynolds, J., Deizer, N., Peterson, M, & Bakitas, M. (2009). Putting evidence into practice: What are the pharmacological interventions for nociceptive and neuropathic cancer pain in adults? *Clinical Journal of Oncology Nursing, 13*(6), 649–655.

Ajzen, I. (1985). From intentions to actions: A theory of planned behaviour. In J. Kuhland & J. Beckman (Eds.), *Action-control: From cognitions to behavior* (pp. 11–39). Heidelberg, Germany: Springer.

Ajzen, I. (1991). The theory of planned behavior. *Organizational Behavior and Human Decision Processes, 50,* 179–211.

Ajzen, I., & Fishbein, M. (1980). *Understanding attitudes and predicting social behaviour.* Englewood Cliffs, NJ: Prentice-Hall.

Akil, H., Owens, C., Gutstein, H., Taylor, L., Curran, E., & Watson, S. (1998). Endogenous opioids: overview and current issues. *Drug and Alcohol Dependence, 51,*127–140.

Akil, H., Watson, S.J., Young, E., Lewis, M.E., et al. (1984). Endogenous opioids: Biology and function. *Annual Review of Neuroscience, 7,* 223–255.

Alberta Alcohol and Drug Abuse Commission. (2003). Beyond the ABCs: Information for professionals. www.gov.ab.ca/aadac/addictions/beyond/beyond

Albertsen, P. (1998, November). A competing risk analysis of outcomes associated with men treated conservatively for clinically localized prostate cancer. Paper presented at the *Cancer Care: Quality of Life and Outcomes Symposium,* Chicago, IL.

Alcohol and drug abuse among treaty Indians in Saskatchewan: Needs assessment and recommendations for change. (1984). Federation of Saskatchewan Indian Nations.

Alderman, B.A., Rogers, T.J., Landers, D.M., Arent, S.M. & Johnson, T.A. (2006). *The influence of physical activity and fitness on stress: A meta-analysis.* Unpublished manuscript.

Aldwin, C.M. (1994). *Stress, coping and development: An integrative perspective.* New York: Guilford Press.

Alexander, C.N., Robinson, P., Orme-Johnson, D.W., Schneider, R.H., & Walton, K.G. (1994). The effects of transcendental meditation compared to other methods of relaxation and meditation in reducing risk factors, morbidity, & mortality. *Homeostasis, 35,* 243–263.

Ali, J. (2002). *Mental health of Canada's immigrants.* Supplement to Health Reports, Statistics Canada, Catalogue 82-003-SIE, pp. 1–11.

Alon, E., Jaquenod, M., & Schaeppi, B. (2003). Post-operative epidural versus intravenous patient-controlled analgesia. *Minerva Anestesiol, 69*(5), 443–437.

Alonso, J., Black, C., Norregaard, J.C., Dunn, E., et al. (1998). *Medical Care, 36,* 868–878.

Alvord, M.K., & Grados, J.J. (2005). Enhancing resilience in children: A proactive process. *Professional Psychology: Research and Practice, 36,* 238–245.

Amelang, M. (1997). Using personality variables to predict cancer and heart disease. *European Journal of Personality, 11,* 319–342.

American Cancer Society. (2006). Approaches for smoking cessation. Cancer Medicine. Retrieved August 30, 2006 from www.ncbi.nlm.nih.gov/entrez/query.fcgi?CMD=search&DB=books&doptcmdl=GenB

American Psychiatric Association. (1994). Practice guideline for the treatment of patients with eating disorders. Retrieved July 21, 2003 from www.psych.org/clin_res/guide.bk-4.cfm

American Psychiatric Association. (1997). *Diagnostic and statistical manual of mental disorders.* (4th ed.). Washington, DC: Author.

Anand, B.K., & Chhina, G.S. (1961). Investigations on yogis claiming to stop their heart beats. *Indian Journal of Medical Research, 49,* 90–94.

Anand, B.K., Chhina, G.S., & Singh, B. (1961a). Studies on Shri Ramand Yogi during his stay in an air-tight box. *IndianJournal of Medical Research, 49,* 82–89.

Anand, B.K., Chhina, G.S., & Singh, B. (1961b). Some aspects of electroencephalographic studies in yogis. *EEG and Clinical Neurophysiology, 13*, 452–456.

Andersen, B.L., Cacioppo, J.T., & Roberts, D.C. (1995). Delay in seeking a cancer diagnosis: Delay stages and psychophysiological comparison processes. *British Journal of Social Psychology, 34*, 33–52.

Anderson, B.L., Farrar, W.B., Golden-Kreutz, D., Kutz, L.A., MacCallum, R., Courtney, M.E., & Glaser, R. (1998). Stress and immune responses after surgical treatment for regional breast cancer. *Journal of the National Cancer Institute, 90*, 30–36.

Anderson, E.A. (1987). Preoperative preparation for cardiac surgery facilitates recovery, reduces psychological distress, and reduces the incidence of acute postoperative hypertension. *Journal of Consulting and Clinical Psychology, 55*, 513–520.

Anderson, J.C., Linden, W., & Habra, M. (2005). The importance of examining blood pressure reactivity and recovery in anger provocation research. *International Journal of Psychophysiology, 57*(3), 159–163.

Anderson, J.G. (1999). The business of cyberhealthcare. *MD Computing, 16*(6), 23–25.

Anderson, K.O., Bradley, L.A., Young, L.D., McDaniel, L.K., & Wise, C.M. (1985). Rheumatoid arthritis: Review of psychological factors related to etiology, effects, and treatment. *Psychological Bulletin, 98*, 358–387.

Anderson, P. (2000). The evidence of health promotion effectiveness: Shaping public health in a new Europe: Part two. A report for the European Commission by the International Union for Health Promotion and Education. Brussels.

Anderson, R., Freedland, K., Clouse, R., & Lustman, P. (2001). Prevalence of comorbid depression in adults with diabetes. A meta-analysis. *Diabetes Care, 24*, 1069–1078.

Andreoli, A.V., Keller, S.E., Rabaeus, M., Marin, P., Bartlett, J.A., & Taban, C. (1993). Depression and immunity: Age, severity, and clinical course. *Brain, Behavior, and Immunity, 7*, 279–292.

Anshell, M.H. (2006). *Applied exercise psychology*. New York: Springer.

Antall, G.F., & Kresevic, D. (2004). The use of guided imagery to manage pain in an elderly orthopaedic population. *Orthopaedic Nursing, 23*, 335–340.

Antoni, M.H., August, S., LaPerriere, A., Baggett, H.L., Klimas, N., et al. (1990). Psychological and neuroendocrine measures related to functional immune changes in anticipation of HIV-1 serostatus notification. *Psychosomatic Medicine, 52*, 496–510.

Antoni, M.H., Kumar, M., Ironson, G., Cruess, D.G., Cruess, S., Lutgendorf, S., Klimas, N., Fletcher, M., and Schneiderman, N. (2000). Cognitive-behavioral stress management intervention effects on anxiety, 24-hr urinary norepinephrine output, and T-cytotoxic/suppressor cells over time among symptomatic HIV-infected gay men. *Journal of Consulting and Clinical Psychology, 68*, 31–45.

Antshel, K.M. (2002). Integrating culture as a means of improving treatment adherence in the Latino population. *Psychology, Health & Medicine, 7*, 435–449.

Antorini, M.H. (2003). Stress management effects on psychological, endocrinological, and immune functioning in men with HIV infection: Empirical support for a psychoneuroimmunological model. *Stress: The International Journal on the Biology of Stress, 6*(3), 173–188.

Arborelius, E., & Bremberg, S. (1992). What can doctors do to achieve a successful consultation? Videotaped interviews analyzed by the 'consultation map' method. *Family Practice, 9*, 61–66.

Ariely, D., & Loewenstein, G. (2006). The heat of the moment: The effect of sexual arousal on sexual decision making. *Journal of Behavioral Decision Making, 19*, 87–98.

Armitage, C.J., Norman, P., and Conner, M. (2002). Can the Theory of Planned Behaviour mediate the effects of age, gender and multidimensional health locus of control? *British Journal of Health Psychology, 7*, 299–316.

Arnett, J.L., Martin, R.M., Streiner, D.L., & Goodman, J.T. (1987). Hospital psychology in Canada. *Canadian Psychology, 28*, 161–171.

Arnsberger, P., Fox, P., Ryder, P., Nussey, B., Zhang, X., & Otero-Sabogal, R. (2006). Timely follow-up among multicultural women with abnormal mammograms. *American Journal of Health Behavior, 30*(1), 51–61.

Aronoff, G.M. (2000). Opioids in chronic pain management: Is there a significant risk of addiction? *Current Review of Pain, 4*, 112–121.

Aronoff, G.M., Wagner, J.M., & Spangler, A.S. (1986). Chemical interventions for pain. *Journal of Consulting and Clinical Psychology, 54*, 769–775.

Ary, D.V., & Biglan, A. (1988). Longitudinal changes in adolescent cigarette smoking behavior: Onset and cessation. *Journal of Behavioral Medicine, 11*, 361–382.

Asmundson, G.J.G., Norton, G.R., Allerdings, M.D., Norton, P.J., & Larsen, D.K. (1998). Posttraumatic stress disorder and work-related injury. *Journal of Anxiety Disorders, 12*, 57–69.

Aspinwall, L.G., & Taylor, S.E. (1997). A stitch in time: Self-regulation and proactive coping. *Psychological Bulletin, 121*, 417–436.

Astin, J.A. (2004). Mind-body therapies for the management of pain. *Clinical Journal of Pain, 20*, 27–32.

Astle, S.J. (1996). The experience of loss in athletes. *Journal of Sports Medicine and Physical Fitness, 26*, 279–284.

Auslander, G.K., Netzer, D., & Arad, I. (2003). Parental anxiety following discharge from hospital of their very low birth weight infants. *Family Relations: Interdisciplinary Journal of Applied Family Studies, 52*(1), 12–21.

Austenfeld, J.L., & Stanton, A.L. (2004). Coping through emotional approach: A new look at emotion, coping, and health-related outcomes. *Journal of Personality, 72*(6), 1335–1363.

Avitsur, R., Stark, J.L., Dhabhar, F.S., & Sheridan, J.F. (2002). Social stress alters splenocyte phenotype and function. *Journal of Neuroimmunology, 132*, 66–71.

Ayanian, J.Z., & Cleary, P.D. (1999). Perceived risks of heart disease and cancer among cigarette smokers. *Journal of the American Medical Association, 281,* 1019–1021.

Azar, B. (1999, February). Sex differences in pain reports may be smaller than previously thought. *APA Monitor,* 7.

Aziz, A. (2004). Sources of perceived stress among American medical doctors: A cross-cultural perspective. *Cross-Cultural Management, 11*(4), 28–39.

B

Badgley, R.F. (1994). Health promotion and social change in the health of Canadians. In A. Pederson, M. O'Neill, & I. Rootman, (Eds.), *Health promotion in Canada: Provincial, national and international perspectives* (pp. 200–239). Toronto: Saunders.

Bagozzi, R.P. (1992). The self-regulation of attitudes, intentions, and behavior. *Social Psychology Quarterly, 29,* 178–204.

Bahrke, M.S., & Morgan, W.P. (1978). Anxiety reduction following exercise and meditation. *Cognitive Therapy and Research, 2,* 323–334.

Bailey, R.K., Geyen, D.J., Scott-Gurnell, K., Hipolito, M.M.S., Bailey, T.A., & Beal, J.M. (2005). Understanding and treating depression among cancer patients. *International Journal of Gynecological Cancer, 15*(2), 203–208.

Bair, M.J., Robinson, R.L., Eckert, G.J., Stang, P.E., Croghan, T.W., & Kroenke, K. (2004) Impact of pain on depression treatment response in primary care. *Psychosomatic Medicine, 66,* 17–22.

Baker, C., & Melby, V. (1996). An investigation into the attitudes and practices of intensive care nurses toward verbal communication with unconscious patients. *Journal of Clinical Nursing, 5,* 185–192.

Baker, L., Wagner, T.H., Singer, S., & Bundorf, M.K. (2003). Use of the Internet and e-mail for health care information: Results from a national survey. *JAMA: Journal of the American Medical Association, 289*(18), 2400–2406.

Balfour, L., Silverman, A., Tasca, G., Kowal, J., Seatter, R., & Cameron, W. (2003). Stress and depression related to lower immune system functioning among people with HIV (PHAS). Presentation to the 64th Annual Conference of the Canadian Psychological Association, June 12, Hamilton, Ontario.

Ball, G.D.C., & McCargar, L.J. (2003). Childhood obesity in Canada: A review of prevalence estimates and risk factors for cardiovascular diseases and type 2 diabetes. *Canadian Journal of Applied Physiology, 28,* 117–140.

Balla, J.I. (1982). The late whiplash syndrome: A study of an illness in Australia and Singapore. *Culture, Medicine and Psychiatry, 6,* 191–210.

Bandura, A. (1977). Self-efficacy: Toward a unifying theory of behavior change. *Psychological Review, 84,* 191–215.

Bandura, A. (1986). *Social foundations of thought and action: A social cognitive theory.* Englewood Cliffs, New Jersey: Prentice-Hall.

Bandura, A. (1990). Perceived self-efficacy in the exercise of personal agency. *Journal of Applied Sport Psychology, 2,* 128–163.

Bandura, A. (1991). Self-efficacy mechanism in physiological activation and health-promotion behavior. In J. Madden IV (Ed.), *Neurobiology of learning, emotion, and affect* (pp. 229–269). New York: Raven Press.

Bandura, A. (1997). *Self-efficacy: The exercise of control.* New York: Freeman.

Bannister, R. (1955). *The four-minute mile.* New York: Dodd, Mead.

Barling, N.R., & Moore, S.M. (1996). Prediction of cervical cancer screening using the theory of reasoned action. *Psychological Reports, 79,* 77–78.

Barnes, E. (2005). Caring and curing: Paediatric cancer services since 1960. *European Journal of Cancer Care, 14*(4), 373–380.

Barnes, M.P., & Ward, A.B. (2000). *Textbook of rehabilitation medicine.* Oxford: Oxford University Press.

Barnett, R.C., Steptoe, A., & Gareis, K.C. (2005). Marital-role quality and stress-related psychobiological indicators. *Annals of Behavioral Medicine, 30*(1), 36–43.

Baron, R.S., Cutrona, C.E., Hicklin, D., Russell, D.W., & Lubaroff, D.M. (1990). Social support and immune function among spouses of cancer patients. *Journal of Personality and Social Psychology, 59,* 344–352.

Barraclough, J., Pinder, P., Cruddas, M., Osmond, C., Taylor, I., & Perry, M. (1992). Life events and breast cancer prognosis. *British Medical Journal, 304,* 1078–1081.

Barrett, L., & Yates, P. (2002). Oncology/haematology nurses: A study of job satisfaction, burnout, and intention to leave the specialty. *Australian Health Review: A Publication of the Australian Hospital Association, 25*(3), 109–121.

Barton, J., Chassin, L., Presson, C.C., & Sherman, S.J. (1982). Social image factors as motivators of smoking initiation in early and middle adolescence. *Child Development, 53,* 1499–1511.

Battino, R. (2000). *Guided imagery and other approaches to healing.* Carmarthen, UK: Crown House.

Bauchner, H., Vinci, R., Bak, S., Pearson, C., & Corwin, M.J. (1996). Parents and procedures: A randomized controlled trial. *Pediatrics, 98,* 861–867.

Bauer, M., Fitzgerald, L., Haesler, E., & Manfrin, M. (2009). Hospital discharge planning for frail older people and their family. Are we delivering best practice? A review of the evidence. *Journal of Clinical Nursing, 18,* 2539–2546.

Baum, A., & Posluszny, D.M. (1999). Health psychology: Mapping biobehavioral contributions to health and illness. *Annual Review of Psychology, 50,* 137–163.

Baxter, N., Cohen, R., & McLeod, R. (1996). The impact of gender on the choice of surgery as a career. *American Journal of Surgery, 172,* 373–376.

Beard, H. (2005). Does intermediate care minimize relocation stress for patients leaving the ICU? *Nursing in Critical Care, 10*(6), 272–278.

Beck, A. (1963). Thinking and depression: 1. Idiosyncratic content and cognitive distortions. *Archives of General Psychiatry, 9,* 324–333.

Beck, A. (1976). *Cognitive therapy and the emotional disorders.* New York: International Universities Press.

Becker, M.H. (1974). The health belief model and sick role behavior. *Health Education Monographs, 2,* 409–419.

Becker, M.H., & Janz, N.K. (1987). On the effectiveness and utility of health hazard/health risk appraisal in clinical and nonclinical settings. *Health Services Research, 22,* 537–551.

Becker, M.H., & Maiman, L.A. (1975). Sociobehavioral determinants of compliance with health care and medical care recommendations. *Medical Care, 13,* 10–24.

Beckett, K. (2005). Choosing Cesarean: Feminism and the politics of childbirth in the United States. *Feminist Theory, 6*(3), 251–275.

Beckman, H.B., & Frankel, R.M. (1984). The effect of physician behavior on the collection of data. *Annals of Internal Medicine, 101,* 692–696.

Beecher, H.K. (1959). *Measurement of subjective responses.* New York: Oxford University Press.

Begun, F.P. (1993). Epidemiology and natural history of prostate cancer. In H. Lepor & R.K. Lawson (Eds.), *Prostate disease* (pp. 257–268). Philadelphia: W.B. Saunders.

Behar, R. (2006). Gender-related aspects of eating disorders: A psychosocial view. In P.I. Swain (Ed.), *New developments in eating disorders research* (pp. 37–63). Hauppauge, NY: Nova.

Beisecker, A., & Beisecker, T. (1990). Patient information-seeking behaviors when communicating with doctors. *Medical Care, 28,* 19–28.

Bender, R., Trautner, C., Spraul, M., & Berger, M. (1998). Assessment of excess mortality in obesity. *American Journal of Epidemiology, 147,* 42–48.

Ben-Eliyahu, S., Page, G.G., & Schleifer, S.J. (2007). Stress, NK cells, and cancer: Still a promissory note. *Brain, Behavior, and Immunity, 21,* 881–887.

Bennenbroek, F.T.C., Buunk, B.P., van der Zee, K.I., & Grol, B. (2002). Social comparison and patient information: What do cancer patients want? *Patient Education & Counseling, 47,* 5–12.

Bennett, K.K., Compas, B.E., Beckjord, E., & Glinder, J.G. (2005). Self-blame and distress among women with newly diagnosed breast cancer. *Journal of Behavioral Medicine, 28*(4), 313–323.

Bensing, J.M., Roter, D.L., & Hulsman, R.L. (2003). Communication patterns of primary care physicians in the United States and the Netherlands. *Journal of General Internal Medicine, 18,* 335–342.

Benson, H. (1975). *The Relaxation Response.* New York: William Morrow.

Benson, H., Beary, J.F., & Carol, M.P. (1974). The relaxation response. *Psychiatry, 37,* 37–46.

Ben-Zur, H. (2002). Monitoring/blunting and social support: Associations with coping and affect. *International Journal of Stress Management, 9*(4), 357–373.

Berger, B.G., & Tobar, D.A. (2007). Physical activity and quality of life: Key considerations. In G. Tenenbaum & R.C. Eklund (Eds.), *Handbook of Sport Psychology.* (3rd ed.) (pp. 598–620). New Jersey: John Wiley & Sons.

Bergman, B., Ahmad, F., & Stewart, D.E. (2003). Physician health, stress and gender at a university hospital. *Journal of Psychosomatic Research, 54*(2), 171–178.

Berkowitz, R.I., Agras, W.S., Korner, A.F., Kraemer, H.C., & Zeanah, C.H. (1985). Physical activity and adiposity: A longitudinal study from birth to childhood. *Journal of Pediatrics, 106,*734–738.

Bernstein, D.A., & Borkovec, T.D. (1978) *Progressive relaxation training: A manual for the helping professions.* Champaign, IL: Research Press.

Bernstein, D.A., & Given, B.A. (1984). Progressive relaxation: Abbreviated methods. In R. Woolfolk and P. Lehrer (Eds.), *Principles and practice of stress management.* New York: Guilford Press.

Beyerstein, B. (1997). Alternative medicine: Where's the evidence? *Canadian Journal of Public Health, 88,* 149–152.

Bigatti, S., & Cronan, T.A. (2002). A comparison of pain measures used with patients with fibromyalgia. *Journal of Nursing Measurement, 10,* 5–14.

Bigby, J., & Perez-Stable, E.J. (2004). The challenges of understanding and eliminating racial and ethnic disparities in health. *Journal of General Internal Medicine, 19,* 201–203.

Biddle, S.J.H., & Mutrie, N. (2001). *Psychology of physical activity: Determinants, well-being and interventions.* New York: Routledge.

Biglan, A., Duncan, T.E., Ary, D.V., & Smolkowski, K. (1995). Peer and parental influences on adolescent tobacco use. *Journal of Behavioral Medicine, 18,* 315–330.

Bilney, C., & D'Ardenne, P. (2001). The truth is rarely pure and never simple: A study of some factors affecting history-sharing in the GUM clinic setting. *Sexual and Relationship Therapy, 16,* 349–374.

Bingefors, K., & Isacson, D. (2004). Epidemiology, co-morbidity, and impact on health-related quality of life of self-reported headache and musculoskeletal pain—a gender perspective. *European Journal of Pain, 8,* 435–450.

Birk, L. (Ed.) (1973). *Biofeedback: Behavioral medicine.* New York: Grune and Stratton.

Birmingham, C.L., Su, J., Hlynsky, J.A., Goldner, E.M., & Gao, M. (2005). The mortality rate from anorexia nervosa. *International Journal of Eating Disorders, 38*(2), 143–146.

Birnbaum, M.H., Wong, R., & Wong, L.K. (1976). Combining information from sources that vary in credibility. *Memory and Cognition, 4,* 330–336.

Bish, A., Ramirez, A., Burgess, C., & Hunter, M. (2005). Understanding why women delay in seeking help for breast cancer symptoms. *Journal of Psychosomatic Research, 58*(4), 321–326.

Bishop, F.L., Yardley, L., & Lewith, G.T. (2008). Treat or treatment: A qualitative study analyzing patients' use of complementary and alternative medicine. *American Journal of Public Health, 98*(9), 1700–1705.

Bishop, S.R., & Warr, D. (2003). Coping, catastrophizing and chronic pain in breast cancer. *Journal of Behavioral Medicine, 26*(3), 265–281.

Bjordal, J.M., Johnson, M.I., & Ljunggreen, A.E. (2003). Transcutaneous electrical nerve stimulation (TENS) can reduce postoperative analgesic consumption. A meta-analysis with assessment of optimal treatment parameters for postoperative pain. *European Journal of Pain, 7*(2), 181–188.

Blair, M.J., Robinson, R.L., Eckert, G.J., Stang, P.E., Croghan, T.W., & Kroenke, K. (2004). Impact of pain on depression treatment response in primary care. *Psychosomatic Medicine, 66,* 17–22.

Blair, S.N., Kohl, H.W., Paffenberger, R.S., Clark, D.G., Cooper, K.H., & Gibbons, L.W. (1989). Physical fitness and all-cause mortality: A prospective study of healthy men and women. *Journal of the American Medical Association, 262,* 2395–2401.

Blanchard, E.B. (1977). Behavioral medicine: A perspective. In R.B. Williams and W.D. Gentry (Eds.), *Behavioral approaches to medical treatment.* Cambridge, MA: Ballinger.

Blanchard, E.B. (1987). Long-term effects of behavioral treatment of chronic headache. *Behavior Therapy, 18,* 375–385.

Blanchard, E.B. (2000). Headaches. In A.E. Kazdin (Ed.), *Encyclopedia of psychology: Vol. 4* (pp. 67–70). Washington, DC: American Psychological Association.

Blanchard, E.B., Andrasik, F., Guarnieri, P., Neff, D.F., & Rodichok, L.D. (1987). Two-, three-, and four-year follow-up on the self-regulatory treatment of chronic headache. *Journal of Consulting and Clinical Psychology, 55,* 257–259.

Blanchard, E.B., Appelbaum, K.A., Guarnieri, P., Morrill, B., & Dentinger, M.P. (1987). Five year prospective follow-up on the treatment of chronic headache with biofeedback and/or relaxation. *Headache, 27,* 580–583.

Blanchard, E.B., & Haynes, M.R. (1975). Biofeedback treatment of a case of Raynaud's disease. *Journal of Behavior Therapy and Experimental Psychiatry, 6,* 230–234.

Blanchard, E.B., & Young, L.B. (1973). Self-control of cardiac functioning: A promise as yet unfulfilled. *Psychological Bulletin, 79,* 145–163.

Blanchard, J., & Lurie, N. (2004). R-E-S-P-E-C-T: Patient reports of disrespect in the health care setting and its impact on care. *Journal of Family Practice, 53,* 721–730.

Blane, C., Hughes, C.M., & McElnay, J.C. (2006). The impact of depressive symptoms and psychosocial factors on medication adherence in cardiovascular disease. *Patient Education and Counseling, 60*(2), 187–193.

Bleil, M.E., McCaffery, J.M., Sutton-Tyrrell, K., & Manuck, S.B. (2004). Anger-related personality traits and carotid artery atherosclerosis in untreated hypertensive men. *Psychosomatic medicine, 66*(5), 633–639.

Bloom, J.R., & Kessler, L. (1994). Emotional support following cancer: A test of the stigma and social activity hypothesis. *Journal of Health and Social Behavior, 35,* 118–133.

Boey, K.W. (1999). Distressed and stress resistant nurses. *Issues in Mental Health Nursing, 20,* 33–54.

Bogart, L.M., & Delahanty, D.L. (2004). Psychosocial models. In T. Boll, R.G. Frank, A. Baum, & J.L. Wallander (Eds.), *Handbook of clinical health psychology: Volume 3. Models and perspectives in health psychology* (pp. 201–248). Washington, DC: American Psychological Association.

Bogart, L.M., & Helgeson, V.S. (2000). Social comparisons among women with breast cancer: A longitudinal investigation. *Journal of Applied Social Psychology, 30*(3), 547–575.

Bogg, T., & Roberts, B.W. (2004). Conscientiousness and health-related behaviours: A meta-analysis of the leading behavioural contributors to mortality. *Psychological Bulletin, 130,* 887–919.

Boldt, J., Thaler, E., Lehmann, A., Papsdorf, M., & Isgro, F. (1998). Pain management in cardiac surgery patients: Comparison between standard therapy and patient-controlled analgesia regimen. *Journal of Cardiothoracic and Vascular Anesthiology, 12,* 654–658.

Bonham, V.L. (2001). Race, ethnicity, and pain treatment: Striving to understand the causes and solutions to the disparities in pain treatment. *Journal of Law, Medicine and Ethics, 29,* 52–68.

Booth, M.J. (1998). Nurse anesthetist reaction to the unexpected or untimely death of patients in the operating room. *Holistic Nursing Practice, 13,* 51–58.

Borland, R., Wilson, N., Fong, G.T., Hammond, D., Cummings, K. M., et al. (2009). Impact of graphic and text warnings on cigarette packs: Findings from four countries over five years. *Tobacco Control: An International Journal, 18*(5), 358–364.

Boroditsky, R., Fisher, W., & Sand, M. (1996). The 1995 Canadian contraception study. *Journal SOGC, 18 Supplement,* 1–31.

Boscarino, J.A. (1997). Diseases among men 20 years after exposure to severe stress: Implications for clinical research and medical care. *Psychosomatic Medicine, 59,* 605–614.

Bottomley, A., Hunton, S., Roberts, G., Jones, et al. (1996). A pilot study of cognitive behavioral therapy and social support group interventions with newly diagnosed cancer patients. *Journal of Psychosocial Oncology, 14,* 65–83.

Boulanger, A., Clark, A.J., Squire, P., Cui, E., & Horbay, G.L.A. (2007). Chronic pain in Canada: Have we improved our management of chronic noncancer pain? *Pain Research and Management, 12*(1), 39–47.

Bower, J.E., Kemeny, M.E., Taylor, S.E., & Fahey, J.L. (1998). Cognitive processing, discovery of meaning, CD4 decline, and AIDS–related mortality among bereaved HIV-seropositive men. *Journal of Consulting and Clinical Psychology, 66,* 979–986.

Bowler, D.F. (2001). "It's all in your mind": The final common pathway. *Work: Journal of Prevention, Assessment & Rehabilitation, 17,* 167–174.

Bozoian, S., Rejeski, W.J., & McAuley, E. (1994). Self–efficacy influences feeling states associated with acute exercise. *Journal of Sport and Exercise Psychology, 16,* 326–333.

Bracegirdle, H. (1995). Children's stereotypes of visibly physically impaired targets: An empirical study. *British Journal of Occupational Therapy, 58*, 25–27.

Brady, J.V., Porter, R.W., Conrad, D.G., & Mason, J.W. (1958). Avoidance behavior and the development of duodenal ulcers. *Journal of the Experimental Analysis of Behavior, 1*, 69–72.

Brain, K., Henderson, B. J., Tyndel, S., Bankhead, C., Watson, E., Clements, A., Austoker, J. (2008). Predictors of breast cancer-related distress following mammography screening in younger women on a family history breast screening programme. *Psycho-Oncology, 17*, 1180–1188.

Brand, R.J., Paffenberger, R.S., Scholtz, R.I., & Kampert, J.B. (1979). Work activity and fatal heart attack studied by multiple logistic risk analysis. *American Journal of Epidemiology, 110*, 52–56.

Brannon, L., & Feist, J. (2000). *Health psychology: An introduction to behavior and health.* Belmount, CA: Wadsworth/ Thompson Learning.

Brannon L., & Feist, J. (2007). *Health psychology: An introduction to behavior and health.* (6th ed.). Toronto: Thomson Wadsworth.

Bray, G.A. (1998). *Contemporary diagnosis and management of obesity.* Newton, PA: Handbooks in Health Care.

Bray, G.A., & Tartaglia, L.A. (2000). Medicinal strategies in the treatment of obesity. *Nature, 404*, 672–677.

Breivik, H., Collett, B., Ventafridda, V., Cohen, R., & Gallacher, D. (2005). Survey of pain in Europe: Prevalence, impact on daily life, and treatment. *European Journal of Pain, 10*, 287–233.

Brett, J., Bankhead, C., Henderson, B., Watson, E., & Austoker, J. (2005). The psychological impact of mammographic screening. A systematic review. *Psycho-Oncology, 14*(11), 917–938.

Brewer, B.W. (2001). Psychology of sport injury rehabilitation. In R.N. Singer, H.A. Hausenblas, & C.M. Janelle (Eds.), *Handbook of Sport Psychology.* (2nd ed.) (pp. 767–809). New York: Wiley.

Brewer, B.W. (2010). The role of psychological factors in sport injury rehabilitation outcomes. *International Review of Sport and Exercise Psychology, 3*, 40–61.

Brewer, B.W., Van Raalte, J.L., & Linder, D.E. (1991). Peak performance and the perils of retrospective introspection. *Journal of Sport and Exercise Psychology, 10*, 45–61.

Brewin, C.R., Watson, M., McCarthy, S., Hyman, P., & Dayson, D. (1998). Intrusive memories and depression in cancer patients. *Behaviour Research and Therapy, 36*, 1131–1142.

Brewster, J.M. (2001). Helping physicians with alcohol problems. *CMAJ, 164*(2), 179.

Brinchmann, B.S., Forde, R., & Nortvedt, P. (2002). What matters to the parents? A qualitative study of parents' experiences with life-and-death decisions concerning their premature infants. *Nursing Ethics, 9*(4), 388–404.

Brink, E., Karlson, B.W., & Hallberg, L.R.-M. (2002). To be stricken with acute myocardial infarction: A grounded theory study of symptom perception and care-seeking behaviour. *Journal of Health Psychology, 7*(5), 533–543.

British Columbia Eating Disorder Association. (1998). *School outreach program training manual.* Victoria, BC: Author.

Broderick, J.E., Junghaenel, D.U., & Turk, D.C. (2004). Stability of patient adaptation classifications on the multidimensional pain inventory. *Pain, 109*, 94–102.

Brondolo, E., & Mas, F. (2001). Cognitive-behavioral strategies for improving medication adherence in patients with bipolar disorder. *Cognitive and Behavioral Practice, 8*(2), 137–147.

Brousse, T. (1946). A psycho-physiological study. *Main Currents in Modern Thought, 4*, 77–84.

Brown, C. (2005). Injuries: The psychology of recovery and rehab. In S. Murphy (Ed.), *The sport psych handbook* (pp. 215–236). Champaign, IL: Human Kinetics.

Brown, D.L. (1988). No pretending not to know. *Journal of the American Medical Association, 260*, 2720.

Brown, M.A., & Stetz, K. (1999). The labor of caregiving: A theoretical model of caregiving during potentially fatal illness. *Qualitative Health Research, 9*, 182–197.

Browning, G., & Warren, N.A. (2006). Unmet needs of family members in the medical intensive care waiting room. *Critical Care Nursing Quarterly, 29*(1), 86–95.

Bruch, H. (1973). Eating disorders. *Obesity, anorexia nervosa and the person within.* New York: Basic Books.

Bruch, H. (1978). *The golden cage: The enigma of anorexia nervosa.* Cambridge, MA: Harvard University Press.

Bruch, H. (1982). Anorexia nervosa: Therapy and theory. *American Journal of Psychiatry, 139*, 1531–1538.

Bruch, H. (2001). *The golden cage: The enigma of anorexia nervosa.* Cambridge, MA: Harvard University Press.

Brucker, P.S., Yost, K., Cashy, J., Webster, K., & Cella, D. (2005). General population and cancer patients norms for the Functional Assessment of Cancer Therapy—General (FACT-G). *Evaluation & the Health Professions, 28*(2), 192–211.

Brunton, P. (1972). *A search in secret India.* New York: Samuel Weiser.

Bryant, J. (1999). Social determinants of participation in preventive screening services in Prince George, British Columbia. Unpublished Masters Thesis, The University of Northern British Columbia.

Buckalew, L.W. (1991). Patients' compliance: The problem and directions for psychological research. *Psychological Reports, 68*, 348–350.

Buckworth, J. & Dishman, R.K. (2007). Exercise adherence. In G. Tenenbaum & R.C. Eklund (Eds.), *Handbook of sport psychology.* (3rd ed.) (pp. 509–536). New Jersey: John Wiley & Sons.

Bulik, C.M., Sullivan, P.F., & Kendler, K.S. (2003). Genetic and environmental contributions to obesity and binge eating. *International Journal of Eating Disorders, 33*, 293–298.

Bulik, C.M., Sullivan, P.F., Tozzi, F., Furberg, H., Lichtenstein, P., & Pedersen, N.L. (2006). Prevalence, heritability, and prospective risk factors for anorexia nervosa. *Archives of General Psychiatry, 63*, 305–312.

Burack, J.H., Young, L.D., Anderson, K.O., Turner, R.A., Agudelo, C.A., et al. (1993). Depressive symptoms and CD4 lymphocyte decline among HIV-infected men. *Journal of the American Medical Association, 270,* 2568–2573.

Burack, R.C., & Carpenter, R.R. (1983). The predictive value of the presenting complaint. *Journal of Family Practice, 16,* 749–754.

Burgess, C.C., Potts, H.W., Hamed, H., Bish, A.M., Hunter, M.S., Richards, M.A., & Ramirez, A.J. (2006). Why do older women delay presentation with breast cancer symptoms? *Psycho-Oncology, 15* (11), 962–968.

Burgess, C., & Ramirez, A. (2006). Response to the letter to the editor from Professor Friedrich Stiefel on "Understanding why women delay in seeking help for breast cancer symptoms." *Journal of Psychosomatic Research, 60*(3), 309–310.

Burgoon, M., Callister, M., & Hunsaker, F.G. (1994). Patients who deceive: An empirical investigation of patient-physician communication. *Journal of Language and Social Psychology, 13,* 443–468.

Burke, R.J., & Richardsen, A.M. (1990). Sources of satisfaction and stress among Canadian physicians. *Psychological Reports, 67,* 1335–1344.

Burns, J.W., Sherman, M.L., Devine, J., Mahoney, N., & Pawl, R. (1995). Association between workers' compensation and outcome following multidisciplinary treatment of chronic pain: Roles of mediators and moderators. *Clinical Journal of Pain, 11,* 94–102.

Burt, R. D., Dinh, K. T., Peterson, A. V. Jr., & Sarason, I. G. (2000). Predicting adolescent smoking: A prospective study of personality variables. *Preventive Medicine, 30*(2), 115–125.

Burte, J.M., Burte, W.D., & Araoz, D.L. (1994). Hypnosis in the treatment of back pain. *Australian Journal of Clinical Hypnotherapy andHypnosis, 15,* 93–115.

Burton, D., Naylor, S., & Holliday, B. (2001). Goal setting in sports: Investigating the goal effectiveness paradox. In R.N. Singer, H.A. Hausenblas, & C.M. Janelle (Eds.), *Handbook of Sport Psychology.* (2nd ed.) (pp. 497–528). New York: Wiley.

Burton, K.R., & Wong, I.K. (2004). A force to contend with: The gender gap closes in Canadian medical schools. *Canadian Medical Association Journal, 170*(9), 1385–1386.

Bush, D.E., Ziegelstein, R.C., Tayback, M., Richter, D., Stevens, S., Zahalsky, H., & Fauerbach, J.A. (2002). Even minimal symptoms of depression increase mortality risk after acute myocardial infarction. *American Journal of Cardiology, 89,* 112–113.

Byrne, D. (1977). Social psychology and the study of sexual behavior. *Personality and Social Psychology Bulletin, 3,* 3–30.

C

Cafri, G. Olivardia, R., & Thompson, J. K. (2008). Symptom characteristics and psychiatric comorbidity among males with muscle dysmorphia. *Comprehensive Psychiatry, 49,* 374–379.

Calhoun, E. (1998, November). Reimbursement dilemmas for patients with refractory ovarian cancer. Paper presented at the Cancer Care: Quality of Life and Outcomes Symposium, Chicago, IL.

Calle, E.E., Thun, M.J., Petrelli, J.M., Rodriguez, C., & Heath, C.W. (1999). Body-mass index and mortality in a prospective cohort of U.S. adults. *The New England Journal of Medicine, 341,*1097–1105.

Calzavara, L.M., Bullock, S.L., Myers, T., Marshall, V.W., Cockerill, R. (1999). Sexual partnering and risk of HIV/STD among Aboriginals. *Canadian Journal of Public Health, 90,* 186–191.

Cameron, L. (1997). Screening for cancer: Illness perceptions and illness worry. In K.J. Petrie & J.A. Weinman (Eds.), *Perceptions of health and illness: Current research and applications* (pp. 291–322).

Campbell, C.M., Edwards, R.R., & Fillingim, R.B. (2005). Ethnic differences in responses to multiple experimental pain stimuli. *Pain, 113,* 20–26.

Campbell, S.H., & Birdsell, J.M. (1994). Knowledge, beliefs, and sun protection behaviors of Alberta adults. *Preventive Medicine, 23,* 160–166.

Campbell-Heider, N., & Knapp, T.R. (1993). Toward a hierarchy of adaptation to biomedical technology. *Crit Care Nurs Q, 16*(3), 42–50.

Canadian Cancer Society. (2003, April 8). Cigarette package warning labels. Retrieved November 3, 2010, from www.cancer.ca/Canada-wide/How%20you%20can%20help/Take%20action/Advocacy%20what%20were%20doing/Tobacco%20control%20advocacy/Progress%20in%20tobacco%20control/Cigarette%20package%20warning%20labels.aspx?sc_lang=en

Canadian Cancer Society. (2006). *Canadian cancer statistics: 2006.* Retrieved May 30, 2006, from www.cancer.ca

Canadian Cancer Society/National Cancer Institute of Canada. (2005). *Cancer statistics, 2005.* Toronto: Author.

Canadian Centre on Substance Abuse. (1999). Retrieved August 25, 2003, from www.ccsa.ca/

Canadian Centre on Substance Abuse. (2005). Canadian addiction survey. Retrieved June 10, 2006, from www.ccsa.ca/CCSA/EN/Research/Research_Activities/CanadianAddictionSurvey.htm

Canadian Fitness and Lifestyle Research Institute. (2009). Barriers to physical activity in children. *2009 Physical Activity Monitor: Facts and Figures, Bulletin 3.*

Canadian Institute for Health Information. (1998). *National health expenditure trends, 1975–1998.* Ottawa: Author.

Canadian Institute for Health Information. (2001). *Full-time equivalent physicians report: Canada, 1996/97 to 1998/99.* Ottawa: Author.

Canadian Institute for Health Information. (2005a). For the first time, more Canadian physicians are returning to the country than leaving. Media Advisory. Retrieved May 23,

2006, from www.cihi.ca/cihiweb/dispPage.jsp?cw_page=media_24aug2005_e

Canadian Institute for Health Information. (2005b). *Inpatient hospitalizations and average length of stay: Trends in Canada, 2003–2004 and 2004–2005*. Ottawa: Author.

Canadian Institute for Health Information. (2005c). Public health programs and prevention account for, on average, only 3% of health spending, says OECD. Retrieved April 24, 2006, from secure.cihi.ca/cihiweb/dispPage.jsp?cw_page=media_08nov2005_e

Canadian Institute for Health Information. (2006). *Full-time equivalent physicians report: Canada, 2002–2003 and 2003–2004*. Ottawa: Author.

Canadian Institute for Health Information. *National Health Expenditure Trends*, 1975 to 2009. (Ottawa, Ont.: CIHI, 2009).

Canadian Institutes of Health Research. (2004). Obesity. Retrieved August 10, 2006, from www.cihr-irsc.gc.ca/e/24942.html

Canadian Mental Health Association (2005). Eating disorsders. Retrieved June 5, 2010 from http://download.cmha.ab.ca/Edmonton/Eating%20Disorders.pdf

Canadian Nurses Association. (1997a). Out in front—Advanced nursing practice. *Nursing Now: Issues and Trends in Canadian Nursing*, January.

Canadian Nurses Association (CNA) and Canadian Institute for Health Information (CIHI) (2006). The Regulation and Supply of Nurse Practitioners in Canada: 2006. Cited in DiCenso, A., Auffrey, L., Bryant-Lukosius, D., Donald, F., Martin-Misener, R., Matthews, S., & Opsteen, J. (2007). Primary health care nurse practitioners in Canada. *Contemporary Nurse*, 26, 104–115.

Canadian Nurses Association. (1997b). *The future supply of registered nurses: A discussion paper*. Ottawa, Author.

Canam, C. (2005). Illuminating the clinical nurse specialist role of advanced nursing practice: A qualitative study. *Canadian Journal of Nursing Leadership*, 18(4), 70–89.

Cannon, W.B. (1939). *The wisdom of the body*. New York: Norton.

Cano, A., & de C. Williams, A.C. (2010). Social interaction in pain: Reinforcing pain behaviors or building intimacy? *Pain*, 149, 9–11.

Cappelli, M., Surh, L., Walker, M., Korneluk, Y., Humphreys, L., Verma, S., Hunter, A., Allanson, J., & Logan, D. (2001). Psychological and social predictors of decisions about genetic testing for breast cancer in high-risk women. *Psychology, Health & Medicine*, 6(3), 321–333.

Cardenas, V. (2006). The relationship between social support and depression among Latina and Caucasian dementia caregivers. *Dissertation Abstracts International: Section B; The Sciences and Engineering*, 66 (7–B), 39–42.

Carlson, C.R., & Hoyle, R.H. (1993). Efficacy of abbreviated progressive muscle relaxation training: A quantitative review of behavioral medicine research. *Journal of Consulting and Clinical Psychology*, 61, 1059–1067.

Carlsson, C.P.O., & Sjolund, B.H. (1994). Acupuncture and subtypes of chronic pain: Assessment of long-term results. *Clinical Journal of Pain*, 10, 290–295.

Carlsson, C.P.O., & Sjolund, B.H. (2001). Acupuncture for chronic low back pain: A randomized placebo-controlled study with long-term follow-up. *Clinical Journal of Pain*, 17, 296–305.

Carney, R.M., Freedland, K.E., & Veith, R.C. (2005). Depression, the autonomic nervous system, and coronary heart disease. *Psychosomatic Medicine*, 67(Supp 1), S29–S33.

Carney, R.M., & Jaffe, A.S. (2002). Treatment of depression following acute myocardial infarction. *Journal of the American Medical Association*, 288(6), 750–751.

Carpenter, D.J., Gatchel, R.J., & Hasegawa, T. (1994). Effectiveness of a video-taped behavioral intervention for dental anxiety: The role of gender and need for information. *Behavioral Medicine*, 20, 123–132.

Carpenter, K.M., Hasin, D.S., Allison, D.B., & Faith, M.S. (2000). Relationships between obesity and DSM-IV major depressive disorder, suicide ideation, and suicide attempts: Results from a general population study. *American Journal of Public Health*, 90, 251–257.

Carter, B.S., & Leuthner, S.R. (2002). Decision making in the NICU—Strategies, statistics, and "satisficing." *Bioethics Forum*, 18(3–4), 7–15.

Casperson, C.J., Powell, K.E., & Christenson, G.M. (1985). Physical activity, exercise, and physical fitness: Definitions and distinctions for health-related research. *Public Health Reports*, 100, 126–131.

Cassidy, K., Reid, G.J., McGrath, P.J., Finely, G.A., Smith, D.J., Morley, C., et al. (2002). Watch needle, watch TV: Audiovisual distraction in preschool immunization. *Pain Medicine*, 3, 108–118.

Castro, C. M., Wilson, C., Wang, F., Scillinger, D. (2007). Babel babble: Physicians' use of unclarified medical jargon with patients. *American Journal of Health Behavior*, 31(Suppl 1), S85–S95.

Catania, J.A., Kegeles, S.M., & Coates, T.J. (1990). Towards an understanding of risk behavior: An AIDS risk reduction model (ARRM). *Health Education Quarterly*, 17, 53–72.

Catz, S.L., Kelly, J.A., Bogart, L.M., Genosch, E.G., & McAuliffe, T.L. (2000). Patterns, correlates, and barriers to medication adherence among persons prescribed new treatments for HIV disease. *Health Psychology*, 19, 124–133.

CCSA (2008). CCSA roadside survey shows more drivers using drugs than alcohol. Retrieved on July 1, 2010 from www.ccsa.ca/2008%20CCSA%20Documents2/ccsa-newrel-20081210e.pdf

CCSA. (2010). Clearing the smoke on cannabis series highlights. Retrieved on July 1, 2010 from www.ccsa.ca/2010%20CCSA%20Documents/ccsa-011817-2010.pdf

CCSA. (2010). Canadian Alcohol and Drug Use Monitoring Survey (CADUMS): Summary of results for 2009.

Retrieved July 1, 2010 from www.hc-sc.gc.ca/hc-ps/drugs-drogues/stat/_2009/summary-sommaire-eng.php#alc

Cella, D.F., Tulsky, D.S., Gray, G., Saraflan, B., Linn, E., Bonomi, A., Silberman, M., Yellen, et al. (1993). The Functional Assessment of Cancer Therapy Scale: Development and validation of the general measure. *Journal of Clinical Oncology, 11*, 570–579.

Centers for Disease Control and Prevention (CDC). (1993). Cigarette smoking: Attributable mortality and years of potential life lost—United States, 1990. *Morbidity and Mortality Weekly Report, 42*, 645–649.

Centers for Disease Control and Prevention. (2005). Meningococcal disease. Retrieved March 26, 2006, from www.cdc.gov/ncidod/dbmd/diseaseinfo/meningococcal_g.htm

Chamberlain, J., Clifford, R.E., Nathan, B.E., Price, J.L., & Burn, I. Repeated screening for breast cancer. *Journal of Epidemiology and Community Health, 38*, 54–57.

Chambers, C.T., Cassidy, K.L., McGrath, P. J., et al. (1996). *Child Facial Coding System: A manual*. Nova Scotia and Vancouver: Dalhousie University and University of British Columbia.

Chan, B. (2002). *From perceived surplus to perceived shortage.* Ottawa: Canadian Institute for Health Information.

Chang, Y., & Etnier, J.L. (2009). Exploring the dose-response relationship between resistance exercise intensity and cognitive function. *Journal of Sport and Exercise Psychology, 31*, 640–656.

Chapman, C.R. (1984). New directions in the understanding and management of pain. *Social Science and Medicine, 19*, 1261–1277.

Chapman, C.R., Casey, K.L., Dubner, R., Foley, K.M., et al. (1985). Pain measurement: An overview. *Pain, 22*, 1–31.

Chapple, A., Ziebland, S., & McPherson, A. (2004). Stigma, shame, and blame experienced by patients with lung cancer: Qualitative study. *British Medical Journal, 328*(7454), n.p.

Charnley, F. (1999). Occupational stress in the newly qualified staff nurse. *Nursing Standard, 13*(29), 33–36.

Chassin, L., Presson, C.C., Pitts, S.C., & Sherman, S.J. (2000). The natural history of cigarette smoking from adolescence to adulthood in a Midwestern community sample. Multiple trajectories and their psychosocial correlates. *Health Psychology, 19*, 223–231.

Chaves, I.F., & Barber, T.X. (1976). Hypnotism and surgical pain. In D. Mostofsky (Ed.), *Behavioral control and modification of physiological activity*. Englewood Cliffs, NJ: Prentice-Hall.

Chavez, M. & Insel, T.R. (2007). Eating disorders. *American Psychologist, 62*(3), 159–166.

Chen, E.H., Shofer, F.S., Dean, A.J., Hollander, J.E., Baxt, W.G., Robey, J.L., Sease, K.L. & Mills, A.M. (2008). Gender disparity in analgesic treatment of emergency department patients with acute abdominal pain. *Academic Emergency Medicine, 15*, 414–418.

Chen, J., Fair, M., Wilkins, R., & Cyr, M. (1998). Maternal education and fetal and infant mortality in Quebec. *Health Reports, 10*(2), 53–64.

Chen, J., & Millar, W.J. (1998). Age of smoking initiation: Implications for quitting. *Health Reports, 9*(4), 39–46.

Chen, J., Ng, E., & Wilkins, R. (1996). The health of Canada's immigrants in 1994–1995. *Health Reports, 7*, 42.

Chen, J., & Wilkins, R. (1998). Seniors' needs for health-related personal assistance. *Health Reports, 10*(1), 39–50.

Chen, X., & Siu, L.L. (2001). Impact of the media and the Internet on oncology: Survey of cancer patients and oncologists in Canada. *Journal of Clinical Oncology, 19*(23), 4291–4297.

Cherny, N.I. (1996). The problem of inadequately relieved suffering. *Journal of Social Issues, 52*, 13–30.

Christianson, S. (1992). Emotional stress and eyewitness memory: A critical review. *Psychological Bulletin, 112*, 284–309.

CHSRF–Canadian Health Services Research Foundation. (2006). Myth: Medical malpractice lawsuits plague Canada. Mythbusters. Retrieved June 30, 2010, from www.chsrf.ca/mythbusters/html/myth21_e.php

Chung, B. (2001). Muscle dysmorphia: A critical review of the proposed criteria. *Perspectives in Biology and Medicine, 44*(4), 565–574.

Chyun, D.A., Melkus, G.D., Katten, D.M., Price, W.J., Davey, J.A., Grey, N., Heller, G., & Wacker, F.J. (2006). The association of psychological factors, physical activity, neuropathy, and quality of life in type 2 diabetes. *Biological Research for Nursing, 7*(4), 279–288.

Cinciripini, P.M., & Floreen, A. (1982). An evaluation of a behavioral program for chronic pain. *Journal of Behavioral Medicine, 5*, 375–389.

Clark, J. (1998, November). Prostate cancer quality of life: Patient centered measures of health outcomes. Paper presented at the *Cancer Care: Quality of Life and Outcomes Symposium*, Chicago, IL.

Clark, N.M., Gong, M., Schork, M.A., Evans, D., et al. (1998). Impact of education for physicians on patient outcomes. *Pediatrics, 101*, 831.

Clarke, J.N. (2000). *Health, illness, and medicine in Canada.* Don Mills, ON: Oxford University Press.

Classen, C., Butler, L.D., Koopman, C., Miller, E., DiMiceli, S., Giese-Davis, J., Fobair, P., Carlson, R.W., Kraemer, H.C., & Spiegel, D. (2001). Supportive-expressive group therapy and distress in patients with metastatic breast cancer. *Archives of General Psychiatry, 58*(5), 494–501.

Clements, P.T., DeRanieri, J.T., Vigil, G.J., & Benasutti, K.M. (2004). Life after death: Grief therapy after the sudden traumatic death of a family member. *Perspectives in Psychiatric Care, 40*(4), 149–154.

Clowers, M. (2002). Young women describe the ideal physician. *Adolescence, 37*, 695–704.

Coambs, R.B., Jensen, P., Her, M.H., Ferguson, B.S., et al. (1995). *Review of the scientific literature on the prevalence, consequences, and health costs of noncompliance and inappropriate use of prescription medication in Canada.* Ottawa:

Pharmaceutical Manufacturers Association of Canada (University of Toronto Press).

Cockerham, W.M. (1998). *Medical sociology.* (7th ed.). Upper Saddle River, NJ: Prentice Hall.

Cohen, H.J. (2000). Editorial: In search of the underlying mechanisms of frailty. *Journals of Gerontology Series A—Biological Sciences & Medical Sciences, 55,* M706–708.

Cohen, L., Rouladi, R.T., & Katz, J. (2005). Preoperative coping strategies and distress predict postoperative pain and morphine consumption in women undergoing abdominal gynecologic surgery. *Journal of Psychosomatic Research, 58*(2), 201–209.

Cohen, M.R., & Smetzer, J. (2005). Patient-controlled analgesia safety issues. *Journal of Pain & Palliative Care Pharmacotherapy, 19*(1),45–50.

Cohen, S., Doyle, W.J., Skoner, D.P., Fireman, P., Gwaltner, J.M. Jr., & Newsom, J.T. (1995). State and trait negative affect as predictors of objective and subjective symptoms of respiratory viral infections. *Journal of Personality and Social Psychology, 68,* 139–169.

Cohen, S., Doyle, W.J., Skoner, D.P., Rabin, B.S., & Gwaltney, J.M. (1997). Social ties and susceptibility to the common cold. *Journal of the American Medical Association, 277,* 1940–1944.

Cohen, S., & Herbert, T.B. (1996). Health psychology: Psychological factors and physical disease from the perspective of human psychoneuroimmunology. *Annual Review of Psychology, 47,* 113–142.

Cohen, S., Rodriguez, M.S., Feldman, P.J., Rabin, B.S., & Manuck, S.B. (2002). Reactivity and vulnerability to stress-associated risk for upper respiratory illness. *Psychosomatic Medicine, 64,* 302–310.

Cohen, S., Tyrrell, D.A.J., & Smith, A.P. (1993). Negative life events, perceived stress, negative affect, and susceptibility to the common cold. *Journal of Personality and Social Psychology, 64,* 131–140.

Cohen, S., & Wills, T.A. (1985). Stress, social support, and the buffering hypothesis. *Psychological Bulletin, 98,* 310–357.

Coiagluri, B., Roscoe, J.A., Morrow, G.R., Atkins, J.N., Giguere, J.K., & Colman, L.K. (2008). How do patient expectancies, quality of life, and postchemotherapy nausea interrelate? *Cancer, 113*(3), 654–661.

Cole, B. (1998, November). An overview of the Q-Twist method for evaluating trade-offs in clinical trials. Paper presented at the *Cancer Care: Quality of Life and Outcomes Symposium,* Chicago, IL.

Concheiro, A., Diaz, E., Luaces, C., Pou, J., & Garcia, J. (2001). Triage criteria in a emergency department. *An Esp Pediatr, 54*(3), 233–237.

Conn, K. (2000). *CP's role in First Nations and Inuit health care.* Ottawa: First nations and Inuit Health Branch.

Constable, R.T. (2003). MR physics of body MR imaging. *Radiol Clin North Am, 41*(1), 1–15.

Cook, J.A., Grey, D., Burke, J., Cohen, M.H., Gurtman, A.C., Richardson, J.L., Wilson, T.E., Young, M.A., & Hessol, N.A. (2004). Depressive symptoms and AIDS-related mortality among a multisite cohort of HIV-positive women. *American Journal of Public Health, 94*(7), 1133–1140.

Cooke, M.W., Arora, P., & Mason, S. (2003). Discharge from triage: Modelling the potential in different types of emergency department. *Emerg Med J, 20*(2), 131–133.

Coombs, R.H. (1998). *Surviving medical school.* Thousand Oaks, CA: Sage.

Coombs, R.H., & Fawzy, F.I. (1993). Surgeons' personalities: The influence of medical school. *Medical Education, 27,* 337–343.

Cooper, C.L., & Baglioni, A.J. (1988). A structural model approach toward the development of a theory of the link between stress and mental health. *British Journal of Medical Psychology, 61,* 87–102.

Cooper, L.A., Roter, D.L., Johnson, R.L., Ford, D.E., Steinwachs, D.M., & Powe, N.R. (2003). Patient-centered communication, ratings of care, and concordance of patient and physician race. *Annals of Internal medicine, 139,* 907–915.

Cordova, M.J., Cunningham, L.L.C., Carlson, C.R., & Andrykowski, M.A. (2001). Posttraumatic growth following breast cancer: A controlled comparison study. *Health Psychology, 20*(3), 176–185.

Coulter, A. (2002). Patients' views of the good doctor. *British Medical Journal, 325,* 668–669.

Courneya, K.S., Friedenreich, C.M., Sela, R.A., Quinney, H.A., Rhodes, R.E., & Handman, M. (2003). The group psychotherapy and home-based physical exercise (group-hope) trial in cancer survivors: Physical fitness and quality of life outcomes. *Psycho-Oncology, 12*(4), 357–374.

Cousins, N. (1988). Intangibles in medicine: An attempt at a balancing perspective. *Journal of the American Medical Association, 260,* 1610–1612.

Cousson-Gélie, F., Irachabal, S., Bruchon-Schweitzer, M., Dihuydy, J.M., & Lakdja, F. (2005). Dimensions of Cancer Locus of Control Scale as predictors of psychological adjustment and survival in breast cancer patients. *Psychological Reports, 97*(3), 699–711.

Coyne, J., Aldwin, C., & Lazarus, R.S. (1981). Depression and coping in stressful episodes. *Journal of Abnormal Psychology, 90,* 439–447.

Coyne, J.C., & Racioppo, M.W. (2000). Never the twain shall meet? Closing the gap between coping research and clinical intervention research. *American Psychologist, 55,* 655–664.

Coyne, J.C., Thombs, B.D., Stefanek, M., & Palmer, C. (2009). Time to let go of the illusion that psychotherapy extends the survival of cancer patients: Reply to Kraemer, Kuchler, and Spiegel (2009). *Psychological Bulletin, 135*(2), 179–182.

Cox, H. (1973). *The seduction of the spirit.* New York: Simon and Schuster.

Cox, R.H. (2007). *Sport psychology: Concepts and applications.* (6th ed.). New York: McGraw-Hill.

Cozby, P.C. (1993). *Methods in behavioral research.* (5th ed.). Mountain View, CA: Mayfield.

Cramer, J.A., Mattson, R.H., Prevey, M.L., Scheyer, R.D., & Ouellette, V.L. (1989). How often is medication taken as prescribed? *Journal of the American Medical Association, 261,* 3273–3277.

Creating a consistent health promotion approach in a national network. Ontario Health Promotion e-Bulletin, No. 453, Volume 2006. Retrieved March 1, 2010 from www.ohpe.ca/node/7231

Crepaz, N., & Marks, G. (2002). Towards an understanding of sexual risk behavior in people living with HIV: A review of social, psychological, and medical findings. *AIDS, 16,* 135–149.

Critchley, J.A., & Capewell, S. (2003). Mortality risk reduction associated with smoking cessation in patients with coronary heart disease. *Journal of the American Medical Association, 290,* 86–97.

Crossley, M.L., & Mubarik, A. (2002). A comparative investigation of dental and medical students' motivation towards career choice. *Br Dent J, 193*(8), 471–473.

Croyle, R.T., & Hunt, J.R. (1991). Coping with health threat: Social influence processes in reactions to medical test results. *Journal of Personality and Social Psychology, 60,* 382–389.

Csikszentmihalyi, M. (1997). *Finding flow.* New York: Basic Books.

Cullinane, C.A., Chu, D.Z.J., & Mamelak, A.N. (2002). Current surgical options in the control of cancer pain. *Cancer Practice, 10,* s21–s26.

Cummings, G.G., Fraser, K., & Tarlier, D.S. (2003). Implementing advanced nurse practitioner roles in acute care: an evaluation of organizational change. *J Nurs Adm, 33*(3), 139–145.

Curt, G.A., Breitbart, W., Cella, D., Groopman, J.E., Horning, S.J., Itri, L.M., Johnson, D.H., Miaskowski, C., Scherr, S., Portenoy, R.K., & Vogelzang, N.J. (2000). Impact of cancer-related fatigue on the lives of patients: New findings from the Fatigue Coalition. *The Oncologist,* 353–360.

Cuthbertson, B.H., Hull, A., Strachan, M., & Scott, J. (2004). Post-traumatic stress disorder after critical illness requiring general intensive care. *Intensive Care Medicine, 30,* 450–455.

D

Dalal, S., & Melzack, R. (1998). Potentiation of opioid analgesia by psychostimulant drugs: A review. *Journal of Pain and Symptom Management, 16,* 245–253.

Dando, T.M., & Perry, C.M. (2004). Aprepitant: A review of its use in the prevention of chemotherapy-induced nausea and vomiting. *Drugs, 64*(7), 777–794.

Danish, S.J., Nellen, V.C., & Owens, S.S. (1996). Teaching life skills through sport: Community-based programs for adolescents. In J.L. Van Raalte & B. Brewer (Eds.), *Exploring sport and exercise psychology* (pp. 205–225). New York: American Psychological Association.

Danish, S.J., Pettipas, A.J., & Hale, B.D. (1993). Life development intervention for athletes: Life skills through sports. *The Counseling Psychologist, 21,* 352–385.

Dare, C., & Eisner, I. (1995). Family therapy and eating disorders. In K. Brownell & C. Fairburn (Eds.), *Eating disorders and obesity: A comprehensive handbook* (pp. 318–323). New York: The Guilford Press.

Dantendorfer, K., Amering, M., Bankier, A., Helbich, T., Prayer, D., Youssefzadeh, S., Alexandrowicz, R., Imhof, H., & Katschnig, H. (1997). A study of the effects of patient anxiety, perceptions and equipment on motion artifacts in magnetic resonance imaging. *Magnetic Resonance Imaging, 15,* 301–306.

David, D., Ruttenberg, D.H., & Bovberg, D.H. (2006). Relations between coping responses and optimism-pessimism in predicting anticipatory psychological distress in surgical breast cancer patients. *Personality and Individual Differences, 40,* 203–213.

Davidson, R.J., Kabat-Zinn, J., Schumacher, J., Rosenkranz, M., Muller, D., Santorelli, S.F., et al. (2003). Alterations in brain and immune function produced by mindfulness meditation. *Psychosomatic Medicine, 65,* 564–570.

de Bruyn, T. (2000). *Taking stock: Policy issues associated with complementary and alternative health care.* Ottawa: Health Systems Division, Health Promotion and Programs Branch, Health Canada.

Deinzer, R., & Schüller, N. (1998). Dynamics of stress-related decrease of salivary immunoglobulin A (sIgA): Relationship to symptoms of the common cold and studying behavior. *Behavioral Medicine, 23,* 161–169.

De Koninck, M., Bergeron, P., & Bourbonnais, R. (1997). Women physicians in Québec. *Social Science and Medicine, 44,* 1825–1832.

De Kooker, M. (2008). Mind, immunity and health: The science and clinical applications of psychoneuroimmunology. *Continuing Medical Education, 26*(1), 18–20.

Denis, M.A., Ecochard, R., Bernadet, A., Forissier, M.F., Porst, J.M., Robert, O., Volckmann, C., & Bergeret, A. (2003). Risk of occupational blood exposure in a cohort of 24,000 hospital healthcare workers: position and environment analysis over three years. *J Occup Environ Med, 45*(3), 283–288.

Desbiens, N.A., Mueller-Rizner, N., Haniel, M.B., & Connors, A.F., Jr. (1998). Preference for comfort care does not affect the pain experience of seriously ill patients. The SUPPORT Investigators Study to Understand Prognoses and Preferences for Outcomes and Risks of Treatment. *Journal of Pain and Symptom Management, 16,* 281–289.

Deveugele, M., Derese, A., De Bacquer, D., van den Brink-Muinen, A., Bensing, J., & De Maesener, J. (2004). Is the communicative behavior of GPs during the consultation related to diagnosis? A cross-sectional study in six European countries. *Patient Education and Counseling, 54*(3), 283–289.

Devine, E.C. (2003). Meta-analysis of the effect of psychoeducational interventions on pain in adults with cancer. *Oncol Nurs Forum, 30*(1), 75–89.

De Wit, R., Herrstedt, J., Rapoport, B., Carides, A.D., Guoguang-Ma, J., Elmer, M., Schmidt, C., Evans, J.K., & Horgan, K.J. (2004). The oral NK1 antagonist, aprepitant, given with standard antiemetics provides protection against nausea and vomiting over multiple cycles of cisplatin-based chemotherapy: A combined analysis of two randomised, placebo-controlled phase III clinical trials. *European Journal of Cancer, 40*(3), 403–510.

Dialogue on Health Reform. (1996). Ontario Nurses Association.

Dickinson, L.M., deGruy, F.V., Dickinson, W.P., & Candib, L.M. (1999). Health-related quality of life and symptom profiles of female survivors of sexual abuse. *Archives of Family Medicine, 8*(1), 35–43.

DiFranceisco, W., Kelly, J.A., Sikkema, K.J., Somlai, A.M., Murphy, D.A., & Stevenson, L.Y. (1998). Differences between completers and early dropouts from 2 HIV intervention trials: A health belief approach to understanding prevention program attrition. *American Journal of Public Health, 88*, 1068–1073.

DiGirolamo, A., Thompson, N., Martorell, R., Fein, S., & Grummer-Strawn, L. (2005). Intention or experience? Predictors of continued breastfeeding. *Health Education & Behavior, 32*(2), 208–226.

Dillard, J., & Hirchman, L.A. (2002). *The chronic pain solution.* New York: Bantam.

Dillbeck, M.C., & Orme-Johnson, D.W. (1987). Physiological differences between transcendental meditation and rest. *American Psychologist, 42*, 879–880.

DiMatteo, M.R. (1994). Enhancing patient adherence to medical recommendations. *Journal of the American Medical Association, 271*, 79–83.

DiMatteo, M.R. (1995). Health psychology research: The interpersonal challenges. In G.G. Brannigan & M.R. Merrens (Eds.), *The social psychologists: Research adventures* (pp. 207–221). New York: McGraw-Hill.

DiMatteo, M.R. (2004a). Social support and patient adherence to medical treatment: A meta-analysis. *Health Psychology, 23*, 207–218.

DiMatteo, M.R. (2004b). Variations in patients' adherence to medical recommendations: A quantitative review of 50 years of research. *Medical Care, 42*(3), 200–209.

DiMatteo, M.R., & DiNicola, D.D. (1982). *Achieving patient compliance: The psychology of the medical practitioner's role.* New York: Pergamon.

DiMatteo, M.R., Giordani, P.J., Lepper, H.S., & Croghan, T.W. (2002). Patient adherence and medical treatment outcomes: A meta-analysis. *Medical Care, 40*(9), 794–811.

DiMatteo, M.R., Lepper, H.S., & Croghan, T.W. (2001). Depression is a risk factor for noncompliance with medical treatment: Meta-analysis of the effects of anxiety and depression on patient adherence. *Archives of Internal Medicine, 160*, 2101–2107.

DiMatteo, M.R., & Martin, L.R. (2002). *Health psychology.* Boston: Allyn & Bacon.

Dimeo, F. (2002). Radiotherapy-related fatigue and exercise for cancer patients: A review of the literature and suggestions for future research. *Front Radiat Ther Oncol, 37*, 49–56.

Dimeo, F.C. (2001). Effects of exercise on cancer-related fatigue. *Cancer, 92*(6 Suppl), 1689–1693.

Dimeo, F.C., Stieglitz, R.D., Novelli-Fischer, U., Fetscher, S., & Keul, J. (1999). Effects of physical activity on the fatigue and psychologic status of cancer patients during chemotherapy. *Cancer, 85*, 2273–2277.

Dinh, K.T., Sarason, I.G., Peterson, A.V., & Onstad, L.E. (1995). Children's perception of smokers and nonsmokers: A longitudinal study. *Health Psychology, 14*, 32–40.

Dirkzwager, A.J., van der Velden, P.G., Grievink, L., & Yzermans, C.J. (2007). Disaster-related posttraumatic stress disorder and physical health. *Psychosomatic Medicine, 69*, 435–440.

Dishman, R.K. (Ed.). (1988). *Exercise adherence: Its impact on public health.* Champaign, IL: Human Kinetics.

Dishman, R.K. (2001). The problem of exercise adherence: The problem of sloth in nations with market economies. *Quest, 53*, 279–294.

Dishman, R.K., & Buckworth, J. (1997). Adherence to physical activity. In W.P. Morgan (Ed.), *Physical activity and mental health* (pp. 63–80). Washington, DC: Taylor and Francis.

Distefan, J.M., Pierce, J.P., & Gilpin, E.A. (2004). Do favorite movie stars influence adolescent smoking initiation? *American Journal of Public Health, 94*(7), 1239–1244.

DiTomasso, R.A., & Kovnat, K.D. (1994). Medical patients. In F.D. Dattilio & A. Freeman (Eds.), *Cognitive-behavioral strategies in crisis intervention* (pp. 325–344). New York: Guilford Press.

Diverty, B., & Pérez, C. (1998). The health of Northern residents. *Health Reports, 9*(4), 49–58.

Dlin, B.M. (1980). The experience of surviving almost certain death. *Advances in psychosomatic medicine, 10*, 111–118.

Doll, R., Stephen, J., Barroetavena, M.C., Linden, W., Poole, G., Ng, E., Fyles, G., & Habra, M. (2003). Patient navigation in cancer care: Program delivery and research in British Columbia. *Canadian Oncology Nursing Journal, 13*(3), 193.

Doll, R., Stephen, J., Barroetavena, M.C., Linden, W., Poole, G. & Fyles, G. (2005). Patient Navigation in Cancer Care. Final Report. Vancouver: BC Cancer Agency.

Donnelly, G. (2003). Clinical expertise in advanced practice nursing: A Canadian perspective. *Nurse Educ Today, 23*(3), 168–173.

Dorner, T. E., Stronegger, W. J., Rebhandl, E., Rieder A., & Freidl, W. (2010). The relationship between various psychosocial factors and physical symptoms reported during primary-care health examinations. *Wiener Klinische Wochenschrift, 122*, 103–9.

Doucet, M.D., Purdy, R.A., Kaufman, D.M., & Langille, D.B. (1998). Comparison of problem-based learning and lecture format in continuing medical education on headache diagnosis and management. *Medical Education, 32*, 590–596.

Douglas Mental Health Institute. (2010) Ask the expert. Retrieved June 5, 2010 from www.douglasresearch.qc.ca/expert_advices?id=91

Doyle, W.J., Gentile, D.A., & Cohen, S. (2006). Emotional style, nasal cytokines, and illness expression after experimental rhinovirus exposure. *Brain, Behavior, and Immunity, 20*(2), 175–181.

Dracup, K. (2009). The challenge of reducing prehospital delay in patients with acute coronary syndrome. *Circulation. Cardiovascular Quality and Outcomes, 2*, 144–145.

Driskell, J.E., Copper, C., Moran, A. (1994). Does mental practice enhance performance? *Journal of Applied Psychology, 79*, 481–492.

Drozda, D.J., Allen, S.R., Standiford, D.A., Turner, A.M., & McCain, G.C. (1997). Personal illness models of diabetes: Parents of preadolescents and adolescents. *Diabetes Education, 23*, 550–557.

Dubbert, S. (2002). Physical activity and exercise: Recent advances and current challenges. *Journal of Consulting and Clinical Psychology, 70*, 526–536.

Duda, J.L. (1992). Motivation in sport settings: A goal perspective approach. In G. Roberts (Ed.), *Motivation in sport and exercise*(pp. 57–91). Champaign, IL: Human Kinetics.

Duda, J.L., & Hall, H. (2001). Achievement goal theory in sport: Recent extensions and future directions. In R.N. Singer, H.A. Hausenblas, & C.M. Janelle (Eds.), *Handbook of sport psychology*. (2nd ed.) (pp. 417–443). New York: Wiley.

Dugan, J., Lauer, E., Bouquot, Z., Dutro, B.K., Smith, M., & Widmeyer, G. (1996). Stressful nurses: The effect on patient outcomes. *Journal of Nursing Care Quality, 10*(3), 46–58.

Dumont, C., St. Onge, M., Fougeyrollas, P., & Renaud, L.A. (1998). Perceived burden in family caregivers with physical disabilities. *Canadian Journal of Occupational Therapy, 65*, 258–270.

Dunkel-Schetter, C. (1984). Social support and cancer: Findings based on patient interviews and their implications. *Journal of Social Issues, 40*(4), 77–98.

Dunn, J., Steginga, S.K., Occhipinti, S., & Wilson, K. (1999). Evaluation of a peer support program for women with breast cancer—Lessons for practitioners. *Journal of Community and Applied Social Psychology, 9*, 13–22.

E

Eaton, D.K., Kann, L., Kinchen, S., Shanklin, S., Ross, J. et al. (2010). Youth risk behavior surveillance–United States, 2009. MMWR. *Surveillance Summaries: Morbidity And Mortality Weekly Report. Surveillance Summaries/CDC, 59*(5), 1–142.

Edelman, S. (2005). Relationship between psychological factors and cancer: An update of the evidence. *Clinical Psychologist, 9*(2), 45–53.

Edwards, C.L., Fillingim, R.B., & Keefe, F. (2001). Race, ethnicity and pain. *Pain, 94*, 133–137.

Edwards, G., & Gross, M.M. (1976). Alcohol dependence: Provisional description of a clinical syndrome. *British Medical Journal*, 1058–1061.

Edwards, R.R., & Fillingim, R.B. (2003). Ethnic differences in thermal pain responses. *Psychosomatic Medicine, 6*, 346–354.

Edwards, R. R., Haythornthwaite, J.A., Sullivan, M.J., & Filingim, R.B. (2004). Catastrophizing as a mediator of sex differences in pain: Differential effects for daily pain versus laboratory-induced pain. *Pain, 111*, 335–341.

Eisenberg, D.M., Davis, R.B., Eltner, S.L., Appel, S., Wilkey, S., Van Rompay, M., et al. (1998). Trends in alternative medicine use in the United States 1990–1997. *Journal of the American Medical Association, 280*, 1569–1575.

Eisler, I., Dare, C., Russell, G.F., Szmukler, G., le Grange, D., & Dodge, E. (1997). Family and individual therapy in anorexia nervosa. A 5-year follow-up. *Archives of General Psychiatry, 54*, 1025–1030.

Elkins, G., White, J., Patel, P., Marcus, J., & Perfect, M.M. (2006). Hypnosis to manage anxiety and pain associated with colonoscopy for colorectal cancer screening: Case studies and possible benefits. *International Journal of Clinical and Experimental Hypnosis, 54*(4), 416–431.

Ellingson, L.A., & Yarber, W.L. (1997). Breast self-examination, the health belief model and sexual orientation in women. *Journal of Sex Education and Therapy, 22*, 29–24.

Ellis, A. (1962). *Reason and emotion in psychotherapy*. New York: Lyle Stuart.

Ellis, A. (1975). *How to live with a "neurotic."* (rev. ed.). New York: Crown.

Ellis, A. (1977). The basic clinical theory of rational-emotive therapy. In A. Ellis & R. Grieger (Eds.), *Handbook of rational-emotive therapy*. New York: Springer.

Ellis, A. (1994). The sport of avoiding sports and exercise: A rational emotive behavior therapy perspective. *The Sport Psychologist, 8*, 248–261.

Ellis, A., & Harper, B.A. (1975). *A new guide to rational living*. North Hollywood, CA: Wilshire.

Ellis, D.A., Naar-King, S., Frey, M., Templin, T., Rowland, M., & Cakan, N. (2005). Multisystemic treatment of poorly controlled Type 1 diabetes: Effects on medical resource utilization. *Journal of Pediatric Psychology, 30*(8), 656–666.

Elmore, J.G., Armstrong, K., Lehman, C.D., & Fletcher, S.W. (2005). Screening for breast cancer. *Journal of the American Medical Association, 293*(10), 1245–1256.

Emanuel, E.J., & Emanuel, L.L. (1992). Four models of the physician-patient relationship. *Journal of the American Medical Association, 267*, 2221–2226.

Emmons, K.M., Wechsler, H., Dowdall, G., & Abraham, M. (1998). Predictors of smoking among U.S. college students. *American Journal of Public Health, 88*, 104–107.

Engebretson, T.O., Clark, M.M., Niaura, R.S., Phillips, T., Albrecht, A., & Tilkemeier, P. (1999). Quality of life and anxiety in a phase II cardiac rehabilitation program. *Medical Science in Sports Exercise, 31*, 216–223.

Engel, G.L. (1977). The need for a new medical model: A challenge for biomedicine. *Science, 196*, 129–136.

Enns, M.W., Cox, B.J., Sareen, J., & Freeman, P. (2001). Adaptive and maladaptive perfectionism in medical students: A longitudinal investigation. *Medical Education, 35*(11), 1034–1042.

Environics Research Group. (2001). Baseline surveys: The health effects of tobacco and health warning messages on cigarette packages. Report to Health Canada. Accessed on October 28, 2010 from www.hc-sc.gc.ca/hl-vs/pubs/tobac-tabac/smoking-tabagisme/index_e.html

Ephraim, P.L., Wegener, S.T., MacKenzie, E.J., Dillingham, T.R., & Pezzin, L.E. (2005). Phantom pain, residual limb pain, and back pain in amputees: Results of a national survey. *Phys Med Rehabil, 86*, 1910–1919.

Epp, J. (1986). Achieving health for all: A framework for health promotion. *Canadian Journal of Public Health, 77*, 393–430.

Epstein, L.H., & Cluss, P.A. (1982). A behavioral medicine perspective on adherence to long-term medical regimens. *Journal of Consulting and Clinical Psychology, 50*, 950–971.

Erickson, M.H. (1967). An introduction to the study and application of hypnosis for pain control. In J. Lassner (Ed.), *Hypnosis and psychosomatic medicine* (p. 83). New York: Springer.

Estabrooks, P.A. (2000). Sustaining exercise participation through group cohesion. *Sport Science Reviews, 28*, 63–67.

Esterling, B.A., Kiecolt-Glaser, J.K., Bodnar, J.C., & Glaser, R. (1994). Chronic stress, social support, and persistent alterations in the natural killer cell response to cytokines in older adults. *Health Psychology, 13*, 291–298.

Etnier, J.L., Salazar, W., Landers, D.M., Petruzzello, S.J., Han, M., & Nowell, P. (1997). The influence of physical fitness and exercise upon cognitive functioning: A meta-analysis. *Journal of Sport and Exercise Psychology, 19*, 249–277.

Etter, J.F., & Perneger, T.V. (2001). Attitudes toward nicotine replacement therapy in smokers and ex-smokers in the general public. *Clinical Pharmacology and Therapeutics, 69*, 175–183.

Evans, B., Duggan, W., Baker, J., Ramsay, M., & Abiteboul, D. (2001). Exposure of healthcare workers in England, Wales, and Northern Ireland to bloodborne viruses between July 1997 and June 2000: Analysis of surveillance data. *British Medical Journal, 322*, 397–398.

Evans, D.L., Folds, J.D., Petitto, J.M., Golden, R.N., Pedersen, C.A., Corrigan, M., Gilmore, J.H., Silva, S.G., Quade, D., & Ozer, H. (1992). Circulating natural killer cell phenotypes in men and women with major depression. *Archives of General Psychiatry, 49*, 388–395.

Evans, P.D., Doyle, A., Hucklebridge, F., & Clow, A. (1997). Positive but not negative life-events predict vulnerability to upper respiratory illness. *British Journal of Health Psychology, 2*, 339–348.

Evans, P., Hucklebridge, K., & Clow, A. (2003). *Mind, immunity and health: The science of pschoneuroimmunology*. London: Free Association Books.

Evans, R.L., & Connis, R.T. (1995). Comparison of brief group therapy for depressed cancer patients receiving radiation treatment. *Public Health Reports, 110*, 306–311.

Evans, R.L., & Hendricks, R.D. (1993). Evaluating hospital discharge planning: A randomized clinical trial. *Medical Care, 31*, 358–370.

Evans, R.W., & Penzien, D.B. (2003). Your headache is a cow. *Headache, 43*, 168–169.

F

Facione, N.C., Miaskowski, C., Dodd, M.J., & Paul, S.M. (2002). The self-reported likelihood of patient delay in breast cancer: New thoughts for early detection. *Preventive Medicine, 34*, 397–407.

Farooqui, I.S., Matarese, G., Lord, G.M., Keogh, J.M., Lawrence, E., Agwu, C., et al. (2002). Beneficial effects of leptin on obesity, T cell hyporesponsiveness, and neuroendocrine/metabolic dysfunction of human congenital leptin deficiency. *The Journal of Clinical Investigation, 110*, 1093–1103.

Faulkner, M. (2001). The onset and alleviation of learned helplessness in older hospitalized people. *Aging & Mental Health, 5*(4), 379–386.

Fawcett, S.B., Paine-Andrews, A., Francisco, V.T., Schultz, J., Richter, K.P., Berkley-Patton, J., Fisher, J.L., Lewis, R.K., Lopez, C.M., Russos, S., Williams, E.L., Harris, K.J., & Evansen, P. (2001). Evaluating community initiatives for health and development. In I. Rootman, M. Goodstadt, B. Hyndman, D.V. McQueen, L. Potvin, J. Springett, & E. Ziglio (Eds.), *Evaluation in health promotion: Principles and perspectives*. World Health Organization Regional Publications, European Series, No. 92.

Fawzy, N.W., Secher, L., Evans, S., & Giuliano, A.E. (1995). The Positive Appearance Centre: An innovative concept in comprehensive psychosocial cancer care. *Cancer Practice, 3*(4), 233–238.

Felton, G.M., Parsons, M., & Bartoces, M.G. (1997). Demographic factors: Interaction effects on health promoting behavior and health related factors. *Public Health Nursing, 14*, 361–367.

Felton, J.S. (1998). Burnout as a clinical entity—Its importance in health care workers. *Occupational Medicine, 48*, 237–250.

Feltz, D.L. (1988). Self-confidence and sports performance. In K.B. Pandolf (Ed.), *Exercise and sport sciences reviews* (pp. 423–457). New York: MacMillan.

Feltz, D.L., & Landers, D.M. (1983). The effects of mental practice on motor skill learning and performance: A meta-analysis. *Journal of Sport Psychology, 5*, 25–57.

Feltz, D.L., & Lirgg, C.D. (2001). Self-efficacy beliefs in athletes, teams, and coaches. In R.N. Singer, H.A. Hausenblas, & C.M. Janelle (Eds.), *Handbook of sport psychology*. (2nd ed.) (pp. 340–361). New York: Wiley.

Ferguson, E., & Cassaday, H.J. (1999). The Gulf War and illness by association. *British Journal of Psychology*, 90, 459–475.

Ferguson, E., & Cassaday, H.J. (2002). Theoretical accounts of Gulf War Syndrome: From environmental toxins to psychoneuroimmunology and neurodegeneration. *Behavioral Neurology*, 13, 133–147.

Ferguson, E., James, D., & Madeley, L. (2002). Factors associated with success in medical school: Systematic review of the literature. *British Medical Journal*, 324(7343), 952–957.

Ferguson, E., James, D., O'Hehir, F., & Sanders, A. (2003). Pilot study of the roles of personality, references, and personal statements in relation to performance over the five years of a medical degree. *British Medical Journal*, 326(7386), 429–431.

Ferrell, B., Smith, S., Cullinane, C., & Melancon, C. (2003). Symptom concerns of women with ovarian cancer. *J Pain Symptom Manage*, 25(6), 528–538.

Ferrell, B.R., Novy, D., Sullivan, M.D., Banja, J., Dubois, M.Y., Gitlin, M.C., Hamaty, D., Lebovich, A., Liman, A., Lippe, P.M., & Livovich, A.G. (2001). Ethical dilemmas in pain management. *Journal of Pain*, 2, 171–180.

Festinger, L. (1954). A theory of social comparison processes. *Human Relations*, 7, 117–140.

Fillingim, R.B. (2003). Sex-related influences on pain: A review of mechanisms and clinical implications. *Rehabilitation Psychology*, 48, 165–174.

Fillingim, R.B. & Edwards, R. R. (2001). The association of hormone replacement therapy with experimental pain responses in postmenopausal women. *Pain*, 92, 229–234.

Fillingim, R. B., King, C. D., Ribeiro-Dasilva, M.C., Rahim-Williams, B., & Riley, J.L. III. (2009). Sex, gender, and pain: A review of recent clinical and experimental findings. *The Journal of Pain*, 10, 447–485.

Fillmore, K.M., Kerr, W.C., & Stockwell, T. (2006). Moderate alcohol use and reduced mortality risk: Systematic error in prospective studies. *Addiction Research and Theory*, 14(2), 101–132.

Finkelstein, P. (1986). Studies in the anatomy laboratory: A portrait of individual and collective defense. In R.H. Coombs, D.S. May, & G.W. Small (Eds.), *Inside doctoring: Stages and outcomes in the professional development of physicians* (pp. 22–42). New York: Praeger.

Finley, A., Chambers, C.T., McGrath, P.J., & Walsh, T. (1999, October). Further validation of the Parents' Postoperative Pain Measure. Poster session presented at the annual meeting of the American Pain Society, Fort Lauderdale, FL.

Fischer, S., Smith, G.T., & Anderson, K.G. (2003). Clarifying the role of impulsivity in bulimia nervosa. *International Journal of Eating Disorders*, 33(4), 406–411.

Fishbein, M., & Ajzen, I. (1975). *Belief, attitude, intention, and behavior: An introduction to theory and research*. Reading, MA: Addison-Wesley.

Fisher, J.D., & Fisher, W.A. (1992). Changing AIDs risk behavior. *Psychological Bulletin*, 111, 455–474.

Fisher, J.D., & Fisher, W.A. (1998). Theoretical approaches to individual level change in HIV risk behavior. In J. Peterson & R. Diclemente (Eds.), *HIV prevention handbook*. New York: Plenum.

Fisher, J. D., Fisher, W. A., & Shuper, P. A. (2009). The information-motivation-behavioural skills model of HIV preventive behavior. In R. J. DiClemente, R. A. Crosby, & M. C. Kegler (Eds.), *Emerging theories in health promotion practice and research*. (2nd ed.) (pp. 21–63). San Francisco: Jossey-Bass.

Flaherty, J.A., & Richman, J.A. (1993). Substance use and addiction among medical students, residents, and physicians. *Psychiatric Clinics of North America*, 16, 189–197.

Flakus, B.J. (1998). Stress relief for critical care nurses. *Nursing Management*, 29, 48D, 48H–48J.

Flanagan, W.M., Le Petit, C., Berthelot, J.M., White, K.J., Coombs, B.A., & Jones-McLean, E. (2003). Potential impact of population-based colorectal cancer screening in Canada. *Chronic Diseases in Canada*, 24(4), 81–88.

Flor, H. (2001). Psychophysiological assessment of the patient with chronic pain. In D.C. Turk & R. Melzack (Eds.), *Handbook of pain assessment*. (2nd ed.) (pp. 70–96). New York: Guilford Press.

Folkins, C.H., & Syme, W.E. (1981). Physical fitness training and mental health. *American Psychologist*, 373–389.

Folkman, S., & Lazarus, R.S. (1985). If it changes it must be a process: Study of emotion and coping during three stages of a college examination. *Journal of Personality and Social Psychology*, 48,150–170.

Folkman, S., Lazarus, R.S., Dunkel-Schetter, C., DeLongis, A., & Gruen, R.J. (1986). Dynamics of a stressful encounter: Cognitive appraisal, coping and encounter outcomes. *Journal of Personality and Social Psychology*, 50,992–1003.

Fong, G.T., Hammond, D., Laux, F.L., Zanna, M.P., Cummings, K.M., Borland, R., & Ross, H. (2004). The near-universal experience of regret among smokers in four countries: Findings from the International Tobacco Control Policy Evaluation Survey. *Nicotine Tobacco Research*, 6(3), S341–S451.

Fontaine, K.R., Redden, D., Wang, C., Westfall, A.O., & Allison, D.B. (2003). Years of life lost due to obesity. *Journal of the American Medical Association*, 289(2), 187–193.

Fordyce, W.E. (1976). *Behavioral methods for chronic pain and illness*. St. Louis: C.V. Mosby.

Forester, B., Kornfeld, D.S., Fleiss, J.L., & Thompson, S. (1993). Group psychotherapy during radiotherapy: Effects on emotional and physical distress. *American Journal of Psychiatry*, 150, 1700–1706.

Fox, K.R. (2000). The effects of exercise on physical self-perceptions and self-esteem. In S.J.H. Biddle, K.R. Fox, & S.H. Boutcher (Eds.), *Physical activity and psychological well-being* (pp. 88–117). London: Routledge & Kegan Paul.

Fox, R., & Gourlay, Y.J. (2000). The impact of highly active antiretroviral combination therapy in HIV infected patients in Glasgow. *Health Bull (Edinb)*, 58(4), 309–315.

Fraguela, J.A.G., Martin, A.L., & Trinanes, E.R. (2003). Drug abuse prevention in the school: Four-year follow-up of a programme. *Psychology in Spain, 7*, 29.

Fraley, S.S., & Altmaier, E.M. (2002). Correlates of patient satisfaction among menopausal women. *Journal of Clinical Psychology in Medical Settings, 9*, 235–243.

Francis, L., & Barling, J. (2005). Organizational injustice and psychological strain. *Canadian Journal of Behavioural Science, 37*, 250–261.

Frank, M.G., Hendricks, S.E., Johnson, D.R., Wieseler, J.L., & Burke, J.W. (1999). Antidepressants augment natural killer cell activity: In vivo and in vitro. *Neuropsychobiology, 39*, 18-24.

Franco-Bronson, K. (1996). The management of treatment-resistant depression in the medically ill. *Psychiatric Clinics of North America, 19*, 329–350.

Frankel, R., & Beckman, H. (1989). Evaluating the patient's primary problem(s). In M. Stewart & D. Roter (Eds.), *Communicating with medical patients* (pp. 86–98). Newbury Park, CA: Sage Publications.

Frankish, C.J., Milligan, C.D., & Reid, C. (1998). A review of relationships between active living and determinants of health. *Social Science and Medicine, 47*, 287–301.

Franks, P., & Bertakis, K.D. (2003). Physician gender, patient gender, and primary care. *Journal of Women's Health, 12*, 73–80.

Frasure-Smith, N., & Lesperance, F. (2003). Depression and other psychological risks following myocardial infarction. *Archives of General Psychiatry, 60*(6), 627–636.

Frasure-Smith, N., & Lespérance, F. (2008). Depression and anxiety as predictors of 2-year cardiac events in patients with stable coronary artery disease. *Archives of General Psychiatry, 65*(1), 62–71.

Frasure-Smith, N., Lesperance, F., & Talajic, M. (1993). Depression following mycardial infarction: Impact on 6-month survival. *Journal of the American Medical Association, 270*, 1860–1861.

Frasure-Smith, N., & Prince, R. (1985). The Ischemic Heart Disease Life Stress Monitoring Program: Impact on mortality. *Psychosomatic Medicine, 47*, 431–445.

Fredericks, L.E., & Evans, F.J. (2001). *The use of hypnosis in surgery and anesthesiology: Psychological preparation of the surgical patient.* Springfield, IL: Charles C. Thomas.

Fredrickson, B.L. (2001). The role of positive emotions in positive psychology: The broaden-and-build theory of positive emotions. *American Psychologist, 56*,218–226.

Freeman, N., Friedman, R.S., Bartholow, B.D., & Wulfert, E. (2010). Effects of alcohol priming on social disinhibition. *Experimental and Clinical Psychopharmacology, 18*(2), 135-144.

Frey Law, L.A., Evans, S., Knudtson, J., Nus, S., Scholl, K., & Sluka, K.A. (2008). Massage reduces pain perception and hyperalgesia in experimental muscle pain: A randomized, controlled trial. *The Journal of Pain, 9*(8), 714–721.

Friedman, J.M. (2000). Obesity in the new millenium. *Nature, 404*, 632–634.

Friedman, J.M. (2003). A war on obesity, not the obese. *Science, 299*, 856–858.

Friedman, L.C., Kalidas, M., Elledge, R., Dulay, M.F., Romero, C., Chang, J., & Liscum, K.R. (2006). Medical and psychosocial predictors of delay in seeking medical consultation for breast symptoms in women in a public sector setting. *Journal of Behavioral Medicine, 29*, 327–334.

Friedman, M., & Rosenman, R.H. (1959). Association of specific overt behavior pattern with blood and cardiovascular findings—Blood cholesterol level, blood clotting time, incidence of arcus senilis, and clinical coronary artery disease. *Journal of the American Medical Association, 162*, 1286–1296.

Friedman, M., & Rosenman, R.H. (1974). *Type A behavior and your heart.* New York: Knopf.

Frigon, J-Y. (2004). Biobehavioural and cognitive determinants of adolescent girls' involvement in sexual risk behaviours: A test of three theoretical models. *Canadian Journal of Human Sexuality, 13*(1), 29–44.

Frisoni, G.B., Fedi, V., Geroldi, C., & Trabucchi, M. (1999). Cognition and perception of physical symptoms in the community-dwelling elderly. *Behavioral Medicine, 25*, 5–12.

Fuchs-Lacelle, S. & Hadjistavropoulos, T. (2004). Development and preliminary validation of the pain assessment checklist for seniors with limited ability to communicate. *Pain Management Nursing, 5*, 37–49.

Fuchs-Lacelle, S., Hadjistavropoulos, T., & Lix, L. (2008). Pain assessment as intervention: A study of older adults with severe dementia. *Clinical Journal of Pain, 24*, 697–707.

Fukunger, T., Mizou, Y., Yamashita, A., Yamada, M., Yamamoto, Y., Tatsuno, Y., et al. (1992). Thymus of abused neglect children. *Forensic Science International, 53*(1), 69–79.

Fulton, T.R. (1996). Nurses' adoption of patient-controlled analgesia approach. *Western Journal of Nursing Research, 18*, 383–396.

G

Gagliese, L., & Katz, J. (2003). Age differences in postoperative pain are scale dependent: A comparison of measures of pain intensity and quality in younger and older surgical patients. *Pain, 103*, 11–20.

Gagliese, L., & Melzack, R. (1997). Age differences in the quality of chronic pain: A preliminary study. *Pain Research and Management, 2*, 157–162.

Gagliese, L, Weizblit, N., Ellis, W., & Chan, V.W.S. (2005). The measurement of postoperative pain: A comparison of intensity scales in younger and older surgical patients. *Pain, 117*(3), 412–420.

Gagnon, E.M., & Recklitis, C.J. (2003). Parents' decision-making preferences in pediatric oncology: the relationship to health care involvement and complementary therapy use. *Psychooncology, 12*(5), 442–452.

Galdas, P.M., Cheater, F., & Marshall, P. (2005). Men and health help-seeking behavior: Literature review. *Journal of Advanced Nursing, 49*, 616–623.

Gall, T.L., Charbonneau, C., Clarke, N.H., Grant, K., Joseph, A., & Shouldice, L. (2005). Understanding the nature and role of spirituality in relation to coping and health: A conceptual framework. *Canadian Psychology, 46,* 88–104.

Gall, T.L., & Cornblat, M.W. (2002). Breast cancer survivors give voice: A qualitative analysis of spiritual factors in long-term adjustment. *Psycho-Oncology, 11*(6), 524–535.

Garber, M.C. (2004). The concordance of self-report with other measures of medication adherence: A summary of the literature. *Medical Care, 42,* 649–652.

Gard, M.C.E., & Freeman, C.P. (1996). Dismantling of a myth: Review of eating disorders and socioeconomic status. *International Journal of Eating Disorders, 20,* 1–12.

Gareis, K.C., & Barnett, R.C. (2002). Under what conditions do long work hours affect psychological distress: A study of full-time and reduced-hours female doctors. *Work & Occupations, 29*(4), 483–497.

Gatchel, R.J. (2005). *Clinical essentials of pain management.* Washington, DC: American Psychological Association.

Gathchel, R.J., & Oordt, M.S. (2003). Coping with chronic or terminal illness. In R.J.O. Gatchel & M.S. Oordt (Eds.), *Clinical health psychology and primary care: Practical advice and clinical guidance for successful collaboration* (pp. 213–233). Washington, DC: American Psychological Association.

Gaudette, L.A., Richardson, A., & Huang, S. (1998). Which workers smoke? *Health Reports, 10*(3), 35–45.

Gauvin, L. (1990). An experiential perspective on the motivational features of exercise and lifestyle. *Canadian Journal of Sport Sciences, 15,* 51–58.

Gauvin, L., Levesque, L., & Richard, L. (2001). Helping people initiate and maintain a more active lifestyle: A public health framework for physical activity promotion research. In R.N. Singer, H.A. Hausenblas, & C.M. Janelle (Eds.), *Handbook of sport psychology.* (2nd ed.) (pp. 718–739). New York. Wiley.

Gauvin, L., & Spence, J.C. (1995). Psychological research on exercise and fitness: Current research trends and future challenges. *The Sport Psychologist, 9,* 434–448.

Gavin, L., Steiger, H., & Brodeur, (2008). Eating-disorder symptoms and syndromes in a sample of urban-dwelling Canadian women: Contributions toward a population health perspective. *International Journal of Eating Disorders, 42*(2), 158–165.

Gay, M., Philippot, P., & Luminet, O. (2002). Differential effectiveness of psychological interventions for reducing osteoarthritis pain: A comparison of Erickson hypnosis and Jacobson relaxation. *European Journal of Pain, 6,* 1–16.

Gellaitry, G., Cooper, V., Davis, C., Fisher, M., Date, H.L., & Horne, R. (2005). Patients' perception of information about HAART: Impact on treatment decisions. *AIDS Care, 17,* 367–376.

Gendolla, G. H., Abele, A. E, Andrei, A., Spurk, D., & Richter, M. (2005). Negative *mood,* self-focused attention, and the experience of physical symptoms: the joint impact *hypothesis.Emotion, 5* (2), 131–44.

George, T.R. (1994). Self-confidence and baseball performance: A causal examination. *Journal of Sport and Exercise Psychology, 16,* 3181–399.

Georgiades, K., Boyle, M.H., Duku, E., & Racine, Y. (2006). Tobacco use among immigrant and nonimmigrant adolescents: Individual and family level influences. *Journal of Adolescent Health, 38*(4), e1–e7.

Geyer, S. (1991). Life events prior to manifestation of breast cancer: A limited prospective study covering eight years before diagnosis. *Journal of Psychosomatic Research, 35,* 335–363.

Gibson, S.J., & Chambers, C.T. (2004). Pain over the lifespan: A developmental perspective. In T. Hadjistavropoulos & K.D. Craig (Eds.), *Pain: Psychological perspectives* (pp. 113–153). Mahwah, NJ: Erlbaum.

Gilbar, O. (1989). Who refuses chemotherapy: A profile. *Psychological Reports, 64,* 1291–1297.

Giles, B.E., & Walker, J.S. (2000). Sex differences in pain and analgesia. *Pain Reviews, 7,* 181–193.

Gill, D. (2006). Sport psychology and fitness activities. In J. Doasil (Ed.), *The sport psychologist's handbook* (pp. 589–615). Chichester, England. John Wiley & Sons.

Gilpin, E.A., Pierce, J.P., & Parkas, A.J. (1997). Duration of smoking abstinence and success in quitting. *Journal of the National Cancer Institute, 89,* 572–576.

Gilpin, E.A., White, V.M., & Pierce, J.P. (2005). What fraction of young adults are at risk for future smoking, and who are they? *Nicotine & Tobacco Research, 7*(5), 747–759.

Girdano, D.A., Dusek, D.E., & Everly, G.S. (2005). *Controlling stress and tension.* San Francisco: Pearson Education.

Glantz, S.A. (2004). 'Smoking in movies: A major problem and a real solution.' Erratum. *Lancet, 363*(9404), 250.

Glantz, S.A. (2004). Back to the future. Smoking in movies in 2002 compared with 1950 levels. *American Journal of Public Health, 94,* 261–262.

Glantz, S. (June, 2009). Smoking in the movies. Paper presented at the UK National Smoking Cessation Conference, London, UK. Retrieved July 1, 2010 from www.uknscc.org/2009_UKNSCC/mp3/stanton_glantz.html

Glaser, R., Kiecolt-Glaser, J.K., Bonneau, R., Malarkey, W., & Hughes, J. (1992). Stress-induced modulation of the immune response to recombinant hepatitis B vaccine. *Psychosomatic Medicine, 54,* 22–29.

Glaser, R., Kiecolt-Glaser, J.K., Speicher, C.E., & Holliday, J.E. (1985). Stress, loneliness, and changes in herpesvirus latency. *Journal of Behavioral Medicine, 8,* 249–260.

Glaser, R., Pearson, G.R., Bonneau, R.H., Esterling, B.A., et al. (1993). Stress and memory T-cell response to the Epstein-Barr virus in healthy medical students. *Health Psychology, 12,* 435–442.

Glaser, R., & Kiecolt-Glaser, J.K. (2005). Science and society: Stress-induced immune dysfunction: Implications for health. *Nature Reviews: Immunology, 5*(3), 243–251.

Glaser, R., Padgett, D.A., Litsky, M.L., Baiocchi, R.A., Yang, E.V., Chen, M., Yeh, P-E, Klmas, N.G., Marshall, G.D., Whiteside, T., Herberman, R., Kiecolt, Glaser, J., & Williams, M.V. (2005). Stress-associated changes in the steady-state expression of latent Epstein-Barr virus: Implications for chronic fatigue syndrome and cancer. *Brain, Behavior, and Immunity*, 19, 91–103.

Glassman, A.H., & Shapiro, P.A. (1998). Depression and the course of coronary artery disease. *American Journal of Psychiatry*, 155, 4–11.

Gmel, G., Gutjahr, E., & Rehm, J. (2003). How stable is the risk curve between alcohol and all-cause mortality and what factors influence the shape? A precision-weighted hierarchical meta-analysis. *European Journal of Epidemiology*, 18, 631–642.

Godin, G., Maticka-Tyndale, E., Adrien, A., Manson-Singer, S., et al. (1996). Cross-cultural testing of three social cognitive theories: An application to condom use. *Journal of Applied Social Psychology*, 26, 1556–1586.

Goffman, E. (1961). *Asylums*. New York: Anchor.

Gold, M.S. (2004). Physician health and impairment. *Psychiatric Annals*, 34(10), 736–741.

Goldberg, R.J., Gurwitz, J.H., & Gore, J.M. (1999). Duration of, and temporal trends (1994–1997) in, prehospital delay in patients with acute myocardial infarction. *Archives of Internal Medicine*, 159, 2141–2146.

Goldsmith, D.J. (2004). *Communicating social support*. New York: Cambridge University Press.

Goldstein, D.S., & McEwan, B. (2002). Allostasis, homeostasis, and the nature of stress. *Stress*, 193, 1081–1086.

Gollwitzer, P.M. (1993). Goal achievement: The role of intentions. In W. Stroebe & M. Hewstone (Eds.), *European Review of Social Psychology*, Vol. 4 (pp. 141–185). Chichester, UK: Wiley.

Gollwitzer, P.M. (2003). Goal achievement: The role of intentions. In W. Stroebe & M. Hewstone (Eds.), *European Review of Social Psychology*, Vol. 4 (pp. 141–185). Chichester, UK: Wiley.

Goodheart, C.D., & Lansing, M.H. (1997). *Treating people with chronic disease: A psychological guide*. Washington, DC: American Psychological Association.

Goodman, G., & Dooley, D. (1976). A framework for help-intended communication. *Psychotherapy: Theory, Research and Practice*, 13, 106–117.

Goodwin, P.J., Leszcz, M., Ennis, M., Koopmans, J., Vincent, L., Guther, H., Drysdale, E., Hundleby, M., Chochinov, H.M., Navarro, M., Speca, M., & Hunter, J. (2001). The effect of group psychosocial support on survival in metastatic breast cancer. *New England Journal of Medicine*, 345(24), 1719–1726.

Gott, C.M., Rogstad, K.E., Riley, V., & Ahmed-Jushuf, I. (1999). Delay in symptom presentation among a sample of older GUM clinic attenders. *International Journal of STD & AIDS*, 10, 43–46.

Gøtzsche P.C., Nielsen M. (2005). Screening for breast cancer with mammography. *Cochrane Database of Systematic Reviews* 2006, Issue 4. Art. No.: CD001877. DOI: 10.1002/14651858.CD001877.pub2.

Gould, D., & Damarjian, N. (1996). Imagery training for peak performance. In J.L. Van Raaalte & B.W. Brewer (Eds.), *Exploring sport and exercise psychology* (pp. 25–50). Washington, DC: American Psychological Association.

Grams, G.D., Herbert, C., Heffernan, C., Calam, B., Wilson, M.A., Grzybowski, S., & Brown, D. (1996). Haida perspectives on living with non-insulin-dependent diabetes. *Canadian Medical Association Journal*, 155, 1563–1568.

Gravely-Witte, S., Leung, Y.W., Nariani, R., Tamim, H., Oh, P., Chan, V.M., & Grace, S.L. (2010). Effects of cardiac rehabilitation referral strategies on referral and enrollment rates. Nature Reviews. *Cardiology*, 7(2), 87–96.

Gray, F., Chretien, F., Vallat-Decouvelaere, A.V., & Scaravilli, F. (2003). The changing pattern of HIV neuropathology in the HAART era. *J Neuropathol Exp Neurol*, 62(5), 429–440.

Gray, R.E., Fitch, M., Davis, C., & Phillips, C. (1997). Interviews with men with prostate cancer about their self-help group experiences. *Journal of Palliative Care*, 13, 15–21.

Green, E.E., Green, A.M., & Walters, E.D. (1972). Biofeedback for mind-body self-regulation: Healing and creativity. *Fields . . . Within Fields*, 5, n131–144.

Green, L., & Kreuter, M. (1991). *Health promotion planning: An educational and environmental approach*. Mountain View, CA: Mayfield Publishing.

Green, S., & Poole, G. (in press). Resident work hours: Examining work hours, sleep hours, and attitudes towards work hour limitations in residents in general surgery, orthopaedics, and internal medicine. *British Columbia Medical Journal*.

Greenwood, J. (1998). Meeting the needs of patients' relatives. *Professional Nurse*, 14, 156–158.

Gregoire, I., Kalogeropoulos, D., & Corcos, J. (1997). The effectiveness of a professionally led support group for men with prostate cancer. *Urological Nursing*, 17, 58–66.

Greist, J.H. (1984). Exercise in the treatment of depression. Coping with mental stress: The potential and limits of exercise intervention. Washington, DC: National Institute of Mental Health.

Griffin, M.J., Brennan, L., & McShane, A.J. (1998). Preoperative education and outcome of patient controlled analgesia. *Canadian Journal of Anaesthiology*, 45, 943–948.

Griffin, J.A., Umstattd, M.R., & Usdan, S.L. (2010). Alcohol use and high-risk sexual behavior among collegiate women: a review of research on alcohol myopia theory. *Journal of American College Health*, 58(6), 523–532.

Grippo, A.J., & Johnson, A.K. (2002). Biological mechanisms in the relationship between depression and heart disease. *Neuroscience & Biobehavioral Reviews*, 26(8), 941–962.

Gross, R., Bilker, W.B., Friedman, H.M., Coyne, J.C., & Strom, B.L. (2002). Provider inaccuracy in assessing adherence and outcomes with newly initiated antiretroviral therapy. *AIDS, 16,* 1835–1837.

Grossman, P., Niemann, L., Schmidt, S., & Walach, H. (2004). Mindfulness-based stress reduction and health benefits: A meta-analysis. *Journal of Psychosomatic Research, 57,* 35–43.

Grunau, R.V.E., & Craig, K.D. (1987). Pain expression in neonates: Facial action and cry. *Pain, 28,* 395–410.

Grusser, S.M., Winter, C., Muhlnickel, W., et al. (2001). The relationship of perceptual phenomena and cortical reorganization in upper extremity amputees. *Neuroscience, 102,* 263–272.

Gruzelier, J. (2003). Self-hypnosis and immune function, health, wellbeing, and personality. *Australian Journal of Clinical & Experimental Hypnosis, 31*(2), 153–161.

Gunzerath, L., Faden, V., Zakhari, S., & Warren, K. (2004). National Institute on Alcohol Abuse and Alcoholism report on moderate drinking. *Alcoholism: Clinical and Experimental Research, 28,* 829–847.

Gura, T. (2003). Cellular warriors at the battle of the bulge. *Science, 299,* 846–849.

Gushue, G.V., & Brazaitis, S.J. (2003). Lazarus and group psychotherapy: AIDS in the era of protease inhibitors. *Counseling Psychologist, 31*(3), 314–342.

Gutkin, C. (2003). Medical schools' accountability for physician resources. *Canadian Family Physician, 49,* 263.

H

Haan, N. (1993). The assessment of coping, defense, and stress. In L. Goldberger & S. Breznitz (Eds.), *Handbook of stress: Theoretical and clinical aspects.* (2nd ed.) (pp. 258–273). New York: Free Press.

Hadjistavropoulos, H.D., Craig, K.D., Grunau, R.E., & Johnston, C.C. (1994). Judging pain in newborns: Facial and cry determinants. *Journal of Pediatric Psychology, 19,* 485–491.

Hadjistavropoulos, H.D., Craig, K.D., Grunau, R.E., & Whitfield, M.F. (1997). Judging pain in infants: Behavioural, contextual, and developmental determinants. *Pain, 73,* 319–324.

Hadjistavropoulos, H.D., & de C. Williams, A.C. (2004). Psychological interventions in chronic pain. In T. Hadjistavropoulos & K.D. Craig (Eds.), *Pain: Psychological perspectives* (pp. 271–301). Mahwah, NJ: Erlbaum.

Hadjistavropoulos, T. (2004). Ethics for psychologists who treat, assess, and/or study pain. In T. Hadjistavropoulos & K.D. Craig (Eds.), *Pain: Psychological perspectives* (pp. 327–344). Mahwah, NJ: Erlbaum.

Hadjistavropoulos, T., LaChapelle, D., MacLeod, F., Snider, B., & Craig, K.D. (2000). Measuring movement–exacerbated pain in cognitively impaired frail elders. *Clinical Journal of Pain, 16,* 54–63.

Hadjistavropolous, T., von Baeyer, C., & Craig, K.D. (2001). Pain assessment in persons with limited ability to communicate. In D.C. Turk & R. Melzack (Eds.), *Handbook of pain assessment.* (2nd ed.) (pp. 134–152). New York: Guilford.

Hadlow, J., & Pitts, M. (1991). The understanding of common terms by doctors, nurses and patients. *Social Science and Medicine, 32,* 193–196.

Hahn, D.B., Payne, W.A., Gallant, M., & Crawford, S. (2003). *Focus on health.* Toronto: McGraw-Hill Ryerson.

Halfens, R.G. (1995). Effect of hospital stay on health locus-of-control beliefs. *Western Journal of Nursing Research, 17,* 156–167.

Hall, C.R. (2001). Imagery in sport and exercise. In R.N. Singer, H.A. Hausenblaus, & C.M. Janelle (Eds.), *Handbook of sport psychology.* (2nd ed.) (pp. 529–549). New York: Wiley.

Hall, J. A., & Roter, D. L. (2007). Physician-patient communication. In H.S. Friedman & R. Cohen Silver (Eds.) *Foundations of health psychology* (pp. 325–357). New York: Oxford University Press.

Hall, L.M., & Kiesners, D. (2005). A narrative approach to understanding the nursing work environment in Canada. *Social Science & Medicine, 61*(12), 2482–2491.

Hall, S., & Smith, A. (1996). Investigation of the effects and aftereffects of naturally occurring upper respiratory tract illness on mood and performance. *Physiology and Behavior, 59,* 569–577.

Hallowell, L.M., Stewart, S.E., de Amorim, E., Silva, C.T., Ditchfield, M.R. (2007). Reviewing the process of preparing children for MRI. *Pediatric Radiology, 38*(3), 271–279.

Halmi, K. A., Agras, W. S., Crow, S., Mitchell, J., Wilson, G. T., Bryson, S. W., & Kraemer, H. C. (2005). Predictors of treatment acceptance and completion in anorexia nervosa: Implications for future study designs. *Archives of General Psychiatry, 62,* 776–781.

Hamill, S., & Dickey, M. (2005). Cultural competence: What is needed in working with Native Americans with HIV/AIDS? *Journal of the Association of Nurses in AIDS Care, 16,* 64–69.

Hamm, R.M., & Smith, S.L. (1998). The accuracy of patients' judgments of disease probability and test sensitivity and specificity. *Journal of Family Practice, 47,* 44–52.

Hammond, D. (2005). Smoking behaviour among young adults: Beyond youth prevention. *Tobacco Control, 14,* 181–185.

Hammond, D., Fong, G.T., McDonald, P.W., Brown, K.S., & Cameron, R. (2004). Graphic Canadian cigarette warning labels and adverse outcomes: Evidence from Canadian smokers. *American Journal of Public Health, 94*(8), 1442–1445.

Hammond, D., Fong, G.T., McDonald, P.W., Cameron, R., & Brown, K.S. (2003). Impact of the graphic Canadian warning labels on adult smoking behaviour. *Tobacco Control, 12,* 391–395.

Hammond, D., McDonald, P.W., Fong, G.T., & Borland, R. (2004). Do smokers know how to quit? Knowledge and perceived effectiveness of cessation assistance as predictors of cessation behaviour. *Addiction, 99,* 1042–1048.

Hammond, D., McDonald, P.W., Fong, G.T., Brown, K.S., & Cameron, R. (2004). The impact of cigarette warning labels and smoke-free bylaws on smoking cessation: Evidence from former smokers. *Canadian Journal of Public Health, 95*(3), 201–204.

Hansen, R.G. (1986). *The joy of stress*. Fairway, KS: Andrews, McMeel and Parker.

Hansen, W.B., Graham, J.W., Sobel, J.L., Shelton, D.R., Flay, B.R., & Johnson, C.A. (1987). The consistency of peer and parent influences on tobacco, alcohol, and marijuana use among young adolescents. *Journal of Behavioral Medicine, 10,* 559–579.

Harandi, A.A., Esfandani, A., & Shakibaei, F. (2004). The effect of hypnotherapy of procedural pain and state anxiety related to physiotherapy in women hospitalized in a burn unit. *Contemporary Hypnosis, 21,* 28–34.

Hardy, J., Roberts, R., & Hardy, L. (2004). Awareness and motivation to change negative self-talk. *The Sport Psychologist, 23,* 435–450.

Hardy, L., Jones, G., & Gould, D. (1996). *Understanding psychological preparation for sport: Theory and practice of elite performers*. Chichester, England: John Wiley and Sons.

Harper, D.C. (1999). Presidential address: Social psychology of difference: Stigma, spread, and stereotypes in childhood. *Rehabilitation Psychology, 44,* 131–144.

Harris, L.M., Robinson, J., & Menzies, R.G. (1999). Evidence for fear of restriction and fear of suffocation as components of claustrophobia. *Behaviour Research and Therapy, 37,* 155–159.

Harrison, D., & Chick, J. (1994). Trends in alcoholism among male doctors in Scotland. *Addiction, 89,* 1613–1617.

Harrison, M.J., Kushner, K.E., Benzies, K., Rempel, G., & Kimak, C. (2003). Women's satisfaction with their involvement in health care decisions during a high-risk pregnancy. *Birth, 30*(2), 109–115.

Hart, I., & Poole, G.D. (1995). Individualism and collectivism and considerations in cross-cultural health research. *Journal of Social Psychology, 135,* 97–99.

Hart, T. A., & Heimberg, R. G. (2005). Social anxiety as a risk factor for unprotected intercourse among gay and bisexual male youth. *AIDS and Behavior, 9*(4), 505–512.

Hashmi, J.A., & Davis, K.D. (2010). Women experience greater heat pain adaptation and habituation than men. *Pain, 145,* 350–357.

Haskard Zolnierek, K. B., & DiMatteo, M. R. (2009). Physician communication and patient adherence to treatment: A meta-analysis. *Medical Care, 47*(8), 826–834.

Haskard Zolnierek, K. B., & DiMatteo, M. R., Mondala, M.M., Zhang, Z., Martin, L. R., & Messiha, A. H. (2009). Development and validation of the Physician-Patient Humor Rating Scale. *Journal of Health Psychology, 14*(8), 1163–1173.

Haskell, W.L., Alderman, E.L., Fair, J.M., et al. (1994). Effects of intensive multiple risk factor reduction on coronary atherosclerosis and clinical cardiac events in men and women with coronary artery disease: The Stanford Coronary Risk Intervention Project (SCRIPT). *Circulation, 89,* 975–990.

Hass, J. (2006). Nurse practitioners now able to work across Canada. *Canadian Medical Association Journal, 174*(7), 911–912.

Haug, M.R., Musil, C.M., Warner, C.D., & Morris, D.L. (1997). Elderly persons' interpretation of a bodily change as an illness symptom. *Journal of Aging Research, 9,* 529–552.

Haupt, E., Herrmann, R., Benecke-Timp, A., Vogel, H., Haupt, A., & Walter, C. (1996). The KID Study II: Socioeconomic baseline characteristics, psycho-social strain, standard of current medical care education of the Federal Insurance for Salaried Employees' Institution (BfA) diabetic patients in inpatient rehabilitation. Kissingen Diabetes Intervention Study. *Experimental Clinics in Endocrinology and Diabetes, 104,* 378–386.

Hawton, K., Clements, A., Sakarovitch, C., Simkin, S., & Deeks, J.J. (2001). Suicide in doctors: A study of risk according to gender, seniority and specialty in medical practitioners in England and Wales, 1979–1995. *Journal of Epidemiology & Community Health, 55*(5), 296–300.

Hayden, J.A., van Tulder, M.W., & Tomlinson, G. (2005). Systematic review: Strategies for using exercise therapy to improve outcomes in chronic low back pain. *Annals of internal Medicine, 142,* 776–785.

Hayes, L.J., O'Brien-Pallas, Duffield, C., Shamain, J., Buchan, J., Hughes, F., Laschinger, H.K.S., North, N., & Stone, P.W. (2006). Nursing turnover: A literature review. *International Journal of Nursing Studies, 43*(2), 237–263.

Haynes, R.B., Ackloo, E., Sahota, N., McDonald, H. P., & Yao, X. (2008). Interventions for enhancing medication adherence. *Cochrane Database of Systematic Reviews, 2.* Retrieved June 30, 2010, from www.mrw.interscience.wiley.com/cochrane/clsysrev/articles/CD000011/frame.html

Haynes, R.B., McKibbon, K.A., & Kanani, R. (1996). Systematic review of randomized trials of interventions to assist patients to follow prescriptions for medications. *Lancet, 348,* 383–386.

Haynes, S.G., Feinleib, M., & Kannel, W.B. (1980). The relationship of psychosocial factors to coronary heart disease in the Framingham Study: I. Methods and risk factors. *American Journal of Epidemiology, 107,* 362–383.

Hays, K. (1999). *Working it out: Using exercise in psychotherapy*. Washington, DC: American Psychological Association.

Hays, K.F. (2002). The enhancement of performing excellence among performing artists. *Journal of Applied Sport Psychology, 14,* 299–312.

Health Canada. (2000a). *Preventing substance use problems among young people: A compendium of best practices*. Ottawa: Health Canada Publications.

Health Canada. (2000b). *Straight facts about drugs and drug abuse*. Ottawa: Health Canada Publications.

Health Canada. (2002). *AIDS: The AIDS/HIV files*. Retrieved July 25, 2003, from www.hc-sc.gc.ca/english/feature/aids/symptoms_main.html

Health Canada. (2003). *Diabetes in Canada*. (2nd ed.). Ottawa: Author.

Health Canada. (2003a). *Body mass index (BMI) nomogram*. Retrieved July 6, 2003, from www.hc-sc.gc.ca/hpfb-dgpsa/onpp-bppn/bmi_chart_java_e.html

Health Canada. (2003b). *Canadian tobacco use monitoring survey 2002: Environmental tobacco smoke: At home, at work and in public places.* Retrieved July 17, 2003, from www.hc-sc.gc.ca/hecs-sesc/tobacco/research/ctums/2001/2001ets.html

Health Canada (2003c). Canadian guidelines for body weight classification in adults. Retrieved June 1, 2010 from www.hc-sc.gc.ca/fn-an/nutrition/weights-poids/guide-ld-adult/weight_book-livres_des_poids-13-eng.php

Health Canada. (2004a). Best practices—Treatment and rehabilitation for driving while impaired offenders. Retrieved June 10, 2006, from www.hc-sc.gc.ca/ahc-asc/pubs/drugs-drogues/bp_treatment-mp_traitement/overview-apercu_e.html

Health Canada. (2004b). Quitting smoking. Retrieved April 24, 2006, from www.hc-sc.gc.ca/hl-vs/tobac-tabac/research-recherche/stat/ctums-esutc/fs-if/2003/2003-quit-cess_e.html

Health Canada. (2005a). It's your health: Breast implants. Retrieved June 27, 2006, from www.hc-sc.gc.ca/iyh-vsv/med/implants_e.html

Health Canada. (2005b). Healthy living: Canadian tobacco use monitoring survey (CTUMS). Retrieved May 17, 2006, from www.hc-sc.gc.ca/hl-vs/tobac-tabac/research-recherche/stat/ctums-esutc/prevalence/index_e.html

Health Canada. (2005c). Healthy living: Nicotine addiction. Retrieved September 1, 2006, from www.hc-sc.gc.ca/hl-vs/tobac-tabac/res/news-nouvelles/fs-if/nicotine_e.html

Health Canada. (2006a). Diseases & conditions: HIV and AIDS. Retrieved June 6, 2006, from www.hc-sc.gc.ca/dc-ma/aids-sida/index_e.html

Health Canada. (2006b). Healthy living: Overview of health risks of smoking. Retrieved September 1, 2006, from www.hc-sc.gc.ca/hl-vs/tobac-tabac/res/news-nouvelles/fs-if/nicotine_e.html

Health Canada. (2006c). Women and cancer. Retrieved April 9, 2006, from www.hc-sc.gc.ca/hl-vs/pubs/women-femmes/cancer_e.html

Health Canada. (2009a). The Canadian Alcohol and Drug Use Monitoring Survey (CADUMS) summary of results for 2009. Retrieved July 1, 2010, from www.hc-sc.gc.ca/hc-ps/drugs-drogues/stat/_2009/summary-sommaire-eng.php

Health Canada (2009b). Straight facts about drugs and drug abuse. Retrieved November 3, 2010, from www.hc-sc.gc.ca/hc-ps/pubs/adp-apd/straight_facts-faits_mefaits/tables-tableaux-eng.php

Health Canada. (2010). Drug and alcohol use statistics: Major findings from the Canadian Alcohol and Drug Use Monitoring Survey (CADUMS) 2009. Retrieved July 1, 2010, from www.hc-sc.gc.ca/hc-ps/drugs-drogues/stat/index-eng.php

Hearn, J., & Higginson, T.J. (1998). Do specialist palliative care teams improve outcomes for cancer patients? A systematic literature review. *Palliative Medicine, 12,* 317–332.

Heatherton, T.F., Herman, C.P., & Polivy, J. (1992). Effects of distress on eating: The importance of ego-involvement. *Journal of Personality and Social Psychology 62,* 81–803

Hebebrand, J., & Hinney, A. (2009). Environmental and genetic risk factors in obesity. *Child and Adolescent Psychiatric Clinics of North America, 18,* 83–94.

Hemingway, H., & Marmot, M. (1999). Psychosocial factors in the aetiology and prognosis of coronary heart disease: Systematic review of prospective cohort studies. *British Medical Journal, 318,* 1460–1467.

Helft, P.R., Hlubocky, F., & Daugherty, C.K. (2003). American oncologists' views of Internet use by cancer patients: A mail survey of American Society of Clinical Oncology members. *Journal of Clinical Oncology, 21*(5), 942–947.

Henbest, R.J., & Fehrsen, G.S. (1992). Patient-centredness: Is it applicable outside the west? Its measurement and effect on outcomes. *Family Practice, 9,* 311–317.

Hendricks, L.E., & Hendricks, R.T. (1998). Greatest fears of type 1 and type 2 patients about having diabetes: Implications for diabetes educators. *Diabetes Education, 24,* 168–173.

Henry, J.L. (2008). The need for knowledge translation in chronic pain. *Pain Research and Management, 13*(6), 465–476.

Henthorne, T.L., LaTour, M.S., & Nataraajan, R. (1993). Fear appeals in print advertising: An analysis of arousal and ad response. *Journal of Advertising, 22,* 59–69.

Herbert, H.D., Butera, J.N., Castillo, J., & Mega, A.E. (2009). Are we training our fellows adequately in delivering bad news to patients? A survey of hemoatology/oncology program directors. *Journal of Palliative Medicine, 12*(12), 1119–1124.

Herbert, T.B., & Cohen, S. (1993). Stress and immunity in humans: A meta-analytic review. *Psychosomatic Medicine, 55,* 364–379.

Herbert, T.B., Cohen, S., Marsland, A.L., Bachen, E.A., Rabin, B.S., et al. (1994). Cardiovascular reactivity and the course of immune response to an acute psychological stressor. *Psychosomatic Medicine, 56,* 337–344.

Herman, C.P., Fitzgerald, N.E., & Polivy, J. (2003). The influence of social norms on hunger ratings and eating. *Appetite, 41,* 15–20.

Herman, C.P., Koenig-Nobert, S., Peterson, J.B., & Polivy, J. (2005). Matching effects on eating: Do individual differences make a difference? *Appetite, 45,* 108–109.

Herman, C.P., & Polivy, J. (1975). Anxiety, restraint, and eating behavior. *Journal of Abnormal Psychology, 84,* 666–672.

Herman, C.P., & Polivy, J. (1980). *Restrained eating.* In A.J. Stunkard (Ed.), *Obesity* (pp. 593–606). Philadelphia: Saunders.

Herman, C.P., Roth, D.A., & Polivy, J. (2003). Effects of the presence of others on food intake: A normative interpretation. *Psychological Bulletin, 129,* 873–886.

Herrmann, C.K., Brand-Driehorst, S., Kaminsky, B., Leibing, E., Staats, H., & Rüger, U. (1998). Diagnostic groups and depressed mood as predictors of 22-month mortality in medical inpatients. *Psychosomatic Medicine, 60,* 570–577.

Hewitt, M., & Rowland, J.H. (2002). Mental health service use among adult cancer survivors: Analysis of the National Health Interview Survey. *Journal of Clinical Oncology, 20,* 4581–4590.

Hickok, J.T., Roscoe, J.A., Morrow, G.R., King, D.K., Atkins, J.N., & Fitch, T.R. (2003). Nausea and emesis remain significant problems of chemotherapy despite prophylaxis with 5-hydroxytryptamine-3 antiemetics: A University of Rochester James P. Wilmot Cancer Center Community Clinical Oncology Program Study of 360 cancer patients treated in the community. *Cancer, 97*(11), 2880–2886.

Hicks, C.L., von Baeyer, C.L., Spafford, P.A., van Korlaar, I., & Goodenough, B. (2001). The Faces Pain Scale—revised: Toward a common metric in pediatric pain measurement. *Pain, 93*(2), 173–183.

Hilgard, E.R., & Hilgard, J.R. (1975). *Hypnosis in the relief of pain.* Los Altos, CA: Kaufman.

Hill, J.O., Wyatt, H.R., Reed, G.W., & Peters, J.C. (2003). Obesity and the environment: Where do we go from here? *Science, 299,* 853–855.

Hilsden, R.J., Verhoef, M.J., Best, A., & Pocobelli, G. (2003). Complementary and alternative medicine use by Canadian patients with inflammatory bowel disease: Results from a national survey. *Am J Gastroenterol, 98*(7), 1563–1568.

Hilton, S., Hunt, K., Emslie, C, Salinas, M., & Ziebland, S. (2008). Have men been overlooked? A comparison of young men and women's experiences of chemotherapy-induced alopecia. *Psycho-Oncology, 17,* 577–583.

Hinds, P.S., Sanders, C.B., Srivastava, D.K., Hickey, S., Jayawardene, D., Milligan, M., Olson, M.S., Puckett, P., Quargnenti, A., Randall, E.A., & Tye, V. (1998). Testing the stress-response sequence model in paediatric oncology nursing. *Journal of Advanced Nursing, 28,* 1146–1157.

HIV/AIDS among Aboriginal persons in Canada: A continuing concern. (2003). Ottawa: Health Canada, Centre for Infectious Disease Prevention and Control.

Hoek, H.W. (2006). Incidence, prevalence and mortality of anorexia nervosa and other eating disorders. *Current Opinion in Psychiatry, 19*(4), 389–394.

Hoeyymans, N., Feskens, E., Kromhout, D., & Van Den Bos, G. (1997). Aging and the relationship between functional status and self-rated health in elderly men. *Social Science and Medicine, 45*(1), 1527–1536.

Hoffman, A.J., & Scott, L.D. (2003). Role stress and career satisfaction among registered nurses by work shift patterns. *J Nurs Adm, 33*(6), 337–342.

Hoffmann, D.E., & Tarzian, A.J. (2001). The girl who cried pain: A bias against women in the treatment of pain. *The Journal of Law, Medicine and Ethics, 29,* 13–27.

Hoffman, H.G. (2004). Virtual-reality therapy. *Scientific American, 291*(2), 58–65.

Hoffman, H.G., Richards, T.L., Bills, A.R., Van Oostrom, T. Magula, J., Seibel, E.J., & Sharar, S.R. (2006). Using MRI to study the neural correlates of virtual reality analgesia. *CNS Spectrums, 11*(1), 45–51.

Hoffman, H.G., Patterson, D.R., Magula, J., Carrougher, G.J., Zeltzer, K., Dagadakis, S., & Sharar, S.R. (2004). Water-friendly virtual reality pain control during wound care. *Journal of Clinical Psychology, 60*(2), 189–195.

Hoffman, H.G., Sharar, S.R., Coda, B., Everett, J.J. Ciol, M., Richards, T., & Patterson, D.R. (2004). Manipulating presence influences the magnitude of virtual reality analgesia. *Pain, 111,* 162–168.

Hogan, B.E., & Linden, W. (2004). Anger response styles and blood pressure: At least don't ruminate about it! *Annals of Behavioral Medicine, 27*(1), 38–49.

Holdcraft, L.C., Assefi, N., & Buchwald, D. (2003). Complementary and alternative medicine in fibromyalgia and related syndromes. *Best Pract Res Clin Rheumatol, 17*(4), 667–683.

Holland, C.K. (1993). An ethnographic study of nursing culture as an exploration for determining the existence of a system of ritual. *Journal of Advances in Nursing, 18,*1461–1470.

Holland, J.C., Romano, S.J., Heiligenstein, J.H., Tepner, R.G., & Wilson, M.G. (1998). A controlled trial of fluoxetine and desipramine in depressed women with advanced cancer. *Psychooncology, 7,* 291–300.

Holland, K.D., & Holahan, C.K. (2003). The relation of social support and coping to positive adaptation to breast cancer. *Psychology & Health, 18,* 15–29.

Holly, P., Kennedy, P., Taylor, A., & Beedie, A. (2003). Immediate breast reconstruction and psychological adjustment in women who have undergone surgery for breast cancer: A preliminary study. *Psychology, Health & Medicine, 8*(4), 441–452.

Holmich, L.R., Friis, S., Fryzek, J.P., Vejborg, I.M., Conrad, C., Sletting, S., Kjoller, K., McLaughlin, J.K., & Olsen, J. H. (2003). Incidence of silicone breast implant rupture. *Arch Surg, 138*(7), 801–806.

Homo-Delarche, F., Fitzpatrick, F., Christeff, N., Nunez, E.A., Bach, J.F., & Dardenne, M. (1991). Sex steroids, glucocorticoids, stress and autoimmunity. *Journal of Steroid Biochemistry and Molecular Biology, 40,* 619–637.

HON Code of Conduct for Medical and Health Web Sites. (2003, April 23). [Web site]. Health on the Net Foundation. Retrieved July 1, 2003, from www.hon.ch/

Hong, T.B., Oddone, E.Z., Dudley, T.K., & Bosworth, H.B. (2006). Medication barriers and anti-hypertensive medication adherence: The moderating role of locus of control. *Psychology, Health & Medicine, 11*(1), 20–28.

Hornberger, J., Thom, D., & MacCurdy, T. (1997). Effects of a self-administered previsit questionnaire to enhance awareness of patients' concerns in primary care. *Journal of General Internal Medicine, 12,* 597–606.

Hoskins, C.N., Baker, S., Sherman, D., & Bohlander, J. (1996). Social support and patterns of adjustment to breast cancer. *Scholarly Inquiry For Nursing Practice, 10,* 99–123.

Hospital days and average length of stay for Canada, Provinces and Territories, 1994/95 to 1999/00. (2001, Sept 26). [web site]. Hospital Morbidity Database, Canadian Institute for Health Information. Retrieved July 8, 2003, from secure.cihi.ca/chihweb/en/media_26sep2001_tab3_e.html

House, J.S. (1981). *Work stress and social support.* Reading, MA: Addison-Wesley.

House, J.S., Landis, K.R., & Umberson, D. (1988). Social relationships and health. *Science, 241,* 540–545.

Hovland, C.I., Janis, I.L., & Kelley, H.H. (1953). *Communication and persuasion: Psychological studies of opinion change.* New Haven, CT: Yale University Press.

How Canadians Find Health Information on the Internet. (2003, March 15). [Web site]. Canadian Health Network. Retrieved June 29, 2003, from www.canadian-health-network.ca/html/newnotable/mar15a_2003e.html

Howard, G., Wagenknecht, L.E., Burk, G.L., Diez-Roux, A., et al. (1998). Cigarette smoking and progression of atherosclerosis: The Atherosclerosis Risk in Communities (ARIC) Study. *Journal of the American Medical Society, 279,* 119–124.

Howard, V.A., & Thurber. (1998). The interpretation of infant pain: Physiological and behavioral indicators. *Pediatric Nursing, 13(3),* 164–174.

Howie, J.G., Porter, A.M., Heaney, D.J., & Hopton, J.L. (1991). Long to short consultation ratio: A proxy measure of quality of care for general practice. *British Journal of General Practice, 41(343),* 48–54.

Humbke, K.L., Brown, D.L., Welder, A.N., Fillion, D.T., Dobson, K.S., & Arnett, J.L. (2004). A survey of hospital psychology in Canada. *Canadian Psychology, 45(1),* 31–41.

Hunter, M., & Philips, C. (1981). The experience of headache: An assessment of the qualities of tension headache pain. *Pain, 10,* 209–219.

Hunter, J.P., Katz, J., & Davis, K.D. (2005). Dissociation of phantom limb phenomena from stump tactile spatial acuity and sensory thresholds. *Brain, 128,* 308–320.

Hurley, A.D., Tomasulo, D.J., & Pfadt, A.G. (1998). Individual and group psychotherapy approaches for persons with mental retardation and developmental disabilities. *Journal of Developmental and Physical Disabilities, 10,* 365–386.

Huth, M.M., Broome, M.E., & Good, M. (2004). Imagery reduces children's post-operative pain. *Pain, 110,* 4399–448.

Hwang, S.W. (2006). Discharge day. *Canadian Medical Association Journal, 174(8),* 1138–1139.

I

Igartua, J.J., Cheng, L., & Lopes, O. (2003). To think or not to think: Two pathways towards persuasion by short films on AIDS prevention. *Journal of Health Communication, 8(6),* 513–528.

Ilacqua, G.E. (1994). Migraine headaches: Coping efficacy of guided imagery training. *Headache, 34,* 99–102.

Inman, J.J., & Zeelenberg, M. (2002). Implementation regret in repeat purchase versus switching decisions: The attenuating role of decision justifiability. *Journal of Consumer Research, 29,* 116–128.

International Centre for Health and Society. (2003). *Social determinants of health: The solid facts.* (2nd ed.). World Health Organization, Europe.

Irwin, M., Daniels, M., Smith, T.L., Bloom, E., & Weiner, H. (1987). Impaired natural killer cell activity during bereavement. *Brain, Behavior, and Immunity, 1,* 98–104.

Irwin, M., Lacher, U., & Caldwell, C. (1992). Depression and reduced natural killer cytotoxicity: A longitudinal study of depressed patients and control subjects. *Psychological Medicine, 22,* 1045–1050.

Irwin, M., Patterson, T., Smith, T.L., Caldwell, C., Brown, S.A., Gillin, J.C., & Grant, I. (1990). Reduction of immune function in life stress and depression. *Biological Psychiatry, 27,* 23–30.

Irwin, M.R., Pike, J.L., Cole, J.C., & Oxman, M.N. (2003). Effects of a behavioral intervention, tai chi chih, on varcella-zoster virus specific immunity and health functioning in older adults. *Psychosomatic Medicine, 65,* 823–830.

Iverson, G. (1998). Mild head trauma: Epidemic in nature. *Recovery, 9,* 4–7.

Iwai, K. (1996). 1: The self-image of muscular dystrophy inpatients and the psychological effects of their disease. *Japanese Journal of Special Education, 33(5),* 1–6.

J

Jackson, S.A., & Csikszentmihalyi. M. (1999). *Flow in sports.* Champaign, IL: Human Kinetics.

Jacobs, G.D. (2001). Clinical applications of the relaxation response and mind-body interventions. *Journal of Alternative and Complementary Medicine, 7* (Suppl. 1), 92–101.

Jacobsen, P.B., & Hann, D.M. (1998). Cognitive-behavioral interventions. In J.C. Holland (Ed.), *Psycho-oncology* (pp. 717–729). New York: Oxford University Press.

Jacobson, A.M., & Weinger, K. (1998). Treating depression in diabetic patients; Is there an alternative to medications? *Annals of Internal Medicine, 129,* 656–657.

Jacobson, E. (1938). *Progressive relaxation: A physiological and clinical investigation of muscle states and their significance in psychology and medical practice.* (2nd ed.). Chicago: University of Chicago Press.

Jacobson, P.D., Bovbjerg, D.H., Schwartz, M.D., Hudis, C.A., Gilewski, T.A., & Norton, L. (1995). Conditioned emotional distress in women receiving chemotherapy for breast cancer. *Journal of Consulting and Clinical Psychology, 63,* 108–114.

Jacox, A., Carr, D.B., & Payne, R. (1994). New guidelines for management of pain in patients with cancer. *New England Journal of Medicine, 330(9),* 651–655.

JAMA. (1998). NIH Consensus Conference. Acupuncture. *Journal of the American Medical Association, 280(17),* 1518–1524.

Jamsa, K., & Jamsa, T. (1998). Technology in neonatal intensive care—A study on parents' experiences. *Technology and Health Care, 6,* 225–230.

Jasnowski, M.L., Holmes, D.S., & Banks, D.L. (1988). Changes in personality associated with changes in aerobic and anaerobic fitness in women and men. *Journal of Psychosomatic Research, 32,* 273–276.

Jellinek, E.M. (1960). *The disease concept of alcoholism.* New Haven, CT: College and University Press.

Jemmott, J.B., III, Borysenko, M., Chapman, R., et al. (1983). Academic stress, power motivation, and decrease in secretion rate of salivary secretory Immunoglobulin A. *Lancet,* 1400–1402.

Jenkins, C.D. (1996). Where there's hope, there's life. *Psychosomatic Medicine, 58,* 122–124.

Jensen, M.P., & Karoly, P. (2001). Self-report scales and procedures for assessing pain in adults. In D.C. Turk & R. Melzack (Eds.), *Handbook of pain assessment.* (2nd ed.) (pp. 15–34). New York: Guilford.

Jensen, M.P., Turner, J.A., Romano, J.M., & Strom, S.E. (1995). The Chronic Pain Coping Inventory: Development and preliminary validation. *Pain, 60,* 203–216.

Joachim, G., & Acorn, S. (2000). Stigma of visible and invisible chronic conditions. *J Adv Nurs, 32*(1), 243–248.

Job, E. (2003). *Learning to show "it hurts": The role of developmental factors in predicting young children's use of self-report scales for pain.* Unpublished master's thesis, University of British Columbia, Vancouver, British Columbia.

Johnson, M., & Vögele, C. (1993). Benefits of psychological preparation for surgery: A meta-analysis. *Annals of Behavioral Medicine, 15,* 245–256.

Johnson, R.L., Roter, D., & Powe, D.R. (2004). Patient race/ethnicity and quality of patient-physician communication during medical visits. *American Journal of Public Health, 94,* 2084–2090.

Johnson, R.L., Saha, S., Arbelaez, J.J., Beach, M.C., & Cooper, L. (2004). Racial and ethnic differences in patient perceptions of bias and cultural competence in health care. *Journal of General Internal Medicine, 19,* 101–110.

Johnston, K.L., & White, K.M. (2003). Binge-drinking: A test of the role of group norms in the theory of planned behaviour. *Psychology and Health, 18,* 63–77.

Joint United Nations Programs on HIV/AIDS. (2006). *Report on the global AIDS epidemic.* Geneva, Switzerland: UNAIDS.

Jolly, A.M., Orr, P.H., Hammond, G., & Young, T.K. (1995). Risk factors for infection in women undergoing testing for Chlamydia trachomatis and Neisseria gonorrhoeae in Manitoba, Canada. *Sexually Transmitted Diseases, 22,* 289–295.

Jonasson, G., Carlsen, K.H., Sodal, A., Jonasson, C., & Mowinckel, P. (1999). Patient compliance in a clinical trial with inhaled budesonide in children with mild asthma. *European Respiratory Journal, 14,* 150–154.

Jones, G. (2002). Performance excellence: A personal perspective on the link between sport and business. *Journal of Applied Sport Psychology, 14,* 268–281.

Jones, L.W., Courneya, K.S., Fairey, A.S., & Mackey, J.R. (2005). Does the theory of planned behavior mediate the effects of an oncologist's recommendation to exercise in newly diagnosed breast cancer survivors? Results from a randomized controlled trial. *Health Psychology, 24*(2), 189–197.

Jones, L.W., Sinclair, R.C., & Courneya, K.S. (2003). The effects of source credibility and message framing on exercise intentions, behaviors and attitudes: An integration of the elaboration likelihood model and prospect theory. *Journal of Applied Social Psychology, 33,* 179–196.

Jones, S. (1996). Demographic distributions of literacy in Canada. In *Reading the future: A portrait of literacy in Canada.* Ottawa: Ministry of Industry.

Jorenby, D.E., Leischow, S.J., Nides, M.A., Rennard, S.I., et al. (1999). A controlled trial of sustained-release bupropion, a nicotine patch, or both for smoking cessation. *New England Journal of Medicine, 340,* 685–691.

Judd, J., Frankish, & Moulton, G. (2001). Setting standards in the evaluation of community-based health promotion programs—A unifying approach. *Health Promotion International, 16*(4), 367–380.

Julien, R.M. (2005). *A primer of drug action.* (10th ed.). New York: Worth.

Jurgens, C.Y. (2003). Somatic awareness, uncertainty, and delay in care-seeking in acute heart failure. *Research in Nursing and Health, 29*(2), 74–86.

K

Kaasa, S., & Loge, J.H. (2003). Quality of life in palliative care: principles and practice. *Palliat Med, 17*(1), 11–20.

Kabat-Zinn, J. (1993). Mindfulness meditation: Health benefits of an ancient Buddhist practice. In D. Goleman & J. Gurin (Eds.), *Mind/body medicine: How to use your mind for better health* (pp. 259–275). Yonkers, NY: Consumer Reports Books.

Kaegi, E. (1998a). Unconventional therapies for cancer: 5. Vitamins A, C and E. Task Force on Alternative Therapies of the Canadian Breast Cancer Research Initiative. *Canadian Medical Association Journal, 158,* 1483–1488.

Kaegi, E. (1998b). A patient's guide to choosing unconventional therapies. *Canadian Medical Association Journal, 158,* 1161–1165.

Kahn, B.E., & Wansink, B. (2004). The influence of assortment structure on perceived variety and consumption quantities. *Journal of Consumer Research, 30,* 519–533.

Kahneman, D., & Miller, D.T. (1986). Norm theory: Comparing reality to its alternatives. *Psychological Review, 80,* 136–153.

Kalisch, P.A., & Kalisch, B.J. (1987). *The changing image of the nurse.* Menlo Park, CA: Addison-Wesley.

Kanerva, M., Tarkkila, P., & Pitkaranta, A. (2003). Day-case tonsillectomy in children: Parental attitudes and consultation rates. *Int J Pediatr Otorhinolaryngol, 67*(7), 777–784.

Kangas, M., Henry, J.L. & Bryant, R.A. (2002). Posttraumatic stress disorder following cancer: A conceptual and empirical review. *Clinical Psychology Review, 22,* 499–524.

Ka'opua, L.S.I., & Mueller, C.W. (2004). Treatment adherence among Native Hawaiians living with HIV. *Social Work, 49,* 55–62.

Kappesser, J., Williams, A.C., & Prkachin, K.M. (2006). Testing two accounts of pain underestimation. *Pain, 124,* 109–116.

Kaplan, R.M., Sallis, J.F., & Patterson, T.L. (1993). *Health and human behavior.* New York: McGraw-Hill.

Kaplan, S.H., Gandek, B., Greenfield, S., Rogers, W., & Ware, J.E. (1995). Patient and visit characteristics related to physicians' participatory decision-making style: Results from the Medical Outcomes Study. *Medical Care, 33,* 1176–1187.

Kaps, E.C. (1994). The role of the support group, "Us Too." *Cancer, 74,* 2188–2189.

Karaca, I., Ilkay, E., Akbulut, M., & Yavuzkir, M. (2003). Treatment of in-stent restenosis with excimer laser coronary angioplasty. *Jpn Heart J, 44*(2), 179–186.

Karasek, R. (1979). Job demands, job decision latitude, and mental strain: Implications for job design. *Administrative Science Quarterly, 24,* 285–310.

Karl, A., Muhlnickel, W., Kurth, R., & Flor, H. (2004). Neuroelectric source imaging of steady-state movement-related cortical potentials in human upper extremity amputees with and without phantom limb pain. *Pain, 110,* 90–102.

Kashani, J., & Hakami, N. (1982). Depression in children and adolescents with malignancy. *Canadian Journal of Psychiatry, 27,* 474–477.

Katz, J., Wowk, A., Culp, D., & Wakeling, H. (1999). A randomized, controlled study of the pain- and tension-reducing effects of 15 minute workplace massage treatments versus seated rest for nurses in a large teaching hospital. *Pain Research and Management, 4*(2), 81–88.

Katz, R.C., Flasher, L., Cacciapaglia, H., & Nelson, S. (2001). The psychosocial impact of cancer and lupus: A cross validation study that extends the generality of "benefit finding" in patients with chronic disease. *Journal of Behavioral Medicine, 24*(6), 561–571.

Katz, R.C., Wilson, L., & Frazer, N. (1994). Anxiety and its determinants in patients undergoing magnetic resonance imaging. *Journal of Behavior Therapy and Experimental Psychiatry, 25,* 131–134.

Katzmarzyk, P.T. & Janssen, I. (2004). The economic costs associated with physical inactivity and obesity in Canada: An update. *Canadian Journal of Applied Physiology, 29*(2), 90–115.

Kavussanu, M., & McAuley, E. (1996). Exercise and optimism: Are highly active individuals more optimistic? *Journal of Sport and Exercise Psychology, 18,* 264–280.

Kawachi, I., Sparrow, D., Spiro, A., Vokonas, P., & Weiss, S.T. (1996). A prospective study of anger and coronary heart disease: The Normative Aging Study. *Circulation, 94,* 2090–2095.

Keefe, F.J., Williams, D.A., & Smith, S.J. (2001). Assessment of pain behaviors. In D.C. Turk & R. Melzack (Eds.), *Handbook of pain assessment.* (2nd ed.) (pp. 170–189). New York: Guilford.

Keefler, J., Duder, S., & Lechman, C. (2001). Predicting length of stay in an acute care hospital: The role of psychosocial problems. *Social Work in Health Care, 33*(2), 1–16.

Kehr, B.A. (2004). Computer-enhanced treatment compliance. *Behavioral Health Management, 24*(2), 44–48.

Kelly, B., Raphael, B., Judd, F., Perdices, M., Kernutt, G., Burnett, P., Dunne, M., & Burrows, G. (1998). Posttraumatic stress disorder in response to HIV infection. *General Hospital Psychiatry, 20,* 345–352.

Kelly, J.A. (1998). Group psychotherapy for persons with HIV and AIDS-related illnesses. *International Journal of Group Psychotherapy, 48,* 143–162.

Kelner, K., & Helmuth, L. (2003). Obesity—What is to be done? *Science, 299,* 845.

Kelner, M. (1995). Activists and delegators: Elderly patients' preferences about control at the end of life. *Social Science & Medicine, 41*(4), 537–545.

Kemeny, M.E. (2005). The psychobiology of stress. In G. Miller & E. Chen (Eds.), *Current directions in health psychology* (pp. 55–63). Washington, DC: Pearson Education.

Kendall, C., & Hailley, B.J. (1993). The relative effectiveness of three reminder letters on making and keeping mammogram appointments. *Behavioral Medicine, 19,* 29–34.

Kendall-Tackett, K. (2009). Psychological trauma and physical health: A psychoneuroimmunology approach to etiology of negative health effects and possible interventions. *Psychological Trauma: Theory, Practice, and Policy, 1,* 35-48.

Kendler, K.S., Kessler, R.C., Heath, A.C., Neale, M.C., & Eaves, L.J. (1991). Coping: A genetic epidemiological investigation. *Psychological Medicine, 21,* 337–346.

Kennedy, J. & Morgan, S. (2009). Cost-related prescription nonadherence in the United States and Canada: A system-level comparison using the 2007 International Health Policy Survey in Seven Countries. *Clinical Therapy, 31*(1), 213–219.

Kenkel, M.B., Deleon, P.H., Mantell, E.O., & Steep, A.E. (2005). Divided no more: Psychology's role in integrated health care. *Canadian Psychology, 46*(4), 189–202.

Keogh, E. (2006). Sex and gender differences in pain: A selective review of biological and psychosocial factors. *Journal of Men's Health and Gender 3,* 236–243.

Keogh, E. (2009). Sex differences in pain. In R.J. Moore (Ed.), *Biobehavioral approaches to pain* (pp. 125–148). New York: Springer Science and Business Media.

Keogh, E., Bond, F.W., Hanmer, R., & Tilson, J. (2005). Comparing acceptance- and control-based coping instructions on the cold-pressor pain experiences of healthy men and women. *European Journal of Pain, 9*(5), 59–81.

Kern, M.L., & Friedman, H.S. (2008). Do conscientious individuals live longer? A quantitative review. *Health Psychology, 27,* 505–512.

Kerns, R.D., Turk, D.C., & Rudy, T.E. (1985). The West Haven-Yale Multidimensional Pain Inventory. *Pain, 23,* 345–356.

Kerr, D.P., Walsh, D.M., & Baxter, D. (2003). Acupuncture in the management of chronic low back pain: A blinded randomized controlled trial. *Clinical Journal of Pain, 19*(6), 364–370.

Kerssens, J.J., Bensing, J.M., & Andela, M.G. (1997). Patient preference for genders of health professionals. *Social Science and Medicine, 44,* 1531–1540.

Kerzman, H., Baron-Epel, O., & Toren, O. (2005). What do discharged patients know about their medication? *Patient Education and Counseling, 56*(3), 276–282.

Keski-Rahkonen, A., Viken, R.J., Kaprio, J., Rissanen, A., & Rose, R.J. (2004). Genetic and environmental factors in breakfast eating patterns. *Behavior Genetics, 34*(5), 503–514.

Kiecolt-Glaser, J.K., Dura, J.R., Speicher, C.E., Trask, O.J., & Glaser, R.G. (1991). Spousal caregivers of dementia victims: Longitudinal changes in immunity and health. *Psychosomatic Medicine, 53,* 345–362.

Kiecolt-Glaser, J.K., Fisher, J.D., Ogrocki, P., Stout, J.C., Speicher, C.E., & Glaser, R. (1987a). Marital quality, marital disruption, and immune function. *Psychosomatic Medicine, 49,* 13–34.

Kiecolt-Glaser, J.K., Garner, W., Speicher, C., Penn, G.M., Holliday, J., & Glaser, R. (1984). Psychosocial modifiers of immunocompetence in medical students. *Psychosomatic Medicine, 46,* 7–14.

Kiecolt-Glaser, J.K., & Glaser, R. (1995). Psychoneuroimmunology and health consequences: Data and shared mechanisms. *Psychosomatic Medicine, 57,* 269–274.

Kiecolt-Glaser, J.K., & Glaser, R. (2001). Stress and immunity: Age enhances the risks. *Current Directions in Psychological Science, 10,* 18–21.

Kiecolt-Glaser, J.K., Glaser, R., Shuttleworth, E.C., Dyers, C.S., Ogroki, P., & Speicher, C.E. (1987b). Chronic stress and immunity in family caregivers of Alzheimer's disease victims. *Psychosomatic Medicine, 49,* 523–535.

Kiecolt-Glaser, J.K., Kennedy, S., Malkoff, S., Fisher, L., Speicher, C.E., & Glaser, R. (1988). Marital discord and immunity in males. *Psychosomatic Medicine, 50,* 213–229.

Kiecolt-Glaser, J.K., Marucha, P.T., Atkinson, C., & Glaser, R. (2001). Hypnosis as a modulator of cellular immune dysregulation during acute stress. *Journal of Consulting & Clinical Psychology, 69,* 674–682.

Kiecolt-Glaser, J.K., McGuire, L., Robles, T.F., & Glaser, R. (2002a). Psychoneuroimmunology: Psychological influences on immune function and health. *Journal of Consulting and Clinical Psychology, 70,* 537–547.

Kiecolt-Glaser, J.K., McGuire, L., Robles, T.F., & Glaser, R. (2002b). Emotions, morbidity, and mortality: new perspectives from psychoneuroimmunology. *Annual Review of Psychology, 53,* 83–107.

Kiecolt-Glaser, J.K., Preacher, K.J., MacCallum, R.C., Atkinson, C., Malarkey, W.B., & Glaser, R. (2003). Chronic stress and age-related increases in proinflammatory cytokine IL-6. *Proceedings of the National Academy of Sciences,* Washington, DC.

Kiecolt-Glaser, J.K., Robles, T.F., Heffner, K.L., Loving, T.J., & Glaser, R. (2002). Psycho-oncology and cancer: Psychoneuroimmunology and cancer. *Annals of Oncology, 13* (Suppl 4), 165–169.

Kiene, S.M., Barta, W.D., Zelenski, J.M., & Cothran, D.L. (2005). Why are you bringing up condoms now? The effect of message content on framing effect. *Health Psychology, 24*(3), 321–326.

Kiesler, D.J. (1966). Some myths of psychotherapy research and the search for a paradigm. *Psychological Bulletin, 65,* 110–136.

Kilborn, L.C., & Labbe, E.E. (1990). Magnetic resonance imaging scanning procedures: Development of phobic response during scan and at one-month follow-up. *Journal of Behavioral Medicine, 13,* 391–401.

Kinder, L.S., Bradley, K.A., Katon, W.J., Ludman, E., McDonell, M.B., & Bryson, C.L. (2008). Depression, posttraumatic stress disorder, and mortality. *Psychosomatic Medicine, 70,* 20–26.

King, A.J.C., Boyce, W.F., & King, M.A. (1999). Trends in the health of Canadian youth. Health Behaviors in School-Aged Children, a World Health Organization Cross-National Study. Canada: Health Canada.

King, K.M., & Teo, K.K. (1998). Cardiac rehabilitation referral and attendance: Not one and the same. *Rehabilitation Nursing, 23,* 246–251.

Kingston, G. (1999). Concussion leaves a gap in Long's memory. *Vancouver Sun,* October 18.

Kinsey, A.C., Pomeroy, W.B., & Martin, C.C. (1948). *Sexual behavior in the human male.* Philadelphia: Saunders.

Kinsey, A.C., Pomeroy, W.B., Martin, C.C., & Gebhard, P.H. (1953). *Sexual behavior in the human female.* Philadelphia: Saunders.

Kircaldy, B.D., & Shephard, R.J. (1990). Therapeutic implications of exercise. *International Journal of Sport Psychology, 21,* 165–184.

Kirkley, B.G., Schneider, J.A., Agras, W.J., & Bachman, J.A. (1985). Comparison of two group treatments for bulimia. *Journal of Consulting and Clinical Psychology, 53,* 43–48.

Kirschenbaum, D. (1998). Using sport psychology interventions to improve health psychology outcomes. *The Health Psychologist, 20,* 16–23.

Kirschenbaum, K.S. (1997). Prevention of sedentary lifestyles: Rationale and methods. In W.P. Morgan (Ed.), *Physical activity and mental health* (pp. 33–48). Washington, DC: Taylor and Francis.

Kishchuk, N., Tremblay, M., Lapierre, J., Heneman, B., & O'Loughlin, J. (2004). Qualitative investigation of young smokers' and ex-smokers' view on smoking cessation methods. *Nicotine and Tobacco Research, 6,* 491–500.

Kissane, D. (2009). Beyond the psychotherapy and survival debate: The challenge of social disparity, depression and treatment adherence in psychosocial cancer care. *Psycho-Oncology, 18*(1), 1–5.

Kleinke, C.L., & Spangler, A.S. (1988). Psychometric analysis of the audiovisual taxonomy for assessing pain behavior in chronic back-pain patients. *Journal of Behavioral Medicine, 11,* 83–94.

Klump, K., McGue, M., & Iacono, W.G. (2000). Age differences in genetic and environmental influences on eating attitudes and behaviors in preadolescent and adolescent female twins. *Journal of Abnormal Psychology, 109,* 239–251.

Knight, J.R., Sanchez, L.T., Sherritt, L., Bresnahan, L.R., Silveria, J.M., & Fromson, J.A. (2002). Monitoring physician drug problems: Attitudes of participants. *Journal of Addictive Diseases, 21*(4), 27–36.

Knoerl, D.V., Faut-Callahan, M., Paice, J., & Shoot, S. (1999). Preoperative PCA teaching program to manage postoperative pain. *Medsurgical Nursing, 8,* 25–33, 36.

Komaroff, A.L. (2003, March 7). *An update on the obesity problem.* Journal Watch (General). Retrieved July 9, 2003, from general-medicine.jwatch.org/cgi/content/full/2003/307/8

Komproe, I.H., Rijken, M., Ros, W.J.G., Winnubst, J.A.M., & Harm't, H. (1997). Available support and received support: Different effects under stressful circumstances. *Journal of Social and Personal Relationships, 14,* 59–77.

Kop, W.J., & Gottdiener, J.S. (2005). The role of immune system parameters in the relationship between depression and coronary artery disease. *Psychosomatic Medicine, 67*(Supp 1), S37–S41.

Korol, C. T., & Craig, K.D. (2001). Pain from the perspectives of health psychology and culture. In S.S. Kazarian & E.R. Evans (Eds.), *Handbook of cultural health psychology* (pp. 241–265). San Diego: Acadmic Press.

Kowalcek, I., Muhlhoff, A., Bachmann, S., & Gembruch, U. (2002). Depressive reactions and stress related to prenatal medicine procedures. *Ultrasound Obstet Gynecol, 19*(1), 18–23.

Kraemer, H.C., Kuchler, T., & Spiegel, D. (2009). Use and misuse of the CONSORT guidelines to assess research findings: Comment on Coyne, Stefanek, and Palmer (2007). *Psychological Bulletin, 135,* 173–178.

Kraetschmer, N., Sharpe, N., Urowitz, S., & Deber, R.B. (2004). How does trust affect patient preferences for participation in decision-making? *Health Expectations: An International Journal of Public Participation in Health Care & Health Policy, 7*(4), 317–326.

Kramer, M. (1974). *Reality shock—Why nurses leave nursing.* St. Louis, MO: CV Mosby.

Kramer, M., & Schmalenberg, C.E. (2003). Magnet hospital staff nurses describe clinical autonomy. *Nursing Outlook, 51,* 13–19.

Krantz, D.S., Grunberg, N.E., & Baum, A. (1985). Health psychology. *Annual Review of Psychology, 36,* 349–383.

Krebs, L.U., Myers, J., Decker, G., Kinzler, J., Asfahani, P., & Jackson, J. (1996). The oncology nursing image: Lifting the mist. *Oncology Nursing Forum, 23,* 1297–1304.

Kruger, J., Galuska, D.A., Serdula, M.K., & Jones, D.A. (2004). Attempting to lose weight: Specific practices among U.S. adults. *American Journal of Preventive Medicine, 26,* 402–406.

Krupat, E., Fancey, M., & Cleary, P.D. (2000). Information and its impact on satisfaction among surgical patients. *Social Science & Medicine, 51*(12), 1817–1825.

Kübler-Ross, E. (1969). *On death and dying.* New York: Macmillan.

Kubzansky, L.D., Martin, L.T., & Buka, S.L. (2009). Early manifestations of personality and adult health: A life course perspective. *Health Psychology, 28,* 364–372.

Kuehn, B.M. (2006). Report reviews secondhand smoke risks: some scientists question level. *Journal of the American Medical Association, 296*(8), 922–953.

Kuhl, D. (2003). *What dying people really want: Practical wisdom for the end of life.* New York: Public Affairs Publishing.

Kunz, M., Scharmann, S., Hemeter, U., Schepelmann, K., Lautenbacher, S. (2007). The facial expression of pain in patients with dementia. *Pain, 133,* 221–228.

Kurtz, S.M. (2002). Doctor-patient communication: Principles and practices. *Canadian Journal of Neurological Sciences, 29*(2), S23–S29.

Kurtz, S.M., Silverman, J., Benson, J., & Draper, J. (2003). Marrying content and process in clinical method teaching: Enhancing the Calgary Cambridge guides. *Academic Medicine, 78*(8), 802–809.

Kuuppelomäki, M., & Lauri, S. (1998). Cancer patients' reported experiences of suffering. *Cancer Nursing, 21,* 364–369.

Kwong, J.C., Dhalla, I.A., Streiner, D.L., Baddour, R.E., Waddell, A.E., & Johnson, I.L. (2002). Effects of rising tuition fees on medical school class composition and financial outlook. *Canadian Medical Association Journal, 166*(8), 1023–1028.

L

La Via, M.F., Munno, I., Lydiard, R.B., Workman, E.W., Hubbard, J.R., Michel, Y., & Paulling, E. (1996). The influence of stress intrusion on immunodepression in generalized anxiety disorder patients and controls. *Psychosomatic Medicine, 58,* 138–142.

Labonte, R. (1987). Community health promotion strategies. *Health Promotion, 16,* 5–10, 32.

Labonte, R. (1990). Health promotion: From concepts to strategies. In G. Eikenberg (Ed.), *The seeds of health: Promoting wellness in the '90s.* (pp. 129–146). Ottawa: Canadian College of Health Service Executives.

Ladwig, K. H., & Dammann, G. (1997). Psychological adaptation after successful out-of-hospital resuscitation. *Journal of Psychosomatic Research, 43*(6), 559–564.

Ladwig, K.H., Schoefinius, A., Dammaun, G., Danner, R., Gurtler, R., & Herrmann, R. (1999). Long-acting psychotraumatic properties of a cardiac arrest experience. *American Journal of Psychiatry, 156,* 912–919.

Laforge, R.G., Greene, G.W., & Prochaska, J.O. (1994). Psychosocial factors influencing low fruit and vegetable consumption. *Journal of Behavioral Medicine, 17,* 361–374.

Lalonde, M. (1974). *New perspectives on the health of Canadians.* Ottawa: Information Canada.

Landers, D.M., & Arent, S.M. (2001) In R.N. Singer, H.A. Hausenblas, & C.M. Janelle (Eds.), *Handbook of sport psychology.* (2nd ed.) (pp. 740– 765). New York: Wiley.

Landers, D.M., & Arent. S.M. (2007). Physical activity and mental health. In G. Tenenbaum, & R.C. Eklund (Eds.),

Handbook of sport and exercise psychology. (3rd ed.) (pp. 469–491). New Jersey: John Wiley & Sons.

Landers, D.M., & Peruzzello, S.J. (1994). Physical activity, fitness, and anxiety. In C. Bouchard, R.J. Shephard, & T. Stephens (Eds.), *Physical activity, fitness, and health: International proceedings and consensus statement* (pp. 868–882). Champaign, IL: Human Kinetics.

Lang, E.V., Benotsche, E.G., Fick, L.J., Lutgendorf, S., Bebaum, M.L., Berbaum, K.S., et al. (2000). Adjunctive non-pharmacological analgesia for invasive medical procedures: A randomized trial. *Lancet, 355*, 1486–1480.

Larocque, D. (1996). Absenteeism. *Canadian Nurse, 92*(9), 42–46.

Larson, P.J., & Ferketich, S.L. (1993). Patients' satisfaction with nurses' caring during hospitalization. *Western Journal of Nursing Research, 15*, 690–707.

Larson, R., & Sutker, S. (1966). Value differences and value consensus by socioeconomic levels. *Social Forces, 44*, 563–569.

Laschinger, H.K.S., Finegan, J.E., Shamian, J., & Wilk, P. (2004). A longitudinal analysis of the impact of workplace empowerment on work satisfaction. *Journal of Organizational Behavior, 25*(4), 527–545.

Lau, R.R., Hartman, K.A., & Ware, J.E. Jr. (1986). Health as a value: Methodological and theoretical considerations. *Health Psychology, 5*, 25–43.

Lavie, C.J., Milani, R.V., Cassidy, M.M., & Gilliland, Y.E. (1999). Effects of cardiac rehabilitation and exercise training programs in women with depression. *American Journal of Cardiology, 83*, 1480–1483.

Lavin, D., & Groarke, A. (2005). Dental floss behaviour: A test of the predictive utility of the Theory of Planned Behaviour and the effects of making implementation intentions. *Psychology, Health & Medicine, 10*(3), 243–252.

Layne, N. (1987). *Solvent use/abuse among the Canadian Registered Indian and Inuit population. An overview paper. Unpublished report.* Ottawa: National NativeAlcohol and Drug Abuse Program.

Lazarus, R.S. (1999). *Fifty years of the research and theory of R.S. Lazarus: An analysis of historical and perennial issues.* Mahwah, NJ: Erlbaum.

Lazarus, R.S. (2006). *Stress and emotion.* New York: Springer.

Lazarus, R.S., & Folkman, S. (1984). *Stress, appraisal, and coping.* New York: Springer.

Leathart, A. (1994). Communication and socialisation (1): An exploratory study and explanation for nurse-patient communication in ITU. *Intensive and Critical Care Nursing, 10*, 93–104.

Leatherdale, S.T., Cameron, R., Brown, K., Jolin, M.A., & Kroeker, C. (2006). The influence of friends, family, and older peers on smoking among elementary school students: Low-risk students in high-risk schools. *Preventive Medicine: An International Journal Devoted to Practice and Theory, 42*(3), 218–222.

Leatherdale, S.T., Maske, S., & Kroder, C. (2006). Sex differences in how older students influence younger student smoking behaviour. *Addictive Behaviors, 31*(8), 1308–1318.

Lee, A., & Poole, G. (2005). An application of the transactional model to the analysis of chronic illness narratives. *Qualitative Health Research, 15*(3), 346–364.

Lee, F.J., Stewart, M., & Brown, J.B. (2008). Stress, burnout, and strategies for reducing them: What's the situation among Canadian family physicians? *Canadian Family Physician, 54*, 234.

Lee, I-M., Paffenberger, R.S., & Hsieh, C-C. (1992). Physical activity and risk of prostatic cancer among college alumni. *American Journal of Epidemiology, 146*, 413–417.

Lee, J., Parsons, G.F., & Gentleman, J.F. (1998). Falling short of the Pap test guidelines. *Health Reports, 10*(1), 9–19.

Lee, R.S., Kochman, A., & Sikkema, K.J. (2002). Internalized stigma among people living with HIV-AIDS. *AIDS & Behavior, 6*(4), 309–319.

Leit, R.A., Gray, J.J., & Pope, H.G., Jr. (2002). The media's representation of the ideal male body: A cause for muscle dysmorphia? *International Journal of Eating Disorders, 13*(3), 334–338.

Leit, R.A., Pope, H.G., Jr., & Gray, J.J. (2000). Cultural expectations of muscularity in men: The evolution of playgirl centerfolds. *International Journal of Eating Disorders, 29*(1), 90–93.

Leiter, M., Harvie, P., & Frizzel, C. (1998). The correspondence of patient satisfaction and nurse burnout. *Social Science and Medicine, 47*, 1611–1617.

Lemos, K., Suls, J., Jenson, M., Lounsbury, P., & Gordon, E.E.I. (2003). How do female and male cardiac patients and their spouses share responsibilities after discharge from the hospital? *Annals of Behavioral Medicine, 25*(1), 8–15.

Lenz, E.R., & Perkins, S. (2000). Coronary artery bypass graft surgery patients and their family member caregivers: Outcomes of a family-focused staged psychoeducational intervention. *Appl Nurs Res, 13*(3), 142–150.

Lepnurm, R., Lockhart, W.S., & Keegan, D. (2009). A measure of daily distress in practicing medicine. *Canadian Journal of Psychiatry, 54*(3), 170–180.

LeResche, L. (2000). Epidemiologic perspectives on sex differences in pain. In R.B. Fillingim (Ed.), *Sex, gender, and pain* (pp. 233–249). Seattle, WA: IASP Press.

Le Scanff, C., & Taugis, T. (2002). Stress management for police special forces. *Journal of Applied Sport Psychology, 14,*330–343.

Leserman, J., Jackson, E.D., Petitto, J.M., Golden, R.N., Silva, S.G., Perkins, D.O., Cai, J., Folds, J.D., & Evans, D.L. (1999). Progression to AIDS: The effects of stress, depressive symptoms, and social support. *Psychosomatic Medicine, 61*(3), 397–406.

Lester, N., Lefebvre, J.C., & Keefe, F.J. (1994). Pain in young adults: 1. Relationship to gender and family pain history. *Clinical Journal of Pain, 19*, 282–289.

Leszcz, M., & Goodwin, P.J. (1998). The rationale and foundations of group psychotherapy for women with metastatic breast cancer. *International Journal of Group Psychotherapy, 48*, 245–273.

Letizia, M., Creech, S., Norton, E., Shanahan, M., & Hedges, L. (2004). Barriers to caregiver administration of pain medication in hospice care. *Journal of Pain and Symptom Management, 27*(2), 114–124.

Lett, H.S., Davidson, J., & Blumenthal, J.A. (2005). Nonpharmacologic treatments for depression in patients with coronary heart disease. *Psychosomatic Medicine, 67*(Supp 1), S58–S62.

LeUnes, A., & Nation, J.R. (2002). *Sport psychology.* (3rd ed.). Pacific Grove, CA: Wadsworth.

LeUnes, A.D., & Nation, J.R. (1989). *Sport psychology: An introduction.* Chicago, IL: Nelson-Hall.

Leuthner, S.R. (2001). Decisions regarding resuscitation of the extremely premature infant and models of best interest. *Journal of Perinatology, 21*(3), 193–198.

Levant, R.F. (2005). Graduate education in clinical psychology for the twenty-first century: Educating psychological health care providers. *Journal of Clinical Psychology, 61*(9), 1087–1090.

Leventhal, E.A., Hansell, S., Diefenbach, M., Leventhal, H., & Glass, D.C. (1996). Negative affect and self-report of physical symptoms: Two longitudinal studies of older adults. *Health Psychology, 15*, 193–199.

Leventhal, H., Weinman, J., Leventhal, E.A., & Phillips, L.A. (2008). Health psychology: The search for pathways between behavior and health. *Annual Review of Psychology, 59*, 477–505.

Levin, J.S., & Puchalski, C.M. (1997). Religion and spirituality in medicine: Research and education. *Journal of the American Medical Association, 278*, 792–793.

Levine, R.L., & Levy, L.A. (2006). Relationship between self-reported intensity of headache and magnitude of surface EMG. *Psychological Reports, 1*, 91–94.

Levinson, W. (1994). Physician-patient communication. A key to malpractice prevention. *Journal of the American Medical Association, 272*, 1619–1620.

Levinson, W., & Lurie, N. (2004). When most doctors are women: What lies ahead? *Annals of Internal Medicine, 141*, 271–474.

Levinson, W., Roter, D.L., Mullooly, J.P., Dull, V.T., & Frankel, R.M. (1997). Physician-patient communication. The relationship with malpractice claims among primary care physicians and surgeons. *Journal of the American Medical Association, 277*, 553–559.

Lewin, A.B., Heidgerken, A.D., Geffken, G.R., Williams, L.B., Storch, E.A., Gelfand, K.M., & Silverstein, J.H. (2006). The relation between family factors and metabolic control: The role of diabetes adherence. *Journal of Pediatric Psychology, 31*(2), 174–183.

Lewis, C.C., Brimacombe, C.A.E., & Matheson, D.H. (at press, 2011). *Factors influencing patient disclosure to physicians in birth control clinics: An application of the Communication Privacy Management Theory Health Communication.* University of Victoria, Victoria, British Columbia.

Ley, P. (1977). Psychological studies of doctor-patient communication. In S. Rachman (Ed.), *Contributions to medical psychology, 1.* Oxford: Pergamon.

Ley, P. (1982). Satisfaction, compliance, and communication. *British Journal of Clinical Psychology, 21*, 241–254.

Li, C., Unger, J.B., Schuster, D., Rohrbach, L.A., Howard-Pitney, B., & Norman, G. (2003). Youths' exposure to environmental tobacco smoke (ETS) associations with health beliefs and social pressure. *Addictive Behaviors, 28*, 39–53.

Li, M.D., Ma, J.Z., & Beuten, J. (2004). Progress in searching for susceptibility loci and genes for smoking related behaviour. *Clinical Genetics, 66*, 382–392.

Lieberman, A. (2006). Depression in Parkinson's disease—A review. *Acta Neurological Scandinavica, 113*(1), 1–8.

Lin, L., Halgin, R.P., Well, A.D., & Ockene, I. (2008). The relationship between depression and occupational, household, and leisure-time physical activity. *Journal of Clinical Sport Psychology, 2*, 95–107.

Ling, D., Niu, T., Feng, Y., Xing, H., & Xu, X. (2004). Association between polymorphism of the dopamine transporter gene and early smoking onset: An interaction risk on nicotine dependence. *Journal of Human Genetics, 49*, 35–39.

Liossi, C., & Hatira, P. (2003). Clinical hypnosis in the alleviation of procedure-related pain in pediatric oncology patients. *International Journal of Clinical and Experimental Hypnosis, 51*(1), 4–28.

Liu, H., Golin, C.E., Miller, L.G., Hays, R.D., Beck, C.K., Sanadji, S., et al. (2001). A comparison study of multiple measures of adherence to HIV protease inhibitors. *Annals of Internal Medicine, 134*, 968–977.

Literature Review: Evaluation Strategies in Aboriginal Substance Abuse Programs: A Discussion. (2002). Ottawa: Health Canada.

Litt, M.D., Nye, C., & Shafer, D. (1995). Preparation for oral surgery: Evaluating elements of coping. *Journal of Behavioral Medicine, 18*, 435–459.

Lloyd, C., Joyce, R., Hurry, J., & Ashton, M. (2000). The effectiveness of primary school drug education. *Drugs: Education, Prevention & Policy, 7*(2), 109–126.

Lloyd, E.C., Mathews, K.A., Wing, R.R., & Orchard, T.I. (1992). Psychosocial factors and complications of IDDM. The Pittsburgh Epidemiology of Diabetes Complications Study VIII. *Diabetes Care, 15*, 166–172.

Locke, E.A. (1968). Toward a theory of task motivation and incentives. *Organizational Behaviour and Human Performance, 3*, 157–189.

Locke, E.A., & Latham, G.P. (1985). The application of goal setting to sports. *Journal of Sports Psychology, 7*, 205–222.

Locke, E.A., & Latham, G.P. (1990) *A theory of goal-setting and task performance.* Englewood Cliffs, NJ: Prentice-Hall.

Logan, D.E., & Rose, J.B. (2005). Is postoperative pain a self-fulfilling prophecy? Expectancy effects on postoperative pain and patient-controlled analgesia use among adolescent surgical patients. *Journal of Pediatric Psychology, 30*(2), 187–196.

Logan, D.E., & Rose, J.B. (2004). Gender differences in postoperative pain and patient controlled analgesia use among adolescent surgical patients. *Pain, 109*(3), 481–487.

Lollis, C.M., Johnson, E.H., & Antoni, M.H. (1997). The efficacy of the health belief model for predicting condom usage and risky sexual practices in university students. *AIDS Education and Prevention, 9*, 551–563.

Lorber, J. (1975). Good patients and problem patients: Conformity and deviance in a general hospital. *Journal of Health and Social Behavior, 16*, 213–225.

Lower, J.S., Bonsack, C., & Guion, J. (2003). Peace and quiet. *Nurs Manage, 34*(4), 40A–40D.

Lowery, D., Fillingim, R.B., & Wright, R.A. (2003). Sex differences and incentive effects on perceptual and cardiovascular responses to cold pressor pain. *Psychosomatic Medicine, 65*, 284–291.

Lu, D.P., Lu, G.P., & Kleinman, L. (2001). Acupuncture and clinical hypnosis for facial and head and neck pain: A single crossover comparison. *The American Journal of Clinical Hypnosis, 44*, 141–148.

Luce, G., & Peper, E. (1971). Mind over body, mind over mind. *New York Times Magazine*, September.

Ludwick-Rosenthal, R., & Neufeld, R.W.J. (1988). Stress management during noxious medical procedures: An evaluative review of outcome studies. *Psychological Bulletin, 104*, 326–342.

Lukins, R., Davan, I.G.P., & Drummond, P.D. (1997). A cognitive behavioural approach to preventing anxiety during magnetic resonance imaging. *Journal of Behavior Therapy and Experimental Psychiatry, 28*, 97–104.

Lung Association. (2004). Chronic obstructive pulmonary disease (COPD) fact sheet. Retrieved April 5, 2006, from www.proresp.com/tla_copd_factsheet.asp

Lurie, J.D., & Sox, H.C. (1999). Principles of medical decision making. *Spine, 24*, 493–498.

Lurie, N., Rank, B., Parenti, C., Woolley, T., & Snoke, W. (1989). How do house officers spend their nights? A time study of internal medicine staff on call. *New England Journal of Medicine, 320*, 1673–1677.

Luschen, G., Cockerham, W., & Kunz, G. (1996). The sociocultural context of sport and health problems of causal relations and structural interdependence. *Sociology of Sport Journal, 13*, 197–213.

Lussier, M.-T., & Richard, C. (2006). Complaints and legal actions: Role of doctor-patient communication. *Canadian Family Physician, 51*, 37–39.

Lustman, P.J., Freedland, K.E., Griffith, L.S., & Clouse, R.E. (1998a). Predicting response to cognitive behavior therapy of depression in type 2 diabetes. *General Hospital Psychiatry, 20*, 302–306.

Lustman, P.J., Griffith, L.S., Freedland, K.E., & Clouse, R.E. (1998b). Cognitive behavior therapy for depression in type 2 diabetes mellitus. A randomized, controlled trial. *Annals of Internal Medicine, 129*, 613–621.

Lutsky, I., Hopwood, M., Abram, S.E., Jacobson, G.R., Haddox, J.D., & Kampine, J.P. (1993). Psychoactive substances use among American anesthesiologists: A 30-year retrospective study. *Canadian Journal of Anaesthesiology, 40*, 915–921.

Lynch, G.P. (1988). Athletic injuries and the practicing sport psychologist: Practical guidelines for assisting athletes. *The Sport Psychologist, 2*, 161–167.

Lynch, M.E., Clark, A.J., & Sawynok, J. (2003). Intravenous adenosine alleviates neuropathic pain: A double blind placebo controlled crossover trial using an enriched enrolment design. *Pain, 103*, 111–117.

Lynch, M.E., & Watson, C.P.N. (2006). The pharmacotherapy of chronic pain: A review. *Pain Research and Management, 11*, 11–38.

Lynge, E., Olsen, A.H., Fracheboud, J., & Patnick, J. (2003). Reporting of performance indicators of mammography screening in Europe. *Eur J Cancer Prev, 12*(3), 213–222.

Lyubomirsky, S. (2001). Why are some people happier than others? The role of cognitive and motivational processes in well-being. *American Psychologist, 56*, 239–249.

Lyubomirsky, S., King, L., & Diener, E. (2005). The benefits of frequent positive affect: Does happiness lead to success. *Psychological Bulletin, 131*, 803–855.

M

Macciocchi, S.N., Barth, J.T., Alves, W.A., Rimel, R.W., & Jane, J.J. (1996). Neuropsychological functioning and and recovery after mild head injury in collegiate athletes. *Neurosurgery, 39*, 510–514.

MacDonald, N.E., Wells, G.A., Fisher, W.A., Warren, W.K., et al. (1990). High-risk STD/HIV behavior among college students. *Journal of the American Medical Association, 263*, 3155–3159.

MacDonald, T.K., MacDonald, N.E., Zanna, M.P., & Fong, G.T. (2000). Alcohol, sexual arousal, and intentions to use condoms: Applying alcohol myopia to risky sexual behavior. Manuscript submitted for publication.

MacDonald, T.K., Zanna, M.P., & Fong, G.T. (1996). Why common sense goes out the window: Effects of alcohol on intentions to use condoms. *Personality and Social Psychology Bulletin, 22*, 763–775.

MacDonald, T.K., Zanna, M.P., & Fong, G.T. (1998). Alcohol and intentions to engage in risky behaviors: Experimental evidence for a causal relationship. In J.G. Adair, D. Belanger, & K. Dion (Eds.), *Advances in psychological science: Vol. 1. Social, personal, and cultural aspects* (pp. 407–428). East Sussex, UK: Psychology Press.

MacDonald, T.K., Zanna, M.P., & Fong, G.T. (1995). Decision making in altered states: Effects of alcohol on attitudes toward drinking and driving. *Journal of Personality and Social Psychology, 68*, 973–985.

MacKean, P., & Gutkin, C. (2003). Fewer medical students selecting family medicine. Can family practice survive? *Can Fam Physician, 49*, 408–409, 415–407.

Maclean, N., & Pound, P. (2000). A critical review of the concept of patient motivation in the literature on physical rehabilitation. *Social Science & Medicine, 50*(4), 495–506.

MacLeod, S. (September 23, 2002). Research, education, and the impact of prescription compliance on better medicine. Paper presented at the 2003 Conference entitled Toward a National Strategy on Drug Insurance: Challenges and Priorities. www.irpp.org/events/archive/sep02/macleod.pdf [June 9, 2003].

Madsen, M.V., Gotzsche, P.C., & Hrobjartsson, A. (2009). Acupuncture treatment for pain: systematic review of randomized clinical trials with acupuncture, placebo acupuncture, and no acupuncture groups. *British Medical Journal, 338,* 1–8.

Maes, M. (1995). Evidence for an immune response in major depression: A review and hypothesis. *Progress in Neuro-Psychopharmacology & Biological Psychiatry, 19,* 11–38.

Maes, M., Christophe, A., Bosmans, E., Lin, A., & Neels, H. (2000). In humans, serum polyunsaturated fatty acid levels predict the response of proinflammatory cytokines to psychologic stress. *Biological Psychiatry, 47,* 910–920.

Magarey, J.M., & McCutcheon, H.H. (2005). "Fishing with the dead"—Recall of memories from the ICU. *Intensive and Critical Care Nursing, 21*(6), 344–354.

Magni, G., Rossi, M.R., Rigatti-Luchini, S., & Merskey, H. (1992). Chronic abdominal pain and depression. Epidemiologic findings in the United States. Hispanic Health and Nutrition Examination Survey. *Pain, 49,* 549–559.

Mahoney, M. (1996). Foreword. In J.L. Van Raalte & B.W. Brewer (Eds.), *Exploring sport and exercise psychology.* Washington, DC: American Psychological Association.

Mahoney, M.J., Gabriel, T.J., & Perkins, T.S. (1987). Psychological skills and exceptional athletic performance. *The Sport Psychologist, 1,* 181–199.

Mangelli, L., Gribbin, N., Buchi, S., Allard, S., & Sensky, T. (2002). Psychological well-being in rheumatoid arthritis: Relationship to "disease" variables and affective disturbance. *Psychother Psychosom, 71*(2), 112–116.

Manne, S.L., Jacobsen, P.B., Gorfinkle, K., Gerstein, F., & Redd, W.H. (1993). Treatment adherence difficulties among children with cancer: The role of parenting style. *Journal of Pediatric Psychology, 18,* 47–62.

Marcoux, B.C., & Shope, J.T. (1997). Application of the theory of planned behavior to adolescent use and misuse of alcohol. *Health Education Research, 12,* 323–331.

Marlatt, G.A., & Gordon, J.R. (1980). Determinants of relapse: Implications for the maintenance of behavior change. In P.O. Davidson & S.M. Davidson (Eds.), *Behavioral medicine: Changing health lifestyles.* (pp. 410–452). New York: Brunner/Mazel.

Marquie, L., Raufaste, E., Lauque, D., Marine, C., Ecoiffier, M., & Sorum, P. (2003). Pain rating by patients and physicians: Evidence of systematic miscalibration. *Pain, 102,* 289–296.

Marrero, D.G., Guare, J.C., Vandagriff, J.L., & Fineberg, N.S. (1997). Fear of hypoglycemia in the parents of children and adolescents with diabetes: Maladaptive or health response? *Diabetes Education, 23,* 281–286.

Marrett, L.D., De, P., Airia, P., Dryer, D. (2008). Cancer in Canada in 2008. Canadian Medical Association Journal, 179(11), 1163.

Marrett, L.D., De, P., Airia, P., Dryer, D. (2008). Cancer in Canada in 2008. *Canadian Medical Association Journal, 179*(11), Retrieved October 28, 2009 from www.cmaj.ca/cgi/content/full/179/11/1163

Marshall, S.P., Smith, M.S., & Weinberger, E. (1995). Perceived anxiety of pediatric patients to magnetic resonance. *Clinical Pediatrics, 34,* 59–60.

Marsland, A.L., Manuck, S.B., Fazzari, T.V., Steward, C.J., & Rabin, B.S. (1995). Stability of individual differences in cellular immune responses to acute psychological stress. *Psychosomatic Medicine, 57,* 295–298.

Martens, P., Bond, R., Jebamani, L., Brurchill, C., Noralou, R., Derksen, S., Beaulieu, M., Steinbach, C., MacWilliam, L., Walld, R., Dik, N., Sanders, D., Tanner-Spence, M., Leader, A., Elias, B., & O-Neil, J. (2002). *The health and health care use of registered First Nations people living in Manitoba: A population-based study.* Winnipeg: Manitoba Centre for Health Policy, University of Manitoba.

Martin, D.P., Diehr, P., Conrad, D.A., Davis, J.H., Leickly, R., & Perrin, E.B. (1998). Randomized trial of a patient-centered hospital unit. *Patient Education and Counseling, 34,* 125–133.

Martin, J.J., & Cutler, K. (2002). An exploratory study of flow and motivation in theater actors. *Journal of Applied Sport Psychology, 14,* 344–352.

Martin, P.D., & Brantley, P.J. (2004). Stress, coping, and social support in health and behavior. In J.M. Raczynsky & L.C. Leviton (Eds.), *Handbook of clinical health psychology,* Vol. 2 (pp. 233–267). Washington, DC: American Psychological Association.

Martin, R., Lemos, K., Rothrock, N., Bellman, S.B., Russell, D. Trip-Reimer, T., et al. (2004). Gender disparities in common sense models of illness among myocardial infarction victims. *Health Psychology, 23,* 345–353.

Martinsen, E.W. (1990). Benefits of exercise for the treatment of depression. *Sports Medicine, 9,* 380–389.

Martinsen, E.W. (1993). Therapeutic implications of exercise for clinically anxious and depressed patients. *International Journal of Sport Psychology, 24,* 185–199.

Martinsen, E.W. (1994). Physical activity and depression: Clinical experience. *Actua Psychiatrca Scandinavica, 377,* 23–27.

Martinson, E.W., & Morgan, W.P. (1997). Antidepressant effects of physical activity. In W.P. Morgan (Ed.), *Physical activity and mental status* (pp. 93–106). Washington, DC: Taylor and Francis.

Martz, E. (2005). Associations and predictors of posttraumatic stress levels according to person-related, disability-related, and trauma-related variables among individuals with spinal cord injuries. *Rehabilitation Psychology, 50*(2), 149–157.

Marvel, M.K. (1993). Involvement with the psychosocial concerns of patients. *Archives of Family Medicine, 2,* 629–633.

Marvel, M.K., Epstein, R.M., Flowers, K., & Beckman, H.B. (1999). Soliciting the patient's agenda: Have we improved? *Journal of the American Medical Association, 281*, 283–287.

Maslach, C. (1979). The burn-out syndrome and patient care. In C. Garfield (Ed.), *The emotional realities of life-threatening illness* (pp. 111–120). St. Louis, MO: CV Mosby.

Maslach, C., & Leiter, M.P. (1997). *The truth about burnout.* San Francisco: Jossey-Bass.

Masten, A.S. (2001). Ordinary magic: Resilience processes in development. *American Psychologist, 56,*227–238.

Matarazzo, J.D. (1980). Behavioral health and behavioral medicine. *American Psychologist, 35*, 807–817.

Matarazzo, J.D., Weiss, S.M., Herd, J.A., Miller, N.E., & Weiss, S. (Eds.). (1984). *Behavioral health: A handbook of health enhancement and disease prevention.* New York: Wiley.

Matheson, D.H. (1997). The painful truth: Interpretation of facial expressions of pain in older adults. *Journal of Nonverbal Behaviour, 21*, 223–238.

Maticka-Tyndale, E. (2001). Sexual health and Canadian youth: How do we measure up? *Canadian Journal of Human Sexuality, 10*, 1–17.

Matrunola, P. (1996). Is there a relationship between job satisfaction and absenteeism? *Journal of Advanced Nursing, 23*, 827–834.

Matsunaga, H., Kiriike, N., Iwasaki, Y., Miyata, A., & Matsui, T. (2000). Multi-impulsivity among bulimic patients in Japan. *International Journal of Eating Disorders, 27*, 348–352.

Mauer, M.H., Burnett, K.F., Ouellette, E.A., Ironson, G.H., & Dandes, H.M. (1999). Medical hypnosis and orthopedic hand: Pain perception, postoperative recovery, and therapeutic comfort. *International Journal of Clinical and Experimental Hypnosis, 47*(2), 144–161.

Mayled, A. (1998). Medical admissions units: The role of the nurse practitioner. *Nursing Standard, 12*, 44–47.

Mayne, T.J., & Ambrose, T.K. (1999). Research review on anger in psychotherapy. *Journal of Clinical Psychology, 55*, 353–363.

Mazullo, J.M., Lasagna, L., & Griner, P.F. (1974). Variations in interpretation of prescription instructions. *Journal of the American Medical Association, 227*, 929–931.

McAuley, E., & Courneya, K.S. (1992). Self-efficacy relationships with affective and exertion responses to exercise. *Journal of Applied Social Psychology, 22*, 312–326.

McAuley, E., Schaffer, S.M., & Rudolph, D. (1995). Affective responses to acute exercise in elderly impaired males: The moderating effects of self-efficacy and age. *International Journal of Aging and Human Development, 41*, 13–35.

McCaul, K.D., Schroeder, D.M., & Reid, P.A. (1996). Breast cancer worry and screening. Some prospective data. *Health Psychology, 15*, 430–433.

McCorkle, R., Tang, S.T., Greenwald, H., Holcombe, G., & Lavery, M. (2006). Factors related to depressive symptoms among long-term survivors of cervical cancer. *Health Care for Women International, 27*, 45–58.

McDaniel, J.S. (1996). Stressful life events and psychoneuroimmunology. In T.W. Miller (Ed.), *Theory and assessment of stressful life events* (pp. 3–36). Madison, CT: International Universities Press.

McDonald, D. D. & Fedo, J. (2009). Older adults' pain *communication*: the effect of interruption. *Pain Management Nursing, 10*(3), 149–53.

McDonald, H.P., Garg, A.X., & Haynes, R.B. (2002). Interventions to enhance patient adherence to medication prescriptions: Scientific review. *Journal of the American Medical Association, 288*, 2868–2879.

McDonald, J.T., & Kennedy, S. (2005). Is migration to Canada associated with unhealthy weight gain? Overweight and obesity among Canada's immigrants. *Social Science & Medicine, 61*, 2469–2481.

McEwen, B.S. (1998). Protective and damaging effects of stress mediators. *New England Journal of Medicine, 338*, 171–1179.

McEwen, B.S. (2000). Allostasis and allostatic load: Implications for neuropsychopharmacology. *Neuropsychopharmacology, 22*, 108–124.

McEwen, B.S., & Stellar, E. (1993). Stress and the individual: Mechanisms leading to disease. *Archives of General Medicine, 153*, 2093–2101.

McFarland, K.F., & Rhoades, D.R. (1998). Gender-related values and medical specialty choice. *Academic Psychiatry, 22*, 236–239.

McFarlane, T., Polivy, J., & Herman, C.P. (1998). Effects of false weight feedback on mood, self-evaluation, and food intake in restrained and unrestrained eaters. *Journal of Abnormal Psychology, 107*, 312–318.

McFarlane, T., Polivy, J., & McCabe, R.E. (1999). Help, not harm: Psychological foundation for a nondieting approach toward health. *Journal of Social Issues, 55*, 261–276.

McGovern, R.J., Heyman, E.N., & Resnick, M.I. (2002). An examination of coping style and quality of life of cancer patients who attend a prostate cancer support group. *Journal of Psychosocial Oncology, 20*(3), 57–68.

McGrath, P.A. (1987). An assessment of children's pain: A review of behavioral, physiological and direct scaling techniques. *Pain, 31*, 147–176.

McGrath, P.A., & Gillespie, J. (2001). Pain assessment in children and adolescents. In D.C. Turk & R. Melzack (Eds.), *Handbook of pain assessment.* (2nd ed.) (pp. 97–118). New York: Guilford.

McGrath, P.J., Latimer, M., Finley, G.A., & Chambers, C.T. (2009). Measurement of pain in children. *Pain Research and Management, 14*, 11–12.

McGuire, W.J. (1985). Attitudes and attitude change. In G. Lindzey & E. Aronson (Eds.), *Handbook of social psychology.* (3rd ed.). Vol. 2 (pp. 233–346). New York: Random House.

McIsaac, H.K., Thordarson, D.S., Shafran, R., Rachman, S., & Poole, G. (1998). Claustrophobia and the magnetic imaging procedure. *Journal of Behavioral Medicine, 21*, 255–268.

McKinlay, J.B., Burns, R.B., Feldman, H.A., Freund, K.M., Irish, J.T., Kasten, L.E., Moskowitz, M.A., Potter, D.A., & Woodman, K. (1998). Physician variability and uncertainty in the management of breast cancer: Results from a factorial experiment. *Medical Care, 36,* 385–396.

McKinstry, B. (2000). Do patients wish to be involved in decision making in the consultation? A cross sectional survey with video vignettes. *British Medical Journal, 321,* 867–871.

McNamara, S., Giguère, V., St. Louis, L., & Boileau, J. (2009). Development and implementation of the specialized nurse practitioner role: Use of the PEPPA framework to achieve success. *Nursing & Health Sciences, 11*(3), 318–325.

McPherson, A. (2005). Sustainability of family medicine. *Canadian Medical Association Journal, 172*(2), 157.

McWilliam, C.L., Brown, J.B., & Stewart, M. (2000). Breast cancer patients' experiences of patient-doctor communication: A working relationship. *Patient Education and Counseling, 39,* 191–204.

Meechan, G., Colins, J., & Petrie, K.J. (2003). The relationship of symptoms and psychological factors to delay in seeking medical care for breast symptoms. *Preventive Medicine, 36,* 374–378.

Mehler, P.S. (2003). Osteoporosis in anorexia nervosa: Prevention and treatment. *International Journal of Eating Disorders, 33*(2), 113–126.

Meichenbaum, D. (1975). Enhancing creativity by modifying what subjects say to themselves. *American Educational Research Journal, 12,* 129–145.

Meichenbaum, D. (1977). *Cognitive-behavior modification: An integrative approach.* New York: Plenum Press.

Meichenbaum, D.H. (1985). *Stress innoculation training.* New York: Pergamon Press.

Melamed, B.G., & Siegal, L.J. (1975). Reduction of anxiety in children facing surgery by modeling. *Journal of Consulting and Clinical Psychology, 43,* 511–521.

Melendez, J.C., & McCrank, E. (1993). Anxiety-related reactions associated with magnetic resonance imaging examinations. *Journal of the American Medical Association, 270,* 745–747.

Melzack, R. (1973). *The puzzle of pain.* New York: Basic Books.

Melzack, R. (1975). The McGill Pain Questionnaire: Major properties and scoring methods. *Pain, 1,* 277–299.

Melzack, R. (1987). The short-form McGill Pain Questionnaire. *Pain, 30,* 191–197.

Melzack, R. (1989). Folk medicine and the sensory modulation of pain. In P.D. Wall & R. Melzack (Eds.), *Textbook of pain.* (2nd ed.). Edinburgh: Churchill Livingstone.

Melzack, R. (1991). The gate control theory 25 years later: New perspectives on phantom limb pain. In M.R. Bond, J.E. Charloton, & C.J. Woolf (Eds.), *Proceedings of the VIth World Congress on Pain* (pp. 9–21). Amsterdam: Elsevier Science Publishers.

Melzack, R. (1992). Phantom limbs. *Scientific American, 266,* 120–126.

Melzack, R. (1998). Pain and stress: Clues toward understanding chronic pain. In M. Sabourin, F. Craik, & M. Robert (Eds.), *Advances in psychological science: Vol. 2. Biological and cognitive aspects.* Hove: Psychology Press Limited.

Melzack, R. (1999). Pain—An overview. *Acta Anaesthesiologica Scandinavica, 43,* 880–884.

Melzack, R. (2001). Pain and the neuromatrix in the brain. *Journal of Dental Education, 65,* 1378–1382.

Melzack, R., & Katz, J. (2001). The McGill pain questionnaire: Appraisal and current status. In D.C. Turk & R. Melzack (Eds.), *Handbook of pain assessment.* (2nd ed.) (pp. 35–52). New York: Guilford.

Melzack, R., & Katz, J. (2004). The gate control theory: Reaching for the brain. In T. Hadjistavropoulos & K.D. Craig (Eds.), *Pain: Psychological perspectives* (pp. 13–34). Mahwah, NJ: Erlbaum.

Melzack, R., & Wall, P.D. (1965). Pain mechanisms: A new theory. *Science, 150,* 971–979.

Melzack, R., Israel, R., Laxroix, R., & Schultz, G. (1997). Phantom limbs in people with congenital limb deficiency or amputation in early childhood. *Brain, 120,* 1603–1620.

Mendes-de-Leon, C.F., Powell, L.H., & Kaplan, B.H. (1991). Change in coronary-prone behaviors in the Recurrent Coronary Prevention Project. *Psychosomatic medicine, 53,* 407–419.

Mercado, A.M., Quan, N., Padgett, D.A., Sheridan, J.F., & Marucha, P.T. (2002). Restraint stress alters the expression of interleukin-1 and keratinocyte growth factor at wound site: An in situ hybridization study. *Journal of Neuroimmunology, 129,* 74–83.

Mercken, L., Candel, M., Willems, P., & de Vries, H. (2007). Disentangling social selection and social influence effects on adolescent *smoking:* The importance of reciprocity in friendships. *Addiction, 102*(9), 1483–1492.

Merskey, H. (1986). Psychiatry and pain. In R.A. Sternbach (Ed.), *The psychology of pain.* (2nd ed.). New York: Raven Press.

Metz, J.M., Devine, P., DeNittis, A., Jones, H., Hampshire, M., Goldwein, J., & Whittington, R. (2003). A multi-institutional study of Internet utilization by radiation oncology patients. *Int J Radiat Oncol Biol Phys, 56*(4), 1201–1205.

Myers, C.D., Riley, J.L., & Robinson, M.E. (2003). Psychosocial contributions to sex-correlated differences in pain. *The Clinical Journal of Pain, 19,* 225–232.

Michalko, S.L., McAuley, E., & Bane, S. (1996). Self-efficacy and affective responses to acute exercise in middle-aged adults. *Journal of Social Behavior and Personality, 11,* 375–385.

Miles, F., & Meehan, J.W. (1995). Visual discrimination of pigmented skin lesions. *Health Psychology, 14,* 171–177.

Miller, B.M., Bartholomew, J.B., & Springer, B.A. (2005). Post-exercise affect: The effect of mode preference. *Journal of Applied Sport Psychology, 17,* 263–262.

Millar, M.G. (1997). The effects of emotion on breast self-examination: Another look at the Health Belief Model. *Social Behavior and Personality, 25,* 223–232.

Miller, D.L., & Stark, L.J. (1994). Contingency contracting for improving adherence in pediatric populations. *Journal of the American Medical Association, 271,* 81–83.

Miller, G.E., & Cohen, S. (2001). Psychological interventions and the immune system: A meta-analytic review and critique. *Health Psychology, 20*(1), 47–63.

Miller, G.E., Cohen, S., Pressman, S., Barkin, A., Rabin, B.S., & Treanor, J. J. (2004). Psychological stress and antibody response to influenza vaccination: When is the critical period for stress, and how does it get inside the body? *Psychosomatic Medicine, 66*(2), 215–223.

Miller, L.G., Liu, H., Hays, R.D., Golin, C.W., Beck, C.K., Asch, S.M., et al. (2002). How well do clinicians estimate patients' adherence to combination antiretroviral therapy? *Journal of General Internal Medicine, 17,* 1–11.

Miller, N.E. (1983). Behavioral medicine: Symbiosis between laboratory and clinic. *Annual Review of Psychology, 34,* 1–31.

Miller, P.S., & Kerr, G.A. (2002). Conceptualizing excellence: Past, present, and future. *Journal of Applied Sport Psychology, 14,* 140–153.

Miller, S.M. (1980). When is a little information a dangerous thing? Coping with stressful life-events by monitoring vs. blunting. In S. Levine & H. Ursin (Eds.), *Coping and health.* New York: Plenum Press.

Miller, S.M. (1996). Monitoring/blunting of threatening information: Cognitive interference and facilitation in the coping process. In I.G. Sarison, G.R. Pierce, & S.B.R. (Eds.), *Cognitive interference: Theories, methods and findings* (pp. 175–190). Mahwah, NJ: Lawrence Erlbaum.

Miller, S.M., & Mangan, C.E. (1983). Interacting effects of information and coping style in adapting to gynecologic stress: Should the doctor tell all? *Journal of Personality and Social Psychology, 45,* 223–236.

Miller, T.D., Balady, G.J., & Fletcher, G.F. (1997). Exercise and its role in the prevention and rehabilitation of cardiovascular disease. *Annals of Behavioral Medicine, 19,* 220–229.

Miller, V.A., & Drotar, D. (2003). Discrepancies between mother and adolescent perceptions of diabetes-related decision-making autonomy and their relationship to diabetes-related conflict and adherence to treatment. *Journal of Pediatric Psychology, 28,*265–274.

Millstein, S.G. (1996). Utility of the theories of reasoned action and planned behavior for predicting physician behavior: A prospective analysis. *Health Psychology, 15,* 398–402.

Milton, B., Cook, P.A., Dugdill, L., Porcellato, L., Spsringett, J., & Woods, S.W. (2004). Why do primary school children smoke? A longitudinal analysis of predictors of smoking uptake during pre-adolescence. *Public Health, 118,* 247–255.

Minore, B., & Boone, M. (2002). Realizing potential: Improving interdisciplinary professional/paraprofessional health care teams in Canada's northern aboriginal communities through education. *Journal of Interprofessional Care, 16*(2), 139–147.

Minore, B., Jacklin, K., Boon, M., & Cromarty, H. (2009). Realistic expectations: The changing role of paraprofessional health workers in the First Nation communities in Canada. *Education for Health, 22*(2), 1–9.

Minton, C., & Carryer, J. (2005). Memories of former intensive care patients six months following discharge. *Contemporary Nurse, 20*(2), 152–158.

Miró, J., Turk, D.C., & Rudy, T.E. (1991). *Chronic pain management. Against the uniformity myth.* Paper presented at the *II congr´s Internacional Latini Dies, Sitges,* Spain.

Miró, J.R., & Rosa, M. (1999). Preoperative preparation for surgery: An analysis of the effects of relaxation and information provision. *Clinical Psychology & Psychotherapy, 6*(3), 202–209.

Misovich, S.J., Fisher, J.D., & Fisher, W.A. (1996). The perceived AIDS-preventive utility of knowing one's partner well: A public health dictum and individuals' risky sexual behaviour. *The Canadian Journal of Human Sexuality, 5,* 83–90.

Mitchell, J.E., & Crow, S. (2006). Medical complications of anorexia nervosa and bulimia nervosa. *Current Opinion in Psychiatry, 19,* 438–443.

Miyazaki, T., Ishikawa, T., Iimori, H., Miki, A., Wenner, M., Fukunishi, I., & Kawamura, N. (2003). Relationship between perceived social support and immune function. *Stress & Health: Journal of the International Society for the Investigation of Stress, 19,* 3–7.

Mkanta, W.N., Mejia, M.C., & Duncan, R.P. (2010). Race, outpatient mental health service use, and survival after an AIDS diagnosis in the highly active antiretroviral therapy era. *AIDS Patient Care and STDS,24*(1), 31–37.

Moffett, J.K., Torgerson, D., Bell-Syer, S., Jackson, D., Llewlyn-Phillips, H., Farrin, A., & Barber, J. (1999). Randomized controlled trial of exercises for low back pain: Clinical outcomes, costs, and preferences. *British Medical Journal, 319,* 279–283.

Mollema, E.D., Snoek, F.J., Ader, H.J., Heine, R.J., & van der Ploeg, H.M. (2001). Insulin-treated diabetes patients with fear of self-injecting or fear of self-testing: Psychological comorbidity and general well-being. *Journal of Psychosomatic Research, 51*(5), 665–672.

Montgomery, C., Pocock, M., Titley, K., & Lloyd, K. (2003). Predicting psychological distress in patients with leukaemia and lymphoma. *Journal of Psychosomatic Research, 54*(4), 289–292.

Montgomery, G.H. (2004). Cognitive factors in health psychology and behavioral medicine. *Journal of Clinical Psychology, 60*(4), 405–413.

Montgomery, G.H., & Bovbjerg, D.H. (2003). Expectations of chemotherapy-related nausea: Emotional and experiential predictors. *Annals of Behavioral Medicine, 25,* 48–54.

Monti, D.A., Mago, R., & Kunkel, E.J.S. (2005). Depression, cognition, and anxiety among postmenopausal women with breast cancer. *Psychiatric Services, 56*(11), 1353–1355.

Moore, S.M., Barling, N.R., & Hood, B. (1998). Predicting testicular and breast self-examination behaviour: A test of the theory of reasoned action. *Behaviour Change, 15,* 41–49.

Moos, R.H., & Moos, B.S. (2006). Rates and predictors of relapse after natural and treated remission from alcohol use disorders. *Addiction, 101* (2), 212–222.

Moraska, A., Campisi, J., Nguyen, K.T., Maier, S.F., Watkins, L.R., & Fleshner, M. (2002). Elevated IL-1beta contributes to antibody suppression produced by stress. *Journal of Applied Physiology, 93*, 207–215.

Morgan, W.P. (Ed.). (1997). *Physical activity in mental health.* Washington, DC: Taylor and Francis.

Morgan, W.P., & Ellickson, K.A. (1989). Health, anxiety and physical exercise. In D. Hackfort & C. Spielberger (Eds.), *Anxiety in sports: An international perspective.* New York: Hemisphere Publishing.

Morris, E. (1999). Reflections on the NICU. A nurse's perspective. *American Journal of Nursing, 99*(3), 23.

Morrison, D.M., Baker, S.A., & Gillmore, M.R. (2000). Using the Theory of Reasoned Action to predict condom use among high-risk heterosexual teens. In P. Norman & C. Abraham (Eds.), *Understanding and changing health behaviour: From health beliefs to self-regulation* (pp. 27–49).

Moulin, D.W., Clark, A.H., Speechley, M., & Morley-Forster, P.K. (2002). Chronic pain in Canada—Prevalence, treatment, impact and the role of opioid analgesia. *Pain Research and Management, 7*, 179–184.

Moyer, A. (1997). Psychosocial outcomes of breast-conserving surgery versus mastectomy: A meta-analytic review. *Health Psychology, 16*, 284–298.

Mpofu, E., & Houston, E. (1998). Assessment of value change in persons with acquired physical disabilities: Current and prospective applications for rehabilitation counselors. *Canadian Journal of Rehabilitation, 12*, 53–61.

Mulvihill, C.K. (1996). AIDS education for college students: Review and proposal for a research-based curriculum. *AIDS Education and Prevention, 8*, 11–25.

Mulvihill, D. (2005). The health impact of childhood trauma: An interdisciplinary review, 1997–2003. *Issues in Comprehensive Pediatric Nursing, 28*, 115-136.

Munafo, M., Johnstone, E., Murphy, M., & Walton, R. (2001). New directions in the genetic mechanisms underlying nicotine addiction. *Addiction Biology, 6*(2), 109–117.

Munro, L., Rodwell, J., & Harding, L. (1998). Assessing occupational stress in psychiatric nurses using the full job strain model: The value of social support to nurses. *International Journal of Nursing Studies, 35*, 339–345.

Murgraff, V., Walsh, J., & McDermott, M.R. (2000). The application of Batozzi and Edwards' theory of self-regulation to the prediction of low-risk single-occasion drinking. *Psychology, Health & Medicine, 5*(4), 451–466.

Murphy, H., Dickens, C., Creed, F., & Bernstein, R. (1999). Depression, illness perception and coping in rheumatoid arthritis. *Journal of Psychosomatic Research, 46*, 155–164.

Murphy, K.J., & Brunberg, J.A. (1997). Adult claustrophobia, anxiety and sedation in MRI. *Magnetic Resonance Imaging, 15*, 51–54.

Murphy, S., Nordin, S., & Cumming, J. (2008). Imagery in sport, exercise and dance. In T.S. Horn (Ed.), *Advances in sport psychology.* (3rd ed.) (pp. 297–324). Champaign, Illinois: Human Kinetics.

Murry, M. (1980). *Seeking the master.* London: Neville Spearman.

Musclow, S.L., Sawhney, M., & Watt-Watson, J. (2002). The emerging role of advanced nursing practice in acute pain management throughout Canada. *Clin Nurse Spec, 16*(2), 63–67.

Muscroft, J., & Hicks, C. (1998). A comparison of psychiatric nurses' and general nurses' reported stress and counselling needs: A case study approach. *Journal of Advanced Nursing, 27*, 1317–1325.

Mushlin, A.I., Kouides, R.W., & Shapiro, D.E. (1998). Estimating the accuracy of screening mammography: A meta-analysis. *American Journal of Preventative Medicine, 14*, 143–153.

Musselman, D.L., Evans, D.L., & Nemeroff, C.B. (1998). The relationship of depression to cardiovascular disease. *Archives of General Psychiatry, 55*, 580–592.

Muustedt, K., Muller, H., Blauth-Eckmeyer, E., Stenger, K., Zygmunt, M., & Vahrson, H. (1999). Role of dexamethasone dosage in combination with 5-HT3 antagonists for prophylaxis of acute chemotherapy-induced nausea and vomiting. *British Journal of Cancer, 79*, 637–639.

N

Nabalamba, A., & Millar, W. J. (2007). Going to the doctor. *Health Reports, 18*(1), 23–35 (Statistics Canada Catalogue 82–003). Retrieved June 1, 2010, from www.statcan.gc.ca/pub/82-003-x/82-003-x2006003-eng.pdf

Naimi, T.S., Brown, D.W., Brewer, R.D., Giles, W.H., Mensah, G., et al. (2005). Cardiovascular risk factors and confounders among non-drinking and moderate drinking U.S. adults. *American Journal of Preventive Medicine, 28*(4), 369–373.

Nakamura, M., Tanaka, M., Kinukawa, N., Abe, S., Itoh, K., Imai, K., et al. (2000). Association between basal serum and leptin levels and changes in abdominal fat distribution during weight loss. *Journal of Atherosclerosis and Thrombosis, 6*, 28–32.

Nam, R.K., Fleshner, N., Rakovitch, E., Klotz, L., Trachtenberg, J., Choo, R., Morton, G., & Danjoux, C. (1999). Prevalence and patterns of the use of complementary therapies among prostate cancer patients: An epidemiological analysis. *Journal of Urology, 161*, 1521–1524.

Naqvi, T.Z., Naqvi, S.S.A., & Marz, C.N.B. (2005). Gender differences in the link between depression and cardiovascular disease. *Psychosomatic Medicine, 67*(Suppl 1), S15–S18.

National Cancer Institute of Canada. (2001). *Canadian cancer statistics: Current incidence and mortality.* Toronto: Author.

National Institute on Alcohol Abuse and Alcoholism. (2000, October). Alcohol alert: New advances in alcoholism treatment. Bethesda, MD. Retrieved August 25, 2003, from www.niaaa.nih.gov

National Institute of Health. (2002). *What is complementary and alternative medicine?* Retrieved June 22, 2006, from www.nccam.nih.gov/health/whatiscam/

Nayak, S., Shiflett, S.C., Eshun, S., & Levine, F.M. (2000). Culture and gender effects in pain beliefs and the prediction of pain tolerance. *Cross-Cultural Research, 34*(2), 135–151.

The Need for an Aboriginal Health Institute in Canada. (2003). Ottawa: Health Canada.

Nerenz, D.R., & Leventhal, H. (1983). Self-regulation theory in chronic illness. In T.G. Burish & L.A. Bradley (Eds.), *Coping with chronic disease: Research and applications* (pp. 13–87). New York: Academic Press.

Newbold, K.B. (2005). Self-rated health within the Canadian immigrant population: Risk and the healthy immigrant effect. *Social Science and Medicine, 60,* 1359–1370.

Ng, E., Wilkins, R., Pole, J., & Adams, O.B. (1997). How far to the nearest physician? *Health Reports, 8*(4), 19–31.

Nguyen, H. L., Saczynski, J. S., Gore, J. M., & Goldberg, R. J. (2010). Age and sex differences in duration of prehospital delay in patients with acute myocardial infarction: A systematic review. *Circulation: Cardiovascular Quality and Outcomes, 3,* 82–92.

Niaura R., & Abrams, D.B. (2002). Smoking cessation: Progress, priorities, and prospectus. *Journal of Consulting and Clincial Psychology, 70,* 494–509.

Nicholas, D.R. (2000). Men, masculinity, and cancer: Risk-factor behaviors, early detection, and psychosocial adaptation. *Journal of American College Health, 49,* 27–33.

Nickel, C., Widermann, C., Harms, D., Leiberich, P.L., Tritt, K., et al. (2005). Patients with extreme obesity: Change in mental symptoms three years after gastric banding. *International Journal of Psychiatry in Medicine, 35,* 109–122.

Nideffer, R.M. (1985). *Athlete's guide to mental training.* Champaign, IL: Human Kinetics.

Nieman, d.C., Nehlsen-Cannarella, S.L., Markoff, P.A., Balk-Lamberton, A.J., Yang, H., Chritton, D.B.W., Lee, J.W. & Arabatzis, K. (1990). The effects of moderate exercise training on natural killer cells and acute upper respiratory tract infections. *International Journal of Sports Medicine, 11,* 467–473.

Nimbarte, A., Aghazedeh, F., & Harvey, C. (2006). Comparison of current U.S. and Canadian cigarette pack warnings. *International Quarterly of Community Health Education, 24*(1), 3–27.

North, T.C., McCullagh, P., & Tran, Z.V. (1990). Effects of exercise on depression. *Exercise and Sport Science Reviews, 18,* 379–415.

Norton, G.R., Norton, P.J., Asmundson, G.J.G., Thompson, L.A., & Larsen, M.A. (in press). Neurotic butterflies in my stomach: The role of anxiety, anxiety sensitivity and depression in functional gastrointestinal disorders. *Journal of Psychosomatic Research.*

Novins, D.K., Beals, J., Moore, L.A., Spicer, P., & Manson, S.M. (2004). Use of biomedical services and traditional healing options among American Indians: Sociodemographic correlates, spirituality and ethnic identity. *Medical Care, 42,* 670–679.

O

O'Brien-Pallas, L., Alksnis, C., & Wang, S. (2003). *Bringing the future into focus: Projecting RN retirement in Canada.* Ottawa: Canadian Institute for Health Information.

Ockene, J.K. (2001). Strategies to increase adherence to treatment. In L.E. Burke & I.S. Ockene (Eds.), *Compliance in healthcare and research* (pp. 43–55). Armonk, NY: Futura.

Ockene, J.K., Emmons, K.M., Mermelstein, R.J., Perkins, K.A., Bonollo, D.S., Voorhees, C.C., & Hollis, J.F. (2000). Relapse and maintenance issues for smoking cessation. *Health Psychology, 19,* 17–31.

O'Connor, P.G., & Spickard, A. Jr. (1997). Physician impairment by substance abuse. *Medical Clinics of North America, 81,* 1037–1052.

Oliver, L.N., & Hayes, M.V. (2008). Effects of neighbourhood income on reported body mass index: An eight-year longitudinal study of Canadian children. *BMC Public Health, 8,* 16.

Olivardia, R. (2001). Mirror, mirror on the wall, who's the largest of them all? The features and phenomenology of muscle dysmorphia. *Harvard Review of Psychiatry, 9,* 254–259.

Olivardia, R., Pope, H.G., Jr., Hudson, J.I. (2000). Muscle dysmorphia in male weightlifters: A case-control study. *American Journal of Psychiatry, 157*(8), 1291–1296.

Olson, J.M., & Maio, G.R. (2003). Attitudes in social behavior. In T. Millon & M.J. Lerner (Eds.), *Handbook of psychology: Personality and social psychology,* Vol. 5 (pp. 299–325). New York: Wiley & Sons.

O'Neill, M., Rootman, I., & Pederson, A. (1994). Beyond Lalonde: Two decades of Canadian health. In A. Pederson, M. O'Neill, & I. Rootman (Eds.), *Health promotion in Canada: Provincial, national and international perspectives* (pp. 374–386). Toronto: Saunders.

Ong, L.M.L., Visser, M.R.M., Lammes, F.B., & de Haes, J.M. (2000). Doctor-patient communication and cancer patients' quality of life and satisfaction. Patient Education and Counselling, 41, 145–156.

Ontario, Ministry of Transportation (2009). Impaired driving. Retrieved July 1, 2010, from www.mto.gov.on.ca/english/safety/impaired/interlock.shtml

Orlick, T., & Partington, J. (1988). Mental links to excellence. *The Sport Psychologist, 2,* 105–130.

Orne, M.T. (1962). On the social psychology of the psychological experiment: With particular reference to demand characteristics and their implications. *American Psychologist, 17,* 776–783.

Orne, M.T. (1989). On the construct of hypnosis: How its definition affects research and its clinical application. In G.D. Burrows & L. Dennerstein (Eds.), *Handbook of hypnosis and psychosomatic medicine.* Amsterdam: Elsevier.

Ortner, C.N.M., MacDonald, T.K., & Olmstead, M.C. (2003). Alcohol intoxication reduces impulsivity in the delay-discounting paradigm. *Alcohol & Alcoholism, 38,* 151–156.

Osowiecki, D., & Compas, B.E. (1998). Psychological adjustment to cancer: Control beliefs and coping in adult cancer patients. *Cognitive Therapy and Research, 22*, 483–499.

Out, J.W., & Lafreniere, K.D. (2001). Baby Think It Over®: Using role-play to prevent teen pregnancy. *Adolescence, 36*(143), 571–582.

Owen, H., & Plummer, J. (1997). Patient-controlled analgesia: Current concepts in acute pain management. *CNS Drugs, 8*, 203–218.

P

Paffenbarger, R.S., Wing, A.L., & Hyde, R.T. (1978). Physical activity as an index of heart attack risk in college alumni. *American Journal of Epidemiology, 108*, 161–175.

Paice, J.A., Toy, C., & Shott, S. (1998). Barriers to cancer pain relief: Fear of tolerance and addiction. *Journal of Pain Symptom Management, 16*, 1–9.

Pallavicini-Gonzalez, J., Venegas-Ramirez, L., & Espinoza, M.A. (1995). The experience of intensive care patients of J.J. Aguirre Hospital: 1989–1992. *Revista de Psiquiatria Clinica, 32*(1–2), 25–36.

Papacharisis, V., Goudas, M., Danish, S., & Theodorakis, Y. (2005). The effectiveness of teaching a life skills program in a sport context. *Journal of Applied Sport Psychology, 17*, 247–254.

Paparizos, A.L., Tripp, D.A., Sullivan, M.J.L., & Rubenstein, M.L. (2005). Catastrophizing and pain perception in recreational ballet dancers. *Journal of Sport Behavior, 28*(1), 35–50.

Parboosingh, E.J., Anderson, G., Clark, E.A., et al. (1996). Cervical cancer screening: Are the 1989 recommendations still valid? *Canadian Medical Association Journal, 154*, 1867–1869.

Pargman, D. (1998). *Understanding sport behavior.* Upper Saddle River, NJ: Prentice-Hall.

Park, D.C., Hertzog, C., Leventhal, H., Morrell, R.W., et al. (1999). Medication adherence in rheumatoid arthritis patients: Older is wiser. *Journal of the American Geriatric Society, 47*(2), 172–183.

Parker, G., Heruc, G., Hilton, T., Oiley, A., Brotchie, H., Hadzi-Pavlovic, D., Owen, C., Friend, C., & Walsh, W.F. (2006). Explicating links between acute coronary syndrome and depression: Study design and methods. *Australian and New Zealand Journal of Psychiatry, 40*(3), 245–252.

Parker, P.A., & Kulik, J.A. (1995). Burnout, self- and supervisor-related job performance, and absenteeism among nurses. *Journal of Behavioral Medicine, 18*, 581–599.

Parrish, J.M. (1986). Parent compliance with medical and behavioral recommendations. In N.A. Krasnegor, J.D. Arasteh, & M.F. Cataldo (Eds.), *Child health behavior: A behavioral pediatrics perspective.* New York: Wiley.

Parsons, T. (1951). *The social system.* Glencoe, IL: Free Press.

Paskett, E.D., & Rimer, B.K. (1995). Psychosocial effects of abnormal Pap tests and mammograms: A review. *Journal of Women's Health, 4*, 73–82.

Passik, S.D., & Weinreb, H.J. (2000). Managing chronic non-malignant pain: Overcoming obstacles to the use of opioids. *Advances in Therapy, 17*, 70–83.

Pate, R.R., Pratt, M., Blair, S.N., Haskell, W.L., et al. (1995). Physical activity and public health: A recommendation from the Centers for Disease Control and Prevention and the American College of Sports Medicine. *Journal of the American Medical Association, 273*, 402–407.

Patterson, D.R. (2004). Treating pain with hypnosis. *Current Directions in Psychological Science, 13*(6), 252–255.

Patterson, D.R. (2005). Behavioral methods for chronic pain and illness: A reconsideration and appreciation. *Rehabilitation Psychology, 50*(3), 312–315.

Patterson, D.R., Hoffman, H.G., Weichman, S.A., Jensen, M.P., & Shara, S.R. (2004). Optimizing control of pain from severe burns: A literature review. *American Journal of Clinical Hypnosis, 47*(1), 43–54.

Patterson, J.M., Novak, C.B., Mackinnon, S.E., & Ellis, R.A. (2003). Needlestick injuries among medical students. *American Journal of Infection Control, 31*(4), 226–230.

Pavlin, D.J., Sullivan, M.J.L., Freund, P.R., & Roesen, K. (2005). Catastrophizing: A risk factor for postsurgical pain. *Clinical Journal of Pain, 21*(1), 83–90.

Payne, S.A., Dean, S.J., & Kalus, C. (1998). A comparative study of death anxiety in hospice and emergency nurses. *Journal of Advanced Nursing, 28*, 700–706.

Pearlin, L.I. (1993). The social contexts of stress. In L. Goldberger & S. Breznitz (Eds.), *Handbook of stress: Theoretical and clinical aspects.* (2nd ed.) (pp. 303–315). New York: Free Press.

Peng, P., Stinson, J. N., Choiniere, M., Dion, D., Intrater, H., LeFort, S., Lynch, M., Ong, M. et al. (2008). Role of health care professionals in multidisciplinary pain treatment facilities in Canada. *Pain Research and Management, 13*(6), 484–488.

Pennebaker, J.W. (1994). Psychological bases of symptom reporting: Perceptual and emotional aspects of chemical sensitivity. *Toxicology and Industrial Health, 10*, 497–511.

Pennebaker, J.W. (2000). Psychological factors influencing the reporting of physical symptoms. In A.A. Stone, J.S. Turkkan, C.A. Bachrach, J.B. Jobe, H.S. Kurtzman & V.S. Cain (Eds.), *The science of self-report: Implications for research and practice.* Mahwah, NJ: Lawrence Erlbaum.

Penninx, B.W., Guralnik, J.M., Mendes de Leon, C.F., Pahor, M., Visser, M., Corti, M.C., & Wallace, R.B. (1998). Cardiovascular events and mortality in newly and chronically depressed persons > 70 years of age. *American Journal of Cardiology, 81*, 988–94.

Perneger, T.V., Charvet-Bérard, A., & Perrier, A. (2008). *Patient* assessments of the most important medical *decision* during a hospitalization. *Journal of General Internal Medicine, 23*(10), 1659–1665.

Persky, V.W., Kempthorne-Rawson, J., & Shekelle, R.B. (1987). Personality and risk of cancer: 20-year follow-up of the Western Electric Study. *Psychosomatic Medicine, 49*, 435–449.

Peterkin, A.D. (1998). *Staying human during residency training.* Toronto: University of Toronto Press.

Petticrew, M., Bell, R., & Hunter, D. (2002). Influence of psychological coping on survival and recurrence in people with cancer: Systematic review. *British Medical Journal, 325*(7372), 1066–1069.

Petty, R.E., & Cacioppo, J.T. (1981). *Attitudes and persuasion: Classic and contemporary approaches.* Dubuque, IA: Brown.

Phillips, A.C., Carroll, D., Evans, P., Bosch, J.A., Clow, A., Hucklebridge, F., & Der, G. (2006). Stressful life events are associated with low secretion rates of immunoglobulin A in saliva in the middle aged and elderly. *Brain, Behavior, and Immunity, 20*(2), 191–197.

Phillips, K.D., & Morrow, J.H. (1998). Nursing management of anxiety in HIV infection. *Issues in Mental Health Nursing, 19,* 375–397.

Phillips, S. (1996). Sexual harassment of female physicians by patients. What is to be done? *Canadian Family Physician, 42,* 73–76.

Physicians for a Smoke-Free Canada. (2004). Questions and answers about second-hand smoke and occupational health and safety laws in Canada. Ottawa, Ontario. Retrieved May 17, 2006, from www.smoke-free.ca

Pierce, J.P. (2005). Influence of movie stars on the initiation of adolescent smoking. *Pediatric Dentistry, 27,* 149.

Pike, K. M., Walsh, B. T., Vitousek, K., Wilson, G. T., & Bauer, J. (2003). Cognitive behavior therapy in the posthospitalization treatment of anorexia nervosa. *American Journal of Psychiatry, 160,* 2046–2049.

Pinckney, R.G., Geller, B.M., Burman, M., & Littenberg, B. (2003). Effect of false-positive mammograms on return for subsequent screening mammography. *American Journal of Medicine, 114*(2), 120–125.

Pinder, R. (1990). *The management of chronic disease: Patient and doctor perspectives on Parkinson's disease.* London: MacMillan Press.

Pinquart, M., & Frohlich, C. (2009). Psychosocial resources and subjective well-being of cancer patients. *Psychology & Health, 24*(4), 407–421.

Pistrang, N., Barker, C., & Rutter, C. (1997). Social support as conversation: Analysing breast cancer patients' interactions with their partners. *Social Science and Medicine, 45,* 773–782.

Pi-Sunyer, X. (2003). A clinical view of the obesity problem. *Science, 299,* 859–860.

Pitts, M.K., Wooliscroft, J., Cannon, S., Johnson, I., & Singh, G. (2000). Factors influencing delay in treatment seeking by first-time attenders at a genitourinary clinic. *International Journal of STD & AIDS, 11,* 375–378.

Playford, E.D., Dawson, L., Limbert, V., Smith, M., Ward, C.D., & Wells, R. (2000). Goal-setting in rehabilitation: Report of a workshop to explore professionals' perceptions of goal-setting. *Clinical Rehabilitation, 14,* 491–496.

Plomin, R., DeFries, J.C., McClearn, G.E., & McGuffin, P. (2001). *Behavioral genetics.* (4th ed.). New York: Worth.

Plotkin, S.A. (2001). Immunologic correlates of protection induced by vaccination. *Pediatric Infectious Disease, 20,* 73–75.

Poczwarsdowski, A., & Conroy, D.E. (2002). Coping responses to failure and success among elite athletes and performing artists. *Journal of Applied Sport Psychology, 14,*313–329.

Polatin, P.B., & Mayer, T.G. (2001). Quantification of function in chronic low back pain. In D.C. Turk & R. Melzack (Eds.), *Handbook of pain assessment.* (2nd ed.) (pp. 191–203). New York: Guilford.

Polimeni, A.-M., & Moore, S. (2002). Insights into women's experiences of hospital stays: Perceived control, powerlessness and satisfaction. *Behaviour Change, 19*(1), 52–64.

Polivy, J. (1996). Psychological consequences of food restriction. *Journal of the American Dietetic Association, 96,* 859–592.

Polivy, J., & Herman, C.P. (2002). Causes of eating disorders. *Annual Review of Psychology, 53,* 187–213.

Polivy, J., & Herman, C.P. (2004). Sociocultural idealization of thin female body shapes: An introduction to the special issue on body image and eating disorders. *Journal of Social and Clinical Psychology, 23,* 1–6.

Polivy, J., & Herman, C.P. (2006). An evolutionary perspective on dieting. *Appetite, 47,* 30–35.

Polivy, J., Herman, C.P., & Boivin, M. (2005). Eating disorders. In J.E. Maddux & B.A. Winstead (Eds.), *Psychopathology: Foundations for a contemporary understanding* (pp. 229–254). Mahwah, NJ: Erlbaum.

Pomerleau, O.F. (1979). Behavioral factors in the establishment, maintenance, and cessation of smoking. In *Smoking and health: A report of the Surgeon General* (pp. 16–31). Washington, DC: GPO.

Pomeroy, W.B. (1972). *Dr. Kinsey and the institute for sex research.* New York: Harper & Row.

Ponte, P.R., Conlin, G., Conway, J.B., Grant, S., Medeiros, C., Nies, J., Shulman, L., Branowicki, P., & Conley, K. (2003). Making patient-centered care come alive: Achieving full integration of the patient's perspective. *J Nurs Adm, 33*(2), 82–90.

Poole, G.D., & Kallhood, L. (1996, April). Technologists' perceptions of patient stress and technologists' helping strategies: Survey results. *Radiaction,* 19–20.

Poole, G.D., Poon, C., Achille, M., White, K., Franz, N., Jittler, S., Watt, K., Cox, D. N., & Doll, R. (2001). Social support for prostate cancer patients: The effect of support groups. *Journal of Psychosocial Oncology, 19*(2), 1–16.

Poole, G.D., & Ting, K. (1995). Cultural differences between Euro-Canadian and Indo-Canadian maternity patients. *Journal of Social Psychology, 135,* 631–644.

Pope, H.G., Jr. (2001). Unraveling the Adonis complex. *Psychiatric Times, 18*(3), 22–26.

Pope, H.G., Jr., Olivardia, R., Gruber, A.J., & Borowiecki, J. (1999). Evolving ideals of male body image as seen through action toys. *International Journal of Eating Disorders, 26,* 65–72.

Pope, C. G., Pope, H. G., Jr., Menard, W., Fay, C., Olivardia, R., & Phillips, K. A. (2005). Clinical features of muscle dysmorphia among males with body dysmorphic disorder. *Body Image, 2*, 395–400.

Porteous, A. & Tyndall, J. (1994). Yes, I want to walk to the OR. *Canadian Operating Room Nursing Journal, 12*, 15–25.

Potts, H.W., & Wyatt, J.C. (2002). Survey of doctors' experience of patients using the Internet. *J Med Internet Res, 4*(1), e5.

Powell, L. H., Calvin, J. E., III., & Calvin, J. E., Jr. (2007). Effective obesity treatments. *American Psychologist, 62*, 234–246.

Powers, P. S., & Bruty, H. (2009). Pharmacotherapy for eating disorders and obesity. *Child and Adolescent Psychiatric Clinics of North America, 18*, 175–187.

Prapavessis, H., Maddison, R., Ruygrok, P.N., Bassett, S., Harper, T., & Gillanders, L. (2005). Using Theory of Planned Behavior to understand exercise motivation in patients with congenital heart disease. *Psychology, Health & Medicine, 10*(4), 335–343.

Prescott, L.M., Harley, J.P., & Klein, D.A. (1999). *Microbiology.* (4th ed.). Boston: WCB/McGraw-Hill.

Pressman, S.D., & Cohen, S. (2005). Does positive affect influence health? *Psychological Bulletin, 131*(6), 925–971.

Pressman, S.D., Cohen, S., Miller, G.E., Barkin, A., Rabin, B.S., & Treanor, J.J. (2005). Loneliness, social network size, and immune response to influenza vaccination in college freshmen. *Health Psychology, 24*(3), 297–306.

Price, R.A. (2002). Genetics and common obesities: Background, current status, strategies and future prospects. In T.A. Wadden & A.J. Stunkard (Eds.), *Handbook of obesity treatment* (pp. 73–94). New York: Guilford Press.

Prickett, C. Lister, E.C., Trevithick-Sutton, C., Hirst, M., Vinson, J., Noble, E., & Trevithick, R. (2004). Alcohol: Friend or foe? Alcoholic beverage hormesis for cataract and atherosclerosis is related to plasma antioxidant activity. *Nonlinearity in Biology, Toxicology and Medicine, 2*(4), 353–370.

Prkachin, K.D. (2007). The coming of age of pain expression. *Pain, 133*, 3–4.

Prkachin, K.D., Hughes, E.A., Schultz, I., Joy, P., & Hunt, D. (2002). Real-time assessment of pain behavior during clinical assessment of low-back pain patients. *Pain, 95*, 23–30.

Prkachin, K.M., Solomon, P.E., & Ross, J. (2007). Underestimation of pain by health-care providers: Towards a model of the process of inferring pain in others. *Canadian Journal of Nursing Research, 39*, 88–106

Prochaska, J.O., & DiClemente, C.C. (1983). Stages and processes of self-change of smoking: Toward an integrative model of change. *Journal of Consulting and Clinical Psychology, 51*, 390–395.

Prochaska, J.O., & DiClemente, C.C. (1986). Toward a comprehensive model of change. In W.R. Miller, N. Heather, et al. (Eds.), *Treating addictive behaviors: Processes of change. Applied clinical psychology.* (pp. 3–27). New York: Plenum Press.

Prochaska, J.O., & Velicer (1997). The transtheoretical model of health behavior change. *American Journal of Health Promotion, 12*, 38–48.

Pruzinsky, T., Levine, E., Persing, J.A., Barth, J.T., & Obrecht, R. (2006). Facial trauma and facial cancer. In D.B. Sarwer, T. Pruzinsky, T.F. Cash, R.M. Goldwyn, J.A. Persing, & L.A. Whitaker (Eds.), *Psychological aspects of reconstructive and cosmetic plastic surgery: Clinical empirical and ethical perspectives* (pp. 125–143). Philadelphia: Lippincott Williams & Wilkins.

Pryse-Phillips, W., Findlay, H., Tugwell, P., Edmeads, J., et al. (1992). A Canadian population survey on the clinical, epidemiological and societal impact of migraine and tension-type headache. *Canadian Journal of Neurol Sci, 19*, 333–339.

Ptacek, J.T., Fries, E.A., Eberhardt, T.L., & Ptacek, J.J. (1999). Breaking bad news to patients: Physicians' perceptions of the process. *Support and Care for Cancer, 7*(3), 113–120.

Public Health Agency of Canada. (2002). Environmental tobacco smoke and deaths from coronary heart disease in Canada. *Chronic Diseases in Canada, 23*(1). Retrieved September 1, 2006, from www.phac-aspc.gc.ca/publicat/cdic-mcc/23-1/b_e.html

Public Health Agency of Canada. (2003). Centre for Chronic Disease Prevention and Control: Chronic Respiratory Diseases. Retrieved April 5, 2006, from www.phac-aspc.gc.ca/ccdpc-cpcmc/crd-mrc/copd_e.html

Public Health Agency of Canada. (2005a). Diabetes. Retrieved June 4, 2006, from www.phac-aspc.gc.ca/ccdpc-cpcmc/diabetes-diabete/english/index.html

Public Health Agency of Canada. (2005b). Understanding the HIV/AIDS epidemic among Aboriginal Peoples in Canada: The community at a glance. Retrieved June 6, 2006, from www.phac-aspc.gc.ca/publicat/epiu-aepi/epi-note/index.html#2

Public Health Agency of Canada. (2006). *HIV and AIDS in Canada: Surveillance report to December 31, 2005.* Surveillance and Risk Assessment Division, Centre for Infectious Disease Prevention and Control.

Public Health Agency of Canada. (2009). Obesity in Canada—Snapshot. Retrieved June 2, 2010, from www.phac-aspc.gc.ca/publicat/2009/oc/index-eng.php

Q

Quirk, M., & Wagner, S. (1995). Environmental psychology and health. *Environment and Behavior, 27*, 90–99.

R

Rachman, S., & Taylor, S. (1993). Analysis of claustrophobia. *Journal of Anxiety Disorders, 7*, 1-11.

Raglan, J.S., & Morgan, W.P. (1987). Influence of exercise and "distraction therapy" on state anxiety and blood pressure. *Medicine and Science in Sport and Exercise, 19*, 456–463.

Rains, J.C., Penzien, D.B., & Jamison, R.N. (1992). A structured approach to the management of chronic pain. In L. VandeCreek, S. Knapp, & T.L. Jackson (Eds.), *Innovations in clinical practice: A source book,* Vol. 11 (pp. 521–539). Sarasota, FL: Professional Resource Press.

Ramirez, A., Bravo, I.M., & Katsikas, S. (2005). Infant feeding decisions and practices in the U.S. and Colombia. *Journal of Prenatal & Perinatal Psychology & Health, 19*(3), 237–249.

Ramirez, A.J., Craig, T.K., Watson, J.P., Fentiman, I.S., North, W.R., & Rubens, R.D. (1989). Stress and relapse of breast cancer. *British Medical Journal, 298,* 291–293.

Ramirez, A.J., Westcombe, A.M., Burgess, C.C., Sutton, S., Littlejohns, P., & Richards, M.A. (1999). Factors predicting delayed presentation of symptomatic breast cancer: A systematic review. *The Lancet, 353,* 1127–1131.

Rando, T. (1996). Complications in mourning traumatic death. In K. Doka (Ed.), *Living with grief after sudden loss: Suicide, homicide, accident, heart attack, stroke* (pp. 134–159). Washington, DC: Hospice Foundation of America.

Ranney, L., Melvin, C., Lux, L., McClain, E., & Lohr, K.N. (2006). Systematic review: Smoking cessation intervention strategies for adults and adults in special populations. *Annals of Internal Medicine, 145*(11), 845–856.

Raps, C.S., Peterson, C., Jonas, M., & Seligman, M.E.P. (1982). Patient behavior in hospitals: Helplessness, reactance, or both? *Journal of Personality and Social Psychology, 42,* 1036–1041.

Rathmore, S.S., Lenert, L.A., Weinfurt, K.P., Tinoco, A., Taleghani, C.K., Harless, W., & Schulman, K.A. (2000). The effects of patient sex and race on medical students' rating of quality of life. *American Journal of Medicine, 108,* 561–566.

Ratner, P. A., Tzianetas, R., Tu, A. W., Johnson, J. L., Mackay, M., Buller, C. E., Rowlands, M., Reime, B. (2006). Myocardial infarction symptom recognition by the lay public: The role of gender and ethnicity. *Journal of Epidemiology and Community Health, 60*(7), 606–15.

Rattray, J.E., Johnston, M., & Wildsmith, J.A.W. (2005). Predictors of emotional outcomes of intensive care. *Anesthesia, 60*(11), 1985–1092.

Ravaldi, C., Vannacci, A., Zucchi, T. (2003). Eating disorders and body image disturbances among ballet dancers, gymnasium users and body builders. *Psychopathology, 36*(5), 247–254.

Ravindran, A.V., Griffiths, J., Merali, Z., & Anisman, H. (1995). Lymphocyte subsets associated with major depression and dysthymia; Modification by antidepressant treatment. *Psychosomatic Medicine, 57,* 555–563.

Ray, O. (2004). How the mind hurts and heals the body. *American Psychologist, 59,* 29–40.

Reeves, J.L., II, Graff-Radford, S.B., & Shipman, D. (2004). The effects of transcutaneous electrical nerve stimulation on experimental pain and sympathetic nervous system response. *Pain Medicine, 5,* 150–161.

Reiche, E.M.V., Morimoto, H.K., & Nunes, S.O.V. (2005). Stress and depression-induced immune dysfunction: Implications for the development and progression of cancer. *International Review of Psychiatry, 17*(6), 515–527.

Reiche, E.M.V., & Nunes, S.O.V. (2005). Stress and depression—Induced immune dysfunction: Implications for the development and progression of cancer. *International Review of Psychiatry, 17*(6), 515–527.

Reid, J.L., & Hammond, D. (2009). Tobacco use in Canada: Patterns and trends, 2009 edition. Waterloo, ON: Propel Centre for Population Health Impact, University of Waterloo.

Reid, J.L., Hammond, D., & Driezen P. (2010). Socioeconomic status and smoking in Canada, 1999–2006: Has there been any progress on disparities in tobacco use? *Canadian Journal of Public Health, 101*(1), 73–78.

Reid, M.R., Mackinnon, L.T., & Drummond, P.D. (2001). The effects of stress management on symptoms of upper respiratory tract infection, secretory immunoglobulin A, and mood in young adults. *Journal of Psychosomatic Research, 51,* 721–728.

Rejeski, W.J., Hardy, C.H., & Shaw, J. (1991). Psychometric confounds of assessing state anxiety in conjunction with acute bouts of vigorous exercise. *Journal of Sport and Exercise Psychology, 13,* 65–74.

Remick, A. K., Polivy, J., & Pliner, P. (2009). Internal and external moderators of the effect of variety on food intake. *Psychological Bulletin,* (3), 434–451.

Rennick, J.E., Johnston, C.C., Dougherty, G., Platt, R., & Ritchie, J.A. (2002). Children's psychological responses after critical illness and exposure to invasive technology. *Journal of Developmental & Behavioral Pediatrics, 23*(3), 133–144.

Rentsch, D., Luthy, C., Perneger, T.V., & Allaz, A.F. (2003). Hospitalisation process seen by patients and health care professionals. *Soc Sci Med, 57*(3), 571–576.

Research Quarterly for Exercise and Sport. (1995). Physical Activity, Health and Well-being. *Research Quarterly for Exercise and Sport Science,* special issue: Proceedings of the International Scientific Consensus Conference, 66(4): whole.

Resident duty hours language: Final requirements. (2003, February 13). Accreditation Council for Graduate Medical Education Board of Directors. Accessed July 11, 2003 from www.acgme.org

Reynolds, D.V. (1969). Surgery in the rat during electrical anesthesia induced by focal brain stimulation. *Science, 164,* 444–445.

Reynolds, F. (2001). Strategies for facilitating physical activity and wellbeing: A health promotion perspective. *British Journal of Occupational Therapy, 64,* 330–336.

Rice, P.R. (1999). *Stress and health.* (3rd ed.). Pacific Grove, CA: Brooks/Cole.

Richards, J.S., Nepomuceno, C., Riles, M., & Suer, Z. (1982). Assessing pain behavior: The UAB Pain Behavior Scale. *Pain, 14,* 393–398.

Richards, M.A., Westcombe, A.M., Love, S.B., Littlejohns, P., & Ramirez, A.J. (1999). Influence of delay on survival in patients with breast cancer: A systematic review. *The Lancet, 353*, 1119–1126.

Richards, T. (1990). Chasms in communication. *British Medical Journal, 301*, 1407–1408.

Richardsen, A.M., & Burke, R.J. (1991). Occupational stress and job satisfaction among Canadian physicians. *Work and Stress, 5*, 301–313.

Richman, L.S., Kubzansky, L., Maselko, J., Kawachi, I., Choo., P., & Bauer, M. (2005). Positive emotion and health: Going beyond the negative. *Health Psychology, 24*, 422–429.

Riegel, B.J., Dracup, K.A., & Glaser, D. (1998). A longitudinal causal model of cardiac invalidism following myocardial infarction. *Nurs Res, 47*(5), 285–292.

Riley, J.L., III, Wade, J.B., Myers, C.D., Sheffield, D., Papas, R.K., & Price, D.D. (2002). Racial/ethnic differences in the experience of chronic pain. *Pain, 100*, 291–298.

Rintamaki, L.S., & Brashers, D.E. (2005). Social identity and stigma management for people living with HIV. In E. B. Ray (Ed.), *Health communication in practice: A case study approach* (pp.145–156). Mahwah, NJ: Lawrence Erlbaum Associates Publishers.

Rithotz, M.D., & Jacobson, A.M. (1998). Living with hypoglycemia. *Journal of General Internal Medicine, 13*, 799–804.

Rivers, S.E., Salovey, P., Pizarro, D.A., Pizarro, J., & Schneider, T.R. (2005). Message framing and Pap test utilization among women attending a community health clinic. *Journal of Health Psychology, 10*(1), 65–77.

Robinson, D. (1973, July 15). Ten noted doctors answer ten tough questions. *Parade.*

Robinson, G.C., Armstrong, R.W., Brendle-Moczuk, I., & Loock, C.A. (1992). Knowledge of fetal alcohol syndrome among native Indians. *Canadian Journal of Public Health, 83*(5), 337–338.

Robinson, G.E. (2003). Stresses on women physicians: Consequences and coping techniques. *Depression and Anxiety, 17*(3), 180–189.

Robinson, M.E., Riley, J.L. III, Myers, C.D., Papas, R.K., Wise, E.A., et al. (2001). Gender role expectations of pain: Relationship to sex differences in pain. *The Journal of Pain, 2*(5), 251–257.

Robinson, M.E., Wise, E.A., Gagnon, C., Fillingim, R.B., & Price, D.D. (2004). Influences of gender role and anxiety on sex differences in temporal summation of pain. *The Journal of Pain, 5*(2), 77–82.

Robles, T.F., & Kiecolt-Glaser, J.K. (2003). The physiology of marriage. Pathways to health. *Physiology & Behavior, 79*(3), 409–416.

Rodin, J. (1981). Current status of the internal-external hypothesis for obesity: What went wrong? *American Psychologist, 36*, 361–372.

Rodin, J., & Salovey, P. (1989). Health psychology. *Annual Review of Psychology, 40*, 533–579.

Rodrigue, J.R., & Hoffman, R.G. (1994). Caregivers of adults with cancer: multidimensional correlates of psychological distress. *Journal of Clinical Psychology in Medical Settings, 1*, 231–244.

Roelofs, J., Boissevain, M.D., Peters, M.L., de Jong, J.R., & Vlaeyen, J.W.S. (2002). Psychological treatments for chronic low back pain: Past, present, and beyond. *Pain Reviews, 9*, 29–40.

Roesch, S.C., Adams, L., Hines, A., Palmores, A., Vyas, P., Tran, C., Pekin, S., & Vaughn, A.A. (2005). Coping with prostate cancer: A meta-analytic review. *Journal of Behavioral Medicine, 38*(3), 281–293.

Rogg, L., Loge, J.H., Aasland, O.G., & Graugaard, P.K. (2009). Physicians' attitudes towards disclosure of prognostic information: A survey among a representative cross-section of 1605 Norwegian physicians. *Patient Education and Counseling, 77*(2), 242–7.

Rohman, L. (2009). The relationship between anabolic androgenic steroids and muscle dysmorphia: A review. *Eating Disorders, 17*, 187–199.

Rollman, G.B. (2004). Ethnocultural variations in the experience of pain. In T. Hadjistavropoulos & K.D. Craig (Eds.), *Pain: Psychological perspectives* (pp. 155–178). Mahwah, NJ: Erlbaum.

Rollman, G.B., Abdell-Shaheed, J., Gillespie, J.M., & Jones, K.S. (2004). Does past pain influence current pain: Biological and psychosocial models of sex differences. *European Journal of Pain, 8*(5), 427–433.

Romas, J.A., & Sharma, M., (2004) *Practical stress management.* (3rd ed.). San Francisco: Pearson Education.

Rondeau, K.V., Williams, E.S., & Wager, T.H. (2008). Turnover and vacancy rates for registered nurses: Do local labor market factors matter? *Health Care Management Review, 33*(1), 69–78.

Rosengard, C., Chambers, D.B., Tulsky, J.P., Long, H.L., & Chesney, M. (2001). Value on health, health concerns and practices of women who are homeless. *Women & Health, 34*, 29–44.

Rosenstock, I.M. (1974). Historical origins of the health belief model. *Health Education Monographs, 2*, 328–335.

Rosenstock, I.M., Strecher, V.J., & Becker, M.H. (1994). The Health Belief Model and HIV risk behavior change. In R.J. DiClemente & J.L. Peterson (Eds.), *Preventing AIDS: Theories and methods of behavioral interventions* (pp. 5–25). New York: Plenum.

Roseveare, C., Seavell, C., Patel, P., Criswell, J., Kimble, J., Jones, C., & Shepherd, H. (1998). Patient-controlled sedation and analgesia, using propofol and alfentanil, during colonoscopy: A prospective randomized controlled trail. *Endoscopy, 30*, 768–773.

Rosier, E.M., Iadarola, M.J., & Cognill, R.C. (2002). Reproducibility of pain measurement and pain perception. *Pain, 98*, 205–216.

Ross, C.E., & Mirowsky, J. (2002). Family relationships, social support and subjective life expectancy. *Journal of Health & Social Behavior, 43*, 469–489.

Rosser, W.W. (1996). Approach to diagnosis by primary care clinicians and specialists: Is there a difference? *Journal of Family Practice, 42*, 139–144.

Roter, D.L. (2000). The enduring and evolving nature of the patient-physician relationship. *Patient Education and Counseling, 39*, 5–15.

Roter, D.L., Frankel, R.M., Hall, J.A., & Sluyter, D. (2006). The expression of emotion through nonverbal behavior in medical visits. *Journal of Internal Medicine, 21*, S28.

Roter, D.L., Hall, J.A., Merisca, R., Nordstrom, B., et al. (1998). Effectiveness of interventions to improve patient compliance: A meta-analysis. *Medical Care, 36*, 1138–1161.

Roter, D.L., Hall, J.A., & Aoki, Y. (2002). Physician gender effects in medical communication: A meta-analytic review. *Journal of the American Medical Association, 288*, 756–764.

Rotton, J., & Dubitsky, S.S. (2002). Immune function and affective states following a natural disaster. *Psychological Reports, 90*, 521–524.

Rouse, B.A. (Ed.). (1998). Substance abuse and mental health statistics source book. Rockville, MD: Department of Health and Human Services: Substance Abuse and Mental Health Services Administration.

Roux, S., Markle, L., & Diamond, A. (1998). False positive rate for screening mammography. *New England Journal of Medicine, 339*, 561.

Rozanski, A., Blumenthal, J.A., & Kaplan, J. (1999). Impact of psychological factors on the pathogenesis of cardiovascular disease and implications for therapy. *Circulation, 99*, 2192–2217.

Rudolph, D.L., & Butki, B.D. (1998). Self-efficacy and affective responses to short bouts of exercise. *Journal of Applied Sport Psychology, 10*, 268–280.

Rudolph, K.D., Dennig, M.D., & Weisz, J.R. (1995). Determinants and consequences of children's coping in the medical setting: Conceptualization, review and critique. *Psychological Bulletin, 118*, 328–357.

Ruiter, R.A.C., Abraham, C., & Kok, G. (2001). Scary warnings and rational precautions: A review of the psychology of fear appeals. *Psychology and Health, 16*, 613–630.

Rushall, B.S. (1984). The content of competition thinking. In W.F. Straub & J.M. Williams (Eds.), *Cognitive Sport Psychology*. Lansing, MI: Sport Science Associates.

Russell, S. (1999). An exploratory study of patients' perceptions, memories and experiences in an intensive care unit. *Journal of Advanced Nursing, 29*, 783–791.

Rutledge, P.C. & Sher, K.J. (2001). Heavy drinking from the freshman year into early young adulthood: The roles of stress, tension-reduction drinking motives, gender and personality. *Journal of Studies on Alcohol, 62*, 457–466.

Ryan, C.J., & Zerwic, J.J. (2003). Perceptions of symptoms of myocardial infarction related to health care seeking behaviors in the elderly. *Journal of Cardiovascular Nursing, 18*, 184–196.

Rydahl-Hansen, S. (2005). Hospitalized patients experienced suffering in life with incurable cancer. *Scandinavian Journal of Caring Sciences, 19*(3), 213–222.

S

Sabir, S., Godwin, M., & Birtwhistle, R. (1997). Men and women residents' experiences with women's health care in a family medicine center. *Academic Medicine, 72*, 293–295.

Safer, M.A., Tharps, Q.J., Jackson, T.C., & Leventhal, H. (1979). Determinants of three stages of delay in seeking care at a medical care clinic. *Medical Care, 17*, 11–29.

Sainsbury, R., Johnston, C., & Haward, B. (1999). Effect on survival of delays in referral of patients with breast-cancer symptoms: A retrospective analysis. *The Lancet, 353*, 1132–1135.

Salmela, J.H. (1992). *The world sport psychology sourcebook.* (2nd ed.). Champaign, IL: Human Kinetics.

Salmon, P. (2000). Effects of physical exercise on anxiety, depression, and sensitivity to stress: A unifying theory. *Clinical Exercise Review, 21*,33–61.

Salovey, P., Rothman, A. J., Detweiler, J. B., & Steward, W. T. (2000). Emotional states and physical health. American Psychologist, 55, 110–121

Saltz, R. (2004–2005). Preventing alcohol-related problems on college campuses. *Alcohol Research and Health, 28*(4), 249–251.

Saltz, R. (2005). Prevention of college student drinking problems. In B. Galanter (Ed.), *Recent developments in alcoholism: Volume 17. Alcohol problems in adolescents and young adults* (pp. 255–274). New York: Kluwer Academic/Plenum Publishers.

Sands, L.P., Yaffe, K., Covinsky, K., Chren, M.-M., Counsell, S., Palmer, R., Fortinsky, R., & Landefeld, C.S. (2003). Cognitive screening predicts magnitude of functional recovery from admission to 3 months after discharge in hospitalized elders. *Journals of Gerontology: Series A: Biological Sciences & Medical Sciences, 58*(1), 37–45.

Santavirta, N., Bjorvell, H., Solovieva, S., Alaranta, H., Hurskainen, K., & Konttinen, Y.T. (2001). Coping strategies, pain and disability in patients with hemophilia and related disorders. *Arthritis and Rheumatism, 45*, 48–55.

Santos, S.R., Carroll, C.A., Cox, K.S., Teasley, S.L., Simon, S.D., Bainbridge, L., Cunningham, M., & Ott, L. (2003). Baby boomer nurses bearing the burden of care: A four-site study of stress, strain, and coping for inpatient registered nurses. *J Nurs Adm, 33*(4), 243–250.

Sarafino, E.P. (1998). *Health psychology: Biopsychosocial interactions.* New York: John Wiley and Sons.

Sarafino, E.P., & Goehring, P. (2000). Age comparisons in acquiring biofeedback control and success in reducing headache pain. *Annals of Behavioral Medicine, 22*, 10–16.

Sareen, J., Cox, B.J., Stein, M.B., Afifi, T.O., Fleet, C., & Asmundson, G.J. (2007). Physical and mental comorbidity, disability, and suicidal behavior associated with post-traumatic stress disorder in a large community sample. *Psychosomatic Medicine, 69*, 242–248.

Sarna, L., Padilla, G., Holmes, C., Tashkin, D., Brecht, M.L., & Evangelista, L. (2002). Quality of life of long-term survivors of non-small cell lung cancer. *Journal of Clinical Oncology, 20*, 2920–2929.

Sasieni, P., Adams, J., & Cuzick, J. (2003). Benefit of cervical screening at different ages: Evidence from the UK audit of screening histories. *Br J Cancer, 89*(1), 88–93.

Savard, M., Miller, S., Mills, M., O'Leary, A., Harding, H., Douglas, S.D., Mangan, C.E., Belch, R., & Winokur, A. (1999). Association between subjective sleep quality and depression on immunocompetence in low-income women at risk for cervical cancer. *Psychosomatic Medicine, 61*, 496–507.

Sawatzky, J.V., & Naimark, B.J. (2002). Physical activity and cardiovascular health in aging women: A health-promotion perspective. *Journal of Aging & Physical Activity, 10*, 396–412.

Say, R., Murtagh, M., & Thomson, R. (2006). Patients' preference for involvement in medical decision making: A narrative review. *Patient Education and Counseling, 60*(2), 102–114.

Scascighini, L., Toma, V., Dober-Spielmann, S., & Sprott, H. (2008). Multidisciplinary treatment for chronic pain: A systematic review of interventions and outcomes. *Rheumatology, 47*(5), 670–678.

Schackman, B.R., Finkelstein, R., Neukermans, C.P., Lewis, L., & Eldred, L. (2005). The cost of HIV medication adherence support interventions: Results of a cross-site evaluation. *AIDS Care, 17*, 927–937.

Schacter, S. (1971). Some extraordinary facts about obese humans and rats. *American Psychologist, 26*, 129–144.

Schachter, S. (1981). Recidivism and self-cure of smoking and obesity. *American Psychologist, 31*, 436–444.

Scheifer, S.J., Keller, S.E., Camerino, M., Thornton, J.C., & Stein, M. (1983). Suppression of lymphocyte stimulation following bereavement. *Journal of the American Medical Association, 250*, 374–377.

Scheifer, S.J., Keller, S.E., Meyerson, A.T., Raskin, M.J., Davis, K.L., & Stein, M. (1984). Lymphocyte function in major depressive disorder. *Archives of General Psychiatry, 41*, 484–486.

Schilling, L.M., Scatena, L., Steiner, J.F., Albertson, G.A., Lin, C.T., Cyran, L., Ware, L., & Anderson, R.J. (2002). The third person in the room: Frequency, role, and influence of companions during primary medical care encounters. *Journal of Family Practice, 51*(8), 685–690.

Schleifer, S.J., Keller, S.E., & Bartlett, J.A. (1999). Depression and immunity clinical factors and therapeutic course. *Psychiatric Research, 85*, 63–69.

Schmale, A.H., Jr., & Engel, G.L. (1967). The giving up-given up complex illustrated on film. *Archives of General Psychiatry, 17*, 135–145.

Schmidt, H. (2009). Personal responsibility in the NHS constitution and the social determinants of health approach: Competitive or complementary? *Health Economics, Policy and Law, 4*, 129–138.

Schmitz, M.F., & Crystal, S. (2000). Social relations, coping, and psychological distress among persons with HIV/AIDS. *Journal of Applied Social Psychology, 30*(4), 665–683.

Schneider, M., Dunn, A., & Cooper, D. (2009). Affect exercise, and physical activity among healthy adolescents. *Journal of Sport and Exercise Psychology, 31*, 706–723.

Schreiber, L. (2005). The importance of precision in language: Communication research and (so-called) alternative medicine. *Health Communication, 17*(2), 173–190.

Schubert, D., Burns, Paras, W., & Sioson, E. (1992). Increase of medical hospital length of stay by depression in stroke and amputation patients: A pilot study. *Psychotherapy and Psychosomatics, 57*, 61–66.

Schuckit, M.A. (1996). Recent developments in the pharmacotherapy of alcohol dependence. *Journal of Consulting and Clinical Psychology, 64*, 669–676.

Schulz, R., Bookwalla, J., Knapp, J.E., Scheier, M., & Williamson, G.M. (1996). Pessimism, age, and cancer mortality. *Psychology and Aging, 11*, 304–309.

Schutz, J., & Luthe, W. (1959). *Autogenic training: A psychophysiological approach to psychotherapy*. New York: Grune and Stratton.

Schwam, K. (1998). The phenomenon of compassion fatigue in perioperative nursing. *AORN Journal, 68*, 642–645, 647–648.

Schwartz, G.E., & Weiss, S.M. (1978). Behavioral medicine revisited: An amended definition. *Journal of Behavioral Medicine, 1*, 249–251.

Schwartzberg, J.G., Cowett, A., VanGeest, J., & Wolf, M.S. (2007). Communication techniques for patients with low health literacy: A survey of physicians, nurses, and pharmacists. *American Journal of Health Behavior, 31*(Suppl 1), S96–S104.

Schwitzer, G. (2002). A review of features in Internet consumer health decision-support tools. *J Med Internet Res, 4*(2), E11.

Scott, C.G., & Ambroson, D.L. (1994). The rocky road to change: Implications for substance abuse programs on college campuses. *Journal of American College Health, 42*, 291–296.

Scott, K. (1994). *Substance abuse among Indigenous Canadians*. Paper presented at the Joint Research Advisory Meeting, Ottawa.

Sebire, S.J., Standage, M., & Vansteenkiste, M. (2009). Examining intrinsic versus extrinsic exercise goals: Cognitive, affective, and behavioural outcomes. *Journal of Sport and Exercise Psychology, 31*, 189–210.

Segall, A., & Roberts, L.W. (1980). A comparative analysis of physician estimates and levels of medical knowledge among patients. *Sociology of Health and Illness, 2*(3), 317–334.

Segerstrom, S.C., & Miler, G.E. (2004). Psychological stress and the human immune system: A meta-analytic study of 30 years of inquiry. *Psychological Bulletin, 130*(4), 601–630.

Seligman, M.E.P. (1975). *Helplessness*. San Francisco: Freeman.

Sellwood, W., & Tarrier, N. (1994). Demographic factors associated with extreme non-compliance in schizophrenia. *Social Psychiatry and Psychiatric Epidemiology, 29*, 172–177.

Selye, H. (1956). *The stress of life*. New York: McGraw-Hill.

Selye, H. (1974). *Stress without distress*. Philadelphia: Lippincott.

Selye, H. (1976). *Stress in health and disease*. Woburn, MA: Butterworth.

Selye, H. (1993). History of the stress concept. In L. Goldenberger & S. Breznitz (Eds.), *Handbook of stress: Theoretical and clinical aspects* (pp. 7–17). New York: Free Press.

Serprell, L., & Tresure, J. (2002). Bulimia nervosa: Friend or foe? The pros and cons of bulimia nervosa. *International Journal of Eating Disorders, 32*(2), 164–170.

Sexton, M.M. (1979). Behavioral epidemiology. In O.F. Pomerleau & J.P. Brady (Eds.), *Behavioral medicine: Theory and practice*(pp. 3–22). Baltimore, MD: Williams & Wilkins.

Seymour, G.J., Savage, N.W., & Walsh, L.J. (1995). *Immunology: An introduction for the health sciences*. Roseville, NSW: McGraw-Hill Australia.

Shadel, W.G., Shiffman, S., Niaura, R., Nichter, R., Nichter, M., & Abrams, D.B. (2000). Current models of nicotine dependence: What is known and what is needed to advance understanding of tobacco etiology among youth. *Drug and Alcohol Dependence, 59* (Suppl.), S9–S22.

Shamseer, L., Roth, D.E., Tallet, S., Hilliard, R., & Vohra, S. (2008). A comparison of Canadian pediatric resident career plans in 1998 and 2006. *Pediatrics, 112*(6), e1199–1209.

Shapiro, S. (1977). Evidence on screening for breast cancer from randomised trial. *Cancer, 39*, 2772–2782.

Sheffield, D., Biles, P.L., Orom, H., Maixner, W., & Sheps, D.S. (2000). Race and sex differences in cutaneous pain perception. *Psychosomatic Medicine, 62*, 517–523.

Shekelle, R.B., Raynor, W.J., Ostfeld, A.M., Garron, D.C., Bieliauskas, L.A., Liu, S.C., Maliza, C., & Paul, O. (1981). Psychological depression and 17-year risk of death from cancer. *Psychosomatic Medicine, 43*, 117–125.

Sheldon, K.M., & King, L. (2001). Why positive psychology is necessary. *American Psychologist, 56*, 216–217.

Sheps, D.S., & Rozanski, A. (2005). From feeling blue to clinical depression: Exploring the pathogenicity of depressive symptoms and their management in cardiac practice. *Psychosomatic Medicine, 67*(Supp 1), S2–S5.

Sherwood, P.R., Given, B.A., Given, C.W., Schiffman, R.F., Murman, D.L., Lovely, M., von Eye, A., Rogers, L.R., & Remer, S. (2006). Predictors of distress in caregivers of persons with a primary malignant brain tumor. *Research in Nursing & Health, 29*(2), 105–120.

Shields M. (2006). Overweight and obesity among children and youth. *Health Reports, 17*, 27–42.

Shields, M., & Tremblay, M.S. (2008). Sedentary behaviour and obesity. *Health Reports, 19*, pp. 19–30.

Shields-Poe, D., & Pinelli, J. (1997). Variables associated with parental stress in neonatal intensive care units. *Neonatal Network, 16*, 29–37.

Shifren, K., Bauserman, R., & Carter, D.B. (1993). Gender role orientation and physical health: A study among young adults. *Sex Roles, 29*, 421–432.

Shine, K.I. (2002). Health care quality and how to achieve it. *Academic Medicine, 77*, 91–99.

Shlain, L. (1979). Cancer is not a four-letter word. In C.A. Garfield (Ed.), *Stress and survival: The emotional realities of life–threatening illness*. St. Louis: C.V. Mosby.

Shopland, D.R., & Burns, D.M. (1993). Medical and public health implications of tobacco addiction. In C.T. Orleans & J. Slade (Eds.), *Nicotine addiction: Principles and management*. New York: Oxford University Press.

Shrier, D.K., Zucker, A.N., Mercurio, A.E., Landry, L.J., Rich, M., & Shrier, L.A. (2007). Generation to generation: Discrimination and harassment experiences of physician mothers and their physician daughters. *Journal of Women's Health, 16*(6), 883–894.

Sidel, J., et al. (1998). Shaping the healthcare environment through evidence-based medicine: A case study of the ICONS Project. *Hospital Quarterly, 2*, 29–33.

Silverman, J., Kurtz, S., & Draper, J. (2005). *Skills for communicating with patients*. (2nd ed.). Oxford: Radcliffe Medical Press.

Silver Wallace, L. (2002). Osteoporosis prevention in college women: Application of the expanded health belief model. *American Journal of Health Behavior, 26*, 163–172.

Siminoff, L.A., Graham, G.C., & Gordon, N.H. (2006). Cancer communication patterns and the influence of patient characteristics: Disparities in information-giving and affective behaviors. *Patient Education and Counseling, 62*(3), 355–360.

Simon, E.P. (1999). Hypnosis using a communication device to increase magnetic resonance imaging tolerance with a claustrophobic patient. *Military Medicine, 164*(1), 71–72.

Simpson, M., Buckman, R., Stewart, M., Maguire, P., et al. (1991). Doctor-patient communication: The Toronto consensus statement. *British Medical Journal, 303*, 1385–1367.

Simpson, S., Eurich, D.T., Majumdar, S.R., Padwal, R.S., Tsuyuki, R.T., Varney, J., & Johnson, J. (2006). A meta-analysis of the association between adherence to drug therapy and mortality. *British Medical Journal, 332*, 7557.

Sinclair, S. (1997). *Making doctors: An institutional apprenticeship*. Oxford: Berg.

Singh, A.N. (2005). Multidisciplinary management of chronic pain. *International Medical Journal, 12*(2), 111–116.

Single, E. (2005). New directions in alcohol policy. In *Substance abuse in Canada: Current challenges and choices*. Ottawa, ON: Canadian Centre on Substance Abuse.

Sist, T.C., Florio, G.A., Miner, M.F., Lema, M.J., & Zevon, M.A. (1998). The relationship between depression and pain language in cancer and chronic non-cancer pain patients. *Journal of Pain and Symptom Management, 15*, 350–358.

Skevington, S.M. (2004). Pain and symptom perception. In A. Kaptein & J. Weinman (Eds.), *Health psychology* (pp. 182–206). Malden, MA: Blackwell.

Slomkowski, C., Rende, R., Novak, S., Lloyd-Richardson, E., & Niaura, R. (2005). Sibling effects on smoking in adolescence: Evidence for social influence from a genetically informative design. *Addiction, 100*, 430–438.

Slovenko, R. (2006). Patients who deceive. *International Journal of Offender Therapy and Comparative Criminology, 50*(1), 241–244.

Sluijs, E.M., Kerssens, J.J., van der Zee, J., & Myers, L.B. (1998). Adherence to physiotherapy. In L.B. Meyers, K. Midence, et al. (Eds.), *Adherence to treatment in medical conditions.* Amsterdam: Harwood Academic.

Sluka, K.A., & Walsh, D. (2003). Transcutaneous electric nerve stimulation: Basic science mechanisms and clinical effectiveness. *Journal of Pain, 4*(3), 109–121.

Smart, G. (1997). Helping children relax during magnetic resonance imaging. *American Journal of Maternity and Child Nursing, 22,* 236–241.

Smiley, K.A. (2004). A structured group for gay men newly diagnosed with HIV/AIDS. *The Journal for Specialists in Group Work, 29*(2), 207–224.

Smith, A., Stewart D., Peled, M., Poon, C., Saewyc, E. and the McCreary Centre Society. (2009). *A picture of health: Highlights from the 2008 BC adolescent health survey.* Vancouver, BC: McCreary Centre Society.

Smith, A., Vollmer-Conna, U., Bennett, B., Wakefield, D., Kickie, I., & Lloyd, A. (2004). The relationship between distress and the development of a primary immune response to a novel antigen. *Brain, Behavior, and Immunity, 18,* 65–75.

Smith, J.C. (1993). *Understanding stress and coping.* New York: MacMillan.

Smith, R.E. (1980). Development of an integrated coping response through cognitive-affective stress management training. In I.G. Sarason & C.D. Spielberger (Eds.), *Stress and anxiety, Vol.7.* Washington, DC: Hemisphere Publishing Corporation.

Smith, R.E. (1999). Generalization effects in coping skills training. *Journal of Sport and Exercise Psychology, 21,* 189–204.

Smith, T.P., Kennedy, S.L., & Fleshner, M. (2004). Influence of age and physical activity on the primary in vivo antibody and T cell-mediated responses in men. *Journal of Applied Physiology, 97,* 491–498.

Smith, T.W., & Ruiz, J.M. (2002). Psychosocial influences on the development and course of coronary heart disease: Current status and implications for research and practice. *Journal of Consulting and Clinical Psychology, 70,* 548–568

Solomon, G.F., & Moos, R.H. (1964). Emotions, immunity and disease: A speculative theoretical integration. *Archives of General Psychiatry, 11,* 657–674.

Solomon, G.F., Segerstrom, S.C., Grohr, P., Kemeny, M., & Fahey, J. (1997). Shaking up immunity: Psychological and immunologic changes after a natural disaster. *Psychosomatic Medicine, 59,* 114–127.

Song, C., & Leonard, B. (2000). *Fundamentals of psychoneuroimmunology.* New York: John Wiley and Sons Ltd.

Sonstroem, R.J. (1997). Physical activity and self-esteem. In W.P. Morgan (Ed.), *Physical activity and mental health* (pp. 127–143). Washington, DC: Taylor and Francis.

Spence, J.C., McGannon, K.R., & Poon, P. (2005). The effect of exercise on global self-esteem: A quantitative review. *Journal of Sport and Exercise Psychology, 27,* 311–334.

Spencer, J., Young, M.E., Rintala, D., & Bates, S. (1995). Socialization to the culture of a rehabilitation hospital: An ethnographic study. *Journal of Occupational Therapy, 49,* 53–62.

Spickard, A., Gabbe, S.G., & Christensen, J.F. (2002). Mid-career burnout in generalist and specialist physicians. *Journal of the American Medical Association, 288*(12), 1447–1450.

Spiegel, D., & Bloom, J.R. (1983). Group therapy and hypnosis reduce metastatic breast carcinoma pain. *Psychosomatic Medicine, 45,* 333–339.

Spiegel, D., Kraemer, H.C., & Bloom, J.R. (1998). A tale of two methods: Randomization versus matching trials in clinical research. *Psycho-Oncology, 7,* 371–375.

Spiegel, D., Sephton, S.E., Terr, A.I., & Stites, D.P. (1998). Effects of psychosocial treatment in prolonging cancer survival may be mediated by neuroimmune pathways. *Annals of the New York Academy of Sciences, 840,* 674–683.

Spinhoven, P., & ter Kuile, M.M. (2000). Treatment outcome expectancies and hypnotic susceptibility as moderators of pain reduction in patients with chronic tension-type headache. *International Journal of Clinical and Experimental Hypnosis, 48,* 290–305.

Sprague, S., Lutz, K., Bryant, D., Farrokhyar, F., Zlowodzki, M., & Bhandari, M. (2007). Complementary and alternative medicine use in patients with fractures. *Clinical Orthopaedics and Related Research, 463,* 183–178.

Springer, S.A., Chen, S., & Altice, F. (2009). Depression and symptomatic response among HIV-infected drug users enrolled in a randomized controlled trial of directly administered antiretroviral therapy. *AIDS Care, 21*(8), 976–983.

Stack, A.G., & Martin, D.R. (2005). Association of patient autonomy with increased transplantation and survival among new dialysis patients in the United States. *American Journal of Kidney Disease, 45*(4), 730–742.

Stainer, U.M., Grond, S., & Maier, C. (1999). Responders and non-responders to post-operative pain treatment: The loading dose predicts analgesic needs. *European Journal of Anaesthesiology, 16,* 103–110.

Starkweather, A.R. (2007). The effects of exercise on perceived stress and IL-6 levels among older adults. *Biological Research for Nursing, (8)*3, 186–194.

Standl, T., Burmeister, M.A., Ohnesorge, H., Wilhelm, S., Striepke, M., Gottschalk, A., Horn, E.P., & Schulte Am Esch, J. (2003). Patient-controlled epidural analgesia reduces analgesic requirements compared to continuous epidural infusion after major abdominal surgery. *Can J Anaesth, 50*(3), 258–264.

Stanton, W.R., Flay, B.R., Colder, C.R., & Mehta, P. (2004). Identifying and predicting adolescent smokers' developmental trajectories. *Nicotine & Tobacco Research, 6*(5), 843–852.

Starfield, B. (1994). Is primary care essential? *Lancet, 344,* 1129.

Starfield, B., Wray, C., Hess, K., Gross, R., et al. (1981). The influence of patient-practitioner agreement on outcome of care. *American Journal of Public Health, 71,* 127–131.

Starkes, J.L., Helson, W., & Jack, R. (2001). In R.N. Singer, H.A. Hausenblas, & C.M. Janelle (Eds.), *Handbook of Sport Psychology.* (2nd ed.) (pp.174–204). New York: Wiley.

Statistics Canada. (2001, June 22). Impact of smoking on life expectancy and disability. *The Daily.* Retrieved September 1, 2006, from www.statcan.ca/Daily/English/010622/d010622a.htm

Statistics Canada. (2002a). National longitudinal survey of children and youth: Childhood obesity. *The Daily.* Retrieved May 17, 2006, from www.statcan.ca/Daily/English/021018/d021018b.htm

Statistics Canada. (2002b, May 8). Canadian community health survey: A first look. *The Daily.* Retrieved July 9, 2003, from www.statcan.ca/Daily/English/020508/d020508a.htm

Statistics Canada. (2004a). Alcohol and illicit drug dependence. *Health Reports, 9* (Supplement), 9–19.

Statistics Canada. (2005a). Canadian Community Health Survey: Obesity among children and adults. Retrieved August 10, 2006, from www.statcan.ca/Daily/English/050706/d050706a.htm

Statistics Canada. (2005b). Deaths, 2003. *The Daily.* Retrieved April 20, 2006, from www.statcan.ca/Daily/English/051221/d051221b.htm

Statistics Canada. (2005c). International adult literacy and skills survey: Building on our competencies. *The Daily.* Retrieved May 17, 2006, from www.statcan.ca/Daily/English/051130/d051130b.htm

Statistics Canada. (2005d). Adult obesity in Canada: Measured height and weight. Retrieved June 2, 2010 from www.statcan.gc.ca/pub/82-620-m/2005001/article/adults-adultes/8060-eng.htm

Statistics Canada. (2006). Well being. *Health Indicators.* Retrieved April 26, 2006, from www.statcan.ca/english/freepub/82-221-XIE/82-221-XIE2006001.htm

Statistics Canada (2007). Physically active Canadians. *The Daily.* Retrieved April 4, 2010, from www.statcan.gc.ca/daily-quotidien/070822/dq0770822b-eng.htm

Statistics Canada. (2008, Dec 4). Leading causes of death. Retrieved July 1, 2010 from www.statcan.gc.ca/daily-quotidien/081204/dq081204c-eng.htm

Statistics Canada (2008). Organized sports participation among children. *The Daily.* Retrieved April 4, 2010, from www.statcan.gc.ca/daily-quotidien/080603/dq080603a-eng.htm

Statistics Canada (2008). Participation in sports. *The Daily.* Retrieved April 14, 2010, from www.statcan.gc.ca/daily-quotidien/080207/dq080207b-eng.htm

Statistics Canada. (2010, June 15). Canadian Community Health Survey. *The Daily.* Retrieved June 24, 2010, from www.statcan.gc.ca/daily-quotidien/100615/dq100615b-eng.htm

Steele, C.M., & Josephs, R.A. (1990). Alcohol myopia: Its prized and dangerous effects. *American Psychologist, 45,* 921–933.

Steffens, D.C., O'Connor, C.M., Jiang, W.J., Pieper, C.F., Kuchibhatia, M.N., Arias, R.M., Look, A., Davenport, C., Gonzalez, M.B., & Krishnan, K.R. (1999). The effect of major depression on functional status in patients with coronary artery disease. *Journal of the American Geriatric Society, 47,* 319–322.

Stein, P.N., & Motta, R.W. (1992). Effects of aerobic and non-aerobic exercise on depression and self-concept. *Perceptual Motor Skills, 74,* 79–89.

Stein, R. I., Kenardy, J., Wiseman, C. V., Douunchis, J. Z., Arnow, B. A., & Wilfley, D. E. (2007). What's driving the binge in binge eating disorder?: A prospective examination of precursors and consequences. *International Journal of Eating Disorders, 40*(3), 195–203.

Stein, R. I., Saelens, B. E., Dounchis, J. Z., Lewczyk, C. M., Swenson, A. K., Wilfley, D. E. (2001). Treatment of eating disorders in women. *The Counseling Psychologist, 29*(5), 695–732.

Steinbach, J.P., Blaicher, H-P., Herrlinger, U., Wick, W., Nägele, T., Meyermann, R., Tatagiba, M., Bamberg, M., Dichgans, J., Karnath, H.-O., & Weller, M. (2006). Surviving gliobastoma for more than 5 years: The patient's perspective. *Neurology, 66,* 239–242.

Sternbach, R.A. (1968). *Pain: A psychophysiological analysis.* New York: Academic Press.

Sternbach, R.A. (1986). Clinical aspects of pain. In R.A. Sternbach (Ed.), *The psychology of pain.* (2nd ed.). New York: Raven Press.

Sternbach, R.A. (1989). Acute versus chronic pain. In P.D. Wall & R. Melzack (Eds.), *Textbook of pain.* (2nd ed.). Edinburgh: Churchill Livingstone.

Stevens, B. (1997). Pain assessment in children: Birth through adolescence. *Child and Adolescent Psychiatric Clinics of North America, 6,* 725–743.

Stevens, B. (2001). Acute pain management in infants in the neonatal intensive care unit. In G.A. Finley & P.J. McGrath (Eds.), Acute and procedure pain in infants and children. *Progress in pain research and management, 20,*101–128. Seattle: IASP Press.

Stevens, B.J., & Franck, L.S. (2001). Assessment and management of pain in neonates. *PaediatricDrugs, 3,* 539–558.

Stevens, S.L., Colwell, B., Smith, D.W., Robinson, J., & McMillan, C. (2005). An exploration of self-reported negative affect by adolescence as a reason for smoking: Implications for tobacco prevention and intervention programs. *Preventive Medicine, 41,* 589–596.

Stevens, B.J., & Franck, L.S. (2001). Assessment and management of pain in neonates. *Paediatric Drugs, 3,* 539–558.

Stevenson, K. (2002). Health information on the Net. *Canadian Social Trends*, (Autumn), 7–9.

Stewart, K.L. (2004). *Pharmacological and behavioral treatments for migraine headaches: A meta-analytic review.* Dissertation Abstracts International: Section B, 65 (3-B), 1535.

Stewart, L., Reilly, J. J., & Hughes, A. R. (2009). Evidence-based behavioral treatment of obesity in children and adolescents. *Child and Adolescent Psychiatric Clinics of North America, 18,* 189–198.

Stewart, M.A. (1995). Effective physician-patient communication and health outcomes: A review. *Canadian Medical Association Journal, 152,* 1423–1433.

Stewart, M., Brown, J.B., Donner, A., McWhinney, I.R., Oates, J., Weston, W.W., & Jordan, J. (2000). The impact of patient-centered care on outcomes. *The Journal of Family Practice, 49,*796–804.

Stewart, M.A., Brown, J.B., Levenstein, J.H., McCracken, E., & McWhinney, I.R. (1986). The patient-centered clinical method: Changes in residents' performance over two months of training. *Family Practice, 3,* 164–167.

Stewart, M.A., Brown, J.B., Weston, W.W., McWhinney, I.R., et al. (1999). *Patient-centred medicine: Transforming the clinical method.* Thousand Oaks, CA: Sage.

Stewart, M.A., McWhinney, I.R., & Buck, C.W. (1979). The doctor-patient relationship and its effect upon outcome. *Journal of the Royal College of General Practice, 29,* 77–82.

Stice, E. (1994). Relation of media exposure to eating disorder symptomology: An examination of mediating mechanisms. *Journal of Abnormal Psychology, 103,* 836–840.

St. Leger, L. (2005). Questioning sustainability in health promotion projects and programs. *Health Promotion International, 20*(4), 317–319.

Stock Keister, M.C., Green, L.A., Kahn, N.B., Phillips, R.L., McCann, J., & Fryer, G.D. (2004). What people want from their family physician. *American Family Physician, 69*(10), 2310.

Stone, A.A., Cox, D.S., Valdimarsdottir, H., Jandorf, L., & Neale, J.M. (1987). Evidence that secretory IgA antibody is associated with daily mood. *Journal of Personality and Social Psychology, 52,* 988–993.

Story, M., French, S.A., Resnick, M.D., et al. (1995). Ethnic/racial and socioeconomic differences in dieting behaviors and body image perceptions in adolescents. *International Journal of Eating Disorders, 18,* 173–179.

Strahan, E.H.E., & Brown, R.J. (2004). A qualitative study of the experiences of patients following transfer from intensive care. *Intensive and Critical Care Nursing, 21,* 160–171.

Strasser, F., Walker, P., & Bruera, E. (2005). Palliative pain management: When both pain and suffering hurt. *Journal of Palliative Care, 21*(2), 69–79.

Straub, R.O. (2007). *Health psychology.* (2nd ed.). New York: Worth.

Streltzer, J. (1997). Pain. In W.S. Tseng & J. Streltzer (Eds.), *Culture and psychopathology: A guide to clinical assessment*(pp. 87–100). New York: Brunner/Mazel.

Striegel-Moore, R. S., & Bulik, C. M. (2007). Risk factors for eating disorders. *American Psychologist, 62*(3), 181–198.

Struckman-Johnson, C., Struckman-Johnson, D., Gilliland, R.C., & Ausman, A. (1994). Effective persuasive appeals in AIDS PSAs and condom commercials on intentions to use condoms. *Journal of Applied Social Psychology, 24,* 2223–2244.

Stuber, M.L. (1995). Stress responses to pediatric cancer: A family phenomenon. *Family Systems Medicine, 13,* 163–172.

Stuijs, E.M., Kerssens, J.J., van der Zee, J., & Myers, L.B. (1998). Adherence to physiotherapy. In L.B. Myers, K. Midence, et al. (Eds.), *Adherence to treatment in medical conditions* (pp. 363–382). Amsterdam: Harwood Academic Publishers.

Su, J.C., & Brimingham, C.L. (2003). Anorexia nervosa: The cost of long-term disability. *Eating and Weight Disorders, 8*(1), 76–79.

Suinn, R. (1972). Behavioral rehearsal training for ski racers. *Behavior Therapy, 3,* 519.

Sullivan, M.D., LaCroix, A.Z., Spertus, J.A., Hecht, J., & Russo, J. (2003). Depression predicts revascularization for 5 years after coronary angiography. *Psychosomatic Medicine, 65*(2), 229–236.

Sullivan, M.J.L., Adams, H., & Sullivan, M.E. (2004). Communicative dimensions of pain catastrophizing: Social cueing effects on pain behaviour and coping. *Pain, 107*(3), 220–226.

Sullivan, M.J.L., Bishop, S.R., & Pivik, J. (1995). The Pain Catastrophizing Scale: Development and validation. *Psychological Assessment, 7,* 524–532.

Sullivan, M.J.L., Lynch, M.E., & Clark, A.J. (2005). Dimensions of catastrophic thinking associated with pain experience and disability in patients with neuropathic pain conditions. *Pain, 113*(3), 310–315.

Sullivan, M.J.L., Martel, M.O., Tripp, D.A., Savard, A., & Crombez, G. (in press). Catastrophic thinking and heightened perception of pain in others. *Pain.*

Sullivan, M.J.L., Thorn, B., Haythornthwaite, J.A., Keefe, F.J., Martin, M., Bradley, L.A., et al. (2001). Theoretical perspectives on the relation between catastrophizing and pain. *Clinical Journal of Pain, 17,* 52–64.

Sullivan, M.J.L., Tripp, D.A., & Santor, D. (2000). Gender differences in pain and pain behavior: The role of catastrophizing. *Cognitive Therapy and Research, 24,* 121–134.

Sullivan, P., & Buske, L. (1998). Results from CMA's huge 1998 physician survey point to a dispirited profession. *Canadian Medical Association Journal, 159*(5), 525–528.

Suls, J., Martin, R., & Leventhal, H. (1997). Social comparison, lay referral, and the decision to seek medical care. In B.P. Buunk & F.X. Gibbons (Eds.), *Health, coping, and well-being: Perspectives from social comparison theory* (pp. 195–226). Mahwah, NJ: Erlbaum.

Suls, J., & Wallston (Eds.) (2003). *Social psychological foundations of health and illness.* Maiden, MA: Blackwell.

Surtees, P.G., Wainwright, N.W.J., Bockholdt, S.M., Luben, R.N., Warcham, N.J., & Khaw, K.-T. (2008). Major depression, C-reactive protein, and incident ischemic heart disease in healthy men and women. *Psychosomatic Medicine, 70,* 850–855.

Surtees, P.G., Wainwright, N.W.J., Luben, R., Khaw, K-T. & Day, N.E. (2006). Mastery, sense of coherence, and mortality: Evidence of independent associations from the EPIC-Norfolk Prospective Cohort Study. Health Psychology, 25(1), 102-110.

Suskin, N., MacDonald, S., Swabey, T., Arthur, H., Vimr, M.A., & Tihaliani, R. (2003). Cardiac rehabilitation and secondary prevention services in Ontario: Recommendations from a consensus panel. Canadian Journal of Cardiology, 19, 833-838.

Sutton, S.R., & Eiser, J.R. (1984). The effect of fear-arousing communications on cigarette smoking: An expectancy-value approach. Journal of Behavioral Medicine, 7, 13-34.

Szasz, T.S., & Hollender, M.H. (1956). A contribution to the philosophy of medicine. The basic models of the doctor-patient relationship. Archives of Internal Medicine, 97, 585-592.

T

Tabar, L., Fagerberg, G., Duffy, S., & Day, N. (1989). The Swedish two-country trial of mammographic screening for breast cancer: Recent results and calculations of benefit. Journal of Epidemiology and Community Health, 43, 107-114.

Tagliacozzo, D.L., & Mauksch, H.O. (1972). The patient's view of the patient's role. In E.G. Jaco (Ed.), Patients, physicians, and illness. (2nd ed.) (pp. 172-185).

Tannock, I.F., & Warr, D.G. (1998). Unconventional therapies for cancer: A refuge from the rules of evidence? Canadian Medical Association Journal, 159, 801-802.

Tate, A.K., & Petruzzello, S.J. (1995). Varying the intensity of acute exercise: Implications for changes in affect. Journal of Sports Medicine and Physical Fitness, 35, 1-8.

Taylor, C.B., Conrad, A., Wilhelm, F.H., Neri, E., DeLorenzo, A., Kramer, M.A. et al. (2006). Psychophysiolooogical and cortisol responses to psychological stress in depressed and nondepressed older men and women with elevated cardiovascular disease risk. Psychosomatic Medicine, 68, 538-546.

Taylor, J. (1994). On exercise and sport avoidance: A reply to Dr. Albert Ellis. The Sport Psychologist, 8, 262-271.

Taylor, J. (1996). Intensity regulation and athletic performance. In J.L. Van Raalte & B.W. Brewer (Eds.), Exploring sport and exercise psychology (pp. 75-106). Washington, DC: American Psychological Association.

Taylor, N., Hall, G.M., & Salmon, P. (1996). Is patient-controlled analgesia controlled by the patient? Social Science and Medicine, 43, 1137-1143.

Taylor, S. E. (2006). Health psychology. (6th ed.). New York: McGraw-Hill.

Taylor, S.E., Klein, L.C., Lewis, B.P., Gruenewald, T.L., Gurung, R.A.R., & Updegraff, J.A. (2000). Biobehavioral responses to stress in females: Tend-and-befriend, not fight-or-flight. Psychological Review, 107, 411-429.

Taylor, S.M., Goldsmith, C.H., & Best, J.A. (1996). The community intervention trial for smoking cessation (COMMIT). Health and Canadian Society, 2, 179-195.

Taylor, V.M., Anderson, G.M., McNeney, B., Diehr, P., Lavis, J.N., Deyo, R.A., Bombardier, K.C., Malter, A., & Axcell, T. (1998). Hospitalizations for back and neck problems: A comparison between the Province of Ontario and Washington State. Health Services Research, 33, 929-945.

Tedeschi, R.G., & Calhoun, L.G. (1995). Trauma and transformation: Growing in the aftermath of suffering. Thousand Oaks, CA: Sage.

Tedeschi, R.G., & Kilmer, R.P. (2005). Assessing strengths, resilience and growth to guide clinical interventions. Professional Psychology: Research and Practice, 36, 230-237.

Tennen, H., Affleck, G., & Zautra, A. (2006). Depression history and coping with chronic pain: A daily process analysis. Health Psychology, 25(3), 370-379.

Tennier, L.D. (1997). Discharge planning: An examination of the perceptions and recommendations for improved discharge planning at the Montreal General Hospital. Social Work in Health Care, 26(1), 41-60.

Teno, J.M., & Coppola, K.M. (1999). For every numerator, you need a denominator: A simple statement but key to measuring the quality of care of the "dying." Journal of Pain and Symptom Management, 17, 109-113.

Teo, K.K., Ounpuss, S., Hawken, S., Pandey, M.R., Valentin, V., Hunt, D., et al. (2006). Tobacco use and risk of myocardial infarction in 52 countries in the INTERHEART study: A case-control study. The Lancet, 368, 647-658.

Thackwray, D.E., Smith, M.C., Bodfish, J.W., & Meyers, A.W. (1993). A comparison of behavioral and cognitive-behavioral intervention for bulimia nervosa. Journal of Consulting and Clinical Psychology, 61, 639-645.

Thoburn, J., & Hammond-Meyer, A. (2004). Eating disorders. In F.M. Kline & L.B. Silver (Eds.), The educator's guide to mental health issues in the classroom (pp. 141-170). Baltimore, MD: Brookes Publishing.

Thomas, D.B., Gao, D.L., Ray, R.M., Wang, W.W., Allison, C.J., Chen, F.L., Porter, P., Hu, Y.W., Zhao, G.L., Pan, L.D., Li, W., Wu, C., Coriaty, Z., Evans, I., Lin, M.G., Stalsberg, H., & Self, S.G. (2002). Randomized trial of breast self-examination in Shanghai: Final results. Journal of the National Cancer Institute, 94, 1420-1421.

Thomas, I.L., Tyle, V., Webster, J., & Neilson, A. An evaluation of transcutaneous electric nerve stimulation for pain relief in labour. Australian and New Zealand Journal of Obstetrics and Gynaecology, 28, 182-189.

Thomas, N.K. (2004). Resident burnout. Journal of the American Medical Association, 292(23), 2880-2889.

Thomas, P.D., Goodwin, J.M., & Goodwin, J.S. (1985). Effects of social support on stress-related changes in cholesterol level, urine acid level, and immune function in an elderly sample. American Journal of Psychiatry, 142, 735-737.

Thomas, R.E. (1997). Problem-based learning: Measurable outcomes. Medical Education, 31, 320-329.

Thomas, W., White, C.M., Mah, J., Geisser, M.S., et al. (1995). Longitudinal compliance with annual screening for fecal occult blood. *American Journal of Epidemiology, 142*, 176–182.

Thomason, T.E., McCune, J.S., Bernard, S.A., Winer, E.P., Tremont, S., & Lindley, C.M. (1998). Cancer pain survey: Patient-centered issues in control. *Journal of Pain Symptom Management, 15*, 275–284.

Thompson, C.L., & Pledger, L.M. (1993). Doctor-patient communication: Is patient knowledge of medical terminology improving? *Health Communication, 5*, 89–97

Thompson, J.K. (1986, April). Larger than life. *Psychology Today*, pp. 38–44.

Thompson, T.L. (2000). The nature and language of illness explanations. In B.B. Whaley (Ed.), *Explaining illness: Research theory and strategies.* Mahwah, NJ: Lawrence Erlbaum.

Thorne, S., Paterson, B., Russell, C., & Schultz, A. (2002). Complementary/alternative medicine in chronic illness as informed self-care decision making. *International Journal of Nursing Studies, 39*(7), 671–683.

Thornton, L.M., Andersen, B.L., Crespin, T.R., & Carson, W.E. (2007). Individual trajectories in stress covary with immunity during recovery from cancer diagnosis and treatments. *Brain, Behavior, and Immunity, 21*, 185–194.

Tjepkema, M. (2002). The health of the off-reserve Aboriginal population. *Health Reports: How Healthy Are Canadians*, Supplement to Volume 13, 73–88.

Tomasi, T.B., Jr. (1971). *The immune system of secretions.* Englewood Cliffs, NJ: Prentice-Hall.

Tomkins, S.S. (1966). Psychological model for smoking behavior. *American Journal of Public Health, 56* (Suppl. 12), 17–20.

Tomkins, S.S. (1968). A modified model of smoking behavior. In E.F. Borgatta & R.R. Evans (Eds.), *Smoking, health and behavior* (pp. 165–188). Chicago: Aldine.

Tompkins, J.M. (2005). Two decades have passed . . . and still it is her eyes that I remember: Reflections of a pediatric nurse. *Pediatric Nursing, 31*(5), 426, 424–425.

Tomporowski, P.D., & Ellis, N.R. (1986). Effects of exercise on cognitive process: A review. *Psychological Bulletin, 99*, 338–346.

Topaz, O., Minisi, A.J., Bernardo, N., Alimar, R., Ereso, A., & Shah, R. (2003). Comparison of effectiveness of excimer laser angioplasty in patients with acute coronary syndromes in those with versus those without normal left ventricular function. *Am J Cardiol, 91*(7), 797–802.

Toynbee, P. (1977). *Patients.* New York: Harcourt Brace.

Tremblay, S., Ross, N.A., & Berthelot, J-M. (2002). Regional socio-economic context and health. *Health Reports: How Healthy Are Canadians*, Supplement to Volume 13, 33–44.

Triandis, H.C., Bontempo, R., Villareal, M.J., Asai, M., & Lucca, N. (1998). Individualism and collectivism: Cross-cultural perspectives on self-ingroup relationships. *Journal of Personality and Social Psychology, 54*, 323–338.

Trifiletti, L.B., Gielen, A.C., Sleet, D.A., & Hopkins, K. (2005). Behavioral and social sciences theories and models: Are they used in unintentional injury prevention research. *Health Education Research, 20*(3), 298–307.

Trotter, R.T., II. (1991). Ethnographic research methods for applied medical anthropology. In C.E. Hill (Ed.), *Training manual in applied medical anthropology* (pp. 180–212). Washington, DC: American Anthropological Association.

Tsoh, J.Y., McClure, J.B., Skaar, K.L., Wetter, D.W., et al. (1997). Smoking cessation 2: Components of effective intervention. *Behavioral Medicine, 23*, 15–27.

Turk, D.C. (2001). Physiological and psychological bases of pain. In A. Baum, T.A. Revenson, & J.E. Singer (Eds.), *Handbook of health psychology* (pp. 117–131). Mahwah, NJ: Erlbaum.

Turk, D.C., & Meichenbaum, D. (1991). Adherence to self-care regimens: the patient's perspective. In R.H. Rozensky, J.J. Sweet, & S.M. Tovian (Eds.), *Handbook of clinical psychology. I. Medical settings* (pp. 249–266). New York: Plenum.

Turk, D.C., Meichenbaum, D., & Genest, M. (1983). *Pain and behavioral medicine: A cognitive-behavioral perspective.* New York: Guilford Press.

Turk, D.C., & Melzack, R. (2001). The measurement of pain and the assessment of people experiencing pain. In D.C. Turk & R. Melzack (Eds.), *Handbook of pain assessment.* (2nd ed.) (pp. 1–11). New York: Guilford.

Turk, D.C., & Melzack, R. (Eds.). (2001). *Handbook of pain assessment.* (2nd ed.). New York: Guilford.

Turk, D.C., Monarch, E.S., & Williams, A.D. (2004). Assessment of pain sufferers. In T. Hadjistavropoulos & K.D. Craig (Eds.), *Pain: Psychological perspectives* (pp. 209–243). Mahwah, NJ: Erlbaum.

Turk, D.C., & Okifuji, A. (1996). Perception of traumatic onset, compensation status, and physical findings: Impact on pain severity, emotional distress, and disability in chronic pain patients. *Journal of Behavioral Medicine, 19*, 435–454.

Turk, D.C., & Stacey, B.R. (2000). Multidisciplinary pain centers in the treatment of chronic back pain. In J.W. Frymoyer, T.B. Ducker, N.M. Hadler, J.P. Kostuik, J.N. Weinstein, & T.S. Whitcloud (Eds.), *The adult spine: Principles and practice.* (2nd ed.). Philadelphia: Lippincott Williams & Wilkins.

Turk, D.C., Wack, J.T., & Kerns, R.D. (1985). An empirical examination of the "pain-behavior" construct. *Journal of Behavioral Medicine, 8*, 119–130.

Turk, D.C., & Winter, F. (2006). *The pain survival guide: How to reclaim your life.* Washington, DC: American Psychological Association.

Turk, D.C., Zacki, H.S., & Rudy, T.E. (1993). Effects of intraoral appliance and biofeedback/stress management alone and in combination in treating pain and depression in TMD patients. *Journal of Prosthetic Dentistry, 70*, 158–164.

Turncock, C. (1991). Communicating with patients in the ICU. *Nursing Standard, 5*(15), 38–40.

Turner Cobb, J.M., & Steptoe, A. (1998). Psychosocial influences on upper respiratory infectious illness in children. *Journal of Psychosomatic Research, 45,* 319–330.

Tversky, A., & Kahneman, D. (1981). The framing of decisions and the psychology of choice. *Science, 211,* 453–458.

Tyc, V.L., Fairclough, D., Fletcher, B., Leigh, L., et al. (1995). Children's distress during magnetic resonance imaging procedures. *Children's Health Care, 24,* 5–19.

Tzeng, H.M., Ketefian, S., & Redman, R.W. (2002). Relationship of nurses' assessment of organizational culture, job satisfaction, and patient satisfaction with nursing care. *International Journal of Nursing Studies, 39*(1), 79–84.

U

Udry, E., & Anderson, M.B. (2008). Athletic injury and sport behaviour. In T.S. Horn (Ed.), *Advances in sport psychology.* (3rd ed.) (pp. 401– 422). Champaign, Illinois: Human Kinetics.

Unruh, A.M. (1996). Gender variations in clinical pain experience. *Pain, 65,* 123–167.

Unruh, A.M., Ritchie, J., & Merskey, H. (1999). Does gender affect appraisal of pain and pain coping strategies? *Clinical Journal of Pain, 15*(1), 31–40.

Urbszat, D., Herman, C.P., & Polivy, J. (2002). Eat, drink, and be merry, for tomorrow we diet: Effects of anticipated deprivation on food intake in restrained and unrestrained eaters. *Journal of Abnormal Psychology, 111,* 396–401.

V

Vallerand, R.J., & Rousseau, F.L. (2001). Intrinsic and extrinsic motivation in sport and exercise: A review using the hierarchical model of intrinsic and extrinsic motivation. In R.N. Singer, H.A. Hausenblas, & C.M. Janelle (Eds.), *Handbook of sport psychology.* (2nd ed.) (pp. 389–416). New York: Wiley.

Vaillant, G.E., Sobowale, N.C., & McArthur, C. (1972). Some psychologic vulnerabilities of physicians. *New England Journal of Medicine, 287,* 372–375.

Van Dorsten, B. (2006). Psychological considerations in preparing patients for implantation procedures. *Pain Medicine, 7*(S1), S47–S57.

Van Elderen, T., Maes, S., Rouneau, C., & Seegers, G. (1998). Perceived gender differences in physician consulting behaviour during internal examination. *Family Practice, 15,* 147–152.

Van Wel, F., & Knobbout, J. (1998). Adolescents and fear appeals. *International Journal of Adolescence and Youth, 7,* 121–135.

VanIneveld, C.H., Cook, D.J., Kane, S.L., & King, D. (1996). Discrimination and abuse in internal medicine residency. The Internal Medicine Program Directors of Canada. *Journal of General Internal Medicine, 11,* 401–405.

Varni, J.W., & Thompson, K.L. (1986). Biobehavioral assessment and management of pediatric pain. In N.A. Krasnegor, J.D. Arasteh, & M.F. Cataldo (Eds.), *Child health behavior: A behavioral pediatrics perspective.* New York: Wiley.

Vealey, R. (1988). Future directions in psychological skills training. *The Sports Psychologist, 2,* 318–336.

Verberne, T.J.P. (2002). Suicide in doctors. *Journal of Epidemiology & Community Health, 56*(3), 237.

Verhoef, M.J., Casebeer, A.L., & Hilsden, R.J. (2002). Assessing efficacy of complementary medicine: adding qualitative research methods to the "Gold Standard." *J Altern Complement Med, 8*(3), 275–281.

Verhoef, M.J., Hagen, N., Pelletier, G., & Forsyth, P. (1999). Alternative therapy use in neurologic diseases: Use in brain tumor patients. *Neurology, 52,* 617–622.

Verhoef, M.J., Lewith, G., Ritenbaugh, C., Boo, H., Fleishman, S., & Leis, A. (2005). Complementary and alternative medicine whole systems research: Beyond identification of the inadequacies of the RCT. *Complementary Therapies in Medicine, 13*(3), 206–212.

Verhoef, M.J., & White, M.A. (2002). Factors in making the decision to forgo conventional cancer treatment. *Cancer Pract, 10*(4), 201–207.

Veronin, M.A. (2002). Where are they now? A case study of health-related Web site attrition. *J Med Internet Res, 4*(2), E10.

Verplanken, B., & Faes, S. (1999). Good intentions, bad habits and effects of forming implementations in healthy eating. *European Journal of Social Psychology, 29*(5–6), 591–604.

Videon, T.M., & Manning, C.K. (2003). Influences on adolescent eating patterns: The importance of family meals. *Journal of Adolescent Health, 32,* 365–373.

Vidrine, J.I., Anderson, C.B., Pollak, K.I., & Wetter, D.W. (2006). Gender differences in adolescent smoking: Mediator and moderator effects of self-generated expected smoking outcomes. *American Journal of Health Promotion, 20*(6), 383–387.

Viemeroe, V., & Krause, C. (1998). Quality of life in individuals with physical disabilities. *Psychotherapy and Psychosomatics, 67,* 317–322.

Vocks, S., Ockenfels, M., Jurgensen, R., Mussgay, L., & Rudddel, H. (2004). Blood pressure reactivity can be reduced by a cognitive behavioral stress management program. *International Journal of Behavioral Medicine, 11,*63-70.

Volume III: Gathering strength. (1996). Ottawa: Royal Commission on Aboriginal Peoples.

von Baeyer, C.L., Baskerville, S., & McGrath, P.J. (1998). Everyday pain in three- to five-year-old children in day care. *Pain Research and Management, 3*(2), 111–116.

Vuckovic, N. (1999). Fast relief: Buying time with medications. *Medical Anthropology Quarterly, 13,* 51–68.

W

Wadden, T.A., Brownell, K.D., & Foster, G.D. (2002). Obesity: Responding to the global epidemic. *Journal of Consulting and Clinical Psychology, 70,* 510–525.

Wadden, T.A., Womble, L.G., Stunkard, A.J., & Anderson, D.A. (2002). Psychosocial consequences of obesity and weight loss. In T.A. Wadden & A.J. Stunkard (Eds.), *Handbook of obesity treatment* (pp. 144–169). New York: Guilford Press.

Wadee, A.A., Kuschke, R.H., Kometz, S., & Berk, M. (2001). Personality factors, stress and immunity. *Stress & Health: Journal of the International Society for the Investigation of Stress, 17*, 25–40.

Wagner, C.C., & McMahon, B.T. (2004). Motivational interviewing and rehabilitation counseling practice. *Rehabilitation Counseling Bulletin, 47*(3), 152–161.

Wahl, C., Gregoire, J.-P., Teo, K., Beaulieu, M., Labelle, S., Leduc, B., Cochrane, B., Lapointe, L., & Montague, T. (2005). Concordance, compliance and adherence in healthcare: Closing gaps and improving outcomes. *Healthcare Quarterly, 8*(1), Retrieved April 20, 2006, from www.longwoods.com/product.php?productid=16941&cat=&page=1

Waitzkin, H. (1984). Doctor-patient communication: Clinical implications of social scientific research. *Journal of the American Medical Association, 252*, 2441–2446.

Waitzkin, H. (1985). Information giving in medical care. *Journal of Health and Social Behavior, 26*, 81–101.

Walker, L.G. (2004). Hypnotherapeutic insights and interventions: A cancer odyssey. *Contemporary Hypnosis, 21*, 35–45.

Walsh, B. T., Kaplan, A. S., Attia, E., Olmstead, M., Parides, M., Carter, J. C., et al. (2006). Fluoxetine after weight restoration in anorexia nervosa: A randomized controlled trial. *Journal of the American Medical Association, 295*, 2605–2612.

Walsh, J.D., Blanchard, E.B., Kremer, J.M., & Blancard, C.G. (1999). The psychosocial effects of rheumatoid arthritis on the patient and the well partner. *Behaviour Research and Therapy, 37*, 259–271.

Walsh, J.C., Lynch, M., Murphy, A.W., & Daly, K. (2004). Factors influencing the decision to seek treatment for symptoms of acute myocardial infarction: An evaluation of the Self-Regulatory Model of illness behaviour. *Journal of Psychosomatic Research, 56*, 67–73.

Walsh-Burke, K. (2000). Matching bereavement services to level of need. *Hospice Journal, 15*(1), 77–86.

Wallston, K.A., Wallston, B.S., & DeVellis, R. (1978). Development of the Multidimensional Health Locus of Control (MHLC) scale. *Health Education Monographs, 6*, 161–170.

Wang, M-Y., Tsai, P-S., Chou, K-R., & Chen, C-M. (2008). A systematic review of the efficacy of non-pharmacological treatments for depression on glycaemic control in type 2 diabetics. *Journal of Clinical Nursing, 17*, 2524–2530.

Wann, D.L. (1997). *Sport psychology.* Upper Saddle River, NJ: Wadsworth.

Wansink, B. (2004). Environmental factors that increase the food intake and consumption volume of unknowing consumers. *Annual Review of Nutrition, 24*, 455–479.

Wansink, B. (2006). *Mindless eating: Why we eat more than we think.* New York: Random House.

Wansink, B., & Kim, J. (2005). Bad popcorn in big buckets: Portion size can influence intake as much as taste. *Journal of Nutrition Education and Behavior, 37*(5), 242–245.

Ward, A., Ramsay, R., & Treasure, J.L. (2000a). Attachment research in eating disorders. *British Journal of Medical Psychology, 73*, 35–51.

Ward, A., Ramsay, R., & Turnbull, S., Benedettini, M., & Treasure, J. (2000b). Attachment patterns in eating disorders: Past in the present. *International Journal of Eating Disorders, 28*, 370–376.

Ward, C.F. (2005). Physicians with opioid dependence. *Journal of the American Medical Association, 293*(3), 294.

Ward, H.E., Tueth, M., & Sheps, D. (2003). Depression and cardiovascular disease. *Current Opinion in Psychiatry, 16*(2), 221–225.

Ward, K.G. (1999). A TEAM approach to NICU care. *RN, 62*(2), 47–49.

Wardle, J., & Pope, R. (1992). The psychological costs of screening for cancer. *Journal of Psychosomatic Research, 36*, 609–624.

Ware, M.A., Doyle, C.R., Woods, R., Lynch, M.E., & Clark, A.J. (2003). Cannabis use for chronic non-cancer pain: Results of a prospective study. *Pain, 102*, 211–216.

Warrick, P.D., Irish, J.C., Morningstar, M., Gilbert, R., Brown, D., & Gullane, P. (1999). Use of alternative medicine among patients with head and neck cancer. *Archives of Otolaryngolical Head and Neck Surgery, 125*, 573–579.

Wartella, J.E., Auerbach, S.M., & Ward, K.R. (2009). Emotional distress, coping and adjustment in family members of neuroscience intensive care unit patients. *Journal of Psychosomatic Research, 66*, 503–509.

Watkins, L.R., & Maier, S.F. (2000). The pain of being sick: Implications of immune-to-brain communication for understanding pain. *Annual Review of Psychology, 51*, 29–57.

Watson, D., Roos, N., Katz, A., & Bogdanovic, B. (2003). Is a 5% decline in physician supply significant? *Canadian Family Physician, 49*(5), 566–567.

Weiger, W.A., Smith, M., Boon, H., Richardson, M.A., Kaptchuk, T.J., & Eisenberg, D.M. (2002). Advising patients who seek complementary and alternative medical therapies for cancer. *Ann Intern Med, 137*(11), 889–903.

Weinberg, R., & McDermott, M. (2002). A comparative analysis of sport and business organizations: Factors perceived critical for organizational success. *Journal of Applied Sport Psychology, 14*, 282–298.

Weinberg, R.S. (1996). Goal setting in sport and exercise: Research to practice. In J.L. Van Raalte & B.W. Brewer (Eds.), *Exploring sport and exercise psychology* (pp. 3–24). Washington, DC: American Psychological Association.

Weinberg, R.S., & Gould, D. (2003). *Foundations of sport and exercise psychology.* (3rd ed.). Champaign, IL: Human Kinetics.

Weiner, D., Peiper, C., McConnell, E., Martinez, S., & Keefe, F.J. (1996). Pain measurement in elders with chronic low back pain: Traditional and alternative approaches. *Pain, 67*, 461–467.

Weiner, E.L., Swain, G.R., Wolf, B., & Gottleib, M. (2001). A qualitative study of physician's own wellness promotion practices. *Western Journal of Medicine, 174*, 19–23.

Weir, E. (2000). Substance abuse among physicians. *CMAJ, 162*(12), 1730.

Weiss, M.R., Wiese, D.M., & Klint, K.A. (1989). Head over heels with success: The relationship between self-efficacy and performance in competitive youth gymnastics. *Journal of Sport and Exercise Psychology, 11*, 444–451.

Weisse, C.S., Sorum, P.C., Sanders, K.N., & Syat, B.L. (2001). Do gender and race affect decisions about pain management? *Journal of General Internal Medicine, 16*, 211–217.

Weller, A., & Hener, T. (1993). Invasiveness of medical procedures and state anxiety in women. *Behavioral Medicine, 19*, 60–65.

Weller, S.C. (1983). New data on intracultural variability: The hot–cold concept of medicine and illness. *Human Organization, 42*, 341–351.

Wells, D. (1997). A critical ethnography of the process of discharge decision-making for elderly patients. *Canadian Journal on Aging, 16*, 682–699.

Wells, K.J., Battaglia, T.A., Dudley, D.J., Garcia, R., Greene, A., Calhoun, E., Mandelblatt, J.S., Paskett, E.D., & Raich, P.C. (2008). Patient navigation: State of the art or is it science? *Cancer, 113*(8), 1999–2010.

Wenger, M., Bagchi, B., & Anand, B. (1961). Experiments in India on "voluntary" control of the heart and pulse. *Circulation, 24,*1319–1325.

Wenzel, L.B., Donnelly, J.P., Fowler, J.M., Habbal, R., Taylor, T.H., Aziz, N., & Cella, D. (2002). Resilience, reflection and residual stress in ovarian cancer survivorship: A gynecologic oncology group study. *Psycho-Oncology, 11*, 142–153.

Weston, W.W., & Brown, J.B. (1995). In M. Stewart, J.B. Brown, W.W. Weston, I.R. McWhinney, C.L. McWilliam, & T.R. Freeman. *Patient-centered medicine: Transforming the clinical method.* Thousand Oaks, CA: Sage.

What Is the Internet, the World Wide Web, and Netscape? (2002, Sept. 27). [Web site]. UC Berkeley Library. Retrieved Octsober 28, 2010, from www.lib.berkeley.edu/TeachingLib/Guides/Internet

While, A.E., & Wilcox, V.K. (1994). Paediatric day surgery: Day-case unit admission compared with general paediatric ward admission. *Journal of Advances in Nursing, 19*, 52–57.

White, S.A., & Duda, J.L. (1991, October). The interdependence between goal perspectives, psychological skill, and cognitive interference among elite skiers. Paper presented at the annual meeting of the Association for the Advancement of Applied Sport Psychology, Savannah, Georgia.

Whitehouse, W.G., Orne, E.C., & Dinges, D.F. (2002). Demand characteristics: Toward an understanding of their meaning and application in clinical practice. *Prevention & Treatment, 5*, Article 34.

Whyte, A., & Niven, C.A. (2004). The illusive phantom: Does primary care meet patient need following limb loss? *Disability and Rehabilitation, 26*(14–15), 894–900.

Wisenfeld, H.Z. (2005). Sex differences in pain perception. *Gender Medicine, 2*(3), 137–145.

Witt, C.M., Jena, S., Brinkhaus, B., Liecker, B., Wegschider, K., & Stefan, N.W. (in press). Acupuncture for patients with chronic neck pain. *Pain.*

WHO. (1999). *Medical products and the internet: A guide to finding reliable information* (WHO/EDM/QSM/99.4). Geneva: World Health Organization.

WHO. (2005). WHO Framework Convention on Tobacco Control. Retrieved September 1, 2006, from www.who.int/tobacco/framework/WHO_FCTC_english.pdf

WHO. (2006). Management of Substance Abuse: Cannabis. Retrieved September 1, 2006, from www.who.int/substance_abuse/facts/cannabis/en/

Wilkins, K. (1995). Causes of death: How the sexes differ. *Health Reports, 7*(2), 33–43.

Wilkins, K., & Beaudet, M.P. (1998). Work stress and health. *Health Reports, 10*(3), 47–62.

Wilkins, K., & Mackenzie, S.G. (2007). Work injuries. *Health Reports, 18*, 1–18.

Wilkins, R., Berthelot, J-M., and Ng, E. (2002). Trends in mortality by neighbourhood income in urban Canada from 1971 to 1996. *Health Reports: How Healthy Are Canadians,* Supplement to Volume 13, 45–71.

Wilkins, K., & Park, E. (1997). Characteristics of hospital users. *Health Reports, 9*(3), 27–36.

Wilkins, R. (1993). The use of postal codes and addresses in the analysis of health data. *Health Reports, 5*(2), 157–177.

Williams, D.M. (2008). Exercise, affect, and adherence: An integrated model and a case for self-paced exercise. *Journal of Sport and Exercise Psychology, 30*, 471–496.

Williams, J. (2001). Psychology of injury risk and prevention. In R.N. Singer, H.A. Hausenblas, & C.M. Janelle (Eds.), *Handbook of sport psychology.* (2nd ed.) (pp. 766–786). New York: John Wiley and Sons.

Williams, J.E., Paton, C.C., Siegler, I.C., Eigenbrot, M.I., Nieto, F.J., & Tyroler, H.A. (2000). Clinical investigation and reports: Anger proneness predicts coronary heart disease risk: Prospective analysis from the Atherosclerosis Risk in Communities (ARIC) Study. *Circulation, 101*, 2034–2039.

Williams, J.M., & Leffingwell, T.R. (1996). Cognitive strategies in sport and exercise psychology. In J.L. Van Raalte & B.W. Brewer (Eds.), *Exploring sport and exercise psychology* (pp. 51–74). Washington, DC: American Psychological Association.

Williams, P., Narcisco, L., Browne, G., Roberts, J., Weir, R., & Gafni, A. (2005). The prevalence, correlates, and costs of depression in people living with HIV/AIDS in Ontario: Implications for service directions. *AIDS Education and Prevention, 17*(2), 119–130.

Williams, P.A., Dominick-Pierre, K., Vayda, E., Stevenson, M., & Burke, M. (1990). Women in medicine: Practice patterns and attitudes. *Canadian Medical Association Journal, 143*, 194–201.

Williams, S.J. (2005). Parson revisited: From the sick role to . . . ? *Health: An International Journal for the Social Study of Health, Illness, and Medicine, 9*(2), 123–144.

Wilson, G.T., Grilo, C. M., & Vitousek, K. M. (2007). Psychological treatment of eating disorders. *American Psychologist, 62*(3), 199–216.

Wilson, P.W.F., D'Agostino, R.B., Levy, D., Belanger, A.M., Silbershatz, H., & Kannel, W.B. (1998). Prediction of coronary heart disease using risk factor categories. *Circulation, 97*, 1837–1847.

Wing, R.R. (2002). Behavioral weight control. In T.A. Wadden & A.J. Stunkard (Eds.), *Handbook of obesity treatment* (pp. 301–316). New York: Guilford Press.

Wipfli, B.M., Rethorst, C.D., and Landers, D. (2008). The anxiolytic effects of exercise: A meta-analysis of randomized trials and dose-response analysis. *Journal of Sport and Exercise Psychology, 30,*392–410.

Witte, K. (1994). Fear control and danger control: A test of the extended parallel process model (EPPM). *Communication Monographs, 61*, 113–134.

Wolf, Z.R. (1993). Nursing rituals: doing ethnography. *NLN Publications*, August, 269–310.

Wolpe, J. (1958). *Psychotherapy by reciprocal inhibition.* Stanford, CA: Stanford University Press.

Wong, H.C. (1999). Educating medical students about alternative therapies. *Canadian Medical Association Journal, 161*, 128–129.

Woodhouse, A. (2005). Phantom limb sensation. *Clinicaland ExperimentalPharmacology and Physiology, 32*, 132–134.

World Health Organization. (1946). Preamble to the Constitution of the World Health Organization as adopted by the International Health Conference, New York, 19–22 June, 1946; signed on 22 July 1946 by the representatives of 61 States (Official Records of the World Health Organization, no. 2, p. 100) and entered into force on 7 April 1948.

World Health Organization. (1986). Ottawa Charter for Health Promotion. Ottawa: Canadian Public Health Association.

World Health Organization. (1998). *Malaria, Fact Sheet No. 94.*

World Health Organization. (2004, October 11). World Health Organization supports global effort to relieve chronic pain. Retrieved May 5, 2010, from www.who.int/mediacentre/news/releases/2004/pr70/en/

Wressle, E.B., Oberg, B., & Henriksson, C. (1999). The rehabilitation process for the geriatric stroke patient—An exploratory study of goal setting and interventions. *Disability and Rehabilitation, 21*(2), 80–87.

Wright, B., Scott, I., Woloschuk, W., & Brenneis, F. (2004). Career choice of new medical students at three Canadian universities: Family medicine versus specialty medicine. *Canadian Medical Association Journal, 170*(13), 1920–1924.

Wright, K.B., & Bell, S.B. (2003). Health-related support groups on the Internet: Linking empirical findings to social support and computer-mediated communication theory. *Journal of Health Psychology, 8*(1), 39–54.

Wright, L. (1988). The Type A behavior pattern and coronary heart disease. *American Psychologist, 43*, 2–14.

Wroth, T.H., & Pathman, D.E. (2006). Primary medication adherence in a rural population: The role of the patient physician relationship and satisfaction with care. *Journal of the American Board of Family Medicine 19*, 478–486.

Wu, Z.H., Freeman, J.L., Greer, A.L., Freeman, D.H., & Goodwin, J.S. (2001). The influence of patients' concerns on surgeons' recommendations for early breast cancer. *European Journal of Cancer Care, 10*(2), 100–106.

Wulsin, L.R., & Singal, B.M. (2003). Do depressive symptoms increase the risk for the onset of coronary disease? A systematic quantitative review. *Psychosomatic Medicine, 65*, 201–210.

Wysocki, T. (2006). Behavioral assessment and intervention in pediatric diabetes. *Behavior Modification, 20*(1), 72–92.

Y

Ye, Z.Q., Lan, R.Z., Du, G.H., Yuan, X.Y., Chen, Z., Ma, Y.Z., et al. (2003). Biofeedback therapy for chronic pelvic pain syndrome. *Asian Journal of Andrology, 5*, 155–158.

Ylinen, E-R., Vehviläinen-Julkunen, K., Pietilä, A-M. (2009). Effects of patients' anxiety, previous pain experience and non-drug interventions on the pain experience during colonoscopy. *Journal of Clinical Nursing, 18*, 1937–1944.

Yogananda, P. (1969). *Autobiography of a yogi.* Bombay, India: Jaico Publishing House.

Z

Zabora, J., Brintzenhofeszoc, K., Curbow, B., Hooker, C., & Piantadosi, S. (2001). The prevalence of psychological distress by cancer site. *Psycho-Oncology, 10*(1), 19–28.

Zachariae, R., Pedersen, C.G., Jensen, A.B., Ehrnrooth, E., Rossen, P.B., & von der Maase, H. (2003). Association of perceived physician communication style with patient satisfaction, distress, cancer-related self-efficacy, and perceived control over the disease. *British Journal of Cancer, 88*, 658–665.

Zajonc, R.B. (1968). Attitudinal effects of mere exposure. *Journal of Personality and Social Psychology Monograph Supplements, 9*, 1–27.

Zakrzewski, P.A., Ho, A.L., & Braga-Mele, R. (2008). Should ophthalmologists receive communication skills training in breaking bad news? *Canadian Journal of Ophthalmology, 43*(4), 419–424.

Zalewski, C., Keller, B., Bowers, C., Miske, P., et al. (1994). Depressive symptomatology and post-stroke rehabilitation outcome. *Clinical Gerontologist, 14*, 62–67.

Zhang, Y., Proenca, R., Maffei, M., Barone, M., Leopold, L., & Friedman, J.M. (1994). Positional cloning of the mouse obese gene and its human homologue. *Nature, 372*, 425–432.

Zanna, M., Cameron, R., Goldsmith, C.H., Poland, B., et al. (1996). Critique of the COMMIT study based on the

Brantford experience. *Health and Canadian Society, 2,* 319–336.

Zatzick, D.F., & Dimsdale, J.E. (1990). Cultural variations in response to painful stimuli. *Psychosomatic Medicine, 52,* 544–557.

Zeitlin, D., Keller, S.E., Shiflett, S.C., Schleifer, S.J., & Bartlett, J.A. (2000). Immunological effects of massage therapy during acute academic stress. *Psychosomatic Medicine, 62,* 83–84.

Zeltzer, L.R., Tsao, J.C.I., Stelling, C., Powers, M., Levy, S., & Waterhouse, M. (2002). A phase I study on the feasibility and acceptability of an acupuncture/hypnosis intervention for chronic pediatric pain. *Journal of Pain & Symptom Management, 24,* 437–446.

Zhuk, M., Hart, T.A., & James, C.A. (2006, August). HIV-knowledge, sexual activity and HIV-testing attitudes and behaviour among immigrant and non-immigrant Canadian university students. Poster session presented at the International AIDS conference. Toronto.

Zifferblatt, S.M. (1975). Increasing patient compliance through applied analysis of behavior. *Preventive Medicine, 4,* 173–182.

Zimlichman, E., Kochba, I., Mimouni, F.B., Chochat, T., Grott, I., Kreiss, Y., et al. (2005). Smoking habits and obesity in young adults. *Addiction, 100,* 1021–1025

Zimmerman, S., Gruber-Baldini, A.L., Hebel, J.R., Sloane, P.D., & Magaziner, J. (2002). Nursing home facility risk factors for infection and hospitalization: Importance of registered nurse turnover, administration, and social factors. *Journal of the American Geriatrics Society, 50*(12), 1987–1995.

Zorilla, E.P., Luborsky, L., McKay, J.R., Rosenthal, R., Houldin, A., Tax, A., McCorkle, R., Seligman, D.A., & Schmidt, K. (2001). The relationship of depression and stressors to immunological assays: A meta-analytic review. *Brain, Behavior, and Immunity, 15,* 199–226.

Zouridakis, E., Avanzas, P., Arroyo-Espliguero, R., Fredericks, S., & Kaski, J.C. (2004). Markers of inflammation and rapid coronary artery disease progression in patients with stable angina pectoris. *Circulation, 10,* 1747–1753.

Zucker, T.P., Flesche, C.W., Germing, U., Schroeter, S., Willers, R., Wolf, H.H., & Hevil, A. (1998). Patient-controlled versus staff-controlled analgesia with pethidine after allogeneic bone marrow transplantation. *Pain, 75,* 305–312.

Zussman, R. (1993). Life in the hospital: A review. *Milbank Quarterly, 71,* 167–185.

Index

Dialogue on Drinking, 329
diarrhea, 47
diastole, 40
diathesis-stress model, 62
diet, 5, 6, 211
digestion, 46–47
digestive system, 44–47
digestive tract, 44
DiMatteo, Robin, 12
discharge planning, 164–165
disease, 371
disease model (of problem drinking), 268
diseases of adaptation, 62
disempowering care, 144
disfigurement, 202
dispositional variables, 89
distraction, 319–322
divorce, 89
"Do Bugs Need Drugs?", 44
doctor-centred care, 126
doctors. *See* physicians
Do Not Resuscitate order (DNR), 167
dopamine, 258
dose-response effect, 93
drinking and driving, 270–271
drive-reduction theory, 338
drug abuse, 271–274
drugs. *See* medication
Dueck, Tyrell, 363
Dugas, Gaetan, 361
duration, 65
dying, stages of, 223, 225

E

Eastern culture, 71–73
eating disorders, 6, 284–290
  anorexia nervosa, 6, 285
  binge eating, 285
  body dysmorphic disorder, 287–288
  bulimia nervosa, 284
  causes of, 286–287
  treatments for, 288–290
ecstasy, 273
education, 133
  diabetes and, 212
  medical school, 171–174
  obesity and, 277, 282
  as social determinant of
    health, 374
effectiveness, 83, 333
efferent, 34
efferent neurons, 29
efficacy beliefs, 190–191, 339
effleurage, 317

ego orientation, 250
elaboration likelihood model of
  persuasion, 337
elderly. *See* age
electroencephalograph (EEG), 72–74,
  306
electrolytes, 48
electromyography (EMG), 74, 306
Ellis, Albert, 75
embarrassment, 127
emergency department, 141, 156–157
emesis, 45
emotional-approach coping, 200
emotional arousal, 239
emotional support, 69, 335
emotion-focused coping, 68, 145,
  200–201
emotions
"Emotions, Immunity and Disease: A
  Speculative Theoretical
  Integration" (Solomon and Moos),
  87
empathy, 207
emphysema, 43
empowering care, 144
endocrine system, 35–36, 81
endogenous opioids, 297–299
Engels, Friedrich, 370
enumerative assay, 82
environmental factors
  diseases as, 2
  immune system and, 90
  interpretation of symptoms and, 109
  perception of symptoms and, 109–110
environmental tobacco smoke (ETS),
  262
epidemiology, 359–362
  language of, 359–360
  research steps in, 360–361
  of SARS outbreak, 359,
    361–362
epilepsy, 34
epinephrine, 60
Epp, Jake, 329
Epstein-Barr virus, 84, 100
ethanol, 266
ethics, 357–358
ethyl alcohol, 266
eustress, 57
euthanasia, 166
event uncertainty, 65
exercise psychology, 229
exhaustion phase, 62
expanded biomedical communication
  pattern, 117

experiential standards, 345
experimental groups, 352
experimental method, 352–353
experimenter bias, 356
expertise model, 162
external imagery, 249
external reinforcement, 190
extra-cellular fluids (ECFs), 48

F

FACT. *See* functional assessment of
  cancer therapy (FACT) scales
factor analysis, 352
faecal occult blood test (FOBT), 150
false-positive results, 152, 179
family-oriented cancer care, 205
fatigue, 96, 203
fear, 151
  cancer and, 114, 198, 199, 200
  chronic illness and, 196–197
  delays and, 114, 127
  diabetes and, 210–211
  heart attacks and, 213
  intensive care and, 161
  of restriction, 154
  of suffocation, 154
fear appeals, 337–341
feasibility standards, 345
feminist theory, 371
feminization of medicine, 180–183
fetal alcohol spectrum disorder (FASD),
  267, 375
field research, 353
fight-or-flight response, 35, 44, 58, 59,
  60, 71
First Nations and Inuit Health Branch
  (FNIHB), 375
Framework Convention on Tobacco
  Control (FCTC), 261
Framingham Heart Study, 5, 243
Frasure-Smith, Nancy, 215
frontal lobes, 33
Functional Assessment of Cancer
  Therapy (FACT) scale, 222
functional tests of immunity, 83–84

G

gametes, 49
gamma alcoholism, 381
gastric banding, 284
gastric bypass, 283
gastrointestinal illnesses, 88
gate control theory, 296–298

symbolic interactionism, 370–371
sympathetic adrenomedullary (SAM)
    system, 59
sympathetic nervous system, 35–42, 44, 45
    immune functioning and, 103
    stress and, 58, 60
symptoms
    perceiving and interpreting, 108–111
    types of, 110–111
synapses, 29
systematic desensitization, 74
systole, 40

T

tangible support, 69, 335
task orientation, 250
technical care, 148
technologists, 191–192
teen pregnancy, 19
teens. *See* youth
temporal lobes, 33
temporal uncertainty, 65
tending, 58
TENS, 314–315
tension reduction hypothesis, 268
testicular self-examination, 20
thalamus, 32
theory of human becoming, 166
theory of planned behaviour, 20–336
theory of reasoned action, 18–19, 336
therapeutic rituals, 147
threat appraisal, 63
threat perception, 338
thymus, 91
thyroid gland, 36, 61
time urgency, 5, 66
tobacco. *See* smoking
tolerance, 38, 91
total institution, 142
traditional treatments, 364

trait-negative affect, 96–97
traits, 96, 99, 213
tranquillizers, 314
transcendent accomplishments, 238
transcendental meditation (TM), 73
transcript analysis, 370
transcutaneous electrical nerve stimulation
    (TENS), 314–315
translocation stress, 161
transtheoretical model, 22
triage, 157
triglycerides, 47
tropic hormones, 35
tumours, 197
Type A behaviour pattern, 5, 67
Type B personality, 66

U

UAB Pain Behavior Scale, 307
ulcers, 46
uncertainty, 178–180
unconventional therapy (UT), 364
uniformity myth, 145
unit of analysis, 372
unsafe sexual behaviour, 274–275
upper respiratory infections (URI), 88
    colds, 11, 44, 89–91, 97
        depression and, 93
        negative mood and, 96–97
        stress and, 89–91
ureter, 48
urethra, 48
urinary bladder, 48
urinary system, 47–49
URLs (uniform resource locators), 379

V

vaccinations, 90
Valsalva manoeuvre, 72

vectors, 361
vehicles, 361
ventricles, 39
verbal descriptor scale, 308, 312
verbal persuasion, 239
vicarious experience, 239
viral challenge studies, 91–96
virtual reality analgesia,
    312–320
visual analog scale, 308, 312
vomiting, 45
vulnerability, 15, 64, 337

W

Waitzkin, Howard, 6
water, 48
Wernicke's area, 33
Western culture, 71–73, 110
withdrawal, 263
World Health Organization (WHO)
    definition of health of, 3, 372
    framework on tobacco, 259, 261
    health promotion and, 328, 329,
        347, 379
    obesity research of, 276

Y

Yale Conference on Behavioural
    Medicine (1977), 3
yoga, 71
youth
    alcohol abuse and, 266
    cancer and, 203
    drug abuse and, 272, 273
    eating disorders and, 284–285
    physical activity and, 246
    pregnancy and, 19
    smoking and, 257–258
    unsafe sex and, 274

Photo Credits